The Oxford
Dictionary of
Civil War Quotations

The Oxford Dictionary of Civil War Quotations

John D. Wright

OXFORD
UNIVERSITY PRESS
2006

OXFORD
UNIVERSITY PRESS

Oxford University Press, Inc., publishes works that further
Oxford University's objective of excellence in research, scholarship, and education.

Oxford New York
Auckland Cape Town Dar es Salaam Hong Kong Karachi
Kuala Lumpur Madrid Melbourne Mexico City Nairobi
New Delhi Shanghai Taipei Toronto

With offices in
Argentina Austria Brazil Chile Czech Republic France Greece
Guatemala Hungary Italy Japan Poland Portugal Singapore
South Korea Switzerland Thailand Turkey Ukraine Vietnam

Copyright © 2006 by Oxford University Press, Inc.

Published by Oxford University Press, Inc.
198 Madison Avenue, New York, New York, 10016
www.oup.com/us
www.askoxford.com

Oxford is a registered trademark of Oxford University Press

Library of Congress Cataloging-in-Publication Data

Wright, John D., 1938-
  The Oxford dictionary of Civil War quotations / John Wright.
     p. cm.
  Includes bibliographical references and index.
  ISBN-13: 978-0-19-516296-7 (hardcover : alk. paper)
  ISBN-10: 0-19-516296-X (hardcover : alk. paper)
  1. United States—History—Civil War, 1861-1865—Quotations, maxims, etc.   2. Quotations,
American. I. Title.
  E468.9.W757 2006
  973.7—dc22

                              2006010276

ISBN-10: 0-19-516296-X
ISBN-13: 978-0-19-516296-7

9 8 7 6 5 4 3 2 1

Printed in the United States of America on acid-free paper

For my wife,
Inge,
who also has
a delightful way with words.

Introduction

"The wisdom of the wise, and the experience of ages, may be preserved by quotation," according to the British author Isaac Disraeli, father of the famous nineteenth-century prime minister.

This quotation had certainly been repeated by Americans before the Civil War, but participants on both sides hardly needed encouragement to record the language of the world's first modern conflict with trench warfare, land mines, submarines, iron warships, balloon observatories, and the electronic telegraph.

The invention of the latter and the growth of large-circulation newspapers ensured that ample quotations would be preserved for posterity, both to the glory and the chagrin of military officers and government officials. Generals learned to choose their words carefully to use and confuse America's new breed of war correspondent. Indeed, some famous quotes were never said, including Gen. William Tecumseh Sherman's "Hold the fort." (His flag message was "Sherman says hold fast.")

This volume brings together quotations that show the realities, dreams, and passions of those who were caught up in a tragedy happening in our own backyard. Their distant words have come from a variety of sources, from well-planned State of the Union speeches to letters quickly scrawled to loved ones by soldiers in dreary camps. Other thoughts are from such sources as government reports, diaries, biographies, newspaper editorials, military orders, and sermons, revealing the mixed emotions of despair and joy, fear and bravery, prejudice and patriotism.

After all, the true individual is often revealed by his or her words. They certainly show the vast humanity of Abraham Lincoln who could one day produce the eloquence of the Gettysburg Address and on another complain humorously that office seekers were "too many pigs for the tits." We can equally contrast the bombast of Sherman's

"Let us destroy Atlanta and make it a desolation" to the pathetic writing of a dying Confederate soldier at Gettysburg who dipped a twig in his own blood, scratching out a message to assure his father "I died with my face to the enemy."

This collection is a respectful remembrance of those who are telling us about their terrifying, yet hopeful, times in their own words: Americans on both sides who fought Americans in a war that freed Americans. And, back in the twenty-first century, I am indebted to the editorial staff of Oxford University Press, especially to Erin McKean for her enthusiasm and gifted guidance and to Georgia Maas for her good judgment and long hours spent on this project.

———————

Oxford University Press would like to thank Professor Donald R. Shaffer, of the University of Northern Colorado, and Mike Musick, of the National Archives, for their help as advisors to this work. Their suggestions and support are much appreciated. We are very grateful for the time and effort scholars dedicate to helping Oxford publish useful and worthwhile reference works.

The Oxford
Dictionary of
Civil War Quotations

Abbott, Henry

US CAPTAIN

The army generally didn't fight well. The new regiments behaved shamefully, as well **1**
as many of the old ones. The 15th Mass. was seized with a panic at nothing at all and
broke like sheep.
  —letter to his brother, December 17, 1862.

★ This was at the battle of Fredericksburg.

Adams, Charles Francis (1807–1886)

US MINISTER TO THE UNITED KINGDOM AND SON OF PRESIDENT JOHN QUINCY ADAMS

All equally see in the convulsion in America an era in the history of the world, out of **2**
which must come in the end a general recognition of the right of mankind to the produce of their labor and the pursuit of happiness.
  —letter to his son, Charles Francis Adams Jr., who was a captain in the Union
  army, December 25, 1862.

Adams, Charles Francis, Jr. (1838–1915)

US BRIGADIER GENERAL

I maintain that every man in the eleven states seceding from the Union had in 1861, **3**
whether he would or no, to decide for himself whether to adhere to his state or to
the nation; and I finally assert that, whichever way he decided, if only he decided
honestly, putting self-interest behind him, he decided right.
  —dedication speech for the Lee Memorial Chapel in Lexington, Virginia,
  January 7, 1907.

Agassiz, Louis (1807–1873)

ZOOLOGIST

I hope and trust that as soon as the condition of the Negro in the warmer parts of our **4**
states has been regulated according to the laws of freedom, the colored population
in the more northern parts of the country will diminish. By a natural consequence of
unconquerable affinities, the colored people in whom the Negro nature prevails will
tend toward the South, while the weaker and lighter ones will remain and die out
among us.
  —letter to Dr. Samuel Howe.

★ Agassiz was a Swiss-born professor of zoology at Harvard. Howe was a Boston
abolitionist.

Alcott, Louisa May (1832–1888)

WRITER

★ Alcott worked in the Union Hotel Hospital in Washington, D.C. (Georgetown). Her most famous work, *Little Women*, was published in 1868.

1   I've often longed to see a war, and now I have my wish. I long to be a man, but as I can't fight, I will content myself with working for those who can.
      —journal, April 1861.

2   The next hospital I enter will, I hope, be one for the colored regiments, as they seem to be proving their right to the admiration and kind offices of their white relations, who owe them so large a debt, a little part of which I shall be so proud to pay.
      —*Hospital Sketches*, 1863.

3   There they were: "our brave boys," as the papers justly call them, for cowards could hardly have been so riddled with shot and shell, so torn and shattered, nor have borne suffering for which we have no name, with an uncomplaining fortitude, which made one glad to cherish each as a brother.
      —*Hospital Sketches*, 1863.

      ★ Alcott is describing the wounded from the battle of Fredericksburg.

4   For a moment, I felt bitterly indignant at this seeming carelessness of the value of life, the sanctity of death; then consoled myself with the thought that, when the great muster roll was called, these nameless men might be promoted above many whose tall monuments record the barren honors they have won.
      —*Hospital Sketches*, 1863.

      ★ Alcott was saddened by the many lonely deaths of soldiers in her hospital after the battle of Fredericksburg.

Alden, James (1810–1877)

US NAVY CAPTAIN

5   Sunk by a torpedo! Assassination in its worst form!
      —official report, August 5, 1864.

      ★ Alden, captain of the USS *Brooklyn*, was commenting on the sinking of the USS *Tecumseh* that day at the battle of Mobile Bay, in which his ship participated. Torpedoes were underwater mines.

Alexander, Edward Porter (1835–1910)

CS BRIGADIER GENERAL

6   My people are going to war, and war for their liberty. If I don't come and bear my part they will believe me a coward—and I will feel that I am occupying the position of one. I must go and stand my chances.
      —quoted by William C. Davis in *Brothers in Arms*, 1995.

      ★ Alexander was then a lieutenant.

A chicken could not live in that field when we open on it.   1
  —quoted by Randall Bedwell in *Brink of Destruction*, 1999.

★ Alexander, then an artillery commander from Georgia, was referring to the battle of Fredericksburg on December 13, 1862.

We would be like rabbits and partridges in the bushes, and they could not scatter to   2 follow us.
  —quoted by Shelby Foote in *The Civil War*, vol. 3, 1958.

★ This was Alexander's proposal for General Robert E. Lee's troops to disband into the woods to avoid surrender; the proposal was rejected by Lee, who surrendered the same day, April 9, 1865.

Alfriend, Frank H. (1841–1887)

SOUTHERN LITERARY MESSENGER EDITOR

There is nothing whatever in the prospective condition of the Confederacy, either   3 political, commercial, or social, which forbids the sanguine expectation of a permanent advancement of the literary profession.
  —*Southern Literary Messenger*, May 1864.

★ Alfriend remarked on the lack of reading in the South but was correctly optimistic about the region's future literature.

Ammen, Jacob

US COLONEL

The Twenty-fourth Ohio Volunteer Infantry had seen the elephant several times,   4 and did not care about seeing him again unless necessary.
  —quoted by Bell Irvin Wiley in *The Life of Billy Yank*, 1952.

★ "See the elephant" meant to see a battle. It was also used more broadly to mean seeing the world.

Anderson, Robert (1805–1871)

US MAJOR

I abandoned Fort Moultrie because I was certain that if attacked my men must have   5 been sacrificed, and the command of the harbor lost. I spiked the guns and destroyed the carriages to keep the guns from being used against us. If attacked, the garrison would never have surrendered without a fight.
  —telegram to Secretary of War John B. Floyd, December 27, 1860.

★ Anderson, in command of forts in Charleston harbor, moved his troops from Fort Moultrie to the more distant Fort Sumter.

1   The governor of this State [South Carolina] sent down one of his aides to-day and demanded, "courteously, but peremptorily," that I should return my command [from Fort Sumter] to Fort Moultrie. I replied that I could not and would not do so. He stated that when the governor came into office he found that there was an understanding between his predecessor and the President that no re-enforcements were to be sent to any of these forts, and particularly to this one, and that I had violated this agreement by having re-enforced this fort. I remarked that I had not re-enforced this command, but that I had merely transferred my garrison from one fort to another, and that, as the commander of this harbor, I had a right to move my men into any fort I deemed proper.
    —telegram to the adjutant general, Colonel Samuel Cooper, December 27, 1860.

2   [The governor of South Carolina] knows not how entirely the city of Charleston is in my power. I can cut his communications off from the sea, and thereby prevent the reception of supplies, and close the harbor, even at night, by destroying the light-houses. Those things, of course, I would never do, unless compelled to do so in self-defense.
    —letter to the US War Department's adjutant general, Colonel Samuel Cooper, January 1, 1861.

    ★ Cooper soon became the Confederacy's adjutant general.

3   Two of your batteries fired this morning on an unarmed vessel bearing the flag of my government. As I have not been notified that war has been declared by South Carolina against the United States, I can not but think this a hostile act committed without your sanction or authority. Under that hope I refrain from opening a fire on your batteries. I have the honor, therefore, respectfully to ask whether the above-mentioned act—one which I believe without parallel in the history of our country or any other civilized government—was committed in obedience to your instructions, and notify you, if it is not disclaimed, that I regard it as an act of war and I shall not, after reasonable time for the return of my messenger, permit any vessel to pass within the range of the guns of my fort.
    —letter to South Carolina governor Francis Pickens, January 9, 1861.

    ★ Charleston's batteries had fired on the *Star of the West*, a New York steamship hired by the US government to take 200 soldiers to reinforce Fort Sumter, commanded by Major Anderson. The ship aborted the mission and returned to New York.

4   If we do not meet again on earth, I hope we may meet in Heaven.
    —quoted by Carl Sandburg in *Abraham Lincoln: The War Years*, 1939.

    ★ These were Anderson's last words to a Confederate delegation leaving Fort Sumter on April 15, 1861, before it was fired upon.

5   I have the honor to acknowledge the receipt of your communication demanding the evacuation of this fort [Sumter]; and to say in reply thereto that it is a demand with which I regret that my sense of honor and of my obligations to my government prevent my compliance.
    —message to CS brigadier general Pierre G. T. Beauregard.

Having defended Fort Sumter for thirty-four hours, until the quarters were entirely **1** burned, the main gates destroyed by fire, the gorge walls seriously injured, the magazine surrounded by flames, and its door closed from the effects of heat, four barrels and three cartridges of powder only being available, and no provisions remaining but pork, I accepted terms of evacuation offered by General Beauregard, being the same offered by him on the 11th instant, prior to the commencement of hostilities, and marched out of the fort Sunday afternoon, the 14th instant, with colors flying and drums beating, bringing away company and private property, and saluting my flag with fifty guns.

—dispatch to Secretary of War Simon Cameron.

God was pleased to guard my little force [at Fort Sumter] from the shell and shot **2** which were thrown into and against my work, and to Him are our thanks due that I am enabled to report that no one was serious injured by their fire. I regret that I have to add that, in consequence of some unaccountable misfortune, one man was killed, two seriously and three slightly wounded whilst saluting our flag as it was lowered.

—dispatch to the assistant adjutant general, Colonel Lorenzo Thomas.

Andrews, Eliza Frances (1840–1931)

Everybody is cast down and humiliated, and we are all waiting in suspense to know **3** what our cruel masters will do with us. . . . Till it comes, "Let us eat, drink and be merry, for tomorrow we die." Only, we have almost nothing to eat, and to drink, and still less to be merry about.

—*The War-Time Journal of a Georgia Girl, 1864–1865*, 1908.

★ Although Andrews's father had owned some two hundred slaves, he had opposed secession.

About three miles from Sparta we struck the "burnt country," as it is well named by **4** the natives, and then I could better understand the wrath and desperation of these poor people.

—quoted by John D. Wright in *The Language of the Civil War*, 2001.

★ Andrews was talking about the area burned by General William T. Sherman's troops as they marched through Georgia.

Andrews, William H.

CS SERGEANT

★ Andrews was a member of the 1st Georgia Infantry.

There is nothing on this green earth half so grand as the sight of soldiers moving into **5** action. A cavalry charge is superb; artillery dashing on the field carries you away; while the deadly infantry moving into the jaws of death causes you to hold your breath in admiration.

—quoted by Randall Bedwell in *Brink of Destruction*, 1999.

Anonymous

1   The President would like to have God on his side, but he must have Kentucky.
  —anonymous, quoted by Nathaniel W. Stephenson in *Lincoln: An Account of His Personal Life, Especially of Its Springs of Action as Revealed and Deepened by the Ordeal of War*, 1922.

  ★ This was a popular abolitionist saying.

2   We have pulled down the temple that has been built for three quarters of a century. We must now clear the rubbish away and reconstruct another. We are houseless and homeless. We must shelter ourselves from storms.
  —anonymous, quoted by Alfred H. Guernsey and Henry M. Alden in *Harper's Pictorial History of the Great Rebellion in the United States*, 1866.

  ★ This was said by a delegate to the South Carolina State Convention that adopted the Ordinance of Secession.

3   I, _____ _____, do solemnly swear that I will bear true allegiance to the United States of America, and that I will serve them honestly and faithfully against all their enemies and opposers whatsoever, and observe and obey the orders of the President of the United States, and the orders of the officers appointed over me according to the rules and articles for the government of the armies of the United States.
  —anonymous, quoted by John D. Wright in *The Language of the Civil War*, 2001.

  ★ This was the "oath of muster" taken by volunteers for the US Army. The Confederate oath was the same, replacing "United States" with "Confederate States" and changing "orders of the President of the United States" to "orders of the Confederate States."

4   We have no fear of your New York, Troy, Vermont, or Massachusetts men, but I own that we do not want to meet those red-legged devils around our houses or hen-coops.
  —anonymous Confederate soldier, quoted by US major general Joseph B. Carr in *Battles and Leaders of the Civil War*, vol. 2, 1888.

  ★ This private letter was sent in May 1861 to a member of the 5th New York Regiment, Captain Hiram Duryea's Zouaves, and read to all. Zouaves dressed in the fashion of the French Zouaves (Algerians in the French army), a uniform that included red trousers.

5   If we could only get one of the royal race of England to rule over us, we should be content.
  —anonymous, quoted in *Harper's Weekly*, June 22, 1861.

  ★ This quoted a report written on April 30 by William Howard Russell, the most famous war correspondent of the *Times* (London). He said that this was the sentiment he found "repeated to me over and over again" while touring the South.

6   The Virginia, marm? Why, of coase. They warn't no two ways o' thinkin' 'bout that ar rig'ment. They just *kivered* tharselves with glory!
  —anonymous, quoted by Constance Cary Harrison in *A Virginia Girl in the First Year of the War*, 1885.

★ This soldier, returning on July 18, 1861, from skirmishes before the first battle of Bull Run (first Manassas), was answering desperate questions from Richmond ladies.

We are always on the highest pinnacle of hope or in the lowest depths of despair.   **1**
—anonymous writer in the *New York Times*, August 21, 1861.

★ This referred to the editorial hyperbole of war coverage.

Souf Carolina is kinder mad at you Yankees.   **2**
—anonymous, quoted by Charles C. Coffin in *Four Years of Fighting*, 1866.

★ The speaker was an escaped slave with Union soldiers in the summer of 1861. Coffin was a correspondent for the *Boston Journal*.

Only two years and a but.   **3**
—anonymous, quoted by John D. Wright in *The Language of the Civil War*, 2001.

★ This was a popular reply given by Union soldiers in the first year of the war when asked how long they still had to serve. Normal enlistment was for three years, but most thought the war would end much quicker.

The war will be over by Christmas.   **4**
—anonymous, quoted by Stuart Berg Flexner in *I Hear America Talking*, 1976.

★ This was commonly said by soldiers in 1861.

The President is a do-nothing!   **5**
—anonymous, quoted by Nathaniel W. Stephenson in *The Day of the Confederacy: A Chronicle of the Embattled South*, 1919.

★ This was a common complaint during Confederate president Jefferson Davis's first year.

We will give our old clothes, hats, and boots to Greeley, if he will call for them. We   **6**
used to give these articles to the niggers he loved so well; but how much more appropriately can they be given to this nigger-worshipper in distress.
—anonymous writer in the *New York Herald*, December 4, 1861.

★ The *Herald* editorial mocked the competition, Horace Greeley and his *New York Tribune*, which was offering special subscription rates.

You have slain all my men and cattle; and you may take the battery and be damned.   **7**
—anonymous Confederate artillery chief, quoted by Richard B. Harwell in *The Confederate Reader: As the South Saw the War*, 1989.

★ This was said to US private W. W. Worthington during the battle of Shiloh.

Imagine all the earthquakes in the world, and all the thunder and lightnings together   **8**
in a space of two miles, all going off at once. That would be like it.
—anonymous US officer, quoted by Shelby Foote in *The Civil War*, vol. 1, 1958.

★ This was one of General Benjamin Butler's officers who observed the bombardments of Fort Jackson and Fort St. Philip below New Orleans by ships of the Union captain David Farragut on April 18, 1862.

1   Niggers is cheap.
     —anonymous, quoted by William Howard Russell in the *Times* (London),
     May 6, 1862.

     ★ Russell was reporting the only comment he overheard from buyers at a slave market
     in Montgomery, Alabama.

2   We feel bully!
     —anonymous Union soldiers, quoted in *Harper's Weekly*, May 7, 1862.

     ★ This was said to Major General George B. McClellan by members of the 4th
     Michigan after a skirmish near Cold Harbor, Virginia.

3   Gentlemen, we had the honor of being captured by Stonewall Jackson himself.
     —anonymous Union soldier, quoted by CS lieutenant general Daniel H. Hill in
     Battles and Leaders of the Civil War, vol. 2, 1888.

     ★ This was said by a Union soldier leading a small squad behind Confederate lines at
     Cold Harbor, Virginia, during the battle of Gaines's Mill on June 27, 1862. Jackson had
     encountered them alone and demanded their surrender.

4   I don't know.
     —anonymous soldiers of Major General Thomas J. "Stonewall" Jackson, quoted by
     Edward Lee Childe in *Life and Campaigns of General Lee*, 1875.

     ★ The troops were ordered to reply this way to any question asked them as they
     marched in the summer of 1862 before the Seven Days' battles. This was the only reply
     Jackson could elicit when he came upon one of his soldiers stealing cherries and asked
     his name and regiment.

5   The Yankees throwed them lamp-posts about too careless like.
     —anonymous Confederate soldier, quoted by CS lieutenant general Daniel H. Hill
     in *Battles and Leaders of the Civil War*, vol. 2, 1888.

     ★ This comment during the Seven Days' battles referred to the elongated shells fired
     by Union gunboats.

6   Boys, he's not much for looks, but if we'd had him we wouldn't have been caught in
     this trap!
     —anonymous, quoted by CS colonel Henry Kyd Douglas in *Battles and Leaders of
     the Civil War*, vol. 2, 1888.

     ★ This was a comment on September 15, 1862, by a surrendering Union soldier at
     Harper's Ferry as General Thomas J. "Stonewall" Jackson rode by.

7   I caught the pitch of that Minie just now; it was a swell from E flat to F, and as it dis-
     appeared in the distance the note retrograded to D, a very pretty change.
     —anonymous, quoted by Alexander Hunter in *Johnny Reb and Billy Yank*, 1905.

     ★ This Confederate soldier found music in the Minie balls flying at the battle of
     Antietam (Sharpsburg).

We hope and pray that you may be permitted by a kind Providence, after the war is   **1**
over, to return.

> —anonymous, quoted by Charles C. Coffin in *Century Magazine*, June 1886.

★ Coffin, a correspondent for the *Boston Journal*, found this inscription in a Bible resting on the chest of a dead Union soldier at the battle of Antietam (Sharpsburg).

I had no shoes. I tried to barefoot, but somehow my feet wouldn't callous. They just   **2**
kept bleeding. I found it so hard to keep up that though I had the heart of a patriot,
I began to feel I didn't have patriotic feet. Of course, I could have crawled on my
hands and knees, but then my hands would have got so sore I couldn't have fired my
rifle.

> —anonymous Confederate soldier, quoted by Helen Dorich Longstreet in *In the
> Path of Lee's "Old War Horse,"* 1917.

★ The soldier was explaining to his officer why he missed the battle of Antietam
(Sharpsburg).

Nothing has astonished Europe in modern times as the magnitude of the scale on   **3**
which the American republic carries on the war for the maintenance of its own
integrity. For the enormous expenditure of men and money, and the vastness of the
theater on which the military operations are conducted, there is no parallel in the
history of any European nation, not excepting even France, under the regime of
the elder Napoleon. There is no civil war to be compared with it in extent, either in
ancient or modern times.

> —anonymous writer of "The Financial Resources of the United States,"
> *Knickerbocker*, October 1862.

★ The *Knickerbocker* was a popular New York monthly magazine.

When the Civil War broke out, the country was in the very acme of prosperity; and   **4**
soon after the war shall have closed, the prosperity of the republic will rise to a
higher point than it ever did before.

> —anonymous writer of "The Financial Resources of the United States,"
> *Knickerbocker*, October 1862.

★ The *Knickerbocker* was a popular New York monthly magazine.

General Barksdale, my cow has just been killed in my stable by a shell. She is very   **5**
fat, and I don't want the Yankees to get her. If you will send someone down to
butcher her, you are welcome to the meat.

> —anonymous, quoted by CS major Robert Stiles in *Four Years under Marse
> Robert*, 1904.

★ This lady appeared at the headquarters of Brigadier General William Barksdale just
before Fredericksburg temporarily fell to Union forces on December 11, 1862.

I am sick and tired of this war, and I can see no prospects of having peace for a long   **6**
time to come. I don't think it ever will be stopped by fighting. The Yankees can't

whip us and we can never whip them, and I see no prospect of peace unless the Yankees themselves rebel and throw down their arms, and refuse to fight any longer.
—anonymous Confederate soldier, quoted by E. B. Long in *The Civil War Day by Day: An Almanac, 1861–1865,* 1971.

★ This was in a letter written after the battle of Stone's River at Murfreesboro, Tennessee, on January 2, 1863.

1   If we are got to be killed up for niggers then we will kill every nigger in this town.
—anonymous, quoted by Thomas Buckner in *A Thrilling Narrative from the Lips of the Sufferers of the Late Detroit Riot,* 1863.

★ Buckner, who was black, overheard this cry during an anti-Negro riot in Detroit on March 6, 1863.

2   Traitors—traitors—traitors, come and take the flag, the man of you who dares.
—anonymous Pennsylvania girl, quoted by Major General George E. Pickett in a letter to his future wife, Sally, June 24, 1863.

★ He was recalling an incident at Greencastle, Pennsylvania. As the Confederate army marched through town, a young girl came onto her porch wearing the US flag as an apron and yelled this. The men lifted their caps and cheered her. The surprised girl added, "Oh, I wish I had a rebel flag; I'd wave that too."

3   Men of the North! Pennsylvanians, Jerseymen, New Yorkers, New Englanders! The foe is at your doors! Are you true men or traitors? If you are patriots deserving to be free prove it by universal rallying, arming, and marching to meet the Rebel foe! Prove it now!
—anonymous writer in the *New York Tribune,* June 26, 1863.

★ This panic, also occurring in other Northern newspapers, was a response to Confederate troops invading Pennsylvania.

4   Would you mind shooting off the bands a bit?
—anonymous Pennsylvania girls, quoted by Major General George E. Pickett in a letter to his future wife, Sally, June 27, 1863.

★ These girls in Chambersburg, Pennsylvania, were watching the Confederate troops march by. The band did strike up ("shoot off") for them, but not their requested "Dixie."

5   If you can't feed us, you had better surrender us, horrible as the idea is, than suffer this noble army to disgrace themselves by desertion.
—anonymous letter to CS lieutenant general John C. Pemberton, June 28, 1863.

★ This appeal, sent during the siege of Vicksburg, was signed by "Many Soldiers."

6   Yes, it takes a damn big neck to hold his head.
—anonymous Confederate soldier, quoted by Douglas Southall Freeman in *R. E. Lee: A Biography,* vol. 3, 1934.

★ During the Confederate push into Pennsylvania, this was a response to a citizen at Chambersburg who noted that General Robert E. Lee had a large neck.

General Lee, I am a Union woman, yet I ask for bread and your autograph.   1
    —anonymous, quoted by Douglas Southall Freeman in *R. E. Lee: A Biography*,
    vol. 3, 1934.

★ This citizen of Chambersburg, Pennsylvania, had come to Lee's headquarters there
to ask for bread for the town's hungry and insisted on his autograph.

Jackson is not here!   2
    —anonymous Confederate soldier, quoted by Douglas Southall Freeman in
    R. E. Lee: A Biography, vol. 3, 1934.

★ This was a member of Lieutenant General Thomas J. "Stonewall" Jackson's old 2nd
Corps. He was complaining about Lieutenant General Richard S. Ewell, Jackson's
replacement, who was holding the troops uncertainly in Gettysburg.

Run ole hahr; if I was an ole hahr I would run, too.   3
    —anonymous Virginia soldier, quoted by Douglas Southall Freeman in *R. E. Lee:
    A Biography*, vol. 3, 1934.

★ He had spotted an old hare on the third day of the battle of Gettysburg, July 3, 1863.

"Uncle Robert" will get us into Washington yet; you bet he will.   4
    —anonymous Confederate soldier, quoted by Douglas Southall Freeman in
    R. E. Lee: A Biography, vol. 3, 1934.

★ He said this as Lee's troops were retreating at the battle of Gettysburg.

Dag-gone him, dag-gone him, dag-gone his old soul, I'm blamed ef I wouldn't be 5
dag-gone willin' to go right through it all and be killed again with them others to hear
Marse Robert [E. Lee], dag-gone him, say over again as how he grieved bout'n
we'all's losses and honored us for we'all's bravery! Darned ef I wouldn't.
    —anonymous Confederate soldier, quoted by Major General George E. Pickett in
    a letter to his future wife, Sally, July 12, 1863.

★ Pickett had just published to the troops Lee's letter of July 9, in which the general
praised their bravery at Gettysburg.

The war has entirely changed the American character. The lavish profusion in which 6
the old Southern cotton aristocracy used to indulge is completely eclipsed by the
dash, parade and magnificence of the new Northern shoddy aristocracy of this period.
Ideas of cheapness and economy are thrown to the winds. The individual who makes
the most money—no matter how—and spends the most money—no matter for
what—is considered the greatest man. To be extravagant is to be fashionable.
    —anonymous writer in the *New York Herald*, October 6, 1863.

The Constitution as it is and the Union as it was.   7
    —anonymous, quoted by Nathaniel W. Stephenson in *The Day of the
    Confederacy: A Chronicle of the Embattled South*, 1919.

★ This was a catchphrase of the peace movement in North Carolina in 1863.

1   Why, I expect sir, that if those miserable Yankees try to blockade us, and keep you from our cotton, you'll just send their ships to the bottom and acknowledge us.
—anonymous, quoted by William Howard Russell in *My Diary, North and South,* 1863.

★ This was said by a Charleston merchant to Russell, the most famous war correspondent of the *Times* (London).

2   I'm a little sorry I wasn't wounded in front; it looks cowardly to be hit in the back, but I obeyed orders, and it don't matter in the end, I know.
—anonymous Union soldier named John, quoted by Louisa May Alcott in *Hospital Sketches,* 1863.

★ This was said by a dying soldier wounded at the battle of Fredericksburg.

3   "Hallo, old Fits is off again!" "How are you, Rheumatiz?" "Will you trade apples, Rib?" "Miss P. may I give Typus a drink of this?" "Look here, No Toes, lend us a stamp, there's a good fellow," etc.
—anonymous soldier, quoted by Louisa May Alcott in *Hospital Sketches,* 1863.

★ She was describing comments of a patient who gave other hospitalized soldiers the names of their wounds and illnesses.

4   Lord! What a scramble there'll be for arms and legs, when we old boys come out of our graves, on Judgment Day: wonder if we shall get our own again? If we do, my leg will have to tramp from Fredericksburg, my arm from here, I suppose, and meet my body, wherever it may be.
—anonymous Union sergeant, quoted by Louisa May Alcott in *Hospital Sketches,* 1863.

5   Well, 'twas my fust [battle], you see, so I ain't ashamed to say I was a trifle flustered in the beginnin', there was such an all-fired racket; for ef there's anything I do spleen agin, it's noise. But when my mate, Eph Sylvester, caved, with a bullet through his head, I got mad, and pitched in, licketty cut. . . . Our part of the fight didn't last long, so a lot of us larked round Fredericksburg . . . and, fust thing I knew, a shell bust, right in front of us, and I keeled over, feelin' as if I was blowed higher'n a kite . . . Next day I was most as black as that darkey yonder, lickin' plates on the sly.
—anonymous Union soldier, quoted by Louisa May Alcott in *Hospital Sketches,* 1863.

6   My dear Miss, we do not want to take your horses; ours are much better; and besides it goes against our feelings, but military necessity requires this step, and we are merely the agents of unrelenting destiny.
—anonymous Union soldier, quoted in *Harper's Weekly,* March 26, 1864.

★ He was responding to a "very handsome lady, quite young" in Virginia who complained as he took her farm horses.

7   Lee to the rear!
—anonymous, quoted by Shelby Foote in *The Civil War,* vol. 3, 1958.

★ This chant went through the Confederate lines during the battle of the Wilderness on May 5, 1864, when General Robert E. Lee rode to join his troops pursuing Union soldiers across a field. A staff sergeant eventually persuaded him to remain behind.

Well, boys, the rest of us may have developed from monkeys; but I tell you none less **1** than a God could have made such a man as Marse Robert!
>—anonymous, quoted by Charles C. Jones Jr., in *Reminiscences of the Last Days, Death and Burial of General Henry Lee*, 1870.

★ This light discussion by Confederate soldiers of Darwin's theory was overheard at a campfire during the battle of Spotsylvania in May 1864.

There goes the Atlanta Express!   **2**
>—anonymous, quoted by John D. Wright in *The Language of the Civil War*, 2001.

★ This was the yell given by Major General William T. Sherman's troops when they fired a shell at Atlanta during the siege of that city in August 1864.

Great God! is it possible! Are these Yanks? Who ever supposed they would come **3** away down here in Alabama?
>—anonymous Southern planter, quoted by Major General William T. Sherman in *Memoirs of General W. T. Sherman*, revised edition, vol. 2, 1886.

★ A local man, south of Talladega, Alabama, made this comment to Brigadier General Lovell H. Rousseau. The planter had mistaken the Union troops for Confederate troops because they arrived in the summer of 1864 with their uniforms covered in gray dust.

Oh, hell! Don't you know that old Sherman carries a duplicate tunnel along?   **4**
>—anonymous Confederate soldier, quoted by Major General William T. Sherman in *Memoirs of General W. T. Sherman*, revised edition, vol. 2, 1886.

★ This overheard conversation at Kennesaw Mountain, Georgia, was reported to Sherman. The soldier was responding to news that Confederate troops had blown up the tunnel near Dalton to slow Sherman's progress.

We can go where the general can.   **5**
>—anonymous, quoted by Thomas B. Van Horne in *Army of the Cumberland*, 1875.

★ This was shouted by troops near US major general David S. Stanley as they watched him charge forward during the battle of Franklin, Tennessee, on November 30, 1864. Van Horne was chaplain of the 13th Ohio Regiment.

Give us something to eat, Massa Jeff.   **6**
>—anonymous, quoted by John D. Wright in *The Language of the Civil War*, 2001.

★ This was heard by Confederate president Jefferson Davis as he passed troops on Missionary Ridge at Chattanooga, Tennessee, in November 1864. "Massa" was the plantation term for "master," often used in an affectionate way by soldiers.

Ain't we in a hell of a fix: a one-eyed President, a one-legged general, and a one- **7** horse Confederacy!
>—anonymous, quoted by John D. Wright in *The Language of the Civil War*, 2001.

★ This was uttered by a Confederate soldier in General John B. Hood's army as they retreated in December 1864 from defeat at the battle of Nashville. (President Jefferson Davis was virtually blind in one eye and Hood had lost a leg at the battle of Chickamauga.)

1   Blackguard and buffoon as [Lincoln] is, he has pursued his end with an energy as untiring as an Indian and a singleness of purpose that might almost be called patriotic.
—anonymous writer in the *Charleston Mercury*, January 10, 1865.

2   Let the sword have no more bloody work to do. If nothing but reunion can be had, let it come, lest a worse fate befall us.
—anonymous Confederate soldiers' letter to Confederate president Jefferson Davis, February 5, 1865.
★ They signed the letter "Many Soldiers."

3   Army! do you call this mob of retreating cowards an army? Soldiers! if you are soldiers, why don't you stand and fight the savage wolves that are coming upon us defenseless women and children?
—anonymous, quoted by CS major Robert Stiles in *Four Years under Marse Robert*, 1903.
★ Stiles was scolded by a young woman in the countryside as General Lee's army retreated from Petersburg, Virginia.

4   No! you all will drink hot blood before you all get thar!
—anonymous woman, quoted by US private Warren Lee Goss in *Recollections of a Private: A Story of the Army of the Potomac*, 1890.
★ This Virginia woman was responding to Goss's hope that Union forces could take Richmond without much fighting (to alleviate her worry about her son in the Confederate army). Goss was with the 2nd Massachusetts Regiment.

5   Look here, Yank; you *guess*, do you, that we fellows are going home to stay? Maybe we are. But don't be giving us any of your impudence. If you do, we'll come back and lick you again.
—anonymous, quoted by CS major general John B. Gordon in *Reminiscences of the Civil War*, 1904.
★ Gordon overheard this just after the surrender at Appomattox Court House. The Confederate soldier was reacting to a Union soldier's comment: "Well, Johnny, I guess you fellows will go home now to stay."

6   There is no doubt that if Mr. Lincoln had lived that his terms of amnesty to the Southern people would have been far more liberal than any his successor has yet proposed. Even Jefferson Davis and the leaders of the rebellion who are now incarcerated would have been permitted to escape the country. "With malice toward none and charity for all" was the spirit which would have animated Mr. Lincoln in his treatment of the rebellion after its military power had been crushed and the whole people subjugated.
—anonymous writer in the *Indianapolis Daily State Sentinel*, October 6, 1865.
★ The *Sentinel* was a Democratic newspaper.

7   Unless something is done [about worthless receipts given farmers for impressed crops and supplies] and that speedily, there will be thousands of the best citizens of the state and heretofore as loyal as any in the Confederacy, that will not care one cent which army is victorious in Georgia.
—anonymous, quoted by Nathaniel W. Stephenson in *The Day of the Confederacy: A Chronicle of the Embattled South*, 1919.

★ This was in an 1865 letter from Griffin, Georgia, to Confederate president Jefferson Davis.

We, the old servants and tenants of our beloved master, Honorable Jefferson Davis, **1** have cause to mingle our tears over his death, who was always so kind and thoughtful of our peace and happiness. We extend to you our humble sympathy.
    —anonymous "Thirteen Negroes," quoted by Hudson Strode in *Jefferson Davis: Tragic Hero*, 1964.

★ This note was sent to Davis's wife, Varina, after his death on December 5, 1889.

The Yankees are nothing but old scrubs. **2**
    —anonymous, quoted by Charles C. Coffin in *Four Years of Fighting*, 1866.

★ This opinion was given by a ten-year-old Virginia girl to Coffin, a correspondent for the *Boston Journal*.

Boys, look out! Here comes old Stonewall or an old hare! **3**
    —anonymous Confederate soldiers, quoted by Lieutenant Colonel G. F. R. Henderson in *Stonewall Jackson and the American Civil War*, vol. 2, 1898.

★ This was a favorite shout among General Thomas J. "Stonewall" Jackson's marching troops when they could hear a cheer down the line. Hares were greatly prized as a nourishing meal.

Here comes the cavalry, but what's that gun tied to the tail for? **4**
    —anonymous, quoted by CS brigadier general Gilbert Moxley Sorrel in *Recollections of a Confederate Staff Officer*, 1905.

★ This refrain would come from marching soldiers of the Army of Northern Virginia, when artillery horses would pass pulling their guns.

Fire at the fellow on the white horse. **5**
    —anonymous, quoted by CS brigadier general Gilbert Moxley Sorrel in *Recollections of a Confederate Staff Officer*, 1905.

★ This was a popular saying among Confederate soldiers in the Army of Northern Virginia.

Cotton is king! **6**
    —anonymous, quoted by Nathaniel W. Stephenson in *The Day of the Confederacy: A Chronicle of the Embattled South*, 1919.

★ This was a popular expression in the South, expressing hope that pressure from Britain, which needed cotton for its mills, would break the Union blockade of Confederate ports.

Why, you old fool, that's the Cabinet that is a-settin', and them thar big feet are ole **7** Abe's.
    —anonymous White House gardener, quoted by Nathaniel W. Stephenson in *Lincoln: An Account of His Personal Life, Especially of Its Springs of Action as Revealed and Deepened by the Ordeal of War*, 1922.

★ The gardener was responding to a query by the Reverend Robert Collyer who, while strolling through the White House grounds, noticed three pairs of feet resting on the ledge of an open window of the building.

1   Make it "Victory or Damned Badly Wounded," and I'm your huckleberry!
—anonymous, quoted by Lloyd Lewis in *Sherman, Fighting Prophet*, 1932.

★ This was the supposed comment of Mexican War veterans when they saw "Victory or Death" banners in Indiana towns.

2   The Civil War was a battle of ideas interrupted by artillery.
—anonymous, quoted by E. B. Long in *The Civil War Day by Day: An Almanac, 1861–1865*, 1971.

★ This was said by a Union soldier who served in Missouri.

3   I fights mit Sigel.
—anonymous, quoted by Mark Boatner III in *The Civil War Dictionary*, 1988.

★ This declaration became the boast and slogan of thousands of German-born soldiers who served under US major general Franz Sigel, a German native and graduate of the German Military Academy.

4   We thought at first [the USS *Monitor*] was a raft on which one of the *Minnesota's* boilers was being taken to shore for repairs.
—anonymous Confederate sailor, quoted by James M. McPherson in *The Battle Cry for Freedom: The Civil War Era*, 1989.

★ This was the first time that this sailor and his *Virginia* shipmates saw the Union's ironclad ship.

5   We will go home, make three more crops, and try them again.
—anonymous Confederate soldier, quoted by William C. Davis in *Brothers in Arms*, 1995.

6   I fired a cannon. I hope I never kill any one.
—anonymous North Carolina artilleryman, quoted by William C. Davis in *Brothers in Arms*, 1995.

7   Invincible in peace and invisible in war.
—anonymous, quoted by John D. Wright in *The Language of the Civil War*, 2001.

★ This was a popular description of certain politicians and soldiers. Union colonel James E. Mulligan, commander of the 23rd Illinois, called Missouri troops "in peace invincible; in war invisible."

8   It takes a man's weight in lead for every soldier killed in battle.
—anonymous, quoted by John D. Wright in *The Language of the Civil War*, 2001.

★ This was a popular saying.

9   My pen is bad, my ink is pale; my love for you shall never fail.
—anonymous, quoted by John D. Wright in *The Language of the Civil War*, 2001.

★ This was a popular phrase used by soldiers to end a letter.

Pope's headquarters is where his hindquarters belong.   **1**
    —anonymous, quoted by John D. Wright in *The Language of the Civil War*, 2001.

★ This became a popular saying among Union soldiers because Major General John Pope supposedly had been asked by a journalist where his headquarters was, and answered "In the saddle." Pope denied ever saying this.

That's somebody's darling.   **2**
    —anonymous, quoted by John D. Wright in *The Language of the Civil War*, 2001.

★ This was a popular saying among marching soldiers on both sides when they encountered a dead soldier. It was derived from sentimental song.

Armistead, Lewis A. (1817–1863)

CS BRIGADIER GENERAL

I have been a Soldier all my life—I was an officer in the Army of the U.S., which service I left to fight for my own country, and for, and with, my own People—and because they were right, and oppressed.   **3**
    —letter to Samuel Cooper, December 21, 1861.

Boys, do you think you can go up under that? It is pretty hot out there.   **4**
    —quoted by Douglas Southall Freeman in *R. E. Lee: A Biography*, vol. 3, 1934.

★ He said this to his brigade after pulling damaged wood off a tree just hit by a shell at Gettysburg on July 3, 1863. He was referring to the upcoming Pickett's charge, in which he was mortally wounded.

Armistead, Z. J.

CS SOLDIER

The Yankees keep Shooting so I am afraid they will knock over my ink so I will close.   **5**
    —letter to his brother.

★ Armistead was writing from Atlanta during the siege.

Aubrey, Cullen B.

They went like gingerbread at a state fair.   **6**
    —*Reflections of a Newsboy in the Army of the Potomac*, 1904.

★ Aubrey, a young newspaper seller, was referring to copies of the *Philadelphia Inquirer* that he sold to Union troops at Gettysburg. It described the first day of the battle they were still engaged in.

Autry, James L.

CS LIEUTENANT COLONEL

1   Mississippians don't know, and refuse to learn, how to surrender to an enemy. If Commodore Farragut and Brigadier General Butler can teach them, let them come and try.
   —letter to US commander S. Phillips Lee, May 18, 1862.

   ★ Autry, of the 27th Mississippi Regiment, was the military governor and post commandant at Vicksburg. Lee had demanded that he surrender the city.

Averell, William W.

US MAJOR GENERAL

2   Over five thousand dead and wounded men were on the ground in every attitude of distress. A third of them were dead or dying, but enough were alive and moving to give to the field a singular crawling effect.
   —quoted by James M. McPherson in *The Battle Cry of Freedom: The Civil War Era*, 1989.

   ★ He was describing the morning after the battle of Malvern Hill, Virginia, on July 1, 1862.

Avery, Isaac E. (?–1863)

MEMBER OF THE 6TH NORTH CAROLINA REGIMENT

3   Major, tell my father that I died with my face to the enemy.
   —quoted in the *Atlanta Journal*, April 12, 1931.

   ★ Avery wrote these words to Major Samuel M. Tare, after being mortally wounded on July 2, 1863, during the battle of Gettysburg. He used a twig dipped in his blood to scratch the words on a rough piece of paper kept in his pocket.

Bailey, Franklin

US PRIVATE

4   I did not think any more of seeing a man shot down by my side than you would of seeing a dumb beast kiled. Strange as it may seam to you, but the more men I saw kiled the more reckless I became.
   —letter to his parents, April 8, 1862.

   ★ This was written a day after the battle of Shiloh.

Baker, Edward Dickinson (1811–1861)

US SENATOR FROM OREGON

The hour of conciliation has passed, the gathering for battle is at hand, and the coun- 1
try requires that every man shall do his duty.
> —speech at the Union Meeting in Union Square, New York City, April 20, 1861.

I am not here to speak timorous words of peace, but to kindle the spirit of manly, 2
determined war.
> —speech at the Union Meeting in Union Square, New York City, April 20, 1861.

Civil War, for the best of reasons upon the one side and the worst upon the other, is 3
always dangerous to liberty, always fearful, always bloody; but, fellow-citizens, there
are yet worse things than fear, than doubt and dread, and danger and blood. Dishonor is worse. Perpetual anarchy is worse. States forever commingling and forever
severing are worse. Traitors and secessionists are worse.
> —speech at the Union Meeting in Union Square, New York City, April 20, 1861.

Baldwin, Samuel Davies

METHODIST MINISTER IN TENNESSEE

Providence has kept the negro race in a state of singular satisfaction with its lot in the 4
South.
> —*Dominion*, 1858.

Ballou, Sullivan (1827–1861)

US MAJOR

I have, I know, but few and small claims upon Divine Providence, but something 5
whispers to me . . . that I shall return to my loved ones unharmed. If I do not my
dear Sarah, never forget how much I love you, and when my last breath escapes me
on the battle field, it will whisper your name. . . . Sarah do not mourn me dead; think
I am gone and wait for thee; for we shall meet again.
> —letter to his wife, July 14, 1861.

★ Ballou, of the 2nd Rhode Island Volunteers, was killed seven days later at the first
battle of Bull Run (first Manassas).

Banks, Nathaniel P. (1816–1894)

US MAJOR GENERAL

The enemy is weak, demoralised, and depressed. 6
> —quoted by Lieutenant Colonel G. F. R. Henderson in *Stonewall Jackson and the
> American Civil War*, vol. 1, 1898.

★ This was said on February 27, 1862, and Banks then defeated Major General Thomas J. "Stonewall" Jackson's troops on March 23 at Kernstown, Virginia.

1   It is impossible to anticipate what work lies before us; I feel the imperative necessity of making preparations for the worst.
    —quoted by US major general Nathan Kimball in *Battles and Leaders of the Civil War*, vol. 2, 1888.

★ This was said about two weeks before General Thomas J. "Stonewall" Jackson routed Banks's 9,000 men with only 1,500 of his own in the Shenandoah Valley on May 23, 1862.

2   By God, sir! I will not retreat. We have more to fear from the opinions of our friends than the bayonets of our enemies!
    —quoted by Shelby Foote in *The Civil War*, vol. 1, 1958.

★ Banks gave this indignant answer on May 23, 1862, to Colonel George H. Gordon, who had suggested a retreat after losing the battle of Front Royal, Virginia, that day to General Thomas J. "Stonewall" Jackson. Soon afterward, Banks retreated.

3   Their conduct was heroic. No troops could be more determined or more daring. . . . The highest commendation is bestowed upon them by all the officers in command on the right. Whatever doubt may have existed before as to the efficiency of organizations of this character, the history of this day proves conclusively to those who were in a condition to observe the conduct of these regiments, that the Government will find in this class of troops effective supporters and defenders.
    —letter to Major General Henry W. Halleck, May 30, 1863.

★ Banks was praising Negro troops of the 2nd Louisiana regiment, made up of freed slaves, for their part in an unsuccessful attack on Port Hudson, Louisiana, on May 27, 1863.

4   We must constantly feel the enemy, know where he is, and what he is doing. Vigilance, activity, and a precaution that has a considerable mixture of audacity in it will carry you through many difficulties.
    —quoted by Lieutenant Colonel G. F. R. Henderson in *Stonewall Jackson and the American Civil War*, vol. 2, 1898.

Banks, Robert W.

CS PRIVATE

5   If I ever lose my patriotism, and the "secesh" spirit dies out, then you may know the "Commissary" is at fault. Corn meal mixed with water and tough beef three times a day will knock the "Brave Volunteer" under quicker than Yankee bullets.
    —letter home, October 22, 1862.

Barker, Thomas E.

US CAPTAIN

I will not take my regiment in another such charge if Jesus Christ himself should **1**
order it!
—quoted by Randall Bedwell in *Brink of Destruction*, 1999.

★ This was said during the battle of the Wilderness in Virginia, which ended on May 7,
1864.

Barksdale, William (1821–1863)

CS BRIGADIER GENERAL

Tell my wife I am shot, but we fought like hell.   **2**
—quoted by Randall Bedwell in *Brink of Destruction*, 1999.

★ Barksdale said this on July 2, 1863, during the battle of Gettysburg, and died the next
day of his wound.

Barnum, Henry A.

US MAJOR GENERAL

Tell my wife that in my last thoughts were blended herself, my boy, and my flag. . . . **3**
God bless the old fla—.
—quoted by Major General Fitz John Porter in *Battles and Leaders of the Civil
War*, vol. 2, 1888.

★ After these words during the battle of Malvern Hill on July 1, 1862, the wounded and
lifeless Major Barnum was presumed dead. He later recovered to become a major general.

Bartlett, Asa W.

CAPTAIN

It was the first blast of the cyclone that swept the Eleventh Corps from its position **4**
on the right of the Union line like chaff from a threshing floor.
—*History of the Twelfth Regiment New Hampshire Volunteers*, 1897.

★ This referred to an attack by Lieutenant General Thomas J. "Stonewall" Jackson's
regiment on May 2, 1863, the second day of the battle of Chancellorsville.

Barton, Clara (1821–1912)

US NURSE

While our soldiers fight, I can stand and feed and nurse them. My place is anywhere **5**
between the bullet and the battlefield.
—quoted by Randall Bedwell in *Brink of Destruction*, 1999.

★ Barton made this observation during the battle of the Wilderness (May 5–7, 1864).

1   General Sherman was right when addressing an assemblage of cadets he told them war was Hell! Deck it as you will, it is this, and whoever has looked active war full in the face has caught some glimpses of regions as infernal, as he may ever fear to see.
—quoted by Percy H. Epler in *The Life of Clara Barton: The Angel of the Battlefield*, 1915.

2   I shall not essay to enlighten you upon the subject of war. Were I to attempt it, I should doubtless miserably fail, for it has long been said, as to amount to an adage, that "women don't know anything about war." I wish men didn't either. They have always known a great deal too much about it for the good of their kind. They have worshipped at Valkyria's shrine, and followed her siren lead, till it has cost a million times more than the whole world is worth, poured out the best blood and crushed the fairest forms the good God has created.
—quoted by Percy H. Epler in *The Life of Clara Barton: The Angel of the Battlefield*, 1915.

3   If I were to speak of war, it would not be to show you the glories of conquering armies but the mischief and misery they strew in their tracks; and how, while they marched on with tread of iron and plumes proudly tossing in the breeze, some one must follow closely in their steps, crouching to the earth, toiling in the rain and darkness, shelterless themselves, with no thought of pride or glory, fame or praise, or reward; hearts breaking with pity, faces bathed in tears and hands in blood. This is the side which history never shows.
—quoted by Kenneth C. Davis in *Don't Know Much about the Civil War*, 1996.

Bartow, Francis (?–1861)

CS BRIGADIER GENERAL

4   They have killed me, boys, but never give up the fight.
—quoted by Brigadier General Gilbert Moxley Sorrel in *Recollections of a Confederate Staff Officer*, 1905.

★ These were the last words of Bartow, who was killed at the first battle of Bull Run (first Manassas).

Bayard, James A. (1799–1880)

US SENATOR FROM DELAWARE

5   The sole cause of the existing disunion excitement which is about to break up the government is the war which has been carried on for years past by all manner of devices by the antislavery fanatical sentiment upon more than $2,000,000,000 of property.
—letter to his son, December 12, 1860.

Beatty, John (1828–1914)

US BRIGADIER GENERAL

When returning from the front I met a soldier of the Thirty-seventh Indiana, trudg-   1
ing along with his gun on his shoulder. I asked him where he was going; he replied
that his father lived four miles beyond, and he just heard that his brother was home
from the Southern army on sick leave, and he was going to take him prisoner.
—*The Citizen Soldier; or, Memoirs of a Volunteer*, 1879.

★ Beatty began with the 3rd Ohio Volunteer Infantry, and after the war he was a US
congressman.

Beauregard, Pierre G. T. (1818–1893)

CS BRIGADIER GENERAL

★ [See also quotations at Joseph E. Johnston.]

I am ordered by the government of the Confederate States to demand the evacua-   2
tion of Fort Sumter. . . . All proper facilities will be afforded for the removal of yourself and command, together with company arms and property, and all private
property, to any post in the United States which you may elect. The flag which you
have upheld so long and with so much fortitude, under the most trying circumstances, may be saluted by you on taking it down.
—message to Major Robert Anderson, April 11, 1861.

★ Anderson was commander of the fort.

I have the honor to send you . . . the flag which waved on Fort Moultrie during the   3
bombardment of Fort Sumter, and was thrice cut by the enemy's balls. Being the
first Confederate flag thus baptized, I have thought it worth sending to the War
Department for preservation.
—letter to Confederate adjutant general Samuel Cooper, who had recently been
the US War Department's adjutant general, May 1, 1861.

All rules of civilized warfare are abandoned, and they proclaim by their acts, if not   4
on their banners, that their war-cry is "BEAUTY AND BOOTY." All that is dear to
man—your honor and that of your wives and daughters—your fortunes and your
lives, are involved in this momentous contest.
—proclamation, June 1, 1861.

★ The proclamation was issued to warn Virginians about the Union army's invasion.

A reckless and unprincipled tyrant has invaded your soil. Abraham Lincoln, regard-   5
less of all moral, legal, and constitutional restraints, has thrown his Abolitionist hosts
among you, who are murdering and imprisoning your citizens, confiscating and
destroying your property, and committing other acts of violence and outrage, too
shocking and revolting to humanity to be enumerated.
—quoted by Kenneth C. Davis in *Don't Know Much about the Civil War*, 1996.

★ This was said on June 1, 1861.

1   If I could only get the enemy to attack me, as I am trying to have him do, I would stake my reputation on the handsomest victory that could be hoped for.
　　　—letter to Louis T. Wigfall, July 8, 1861.

　　★ This was two weeks before the Confederate victory at the first battle of Bull Run (first Manassas). Wigfall, a former US senator, was later a Confederate brigadier general and congressman.

2   We want cannon as greatly as any people who ever, as history tells you, melted their church-bells to supply them; and I, your general, entrusted with the command of the army embodied of your sons, your kinsmen and your neighbors, do now call on you to send your plantation-bells to the nearest railroad depot, subject to my order, to be melted into cannon for the defence of your plantations.
　　　—order, March 8, 1862.

3   Men of the South! Shall our mothers, our wives, our daughters and our sisters, be thus outraged by the ruffianly soldiers of the North, to whom is given the right to treat, at their pleasure, the ladies of the South as common harlots? Arouse friends, and drive back from our soil, those infamous invaders of our homes and disturbers of our family ties.
　　　—General Order No. 44, May 19, 1862.

　　★ This was Beauregard's answer to Major General Benjamin Butler's order for his troops occupying New Orleans to regard any disrespectful woman as a prostitute.

4   If England would join the South at once, the Southern armies, relieved of the present blockade and enormous Yankee pressure, would be able to march right into the northern states.
　　　—quoted by British lieutenant colonel Arthur James Lyon Fremantle in *Three Months in the Southern States: April-June 1863*, 1863.

　　★ The general said this to Fremantle, an observer with the Confederate army.

Bee, Gernard Elliott (1824–1861)

CS BRIGADIER GENERAL

5   Let us determine to die here, and we will conquer. There is Jackson standing like a stone wall. Rally behind the Virginians!
　　　—quoted in *The Annals of America*, vol. 9, 1968.

　　★ Bee's observation was made during the first battle of Bull Run (first Manassas), July 21, 1861, as he watched the bravery of Brigadier General Thomas J. "Stonewall" Jackson's brigade. On May 30, 1863, the brigade became the only one given an official Confederate nickname: the Stonewall Brigade.

Beecher, Henry Ward (1813–1887)

BROOKLYN PREACHER AND ABOLITIONIST

　　★ Beecher was the brother of Harriet Beecher Stowe, the author of *Uncle Tom's Cabin*.

Not a spark of genius has [Lincoln]; not an element for leadership. Not one particle **1** of heroic enthusiasm.
    —quoted by Carl Sandburg in *Abraham Lincoln: The War Years*, 1939.

The soil has drunk blood and is glutted; millions mourn for millions slain, or, envy- **2** ing the dead, pray for oblivion; towns and villages have been razed; fruitful fields have turned back to wilderness. It came to pass, as the prophet said: *The sun was turned to darkness and the moon to blood.*
    —speech at the ceremonial raising of the US flag at Fort Sumter, April 14, 1865.

★ On this same day, Lincoln was assassinated.

Faint is the echo; but it is coming; we now hear it sighing sadly through the pines, **3** but it shall yet break in thunder upon the shore—no North, no West, no South, but the United States of America!
    —speech at the ceremonial raising of the US flag at Fort Sumter, April 14, 1865.

We have shown by all that we have suffered in war how great is our estimate of the importance of the Southern States to this Union, and we will honor that estimate now in peace by still greater exertions for their rebuilding.
    —speech at the ceremonial raising of the US flag at Fort Sumter, April 14, 1865.

They who refuse education to the black man would turn the South into a vast poor- **4** house, and labor into a pendulum incessantly vibrating between poverty and indo- lence.
    —speech at the ceremonial raising of the US flag at Fort Sumter, April 14, 1865.

There is scarcely a man born in the South who has lifted his hand against this ban- **5** ner, but had a father who would have died for it.
    —speech at the ceremonial raising of the US flag at Fort Sumter, April 14, 1865.

And now the martyr is moving in triumphal march, mightier than when alive. The **6** nation rises up at every stage of his coming. Cities and States are his pallbearers, and the cannon speaks the hours with solemn progression.
    —quoted by Colonel Alexander K. McClure in *Lincoln's Yarns and Stories*, 1904.

★ This was part of Beecher's eulogy for Lincoln.

Pass on, thou that hast overcome. Ye people, behold the martyr whose blood, as so **7** many articulate words, pleads for fidelity, for law, for liberty.
    —quoted by Colonel Alexander K. McClure in *Lincoln's Yarns and Stories*, 1904.

★ This was part of Beecher's eulogy for Lincoln.

Bell, John T.

US LIEUTENANT
    ★ Bell was a member of the 2nd Iowa Regiment.

1   In places dead men lay so closely that a person could walk over two acres of ground and not step off the bodies.
—*Tramps and Triumphs of the Second Infantry, Briefly Sketched*, 1886.

★ This was at the battle of Shiloh.

Belmont, August

DEMOCRATIC PARTY CHAIRMAN

2   Four years of misrule by a sectional, fanatical, and corrupt party have brought our country to the very verge of ruin.
—quoted by John G. Nicolay and John Hay in *Abraham Lincoln: A History*, 1914.

★ Belmont was addressing the Democratic National Convention in August 1864.

Benjamin, Israel (1818–1864)

MOLDAVIAN WRITER

3   The present situation in the Northern states—the misfortunes that they have suffered, blow upon blow, at the beginning of the war just broken out—has encouraged the enemies of the American Constitution to condemn it utterly and to represent it as a vain effort.
—*Drei Jahre in Amerika 1859–1862*, vol. 1, 1863.

★ The two-volume work by Benjamin was translated by Charles Reznikoff and published in 1956 as *Three Years in America 1859–1862*.

4   Future generations will be astounded to learn from history that from 400,000 to 500,000 volunteers took up arms to defend the Constitution of their land and that nowhere could this most enlightened people find a man to lead these mighty columns, this mountain rolling onward to victory, so that it might in a short time shatter its weaker opponent, and that immigrant Germans and Irish had to be summoned to act as spearhead.
—*Drei Jahre in Amerika 1859–1862*, vol. 1, 1863.

Benjamin, Judah P. (1811–1884)

US SENATOR FROM LOUISIANA AND, LATER, CS SECRETARY OF WAR AND SECRETARY OF STATE

5   What may be the fate of this horrible contest none can foretell; but this much I will say—the fortunes of war may be adverse to our arms; you may carry desolation into our peaceful land, and with torch and firebrand may set our cities in flames; you may even emulate the atrocities of those who in the days of our Revolution hounded on the bloodthirsty savage; you may give the protection of your advancing armies to the furious fanatics who desire nothing more than to add the horrors of servile insurrection to civil war; you may do this and more, but you never can subjugate us; you

never can subjugate the free sons of the soil into vassals paying tribute to your power; you can never degrade them into a servile and inferior race—never, never, never!
　　—speech to the Senate, December 31, 1860.

It is of no use to re-enforce [Johnston], he is not going to fight.　**1**
　　—quoted by Rod Graff in *Civil War Quiz and Fact Book*, 1985.

★ This criticism of Major General Joseph E. Johnston came as Johnston avoided direct conflict with the troops of Major General William T. Sherman in Georgia. Although others admired Johnston's maneuvers against an overwhelming force, he was soon relieved of his command by President Jefferson Davis.

Bennett, James Gordon (1795–1872)

NEW YORK HERALD FOUNDER AND EDITOR

But we must recollect that Mr. Davis is a soldier, a graduate of West Point, a hero of　**2** the Mexican War and a statesman of military turn of mind. Mr. Lincoln was a splitter of rails, a distiller of whisky, a storyteller and a joke maker. He afterwards became a stump orator, and used his early experiences as his literary capital. Now we have the rails abandoned, the whisky still stopped, but the scent of both hangs about the manner and the matter of his speeches.
　　—editorial, *New York Herald*, February 19, 1861.

The other President, Mr. Davis, has been received with the greatest enthusiasm during　**3** his journey from Mississippi to Montgomery, Ala. He made five and twenty speeches en route, but we do not hear that he told any stories, cracked any jokes, asked the advice of young women about his whiskers, or discussed political platforms.
　　—editorial, *New York Herald*, February 19, 1861.

Lincoln has proved a failure; McClellan has proved a failure; Fremont has proved a　**4** failure; let us have a new candidate.
　　—quoted by Colonel Alexander K. McClure in *Lincoln's Yarns and Stories*, 1904.

★ All three men had already been nominated for the 1864 presidential election.

Benning, Henry L. (1814–1875)

CS BRIGADIER GENERAL

General Hood killed, my horse killed, my brigade torn to pieces, and I haven't a man　**5** left.
　　—quoted by Lieutenant General James Longstreet in *From Manassas to Appomattox: Memoirs of the Civil War in America*, 1896.

★ Benning said this to Longstreet at the battle of Chickamauga, during which he had two horses killed while riding them.

Bertha

1   I must tell you how shamefully Gen. Wheeler's men acted. Though they have a widespread reputation of being the greatest horse thieves in the country, they never acted worse than they have recently. While the enemy were burning and destroying property, on one side of Briar creek, they were stealing horses, and mules on the other.
—letter to the *Countryman*, January, 1865.

★ The letter writer lived in Screven County, Georgia. Other Southerners had complained that Major General Joseph Wheeler's raiders were as feared as the Yankees.

Bickerdyke, Mary Ann "Mother" (1817–1901)

US SANITARY COMMISSION AGENT

2   You believe yourselves very generous and think because you have voted this petty sum [to the Ladies' Aid Society] you are doing all that is required of you. But I have in my hospital a hundred poor soldiers who have done more than any of you. Who of you would contribute a leg, an arm or an eye, instead of what you have done?
—speech to the Milwaukee Chamber of Commerce.

Bierce, Ambrose (1842–1914?)

US SERGEANT MAJOR

★ Bierce was a member of the 9th Indiana Regiment.

3   During the first day's fighting, wide tracts of woodland were burned . . . and scores of wounded who might have recovered perished in slow torture.
—*What I Saw at Shiloh*, 1881.

★ Bierce later became a famous short-story writer and journalist.

Billings, John D. (1842–1933)

US ARTILLERYMAN

★ Billings was an artilleryman with the Army of the Potomac.

4   It is interesting to note that in 1861 and '62 men were mainly examined to establish their *fitness* for service; in 1863 and '64 the tide had changed, and they were then only anxious to prove their *unfitness*.
—*Hard Tack and Coffee*, 1887.

Blenker, Louis (1812–1863)

US BRIGADIER GENERAL

5   Ordinanz numero eins!
—quoted by John D. Wright in *The Language of the Civil War*, 2001.

★ This mock, meaning "Ordinance No. 1," was proclaimed by Blenker, a native German, when he wanted champagne served.

Blunt, James (1826–1881)

US MAJOR GENERAL

The question that negroes will fight is settled; besides, they make better soldiers in **1** every respect than any troops I have ever had under my command.
　　—letter to a friend, July 27, 1863.

★ This referred to the actions eight days before of the 1st Kansas Regiment of colored soldiers during the battle of Honey Springs in Indian Territory (Oklahoma).

Blunt, Sarah R.

US NURSE AT HARPER'S FERRY

How dreadful the news of yesterday is [about Lincoln's assassination] . . . The sol- **2** diers here are enraged and talk of nothing now but *revenge* and retaliation.
　　—letter to her family, April 16, 1865.

Booth, John Wilkes (1838–1865)

ACTOR AND ASSASSIN OF ABRAHAM LINCOLN

They say [the South] had found that "last ditch" which the North has so long derided **3** and been endeavoring to force her in, forgetting they are our brothers, and that it is impolitic to goad an enemy to madness. Should I reach her in safety, and find it true, I will proudly beg permission to triumph or die in that same "ditch" by her side.
　　—quoted by John D. Wright in *The Language of the Civil War*, 2001.

★ Booth wrote this to his brother-in-law, J. S. Clarke, before he assassinated Lincoln. The North used the "last ditch" as a symbol for the grave of the Confederacy; it referred to the many trenches dug during the war.

Looking upon African slavery from the same standpoint held by the noble framers of **4** our Constitution, I have ever considered it one of the greatest blessings (both for themselves and us) that God ever bestowed upon a favorite nation.
　　—letter to his sister, Asia, April 14, 1865.

★ Booth left this letter with his sister before he assassinated Lincoln that same day.

Sic semper tyrannis! The South is avenged. **5**
　　—quoted in the *New York Times*, April 14, 1865.

★ Booth uttered the words after shooting Lincoln in Ford's Theater and leaping onto the stage. The Latin means "Thus always to tyrants," and is the motto of the state of Virginia. The second sentence is possibly apocryphal. Those in the audience who reported it may have misheard the Latin.

1   God's will be done. I have too great a soul to die like a criminal. May He spare me that and let me die bravely. I bless the entire world; have never hated or wronged any one. This last was not a wrong unless God deems it so, and it's with Him to damn or bless me.
       —diary, April 21, 1865.

   ★ The diary was found on Booth's body after he was cornered by Federal troops and shot dead five days after this entry.

2   Tell mother I die for my country.
       —quoted by Alfred H. Guernsey and Henry M. Alden in *Harper's Pictorial History of the Great Rebellion in the United States*, 1866.

   ★ Booth said this when dying after being shot by Federal troops on April 26, 1865. Revived a final time, he added, "I thought I did for the best." He asked to have his hands raised, looked at them, and muttered, "Useless! Useless!"

Boston, John

3   I had a little truble in giting away But as the lord led the Children of Isrel to the land of Canon So he led me to a land Whare fredom Will rain in spite Of erth and hell Dear you must make your Self content I am free from al the Slavers Lash.
       —letter to his wife, Elizabeth, January 12, 1862.

   ★ Boston had escaped slavery to the safety of the New York 14th Regiment at Uptons Hill, Virginia. His wife was safe in Owensville, Maryland.

Botts, John Minor (1802–1869)

4   If the Federal army has heavier artillery and stronger battalions, the Confederate army has more patriotism: I mean by that, the love of State is stronger in the average man, than love of the Union.
       —quoted by Alexander Hunter in *Johnny Reb and Billy Yank*, 1905.

   ★ Botts, a Virginian, opposed secession, and after the war he was considered a possible candidate for the presidency.

Bowles, Samuel

SPRINGFIELD (ILLINOIS) REPUBLICAN EDITOR

5   Lincoln is a simple Susan.
       —quoted by Nathaniel W. Stephenson in *Lincoln: An Account of His Personal Life, Especially of Its Springs of Action as Revealed and Deepened by the Ordeal of War*, 1922.

Boyd, Cyrus F. (1837-?)

US SOLDIER

★ Boyd was a member of the 15th Iowa Infantry.

[Wounded rebels at Shiloh] had fallen in heaps, and the woods had taken fire and **1**
burned all the clothing off them and the naked bodies and blackened corpses are still
lying there unburied. On the hillside near a deep hollow our men were hauling them
down and throwing them into the deep gully. One hundred and eighty had been
thrown in when I was there. Men were in on top of the dead, straightening out their
legs and arms and trampling them down so as to make the hole contain as many as
possible. Other men on the hillside had ropes with a noose on one end, and they
would attach this to a man's foot or his head and haul him down the hollow and roll
him in.
    —diary quoted in *Iowa Journal of History*, vol. 50, no. 1, 1952.

War is hell broke loose and benumbs all the tender feelings of men and makes of **2**
them brutes. I do not want to see any more such scenes and yet I would not have
missed this for any consideration.
    —quoted by William C. Davis in *Brothers in Arms*, 1995.

Bradford, Susan

DIARIST

★ Bradford was a teenage diarist, whose diary was eventually published under her married name of Susan Bradford Eppes.

Everyone at the table who expressed an opinion was firmly set against the Repub- **3**
lican party. Mother says she wants the negroes freed but she wants the United States
Government to make laws which will free them gradually. All agree on one point, if
the negroes are freed our lands will be worthless.
    —*Through Some Eventful Years*, 1926.

★ This entry was written on January 1, 1861.

Our old friend, Mr. Burgess, says: "If Mrs. Harriet Beecher Stowe had died before **4**
she wrote 'Uncle Tom's Cabin,' this would never have happened." He says, "she has
kindled a fire which all the waters of the earth cannot extinguish." Isn't it strange
how much harm a pack of lies can do?
    —*Through Some Eventful Years*, 1926.

★ This entry was written on January 9, 1861.

Today I have no shoes to put on. All my life I have never wanted to go bare-footed, **5**
as most Southern children do. . . . Until the shoes for the army are finished, Mr.
McDearnmid will not have time to make any shoes for any one else, this is right, for
our dear soldiers must come first in everything.
    —*Through Some Eventful Years*, 1926.

★ She had no shoes, although her father's plantation in Leon County, Florida, had
more than 300 slaves. This entry was written on April 7, 1864.

Bragg, Braxton (1817–1876)

CS GENERAL

1   The only question now is; can we reconstruct any government without bloodshed? I do not think we can, and the question is momentous. . . . Such a chaotic mass to work on has never presented itself to my mind, and I can see nothing but confusion to come of it.
—letter to William T. Sherman, December 25, 1860.

★ At this time, these future Union generals were living in Louisiana, Bragg as a planter and Sherman as superintendent of the Louisiana State Seminary of Learning and Military Academy.

2   Our failure is entirely due to a want of discipline and a want of officers. Universal suffrage, furloughs and whisky have ruined us.
—quoted by Lloyd Lewis in *Sherman, Fighting Prophet*, 1932.

★ Bragg was writing his wife after the battle of Shiloh, Tennessee, which ended on April 7, 1862.

3   With every inch of territory lost, there is a corresponding loss of men and the re-sources of war. Conscripts cannot be got from the region held by the Yankees, and soldiers will desert back to their homes in possession of the enemy. Some do so from disaffection, some from weariness with the war, and some to protect their families against a brutal foe.
—letter to General Samuel Cooper, Confederate army adjutant and inspector general, July 25, 1862.

★ Other officers of the Army of Tennessee joined Bragg in this appeal for more troops.

4   The enemy is before us, devastating our fair country, imprisoning our old and vener-ated men (even the ministers of God), insulting our women, and desecrating our altars. It is our proud lot to be assigned the duty of punishing and driving forth these deluded men, led by desperate adventurers and goaded on by Abolition demagogues and demons. Let us but deserve success and an offended Deity will certainly assure it.
—general order to his troops, August 28, 1862.

5   If you prefer Federal rule, show it by your frowns and we shall return whence we came. If you choose rather to come within the folds of our brotherhood, then cheer us with the smiles of your women and lend your willing hands to secure you in your heritage of liberty.
—proclamation to the people of Kentucky, September 14, 1862.

6   I deem it due to the cause and to myself to ask for relief from command and an investigation into the causes of the defeat.
—quoted by Nathaniel W. Stephenson in *The Day of the Confederacy: A Chronicle of the Embattled South*, 1919.

★ The defeat happened at Chattanooga five days earlier. Bragg was relieved by General Joseph E. Johnston and went to Richmond to become military advisor to President Jefferson Davis.

Breckinridge, John C. (1821–1875)

CS MAJOR GENERAL AND SECRETARY OF WAR

★ A Kentuckian defeated by Lincoln in the 1860 election, Breckinridge had been the US vice president under James Buchanan. He became a Confederate brigadier general in 1861, later became a major general, and near the end of the conflict became the Confederacy's secretary of war.

I exchange, with proud satisfaction, a term of six years in the United States Senate   1
for the musket of a soldier.
  —speech in Bowling Green, Kentucky, October 8, 1861.

The straggling has been great, and the situation is not favorable.   2
  —telegram to Confederate president Jefferson Davis, April 8, 1865.

★ This appraisal of General Robert E. Lee's troops was sent one day before the surrender at Appomattox Court House.

Bright, John (1811–1889)

BRITISH LIBERAL POLITICIAN AND REFORMER

My opinion is that the Northern States will manage somehow to muddle through.   3
  —quoted by Justin McCarthy in *Reminiscences*, vol. 1, 1899.

Brown, George W. (1812–1890)

BALTIMORE MAYOR

When are these scenes to cease? Are we to have a war of sections? God forbid.   4
  —letter to Massachusetts governor John A. Andrew, April 20, 1861.

★ Massachusetts troops marching through Baltimore had been attacked by citizens; three soldiers and eight rioters were killed.

Brown, John (1800–1859)

ABOLITIONIST

I believe that to interfere, as I have done, in the behalf of God's despised poor is not   5
wrong but right. Now, if it is deemed necessary that I should forfeit my life for the furtherance of the ends of justice, and mingle my blood further with the blood of my children and with the blood of millions in this slave country whose rights are disregarded by wicked, cruel, and unjust enactments, I say, let it be done.
  —court statement, November 1, 1859.

★ Brown said these words after being sentenced to death for his raid on the US Armory at Harper's Ferry, Virginia.

1   Had I so interfered in behalf of the rich, the powerful, the intelligent, the so-called great, or in behalf of any of their friends . . . every man in this court would have deemed it an act worthy of reward rather than punishment.
     —last speech of this abolitionist during his trial, November 2, 1859.

2   I am yet too young to understand that God is any respecter of persons.
     —last speech of this abolitionist during his trial, November 2, 1859.

3   I John Brown am now quite certain that the crimes of this guilty land: will never be purged away; but with Blood. I had as I now think: vainly flattered myself that without very much bloodshed; it might be done.
     —last written words from his cell, December 2, 1859.

4   This *is* a beautiful country.
     —remark made as he rode on his coffin to the gallows, December 2, 1859.

Brown, Joseph E. (1821–1894)

GEORGIA GOVERNOR

5   No acts of the Government of the United States prior to the secession of Georgia struck a blow at constitutional liberty so fell as has been stricken by the [Confederate] conscript acts.
     —quoted by Nathaniel W. Stephenson in *The Day of the Confederacy: A Chronicle of the Embattled South*, 1919.

     ★ This was in a letter to Confederate president Jefferson Davis in the fall of 1862.

6   Georgia has the power to act independently but her faith is pledged by implication to her Southern sisters. . . . [Georgia] will triumph with her Southern sisters or sink with them in common ruin.
     —quoted by Nathaniel W. Stephenson in *The Day of the Confederacy: A Chronicle of the Embattled South*, 1919.

     ★ This was said in the autumn of 1864.

7   [Atlanta] is to the Confederacy as important as the heart is to the body. We must hold it.
     —quoted by Shelby Foote in *The Civil War*, vol. 3, 1958.

     ★ This was in a letter to Confederate president Jefferson Davis.

8   I entered into this Revolution to contribute my mite to sustain the rights of states and prevent the consolidation of the Government, and I am *still* a rebel . . . no matter who may be in power.
     —quoted by Geoffrey C. Ward in *The Civil War*, 1991.

     ★ Brown was rebelling against Confederate president Jefferson Davis's request for a day of national fasting.

Brown, William W. (1814?–1884)

"What shall be done with the slaves if they are freed?" You had better ask, "What **1** shall we do with the slaveholders if the slaves are freed?" The slave has shown himself better fitted to take care of himself than the slaveholder.
    —*The Black Man: His Antecedents, His Genius, and His Achievements*, 1863.

★ Brown had been a slave.

Browne, Junius Henry

New York Tribune REPORTER

There was no pause in the battle. The roar of the strife was ever heard. The artillery **2** bellowed and thundered, and the dreadful echoes went sweeping down the river, and the paths were filled with the dying and the dead. The sound was deafening, the tumult indescribable. . . . Death was in the air, and bloomed like a poison-plant on every foot of soil.
    —quoted by Kenneth C. Davis in *Don't Know Much about the Civil War*, 1996.

★ Browne was reporting the battle of Shiloh.

Browning, Eliza (Mrs. Orville)

Just a good man made a great man. **3**
    —quoted by Nathaniel W. Stephenson in *Lincoln: An Account of His Personal Life, Especially of Its Springs of Action as Revealed and Deepened by the Ordeal of War*, 1922.

★ This referred to Lincoln. She was the wife of US senator Orville H. Browning of Illinois.

Browning, Orville Henry (1806–1881)

US SENATOR FROM ILLINOIS

★ Browning was Lincoln's close friend.

Our brethren of the South—for I am willing to call them brethren; my heart yet **4** yearns toward them with a fervency of love which even their treason has not extinguished, which tempts me constantly to say in their behalf, "Father, forgive them, for they know not what they do."
    —quoted by Nathaniel W. Stephenson in *Lincoln: An Account of His Personal Life, Especially of Its Springs of Action as Revealed and Deepened by the Ordeal of War*, 1922.

If slavery can survive the shock of war and secession, be it so. If in the conflict for lib- **5** erty, the Constitution and the Union, it must necessarily perish, then let it perish.
    —quoted by Nathaniel W. Stephenson in *Lincoln: An Account of His Personal Life, Especially of Its Springs of Action as Revealed and Deepened by the Ordeal of War*, 1922.

Brownlow, William G. (1805–1877)

KNOXVILLE WHIG EDITOR AND TENNESSEE GOVERNOR

1   I shall go [to jail], because I have failed to recognize the hand of God in the work of breaking up the American Government, and the inauguration of the most wicked, cruel, unnatural, and uncalled-for war ever recorded in history.
   —editorial, *Knoxville Whig*, October 26, 1861.

   ★ This editorial was written as Brownlow's Tennessee newspaper went out of business following his arrest for his Union sympathies. He spent several months in jail, but in 1865 was elected Republican governor of Tennessee.

Brownson, Orestes A. (1803–1876)

2   Politically, the Southern leaders have for a long time formed their association with the least intelligent, the least advanced classes in the Free states, and these Southern leaders are those our Catholic population have followed with the most alacrity. This fact proves, on the one hand, that the South represents the lowest order of civilization in the country, and that Catholics are more easily engaged in supporting it than in supporting the superior civilization represented by the Northern states.
   —"Catholic Schools and Education," *Brownson's Quarterly Review*, January, 1862.

   ★ Brownson was an ardent Catholic.

Bruce, H. W.

JUDGE

3   The hours I remained in Richmond on that melancholy Sunday, after leaving St. Paul's [Episcopal Church], were among the saddest of my life. I felt that our cause was then the Lost Cause. Many of the scenes witnessed by me as I went to and fro through the streets of that good old city were heartrending. The bad news had spread with lightning speed all over the town. . . . The men, generally, were on the street, and large numbers of the ladies stood in the doors and on the steps of their houses, many bathed in tears, making inquiries and giving utterance to woeful disappointment and anguish. . . . The scene, as a whole, was one of bitterest sadness, such as I trust never again to behold; such as, I am sure, I shall never again witness, since such scenes rarely occur in the lifetime of any people.
   —*Some Reminiscences of the Second of April, 1865*, 1881.

   ★ April 2, 1865, was the day Confederate president Jefferson Davis and his government evacuated Richmond. Federal troops entered the city the next day. Bruce lived in Louisville, Kentucky, and gave this as a speech to the local branch of the Southern Historical Society.

Buchanan, James (1791–1868)

US PRESIDENT

   ★ Buchanan preceded Lincoln as president.

The long-continued and intemperate interference of the Northern people with the 1
question of slavery in the Southern States has at length produced its natural effects.
— State of the Union address, December 4, 1860.

Secession is neither more nor less than revolution. 2
— State of the Union address, December 4, 1860.

The fact is that our Union rests upon public opinion and can never be cemented by 3
the blood of its citizens shed in civil war. If it cannot live in the affections of the
people, it must one day perish. Congress possesses many means of preserving it by
conciliation, but the sword was not placed in their hand to preserve it by force.
— State of the Union address, December 4, 1860.

★ Buchanan, a lame-duck president after Lincoln won the election, suggested compromise to avoid Southern secession. However, South Carolina seceded two weeks
after this speech.

The office of the President of the United States is not fit for a gentleman to hold! 4
— quoted by John D. Wright in *The Language of the Civil War*, 2001.

Buckner, Simon B. (1823–1914)

CS BRIGADIER GENERAL

Were our liberties given us but to be trampled beneath the feet of Abraham 5
Lincoln?
— speech in Russellville, Kentucky, September 12, 1861.

★ Two days later he became a brigadier general.

Burbank, Daniel E.

US PRIVATE

The more I see of slavery the more I believe we have been deceived at the North. 6
You had ought to have seen the darkes going to church, they were as happy as clams
in high water.
— letter to his parents, August 11, 1861.

Burnside, Ambrose E. (1824–1881)

US MAJOR GENERAL

You are going to involve us in war and you will be beaten. One Northern man can 7
whip two of your people.
— quoted in *Harper's Weekly*, January 12, 1861.

★ Burnside, who was then treasurer of the Illinois Central Railroad, made this statement during a visit to New Orleans. He organized the 1st Rhode Island Infantry when
the war began.

1   That, Sir, is the last thing on which I wish to be congratulated.
     —quoted in *Harper's Weekly*, November 29, 1862.

     ★ Someone had congratulated Burnside on being named commander of the Army of
     the Potomac, a position Burnside had tried to avoid, refusing it twice.

Butler, Benjamin (1818–1893)

US MAJOR GENERAL

     ★ Butler was nicknamed "Beast Butler" because of his harsh occupation of New
     Orleans.

2   I believed that Mr. Davis would be the strongest, most available candidate the Dem-
     ocratic party could run; and if nominated he would defeat the Republican candidate.
     —quoted by Hudson Strode in *Jefferson Davis: American Patriot*, 1955.

     ★ This was the 1860 election won by Lincoln. Butler was then a Democratic politician
     from Massachusetts. Ironically, Davis became the Confederate president.

3   No flag, banner, ensign, or device of the so-called Confederate States, or any of
     them, will be permitted to be raised or shown in this department, and the exhibition
     of either of them by evil-disposed persons will be deemed, and taken to be evidence
     of, a design to afford aid and comfort to the enemies of the country.
     —proclamation, May 14, 1861.

     ★ The troops of Butler, then commander of the Department of Annapolis, had occu-
     pied Baltimore the previous day.

4   A detachment of the forces of the federal government under my command have
     occupied the city of Baltimore for the purpose, among other things, of enforcing
     respect and obedience to the laws.
     —proclamation, May 14, 1861.

5   In a state of rebellion, I would confiscate that which was used to oppose my arms,
     and take all that property which constituted the wealth of that state and furnished
     the means by which the war is prosecuted, besides being the cause of the war; and
     if, in so doing, it should be objected that human beings were brought to the free
     enjoyment of life, liberty, and the pursuit of happiness, such objection might not
     require much consideration.
     —report to Secretary of War Simon Cameron, July 30, 1861.

     ★ Butler was justifying his refusal to return fugitive slaves, declaring them "contraband
     of war," when he commanded Fortress Monroe in Virginia.

6   As the Officers and Soldiers of the United States have been subject to repeated
     insults from the women calling themselves ladies of New Orleans, in return for the
     most scrupulous non-interference and courtesy on our part, it is ordered that here-
     after when any Female shall, by word, gesture, or movement, insult or show con-

tempt for any officer of the United States, she shall be regarded and held liable to be treated as a woman of the town plying her avocation.
    —General Orders No. 28, May 15, 1862.

I was always a friend of southern rights but an enemy of southern wrongs.   **1**
    —quoted by Geoffrey C. Ward in *The Civil War: An Illustrated History*, 1990.

Butler, Sarah

What is all this fighting for? This ruin and death to thousands of families?   **2**
    —letter to her husband, Major General Benjamin Butler, June 19, 1864.

Byington, A. Homer

New York Tribune CORRESPONDENT

We've had a most bitterly contested battle—really *worse* than Gettysburg inasmuch   **3**
as the *bullet* has been more destructive than artillery.
    —message to Sydney Howard Gay, May 7, 1864.

★ Byington was reporting to Gay, the managing editor, on the battle of the Wilderness.

Cable, George W.

CS OFFICER

This was the flower of the home guard. The merchants, bankers, underwriters,   **4**
judges, real-estate owners, and capitalists of the Anglo-American part of the city
[New Orleans] were "all present or accounted for" in that long line. Gray heads, hoar
heads, high heads, bald heads.
    —quoted in *Battles and Leaders of the Civil War*, vol. 2, 1888.

Caldwell, Mr.

I give notice now that I have so much objection to the name of Kanawha that I will   **5**
ask for a provision in the Constitution that when the Constitution is submitted to the
people they will then determine whether the name shall be Western Virginia or
Kanawha.
    —*Debates and Proceedings of the First Constitutional Convention of West
    Virginia*, November 30, 1861.

★ Kanawha was the early proposed name for West Virginia, which separated from
Virginia to become a loyal Union state on June 20, 1863.

Calhoun, James M. (1811–1875)

ATLANTA MAYOR

1   . . . we know of no other instance ever having occurred—surely never in the United States—and what has this helpless people done that they should be driven from their homes, to wander as strangers, outcasts and exiles, and to subsist on charity?
    —letter to Major General William T. Sherman, September 11, 1864.

    ★ Calhoun and others were petitioning Sherman to reconsider or modify his order, made during occupation, that civilians evacuate Atlanta.

Calhoun, John C. (1782–1850)

US CONGRESSMAN FROM SOUTH CAROLINA

2   It is through our affiliation with that [Democratic] party in the Middle and Western States that we hold power; but when we cease thus to control this nation through a disjointed democracy, or any material obstacle in that party which shall tend to throw us out of that rule and control, we shall then resort to the dissolution of the Union.
    —quoted by Commodore Charles Stewart in a letter to G. W. Childs of Philadelphia, May 4, 1861.

    ★ Stewart was quoting Calhoun's remarks of December 1812.

Call, Richard K. (1792–1862)

FLORIDA GOVERNOR

3   The institution of slavery is doing more in the agency of the world's great progress, more for the improvement and comfort of human life, more for the preaching of the Gospel to heathen nations, more for the fulfillment of prophecy, than any other institution on earth.
    —letter to John S. Littell, February 12, 1861.

    ★ Littell, of Pennsylvania, became a US brigadier general.

Capers, F. W. (?–1892)

CS MAJOR

4   There was fatigue and blood and death in their ranks but no white feather.
    —report to Major General Henry C. Wayne, October 27, 1864.

    ★ The soldiers mentioned were cadets from the Georgia Military Institute.

Carpenter, Francis B.

PORTRAIT PAINTER

. . . his laugh stood by itself. The neigh of a wild horse on his native prairie is not   **1**
more undisguised and hearty.
> —*The Inner Life of Abraham Lincoln: Six Months at the White House*, 1866.

All familiar with [Lincoln] will remember the weary air which became habitual dur-   **2**
ing his last years. This was more of the mind than of the body, and no rest and recre-
ation which he allowed himself could relieve it. As he sometimes expressed it, "no
remedy seemed ever to reach the tired spot."
> —*The Inner Life of Abraham Lincoln: Six Months at the White House*, 1866.

[Lincoln] continued always the same kindly, genial, and cordial spirit he had been at   **3**
first; but the boisterous laughter became less frequent, year by year; the eye grew
veiled by constant meditation on momentous subjects; the air of reserve and detachment from his surroundings increased. He aged with great rapidity.
> —*The Inner Life of Abraham Lincoln: Six Months at the White House*, 1866.

In repose, [Lincoln's] was the saddest face I ever knew. There were days when I   **4**
could scarcely look into it without crying.
> —*The Inner Life of Abraham Lincoln: Six Months at the White House*, 1866.

Carter, Robert G.

US PRIVATE

★ Carter was a member of the 22nd Massachusetts Infantry.

This climate [in Virginia] is making me terribly lazy. I lose all my strength here, and   **5**
feel dumpish continually; I want to lie down constantly; there seems to be something
in the atmosphere that absorbs all my vitality.
> —*Four Brothers in Blue*, 1913.

★ Carter wrote this to his parents in August 1862.

Casey, Silas (1807–1882)

US BRIGADIER GENERAL

It is very certain that no argument is worth a straw with the Southern rebels but that   **6**
of the bayonet, and we would be recreant to the cause of liberty on this earth if we
did not use it effectually.
> —letter to Secretary of War Edwin M. Stanton, May 31, 1862.

Casler, John O.

CS PRIVATE

1   As we passed by the other regiments the shells were bursting and cutting down the pines all around us, and we were shaking hands and bidding farewell to those we were acquainted with, knowing that in a few moments many of us would be stretched lifeless on the field.
   —*Four Years in the Stonewall Brigade*, 1893.

   ★ This occurred during the first battle of Bull Run (first Manassas) on July 21, 1861.

Cavins, E. H. C.

US COLONEL

2   The Confederates fell back in great disorder, and we advanced in disorder just as great. Over logs, through woods, over hills and fields, the brigades, regiments, and companies advanced, in one promiscuous, mixed, and uncontrollable mass. Officers shouted themselves hoarse in trying to bring order out of confusion, but all their efforts were unavailing along the front line, or rather what ought to have been the front line.
   —quoted in *Battles and Leaders of the Civil War*, vol. 2, 1888.

   ★ This was at the battle of Kernstown, Virginia, on March 23, 1862.

Chamberlain, Joshua L. (1828–1914)

US MAJOR GENERAL AND MAINE GOVERNOR

3   But out of that silence rose new sounds more appalling still; a strange ventriloquism, of which you could not locate the source, a smothered moan, as if a thousand discords were flowing together into a key-note weird, unearthly, terrible to hear and bear, yet startling with its nearness; the writhing concord broken by cries for help, some begging for a drop of water, some calling on God for pity; and some on friendly hands to finish what the enemy had so horribly begun; some with delirious, dreamy voices murmuring loved names, as if the dearest were bending over them; and underneath, all the time, the deep bass note from closed lips too hopeless, or too heroic to articulate their agony.
   —quoted by Henry Steele Commager in *The Civil War Archive: The History of the Civil War in Documents*, 2001.

   ★ This described the battlefield at Fredericksburg. Chamberlain was a colonel at the time.

4   I consider it an officer's first duty to look after the welfare of his men.
   —letter to Governor Abner Coburn of Maine, July 21, 1863.

   ★ Chamberlain was then a colonel. He became governor after the war.

All around, strange, mingled roar—shouts of defiance, rally, and desperation; and   **1**
underneath, murmured entreaty and stifled moans; gasping prayers, snatches of
Sabbath song, whispers of loved names; everywhere men torn and broken, stagger-
ing, creeping, quivering on the earth, and dead faces with strangely fixed eyes staring stark into the sky.
  —*Through Blood and Fire at Gettysburg*, 1913.

★ Chamberlain, then a colonel, was commanding the 20th Maine Regiment at
Gettysburg.

Had slavery been kept out of the fight, the Union would have gone down. . . . We did   **2**
not go into that fight to strike at slavery directly; we were not thinking to solve that
problem, but God, in his providence, in His justice, in his mercy, in His great covenant with our fathers, set slavery in the forefront, and it was swept aside as with a
whirlwind, when the mighty pageant of the people passed on to its triumph.
  —quoted in the *Boston Journal*, January 4, 1878.

In great deeds something abides. On great fields something stays. Forms change and   **3**
pass; bodies disappear, but spirits linger, to consecrate ground for the vision-place of
souls. And reverent men and women from afar, and generations that know us not and
that we know not of, heart-drawn to see where and by whom great things were suffered and done for them, shall come to this deathless field to ponder and dream;
And lo! The shadow of a mighty presence shall wrap them in its bosom, and the power
of the vision pass into their souls.
  —speech at Gettysburg dedicating a monument to the 20th Maine Regiment,
  October 3, 1889.

The inspiration of a noble cause involving human interests wide and far, enables   **4**
men to do things they did not dream themselves capable of before, and which they
were not capable of alone.
  —speech at Gettysburg dedicating a monument to the 20th Maine Regiment,
  October 3, 1889.

But we had with us, to keep and to care for, more than five hundred bruised bodies   **5**
of men,—men made in the image of God, marred by the hand of man, and must we
say in the name of God?
  —*The Passing of the Armies*, 1915.

The striking fact is thus established that we had more men killed and wounded in the   **6**
first six months of Grant's campaign, than Lee had at any one period of it in his whole
army. The hammering business had been hard on the hammer.
  —*The Passing of the Armies*, 1915.

The pageant has passed. The day is over. But we linger, loath to think we shall see   **7**
them no more together—these men, these horses, these colors afield.
  —*The Passing of the Armies*, 1915.

1   It was not uncommon incident that from close opposing bivouacs and across hushed breastworks at evening voices of prayer from over the way would stir our hearts, and floating songs of love and praise be caught up and broadened into a mighty and thrilling chorus by our men softening down in cadences like enfolding wings. Such moments were surely a "Truce of God."
     —*The Passing of the Armies*, 1915.

[Combat] makes bad men worse and good men better.
     —quoted by Geoffrey C. Ward in *The Civil War: An Illustrated History*, 1990.

★ Chamberlain was a lieutenant colonel when he said this.

Chambers, William Pitt

CS SERGEANT

★ Chambers was a member of the 46th Mississippi Infantry.

2   In the streets [of Port Gibson] all was confusion. Men with pale faces were running hither and thither, some with arms and seeking a command, women sobbing on every side, children in open-eyed wonder clinging to their weeping mothers not understanding the meaning of it all, and negroes with eyes protruding like open cotton bolls were jostling each other and everybody else and continuously asking about "dem Yankees."
     —diary quoted by Samuel Carter III in *The Final Fortress: The Campaign for Vicksburg 1862–1863*, 1980.

★ Chambers was describing Port Gibson, Mississippi, just before the battle of May 1, 1863.

Chandler, Zachariah (1813–1879)

US SENATOR FROM MICHIGAN

3   The President is a weak man, too weak for the occasion, and those fool or traitor generals are wasting time and yet more precious blood in indecisive battles and delays.
     —quoted by Geoffrey C. Ward in *The Civil War: An Illustrated History*, 1990.

★ This was said after the battle of Fredericksburg, December 1862.

4   A rebel has sacrificed all his rights. He has no right to life, liberty or the pursuit of happiness.
     —quoted by Nathaniel W. Stephenson in *Lincoln: An Account of His Personal Life, Especially of Its Springs of Action as Revealed and Deepened by the Ordeal of War*, 1922.

Chapman, Horatio D.

US CORPORAL

5   We made no distinction between our own and the confederate wounded [at Gettysburg], but treated them both alike, and although we had been engaged in fierce and

deadly combat all day and weary and all begrimed with smoke and powder and dust, many of us went around among the wounded and gave cooling water or hot coffee to drink. The confederates were surprised and so expressed themselves that they received such kind treatment at our hands, and some of the slightly wounded were glad they were wounded and our prisoners.
    —*Civil War Diary of a 49er*, 1929.

★ The diary entry was for July 3, 1863.

I saw a letter sticking out of the breast pocket of one of the confederate dead [at **1** Gettysburg], a young man apparently about twenty-four. Curiosity prompted me to read it. It was from his young wife away down in the state of Louisiana. She was hoping and longing that this cruel war would end and he could come home, and she says, "Our little boy gets into my lap and says, 'Now, Mama, I will give you a kiss for Papa.' But oh how I wish you could come home and kiss me for yourself." But this is only one in a thousand. But such is war and we are getting used to it and can look on scenes of war, carnage and suffering with but very little feeling and without a shudder.
    —*Civil War Diary of a 49er*, 1929.

★ The diary entry was for July 3, 1863.

Chase, Salmon P. (1808–1873)

US SECRETARY OF THE TREASURY AND CHIEF JUSTICE OF THE US SUPREME COURT

I cannot but feel that giving command to McClellan is equivalent to giving Washing- **2** ton to the rebels.
    —comment to the cabinet, August 31, 1862.

★ Chase was then secretary of the treasury. McClellan was being reinstated as commander in chief of the army, but in September was again relieved of his command.

It will be hereafter counted equally a crime and a folly if the colored loyalists of the **3** rebel states shall be left to the control of restored rebels, not likely in that case to be either wise or just, until taught both wisdom and justice by new calamities.
    —letter to Lincoln, April 11, 1865, when Chase was chief justice.

You are President. May God support, guide, and bless you in your arduous duties. **4**
    —quoted by Claude G. Bowers in *The Tragic Era*, 1929.

★ Chief Justice Chase was swearing in President Andrew Johnson after Lincoln's assassination.

If you bring these leaders to trial it will condemn the North, for by the Constitution **5** secession is not rebellion.
    —quoted by Rod Graff in *Civil War Quiz and Fact Book*, 1985.

★ Chief Justice Chase delivered this opinion in late 1865.

Chesnut, Mary Boykin (1823–1886)

DIARIST

★ Chesnut was the wife of James Chesnut Jr., a US senator from South Carolina who resigned to assist the Confederacy. Her diary of some 400,000 words was published nineteen years after her death.

1   She was playing "Yankee Doodle" on the piano before breakfast to soothe her wounded spirit, and the Judge came in and calmly requested her to "leave out the Yankee while she played the Doodle."
     —*A Diary from Dixie*, 1905.

★ In this entry of February 19, 1861, Mrs. Chesnut was describing a Northern visitor in a hotel in Montgomery during the inauguration celebrations for Confederate president Jefferson Davis.

2   At half-past four, the heavy booming of a cannon. I sprang out of bed. And on my knees—prostrate—I prayed as I never prayed before.
     —*A Diary from Dixie*, 1905.

★ This was written on April 12, 1861, the day that Fort Sumter was fired upon.

3   Not by one word or look can we detect any change in the demeanor of these Negro servants. Lawrence sits at our door, sleepy and respectful and profoundly indifferent. So are they all, but they carry it too far. You could not tell that they even heard the awful roar going on in the bay, though it has been dinning in their ears night and day. People talk before them as if they were chairs and tables. They make no sign. Are they stolidly stupid, or wiser than we are; silent and strong, biding their time?
     —*A Diary from Dixie*, 1905.

★ This entry of April 13, 1861, refers to the bombardment of Fort Sumter.

4   I did not know that one could live such days of excitement.
     —*A Diary from Dixie*, 1905.

★ This entry of April 13, 1861, refers to watching the bombardment of Fort Sumter.

5   Our battle summer. May it be our first and last, so-called. After all, we have not had any of the horrors of war.
     —*A Diary from Dixie*, 1905.

★ This was written on July 9, 1861.

6   The Confederacy has been done to death by politicians.
     —*A Diary from Dixie*, 1905.

★ This was written on April 27, 1862.

7   War seems a game of chess, but we have an unequal number of pawns to begin with. We have knights, kings, queens, bishops, and castles enough. But our skillful gener-

als, whenever they cannot arrange the board to suit them exactly, burn up everything and march away.
—*A Diary from Dixie*, 1905.

★ This was written on April 29, 1862, four days after New Orleans was captured.

Men of the North can wait; they can bear discipline; they can endure forever. Losses **1** in battle are nothing to them. Their resources in men and materials of war are inexhaustible, and if they see fit they will fight to the bitter end.
—*A Diary from Dixie*, 1905.

★ This entry, written on June 10, 1862, was indirectly quoting General Winfield Scott.

This war was undertaken by us to shake off the yoke of foreign invaders, so we con- **2** sider our cause righteous. The Yankees, since the war has begun, have discovered it is to free the slaves that they are fighting, so their cause is noble.
—*A Diary from Dixie*, 1905.

★ This was written on July 8, 1862.

Joe Johnston is their polar star; the redeemer! **3**
—*A Diary from Dixie*, 1905.

★ This entry of January 1, 1864, named General Joseph E. Johnston as the guiding light for those who disliked President Jefferson Davis.

God help my country! I think we are like the sailors who break into the spirit closet **4** when they find out the ship must sink. There seems to be for the first time a resolute determination to enjoy the brief hour, and never look beyond the day.
—quoted by Hudson Strode in *Jefferson Davis: Tragic Hero*, 1964.

★ This was written in early 1864.

The end has come. No doubt of the fact. . . . We are going to be wiped off the face **5** of the earth.
—*A Diary from Dixie*, 1905.

★ The entry was written from Columbia, South Carolina, on March 24, 1864.

Atlanta is gone. That agony is over. . . . There is no hope but we will try to have no **6** fear.
—*A Diary from Dixie*, 1905.

★ Sherman's army occupied Atlanta on September 2, 1864, the date of this entry.

The deep waters are closing over us. **7**
—*A Diary from Dixie*, 1905.

★ This entry of December 19, 1864, was written three days after the Confederate defeat at Nashville.

1   Shame—disgrace—misery. . . . The grand smash has come.
    —*A Diary from Dixie*, 1905.

★ This entry was written on February 25, 1865. Columbia, the capital of South Carolina, had been burned on February 17, and General Robert E. Lee's surrender was only six weeks away.

2   Lincoln—old Abe Lincoln—killed—murdered. . . . I know this foul murder will bring down worse miseries on us.
    —*A Diary from Dixie*, 1905.

★ This was written on April 22, 1865.

Childe, Edward Lee

NEPHEW OF ROBERT E. LEE

3   The whole army felt that this man—so undemonstrative, so simply clad, sleeping like the commonest soldier in his tent, having in the midst of the wood a single blanket—was its guide, its protector, incessantly attentive to its welfare, jealous of its dearly purchased fame, and always ready, as its commander and friend, to defend it.
    —*The Life and Campaigns of General Lee*, 1875.

Christian, William S.

CS OFFICER

4   I felt when I first came here, that I would like to revenge myself upon these people for the desolation they have brought upon our own beautiful home; that home where we could have lived so happy, and that we loved so much, from which their vandalism has driven you and my helpless little ones. But though I had such severe wrongs and grievances to redress, yet when I got among these people I could not find it in my heart to molest them.
    —letter to his wife, June 28, 1863.

★ Christian's camp was near Greenwood, Pennsylvania.

Clark, J. M.

GEORGIA PLANTER

5   Take him all and in all, [Jefferson Davis] is the greatest man I ever saw. While I had a high opinion of him before, I have a still higher one now. He is an honor to the Confederacy.
    —letter to his wife, October 4, 1864.

★ Clark had heard the Confederate president speak the day before in Augusta.

Clarke, Charles (1811–1877)

MISSISSIPPI GOVERNOR

General Taylor informs me that all Confederate armies east of the Mississippi river **1**
are surrendered. . . . Masters are responsible as heretofore for the protection and
conduct of their slaves, and they should be kept at home as heretofore.
    —quoted by Robert Lowry and William H. McCardle in *A History of Mississippi*,
1891.

Clay, Clement C. (1816–1882)

CS SENATOR

Then God help us! If that is true, it is the worst blow that has yet been struck the **2**
South.
    —quoted by his wife in *A Belle of the Fifties*, 1905.

★ Clay, in retreat in Georgia with other Confederate leaders, was reacting to news of
Lincoln's assassination.

Cleburne, Patrick R.

CS MAJOR GENERAL

I am with the South in life or in death, in victory or in defeat . . . I believe the North **3**
is about to wage a brutal and unholy war on a people who have done them no wrong,
in violation of the Constitution and the fundamental principles of government. They
no longer acknowledge that all government derives its validity from the consent of
the governed. They are about to invade our peaceful homes, destroy our property,
and inaugurate a servile insurrection, murder our men and dishonor our women. We
propose no invasion of the North, no attack on them, and only ask to be left alone.
    —letter to his brother, May 7, 1861.

★ Cleburne, a captain when this was written, rose to the rank of major general and was
known as "the Stonewall Jackson of the West."

Clemens, Samuel Langhorne (Mark Twain) (1835–1910)

WRITER

No journalist among us can lay his hand on his heart and say he ever lied with such **4**
pathos, such unction, such exquisite symmetry, such sublimity of conception and such
fidelity of execution, as when he did it through and by the inspiration of this regally
gifted marvel of mendacity, the lamented Reliable Contraband. Peace to his ashes!
    —quoted in *Packard's Monthly*, July 1869.

★ Clemens was making a dinner toast for the New York Press Club on June 5, 1869.
"Contraband" was slang for a slave.

Coan, Titus

1   Is not this a glorious war?
      —letter to his mother, April 21, 1861.

      ★ Coan was a medical student in New York City. The first real battle of the war had not
      yet occurred.

Cobb, Howell (1815–1868)

CS MAJOR GENERAL

2   The separation is perfect, complete, and perpetual.
      —speech to the Provisional Congress of the Confederate States of America,
      February 4, 1861.

      ★ Cobb, of Georgia, joined the Confederate army as a colonel in 1861.

3   The day you make soldiers of [slaves] is the beginning of the end of the revolution.
      If slaves will make good soldiers, our whole theory of slavery is wrong.
      —quoted by William C. Davis in *Brothers in Arms*, 1995.

Cobb, Thomas Reade Rootes (1823–1862)

CS BRIGADIER GENERAL

4   I think I see in the future a gory head rise above our horizon. Its name is Civil War.
      Already I can see the prints of his bloody fingers upon our lintels and doorposts. The
      vision sickens me already.
      —speech in Milledgeville, Georgia, November 12, 1860.

      ★ Cobb was a strong voice leading Georgia out of the Union, serving in the
      Confederate congress before becoming a CS brigadier general.

Cockerill, John A.

US COLONEL

5   The blue and gray were mingled together. This peculiarity I observed all over the
      field. It was no uncommon thing to see the bodies of Federal and Confederate lying
      side by side, as though they had bled to death while trying to aid each other.
      —*A Boy at Shiloh*, 1896.

      ★ Cockerill was recalling the aftermath of the battle of Shiloh when he was a sixteen-
      year-old musician with the 70th Ohio Regiment.

6   Here beside a great oak tree I counted the corpses of fifteen men. One of them sat
      stark against the tree, and others lay about as though during the night, suffering from
      wounds, they had crawled together for mutual assistance.
      —*A Boy at Shiloh*, 1896.

I passed . . . the corpse of a beautiful boy in gray who lay with his blond curls scat-   1
tered about his face and his hands folded peacefully across his breast. He was clad in
a bright and neat uniform, well garnished with gold, which seemed to tell the story
of a loving mother and sisters who had sent their household pet to the field of war.
His neat little hat lying beside him bore the number of a Georgia regiment. . . . He
was about my age. . . . At the sight of the poor boy's corpse, I burst into a regular
boo-hoo, and started on.
   —*A Boy at Shiloh*, 1896.

Cockrill, Sterling

Alabama planter

The bloody conflict between brothers, is closed, and we "come to bury Caesar, not   2
to praise him." The South had $2,000,000,000 invested in Slaves. It was very natural,
that they should desire to protect, and not lose this amount of property. Their action
in this effort, resulted in War. There was no desire to dissolve the Union, but to protect this property. The issue was made and it is decided.
   —letter to President Andrew Johnson, September 18, 1865.

Coffin, Charles C. (1823–1896)

Boston Journal correspondent

Men who at the beginning of the struggle were scarcely known beyond their village   3
homes are numbered now among "the immortal names that were not born to die";
while the names of others who once occupied places of honor and trust, who for-
swore their allegiance to their country and gave themselves to do wickedly, shall be
held forever in abhorrence.
   —*Four Years of Fighting*, 1866.

At one time a captain, whose last command had been a pair of draft-horses on his   4
Pennsylvania farm, on coming to a pit in the road, electrified his company by the
stentorian order to "Gee round that hole."
   —*Four Years of Fighting*, 1866.

"General Scott is watching the Rebels with sleepless vigilance," was the not unfre-   5
quent telegraphic despatch sent from Washington [in June 1861]. But he was seventy-
five years of age. His powers were failing. His old wound troubled him at times. He
could walk only with difficulty, and it tired him to ride the few rods between his house
and the War Department. He was slow and sluggish in all his thoughts and actions.
Yet the people had confidence in him, and he in himself.
   —*Four Years of Fighting*, 1866.

★ Scott was general in chief of the US Army when the war began.

1   Everywhere—in city and town and village, in Boston, New York, and Philadelphia,—
there was the same spirit manifested by old and young, of both sexes, to put down
the Rebellion, cost what it might of blood and treasure.
—*Four Years of Fighting*, 1866.

2   Passing on to Washington [in June 1861] I found it in a hubbub. Troops were pouring
in, raw, undisciplined, yet of material to make the best soldiers in the world,—poets,
painters, artists, artisans, mechanics, printers, men of letters, bankers, merchants, and
ministers were in the ranks.
—*Four Years of Fighting*, 1866.

3   The Confederates had gone down as the grass falls before the scythe. Words are
inadequate to portray the scene. Resolution and energy still lingered in the pallid
cheeks, in the set teeth, in the gripping hand.
—*Century Magazine*, June 1886.

4   When the soldiers are seeking rest, the work of the army correspondent begins. All
through the day eyes and ears have been open. The note-book is scrawled with characters intelligible to him if read at once, but wholly meaningless a few hours later.
He must grope his way along the lines in the darkness, visit the hospitals, hear the
narratives of all, eliminate error, get the probable truth, keeping ever in mind that
each general thinks his brigade, each colonel his regiment, every captain his company, did most of the fighting.
—*Century Magazine*, June 1886.

5   Both before and after a battle, sad and solemn thoughts come to the soldier. Before
the conflict they are of apprehension; after the strife there is a sense of relief; but the
thinned ranks, the knowledge that the comrade who stood by your side in the morning never will stand there again, bring inexpressible sadness.
—*Century Magazine*, June 1886.

6   Every army has its driftwood soldiers—valiant at the mess-table, brave in the story
around the bivouac fire, but faint of heart when battle begins. Some of them were old
skulkers, others fresh recruits, with bright uniforms, who had volunteered under the
pressure of enthusiasm.
—*Century Magazine*, June 1886.

7   It was itself a great army.
—quoted by Kenneth C. Davis in *Don't Know Much about the Civil War*, 1996.

★ Coffin was referring to 2,922 officers and 80,000 men reported to be absent without
leave when General Joseph Hooker assumed command of the Army of the Potomac on
January 26, 1863.

Conkling, Roscoe (1829–1888)

US CONGRESSMAN FROM NEW YORK

8   War is not a question of valor, but a question of money. . . . It is not regulated by the
laws of honor, but by the laws of trade. I understand the practical problem to be

solved in crushing the rebellion of despotism against representative government is who can throw the most projectiles? Who can afford the most iron or lead?
    —quoted by Geoffrey C. Ward in *The Civil War: An Illustrated History*, 1990.

Connolly, James A.

US MAJOR

Mine eyes have beheld the promised land. The "domes and minarets and spires" of **1** Atlanta are glittering in the sunlight before us and only 8 miles distant.
    —letter to his wife, July 5, 1864.

Cook, Thomas

NEW YORK HERALD CORRESPONDENT

On the one hand was a solid column of infantry retreating in double quick from the **2** face of the enemy; on the other was a dense mass of being who had lost their reasoning faculties, and were flying from a thousand fancied dangers.
    —quoted by Steven W. Sears in *Chancellorsville*, 1996.

★ Cook was reporting the retreat and panic of Union forces driven by General Thomas J. "Stonewall" Jackson's men on May 2, 1863, the second day of the battle of Chancellorsville.

Cooke, John Esten (1830–1886)

CS INSPECTOR GENERAL

War is a hard trade.   **3**
    —*Wearing of the Gray: Being Personal Portraits, Scenes, and Adventures of the War*, 1867.

That the Southern army, of less than forty thousand men, repulsed more than eighty **4** thousand in the battle of Sharpsburg [Antietam] was due to the hard fighting of the smaller force, and the skill with which its commander [Lee] manoeuvered it.
    —*A Life of General Robert E. Lee*, 1875.

Cooke, Philip St. George (1809–1895)

US BRIGADIER GENERAL

I owe Virginia little, my country much. She has entrusted me with a distant com- **5** mand, and I shall remain under her flag as long as it waves the sign of the National Constitutional Government.
    —edited by Frank Moore in *The Rebellion Record: A Diary of American Events, with Documents, Narratives, Illustrative Incidents, Poetry, Etc.*, vol. 2, 1862.

★ Cooke was a colonel commanding the cavalry for the Utah Expedition when this was said in June 1861. By November, he was made a brigadier general and later became chief of cavalry for Major General George B. McClellan.

Corse, John M. (1835–1893)

US MAJOR GENERAL

1   I am short a cheekbone and an ear, but am able to whip all hell yet!
   —quoted by Major General William T. Sherman in *Memoirs of W. T. Sherman*, vol. 2, 1875.

   ★ Corse, the garrison commander at Allatoona, Georgia, sent this flag signal to General Sherman on October 6, 1864, the day after the battle there. The signalman politely spelled it "h—l."

Crippin, Edward W.

US PRIVATE

   ★ Crippin was a member of the 27th Illinois Volunteers.

2   Visited today by several Southern ladies [in Gunntown, Mississippi] with such delicacies for our wounded as they could raise. God bless them for their kindness.
   —quoted by Robert J. Kerner in *Transactions of the Illinois State Historical Society*, No. 14, 1910.

   ★ This was a diary entry of Crippin, who was one of the wounded after the battle of Brice's Crossroads on June 10, 1864.

Crittenden, John J. (1786–1863)

US SENATOR FROM KENTUCKY

3   Hold fast to the Union. There is safety, tried safety, known safety; and that same Union is the best assurance you can have of eventually obtaining from your fellow citizens a generous recompense for all the wrongs you have received and a generous remedy against any wrongs hereafter.
   —speech to the US Senate, March 2, 1861.

4   Through this great nation common blood flows. What man is there here that is not of a blood, flowing—meandering—perhaps through every state in the Union? . . . We are one people in blood; in language one; in thoughts one; we read the same books; we feed on the same meats; we go to the same schools; we belong to the same communion.
   —speech to the US Senate, March 2, 1861.

   ★ Crittenden was pleading with his fellow senators the day before Congress adjourned.

Crook, George

US MAJOR GENERAL

[Hunter] would have burned the Natural Bridge could he have compassed it.   **1**
    —quoted by CS brigadier general Gilbert Moxley Sorrel in *Recollections of a*
    Confederate Staff Officer, 1905.

★ Crook served with Major General David Hunter and was commenting on his obses-
sion for burning civilian houses and barns.

Cross, E. E. (1832–1863)

US COLONEL

Charge 'em like hell, boys; show 'em you *are* damned Yankees.   **2**
    —edited by Frank Moore in *The Rebellion Record: A Diary of American Events,*
    with Documents, Narratives, Illustrative Incidents, Poetry, Etc., vol. 5, 1862.

★ Cross commanded the 5th New Hampshire Regiment at the indecisive battle of Fair
Oaks (Seven Pines) just east of Richmond, June 1, 1862.

If any man runs I want the file closers to shoot him; if they don't, I shall myself. That's   **3**
all I have to say.
    —quoted by Thomas L. Livermore in *Days and Events*, 1920.

★ This was at the battle of Antietam (Sharpsburg). File closers were used to make sure
the men advanced in their proper places.

Crummer, Wilbur F.

US PRIVATE

    ★ Crummer was a member of the 45th Illinois Infantry.

All the monument reared to those brave men [at Shiloh] was a board, nailed to a tree   **4**
at the head of the trench, upon which I cut with my pocket knife the words: "125
rebels." We buried our Union boys in a separate trench, and on another board were
these words: "35 Union." Many of our men had been taken away and buried separately by their comrades.
    —*With Grant at Fort Donelson, Shiloh, and Vicksburg, and an Appreciation of*
    General U. S. Grant, 1915.

The soldiers gathered up the bodies [at Shiloh] and placed them in wagons, hauling   **5**
them near to the trench, and piling them up like cord wood. We were furnished with
plenty of whiskey, and the boys believed that it would have been impossible to have
performed the job without it. . . . It was night when we finished the task, some of the
squad, "half seas over" with liquor, but they could not be blamed, for it was a hard
job.
    —*With Grant at Fort Donelson, Shiloh, and Vicksburg, and An Appreciation of*
    General U. S Grant, 1915.

Curtis, George William (1824–1892)

NEW YORK TRIBUNE REPORTER

1   We have undertaken to make war without in the least knowing how.
    —quoted by Carl Sandburg in *Abraham Lincoln: The War Years*, 1939.

    ★ Curtis wrote this in a private letter after the first battle of Bull Run (first Manassas).

Curtis, Samuel R. (1805–1866)

US BRIGADIER GENERAL

2   The scene is silent and sad—the vulture and the wolf now have the dominion and the dead friends and foes sleep in the same lonely graves.
    —letter to his brother, March 8, 1862.

    ★ Curtis had just won the battle of Pea Ridge, Arkansas.

Cusac, Isaac

US CAPTAIN

    ★ Cusac was a member of the 21st Ohio Infantry.

3   The Major gave orders to fix bayonets, which was promptly obeyed, but when the order was given to "forward march," not a man moved.
    —quoted by Randall Bedwell in *Brink of Destruction*, 1999.

    ★ Cusac was recalling the battle of Chickamauga in Georgia, which the Union forces lost on September 20, 1863.

Custer, George Armstrong (1839–1876)

US BRIGADIER GENERAL

4   This is the bulliest day since Christ was born.
    —quoted by Randall Bedwell in *Brink of Destruction*, 1999.

    ★ Custer was celebrating the Union victory at Cedar Creek, Virginia, in October 1864; the victory secured the Shenandoah Valley.

5   In the name of General Sheridan I demand the unconditional surrender of this army.
    —quoted by Lieutenant General James Longstreet in *From Manassas to Appomattox: Memoirs of the Civil War in America*, 1896.

    ★ Custer demanded that Longstreet surrender the Army of Northern Virginia but quickly backed down when Longstreet informed him that General Robert E. Lee was meeting with General Ulysses S. Grant for the surrender on this day, April 9, 1865.

Dabney, Robert Lewis

CS MAJOR

The whole country was full of deserted plunder, army wagons, and pontoon-trains   1
partially burned or crippled; mounds of grain and rice and hillocks of mess beef
smoldering; tens of thousands of axes, picks, and shovels; camp kettles gashed with
hatchets; medicine chests with their drugs stirred into a foul medley, and all the
apparatus of a vast and lavish host; while the mire under foot was mixed with blankets lately new, and with overcoats torn from the waist up. For weeks afterward
agents of our army were busy in gathering in the spoils.
　　—*The Life and Campaigns of Lieut.-Gen. Thomas J. Jackson*, 1865.

★ Dabney was describing items left by a retreating Vermont regiment at Savage's
Station, Virginia, in June 1862.

Dahlgren, John A. (1809–1870)

US REAR ADMIRAL

I have walked about the city [Savannah] several times, and can affirm that its tran-   2
quillity is undisturbed. The Union soldiers who are stationed within its limits are as
orderly as if they were in New York or Boston.
　　—telegram to Secretary of the Navy Gideon Welles, January 4, 1865.

Tidings of the murder of the President have just come, and shocked every mind. Can   3
it be that such a resort finds root in any stratum of American opinion? Evidently it
has not been the act of one man, nor of a madman. Who have prompted him?
　　—telegram to Major General William T. Sherman, April 20, 1865.

Daly, Mary

Can our countrymen be so blind, so stupid as to again place a clod, though an hon-   4
est one, in the presidential chair?
　　—diary edited by Harold E. Hammond in *Diary of a Union Lady, 1861–1865*, 1962.

★ Daly was a New York Democrat who, in the summer of 1862, was already worried
about Lincoln's possible reelection in 1864.

Dana, Charles A. (1819–1897)

US ASSISTANT SECRETARY OF WAR

Chickamauga is as fat a name in our history as Bull Run.   5
　　—telegram to Lincoln, September 20, 1863.

★ Dana, who was at the battle, was informing Lincoln of the Union's defeat on this day.

1   The incapacity of the commander [Rosecrans] is astonishing, and it often seems difficult to believe him of sound mind. His imbecility appears to be contagious.
    —telegram to Lincoln, October 16, 1863.

★ Dana was with Major General William Rosecrans's army under siege in Chattanooga. The same day this was received, Lincoln replaced Rosecrans with Lieutenant General Ulysses S. Grant.

Dana, Richard, Jr. (1815–1882)

WRITER AND LAWYER

2   As to the politics of Washington, the most striking thing is the absence of personal loyalty to the President. It does not exist. He has no admirers, no enthusiastic supports, none to bet on his head.
    —quoted by Geoffrey C. Ward in *The Civil War: An Illustrated History*, 1990.

★ Dana wrote *Two Years Before the Mast* (1840) and became a lawyer.

Daniel, John W. (1842–1910)

CS MAJOR

3   The staff of the Army of Northern Virginia . . . was for the most part an improvised affair, as for the most part was the whole Confederate Army, and indeed the Federal Army was almost as much so.
    —*Recollections of a Confederate Staff Officer*, 1905.

Dargan, Edmund S. (1805–1879)

LEGISLATOR AND JUDGE

4   There are now in the slaveholding States over four millions of slaves; dissolve the relation of master and slave, and what, I ask, would become of that race? To remove them from amongst us is impossible. . . . They therefore must remain with us; and if the relation of master and slave be dissolved and our slaves turned loose amongst us without restraint, they would either be destroyed by our own hands—the hands to which they look, and look with confidence, for protection—or we ourselves would become demoralized and degraded. The former result would take place, and we ourselves would become the executioners of our own slaves.
    —speech to the Secession Convention of Alabama on January 11, 1861, quoted by William R. Smith in *The History and Debates of the Convention of the People of Alabama*, 1861.

Davis, Annie

It is my Desire to be free. to go to see my people on the eastern shore. my mistress   1
wont let me. you will please let me know if we are free. and what i can do. I write to
you for advice. Please send me word this week. Or as soon as possible and oblidge.
   —letter to Lincoln, August 25, 1864.

★ This letter from a distressed slave in Bel Air, Maryland, was apparently filed by the
Bureau of Colored Troops and no reply ever sent. Slaves in the Union state of Maryland
had not been officially freed by the Emancipation Proclamation. Davis would have been
liberated by the new Maryland constitution, which went into effect November 1, 1864.

Davis, J. Bancroft (1822–1907)

AMERICAN LAWYER AND CORRESPONDENT FOR THE *TIMES* (LONDON)

I do not see how secession is now to be avoided. In making this statement, however,   2
it is important to define what secession is. It is easier to say what it is not than what
it is. It is not order and good government. It is not submission to the law, and accepting a President elected in the manner provided by the Constitution and the laws.
It is not a regard for the rights of others. It is nothing, in fact, which law-abiding
Englishmen are taught to respect and observe.
   —*Times* (London), December 19, 1860.

A little contest in the harbour of Charleston has grown into a great civil war.   3
   —*Times* (London), May 6, 1861.

Davis, Jefferson (1808–1889)

CONFEDERATE PRESIDENT

[The Republicans] seceded in the last Presidential election [in 1856], went off as a   4
section, organized for themselves, and attempted to force a sectional candidate, supported entirely by a sectional vote. That was secession, practical secession.
   —quoted by Hudson Strode in *Jefferson Davis: American Patriot*, 1955.

★ Davis was a US senator at this time.

Is [abolition] in the cause of Christianity? It cannot be, for servitude is the only agency   5
through which Christianity has reached the Negro race.
   —speech in Boston, October 11, 1858.

★ Davis was still a US senator at this time.

Though the defense of African slavery (thus it is commonly called) is left to the South,   6
the North are jointly benefited by it. Deduct from their trade and manufactures all
which is dependent upon the products of slave labor, their prosperity would fade.
   —speech to the Mississippi Democratic Convention, July 6, 1859, when Davis was
   a US senator.

1   That word "invasion" once had a signification which carried the mind simply to foreigners alone. God forbid we should ever come to learn that it means likewise a portion of our own brethren.
—speech to the US Senate, December 6, 1859.

★ This was after John Brown's attack on Harper's Ferry, Virginia, and predictions of more abolitionist "invasions."

2   I glory in Mississippi's star! [on the US flag] But before I would see it dishonored I would tear it from its place, to be set on the perilous ridge of battle as a sign around which her bravest and best shall meet the harvest home of death.
—speech, November 5, 1860.

★ The future Confederate president would resign from the US Senate within three months.

3   If the secession of South Carolina should be followed by an attempt to coerce her back into the Union, that act of usurpation, folly, and wickedness would enlist every true Southern man for her defense.
—letter to Robert B. Rhett Jr., November 9, 1860.

★ This was three days after Lincoln was elected president. Davis would resign from the US Senate in January 1861. Rhett was editor of the *Charleston Mercury*.

4   Our government is an agency of delegated and strictly limited powers. Its founders did not look to its preservation by force.
—speech to the US Senate, December 10, 1860.

5   Is there wisdom, is there patriotism in the land? If so, easy must be the solution of this question. If not, then Mississippi's gallant sons will stand like a wall of fire around their State; and I go hence, not in hostility to you, but in love and allegiance to her, to take my place among her sons.
—speech to the US Senate, January 10, 1861.

★ Mississippi had seceded the previous day. Davis resigned from the Senate on January 21.

6   My God have us in His holy keeping, and grant that before it is too late, peaceful councils may prevail.
—quoted by Shelby Foote in *The Civil War*, vol. 1, 1958.

★ The future Confederate president said this on January 20, 1861, and resigned from the US Senate the following day.

7   There will be peace if you so will it, and you may bring disaster on every part of the country if you thus will have it.
—Senate resignation speech, January 21, 1861.

8   Secession is to be justified upon the basis that the States are sovereign.
—Senate resignation speech, January 21, 1861.

9   Our present condition, achieved in a manner unprecedented in the history of nations, illustrates the American idea that governments rest upon the consent of the gov-

erned, and that it is the right of the people to alter or abolish governments whenever they become destructive to the ends for which they were established.
    —inaugural address, February 18, 1861.

The time for compromise has now passed, and the South is determined to maintain **1** her position, and make all who oppose her smell Southern powder and feel Southern steel.
    —inaugural address, February 18, 1861.

The impartial, enlightened verdict of mankind will vindicate the rectitude of our **2** conduct, and He who knows the hearts of men will judge of the sincerity with which we labored to preserve the government of our fathers in its spirit.
    —inaugural address, February 18, 1861.

Actuated solely by a desire to preserve our own rights and promote our own welfare, **3** the separation of the Confederate States has been marked by no aggression upon others and followed by no domestic convulsion.
    —inaugural address, February 18, 1861.

★ This was two months before Fort Sumter was fired upon.

We have changed the constituent parts, but not the system of our government. The **4** Constitution formed by our fathers is that of these Confederate States.
    —inaugural address, February 18, 1861.

The suffering of millions will bear testimony to the folly and wickedness of our ag- **5** gressors.
    —inaugural address, February 18, 1861.

★ Davis was emphasizing the responsibility of the North in attacking the South.

We have entered upon the career of independence, and it must be inflexibly pur- **6** sued. . . . As a necessity, not a choice, we have resorted to the remedy of separation, and henceforth our energies must be directed to the conduct of our own affairs, and the perpetuity of the Confederacy which we have formed.
    —inaugural address, February 18, 1861.

Our present political position has been achieved in a manner unprecedented in the **7** history of nations.
    —inaugural address, February 18, 1861.

I was inaugurated [president of the Confederacy] on Monday. . . . Upon my weary **8** heart was showered smiles, plaudits, and flowers; but beyond them I saw troubles and thorns innumerable.
    —letter to his wife, Varina, February 20, 1861.

We are without machinery, without means, and threatened by a powerful opposition; **9** but I do not despond, and will not shrink from the task imposed upon me.
    —letter to his wife, Varina, February 20, 1861.

1   You cannot transform the negro into anything one-tenth as useful or as good as what slavery enables them to be.
     —quoted by Kenneth C. Davis in *Don't Know Much about the Civil War*, 1996.

     ★ This was said in February 1861.

2   Fort Sumter is ours, and nobody is hurt. With mortar, Paixhan, and petard, we tender "Old Abe" our *Beau-regard*.
     —*Charleston Mercury*, April 16, 1861.

     ★ Paixhans, or Columbiads, were large-caliber cannons used as siege artillery. Brigadier General Pierre G. T. Beauregard commanded the attack on Fort Sumter.

3   Whereas Abraham Lincoln, the President of the United States, has, by proclamation, announced the intention of invading this confederacy with an armed force, for the purposes of capturing its fortresses, and thereby subverting its independence and subjecting the free people thereof to the dominion of a foreign power; and whereas it has thus become the duty of this government to repel the threatened invasion, and to defend the rights and liberties of the people by all the means which the laws of nations and usages of civilized warfare place at its disposal; Now, therefore, I, Jefferson Davis, President of the Confederate States of America, do issue this my proclamation, inviting all those who may desire, by service in private armed vessels on the high seas, to aid this government in resisting so wanton and wicked an aggression, to make application for commission or letters of marque and reprisal, to be issued under the seal of these Confederate States.
     —proclamation, April 17, 1861.

4   We feel that our cause is just and holy. We protest solemnly, in the face of mankind, that we desire peace at any sacrifice save that of honor.
     —speech to a special session of the Confederate congress, April 29, 1861.

5   The war of the Revolution was successfully waged, and resulted in the treaty of peace with Great Britain in 1783, by the terms of which the several states were *each by name* recognized to be independent.
     —speech to a special session of the Confederate congress, April 29, 1861.

     ★ Davis was employing history to assert the right of individual states to leave the Union.

6   In a moral and social condition, they had been elevated from brutal savages into docile, intelligent, and civilized agricultural laborers, and supplied not only with bodily comforts but with careful religious instruction, under the supervision of a superior race.
     —speech to a special session of the Confederate congress, April 29, 1861.

     ★ This particular justification of slavery was often used in the South.

7   In independence we seek no conquest, no aggrandizement, no cession of any kind from the states with which we have lately confederated.
     —speech to a special session of the Confederate congress, April 29, 1861.

The President of the United States calls for an army of 75,000 men, whose first ser- 1
vice was to be to capture our forts. It was a plain declaration of war which I was not
at liberty to disregard because of my knowledge that under the Constitution of the
United States the President was usurping a power granted exclusively to the
Congress.
   —speech to a special session of the Confederate congress, April 29, 1861.

Put not your trust in princes and rest not your hopes on foreign nations. This war is 2
ours; we must fight it out ourselves; and I feel some pride in knowing that so far we
have done it without the good will of anybody.
   —quoted by Rod Graff in *Civil War Quiz and Fact Book*, 1985.

★ This was said after European nations failed to recognize the Confederacy officially.

Battles are not won where several unhurt men are seen carrying off each wounded 3
soldier!
   —quoted by William Swinton in *Campaigns of the Army of the Potomac*, 1866.

★ Davis made this observation after watching Confederate troops at the first battle of
Bull Run (first Manassas).

But for you, there would have been no battle of Bull Run. 4
   —quoted by John D. Wright in *The Language of the Civil War*, 2001.

★ Davis made the remark to Mrs. Rose O'Neal Greenhow, a Confederate spy in Washington, D.C., who sent a message concerning Union troop movements to Brigadier
General Pierre G. T. Beauregard that led him to move toward Bull Run (Manassas) for
the battle.

My hope is reverently fixed on Him whose favor is ever vouchsafed to the cause 5
which is just.
   —inauguration in Richmond, Virginia, as president of the Permanent Government
   of the Confederate States of America, February 22, 1862.

Events have cast on our arms and hopes the gloomiest of shadows. 6
   —quoted by Lieutenant Colonel G. F. R. Henderson in *Stonewall Jackson and the
   American Civil War*, vol. 1, 1898.

★ This was in March 1862, when Union troops were building toward a march on
Richmond, though it never came.

The cause could have spared a whole State better than that great soldier. 7
   —quoted by William C. Davis in *Jefferson Davis: The Man and His Hour*, 1991.

★ Davis wept at the news of General Albert A. Johnston's death at the battle of Shiloh.

It is hard to see incompetence losing opportunity and wasting hard-gotten means, 8
but harder still to bear is the knowledge that there is no available remedy.
   —letter to his wife, Varina, June 3, 1862.

Tender consideration for worthless and incompetent officers is but another name for 9
cruelty toward the brave men who fall sacrifices to these defects of their leaders.
   —message to the Confederate congress, October 8, 1862.

1   We are not engaged in a conflict for conquest, or for aggrandizement, or for the set-
     tlement of a point of international law. The question for you to decide is, Will you be
     slaves or will you be independent?
     —speech to the Mississippi legislature, December 26, 1862.

2   After what has happened during the last two years, my only wonder is that we con-
     sented to live for so long a time in association with such miscreants and have loved
     so much a government rotten to the core. Were it ever to be proposed again to enter
     into a Union with such a people, I could not more consent to do it than to trust
     myself in a den of thieves.
     —speech to the Mississippi legislature, December 26, 1862.

3   Our enemies are a traditionalist and homeless race.
     —speech to the Mississippi legislature, December 26, 1862.

4   These [Northern] people, when separated from the South and left entirely to them-
     selves, have in six months demonstrated their utter incapacity for self-government.
     —speech to the Mississippi legislature, December 26, 1862.

5   Our people have only to be true to themselves to behold the Confederate flag among
     the recognized nations of the earth.
     —speech to the Mississippi legislature, December 26, 1862.

6   I cannot avoid remarking with how much pleasure I have noticed the superior moral-
     ity of our troops and the contrast which in this respect they present to the invader.
     —speech to the Mississippi legislature, December 26, 1862.

7   Never be humble to the haughty. Never be haughty to the humble.
     —response to a serenade in Wilmington, North Carolina, January 4, 1863.

8   I am happy to be welcomed on my return to the capital of the Confederacy—the last
     hope, as I believe, for the perpetuation of that system of government which our fore-
     fathers founded—the asylum of the oppressed, and the home of true representative
     liberty.
     —response to those gathered outside the Confederate White House, January 5,
     1863.

9   For what are they waging war? They say to preserve the Union. Can they preserve
     the Union by destroying the social existence of a portion of the South? Do they hope
     to reconstruct the Union by striking at everything which is dear to man?—by show-
     ing themselves so utterly disgraced that if the question was proposed to you whether
     you would combine with hyenas or Yankees, I trust every Virginian would say: "Give
     me the hyenas."
     —response to a serenade in Richmond, January 5, 1863.

It is true you have a cause which binds you together more firmly than your fathers   **1**
were. They fought to be free from the usurpations of the British crown, but they
fought against a manly foe. You fight against the off-scourings of the earth.
—response to a serenade in Richmond, January 5, 1863.

Here, upon your soil, some of the fiercest battles of the Revolution were fought, and   **2**
upon your soil it closed by the surrender of Cornwallis. Here again are men of every
state; here they have congregated, linked in the defense of a most sacred cause. They
have battled, they have bled upon your soil, and it is now consecrated by blood which
cries for vengeance against the insensate foe of religion as well as of humanity, of the
altar as well as of the hearthstone.
—response to a serenade in Richmond, January 5, 1863.

Every crime which could characterize the course of demons has marked the course   **3**
of the invader . . . from the burning of defenseless towns to the stealing of silver
forks and spoons.
—response to a serenade in Richmond, January 5, 1863.

With such noble women at home and such heroic soldiers in the field, we are invin-   **4**
cible.
—response to a serenade in Richmond, January 5, 1863.

See the increasing power of the enemy, but mark that our own has been proportion-   **5**
ately greater, until we see in the future nothing to disturb the prospect of the independence for which we are struggling.
—response to a serenade in Richmond, January 5, 1863.

The people of this confederacy . . . cannot fail to receive this [emancipation] procla-   **6**
mation as the fullest vindication of their own sagacity in foreseeing the uses to which
the dominant party in the United States intended from the beginning to apply their
power; nor can they cease to remember with devout thankfulness that it is to their
own vigilance in resisting the first stealthy progress of approaching despotism that
they owe their escape from consequences now apparent to the most skeptical.
—speech to the Confederate congress, January 12, 1863.

We have reached the close of the second year of the war, and may point with just   **7**
pride to the history of our young Confederacy. Alone, unaided, we have met and
overthrown the most formidable combination of naval and military armaments that
the lust of conquest ever gathered together for the subjugation of a free people.
—proclamation to the people of the Confederate States, April 10, 1863.

The contrast between our past and present condition is well calculated to inspire full   **8**
confidence in the triumph of our arms. At no previous period of the war have our
forces been so numerous, so well organized, and so thoroughly disciplined, armed,
and equipped as at present.
—proclamation to the people of the Confederate States, April 10, 1863.

1   If I could take one wing and Lee the other, I think we could between us wrest a victory from those people.
       —quoted by Nathaniel W. Stephenson in *The Day of the Confederacy: A Chronicle of the Embattled South*, 1919.

   ★ Davis, a former soldier in the Mexican War and former US secretary of war, made this remark to his wife, Varina, in June 1863. "Those people" was the term used by Lee for the Union enemy.

2   It is meet that when trials and reverses befall us we should seek to take home to our hearts and consciences the lessons which they teach, and profit by the self-examination for which they prepare us.
       —proclamation, July 25, 1863.

3   You know too well, my countrymen, what they mean by success. Their malignant rage aims at nothing less than the extermination of yourselves, your wives and children. They seek to destroy what they cannot plunder.
       —proclamation to the soldiers of the Confederate States, August 1, 1863.

4   Fellow citizens, no alternative is left you but victory, or subjugation, slavery and the utter ruin of yourselves, your families and your country. The victory is within your reach.—You need but stretch forth your hand to grasp it.
       —proclamation to the soldiers of the Confederate States, August 1, 1863.

5   To ask me to substitute you by some one in my judgment more fit to command, or who would possess more of the confidence of the army, is to demand an impossibility.
       —letter to General Robert E. Lee, August 11, 1863.

   ★ Lee had written him three days earlier submitting his resignation. This was just over a month after the Gettysburg defeat.

6   I feel it my duty to express personally, and in the name of the Confederate States, our gratitude for such sentiments of Christian good feeling and love, and to assure Your Holiness that the people, threatened even on their own hearths with the most cruel oppression and terrible carnage, is desirous now, as it has always been, to see the end of the impious war; that we have ever addressed prayers to Heaven for that issue which Your Holiness now desires; that we desire none of our enemy's possessions, but that we fight merely to resist the devastation of our country and the shedding of our best blood, and to force them to let us live in peace under the protection of our own institutions, and under our laws, which not only insure to every one the enjoyment of his temporal rights, but also the free exercise of his religion.
       —letter to Pope Pius IX, September 23, 1863.

   ★ Davis had seen letters written by the pope on October 18, 1862, to the archbishops of New Orleans and New York expressing grief over the war and asking them to exhort people to peace and charity. The pope responded on December 3 with a supportive letter.

7   We are now in the darkest hour of our political existence.
       —quoted by Randall Bedwell in *Brink of Destruction*, 1999.

   ★ This evaluation came after the Confederate defeat at Chattanooga on November 25, 1863.

We now know that the only reliable hope for peace is the vigor of our resistance, 1
while the cessation of their hostility is only to be expected from the pressure of their
necessities.
  —remarks to the Confederate congress, December 8, 1863.

[Northerners] are people without faith or law, without moral principles, living in the 2
depths of depravity and abjectness so deep that words cannot express it.
  —quoted by Charles Girard in *A Visit to the Confederate States of America in
  1863*, 1864.

★ Girard was a French military supplier to the Confederacy.

Anything, except reunion with that nation of miscreants. We should prefer to be gov- 3
erned by the King of Dahomey himself, rather than submit to Yankee enslavement.
  —quoted by Charles Girard in *A Visit to the Confederate States of America in
  1863*, 1864.

★ Girard was a French military supplier to the Confederacy.

If we break up our Government, dissolve the Confederacy, disband our armies, eman- 4
cipate our slaves, take an oath of allegiance binding ourselves to obedience to
[Lincoln], and to disloyalty to our own States, he proposed to pardon us, and not to
plunder us of anything more than the property already stolen from us.
  —letter to North Carolina governor Zebulon B. Vance, January 8, 1864.

While brigade after brigade of our brave soldiers who have endured the trials of the 5
camp and battlefield are testifying their patriotism by voluntary reenlistment, discontent, disaffection, and disloyalty are manifested among those who, through the
sacrifices of others, have enjoyed quiet and safety at home.
  —speech to the Confederate congress, February 3, 1864.

Soldiers! Assured success awaits us in our holy struggle for liberty and independence, 6
and for the preservation of all that renders life desirable to honorable men. . . . The
fruits of that success will not be reaped by you alone, but your children and your children's children, in long generations to come, will enjoy blessings derived from you,
that will preserve your memory ever-living in their hearts.
  —speech to Confederate soldiers, February 9, 1864.

I have been pained to hear of your exposure of your person in various conflicts. The 7
country could not bear the loss of you, and my dear friend, though you are prone to
forget yourself, you will not, I trust, again forget the public interest dependent on
your life.
  —quoted by Hudson Strode in *Jefferson Davis: Tragic Hero*, 1964.

★ David said this to Lee after Lee tried to lead a charge on May 12, 1864, during the
battle of Spotsylvania, Virginia.

[Lee and Jackson] supplemented each other, and together, with any fair opportunity, 8
they were absolutely invincible.
  —quoted by Lieutenant Colonel G. F. R. Henderson in *Stonewall Jackson and the
  American Civil War*, vol. 2, 1898.

1   We are fighting for Independence—and that, or extermination, we will have.
—quoted by Shelby Foote in *The Civil War*, vol. 3, 1958.

★ Davis was speaking to two Northerners who met with him in Richmond on July 16, 1864, to seek terms that might lead to an armistice. They were Colonel James F. Jaquess, a Methodist minister from Illinois, and J. R. Gilmore, a New York businessman. Lincoln had approved of their mission.

2   Sherman, to be sure, is before Atlanta; but suppose he *is*, and suppose he takes it? You know that the farther he goes from his base of supplies, the weaker he grows and the more disastrous defeat will be to him.
—quoted by Hudson Strode in *Jefferson Davis: Tragic Hero*, 1964.

★ Davis said this to two Northern peacemakers visiting him on July 16, 1864.

3   At your door lies all the misery and the crime of this war,—and it is a fearful, fearful account.
—quoted by Hudson Strode in *Jefferson Davis: Tragic Hero*, 1964.

★ Davis said this to two Northern peacemakers visiting him on July 16, 1864.

4   But Amnesty, Sir, applies to criminals. We have committed no crime.
—quoted by Hudson Strode in *Jefferson Davis: Tragic Hero*, 1964.

★ Davis said this to two Northern peacemakers visiting him on July 16, 1864.

5   The first effect of disaster is always to spread a deeper gloom than is due to the occasion.
—letter to Herschel V. Johnson, September 18, 1864.

★ Davis was referring to the fall of Atlanta on September 2. Johnson was a Georgia senator in the Confederate congress.

6   Let no one despond.
—speech in Macon, Georgia, September 25, 1864.

★ He repeated this sentence in other speeches as he toured the South after the fall of Atlanta.

7   If one half the men now absent without leave will return to the front, we can defeat the enemy.
—speech in Macon, Georgia, September 25, 1864.

8   Ours is not a revolution. We are a free and independent people, in States that had the right to make a better government when they saw fit.
—speech in Augusta, Georgia, October 3, 1864.

9   I believe it is in the power of the men of the Confederacy to plant our banners on the banks of the Ohio, where we shall say to the Yankee: "Be quiet, or we shall teach you another lesson."
—speech in Columbia, South Carolina, October 4, 1864.

10   We know ourselves fully competent to maintain our own rights and independence against the invaders of our country, and we feel justified in asserting that without the

aid derived from recruiting their armies from foreign countries the invaders would ere this have been driven from our soil.
  —speech to the Confederate congress, November 7, 1864.

Our people have fought so as to command the admiration of mankind, they have   1
nobly met the sacrifices of their position, never before was there so little despotism
under such severe pressure.
  —letter to his nephew, Hugh P. Davis, January 8, 1865.

Let us then unite our hands and our hearts, lock our shields together, and we may   2
well believe that before another summer solstice falls upon us, it will be the enemy
that will be asking us for conferences and occasions in which to make known our
demands.
  —speech in Richmond, February 6, 1865.

★ Three days earlier the peace conference at Hampton Roads, Virginia, had failed.

It is now becoming daily more evident to all reflecting persons that we are reduced   3
to choosing whether the negroes shall fight for us or against us, and that all arguments as to the positive advantages or disadvantages of employing them are beside
the question.
  —letter to John Forsyth, February 21, 1865.

★ Forsyth was editor of the *Register and Advertiser* in Mobile, Alabama.

I am happy to receive your assurance of success [in raising Negro troops], as well as   4
your promise to seek legislation to secure unmistakable freedom to the slave who
shall enter the Army, with a right to return to his old home, when he shall have been
honorably discharged from military service.
  —letter to Virginia governor William Smith, March 30, 1865.

The question is often asked, will we hold Richmond, to which my only answer is, if   5
we can; it is purely a question of military power. The distrust is increasing and embar-
rasses in many ways.
  —letter to General Robert E. Lee, April 1, 1865.

Let us not then despond, my countrymen, but, relying on the never-failing mercies   6
and protecting care of our God, let us meet the foe with fresh defiance, with uncon-
quered and unconquerable hearts.
  —proclamation to the people of the Confederate States of America, April 4, 1865.

★ This was only five days before General Robert E. Lee surrendered.

It is for us, our countrymen, to show by our bearing under reverses how wretched   7
has been the self-deception of those who have believed us less able to endure misfortune with fortitude than to encounter danger with courage.
  —last speech to the Confederacy, April 4, 1865.

★ Davis and the Confederate government had retreated from Richmond, now under
Union occupation, to Danville, Virginia.

1   I will never consent to abandon to the enemy one foot of soil of any of the States of the Confederacy.
         —public proclamation, April 5, 1865.

     ★ Davis said this after he and his government had retreated from Richmond to Danville, Virginia.

2   Our late disasters are terrible, but I do not think we should regard them as fatal. I think we can whip the enemy yet, if our people will turn out.
         —quoted by Shelby Foote in *The Civil War*, vol. 3, 1958.

     ★ This was said on April 13, 1865, four days after General Robert E. Lee had surrendered.

3   I am sorry. We have lost our best friend in the court of the enemy.
         —quoted by Hudson Strode in *Jefferson Davis: Tragic Hero*, 1964.

     ★ Davis had just been informed of Lincoln's assassination.

4   Certainly I have no special regard for Mr. Lincoln, but there are a great many men of whose end I would rather hear than his. I fear it will be disastrous to our people, and I regret it deeply.
         —quoted by Shelby Foote in *The Civil War*, vol. 3, 1958.

     ★ This was said on April 19, 1865, five days after Lincoln's death.

5   Even after that disaster [of Lee's surrender], if the men who "straggled," say thirty or forty thousand in number, had come back with their arms and with a disposition to fight we might have repaired the damage; but panic has seized the country.
         —letter to his wife, Varina, April 23, 1865.

6   . . . again and again will we return until the baffled and exhausted enemy shall abandon in despair his endless and impossible task of making slaves of a people resolved to be free.
         —quoted by Nathaniel W. Stephenson in *The Day of the Confederacy: A Chronicle of the Embattled South*, 1919.

     ★ Davis and his government were in retreat in Danville, Virginia, in April 1865.

7   If the Confederacy fails, there should be written on its tombstone: *Died of a Theory*.
         —quoted by Geoffrey C. Ward in *The Civil War*, 1991.

     ★ This was said in 1865.

8   We are not fighting for slavery. We are fighting for Independence,—and that, or extermination, we *will* have.
         —quoted by Hudson Strode in *Jefferson Davis: Tragic Hero*, 1964.

9   I tried all in my power to avert this war. I saw it coming, and for twelve years I worked night and day to prevent it, but I could not. And now it must go on till the last man of this generation falls in his tracks, and his children seize his musket and fight his battle.
         —quoted by Hudson Strode in *Jefferson Davis: Tragic Hero*, 1964.

I would give my poor life, gladly, if it would bring peace and good will to the two **1** countries; but it would not. It is *they* who desolate our homes, burn our wheatfields, break the wheels of wagons carrying away our women and children, and destroy supplies meant for our sick and wounded.
    —quoted by Hudson Strode in *Jefferson Davis: Tragic Hero*, 1964.

You may "emancipate" every negro in the Confederacy, but *we will be free!* We will **2** govern ourselves. We will do it, if we have to see every Southern plantation sacked, and every Southern city in flames.
    —quoted by Hudson Strode in *Jefferson Davis: Tragic Hero*, 1964.

All we ask is to be left alone.   **3**
    —quoted by Shelby Foote in *The Civil War*, vol. 3, 1958.

★ Davis frequently made this statement.

That there exists a conspiracy in the States to murder me, and that many persons are **4** engaged in it, I have been assured by letters of various dates and from various places. . . . There is a proverb that threatened men live long. I hope to be an example of it.
    —letter to William Howell, November 6, 1867.

★ Howell was Davis's brother-in-law.

I had a few [slaves] when the war began. I was of some use to them; they never were **5** of much use to me.
    —quoted by Hudson Strode in *Jefferson Davis: Tragic Hero*, 1964.

Were the thing to be done over again, I would do as I then did. Disappointments **6** have not changed my convictions.
    —*The Rise and Fall of the Confederate Government*, 1881.

For an enemy so relentless in the war for our subjugation, we could not be expected **7** to mourn [Lincoln's death]; yet, in view of its political consequences, it could not be regarded otherwise than as a great misfortune to the South. He had power over the Northern people, and was without personal malignity toward the people of the South; his successor was without power in the North, and the embodiment of malignity toward the Southern people, perhaps the more so because he had betrayed and deserted them in their hour of need.
    —*The Rise and Fall of the Confederate Government*, 1881.

It is our duty to keep the memory of our heroes green. Yet they belong not to us **8** alone; they belong to the whole country; they belong to America.
    —quoted by Hudson Strode in *Jefferson Davis: Tragic Hero*, 1964.

★ This was said in 1882.

Our children may forget this war, but *we* cannot.   **9**
    —quoted by Hudson Strode in *Jefferson Davis: Tragic Hero*, 1964.

1   Neither current events nor history shows that the majority rules.
    —quoted by Hudson Strode in *Jefferson Davis: Tragic Hero*, 1964.

2   The safety and honor of a Republic must rest upon the morality, intelligence and
    patriotism of the community.
    —speech to Mississippi legislators, March 10, 1884.

    ★ This was nearly two decades after the defeat of the Confederacy.

3   We are now in a transition state, which is always a bad one, both in society and in
    nature. What is to be the result of the changes which may be anticipated it is not pos-
    sible to forecast, but our people have shown such fortitude and have risen so grandly
    from the deep depression inflicted upon them that it is fair to entertain bright hopes
    for the future.
    —speech to Mississippi legislators, March 10, 1884.

4   Sectional hate concentrating itself upon my devoted head, deprives me of the privi-
    leges accorded to others in the sweeping expression of "without distinction of race,
    color or previous condition," but it cannot deprive me of that which is nearest and
    dearest to my heart, the right to be a Mississippian.
    —speech to Mississippi legislators, March 10, 1884.

5   No one is the arbiter of his own fate.
    —speech to Mississippi legislators, March 10, 1884.

6   It has been said that I should apply to the United States for a pardon. But repen-
    tance must precede the right of pardon, and I have not repented. Remembering, as
    I must, all which has been suffered, all which has been lost—disappointed hopes and
    crushed aspirations—yet I deliberately say, if it were all to do over again, I would
    again do just as I did in 1861.
    —speech to Mississippi legislators, March 10, 1884.

7   The people of the Confederate States did more in proportion to their numbers and
    means than was ever achieved by any in the world's history.
    —speech to Mississippi legislators, March 10, 1884.

8   But never question or teach your children to desecrate the memory of the dead by
    admitting that their brothers were wrong in the effort to maintain the sovereignty,
    freedom and independence which was their inalienable birthright—remembering
    that the coming generations are the children of the heroic mothers whose devotion
    to our cause in its darkest hour sustained the strong and strengthened the weak, I
    cannot believe that the cause for which our sacrifices were made can ever be lost,
    but rather hope that those who now deny the justice of our asserted claims will learn
    from experience that the fathers builded wisely and the Constitution should be con-
    strued according to the commentaries of the men who made it.
    —speech to Mississippi legislators, March 10, 1884.

The war between the states was not revolution, as sovereigns never rebel. **1**
> —speech in Montgomery, Alabama, April 28, 1886.

★ This was when Davis laid the cornerstone of a monument to the Confederate dead at the Capitol near where he had been sworn in as president in 1861.

There are some who take it for granted that when I allude to State sovereignty I want **2** to bring on another war. I am too old to fight again, and God knows I do not want you to have the necessity of fighting again. However, if that necessity *should* arise, I know you will meet it as you always have discharged every duty you felt called upon to perform.
> —speech in Savannah, Georgia, May 6, 1886.

The past is dead; let it bury its dead, its hopes and its aspirations. Before you lies the **3** future—a future full of golden promise; a future of expanding national glory, before which all the world shall stand amazed. Let me beseech you to lay aside all rancor, all bitter sectional feeling, and to take your places in the ranks of those who will bring about a consummation devoutly to be wished—a reunited country.
> —quoted by Hudson Strode in *Jefferson Davis: Tragic Hero*, 1964.

★ This was said at Davis's last public speech, in Mississippi City in March 1888.

I feel no regret that I stand before you a man without a country, for my ambition lies **4** buried in the grave of the Confederacy.
> —quoted by Hudson Strode in *Jefferson Davis: Tragic Hero*, 1964.

★ This was said at Davis's last public speech, in Mississippi City, in March 1888.

Pray excuse me. I cannot take it. **5**
> —quoted by Hudson Strode in *Jefferson Davis: Tragic Hero*, 1964.

★ These were Davis's last words before dying on December 6, 1889. He was referring to the medicine offered by his wife, Varina.

Davis, Nicholas A. (1824–1894)

CS CHAPLAIN

They were representative men from all portions of the State [of Texas]—young, **6** impetuous and fresh, full of energy, enterprise, and fire—men of action—men who, when they first heard the shrill shriek of battle, as it came from the far-off coast of South Carolina, at once ceased to argue with themselves, or with their neighbors, as to the why-fores or the where-fores—it was enough to know that the struggle had commenced, and that they were Southrons.
> —*Campaign from Texas to Maryland, with the Battle of Fredericksburg*, 1863.

Here we had the first realization of the fact, that we were *actual soldiers*, and had the **7** first lesson illustrated to us, that a soldier must be patient under wrong, and that he is remediless under injustice—that he, although the self constituted and acknowledged champion of liberty, has, nevertheless, for the time being, parted with that

boon, and, that he is but the victim of all official miscreants who choose to subject him to imposition.
  —*Campaign from Texas to Maryland, with the Battle of Fredericksburg*, 1863.

Davis, Reuben

CS MAJOR GENERAL AND CONGRESSMAN FROM MISSISSIPPI

1   Gifted with some of the highest attributes of a statesman, [Jefferson Davis] lacked the pliancy which enables a man to adapt his measures to the crisis.
  —quoted by Nathaniel W. Stephenson in *The Day of the Confederacy: A Chronicle of the Embattled South*, 1919.

Davis, Varina H. (1826–1906)

WIFE OF JEFFERSON DAVIS

2   While [in New Orleans], Captain Dreux, at the head of his battalion, came to serenade me, but I could not command my voice to speak to him when he came on the balcony; his cheery words and the enthusiasm of his men depressed me dreadfully. Violets were in season, and the captain and his company brought several immense bouquets. The color seemed ominous. Perhaps Mr. Davis's depression had communicated itself to me, and I could not rally or be buoyed up by the cheerfulness of those who were to do battle for us.
  —*Jefferson Davis: A Memoir by His Wife*, 1890.

  ★ This happened in her father's home just before she left to join her newly inaugurated husband in Montgomery, Alabama.

3   Under [the Confederate flag] we won our victories, and the memory of its glory will never fade. It is enshrined in our hearts forever.
  —*Jefferson Davis: A Memoir by His Wife*, 1890.

4   I think I am the proper person to advise Mr. Davis and if I were he, I would die or be hung before I would submit to the humiliation.
  —quoted by Nathaniel W. Stephenson in *The Day of the Confederacy: A Chronicle of the Embattled South*, 1919.

  ★ Varina Davis supposedly said this in regard to the Confederate congress forcing upon her husband a plan for an overall commanding officer of all the armies. Such a bill was passed on January 26, 1865, and General Robert E. Lee assumed the position on February 9.

5   There is no bond uniting us to the Northerners. A great gulf of blood rolls between us. My spirit shrinks appalled from attempting to cross it.
  —letter to Judge George Shea.

  ★ Davis's husband was being held in prison under horrid conditions. Shea was a Northern lawyer offering to defend Davis.

Dawson, Sarah Morgan (1842–1909)

Nothing can be positively ascertained, save that our gunboats are sunk and theirs are **1** coming up to the city [Baton Rouge, Louisiana]. Everything else has been contradicted until we really do not know whether the city [New Orleans] has been taken or not. We only know we had best be prepared for anything. So day before yesterday, Lilly and I sewed up our jewelry, which may be of use if we have to fly. I vow I will not move one step, unless carried away.
—*A Confederate Girl's Diary*, 1913.

★ This was written on April 26, 1862, when Sarah was nineteen. Lilly was her sister.

And if you [Yankees] want to know what an excited girl can do, just call and let me **2** show you the use of a small seven-shooter and a large carving-knife which vibrate between by belt and my pocket, always ready for emergencies.
—*A Confederate Girl's Diary*, 1913.

★ This was written on April 26, 1862.

Vile old Yankee boats, four in number, passed up [the Mississippi River] this morn- **3** ing without stopping. After all our excitement, this "silent contempt" annihilated me. What in the world do they mean?
—*A Confederate Girl's Diary*, 1913.

★ This was written on May 5, 1862, in Baton Rouge, Louisiana.

This is a dreadful war, to make even the hearts of women so bitter! I hardly know **4** myself these last few weeks. I, who have such a horror of bloodshed, consider even killing in self-defense murder, who cannot wish [Yankees] the slightest evil, whose only prayer is to have them sent back in peace to their own country,—I talk of killing them!
—*A Confederate Girl's Diary*, 1913.

★ This was written on May 9, 1862.

"All devices, signs, and flags of the Confederacy shall be suppressed." So says Pi- **5** cayune Butler. *Good.* I devote all my red, white, and blue silk to the manufacture of Confederate flags. As soon as one is confiscated, I make another, until my ribbon is exhausted, when I will sport a duster emblazoned in high colors, "Hurra! For the Bonny blue flag!" Henceforth, I wear one pinned to my bosom—not a duster, but a little flag; the man who says take it off will have to pull it off himself; the man who dares attempt it—well! A pistol in my pocket fills up the gap. I am capable, too.
—*A Confederate Girl's Diary*, 1913.

★ This was written on May 9, 1862, about General Benjamin Butler's order. "Picayune" is a word, especially popular in Louisiana, meaning "trivial."

O if I was only a man! Then I would don the breeches, and slay them with a will! If **6** some Southern women were in the ranks, they would set the men an example they would not blush to follow! Pshaw! There are *no* women here! We are *all* men.
—*A Confederate Girl's Diary*, 1913.

★ This was written on May 9, 1862.

1   Does it take thirty thousand men and millions of dollars to murder defenseless women and children? O the great nation! Bravo!
     —*A Confederate Girl's Diary*, 1913.

     ★ This was written on May 10, 1862.

2   Fine, noble-looking men they were, showing refinement and gentlemanly bearing in every motion. One cannot help but admire such foes! They set us an example worthy of our imitation, and one we would be benefited by following. They came as visitors without either pretensions to superiority, or the insolence of conquerors; they walk quietly their way, offering no annoyance to the citizens. . . . They prove themselves gentlemen, while many of our citizens have proved themselves boors, and I admire them for their conduct.
     —*A Confederate Girl's Diary*, 1913.

     ★ This was written on May 11, 1862. Sarah had seen Union soldiers occupying her town of Baton Rouge.

3   Four days ago the Yankees left us, to attack Vicksburg, leaving their flag flying in the Garrison without a man to guard it, and with the understanding that the town would be held responsible for it. It was intended as a trap, and it succeeded. For night before last, it was pulled down and torn to pieces.
     —*A Confederate Girl's Diary*, 1913.

     ★ This was written on May 17, 1862.

4   "What a fall was there, my country," from my pretty English glove-kid, to sabots made of some animal closely connected with the hippopotamus!
     —*A Confederate Girl's Diary*, 1913.

     ★ Sarah was complaining about the impoverishment of the Confederacy in this diary entry of May 21, 1862. Her quotation alludes to Shakespeare's *Julius Caesar*: "O, what a fall was there, my countrymen!"

5   Three miles from town [Baton Rouge, Louisiana] we began to overtake the fugitives. Hundreds of women and children were walking alone, some bareheaded, and in all costumes. Little girls of twelve and fourteen were wandering on alone. . . . White and black were all mixed together, and were as confidential as though related. . . . The negroes deserve the greatest praise for their conduct. Hundreds were walking with babies or bundles; ask them what they had saved, it was invariable, "My mistress's clothes, or silver, or baby." Ask what they had for themselves, it was, "Bless your heart, honey. I was glad to get away with mistress's things; I did n't think 'bout mine."
     —*A Confederate Girl's Diary*, 1913.

     ★ This entry of May 30, 1862, concerns an event that occurred two days earlier.

6   So ended the momentous shelling of Baton Rouge, during which the valiant Farragut killed one whole woman, wounded three, struck some twenty houses several

times apiece, and indirectly caused the death of two little children who were drowned in their flight. . . . Hurrah for the illustrious Farragut, the Woman Killer!!!
    —*A Confederate Girl's Diary*, 1913.

★ This was written on May 31, 1862.

A gentleman [Union officer] tells me that no one is permitted to leave without a   1
pass. . . . I saw the "pass," just such as we give our negroes, signed by a Wisconsin colonel. Think of being obliged to ask permission from some low plowman to go in and out of our own house!
    —*A Confederate Girl's Diary*, 1913.

★ This was written on June 1, 1862.

They tried the fascinating, and were much mortified by the coldness they met. Dear   2
me! "Why was n't I born old and ugly?" Suppose I should unconsciously entrap some magnificent Yankee! What an awful thing it would be!
    —*A Confederate Girl's Diary*, 1913.

★ This entry, written on June 3, 1862, refers to soldiers of the Union occupation force in Baton Rouge. Her quotation is from Charles Dickens's *Barnaby Rudge*.

How many good, and how many mean people these trouble have shown us.   3
    —*A Confederate Girl's Diary*, 1913.

★ This was written on June 4, 1862.

These people [Union soldiers occupying Baton Rouge, Louisiana] mean to kill us   4
with kindness. There is such a thing as being too kind. Yesterday General Williams sent a barrel of flour to mother accompanied by a note begging her to accept it "in consideration of the present condition of the circulating currency," and the intention was so kind, the way it was done so delicate, that there was no refusing it.
    —*A Confederate Girl's Diary*, 1913.

★ This was written on June 8, 1862.

This war has brought out wicked, malignant feelings that I did not believe could   5
dwell in woman's heart. I see some of the holiest eyes, so holy one would think the very spirit of charity lived in them, and all christian meekness, go off in a mad tirade of abuse and say, with the holy eyes wondrously changed, "I hope God will send down plague, yellow fever, famine, on these vile Yankees, and that not one will escape death."
    —*A Confederate Girl's Diary*, 1913.

★ This was written on June 16, 1862.

I see no salvation on either side. No glory awaits the Southern Confederacy, even if   6
it does achieve independence; it will be a mere speck in the world, with no weight or authority. The North confesses itself lost without us, and paid an unheard of ransom to regain us.
    —*A Confederate Girl's Diary*, 1913.

★ This was written on June 29, 1862.

1   If I was a man-on, would n't I be in Richmond with the boys! . . . What is the use of all these worthless women, in war times?
      —*A Confederate Girl's Diary*, 1913.

      ★ This was written on July 20, 1862.

2   Wicked as it may seem, I would rather have all I own burned, than in the possession of the negroes. Fancy my magenta organdie on a dark beauty!
      —*A Confederate Girl's Diary*, 1913.

      ★ This was written on August 17, 1862.

3   The Virginia news, after being so great and cheering, has suddenly ceased to come. No one knows the final result. The last report that we had was that we held Arlington Heights. Why not Washington consequently? Cincinnati (at last accounts) lay at our mercy.
      —*A Confederate Girl's Diary*, 1913.

      ★ This was written on September 10, 1862.

4   And what a sad sight the Fourth Louisiana was, that was then parading! Men that had fought at Shiloh and Baton Rouge were barefooted. Rags was their only uniform, for very few possessed a complete suit, and those few wore all varieties of colors and cuts. . . . Yet he who had no shoes looked as happy as he who had, and he who had a cap had something to toss up, that's all.
      —*A Confederate Girl's Diary*, 1913.

      ★ This was written on September 24, 1862.

5   I think old Abe wants to deprive us of all that fun! No more cotton, sugar-cane, or rice! No more old black aunties or uncles! No more rides in mule teams, no more songs in the cane-field, no more steamy kettles, no more black faces and shining teeth around the furnace fires! If Lincoln could spend the grinding season on a plantation, he would recall his [emancipation] proclamation. As it is, he has only proved himself a fool, without injuring us.
      —*A Confederate Girl's Diary*, 1913.

      ★ This was written on November 9, 1862.

6   Well! I boast myself Rebel, sing "Dixie," shout Southern Rights, pray for God's blessing on our cause, without ceasing, and would not live in this country if by any calamity we should be conquered. I am only a woman, and that is the way I feel.
      —*A Confederate Girl's Diary*, 1913.

      ★ This was written on January 23, 1863.

7   They are coming! The Yankees are coming at last! For four or five hours the sound of their cannon has assailed our ears. There!—that one shook my bed! Oh, they are coming! God grant us the victory!
      —*A Confederate Girl's Diary*, 1913.

      ★ This happened near Baton Rouge, Louisiana. The diary entry is from March 14, 1863.

"To be, or not to be, that's the question." Whether 't is nobler in the Confederacy to **1**
suffer the pangs of unappeasable hunger and never-ending trouble, or to take passage to a Yankee port, and there remaining, end them. Which is best?
 —*A Confederate Girl's Diary*, 1913.

★ She and her family went to Union-occupied New Orleans. This diary entry is from
March 31, 1863.

These Arkansas troops have acquired a reputation for roughness and ignorance which **2**
they seem to cultivate as assiduously as most people would their virtues. But rudeness does not affect their fighting qualities.
 —*A Confederate Girl's Diary*, 1913.

★ This was written on April 8, 1863.

. . . I abhor this [assassination of Lincoln], and call it foul murder, unworthy of our **3**
cause—and God grant it was only the temporary insanity of a desperate man that
committed this crime! Let not his blood be visited on this nation, Lord!
 —*A Confederate Girl's Diary*, 1913.

★ This was written on April 19, 1865.

"All things are taken from us, and become portions and parcels of the dreadful **4**
pasts." . . . Thursday the 13th came the dreadful tidings of the surrender of Lee and
his army on the 9th. Everybody cried, but I would not, satisfied that God will still
save us, even though all should apparently be lost.
 —*A Confederate Girl's Diary*, 1913.

★ This was written on April 19, 1865. Her quotation is from Alfred, Lord Tennyson's
The Lotus-Eaters, which used the singular "past." The next line in Tennyson's poem
asks the question, "What pleasure do we have to war with evil?"

Every one proclaimed Peace, and the only matter under consideration was whether **5**
Jeff Davis, all politicians, every man above the rank of Captain in the army and above
that of Lieutenant in the navy, should be hanged immediately, or *some* graciously
pardoned.
 —*A Confederate Girl's Diary*, 1913.

★ This was written on April 19, 1865.

Let historians extol blood-shedding; it is woman's place to abhor it. **6**
 —*A Confederate Girl's Diary*, 1913.

★ This was written on April 19, 1865.

Our Confederacy has gone with one crash—the report of the pistol fired at Lincoln. **7**
 —*A Confederate Girl's Diary*, 1913.

★ This was written on June 15, 1865.

It is a rope of sand, this Confederacy, founded on the doctrine of Secession, and will **8**
not last many years—not five.
 —*A Confederate Girl's Diary*, 1913.

1   I don't believe in Secession, but I do in Liberty.
—*A Confederate Girl's Diary*, 1913.

2   I want the South to conquer, dictate its own terms, and go back to the Union, for I
believe that, apart, inevitable ruin awaits both.
—*A Confederate Girl's Diary*, 1913.

3   The North cannot subdue us. We are too determined to be free. . . . If by power of
overwhelming numbers they conquer us, it will be a barren victory over a desolate
land.
—*A Confederate Girl's Diary*, 1913.

De Fontaine, Felix Gregory (1834–1896)

4   Civil War has at last begun. . . . The excitement in the community is indescribable.
With the very first boom of the gun, thousands rushed from their beds to the harbor
front, and all day every available place has been thronged by ladies and gentlemen,
viewing the solemn spectacle through their glasses.
—dispatch to the *New York Herald*, April 12, 1861.

★ De Fontaine, a friend of Brigadier General Pierre G. T. Beauregard, telegraphed
this account of the bombardment of Fort Sumter.

Dilworth, Caleb J.

US COLONEL

5   Well, we will turkey hunt this morning.
—quoted by Lloyd Lewis in *Sherman, Fighting Prophet*, 1932.

★ Dilworth was urging the troops of the 85th Illinois to find Confederate sharpshoot-
ers as General William T. Sherman's army moved through Georgia toward Atlanta.

Dix, John A. (1798–1879)

US SECRETARY OF THE TREASURY AND MAJOR GENERAL

6   If any one attempts to haul down the American flag, shoot him on the spot.
—telegram to W. Hemphill Jones, January 29, 1861.

★ Jones, a Treasury chief clerk, had informed Dix that the captain of the New Orleans
revenue cutter *McClelland* had refused to obey Dix's order to turn over his ship to the
Federal government.

Doster, William E.

US BRIGADIER GENERAL

7   In conversation, [Lincoln] was a patient, attentive listener, rather looking for the
opinion of others, than hazarding his own, and trying to view a matter in all of its
phases before coming to a conclusion.
—*Lincoln and Episodes of the Civil War*, 1915.

Douglas, Henry Kyd

CS MAJOR

It was a dreadful scene. The dead and dying lay thick on the field like harvest   1
sheaths. . . . Prayers were mingled with oaths, and midnight hid all distinction between blue and gray.
    —*I Rode with Stonewall*, 1940.

★ Douglas, the youngest aide on Major General Thomas J. "Stonewall" Jackson's staff,
was describing the aftermath of the battle of Antietam (Sharpsburg) on September 17,
1862. His memoirs were published thirty-seven years after his death.

Jackson was a man of strategy, and it is this quality of his mind that has attracted the   2
admiration of military critics.
    —*I Rode with Stonewall*, 1940.

Quick to decide and almost inflexible in decision, with a boldness to attack that   3
approached rashness and a tenacity in resisting that resembled desperation [General
Jubal Early] was yet on the field of battle not equal to his own intellect or decision.
    —*I Rode with Stonewall*, 1940.

Douglas, Stephen A. (1813–1861)

US SENATOR FROM ILLINOIS

Every man must be for the United States or against it. There can be no neutrals in   4
this war; *only patriots—or traitors.*
    —speech in Chicago, May 1, 1861.

★ Lincoln defeated Democrat Douglas in the 1860 election.

As between the crocodile and the negro, I take the side of the negro; but as between   5
the negro and the white man—I would go for the white man every time.
    —quoted by Colonel Alexander K. McClure in *Lincoln's Yarns and Stories*, 1904.

Douglass, Frederick (1818–1895)

ABOLITIONIST

★ The son of a slave, Douglass escaped to become an abolitionist.

. . . such is my deep, firm conviction that nothing can be attained for liberty univer-   6
sally by war, that were I to be asked the question as to whether I would have my
emancipation by the shedding of one single drop of blood, my answer would be in
the negative.
    —speech in London, 1846.

The simple way, then, to put an end to the savage and desolating war now waged by   7
the slaveholders, is to strike down slavery itself, the primal cause of that war.
    —"How to End the War," *Douglass' Monthly*, May 1861.

1   The national edifice is on fire. Every man who can carry a bucket of water, or remove a brick, is wanted, but those who have the care of the building, having a profound respect for the feeling of the national burglars who set the building on fire, are determined that the flames shall only be extinguished by Indo-Caucasian hands, and to have the building burnt rather than save it by means of any other. Such is the pride, the stupid prejudice and folly that rules the hour.

    —"Fighting Rebels with Only One Hand," *Douglass' Monthly*, September 1861.

    ★ This was before blacks were allowed to become US soldiers.

2   To let this occasion pass unimproved, for getting rid of slavery, would be a sin against unborn generations.

    —speech in Philadelphia, January 14, 1862.

3   The destiny of the colored American . . . is the destiny of America.

    —speech at the Emancipation League, Boston, February 12, 1862.

4   I hold that the [Emancipation] Proclamation, good as it is, will be worthless—a miserable mockery—unless the nation shall so far conquer its prejudice as to welcome into the army full-grown black men to help fight the battles of the Republic.

    —speech in New York City, February 6, 1863.

5   Once let the black man get upon his person the brass letters U. S., let him get an eagle on his button, and a musket on his shoulder, and bullets in his pocket, and there is no power on earth or under the earth which can deny that he has earned the right of citizenship in the United States.

    —speech on July 6, 1863.

6   I shall never forget the benignant expression of his face, the tearful look of his eye, the quiver in his voice, when [Lincoln] deprecated a resort to retaliatory measures.

    —quoted by Nathaniel W. Stephenson in *Lincoln: An Account of His Personal Life, Especially of Its Springs of Action as Revealed and Deepened by the Ordeal of War*, 1922.

    ★ Douglass had visited Lincoln to ask about revenge for the Fort Pillow massacre on April 12, 1864, in which black Union soldiers surrendered and were reportedly shot.

7   I was present at the inauguration of Mr. Lincoln, the 4th of March, 1865. I felt then that there was murder in the air, and I kept close to his carriage on the way to the Capitol, for I felt that I might see him fall that day. It was a vague presentiment.

    —*Life and Times of Frederick Douglass, Written by Himself*, 1881.

8   How sad and strange the fate of this great and good man, the saviour of his country, the embodiment of human charity, whose heart, though strong, was as tender as a heart of childhood; who always tempered justice with mercy; who sought to supplant the sword with counsel of reason, to suppress passion by kindness and moderation; who had a sigh for every human grief and a tear for every human woe, should at last perish by the hand of a desperate assassin, against whom no thought of malice had ever entered his heart!

    —quoted by Colonel Alexander K. McClure in *Lincoln's Yarns and Stories*, 1904.

Dunn, James L.

US SURGEON

In my feeble estimation, General McClellan, with all his laurels, sinks into insignifi- **1**
cance beside the true heroine of the age—the angel of the battle-field.
    —quoted by John D. Wright in *The Language of the Civil War*, 2001.

★ Dunn was writing about the nurse Clara Barton.

Du Pont, Samuel F. (1803–1865)

US REAR ADMIRAL

Success is not in my hands; to do my duty is.   **2**
    —letter to his wife, March 10, 1863.

Early, Jubal A. (1816–1894)

CS LIEUTENANT GENERAL

I not only wish them all dead but I wish them all in Hell.   **3**
    —quoted by Randall Bedwell in *Brink of Destruction*, 1999.

★ This was said about the Union forces on December 15, 1862, after the battle of
Fredericksburg.

We haven't taken Washington, but we've scared Abe Lincoln like hell!   **4**
    —quoted by Randall Bedwell in *Brink of Destruction*, 1999.

★ This was said on July 13, 1864, a day after Early's troops had withdrawn from the out-
skirts of Washington, D.C.

General Lee had not been conquered in battle, but surrendered because he had no **5**
longer an army with which to give battle. What he surrendered was the skeleton, the
mere ghost of the Army of Northern Virginia, which had been gradually worn down
by the combined agencies of numbers, steam-power, railroads, mechanism, and all
the resources of physical science.
    —speech at Washington and Lee University, January 19, 1872

Editorials and Articles, Newspaper

[Harper's Ferry] was an Abolition plot to free the negroes of Maryland and Virginia **6**
at the point of the bayonet. . . . The "irrepressible conflict" of the free and slave
states, which is preached by the Republican leaders as an orthodox doctrine, is well
calculated to lead to such results . . . The danger of having a Republican-Abolition
President can now be readily appreciated.
    —editorial, *Cincinnati Enquirer*, October 19, 1859.

The telegraphic dispatches yesterday morning [about Harper's Ferry] startled the **7**
public with an account of one of the most monstrous villainies ever attempted in this

country. . . . Who is so blind as not to see the inevitable tendency of black republican teaching? Now we have a bloody, glaring, ghastly fact before us. The "conflict" by blows has commenced. The proofs of an extensive and ramified organization is disclosed, the object of which is to stir the southern slaves to bathe their hands in the blood of the whites of the south. Traitorous scoundrels, with white faces, but black hearts, lead them, and the country is stunned with their deeds of infamy, treason and blood.

  —editorial, *Illinois State Register*, October 20, 1859.

1   This most fiendish plot [at Harper's Ferry], of these fanatics—if successful in Virginia and Maryland—we have no doubt was intended to be carried throughout the entire Southern States—having for its object plunder, violations of female chastity, and an indiscriminate slaughter of all who should oppose its fearful march.

  —editorial, *Indianapolis Locomotive*, October 22, 1859.

2   John Brown will meet his fate, whether as a bad man or as a madman, with comparative little sympathy. Our own belief is that he should not be executed; but if the seeds of future excitement are planted on his tomb, we do not doubt it will be found that they were placed there as well by his Southern enemies as by his Northern sympathisers.

  —editorial, *Albany* (New York) *Evening Journal*, November 30, 1859.

3   Though we "would that all men" were Free, we should as readily go to Virginia to run off their Horses and Cattle, as their Slaves. By the Constitution and Laws, Slavery is recognized and tolerated. It was a compact made by our fathers, and one that binds their heirs. We will oppose both its extension and its encroachments. Thus far, and no farther, goes our sense of duty to Freedom.

  —editorial, *Albany* (New York) *Evening Journal*, November 30, 1859.

4   The Speech of Abraham Lincoln at the Cooper Institute last evening was one of the happiest and most convincing political arguments ever made in this City, and was addressed to a crowded and most appreciating audience.

  —editorial, *New York Tribune*, February 28, 1860.

  ★ The speech referred to concerned slavery.

5   Whenever any considerable section of our Union shall deliberately resolve to go out, we shall resist all coercive measures designed to keep it in.

  —editorial, *New York Tribune*, November 9, 1860.

6   Can any sane man believe that England and France will consent, as is now suggested, to stultify the policy of half a century for the sake of an extended cotton trade, and to purchase the favors of Charleston and Milledgeville by recognizing what has been called the isothermal law, which impels African labor toward the tropics on the other side of the Atlantic?

  —editorial, *Times* (London), November 29, 1860.

  ★ The London newspaper was ridiculing the Southern hope that England and France would support the Confederacy in order to save cotton supplies.

... we cannot disguise from ourselves that, apart from all political complications, 1
there is a right and a wrong in this question, and that the right belongs, with all its
advantages, to the States of the North.
  —editorial, *Times* (London), January 4, 1861.

★ The London newspaper was commenting on South Carolina's secession.

Some journals have so far forgotten themselves as to censure Major Anderson for his 2
removal from the defenseless work called Fort Moultrie to the strong fortification
known as Fort Sumter. . . . In forty-five minutes he can destroy Fort Moultrie; in
forty-five weeks the South Carolinians can not take Fort Sumter.
  —editorial, *Harper's Weekly*, January 12, 1861.

★ They took it in thirteen weeks.

The South *might*, after uniting, under a new confederacy, treat the disorganized and 3
demoralized Northern states as *insurgents*, and deny them recognition.
  —editorial, *Charleston Courier*, February 12, 1861.

The enthusiasm and fearlessness of the spectators knew no bounds. 4
  —journalist, quoted by Nathaniel W. Stephenson in *The Day of the Confederacy:
  A Chronicle of the Embattled South*, 1919.

★ This report in the *Charleston Mercury* described the public during the bombardment of Fort Sumter.

Let us learn from the Confederate States what they demand, and if consistent with 5
national honor, grant it, and let them go in peace.
  —editorial, *Journal of Commerce*, April 15, 1861.

★ This New York publication was responding to the fall of Fort Sumter the previous day.

If this Union of ours is a confederacy of States which is liable to be dissolved at the 6
will of any of the States, and if no power rests with the General Government to
enforce its laws, it would seem that we have been laboring under a delusion these
eighty years in supposing we were a nation and the fact would appear to be that the
several States of the union have really been united by no closer bond than that which
connects us with Great Britain and France—a mere treaty stipulation, which any of
the parties were at liberty to annul at pleasure.
  —editorial, *Harper's Weekly*, April 20, 1861.

Peaceable secession is organized anarchy.
  —editorial, *Harper's Weekly*, April 20, 1861.

The Storm Cometh—we hope the infatuated rebels like the appearance of the north- 7
ern horizon. The storm of patriotism may shortly become the hurricane of vengeance,
and they have only themselves to thank. . . . Those who sow the wind must reap the
whirlwind.
  —editorial, *Milwaukee Sentinel*, April 20, 1861.

1   From the mountain-tops and valleys to the shores of the sea, there is one wild shout of fierce resolve to capture Washington City, at all and every human hazard. That filthy cage of unclean birds must and will assuredly be purified by fire.
    —editorial, *Richmond Examiner*, April 23, 1861.

2   It is not to be endured that this flight of abolition harpies shall come down from the black North for their roosts in the heart of the South, to defile and brutalize the land.
    —editorial, *Richmond Examiner*, April 23, 1861.

3   The just indignation of an outraged and deeply injured people will teach the Illinois Ape to repeat his race and retrace his journey across the borders of the free negro States still more rapidly than he came.
    —editorial, *Richmond Examiner*, April 23, 1861.

    ★ The newspaper was saying that Lincoln should leave Washington, D.C.

4   Great cleansing and purification are needed and will be given to that festering sink of iniquity,—that wallow of Lincoln and Scott,—the desecrated city of Washington; and many indeed will be the carcasses of dogs and caitiffs that will blacken the air upon the gallows before the work is accomplished. So let it be.
    —editorial, *Richmond Examiner*, April 23, 1861.

5   War is declared. President Lincoln's proclamation . . . is an absolute proclamation of war against the Gulf States. The die is now cast, and men must take their sides, and hold to them.
    —editorial, *Harper's Weekly*, April 27, 1861.

    ★ Lincoln's proclamation that same day called for 75,000 soldiers.

6   There are some among us still who whine about the evils of civil war. These are they who, with a burglar in their house, his hand on the throat of their wife or daughter, would quote texts on the loveliness of Christian forbearance and charity.
    —editorial, *Harper's Weekly*, April 27, 1861.

7   Among all the brave men from the Rio Grande to the Potomac, and stretching over into insulted, indignant, and infuriated Maryland, there is but one word on every lip—"*Washington;*" and one sentiment on every heart—vengeance on the tyrants who pollute the capital of the republic!
    —editorial, *Richmond Whig*, May 22, 1861.

8   We are not enough in the secrets of our authorities to specify the day on which Jeff. Davis will dine at the White House, and Ben. McCullough take his siesta in General Sickles's gilded tent. We should dislike to produce any disappointment by naming too soon or too early a day; but it will save trouble if the gentlemen will keep themselves in readiness to dislodge at a moment's notice!
    —editorial, *Richmond Whig*, May 22, 1861.

    ★ Jefferson Davis was the Confederate president, Ben McCulloch was a CS brigadier general, and Sickles was actually a US colonel at that time, later rising to the rank of major general.

If the rebels are not virtually whipped when the next spring opens, and if they shall   1
meanwhile have steadily confronted our troops without losing ground, we may consider that the republic has been betrayed by the folly or incompetence of its trusted
leaders, and that disunion is a fixed fact.

   —editorial, *New York Tribune*, June 27, 1861.

If the men in Washington wish to convince the public that they have really repented,   2
and are ready to do their duty, let them see to it that the national flag floats over
Richmond before the 20th of July.

   —editorial, *New York Tribune*, June 27, 1861.

The war can not much longer be conducted and held in check by politicians,   3
whether in uniform or out.

   —editorial, *New York Tribune*, June 27, 1861.

Forward, then, and anticipate the rebel force, which only awaits our approach to   4
flee. Forward to Richmond, and place the national foot on the neck of the traitor
who already sues for peace.

   —editorial, *New York Tribune*, July 1, 1861.

The real question is this: *Does General Scott* (or whoever it may be) *contemplate the*   5
same end, and is he animated by like impulses with the great body of the loyal, liberty-
loving people of the country? . . . Does he want the rebels routed, or would he have
them conciliated?

   —editorial, *New York Tribune*, July 1, 1861.

If the national forces shall be beaten in a fair stand-up fight—which we do not   6
believe possible—the patriot millions will acknowledge the corn and the independence of Secessia. If our side beats, the rebel leaders must abscond.

   —editorial, *New York Tribune*, July 1, 1861.

★ To "acknowledge the corn" meant to admit that one had done something wrong.

Unfortunately, the credit to be given to declarations from the State Department is   7
much impaired.

   —editorial, *New York Tribune*, July 2, 1861.

Forward to Richmond! Forward to Richmond! The Rebel Congress must not be   8
allowed to meet there on the 20th of July! BY THAT DAY THE PLACE MUST BE
HELD BY THE NATIONAL ARMY!

   —editorial, *New York Tribune*, June 26 to July 3, 1861.

A few more Bull Run thrashings will bring [Northerners] once more under the yoke   9
as docile as the most loyal of our Ethiopian "chattels."

   —editorial, *Louisville Courier*, quoted by Alfred H. Guernsey and Henry M.
   Alden in *Harper's Pictorial History of the Great Rebellion in the United States*,
   1866.

1   It is not characteristic of Americans to sit down despondently after a defeat. . . . Let us go to work, then, with a will.
     —editorial, *New York Tribune*, July 30, 1861.

     ★ This was nine days after the first battle of Bull Run (first Manassas).

2   The ladies of Virginia and Maryland have been, as a rule, fiercer in their secessionism than the men.
     —article, *Harper's Weekly*, August 3, 1861.

3   Men and presses who are today preaching "Compromise" and "Peace," are doing more to cripple the Government and help treason than the Rebel armies themselves.
     —editorial, *Albany* (New York) *Evening Journal*, August 21, 1861.

4   The painful intelligence reaches us, in such form that we are not at liberty to disclose it, that General William T. Sherman, late commander of the Department of the Cumberland, is insane. It appears that he was at the time while commanding in Kentucky, stark mad.
     —article, *Cincinnati Commercial*, December 11, 1861.

     ★ Sherman said he had once imprisoned the reporter writing the article, because the man visited his military camp against orders.

5   There never was, and probably never will be, a more interesting subject of political study than the present condition of America. Every problem of the past, and every political difficulty of the present, is there working itself out visibly before our eyes. . . . And, amidst all these difficulties, the American people alone in history have to work out, not in the course of ages but at once, the problem which is older than any form of government now in existence, the extinction of human slavery.
     —article, *Spectator* (London), December 28, 1861.

6   When the defection of eleven states and the distractions of our country are taken into consideration, it is not too much to assert that our inventors have done better last year than ever before, and that inventions are perhaps the most safe and profitable sources of investment in times of war as well as peace.
     —"The Old Year's Progress," *Scientific American*, December 28, 1861.

     ★ This New York publication's optimistic summary of the year listed sixty-six new inventions, most related to warfare.

7   The Southern people are not sufficiently alive to the necessity of exertion in the struggle they are involved in.
     —editorial, *Richmond Examiner*, February 4, 1862.

8   Better to fight even at the risk of losing battles, than remain inactive to fill up inglorious graves.
     —editorial, *Richmond Examiner*, February 4, 1862.

To shake confidence in Jefferson Davis is . . . to bring "hideous ruin and combustion" 1
down upon our dearest hopes and interests.
    —editorial, quoted by Nathaniel W. Stephenson in *The Day of the Confederacy: A*
    Chronicle of the Embattled South, 1919.

★ This appeared in a February 1862 edition of the *Charleston Courier*. The phrase
"hideous ruin and combustion" comes from John Milton's *Paradise Lost*, where it
describes God hurling Satan into hell.

Far better would it be for the Atlantic Ocean with one swell surge to rise up and 2
sweep us and all we have into the Pacific than for the infernal hell-hounds who wage
this wicked war on us to triumph. Let any cruelties, any torments, any death that
earth can inflict, come upon us in preference to the triumph of the Yankees!
    —editorial, *Atlanta Confederacy*, March 20, 1862.

The rebels can afford to give up all their church bells, cow bells and dinner bells to 3
Beauregard, for they never go to church now, their cows have all been taken by for-
aging parties, and they have no dinner to be summoned to.
    —editorial, *Louisville Courier*, March 1862.

One of the greatest and bloodiest battles of modern days has just closed, resulting in 4
the complete rout of the enemy, who attacked us at daybreak Sunday morning. . . .
The slaughter on both sides is immense . . .
    —article, *New York Herald*, April 9, 1862.

★ This was the first word about the battle of Shiloh.

At the 10-inch mortar battery, fuse-plugs were still wanting, and the ordnance offi- 5
cer [Horace Porter] was in despair. . . . Finally, a happy thought struck him: there
was a Yankee [New England] regiment on the island; all Yankees are whittlers; if this
regiment could be turned out to-night, they might whittle enough fuse-plugs before
morning to fire a thousand rounds. . . . The 6th Connecticut was ordered out to
whittle, and did whittle to advantage, providing all the plugs that were used in
Battery Totten on the two succeeding days.
    —*New York Times* correspondent quoted in *Battles and Leaders of the Civil War*,
    vol. 2, 1888.

★ This refers to the siege and capture of Fort Pulaski, Georgia, in April 1862.

Impatient critics are still busy with comments upon a policy, the facts leading to 6
which they do not know, and upon which, if they did, they could form no reliable
opinion.
    —editorial, *Richmond Enquirer*, June 26, 1862.

★ This editorial was attacking critics of General Robert E. Lee's plans to defend
Richmond during the Seven Days' battles.

Wall Street does not ardently believe in the present good fortune or the future 7
prospects of the Republic.
    —article, *New York Times*, September 4, 1862.

1   We again return to the subject of the condition of the Army of Northern Virginia . . .
       that many of the troops are covered with vermin and their clothing rotten and dirty
       beyond anything they have ever seen. There is no negro in Virginia who is not better
       off in this respect than some of the best soldiers and first gentlemen in all the land.
       —editorial, *Richmond Whig*, October 21, 1862.

2   It can hardly be in human nature for men to show more valor, or generals to mani-
       fest less judgment, than were perceptible on our side that day.
       —article, *Cincinnati Daily Commercial*, quoted by Shelby Foote in *The Civil War*,
       vol. 1, 1958.

       ★ This article refers to the Union defeat at the battle of Fredericksburg.

3   In fact, the [Emancipation Proclamation] document is no more or no less than Mr.
       Lincoln's formal surrender to the abolition policy of the Radicals.
       —editorial, *New York Irish-American*, quoted by Florence E. Gibson in *The
       Attitudes of New York Irish toward State and National Affairs*, 1951.

4   It has long been known to military men that the insurgents affect no scruples about
       the employment of their slaves in any capacity in which they may be found useful.
       Yet there are people here at the North who affect to be horrified at the enrollment
       of negroes into regiments. Let us hope that the President will not be deterred by any
       squeamish scruples of the kind from garrisoning the Southern forts with fighting
       men of any color that can be obtained.
       —editorial, *Harper's Weekly*, January 10, 1863.

       ★ There had been a recent sighting of two Negroes serving as pickets in a Confederate
       regiment.

5   [Negroes] are more docile than white recruits, and when once they have mastered a
       movement they retain the knowledge perfectly.
       —article, *Harper's Weekly*, March 14, 1863.

6   It is beginning to be doubted whether Jackson really possesses claims to the reputa-
       tion he enjoys. Some of our officers seem to think he is nothing more than a lucky
       soldier and a good disciplinarian.
       —article, *Harper's Weekly*, March 14, 1863.

7   We have all come to the conclusion that they [the American revolutionary soldiers]
       had a right to be independent, and it was best they should be. Nor can we escape
       from the inference that the Federals will one day come to the same conclusion with
       regard to the Southern States.
       —editorial, *Times* (London), May 2, 1863.

8   The Great Ulysses—the Yankee Generalissimo surnamed Grant—has expressed his
       intention of dining in Vicksburg on the Fourth of July. . . . Ulysses must get into the
       city before he dines in it. The way to cook a rabbit is "first *catch* the rabbit."
       —editorial, *Vicksburg* (Mississippi) *Daily Citizen*, July 2, 1863.

       ★ The newspaper was printed on wallpaper because of the Union blockade. Grant
       caught the rabbit two days later when the Confederates surrendered the city.

Like the Scottish chieftain's braves, Lee's men are springing up from the moor and   **1**
brake, crag and dale, with flashing steel and sturdy arm, ready to do or die in the
great cause of national independence, right and honor.
   —editorial, *Vicksburg* (Mississippi) *Daily Citizen*, July 2, 1863.

The omnipresence of our troops and their throwing dust in the eyes, or rather on the   **2**
heels, of the panic-stricken Federals in Maryland and Pennsylvania clearly prove
that Lee just now is the right man in the right place. To-day Maryland is ours; tomorrow Pennsylvania will be; and the next day Ohio . . . will fall.
   —editorial, *Vicksburg* (Mississippi) *Daily Citizen*, July 2, 1863.

To-day the mongrel administration of Lincoln . . . are in search of a father—for their   **3**
old Abe has departed for parts unknown. Terror reigns in their halls. Lee is to the left
of them, the right of them, in front of them, and all around them; and daily do we
expect to hear of his being down on them.
   —editorial, *Vicksburg* (Mississippi) *Daily Citizen*, July 2, 1863.

The red battle flag now waves in New York over streets wet with the gore of Lincoln's   **4**
hated minions.
   —editorial, *Richmond Dispatch*, quoted by Ernest A. McKay in *The Civil War and
   New York City*, 1990.

★ The newspaper was reacting to New York's draft riots July 13–16, 1863.

The Yankee Congress has already passed laws to confiscate the property of the people   **5**
of the Confederacy, and to emancipate their slaves, and the savage malignity of their
conduct, wherever they have secured a foot-hold in the South, shows, beyond per-
adventure that those laws will be enforced if they ever get the power to enforce
them.
   —editorial, *Staunton* (Virginia) *Spectator*, August 4, 1863.

We repeat, *it is idle to talk of peace*. We must talk of war and wage war until the   **6**
enemy tires of war.
   —editorial, *Staunton* (Virginia) *Spectator*, August 4, 1863.

As long as the people practice the sin of extortion upon each other and the officers   **7**
of the Confederacy rob the Government, we cannot expect to be vouch-safed the
boon of freedom and independence.
   —editorial, *Staunton* (Virginia) *Spectator*, August 4, 1863.

The good ladies of Greenville and vicinity have, upon several occasions, furnished   **8**
the sick and wounded soldiers in this place with large supplies of provisions, such as
bread, pies, bacon, chickens, honey, butter, vegetables, &c., &c. These articles were
all of the very best quality, and such as to make some of the well almost wish they were
sick or wounded that they might partake of some of them. It has been so long since
some of us have tasted chicken that we have forgotten whether they are fish, flesh,
or fowl.
   —editorial, *Staunton* (Virginia) *Spectator*, August 11, 1863.

1   Heads up! Why that long face and gloomy countenance? You must be bilious, and should take a blue pill; for there is no cause for discouragement even, much less for despondency. The prospects of the enemy have never been so bad at this moment, and we have never been so near the end of our trials.
     —editorial, *Staunton* (Virginia) *Spectator*, August 11, 1863.

2   A Georgia paper says that the only effectual way to prevent Northern negroes from enlisting, and white officers from commanding them after enlisting, is not to take either prisoners. Leave them on the battlefield.
     —editorial, *Staunton* (Virginia) *Spectator*, August 11, 1863.

3   This is the age of shoddy.
     —editorial, *New York Herald*, October 6, 1863.

     ★ The newspaper was criticizing poor-quality products, such as Union uniforms from suppliers trying to save money.

4   [Negro troops] are not paid as much as white troops. This is all wrong. If they are expected to work and fight as bravely as their white comrades, they deserve to be paid as well.
     —editorial, *Harper's Weekly*, November 14, 1863.

5   The shelling [of Charleston] commenced at midnight, but did little harm beyond terrifying the ladies left in the city.
     —article, *Harper's Weekly*, January 9, 1864.

6   Twenty months ago [Lincoln] was without a party. The Copperheads hated him; the "Conservative Republicans" thought him too fast; the "Radical Republicans" thought him too slow; the War Democrats were looking for the chance of a return to political power. He held steadily upon his way.
     —editorial, *Harper's Weekly*, March 5, 1864.

7   The rebels pretend to have found papers on Colonel DAHLGREN'S body, directing a massacre of DAVIS and all the officials in Richmond; but it is denied by Federal officers that any such orders were ever issued or suggested.
     —article, *Harper's Weekly*, March 12, 1864.

     ★ The papers were found by a thirteen-year-old after Ulric Dahlgren was killed on March 3, during an attempted raid on Richmond.

8   [Lee] is said to be popular with his army, but the conviction is growing that in General Grant he has met his match, and the confidence entertained in him is not, probably, as great as formerly. In the present campaign he has displayed great tenacity and skill in the management of his army, but in all the elements of strategy Grant has proved more than his equal.
     —article, *Harper's Weekly*, July 2, 1864.

9   The rebel raid in Maryland . . . has vanished, leaving behind as the traces of its devastation desolated homes, empty roosts and stables, and broken communications. . . .

The cost of the work was over twenty-three millions. The damage which the rebels have done will be easily repaired. It is an occasion for regret that they have been able to carry away so much plunder.
    —article, *Harper's Weekly*, July 30, 1864.

Who shall revive the withered hopes that bloomed on the opening of Grant's cam-   1
paign?
    —editorial, *New York World*.

★ This despondent tone followed CS major general Jubal A. Early's raid on Washington, D.C.

We wonder if any spectacle can be more degrading than to see Massachusetts, whose   2
machinations for supremacy in the Union have culminated in the present conflict, sneaking in the rear of the Yankee army to pick up negroes enough to keep her citizens out of the fight. She has received an appropriate rebuke from Sherman.
    —editorial, *Richmond Enquirer*, August 24, 1864.

★ Sherman had written to John Spooner, an agent for Massachusetts, who wanted to recruit freed Negroes into the Union army. Sherman opposed this as being disruptive, adding "it is not fair to our men to count negroes as equals."

The indomitable and irrepressible Mosby is again in the saddle carrying destruction   3
and consternation in his path. . . . If he has not yet won a Brigadier's wreath upon his collar, the people have placed upon his brow one far more enduring.
    —editorial, *The Richmond Whig*, October 18, 1864.

★ Four days earlier, Lieutenant Colonel John Mosby's troops had wrecked and burned a train of the Baltimore and Ohio Railroad, stealing $173,000 of Union funds, in the "Greenback Raid."

Let Mr. Lincoln be *President* for the next term; hitherto he has been a dictator.   4
    —editorial, *New York Daily News*, November 11, 1864.

★ This followed Lincoln's reelection.

New York in ashes would have been more deadly to the Southern cause than New   5
York in the fullness of strength and grandeur.
    —editorial, *New York Daily News*, November 28, 1864.

★ This followed a few small fires set by Confederate saboteurs on November 25.

The desolator of our homes, the destroyer of our property, the Attila of the west,   6
seeks sanctuary. His shrine is the sea.
    —editorial, *Macon* (Georgia) *Telegraph*, November 30, 1864.

★ This invective was aimed at General William T. Sherman during his march through Georgia.

1   They went off up the river, yelling their peculiar mule-like cry which passes for a cheer, with the ill-omened flag waving over them, leaving the proud banner of freedom behind, the love of which, for a time, at least, they have madly rejected.
      —article, *Harper's Weekly*, December 3, 1864.

      ★ This describes Confederate prisoners exchanged for Union ones on the Savannah River.

2   It would seem as if in [Sherman] all the attributes of man were merged in the enormities of the demon, as if Heaven intended in him to manifest depths of depravity yet untouched by a fallen race.
      —editorial, *Macon* (Georgia) *Telegraph*, December 5, 1864.

3   The tendency of the age, the march of the American people, is toward monarchy, and unless the tide is stopped we shall reach something worse than monarchy. Every step we have taken during the past four years has been in the direction of military despotism. Half our laws are unconstitutional.
      —editorial, quoted by Nathaniel W. Stephenson in *The Day of the Confederacy: A Chronicle of the Embattled South*, 1919.

      ★ This appeared in the *Montgomery Mail* in late 1864 and was a criticism of the Confederacy impressing supplies for below market prices.

4   . . . we are not at war with distant provinces, but, unhappily, with our own brothers, whom we prefer to meet on equal terms and as brothers still—not as a victor meets the vanquished.
      —editorial *Harper's Weekly*, March 25, 1865.

5   Sherman has promenaded Georgia and South Carolina. . . . The days of long marches are over, and the days of sharp conflict are already begun. The elements have been hurtling and combining and now comes the storm.
      —editorial, *Harper's Weekly*, April 1, 1865.

6   The arrival [in Richmond] of the President soon got noised abroad, and the colored population turned out in great force, and for a time blockaded the quarters of the President, cheering vociferously.
      —article, *New York Times*, April 4, 1865.

7   The battle of last Saturday before Petersburg shows what Lee may hope to accomplish by hurling his columns against Grant's fortifications. His loss upon that occasion more than decimated his army. Half a dozen more such battles would leave him with no army to fight with.
      —article, *Harper's Weekly*, April 8, 1865.

8   Notwithstanding the fact that thousands of men differed from Mr. Lincoln in reference to measures of public policy, nearly all seemed to feel that, in his untimely death, a great calamity had befallen the nation. . . . On account of the dark deed which has been committed, people express sorrowful forebodings that the prospect of peace, a few days ago so flattering, has been destroyed. We sincerely hope that all

such evil forebodings are unfounded and that the work of pacification and peace may go on.
    —editorial, *Henderson* (Kentucky) *Reporter*, April 17, 1865.

★ This newspaper had been a harsh critic of Lincoln during the war.

The people are full of rejoicing. The war for the Union has been their war, fought in   **1**
their interest, sustained by their patriotism—a patriotism that has withheld neither
property nor life—let the people rejoice, then, in the final triumph, with a consciousness of their own strength, but especially with a conviction of the righteousness of
their victory and a sense of overwhelming gratitude to the God of Battles. Their Hail
Columbia is fitly accompanied by their Te Deums.
    —editorial, *Harper's Weekly*, April 22, 1865.

★ General Robert E. Lee had surrendered two weeks before.

But Mr. Lincoln's death came at a time propitious to the glorification of his mem-   **2**
ory. He died at a time when he was preaching reconciliation and the forgetting of
the past, when he was nobly repressing the blameworthy exultation of the victorious
faction.
    —editorial, *La Patrie* (Paris), April 28, 1865.

Beaten on every field of recognized warfare, treason outdid its very self, and killed   **3**
our President.
    —editorial, *Harper's Weekly*, April 29, 1865.

★ This was two weeks after Lincoln's assassination.

[Lincoln's] death has plunged the nation into deepest mourning, but his spirit still   **4**
animates the people for whom he died.
    —editorial, *Harper's Weekly*, April 29, 1865.

From the height of patriotic vision [Lincoln] beheld the golden fields of the future   **5**
waving in peace and plenty out of sight. He beheld and blessed God, but was not to
enter in. And we with bowed heads and aching hearts move forward to the promised
land.
    —editorial, *Harper's Weekly*, April 29, 1865.

That the successor of Abraham Lincoln will adopt a policy of vengeance is impos-   **6**
sible.
    —editorial, *Harper's Weekly*, April 29, 1865.

★ His successor, Andrew Johnson, had advocated harsh vengeance but did not carry it
out.

Mr. Johnson comes into power through a most melancholy occurrence, but he has   **7**
entered upon the duties of his office with a dignity and firmness that elicits at the
same time the confidence of the American people.
    —editorial, *Harper's Weekly*, May 13, 1865.

★ Lincoln had died on April 15, and Andrew Johnson became president.

1   Give the negroes the vote and they will most certainly be courted by both parties at the South. It may be objected that they will become thus merely the tools of politicians. But it must be remembered that freedom will excite new activities in these black men. They will have leaders of their own; they will have sentiments of their own; and the policy which they will most naturally adopt will be that which will bring them into alliance with the poor loyal whites of the South.
   —editorial, *Harper's Weekly*, May 13, 1865.

2   At about three o'clock yesterday, "all that is mortal" of Jeff'n Davis, late so-called "President of the alleged Confederate States," was duly, but quietly and effectively, committed to that living tomb prepared within the impregnable walls of Fortress Monroe. . . . No more will Jeff'n Davis be known among the masses of men. . . . He is buried alive.
   —editorial, *New York Herald*, May 23, 1865.

3   This has been called a fratricidal war by some, by others an irrepressible conflict between freedom and slavery. We respectfully take issue with the authors of both these ideas. We are not the brothers of the Yankees, and the slavery question is merely the pretext, not the cause of the war. The true irrepressible conflict lies fundamentally in the hereditary hostility, the sacred animosity, the eternal antagonism between the two races engaged.
   —editorial, *Louisville Courier*, quoted by Alfred H. Guernsey and Henry M. Alden in *Harper's Pictorial History of the Great Rebellion in the United States*, 1866.

4   The South loves [Jefferson Davis's] memory as it should love it and as the people of every patriotic country should and ever will respect it. Were the people of the South to forget him, or fail to honor the man who endured so patiently for their sake, they in turn should deserve none of respect or place in the minds of men who have manhood. . . . Jefferson Davis will live longer in history and better than will any who have ever spoken against him.
   —editorial, *New York Times*, quoted by Hudson Strode in *Jefferson Davis: Tragic Hero*, 1964.

   ★ This was written after his funeral on December 11, 1889.

5   [Jefferson Davis] was the chosen chieftain of the new Republic which strove to establish itself, and whose adherents battled for its existence with a heroism the memory of which is everywhere cherished as one that does honor to the American character and name.
   —editorial, *New York World*, quoted by Hudson Strode in *Jefferson Davis: Tragic Hero*, 1964.

   ★ This was written after his funeral on December 11, 1889.

The Americans are making war as no people ever made it before. Their campaigns **1** combine the costliness of modern expeditions with the carnage of barbaric invasions. Grant squanders life like Attila, and money like Louis XIV.

 —editorial, *Times* (London), quoted by Hudson Strode in *Jefferson Davis: Tragic Hero*, 1964.

The cards are in our hands and we intend to play them out to the bankruptcy of **2** every cotton factory in Great Britain and France or the acknowledgement of our independence.

 —editorial, *Charleston Mercury*, quoted by James M. McPherson in *The Battle Cry of Freedom: The Civil War Era*, 1989.

Willing to fight for Uncle Sam but not for Uncle Sambo. **3**

 —Pennsylvania newspaper editorial quoted by John D. Wright in *Language of the Civil War*, 2001.

Erskine, A. N.

CS PRIVATE

I never had a clear conception of the horrors of war until that night and the morn- **4** ing. On going round on that battlefield with a candle searching for my friends I could hear on all sides the dreadful groans of the wounded and their heart piercing cries for water and assistance. Friends and foes all together.

 —letter to his wife, Ann, June 28, 1862.

★ Erskine, with the 4th Texas Regiment, was describing the aftermath of the battle of Gaines's Mill, Virginia.

Everett, Edward (1794–1865)

I should be glad if I could flatter myself that I came as near the central idea of the **5** occasion in two hours as you did in two minutes.

 —letter to Lincoln, November 20, 1863.

★ Everett's two-hour oration had preceded Lincoln's short Gettysburg Address, which actually lasted five minutes.

Ewell, Richard S. (1817–1872)

CS LIEUTENANT GENERAL

You'll be a *dead damsel* in less than a minute. *Get away from here! Get away!* **6**

 —quoted by CS major general John B. Gordon in *Reminiscences of the Civil War*, 1904.

★ Ewell, then a brigadier general, was unsuccessfully trying to shoo a woman from the field before the first battle of Bull Run (first Manassas).

1   It don't hurt a bit to be shot in a wooden leg.
　　—quoted by Carl Sandburg in *Abraham Lincoln: The War Years*, 1939.

　　★ After a bullet struck his false leg at the battle of Gettysburg, Ewell made this comment to Brigadier General John B. Gordon.

2   Certainly; I'm sure he needs it.
　　—quoted by CS colonel Henry Kyd Douglas in *Battles and Leaders of the Civil War*, vol. 2, 1888.

　　★ Ewell was responding to a minister in Carlisle, Pennsylvania, who asked if he could pray for Lincoln.

3   I never saw one of Jackson's couriers approach without expecting an order to assault the North Pole!
　　—quoted by Lieutenant Colonel G. F. R. Henderson in *Stonewall Jackson and the American Civil War*, vol. 1, 1898.

4   We can get along without anything but food and ammunition. The road to glory cannot be followed with much baggage.
　　—quoted by Lieutenant Colonel G. F. R. Henderson in *Stonewall Jackson and the American Civil War*, vol. 1, 1898.

　　★ Ewell was then a major general.

5   I tell you, sir, women would make a grand brigade—if it was not for snakes and spiders! They don't mind bullets—women are not afraid of bullets; but one big blacksnake would put a whole army to flight.
　　—quoted by CS major general John B. Gordon in *Reminiscences of the Civil War*, 1904.

　　★ Ewell was then a brigadier general.

6   Jackson is driving us mad. He don't say a word—no order, no hint of where we're going.
　　—quoted by Rod Graff in *Civil War Quiz and Fact Book*, 1985.

　　★ Ewell, then a major general, was upset that Jackson kept his day-to-day plans secret from even his closest officers.

Farragut, David G. (1801–1870)

US NAVY ADMIRAL

7   We have the stampede on them now, but it will stop if we meet with some reverse through the stupidity of any of our generals.
　　—quoted by Loyall Farragut in *The Life of David Glasgow Farragut: First Admiral of the United States*, 1879.

　　★ This was said on March 10, 1862, a month before Captain Farragut's fleet stormed past the forts defending New Orleans.

My God, is it to end in this way!   **1**
> —quoted by US Navy commander Albert Kautz in *Battles and Leaders of the Civil War*, vol. 2, 1888.

★ Captain Farragut's ship, *Hartford*, was on fire in the Mississippi River on March 24, 1862, but the flames were soon put out.

Any man who is prepared for defeat would be half-defeated before he commenced.   **2**
> —letter to his wife, April 11, 1862.

★ He was a rear admiral at the time.

Capture or be captured.   **3**
> —quoted by John D. Wright in *The Language of the Civil War*, 2001.

★ Rear Admiral Farragut issued this order to his aides on April 18, 1862, as his fleet fought past two forts on the Mississippi River.

I seemed to be breathing flame.   **4**
> —quoted by Marion A. Baker in *Battles and Leaders of the Civil War*, vol. 2, 1888.

★ Captain Farragut was describing the atmosphere of battling up the lower Mississippi River protected by the Confederate forts and fleet. Baker was the mayor's private secretary.

Damn the torpedoes. Full speed ahead.   **5**
> —quoted by Carl Sandburg in *Abraham Lincoln: The War Years*, 1939.

★ Rear Admiral Farragut, lashed to his ship's mast, gave this order during his fleet's victory at Mobile Bay on August 5, 1864. The torpedoes were underwater mines.

Everybody has a weak spot, and the first thing I try to do is to find out where it is,   **6**
and pitch into it with the biggest shell or shot that I have, and repeat that dose until it operates.
> —quoted by A. T. Mahan in *Admiral Farragut*, 1892.

The officers say I don't believe anything. I certainly believe very little that comes in   **7**
the shape of reports. They keep everybody stirred up. I mean to be whipped or to whip my enemy, and not to be scared to death.
> —quoted by A. T. Mahan in *Admiral Farragut*, 1892.

Fenton, William

US COLONEL

My poor boys! My brave boys! Where are my boys?   **8**
> —quoted by Rod Gragg in *Civil War Times Illustrated*, January/February 1994.

★ Fenton was wandering among his decimated troops after their failure on June 16, 1862, to capture an uncompleted fort on James Island near Charleston, South Carolina. His 8th Michigan lost 13 of their 22 officers in the engagement (the battle of Secessionville).

Foote, Andrew H. (1806–1863)

US REAR ADMIRAL

1   Well, I am glad to be done with guns and war.
   —quoted by Rod Graff in *Civil War Quiz and Fact Book*, 1985.

   ★ Foote had been told that the wound he received at the battle of Fort Donelson on February 14, 1862, was not healing; he survived and was appointed rear admiral four months later.

2   You do perfectly right, Sir, in surrendering but you should have blown my boats out of the water before I would have surrendered to you.
   —quoted in *Harper's Weekly*, February 22, 1862.

   ★ Commodore Foote was talking with CS brigadier general Lloyd Tilghman, who had surrendered Fort Henry, Tennessee, on February 6. Tilghman had just told Foote, "I am glad to have surrendered to so gallant an officer."

Forrest, Nathan Bedford (1821–1877)

CS LIEUTENANT GENERAL

3   Boys, these people are talking about surrendering, and I am going out of this place before they do or bust hell wide open.
   —pledge to his men, February 16, 1862.

   ★ Lieutenant Colonel Forrest escaped with several hundred soldiers from Fort Donelson, Tennessee, before dawn on the day it surrendered to Brigadier General Ulysses S. Grant.

4   I will receive 200 able-bodied men if they will present themselves at my headquarters by the first of June with a good horse and gun. I wish none but those who desire to be actively engaged. My headquarters for the present is at Corinth, Miss. Come on, boys, if you want a heap of fun and to kill some Yankees.
   —quoted by Robert S. Henry in *"First with the Most" Forrest*, 1944.

   ★ This was a recruitment advertisement placed in the spring of 1862 when Colonel Forrest was recovering from wounds received at the battle of Shiloh.

5   I must demand an unconditional surrender of your force as prisoners of war or I will have every man put to the sword. You are aware of the overpowering force I have at my command, and this demand is made to prevent the effusion of blood.
   —message to Lieutenant Colonel John G. Parkhurst.

   ★ This resulted in the surrender of Murfreesboro, Tennessee, on July 13, 1862. Lieutenant Colonel Forrest was made a brigadier general a week later.

6   I just took the short cut and got there first with the most men.
   —quoted by Basil W. Duke in *Reminiscences of General Basil W. Duke*, 1911.

★ Brigadier General Forrest was explaining to Colonel John H. Morgan how he had captured an entire Union command and their stores on July 13, 1862.

Shoot up everything blue and keep up the scare. **1**
  —quoted by Shelby Foote in *The Civil War*, vol. 2, 1958.

★ This was said by the brigadier general on April 30, 1863, during an engagement with Union forces at Crooked Creek, Alabama.

The river was dyed with the blood of the slaughtered for two hundred yards. The **2** approximate loss was upward of five hundred killed, but few of the officers escaping. My loss was about twenty killed. It is hope that these facts will demonstrate to the Northern people that negro soldiers cannot cope with Southerners.
  —quoted by General Ulysses S. Grant in *Personal Memoirs of U. S. Grant*, vol. 2, 1886.

★ This dispatch by Forrest came after the Fort Pillow "massacre" in Tennessee on April 12, 1864, in which 231 Union forces died. About half of the fort's defenders were black. Fourteen of Forrest's troops were killed.

I regard captured negroes as I do other captured property and not as captured sol- **3** diers. . . . It is not the policy or the interest of the South to destroy the negro, on the contrary to preserve and protect him, and all who have surrendered to us have received kind and humane treatment.
  —letter to US major general Cadwallader C. Washburn, June 20, 1864.

★ He was responding to Washburn's accusation that Major General Forrest had massacred Negro troops who surrendered at Fort Pillow, Tennessee, on April 12, 1864.

The attempt made to establish a separate and independent confederation has failed, **4** but the consciousness of having done your duty faithfully and to the end will in some measure repay for the hardships you have undergone. . . . You have been good soldiers, you can be good citizens. Obey the laws, preserve your honor, and the government to which you have surrendered can afford to be and will be magnanimous.
  —farewell to his troops, May 9, 1865.

That we are beaten is a self-evident fact, and any further resistance on our part **5** would be justly regarded as the height of folly and rashness. . . . Civil war, such as you have just passed through, naturally engenders feelings of animosity, hatred, and revenge. It is our duty to divest ourselves of all such feelings, and, so far as it is in our power to do so, to cultivate feelings toward those with whom we have so long contested and heretofore so widely but honestly differed. Neighborhood feuds, personal animosities, and private differences should be blotted out, and when you return home a manly, straightforward course of conduct will secure the respect even of your enemies. Whatever your responsibilities may be to government, to society, or to individuals, meet them like men.
  —farewell to his troops, May 9, 1865.

War means fighting and fighting means killing. **6**
  —quoted by Carl Sandburg in *Abraham Lincoln: The War Years*, 1939.

Foster, Ira R.

GEORGIA QUARTERMASTER GENERAL

1   I earnestly desire to secure a pair of socks for every barefooted soldier from Georgia.
—letter to the women of Georgia, February 5, 1864.

Fremantle, Arthur James Lyon (1835–1901)

BRITISH LIEUTENANT COLONEL

★ Fremantle was a British observer with the Confederate army.

2   At the outbreak of the war it was found very difficult to raise infantry in Texas, as no
Texan walks a yard if he can help it. Many mounted regiments were therefore orga-
nized, and afterwards dismounted.
—*Three Months in the Southern States: April–June 1863*, 1863.

★ Fremantle began his trip at Brownsville, Texas.

3   General Lee is, almost without exception, the handsomest man of his age I ever saw.
He is 56 years old, tall, broad shouldered, very well made, well set up, a thorough
soldier in appearance, and his manners are most courteous and full of dignity. He is
a perfect gentleman in every respect. I imagine no man has so few enemies, or is so
universally esteemed. Throughout the South, all agree in pronouncing him to be as
near perfection as man can be. He has none of the small vices, such as smoking,
drinking, chewing or swearing, and his bitterest enemy never accused him of any of
the greater ones.
—*Three Months in the Southern States: April–June 1863*, 1863.

4   The [Confederate] staff-officers . . . spoke of the battle [of Gettysburg] as a certainty; and the universal feeling in the army was one of profound contempt for an
enemy whom they have beaten so constantly, and under so many disadvantages.
—*Three Months in the Southern States: April–June 1863*,1863.

5   I wouldn't have missed this for anything.
—*Three Months in the Southern States: April–June 1863*, 1863.

★ Fremantle said this at Gettysburg to Lieutenant General James Longstreet who
replied, "The devil you wouldn't! I would like to have missed it very much; we've
attacked and been repulsed."

6   The Confederates are now entirely armed with excellent rifles, mostly Enfields.
When they first turned out they were in the habit of wearing numerous revolvers
and bowie-knives. General Lee is said to have mildly remarked "Gentlemen, I think
you will find an Enfield rifle, a bayonet and sixty rounds of ammunition, as much as
you can conveniently carry in the way of arms." They laughed and thought they knew
better; but the six-shooters and bowie-knives gradually disappeared; and now none
are to be seen among the infantry.
—*Three Months in the Southern States: April–June 1863*, 1863.

★ This diary entry was written on June 22, 1863.

I saw, for the first time, the celebrated "Stonewall" Brigade. . . . In appearance the **1**
men do not differ from other Confederate soldiers, except, perhaps, the brigade
contains more elderly men and fewer boys.
    —*Three Months in the Southern States: April–June 1863*, 1863.

★ This diary entry was written on July 1, 1863.

The Southern troops when charging, or to express their delight, always yell in a man- **2**
ner peculiar to themselves. The Yankee cheer is much more like ours [in Britain];
but the Confederate officers declare that the rebel yell has a particular merit, and
always produces a salutary and useful effect upon their adversaries. A corps is sometimes spoken of as a "good yelling regiment."
    —*Three Months in the Southern States: April–June 1863*, 1863.

★ This diary entry was written on July 2, 1863.

The Confederate has no ambition to imitate the regular soldier at all; he looks the **3**
genuine rebel; but in spite of his bare feet, his ragged clothes, his old rug, and tooth-
brush stuck like a rose in his button-hole, he has a sort of devil-may-care, reckless,
self-confident look which is decidedly taking.
    —*Three Months in the Southern States: April–June 1863*, 1863.

★ This diary entry was written on July 9, 1863.

Fremont, Jessie Benton (1824–1902)

WIFE OF MAJOR GENERAL JOHN C. FREMONT

It was a war for a great national idea, the Union, and that General Fremont should **4**
not have dragged the negro into it.
    —quoted by John D. Wright in *The Language of the Civil War*, 2001.

★ Mrs. Fremont was indirectly quoting Lincoln (thus the past tense "It was . . . "), with
whom she had argued. Her husband had provoked Lincoln by declaring slaves to be
free in Missouri on August 30, 1861. The president revoked that declaration.

Fulton, Charles C.

BALTIMORE AMERICAN CORRESPONDENT

The events transpiring at this point, and in the army before Richmond for the past **5**
four days, have been of such varied character and thrilling interest, that I scarcely
know where to commence or end the record in order to make it understandable to
the general reader.
    —article, *Baltimore American*, June 28, 1862.

★ Fulton was describing the Seven Days' battles in Virginia.

Gallegos, J. M.

★ [See quotations at Facundo Pinto.]

Garfield, James A. (1831–1881)

US CONGRESSMAN FROM OHIO

1   God reigns and the government at Washington still lives.
    —quoted in *The Annals of America*, vol. 9, 1968.

    ★ Following Lincoln's death on April 15, 1865, Garfield gave these encouraging words to a crowd on Wall Street in New York. Garfield was also assassinated in 1881 after becoming president.

Garner, John M.

US CHAPLAIN

2   The aim was to group the dead [at Shiloh], by regiments as far as possible, but many isolated ones were buried alone and unmarked. Little red mounds rose rapidly all about in that woods, some covering one man, others several men each. These were all marked, but the marking could not be durable, and the identity of many must have been lost in a short time.
    —quoted in the *Unionville* (Missouri) *Republican*, October 5, 1892.

    ★ Garner was chaplain of the 18th Missouri.

3   The dead animals [horses and mules at Shiloh] were drawn together in piles and ricks of logs and leaves stacked on them; and then fire was applied. . . . Hundreds of such fires in full blast at the same time. The fumes from such quantities of burning, putrid flesh were almost unbearable, and it took so long to reduce these piles to ashes.
    —quoted in the *Unionville* (Missouri) *Republican*, October 5, 1892.

Garnett, Richard B.

CS BRIGADIER GENERAL

4   This is a desperate thing to attempt.
    —quoted by Douglas Southall Freeman in *R. E. Lee: A Biography*, vol. 3, 1934.

    ★ Garnett said this to Brigadier General Lewis A. Armistead on July 3, 1863, at Gettysburg, concerning Pickett's charge, in which Garnett was killed and Armistead mortally wounded.

Garrison, William Lloyd (1805–1879)

ABOLITIONIST AND EDITOR OF *THE LIBERATOR*

5   In firing his gun, John Brown has merely told what time of day it is. It is high noon, thank God.
    —quoted by Geoffrey C. Ward in *The Civil War: An Illustrated History*, 1990.

Fortunate, indeed, was it that [Lincoln] was not a man of hot impulse on the one   **1**
hand, nor a lover of arbitrary power on the other.
    —quoted in the *New York Times*, November 11, 1881.

Gary, Martin W. (1831–1881)

CS BRIGADIER GENERAL

I do not care for white flags. South Carolinians never surrender.   **2**
    —quoted by General Philip H. Sheridan in *Personal Memoirs of P. H. Sheridan,
    General United States Army*, vol. 2, 1888.

★ Sheridan wrongly spells Gary's name "Geary."

All over! Good-bye! Blow her to h—l!   **3**
    —quoted in *Battles and Leaders of the Civil War*, vol. 4, 1888.

★ Gary, the last Confederate general officer to vacate Richmond, was instructing
Captain Clement Sulivane to burn Mayo's Bridge at the foot of 14th Street, over which
his cavalry had passed.

Gay, Sydney Howard (1814–1888)

NEW YORK TRIBUNE MANAGING EDITOR DURING THE WAR

Virginia was not in greater danger of revolution in the winter of 1861 than New York   **4**
is today.
    —letter to Lincoln, July 26, 1863.

★ This referred to the draft riots.

About the only thing I have to show for four years' labor in keeping the *Tribune* a war   **5**
paper while its editor in chief was a copperhead and secessionist, is a chronic diar-
rhea.
    —letter to Edmund Quincy, August 16, 1866.

Gayle, B. B.

CS COLONEL

We are flanked, boys, but let's die in our tracks.   **6**
    —quoted by CS lieutenant general Daniel H. Hill in *Battles and Leaders of the
    Civil War*, vol. 2, 1888.

★ Gayle, of the 12th Alabama, was surrounded at the battle of South Mountain,
Maryland, on September 14, 1862. Ordered to surrender, he uttered these words and
fired his pistol in the enemies' faces before being riddled by the return fire.

Genet, Henry

NEW YORK CITY ALDERMAN

1   Why, you don't pretend that a nigger is a man do you?
     —quoted by Ernest A. McKay in *The Civil War and New York City*, 1990.

     ★ This was said in January 1861 to Alderman John Brady, who had expressed his belief that slaves were not property.

Georgia Delegates to the Confederate Congress

2   Let every man fly to arms. Remove your negroes, horses, cattle, and provisions from before Sherman's army, and burn what you cannot carry. Burn all bridges and block up the roads in his route. Assail the invader in front, flank, and rear, by night and by day. Let him have no rest.
     —quoted by Nathaniel W. Stephenson in *The Day of the Confederacy: A Chronicle of the Embattled South*, 1919.

     ★ This appeal was made to Georgians as Sherman made his march through their state.

Gibbon, John (1827–1896)

US BRIGADIER GENERAL

3   The air was all murderous iron.
     —quoted by Shelby Foote in *The Civil War*, vol. 2, 1958.

     ★ He was referring to the artillery shells coming from the Confederates just before Pickett's charge at the battle of Gettysburg on July 3, 1863.

Gilman, Caroline H. (1794–1888)

4   Fort Sumter looks like a noble stag at bay . . . When will it be surrendered? The men, ours, have finished their work, and are growing impatient of delay. It requires all the wisdom of their superiors to keep them cool. Think of so many thousand men leaving plantations, mercantile life, shops, colleges, and every department of labor, since December, and working like journeymen. . . . Such is my faith in peace, that I carried down a gardener to arrange my flower beds.
     —letter to her daughters in Massachusetts, Mrs. Pickering Dodge of Salem and Mrs. Charles J. Bowen of Kingston, March 31, 1861.

     ★ The fort was taken two weeks later.

Gilmore, J. R. (1822–1903)

UNION JOURNALIST AND LECTURER

5   Let the Northern people once really *feel* the war and they will insist on hanging every one of your leaders.
     —quoted by Hudson Strode in *Jefferson Davis: Tragic Hero*, 1964.

★ He said this to Confederate president Jefferson Davis on a peacemaking mission on July 16, 1864.

[Jefferson Davis] is a man of peculiar ability. Our interview with him explained to me **1** why, with no money and no commerce, with nearly every one of their important cities in our hands, and with an army greatly inferior in numbers and equipment to ours, the Rebels have held out so long. It is because of the sagacity, energy, and indomitable will of Jefferson Davis. Without him the Rebellion would crumble to pieces in a day; with him it may continue to be, even in disaster, a power that will tax the whole energy and resources of the nation.
　　—*Atlantic Monthly*, September 1864.

As [Lincoln] leaned back in his chair, he had an air of unstudied ease, a kind of **2** careless dignity, that well became his station; and yet there was not a trace of self-consciousness about him.
　　—*Personal Recollections of Abraham Lincoln and the Civil War*, 1898.

★ Gilmore was an intermediary between the *New York Tribune* and the White House.

Girard, Charles (1822–1895)

FRENCH MILITARY SUPPLIER TO THE CONFEDERACY

Even the Southern slaves fight with their masters for their way of life, in preference **3** to dying of hunger in Northern cities, as prey of the invader.
　　—*Paris Pays*, May 13, 1861.

We have already been notified of a secessionist movement fermenting in Illinois, Mr. **4** Lincoln's own State. So, perhaps, the day is not too far distant when the Confederacy will contain more States than will the Union, where slavery no longer exists.
　　—*Paris Pays*, August 31, 1861.

In battle, the enthusiasm of Confederate soldiers recalls in several respects that of **5** the French. They march off to death as if they were going to some gala event, singing war songs, tossing off witticisms, seeing in front of them nothing but victory.
　　—*A Visit to the Confederate States of America in 1863*, 1864.

One characteristic is peculiar to [Confederate soldiers]. That is, when there is an **6** order to charge, at first there prevails a deep silence. This silence is succeeded by a rasping yell sent up by the whole column, a cry that strikes horror into the enemy's ranks. All of the prisoners are of one accord in saying that, when they heard that yell, they experienced as a result of it a feeling of terror that they could not describe, except by comparing it to on-coming death.
　　—*A Visit to the Confederate States of America in 1863*, 1864.

War has become a profession, the profession of all [Southerners]. Each person devotes **7** himself to it as though it were his usual occupation.
　　—*A Visit to the Confederate States of America in 1863*, 1864.

1   The Confederate Constitution expressly declares that the slave *trade* is and remains forever abolished. For that matter, these views had prevailed in the Southern States from the beginning of this century and had encountered resistance only in the Northern states, which, having invented the trade, are now using it as a weapon against the Southerners.
   —*A Visit to the Confederate States of America in 1863,* 1864.

Gladstone, William E. (1809–1898)

BRITISH CHANCELLOR OF THE EXCHEQUER AND FUTURE PRIME MINISTER

2   Jefferson Davis and other leaders of the South have made an army; they are making, it appears, a navy; and they have made what is more than either; they have made a nation.
   —speech at Newcastle, October 7, 1862.

3   We may anticipate with certainty the success of the Southern States so far as regards their separation from the North.
   —speech at Newcastle, October 7, 1862.

Gooding, James Henry (1837–1864)

NEGRO SOLDIER OF THE 54TH MASSACHUSETTS REGIMENT

4   All we lack is a paler hue and a better acquaintance with the alphabet.
   —letter to Lincoln, recorded in *National Archives, Record Group 94, Office of the Adjutant General, Colored Troops Division, H133 CTM,* 1863.

   ★ Gooding was asking for equal pay.

Goodwyn, T. J. (1837–1864)

COLUMBIA, SOUTH CAROLINA, MAYOR

5   The Confederate forces having evacuated Columbia, I deem it my duty, as Mayor and representative of the city, to ask for its citizens the treatment accorded by the usages of civilized warfare. I therefore respectfully request that you will send a sufficient guard in advance of the army, to maintain order in the city and protect the persons and property of the citizens.
   —letter to Major General William T. Sherman.

Gordon, George H.

US BRIGADIER GENERAL

6   As cavalry, [Lieutenant Colonel Turner] Ashby's men were greatly superior to ours. In reply to some orders I had given, my cavalry commander replied, "I can't catch

them, sir; they leap fences and walls like deer; neither our men nor our horses are so trained."

> —quoted by Lieutenant Colonel G. F. R. Henderson in *Stonewall Jackson and the American Civil War*, vol. 1, 1898.

★ Henderson was a British officer.

Gordon, John B. (1832–1904)

CS MAJOR GENERAL

Our Southern homes have been pillaged, sacked, and burned; our mothers, wives, **1** and little ones, driven forth amid the brutal insults of your soldiers. Is it any wonder that we fight with such desperation? A natural revenge would prompt us to retaliate in kind, but we scorn to war on women and children.

> —quoted by J. William Jones in *Life and Letters of Robert Edward Lee: Soldier and Man*, 1906.

★ Gordon was addressing women in York, Pennsylvania, about the arrival of his troops.

What seemed reckless audacity was the essence of prudence. [Jackson's] eye had **2** caught at a glance the entire situation, and his genius, with marvellous celerity and accuracy, had weighed all the chances of success or failure. While, therefore, others were slowly feeling their way, or employing in detail insufficient forces, Jackson, without for one moment doubting his success, hurled his army like a thunderbolt against the opposing lines, and thus ended the battle at a single blow.

> —quoted by Lieutenant Colonel G. F. R. Henderson in *Stonewall Jackson and the American Civil War*, vol. 2, 1898.

★ Gordon was a brigadier general at that time.

One of the knightliest soldiers of the Federal army, General Joshua L. Chamberlain **3** of Maine, who afterward served with distinction as governor of his State, called his troops into line [at Appomattox Court House], and as my men marched in front of them, the veterans in blue gave a soldierly salute to those vanquished heroes—a token of respect from Americans to Americans, a final and fitting tribute from Northern to Southern chivalry.

> —*Reminiscences of the Civil War*, 1904.

The Confederates [at Appomattox Court House] who clung to those pieces of bat- **4** tered bunting knew they would never again wave as martial ensigns above embattled hosts; but they wanted to keep them, just as they wanted to keep the old canteen with a bullet-hole through it, or the rusty gray jacket that had been torn by canister. They loved those flags, and will love them forever, as mementoes of the unparalleled struggle. They cherish them because they represent the consecration and courage not only of Lee's army but of all the Southern armies, because they symbolize the bloodshed and glory of nearly a thousand battles.

> —*Reminiscences of the Civil War*, 1904.

1   The South's affections are bound, with links that cannot be broken, around the graves of her sons who fell in her defence, and to the mementoes and memories of the great struggle; but does that fact lessen her loyalty to the proud emblem of a reunited country? Does her unparalleled defence of the now dead Confederacy argue less readiness to battle for this ever-living Republic, in the making and administering of which she bore so conspicuous a part?
    —*Reminiscences of the Civil War*, 1904.

2   During these last scenes at Appomattox some of the Confederates were so depressed in spirit, so filled with apprehensions as to the policy to be adopted by the civil authorities at Washington, that the future seemed to them shrouded in gloom. They knew that burnt homes and fenceless farms, poverty and ashes, would greet them on their return from the war. Even if the administration at Washington should be friendly, they did not believe that the Southern States could recover in half a century from the chaotic condition in which the war had left them.
    —*Reminiscences of the Civil War*, 1904.

3   The meeting of Lee and Grant at Appomattox was the momentous epoch of the century. It marked greater changes, uprooted a grander and nobler civilization, and, in the emancipation of one race and the impoverishment of another, it involved vaster consequences than had ever followed the fall of a dynasty or the wreck of an empire.
    —*Reminiscences of the Civil War*, 1904.

4   It is due to General Sherman to say that he had his peculiar ideas of waging war and making it "hell," but when it was over he declared, "It is our solemn duty to protect and not to plunder."
    —*Reminiscences of the Civil War*, 1904.

5   Unless it be Washington, there is no military chieftain of the past to whom Lee can be justly likened, either in attributes of character or in the impress for good made upon the age in which he lived. Those who knew him best and studied him most have agreed that he was unlike any of the great captains of history. In his entire public career there was a singular absence of self-seeking.
    —*Reminiscences of the Civil War*, 1904.

6   And when the end came and [Lee] realized that Appomattox was the grave of his people's hopes, he regretted that Providence had not willed that his own life should end there also. He not only said in substance, to Colonel Venable of his staff and to others, that he would rather die than surrender the cause, but he said to me on that fatal morning that he was sorry he had not fallen in one of the last battles. Yet no man who saw him at Appomattox could detect the slightest wavering in his marvellous self-poise or any lowering of his lofty bearing.
    —*Reminiscences of the Civil War*, 1904.

7   The strong and salutary characteristics of both Lee and Grant should live in history as an inspiration to coming generations. Posterity will find nobler and more whole-

some incentives in their high attributes as men than in their brilliant careers as warriors.
—*Reminiscences of the Civil War*, 1904.

The lustre of a stainless life is more lasting than the fame of any soldier; and if **1** General Lee's self-abnegation, his unblemished purity, his triumph over alluring temptations, and his unwavering consecration to all life's duties do not lift him to the morally sublime and make him a fit ideal for young men to follow, then no human conduct can achieve such position.
—*Reminiscences of the Civil War*, 1904.

The unseemly things which occurred in the great conflict between the States should **2** be forgotten, or at least forgiven, and no longer permitted to disturb complete harmony between North and South. American youth in all sections should be taught to hold in perpetual remembrance all that was great and good on both sides; to comprehend the inherited convictions for which saintly women suffered and patriotic men died; to recognize the unparalleled carnage as proof of unrivalled courage; to appreciate the singular absence of personal animosity and the frequent manifestation between those brave antagonists of a good-fellowship such as had never before been witnessed between hostile armies.
—*Reminiscences of the Civil War*, 1904.

It will be a glorious day for our country when all the children within its borders shall **3** learn that the four years of fratricidal war between the North and the South was waged by neither with criminal or unworthy intent, but by both to protect what they conceived to be threatened rights and imperilled liberty; that the issues which divided the sections were born when the Republic was born, and were forever buried in an ocean of fraternal blood.
—*Reminiscences of the Civil War*, 1904.

General Grant was not endowed by nature with the impressive personality and sol- **4** dierly bearing of Winfield Scott Hancock, nor with the peculiarly winning and magnetic presence of William McKinley—few men are; but under a less attractive exterior he combined the strong qualities of both.
—*Reminiscences of the Civil War*, 1904.

And the repeated manifestations of General Grant's truly great qualities—his innate **5** modesty, his freedom from every trace of vain-glory or ostentation, his magnanimity in victory, his genuine sympathy for his brave and sensitive foemen, and his inflexible resolve to protect paroled Confederates against any assault, and vindicate, at whatever cost, the sanctity of his pledge to the vanquished—will give him a place in history no less renowned and more to be envied than that secured by his triumphs as a soldier or his honors as a civilian.
—*Reminiscences of the Civil War*, 1904.

1   In looking back now over that valley of death—the period of reconstruction—its waste and its woe, it is hard to realize that the worn and impoverished Confederates were able to go through it.
    —*Reminiscences of the Civil War*, 1904.

Gorgas, Josiah (1818–1883)

CS BRIGADIER GENERAL AND CHIEF OF ORDNANCE

2   Johnston verified all our predictions of him. He is falling back as fast as his legs can carry him. . . . Where he will stop Heaven only knows!
    —quoted by Sarah Woolfolk Wiggins in *The Journals of Josiah Gorgas 1857–1878*, 1995.

    ★ This diary entry was written on May 25, 1864, when Gorgas was a major general. General Joseph E. Johnston was retreating through Georgia before the superior forces of Major General William T. Sherman.

3   The calamity which has fallen upon us in the total destruction of our government is of a character so overwhelming that I am as yet unable to comprehend it. I am as one walking in a dream, & expecting to awake. I cannot see its consequences, nor shape my own course, but am just moving along until I can see my way at some future day. It is marvelous that a people that a month ago had money, armies, and the attributes of a nation should to-day be no more, & that we live, breathe, move, talk as before. Will it be so when the Soul leaves the body behind it?
    —quoted by Sarah Woolfolk Wiggins in *The Journals of Josiah Gorgas 1857–1878*, 1995.

    ★ The diary entry was written on May 4, 1865.

4   The sensation is novel, but we must get used to the presence of our late enemies, now our masters. The town [Montgomery, Alabama] is full of Yankees, & the negros abound everywhere, idle tho not insolent. Three thousand are in camp on the opposite side of the River, & the smallpox is making sad havoc among them. Poor victims of their northern friends.
    —quoted by Sarah Woolfolk Wiggins in *The Journals of Josiah Gorgas 1857–1878*, 1995.

    ★ The diary entry was written on May 26, 1865.

5   The slaves are of course in great commotion. Their freedom has been announced to them, & they are in a state of excitement & jubilee not knowing what responsibilities their new condition brings with it. They are idle but not insubordinate nor disrespectful. It is a curious problem which is being solved by the sword—this freedom of the African race. It will cause many a cruel pang on both sides. The master sees his property suddenly swept away, & the negro does not find in his freedom compensation for the ills it brings upon him. But the world will wag on & his freedom will cling to him and the master will continue to cultivate his land, with black labor

or that failing with white. The energies of the white race will halt but temporarily before this catastrophe.
>   —quoted by Sarah Woolfolk Wiggins in *The Journals of Josiah Gorgas 1857–1878*, 1995.

★ The diary entry was written on June 2, 1865.

[Mr. Walton] is a wealthy planter [in Alabama] owning some 7 or 8 plantations, & is **1** much troubled at the present condition of things—his slaves all freed & his past like as he seems to think wasted. This state of mind is most natural, & leads to despondency in his case, but not so in the case of most planters, and nothing surprises me more than the equanimity with which they meet existing facts. Their slaves are suddenly made their (almost) equals & they contract with them; they are withdrawn from their control & they talk to them & advise them. . . . Where sense & discretion guide & direct the masters they will be sure to regain in time the sway, in some shape which they have at present lost, thro' the total failure of military operations. We may still hope for a future I think.
>   —quoted by Sarah Woolfolk Wiggins in *The Journals of Josiah Gorgas 1857–1878*, 1995.

★ The diary entry was written on June 15, 1865.

Yesterday we rode on the pinnacle of success; today absolute ruin seems to be our **2** portion. The Confederacy totters to its destruction.
>   —edited by Frank Vandiver in *The Civil War Diary of Josiah Gorgas*, 1947.

Dined at Col. Thornton's . . . who is the owner of a very large estate [in Alabama]. It **3** struck me very uncomfortably that his conviction should be so largely interlarded with retrospection of his opposition to the doctrine of secession, & the necessary deduction that we fought so valiantly & bled so freely in a cause radically wrong.
>   —quoted by Sarah Woolfolk Wiggins in *The Journals of Josiah Gorgas 1857–1878*, 1995.

Goss, Warren Lee

US PRIVATE

★ Goss was with the 2nd Massachusetts Regiment.

It was a common expectation among us that we were about to end the rebellion.   **4**
>   —*Recollections of a Private: A Story of the Army of the Potomac*, 1890.

★ This was in April 1862.

The general opinion among us was that at last we were on our way to make an end **5** of the Confederacy.
>   —*Recollections of a Private: A Story of the Army of the Potomac*, 1890.

★ This was in early spring of 1862 when the Army of the Potomac was leaving Washington, D.C.

1   The constant hissing of the bullets, with their sharp *ping* and *bizz* whispering around and sometimes into us, gave me a sickening feeling and a cold perspiration. I felt weak around my knees—a sort of faintness and lack of strength in the joints of my legs, as if they would sink from under me. . . . Seeing I was not killed at once, in spite of all the noise, my knees recovered from their unpleasant limpness, and my mind gradually regained its balance and composure.
   —*Recollections of a Private: A Story of the Army of the Potomac*, 1890.

   ★ This was at the battle of Williamsburg on May 5, 1862.

2   The bullets had cut queer antics among our men. A private, who had a canteen of whisky when he went into the engagement, on endeavoring to take a drink found the canteen quite empty, a bullet having tapped it for him. Another had a part of his thumb-nail taken off. Another had a bullet pass into the toe of his boot, down between two toes, and out along the sole of his foot, without much injury. Another had a scalp-strip of hair about three inches in length from the top of his head.
   —*Recollections of a Private: A Story of the Army of the Potomac*, 1890.

   ★ This was at the battle of Williamsburg on May 5, 1862.

3   At the end of the first day's battle, August 29th, so soon as the fighting ceased, many sought without orders to rescue comrades lying wounded between the opposing lines. There seemed to be an understanding between the men of both armies that such parties were not to be disturbed in their mission of mercy.
   —*Recollections of a Private: A Story of the Army of the Potomac*, 1890.

   ★ This was during the second battle of Bull Run (second Manassas), in 1862.

4   There was a great lack here [second battle of Bull Run (second Manassas)] of organized effort to care for our wounded. Vehicles of various kinds were pressed into service. The removal went on during the entire night, and tired soldiers were roused from their slumbers by the plaintive cries of comrades passing in the comfortless vehicles. In one instance a Confederate and a Union soldier were found cheering each other on the field. They were put into the same Virginia farm-cart and sent to the rear, talking and groaning in fraternal sympathy.
   —*Recollections of a Private: A Story of the Army of the Potomac*, 1890.

5   The murmur of many voices, the mellow, abrupt call of the negro drivers to their mules, the glistening arms of the infantry reflected in the sunlight, the dull rumble of artillery wheels and baggage-wagons, live in memory to-day as one of the pictures of "war's wrinkled front," framed in the routine of more ordinary scenes.
   —*Recollections of a Private: A Story of the Army of the Potomac*, 1890.

6   Without exaggeration, the mud has never been given full credit for the immense help it afford the enemy, as it prevented us from advancing upon them. The ever-present foe, winter and spring, in Old Virginia, was Mud. Summer and fall it was Dust, which was preferable; though marching without water, and with dust filling one's nostrils and throat, was not pleasant
   —*Recollections of a Private: A Story of the Army of the Potomac*, 1890.

No country equals a Virginia road for mud. We stuck it thick, and sometimes knee- 1
deep. It was verily "heavy marching." The foot sank insidiously into the mud, and
came out again reluctantly; it had to be coaxed, and while you were persuading your
left, the willing right was sinking as deep. The noise of walking was like that of a
suction-pump when the water is exhausted. . . . Occasionally a boot or shoe would be
left in the mud, and it would take an exploring expedition to find it. . . . The boys
called their shoes "pontons," "mud-hooks," "soil-excavators," and other names not
quite so polite. . . . Virginia mud has never been fully comprehended. To fully understand it you must march in it, sleep in it, be encompassed round about by it. Great is
mud—Virginia mud.
  —*Recollections of a Private: A Story of the Army of the Potomac*, 1890.

With a nervous tremor convulsing my system, and my heart thumping like muffled 2
drumbeats, I stood before the door of the recruiting office, and before turning the
knob to enter read and reread the advertisement for recruits posted thereon, until I
knew all its peculiarities. The promised chances for "travel and promotion" seem
good, and I thought I might have made a mistake in considering war so serious after
all. "Chances for travel!" I must confess now, after four years of soldiering, that the
"chances for travel" were no myth; but "Promotion" was a little uncertain and slow.
  —*Recollections of a Private: A Story of the Army of the Potomac*, 1890.

Grant, Jesse R. (1794–1873)

FATHER OF ULYSSES S. GRANT

Be careful, Ulyss; you're a general now; it's a good job, don't lose it. 3
  —quoted by Shelby Foote in *The Civil War*, vol. 1, 1958.

  ★ He sent this letter after his son was made a brigadier general on August 7, 1861.

Grant, Ulysses S. (1822–1885)

US GENERAL IN CHIEF OF THE ARMIES

In all this I can see but the doom of slavery. The North do not want, nor will they 4
want, to interfere with the institution. But they will refuse for all time to give it protection unless the South shall return soon to their allegiance.
  —letter to his father-in-law, Frederick Dent, April 19, 1861.

Having served for fifteen years in the regular army, including four years at West 5
Point, and feeling it the duty of every one who has been educated at the
Government expense to offer their service for the support of the Government, I
have the honor, very respectfully, to tender my services until the close of the war, in
such capacity as may be offered. I would say, in view of my present age and length of

service, I feel myself competent to command a regiment, if the President, in his judgment should see fit to entrust one to me.
   —letter to Colonel Lorenzo Thomas, the US Army's adjutant general, May 24, 1861.

   ★ Although Grant addressed this to "Colonel" Thomas, he had been appointed a brigadier general on May 7.

1   I guess I've come to take command.
   —quoted by John D. Wright in *The Language of the Civil War*, 2001.

   ★ Grant was speaking to the men in his first command, the 21st Illinois Volunteers.

2   I determined never to ask for anything, and never have, not even a colonelcy.
   —letter to his father, Jesse, August 3, 1861.

   ★ He had been appointed a colonel in June and put in charge of the 21st Illinois Volunteer Infantry.

3   My inclination is to whip the rebellion into submission, preserving all Constitutional rights. If it cannot be whipped any other way than through a war against slavery, let it come to that legitimately. If it is necessary that slavery should fall that the Republic may continue its existence, let slavery go.
   —letter to his father, Jesse, November 27, 1861, when a brigadier general.

4   Mr. Davis has not made it quite plain who is to furnish the snow for this Moscow retreat through Georgia and Tennessee.
   —quoted by Horace Porter in *Campaigning with Grant*, 1897.

   ★ Grant had read the Confederate president's remarks that Southern troops would be returning to their home states just before Sherman began his march through Georgia in November 1861. Lieutenant Colonel Porter was Grant's aide-de-camp.

5   It is ordered, therefore, that the severest punishment, be inflicted upon every soldier, who is guilty of taking or destroying private property, and any commissioned officer guilty of like conduct, or of countenancing it shall be deprived of his sword and expelled from the camp, not to be permitted to return.
   —General Order No. 3, January 13, 1862.

6   If I had captured [General Pillow], I would have turned him loose, I would rather have him in command of you fellows than as a prisoner.
   —quoted by Shelby Foote in *The Civil War*, vol. 1, 1958.

   ★ Brigadier General Grant was giving CS brigadier general Simon B. Buckner his poor opinion about CS brigadier general Gideon Pillow, who had turned over his command to Buckner and escaped Fort Donelson, Tennessee, before Grant captured it on February 16, 1862.

7   It is much less a job to take them than to keep them.
   —quoted by Shelby Foote in *The Civil War*, vol. 1, 1958.

★ This was after Brigadier General Grant captured more than 12,000 Confederate soldiers at Fort Donelson, Tennessee, on February 16, 1862.

No terms except unconditional and immediate surrender can be accepted. I propose   **1**
to move immediately upon your works.
   —quoted by P. C. Headley in *The Life and Campaigns of General U. S. Grant,*
   1869.

★ These terms were given on February 16, 1862, to CS brigadier general Simon Bolivar Buckner, under siege at Fort Donelson in Tennessee. Buckner accepted, and Grant was nicknamed "Unconditional Surrender" Grant and sometimes called "Old Unconditional."

Retreat? No. I propose to attack at daylight and whip them.   **2**
   —quoted by Harold Holzer in *Witness to War: The Civil War, 1861–1865,* 1996.

★ This was said to his generals after his troops were outfought on April 6, 1862, the first day of the battle of Shiloh.

The Jews, as a class violating every regulation of trade established by the Treasury   **3**
Department and also Department orders, are hereby expelled from the department
[of military operations] within twenty-four hours from receipt of this order.
   —General Order No. 11, December 17, 1862.

★ Lincoln repealed the lieutenant general's order on January 1, 1863, saying that a whole class could not be blamed, "some of whom are fighting in our ranks."

The work of reducing Vicksburg will take time and men, but can be accomplished.   **4**
   —letter to Major General Henry W. Halleck, January 20, 1863.

★ The city did not fall until July 4.

It is expected that all commanders will especially exert themselves in carrying out   **5**
the policy of the administration, not only in organizing colored regiments and rendering them efficient, but also in removing prejudice against them.
   —General Order No. 25, April 22, 1863.

The enemy is badly beaten, greatly demoralized, and exhausted of ammunition. The   **6**
road to Vicksburg is open.
   —letter to Major General William T. Sherman, May 3, 1863.

Impress on the men the importance of going through the State in an orderly man-   **7**
ner, abstaining from taking anything not absolutely necessary for their subsistence
whilst traveling. They should try to create as favorable an impression as possible
upon the people and advise them if it will do any good, to make efforts to have law
and order established within the Union.
   —message to Major General William T. Sherman, August 6, 1863.

★ Sherman was in Vicksburg at the time, before he moved east to Atlanta.

1   I never was an Abolitionist, not even what could be called anti-slavery, but I try to judge farely & honestly and it comes patent to my mind early in the rebellion that the North & South could never live at peace with each other except as one nation, and that without slavery.
   —letter to US congressman Elihu B. Washburne from Illinois, August 30, 1863.

2   Hold Chattanooga at all hazards. I will be there as soon as possible.
   —telegram to Major General George H. Thomas, October 19, 1863.

   ★ Grant was in Louisville, Kentucky, at the time and reached Chattanooga on October 23.

3   It will be all right if it turns out all right.
   —quoted by Rod Graff in *Civil War Quiz and Fact Book*, 1985.

   ★ Grant said this on November 25, 1863, as his troops stormed up Missionary Ridge at Chattanooga before receiving orders to do so. They won the battle.

4   My own opinion is that Lee is averse to going out of Virginia, and if the cause of the South is lost he wants Richmond to be the last place surrendered.
   —telegram to Major General William T. Sherman, December 18, 1863.

5   The gratuitous offerings of our loyal citizens at home, through the agency of the Sanitary Commissions, to our brave soldiers in the field, have been to them the most encouraging and gratifying evidence that whilst they are risking life and health for the suppression of this most wicked rebellion, their friends who cannot assist them with musket and sword are with them in sympathy and heart.
   —letter to the Western Sanitary Commission, January 31, 1864.

6   I have always thought the most slavish life any man could lead was that of a politician. Beside I do not believe any man can be successful as a soldier whilst he has an anchor ahead for other advancement. I know of no circumstances likely to arise which could induce me to accept of any political office whatever.
   —letter to US Navy commander Daniel Ammen, February 16, 1864.

   ★ Grant was elected as president in 1868 and reelected in 1872.

7   I feel much better with this command than I did before seeing it.
   —quoted by Rod Graff in *Civil War Quiz and Fact Book*, 1985.

   ★ Grant was taking over command of the Army of the Potomac on March 12, 1864.

8   I feel the full weight of the responsibilities devolving on me; and I know that if they are met, it will be due to those armies, and above all to the favor of that Providence which leads both nations and men.
   —speech to Lincoln and others, accepting his appointment as lieutenant general of the US Army, March 19, 1864.

9   Really, Mr. Lincoln, I have had enough of this show business.
   —quoted by Rod Graff in *Civil War Quiz and Fact Book*, 1985.

   ★ Grant was ducking a White House party in his honor.

You I propose to move against [General Joseph] Johnston's army, to break it up, and **1**
get into the interior of the enemy's country as far as you can, inflicting all the damage you can against their war resources. I do not propose to lay down for you a plan
of campaign, but simply to lay down the work it is desirable to have done, and leave
you free to execute it in your own way.
        —letter to Major General William T. Sherman, April 4, 1864.

★ This resulted in Sherman's march through Georgia.

Wherever Lee goes, there you will go also.   **2**
        —orders issued to Major General George Meade on April 9, 1864, quoted in
        Personal Memoirs of U. S. Grant, vol. 2, 1886.

Oh! I never maneuver.   **3**
        —quoted by William Swinton in *Campaigns of the Army of the Potomac*, 1866.

★ Grant said this during the battle of the Wilderness in Virginia (May 5–7, 1864). He
was interrupting Major General George Meade's comment about maneuvering, because
Grant intended to use brute force "hammering continuously" to overwhelm General
Robert E. Lee's army, without wasting time on diversions.

The enemy hold our front in very strong force, and evince a strong determination to **4**
interpose between us and Richmond to the last.
        —letter to Major General Henry W. Halleck, May 10, 1864.

★ This message was sent during the Spotsylvania campaign.

I propose to fight it out on this line, if it takes all summer.   **5**
        —dispatch to Washington from his field headquarters at Spotsylvania Court
        House, May 11, 1864.

The enemy are obstinate, and seem to have found the last ditch.   **6**
        —letter to Major General Henry W. Halleck, May 12, 1864.

★ The North used "the last ditch" as a symbol for the grave of the Confederacy; it
referred to the many trenches dug during the war.

Lee's army is really whipped.   **7**
        —dispatch to Major General Henry W. Halleck, May 25, 1864.

★ It would be nearly a year before this would be true.

We are sending congratulations to you, to the young mother and the young recruit. **8**
        —letter to Major General George E. Pickett, July 18, 1864.

★ Grant sent these congratulations through the lines to his enemy (and former friend)
and also lit bonfires and sent a baby's silver service. Pickett's son was born on July 14.

The country has lost one of its best soldiers, and I have lost my best friend.   **9**
        —quoted by Carl Sandburg in *Abraham Lincoln: The War Years*, 1939.

★ Grant was referring to Major General James B. McPherson, killed on July 22, 1864,
during the battle of Atlanta.

1   You people up North now must be of good cheer. . . . If the rebellion is not perfectly and thoroughly crushed it will be the fault and through the weakness of the people North.
—letter to J. Russell Jones, July 24, 1864.

2   Take all provisions, forage, and stock wanted for use of your command. Such as cannot be consumed, destroy.
—letter to Major General Philip H. Sheridan, August 5, 1864.

★ Sheridan was moving up the Shenandoah Valley.

3   If you can possibly spare a division of cavalry, send them through Loudoun County [Virginia] to destroy and carry off the crops, animals, negroes, and all men under fifty years of age capable of bearing arms.
—message to Major General Philip H. Sheridan, August 16, 1864.

4   We ought not to make a single exchange nor release a prisoner on any pretext whatever until the war closes. We have got to fight until the Military power of the South is exhausted and if we release or exchange prisoners captured it simply becomes a war of extermination.
—letter to Secretary of State William H. Seward, August 19, 1864.

5   I am informed by the Assistant Secretary of War that Loudoun County [Virginia] has a large population of Quakers, who are all favorably disposed to the Union. These people may be exempted from arrest.
—message to Major General Philip H. Sheridan, August 21, 1864.

6   Do all the damage to railroads and crops you can. Carry off stock of all descriptions and negroes, so as to prevent further planting. If the war is to last another year we want the Shenandoah Valley to remain a barren waste.
—message to Major General Philip H. Sheridan, August 26, 1864.

7   I have just received your dispatch announcing the capture of Atlanta. In honor of your great victory, I have ordered a salute to be fired with shotted guns from every battery bearing upon the enemy. The salute will be fired within an hour, amid great rejoicing.
—message to Major General William T. Sherman, September 4, 1864.

8   I never held what might be called formal councils or war, and I do not believe in them. They create a divided responsibility, and at times prevent that unity of action so necessary in the field.
—quoted by Horace Porter in *Campaigning with Grant*, 1897.

★ Grant was responding to a proposal in October 1864 that General Sherman conduct a council of war to decide if he should march from Atlanta to the sea.

9   . . . the election having passed off quietly . . . is a victory worth more to the country than a battle won.
—quoted by Colonel Alexander K. McClure in *Lincoln's Yarns and Stories*, 1904.

★ Grant sent this telegram to Lincoln after he was reelected.

Sherman's army is now somewhat in the condition of a ground-mole when he disap- **1**
pears under a lawn. You can here and there trace his track, but you are not quite certain where he will come out till you see his head.
    —quoted by Carl Sandburg in *Abraham Lincoln: The War Years*, 1939.

★ This was said during Sherman's march through Georgia toward the end of 1864.

Everything looks like dissolution in the South. A few more days of success with **2**
Sherman will put us where we can crow loud.
    —letter to US congressman Elihu Washburne, February 23, 1865.

★ Washburne, from Illinois, was a political advisor to Grant and Lincoln.

The results of the last week must convince you of the hopelessness of further resis- **3**
tance on the part of the Army of Northern Virginia in this struggle. I feel that it is so,
and regard it as my duty to shift from myself the responsibility of any further effusion of blood by asking of you the surrender of that portion of the Confederate States
army known as the Army of Northern Virginia.
    —letter to General Robert E. Lee, April 7, 1865.

★ The surrender occurred two days later.

Your note of last evening received. In reply would say that there is but one condition **4**
I would insist upon—namely, that the men and officers surrendered shall be dis-
qualified for taking up arms against the Government of the United States until properly exchanged. I will meet you at any point agreeable to you, for the purpose of
arranging definitely the terms upon which the surrender of the Army of Northern
Virginia will be received.
    —letter to General Robert E. Lee, April 8, 1865.

★ The surrender took place the next day.

The war is over, the Rebels are our countrymen again, and the best sign of rejoicing **5**
after the victory will be to abstain from all demonstrations in the field.
    —quoted in *Battles and Leaders of the Civil War*, vol. 4, 1888.

★ Grant was ordering his troops to stop gun-salute celebrations after General Robert E.
Lee's surrender at Appomattox Court House, Virginia, on April 9, 1865. This quotation
and a detailed description of the surrender were recorded by Grant's aide-de-camp,
Brigadier General Horace Porter.

The suffering that must exist in the South the next year, even with the war ending now, **6**
will be beyond conception. People who talk now of further retaliation and punishment, except of the political leaders, either do not conceive of the suffering endured
already or they are heartless and unfeeling and wish to stay at home, out of danger,
whilst the punishment is being inflicted.
    —letter to his wife, Julia, April 25, 1865.

No matter what Gen. Lee's offenses may have been against the offended dignity of **7**
the Nation, great consideration is due him for his manly course and bearing shown
in his surrender at Appomattox C.H.
    —letter to Secretary of War Edwin M. Stanton, June 20, 1865.

1   Gen. Lee's great influence throughout the whole South caused his example to be followed, and to-day the result is that the Armies lately under his leadership are at their homes desiring peace and quiet, and their Arms are in the hands of our Ordnance officers.
       —letter to Secretary of War Edwin M. Stanton, June 20, 1865.

2   Let [our armies] hope for peace and harmony with that enemy, whose manhood, however mistaken the cause, drew forth such herculean deeds of valor.
       —report to Secretary of War Edwin M. Stanton, July 22, 1865.

3   I am satisfied that the mass of thinking men of the South accept the present situation of affairs in good faith. The questions which have heretofore divided the sentiment of the people of the two sections—slavery and state's rights, or the right of a state to secede from the Union—they regard as having been settled forever by the highest tribunal—arms—that man can resort to.
       —report to President Andrew Johnson, December 18, 1865.

    ★ At the president's request, Grant had recently toured the South to observe conditions during Reconstruction.

4   A military life had no charms for me, and I had not the faintest idea of staying in the army even if I should be graduated, which I did not expect.
       —*Personal Memoirs of U. S. Grant*, vol. 1, 1885.

    ★ Grant was recalling his student days at West Point.

5   The fact is the constitution did not apply to any such contingency as the one existing from 1861 to 1865. Its framers never dreamed of such a contingency occurring. If they had foreseen it, the probabilities are they would have sanctioned the right of a State or States to withdraw rather than that there should be a war between brothers.
       —*Personal Memoirs of U. S. Grant*, vol. 1, 1885.

6   If men make war in slavish obedience to rules, they will fail.
       —*Personal Memoirs of U. S. Grant*, vol. 1, 1885.

7   I regarded it as humane to both sides to protect the persons of those found at their homes, but to consume everything that could be used to support or supply armies.
       —*Personal Memoirs of U. S. Grant*, vol. 1, 1885.

8   *Ifs* defeated the Confederates at Shiloh. There is little doubt that we would have been disgracefully beaten *if* all the shells and bullets fired by us had passed harmlessly over the enemy and *if* all of theirs had taken effect.
       —*Personal Memoirs of U. S. Grant*, vol. 1, 1885.

    ★ He was scoffing at theories about how the Confederates could have won the battle, such as if CS general Albert S. Johnston had not been killed.

9   Four millions of human beings held as chattels have been liberated; the ballot has been given to them; the free schools of the country have been opened to their chil-

dren. The nation still lives, and the people are just as free to avoid social intimacy with the blacks as ever they were, or as they are with white people.
—*Personal Memoirs of U. S. Grant*, vol. 1, 1885.

Up to the battle of Shiloh I, as well as thousands of other citizens, believed that the rebellion against the Government would collapse suddenly and soon, if a decisive victory could be gained over any of its armies. . . . But when Confederate armies were collected which not only attempted to hold a line farther south, from Memphis to Chattanooga, Knoxville and on to the Atlantic, but assumed the offensive and made such a gallant effort to regain what had been lost, then, indeed, I gave up all idea of saving the union except by complete conquest.   **1**
—*Personal Memoirs of U. S. Grant*, vol. 1, 1885.

The battle of Shiloh, or Pittsburg landing, has been perhaps less understood, or, to state the case more accurately, more persistently misunderstood, than any other engagement between National and Confederate troops during the entire rebellion.   **2**
—*Personal Memoirs of U. S. Grant*, vol. 1, 1885.

Shiloh was the severest battle fought at the West during the war, and but few in the East equalled it for hard, determined fighting. I saw an open field, in our possession on the second day, over which the Confederates had made repeated charges the day before, so covered with dead that it would have been possible to walk across the clearing, in any direction, stepping on dead bodies, without a foot touching the ground.   **3**
—*Personal Memoirs of U. S. Grant*, vol. 1, 1885.

I do not recollect having arrested and confined a citizen (not a soldier) during the entire rebellion.   **4**
—*Personal Memoirs of U. S. Grant*, vol. 1, 1885.

As it was, many loyal people despaired in the fall of 1862 of ever saving the Union. The administration at Washington was much concerned for the safety of the cause it held so dear. But I believe there was never a day when the President did not think that, in some way or other, a cause so just as ours would come out triumphant.   **5**
—*Personal Memoirs of U. S. Grant*, vol. 1, 1885.

I always admired the South, as bad as I thought their cause, for the boldness with which they silenced all opposition and all croaking, by press or by individuals, within their control.   **6**
—*Personal Memoirs of U. S. Grant*, vol. 1, 1885.

While a battle is raging one can see his enemy mowed down by the thousand, or the ten thousand, with great composure; but after the battle these scenes are distressing, and one is naturally disposed to do as much to alleviate the suffering of an enemy as a friend.   **7**
—*Personal Memoirs of U. S. Grant*, vol. 1, 1885.

I was rendered insensible, and when I regained consciousness I found myself in a hotel near by with several doctors attending me. My leg was swollen from the knee   **8**

to the thigh, and the swelling, almost to the point of bursting, extended along the body up to the arm-pit. The pain was almost beyond endurance. I lay at the hotel something over a week without being able to turn myself in bed. I had a steamer stop at the nearest point possible, and was carried to it on a litter. I was then taken to Vicksburg, where I remained unable to move for some time afterwards.
    —*Personal Memoirs of U. S. Grant*, vol. 1, 1885.

★ Grant had been injured in occupied New Orleans in August 1863 when his horse shied at a locomotive in the street and fell, as he noted, "probably on me."

1   My son accompanied me throughout the campaign and siege, and caused no anxiety either to me or to his mother, who was at home. He looked out for himself and was in every battle of the campaign. His age, then not quite thirteen, enabled him to take in all he saw, and to retain a recollection of it that would not be possible in more mature years.
    —*Personal Memoirs of U. S. Grant*, vol. 1, 1885.

★ Grant was referring to Frederick, his oldest son, during the Vicksburg campaign in 1862 and 1863.

2   I never knew what to do with a paper except to put it in a side pocket or pass it to a clerk who understood it better than I did.
    —*Personal Memoirs of U. S. Grant*, vol. 1, 1885.

★ Grant was referring to administrative red tape.

3   During the siege [of Vickburg] there had been a good deal of friendly sparring between the soldiers ot the two Armies, on picket where the lines were close together. . . . Often "Johnny" would call, "Well, Yank, when are you coming to town?" The reply was sometimes: "We propose to spend the Fourth of July there."
    —*Personal Memoirs of U. S. Grant*, vol. 2, 1886.

4   On several occasions during the war [Jefferson Davis] came to the relief of the Union army by means of his SUPERIOR military GENIUS. I speak advisedly when I saw Mr. Davis prided himself on his military capacity. He says so himself, virtually, in his answer to the notice of his nomination to the Confederate presidency. Some of his generals have said so in their writings since the downfall of the Confederacy.
    —*Personal Memoirs of U. S. Grant*, vol. 2, 1886.

5   The cause of the great War of the Rebellion against the United States will have to be attributed to slavery. For some years before the war began it was a trite saying among some politicians that "A state half slave and half free cannot exist." All must become slave or all free, or the state will go down. I took no part myself in any such view of the case at the time, but since the war is over, reviewing the whole question, I have come to the conclusion that the saying is quite true.
    —*Personal Memoirs of U. S. Grant*, vol. 2, 1886.

For the present, and so long as there are living witnesses of the great war of sections,   1
there will be people who will not be consoled for the loss of a cause which they
believed to be holy. As time passes, people, even of the South, will begin to wonder
how it was possible that their ancestors ever fought for or justified institutions which
acknowledged the right of property in man.
    —*Personal Memoirs of U. S. Grant*, vol. 2, 1886.

There was no time during the rebellion when I did not think, and often say, that the   2
South was more to be benefited by its defeat than the North. The latter had the people, the institutions, and the territory to make a great and prosperous nation. The
former was burdened with an institution abhorrent to all civilized people not brought
up under it, and one which degraded labor, kept it in ignorance, and enervated the
governing class.
    —*Personal Memoirs of U. S. Grant*, vol. 2, 1886.

The war was expensive to the South as well as to the North, both in blood and trea-   3
sure, but it was worth all it cost.
    —*Personal Memoirs of U. S. Grant*, vol. 2, 1886.

Battles had been fought of as great severity as had ever been known in war . . . but   4
in every instance, I believe, claimed as victories for the South by the Southern press
if not by the Southern generals. The Northern press, as a whole, did not discourage
these claims; a portion of it always magnified rebel success and belittled ours, while
another portion, most sincerely earnest in their desire for the preservation of the
Union and the overwhelming success of the Federal armies, would nevertheless
generally express dissatisfaction with whatever victories were gained because they
were not more complete.
    —*Personal Memoirs of U. S. Grant*, vol. 2, 1886.

As we say out West, if a man can't skin he must hold a leg while somebody else does.   5
    —*Personal Memoirs of U. S. Grant*, vol. 2, 1886.

★ Grant was alluding to Lincoln's vague understanding, but total support, of his military tactics.

General Lee . . . was a very highly estimated man in the Confederate army and States,   6
and filled also a very high place in the estimation of the people and press of the
Northern States. His praise was sounded throughout the entire North after every
action he was engaged in; the number of his forces was always lowered and that of
the National forces exaggerated. To be extolled by the entire press of the South after
every engagement, and by a portion of the press North with equal vehemence, was
calculated to give him the entire confidence of his troops and to make him feared by
his antagonists.
    —*Personal Memoirs of U. S. Grant*, vol. 2, 1886.

In the North the people governed, and could stop hostilities whenever they chose to   7
stop supplies. The South was a military camp, controlled absolutely by the govern-

ment with soldiers to back it up, and the war could have been protracted, no matter to what extent the discontent reached, up to the point of open mutiny of the soldiers themselves.
—*Personal Memoirs of U. S. Grant*, vol. 2, 1886.

1   [Lincoln] always showed a generous and kindly spirit toward the Southern people, and I never heard him abuse an enemy. Some of the cruel things said about President Lincoln, particularly in the North, used to pierce him to the heart.
—*Personal Memoirs of U. S. Grant*, vol. 2, 1886.

2   I felt like anything rather than rejoicing at the downfall of a foe who had fought so long and valiantly, and had suffered so much for a cause, though that cause was, I believe, one of the worst for which a people ever fought, and one for which there was the least excuse. I do not question, however, the sincerity of the great mass of those who were opposed to us.
—*Personal Memoirs of U. S. Grant*, vol. 2, 1886.

★ Grant was describing his feelings when General Lee surrendered on April 9, 1865, at Appomattox Court House, Virginia.

3   What General Lee's feelings were I do not know. As he was a man of much dignity, with an impassible face, it was impossible to say whether he felt inwardly glad that the end had finally come, or felt sad over the result, and was too manly to show it.
—*Personal Memoirs of U. S. Grant*, vol. 2, 1886.

★ Grant was describing his feelings when General Lee surrendered on April 9, 1865, at Appomattox Court House, Virginia.

4   Plans were formed by Northern and Southern citizens to burn our cities, to poison the water supplying them, to spread infection by importing clothing from infected regions, to blow up our river and lake steamers—regardless of the destruction of innocent lives.
—*Personal Memoirs of U. S. Grant*, vol. 2, 1886.

5   The Constitution was not framed with a view to any such rebellion as that of 1861–65. While it did not authorize rebellion it made no provision against it. . . . The Constitution was therefore in abeyance for the time being, so far as it in any way affected the progress and termination of the war.
—*Personal Memoirs of U. S. Grant*, vol. 2, 1886.

6   Mr. Lincoln, I believe, wanted Mr. Davis to escape, because he did not wish to deal with the matter of his punishment. He knew there would be people clamoring for the punishment of the ex-Confederate president, for high treason. He thought blood enough had already been spilled to atone for our wickedness as a nation.
—*Personal Memoirs of U. S. Grant*, vol. 2, 1886.

The armies of Europe are machines: the men are brave and the officers capable; but 1
the majority of the soldiers in most of the nations of Europe are taken from a class of
people who are not very intelligent and who have very little interest in the contest in
which they are called upon to take part. Our armies were composed of men who
were able to read, men who knew what they were fighting for, and could not be
induced to serve as soldiers, except in an emergency when the safety of the nation
was involved, and so necessarily must have been more than equal to men who fought
merely because they were brave and because they were thoroughly drilled and inured
to hardships.
   —*Personal Memoirs of U. S. Grant*, vol. 2, 1886.

[Secretary of War Edwin Stanton] cared nothing for the feelings of others. In fact it 2
seemed to be pleasanter to him to disappoint than to gratify. He felt no hesitation in
assuming the functions of the executive, or in acting without advising with him.
   —*Personal Memoirs of U. S. Grant*, vol. 2, 1886.

All must become slave or all free, or the state will go down.   3
   —*Personal Memoirs of U. S. Grant*, vol. 2, 1886.

★ Grant was commenting on the saying before the war that "A state half slave and half
free cannot exist."

It is probably well that we had the war when we did. We are better off now than we 4
would have been without it, and have made more rapid progress than we otherwise
should have made. . . . But this war was a fearful lesson, and should teach us the
necessity of avoiding wars in the future.
   —*Personal Memoirs of U. S. Grant*, vol. 2, 1886.

It is possible that the question of a conflict between races may come up in the future, 5
as did that between freedom and slavery before. The condition of the colored man
within our borders may become a source of anxiety, to say the least. But he was
brought to our shores by compulsion, and he now should be considered as having as
good a right to remain here as any other class of our citizens.
   —*Personal Memoirs of U. S. Grant*, vol. 2, 1886.

Prior to the rebellion the great mass of the people were satisfied to remain near the 6
scenes of their birth. . . . This is all changed now. The war begot a spirit of independence and enterprise. The feeling now is, that a youth must cut loose from his old
surroundings to enable him to get up in the world.
   —*Personal Memoirs of U. S. Grant*, vol. 2, 1886.

The war has made us a nation of great power and intelligence. We have but little to 7
do to preserve peace, happiness and prosperity at home, and the respect of other
nations. Our experience ought to teach us the necessity of the first; our power
secures the latter.
   —*Personal Memoirs of U. S. Grant*, vol. 2, 1886.

1   I feel that we are on the eve of a new era, when there is to be great harmony between the Federal and Confederate. I cannot stay to be a living witness to the correctness of this prophecy; but I feel it within me that it is to be so.
    —*Personal Memoirs of U. S. Grant*, vol. 2, 1886.

2   The power to command men, and give vehement impulse to their joint action, is something which cannot be defined by words, but it is plain and manifest in battles, and whoever commands an army in chief must choose his subordinates by reason of qualities which can alone be tested in actual combat.
    —quoted by General Philip H. Sheridan in *Personal Memoirs of P. H. Sheridan, General United States Army*, vol. 2, 1888.

3   It would be an unsafe and dangerous rule to hold the commander of an army in battle to a technical adherence to any rule of conduct for managing his command. He is responsible for results, and holds the lives and reputations of every officer and soldier under his orders as subordinate to the great end—victory. The most important events are usually compressed into an hour, a minute, and he cannot stop to analyze his reasons. He must act on the impulse, the conviction, of the instant, and should be sustained in his conclusions, if not manifestly unjust.
    —quoted by General Philip H. Sheridan in *Personal Memoirs of P. H. Sheridan, General United States Army*, vol. 2, 1888.

4   Well, somehow or other, I never learned to swear.
    —quoted by Horace Porter in *Campaigning with Grant*, 1897.

    ★ This was said to Porter, who had just remarked that he had never heard Grant swear.

5   There is too much truth in the old adage, "Councils of war do not fight."
    —quoted by Horace Porter in *Campaigning with Grant*, 1897.

6   Pickett, if there is anything on the top of God's green earth that I can do for you, say so.
    —edited by La Salle Corbell Pickett in *The Heart of a Soldier*, 1913.

    ★ This was after the war, when Major General George E. Pickett visited his old enemy, who offered to write him a check because Union forces had burned his house; the offer was appreciated but refused.

7   Accident often decides the fate of battle.
    —quoted by Carl Sandburg in *Abraham Lincoln: The War Years*, 1939.

Greeley, Horace (1811–1872)

New York Tribune FOUNDER AND EDITOR

8   If the cotton states shall become satisfied that they can do better out of the Union than in it, we insist on letting them go in peace. . . . We hope never to live in a Republic whereof one section is pinned to another by bayonets.
    —editorial, *New York Tribune*, December 17, 1860.

If the Cotton States wish to form an independent nation, they have a clear moral **1** right to do so.

    —editorial, *New York Tribune*, February 23, 1861.

★ Five days earlier Jefferson Davis had been inaugurated as president of the Confederacy.

We think you are unduly influenced by the councils, the representations, the men- **2** aces, of certain fossil politicians hailing from the Border Slave States.

    —editorial, *New York Tribune*, August 19, 1862.

★ Greeley addressed this open-letter editorial to Lincoln.

We complain that the Union cause has suffered, and is now suffering immensely, **3** from mistaken deference to rebel Slavery.

    —editorial, *New York Tribune*, August 19, 1862.

★ This was an open-letter editorial to Lincoln.

We cannot conquer ten millions of people united in solid phalanx against us, power- **4** fully aided by Northern sympathizers and European allies. We must have scouts, guides, spies, cooks, teamsters, diggers, and choppers from the blacks of the South, whether we allow them to fight for us or not, or we shall be baffled and repelled.

    —editorial, *New York Tribune*, August 19, 1862.

The Rebels, from the first, have been eager to confiscate, imprison, scourge, and kill; **5** we have fought wolves with the devices of sheep.

    —editorial, *New York Tribune*, August 19, 1862.

On the face of this wide earth, Mr. President, there is not one disinterested, deter- **6** mined, intelligent champion of the Union cause who does not feel that all attempts to put down the Rebellion and at the same time uphold its inciting cause are preposterous and futile.

    —editorial, *New York Tribune*, August 20, 1862.

Mr. Lincoln is already beaten. He cannot be elected. And we must have another **7** ticket to save us from overthrow.

    —letter to former New York City mayor George Opdyke, August 18, 1864.

★ Lincoln was renominated and reelected that year.

These gentlemen of the South mean to win. They meant it in 1861 when they opened **8** fire on Sumter. They meant it in 1865 when they sent a bullet through the brain of Abraham Lincoln. They mean it now. The moment we remove the iron hand from the Rebels' throats they will rise and attempt the mastery. . . . The first fruits of Reconstruction promise a most deplorable harvest, and the sooner we gather the tares, plow the ground again, and sow new seed, the better.

    —editorial, *New York Tribune*, November 15, 1865.

★ Greeley's editorial called for a harsher Reconstruction policy.

Grover, Cuvier (1828–1885)

US BRIGADIER GENERAL

1   Move slowly forward until the enemy opens fire. Then advance rapidly, give them one volley, and then the bayonet.
    —quoted by Lieutenant Colonel G. F. R. Henderson in *Stonewall Jackson and the American Civil War*, vol. 2, 1898.

    ★ He gave his advice to his troops on August 29, 1862, during the second battle of Bull Run (second Manassas).

Guernsey, Alfred H., and Henry M. Alden

2   Jefferson Davis was not a statesman, not even a high-toned politician; but he was a cool, astute, adroit political manager. He was not a man of either great military capacity or acquirement; but he was a good soldier, and a daring, determined commander.
    —*Harper's Pictorial History of the Great Rebellion in the United States*, 1866.

Gunnison, Norman

US SOLDIER

    ★ Gunnison was with the 2nd New Hampshire Volunteers.

3   With prophetic vision, I look forward to the time when the North and South shall again strike hands. I see our banner waving upon every Southern hill. I see, in the coming day, a vast Republic, stretching from the shores of the Atlantic to the coast of the Pacific—from the frozen regions of Hudson's Bay to the sunny clime of the tropical South, embracing Mexico in its limits, having its centre at New Orleans, and with its power controlling the world, whilst over all, the calm stars of our banner soar triumphant, lighting our Nation's pathway to glory.
    —*Our Stars*, 1863.

4   Though the ark of our national salvation may only come to us over an ocean of blood, still let us pray—God speed its coming.
    —*Our Stars*, 1863.

Gunther, C. Godfrey

NEW YORK CITY MAYOR

5   I do not see how those who have always held that the Federal Government has nothing to do with the domestic institutions of the States, can be expected to rejoice over victories, which whatever they may be, surely are not Union victories.
    —quoted by Ernest A. McKay in *The Civil War and New York City*, 1990.

    ★ Gunther was vetoing his Common Council's resolution in September 1864 to illuminate the city because of the fall of Atlanta and other victories.

The time for rejoicing has come. Let any patriot rejoice. Let any man opposed to the **1**
war, because the war was in conflict with his principles or his feeling rejoice.
    —proclamation, April 12, 1865.

★ Confederate general Robert E. Lee had surrendered three days earlier. Gunther was
one of those opposed to the war.

Haines, Zenas T.

Boston Herald correspondent

A soldier's life is one of curious contrasts. Although *not* always gay, it has the jolliest **2**
kind of episodes. It affords the two emotional extremes. One day finds him in the
midst of hilarity and social enjoyment, the next in the blood and carnage of battle,
with friends falling all about him "Thick as autumnal leaves in Valambrosa."
    —quoted by Richard B. Harwell in *The Civil War Reader*, 1958.

★ Haines wrote this thought on January 23, 1863, with the 44th Massachusetts Regiment in New Bern, North Carolina.

Hall, Henry C.

US sergeant

The country about here [Fredericksburg, Virginia] reminds me more of New En- **3**
gland than any place I have seen, and the climate reminds me more of that infernal
place down below that I have not seen but often heard of.
    —letter to his sister, August 10, 1862.

Hall, James E.

CS corporal

I have the blues terribly . . . undoubtedly there is enough reason for men to feel **4**
melancholy. All my friends are at home—among the Yankees, excepting my brother,
sixteen years old who left the army some time ago. . . . Shall we ever meet again in
the quiet halls of home?
    —edited by Ruth Woods Dayton in *The Diary of a Confederate Soldier: James E.
    Hall*, 1961.

★ This diary entry was written on September 17, 1861. Hall was a member of the 31st
Virginia Infantry. His Barbour County in western Virginia was then occupied by Union
troops.

I have been more discouraged today than I have been since I have been in the army. **5**
I have given up the hope of getting home this winter. I also had good health and a

good constitution before joining the army, but now I begin to feel the effects of so much exposure.
—edited by Ruth Woods Dayton in *The Diary of a Confederate Soldier: James E. Hall*, 1961.

★ This diary entry was written on September 17, 1861.

1   We found a great many of the enemy lying on the field after the fight. I cannot exult over our victory. Such work is a shock to human nature.
—edited by Ruth Woods Dayton in *The Diary of a Confederate Soldier: James E. Hall*, 1961.

★ This diary entry was writtenon September 17, 1861. Hall was describing the aftermath of the battle of Camp Allegheny, Virginia.

2   Surely, if during the revolutions of human affairs we may successfully unite ourselves in the old halls of home, I will never leave again. Could I ever again desire the exciting scenes of war? I have had enough now.
—edited by Ruth Woods Dayton in *The Diary of a Confederate Soldier: James E. Hall*, 1961.

★ This diary entry was written on September 26, 1861.

3   I have heard today that the enemy had shamefully treated some of the citizens of my county, respecting private property and personal violence. May the God of truth and justice forever curse them with His rod, for such infernal enactments.
—edited by Ruth Woods Dayton in *The Diary of a Confederate Soldier: James E. Hall*, 1961.

★ This diary entry was written on September 26, 1861.

4   So common has death become, that when a man dies, he is as soon forgotten. Yesterday I passed by the graveyard of our Regt., it being in a line of the timber which we were felling as a blockade. A few tall hemlock pines were left around them, in respect for the dead. They lie far from the road, in a secluded spot. This may possibly be our fighting ground. The din and clangor of battle may sweep over them, as opposing squadrons meet in terrible combat. But they will sleep on. In that bright sphere their pure souls shall forever stand unmoved during the wreck of time, and crush of worlds.
—edited by Ruth Woods Dayton in *The Diary of a Confederate Soldier: James E. Hall*, 1961.

★ This diary entry was written on September 27, 1861.

5   We found several dead. Among others was a young man who more particularly took attention. He was lying by the edge of the forest—having been struck by a cannon ball. His name was Abbott, from an Indiana Regt. In his portmanteau we found three twists of nicely braided hair, from his sisters. He had a furlough for several days. He had written a letter to his sisters saying he would not start home as soon as he expected, as the army was going down the mountain to whip the rebels, and he

was going to accompany it so he could tell them about it when he came home. Poor fellow. His furlough was exchanged into a *fur-long*.

—edited by Ruth Woods Dayton in *The Diary of a Confederate Soldier: James E. Hall*, 1961.

★ This diary entry was written on October 5, 1861.

War is surely the results of man's ambitions. How clearly it shows the folly of the human heart. Can we still hope for success? Our country, I fear, is lost, forever is lost to me. Can we still be encouraged to fight for a much loved, but now ruined country? **1**

—edited by Ruth Woods Dayton in *The Diary of a Confederate Soldier: James E. Hall*, 1961.

★ This diary entry was written on October 7, 1861.

They have treated me very badly since I have been in the company. I remember well every insult. A day will surely come when they will rue everything they have done against me. **2**

—edited by Ruth Woods Dayton in *The Diary of a Confederate Soldier: James E. Hall*, 1961.

★ This diary entry was written on October 13, 1861.

Our scouts killed three of the enemy. It was a very daring act to go so close to the enemy's camp as to kill some of their pickets, when it was expected they would advance upon our position. I am getting tired of so much foolery. If we have to fight, I wish they would attack us again, and not have so much "bushwacking". **3**

—edited by Ruth Woods Dayton in *The Diary of a Confederate Soldier: James E. Hall*, 1961.

★ This diary entry was written on October 16, 1861.

It is surprising to see how many intelligent and accomplished young men belong to the Southern Army, and merely privates in the ranks. I am going to visit the South when the war is over. **4**

—edited by Ruth Woods Dayton in *The Diary of a Confederate Soldier: James E. Hall*, 1961.

★ This diary entry was written on October 16, 1861.

The weather is most disagreeable here—damp and cold all the time. Couldn't I enjoy the luxuries of home now! How I would like to go to bed at home on such a rainy evening as this, knowing that I could sleep soundly and be perfectly dry until morning. The most disagreeable thing I can think of is to be rained upon at night, when you are very tired and sleepy. I have heard of *swearing* as being characteristic of a soldier,—and he would be very apt to do it then. **5**

—edited by Ruth Woods Dayton in *The Diary of a Confederate Soldier: James E. Hall*, 1961.

★ This diary entry was written on October 17, 1861.

. . . "The old year has gone, and with it many a thought of happy dreams." It has also closed the scenes of many of the darkest periods of history. What great events may **6** transpire in the coming year! A nation will doubtless realize a name and status among other nations of the earth. The United States will rank with the mighty dead—numbered with the fallen greatness of Troy, Greece and Rome. She will then have ceased to exist, but has merely followed the examples of all overthrown Governments. Future ages may read of her greatness and grandeur, but the glory of her arms, and the magnificence of her institutions will forever live in song.

—edited by Ruth Woods Dayton in *The Diary of a Confederate Soldier: James E. Hall*, 1961.

★ This diary entry was written on October 29, 1861.

1   May the young men hereafter in the North, think of the responsibilities of making war upon an innocent people who never did them harm, before they embark in such an enterprise again. Is conscience dead? Is reason dumb?

—edited by Ruth Woods Dayton in *The Diary of a Confederate Soldier: James E. Hall*, 1961.

★ This diary entry was written on October 29, 1861.

2   I have quit hoping to ever see our subjugated county as it was once. I feel more like throwing down my gun and cursing the hour I was born to witness such a condition of affairs, than of doing anything else.

—edited by Ruth Woods Dayton in *The Diary of a Confederate Soldier: James E. Hall*, 1961.

★ This diary entry was written on November 13, 1861.

3   Not to save the life of Gen. Loring, and all the sons of bitches in the Confederate Army, would I volunteer again!

—edited by Ruth Woods Dayton in *The Diary of a Confederate Soldier: James E. Hall*, 1961.

★ This diary entry was written on November 18, 1861.

4   Sickness is more to be dreaded by far in the army, than the bullets. No bravery can achieve anything against it. The soldier may sicken and die, without receiving any attention but from the rough hands of his fellow soldiers. When buried he is as soon forgotten. Not a stone is raised to tell his living name, age or face. But many a bitter tear is shed over his melancholy fate by kind friends far away.

—edited by Ruth Woods Dayton in *The Diary of a Confederate Soldier: James E. Hall*, 1961.

★ This diary entry was written on November 19, 1861.

5   A lady from Ga. came with her husband to see their son in this army. He had died before they came. When I saw her she was weeping bitterly. They planted a white rose over his grave, the only crown of glory received. He lies in a dense pine woods,

and the sad melody of the wind as it continually blows through the branches, seems to sing a requiem full of dark forebodings.

—edited by Ruth Woods Dayton in *The Diary of a Confederate Soldier: James E. Hall*, 1961.

★ This diary entry was written on November 19, 1861.

Today is my birthday (21). . . . I was surely reared for a better destiny than this. It is **1** evidently a condition in which God never intended any human being to be placed. One year of my life has passed away—one that could have been of infinite importance to me. At my age one year is worth three in after life. But instead of being usefully spent, it is in a manner idled away.

—edited by Ruth Woods Dayton in *The Diary of a Confederate Soldier: James E. Hall*, 1961.

★ This diary entry was written on November 27, 1861.

I was assisting in loading logs on a wagon out in the mountains. I had to be walking **2** about in the snow over my shoe tops, and was nearly frozen from handling the logs. I stood it for an hour or so, and then I told the Lieut. that I would see him in hell a mile, before I would stay any longer. So I came away. I expect he will report me.

—edited by Ruth Woods Dayton in *The Diary of a Confederate Soldier: James E. Hall*, 1961.

★ This diary entry was written on November 28, 1861.

I do hope Heaven will stop the further effusion of blood. **3**

—edited by Ruth Woods Dayton in *The Diary of a Confederate Soldier: James E. Hall*, 1961.

★ This diary entry was written on December 18, 1861.

It is horrible to anyone not used to it, to hear the blasphemies of the soldiers. I know **4** there is an apparent special Providence directing the affairs of our country, and over every battle field. His care seems to be doubly manifest, but I could not wonder if He should turn against us—seeing so much wickedness.

—edited by Ruth Woods Dayton in *The Diary of a Confederate Soldier: James E. Hall*, 1961.

★ This diary entry was written on December 29, 1861.

I have come to the conclusion not to volunteer again. Our officers have not given us **5** any encouragement to do so.

—edited by Ruth Woods Dayton in *The Diary of a Confederate Soldier: James E. Hall*, 1961.

★ This diary entry was written on December 29, 1861.

I am so extremely tired of camp life. I long so much to enjoy the pleasures of society. **6** Here, nothing but a collected mass of human beings are assembled, who have lost all

of those finer feelings which makes a man a man, caused by the recklessness of life, and the continual connection with the immediate scenes of death.
>—edited by Ruth Woods Dayton in *The Diary of a Confederate Soldier: James E. Hall*, 1961.

★ This diary entry was written on December 29, 1861.

1   If [the Confederates] never retake Western Virginia, I will say goodbye to Dixie forever.
>—edited by Ruth Woods Dayton in *The Diary of a Confederate Soldier: James E. Hall*, 1961.

★ This diary entry was written on January 14, 1862.

2   Oh, is our country forever lost? Shall our friends forever be in a land of such oppression? What changes have transpired in our history! Truly man is a creature of change.
>—edited by Ruth Woods Dayton in *The Diary of a Confederate Soldier: James E. Hall*, 1961.

★ This diary entry was written on January 27, 1862.

3   We received tolerably doleful news. Our company was paraded and every man mustered into service for the war. No difference whether we reenlisted or not. A considerable damper on our future prospects and expectations. We grumbled about the government doing us injustice, and will continue to do so.
>—edited by Ruth Woods Dayton in *The Diary of a Confederate Soldier: James E. Hall*, 1961.

★ This diary entry was written on April 16, 1862.

Halleck, Henry W. (1815–1872)

US MAJOR GENERAL

4   Instead of relieving you, I wish you, as soon as your new army is in the field, to assume immediate command, and lead it to new victories.
>—letter to Brigadier General Ulysses S. Grant, March 17, 1862.

★ Grant had been in danger of losing his command because he had kept out of touch and was known for probable drunkenness.

5   You will immediately remove from your army all newspaper reporters, and you will permit no telegrams to be sent over the telegraph lines out of your command except those sent by yourself.
>—telegram to Major General John Pope, August 19, 1862.

★ Halleck was general in chief, an administrative post in Washington, D.C., at the time.

I think your staff is decidedly leaky. The substance of my telegrams to you is imme- **1** diately telegraphed back there to the press. . . . Clean out such characters from your headquarters.
    —telegram to Major General John Pope, August 19, 1862.

★ The leak was actually George W. Smalley of the *New York Tribune*, who had a close relationship with Pope. Halleck was general in chief, an administrative post in Washington, D.C., at the time.

The Government seems determined to apply the guillotine to all unsuccessful gen- **2** erals. It seems rather hard to do this where the general is not in fault, but perhaps with us now, as in the French Revolution, some harsh measures are required.
    —letter to Major General Horatio Wright, August 25, 1862.

There is a decided want of legs in our troops. **3**
    —letter to Major General George B. McClellan, October 7, 1862.

★ Halleck was criticizing the lack of movement by the Army of the Potomac.

If we compare the average distances marched per month by our troops for the last **4** year, with that of the rebels, or with European armies in the field, we will see why our troops march no better. They are not sufficiently exercised to make them good and efficient soldiers.
    —letter to Major General George B. McClellan, October 7, 1862.

★ Halleck was criticizing the lack of movement by the Army of the Potomac.

Straggling is the great curse of the army, and must be checked by severe measures. . . . **5** I think, myself, that shooting them while in the act of straggling from their commands, is the only effective remedy that can be applied.
    —letter to Major General George B. McClellan, October 7, 1862.

There is an immobility here that exceeds all that any man can conceive of. It requires **6** the lever of Archimedes to move this inert mass.
    —letter to Missouri governor Hamilton Gamble, October 30, 1862.

★ Halleck was complaining about Major General George B. McClellan's reluctance to attack Confederate forces.

It may be proper to give you some explanation of the revocation of your order ex- **7** pelling all Jews from your department. The President has no objection to your expelling traitors and Jew peddlers, which, I suppose, was the object of your order; but as it in terms proscribed an entire religious class, some of whom are fighting in our ranks, the President deemed it necessary to revoke it.
    —telegram to General Ulysses S. Grant, January 21, 1863.

In my opinion the opening of the Mississippi River will be to us of more advantage **8** than the capture of forty Richmonds.
    —telegram to Major General Ulysses S. Grant, March 20, 1863.

1   Call no council of war. It is proverbial that councils of war never fight.
—telegram to Major General George Meade, July 13, 1863.

★ Lincoln instructed Halleck to send this message.

2   We have five times as many generals here as we want, but are greatly in need of privates. Anyone volunteering in that capacity will be thankfully received.
—quoted by Shelby Foote in *The Civil War*, vol. 3, 1958.

★ Halleck was responding in July 1864 to a telegram from an unattached brigadier general offering his services.

3   The safety of our armies, and a proper regard for the lives of our soldiers, require that we apply to our inexorable foes the severe rules of war.
—letter to Major General William T. Sherman, September 28, 1864.

★ Halleck was approving of Sherman's removal of Atlanta residents from the occupied city.

4   As you suppose, I have watched your movements most attentively and critically and I do not hesitate to say that your [Atlanta] campaign has been the most brilliant of the war. Its results are less striking and less complete than those of General Grant at Vicksburg, but then you have had greater difficulties to encounter, and a longer line of communications to keep up, and a longer and more continuous strain upon yourself and your army.
—telegram to Major General William T. Sherman, September 16, 1864.

★ Halleck was general in chief, an administrative post in Washington, D.C., at the time.

5   I do not approve of General Hunter's course in burning private homes or uselessly destroying private property. That is barbarous. But I approve of taking or destroying whatever may serve as supplies for us or to the enemy's army.
—message to Major General William T. Sherman, September 28, 1864.

6   Should you capture Charleston, I hope that by *some accident* the place may be destroyed, and if a little salt should be sown upon its site, it may prevent the growth of future crops of nullification and secession.
—letter to Major General William T. Sherman, December 18, 1864.

7   Your march [through Georgia] will stand out prominently as the great one of this great war.
—message to Major General William T. Sherman, December 18, 1864.

8   Feigned retreats are "Secesh" tactics.
—quoted by Lieutenant Colonel G. F. R. Henderson in *Stonewall Jackson and the American Civil War*, vol. 2, 1898.

9   It takes more soldiers to enforce it than we get from its enforcement.
—quoted by John D. Wright in *The Language of the Civil War*, 2001.

★ Halleck was complaining about the United States Enrollment Act that enforced the draft.

Halstead, Murat (1829–1908)

CINCINNATI COMMERCIAL EDITOR

Grant, entrusted with our greatest army, is a jackass in the original package. He is a **1** poor drunken imbecile. He is a poor stick sober, and he is most of the time more than half drunk, and much of the time idiotically drunk.
> —letter to Secretary of the Treasury Salmon P. Chase, March 12, 1863.

Hampton, Wade (1818–1902)

CS LIEUTENANT GENERAL

No suffering which can be inflicted by the passage over our country of the Yankee **2** armies can equal what would fall on us if we return to the Union.
> —letter to Confederate president Jefferson Davis, April 19, 1865.

★ General Robert E. Lee had surrendered ten days before.

A return to the Union will brings all the horrors of war, coupled with all the degra- **3** dation that can be inflicted on a conquered people. . . . If I can serve you or my country by any further fighting you have only to tell me so.
> —message to Confederate president Jefferson Davis, April 22, 1865.

Hancock, Winfield Scott (1824–1886)

US MAJOR GENERAL

The Confederate Army could better have lost a corps of thirty thousand men, than **4** Stonewall Jackson.
> —quoted by Alexander Hunter in *Johnny Reb and Billy Yank*, 1905.

These are times when a corps commander's life does not count.   **5**
> —quoted by John D. Wright in *The Language of the Civil War*, 2001.

★ Hancock led the 2nd Corps at Gettysburg and said this as he galloped along the front lines, during which he was seriously wounded.

Handy, A. H. (1809–1883)

MISSISSIPPI HOUSE OF REPRESENTATIVES MEMBER

Secession is not intended to break up the present Government, but to perpetuate it. **6** We do not propose to go out by way of breaking up or destroying the Union as our fathers gave it to us, but we go out for the purpose of getting further guaranties and security for our rights.
> —speech in Baltimore, Maryland, December 19, 1860.

★ Handy was a commissioner of Mississippi at this time.

Hardee, William J. (1815–1873)

CS LIEUTENANT GENERAL

1   We [Confederate soldiers] have seen that there was no real hope of success, except by some extraordinary accident of fortune, and we have also seen that the politicians would never give up till the army was gone. So we have fought with the knowledge that we were to be sacrificed with the result we see to-day, and none of us could tell who would live to see it. We have continued to do our best, however, and have meant to fight as if we were sure of success.
     —quoted by US major general Jacob Dolson Cox in *Military Reminiscences of the Civil War*, vol. 2, 1900.

2   I accept this war as the providence of God. He intended that the slave should be free, and now he is free.
     —quoted in the *New York Herald*, May 9, 1865.

3   Will any of your abolitionists . . . feed and clothe half-a-dozen little children, in order to get the work of a man and woman? Sir, our people can pay the working negroes a fair compensation for their services, and let them take care of their own families, and then have as much left at the end of the year as we had under the old system.
     —quoted in the *New York Herald*, May 9, 1865.

Harney, William (1800–1889)

US BRIGADIER GENERAL

4   It must be apparent to every one who has taken a proper and unbiased view of the subject, that, whatever may be the termination of the unfortunate condition of things in respect to the so-called "cotton states," *Missouri must share the destiny of the Union.*
     —proclamation to the people of the state of Missouri, May 14, 1861.

     ★ Harney, who commanded the Department of the West, actually approved of slavery and was relieved of his command fifteen days after this proclamation

Harris, Isham G. (1818–1897)

TENNESSEE GOVERNOR

5   If this calamity [of secession] shall befall the country, the South will have the consolation of knowing that she is in no manner responsible for the disaster. The responsibility rests alone on the Northern people, who have wilfully broken the band of union, repudiated the obligations and duties it imposes, and only cling to its benefits.
     —speech to the Tennessee General Assembly, quoted in *Public Acts of the State of Tennessee, Passed at the Extra Session of the 33rd General Assembly, for the Year 1861.*

Harris, Wiley P.

MISSISSIPPI JUDGE

They (the colored people) pined for freedom, but did not seek the ballot. It was **1** thrust upon them. They have enjoyed it, or used it for seven years. They are a tractable, and, unless misguided, harmless people. It would be a hard measure to take from them the ballot. Really it rests altogether with them and the American people how long they will keep it.
    —speech in Jackson, Mississippi, August 23, 1875.

★ This was delivered when carpetbaggers had political power in Mississippi.

I assure you that the fact has become known at last to the American people, that the **2** only oppression in the South, is the oppression of the whites by colored majorities led by Radicals.
    —speech in Jackson, Mississippi, August 23, 1875.

Harrison, Constance Cary

In the day-time it seemed impossible to associate suspicion with those familiar tawny **3** or sable faces that surrounded us [in Richmond]. We had seen them for so many years smiling or saddening with the family joys and sorrows; they were so guileless, so patient, so satisfied. What subtle influence was at work that should transform them into tigers thirsting for our blood? The idea was preposterous. But when evening came again, and with it the hour when the colored people (who in summer and autumn weather kept astir half the night) assembled themselves together for dance or prayer-meeting, the ghost that refused to be laid was again at one's elbow. Rusty bolts were drawn and rusty fire-arms loaded. A watch was set where never before had eye or ear been lent to such a service. Peace, in short, had flown from the borders of Virginia.
    —*A Virginia Girl in the First Year of the War*, 1885.

The people in our [Richmond] neighborhood, of one opinion with their dear and **4** honored friend, Colonel Robert E. Lee, of Arlington, were slow to accept the startling suggestion of disruption of the Union.
    —*A Virginia Girl in the First Year of the War*, 1885.

Suddenly the shrill whistle of a locomotive struck the ear, an unwonted sound on **5** Sunday. "Do you know what that means?" said one of the older cousins who accompanied the party [picking wild flowers]. "It is the special train carrying Alexandria volunteers to Manassas, and to-morrow I shall follow with my company." An awe-struck silence fell upon our little band. A cloud seemed to come between us and the sun. It was the beginning of the end too soon to come.
    —*A Virginia Girl in the First Year of the War*, 1885.

Then fairly awoke the spirit that made of Southern women the inspiration of South- **6** ern men for the war. Most of the young fellows we were cheering onward wore the uniform of privates, and for the right to wear it had left homes of ease and luxury. To

such we gave our best homage; and from that time forth, during the four years succeeding, the youth who was lukewarm in the cause or unambitious of military glory, fared uncomfortably in the presence of the average Confederate maiden.
—*A Virginia Girl in the First Year of the War*, 1885.

1   On Saturday evening arrived a message from General Beauregard, saying that early on Sunday an engine and car would be put at our disposal, to take us [ladies] to some point more remote from danger [from the first battle of Bull Run (first Manassas)]. We looked at one another, and, tacitly agreeing that the gallant general had sent not an order, but a suggestion, declined his kind proposal.
—*A Virginia Girl in the First Year of the War*, 1885.

2   Already [in 1862] the pinch of war was felt in the commissariat [in Richmond]; and we had recourse occasionally to a contribution supper, or "Dutch treat," when the guests brought brandied peaches, boxes of sardines, French prunes, and bags of biscuit, while the hosts contributed only a roast turkey or a ham, with knives and forks. Democratic feasts those were, where major-generals and "high privates" met on an equal footing.
—*A Virginia Girl in the First Year of the War*, 1885.

3   The only public event of note [in Richmond] was the inauguration of Mr. Davis as President of the "Permanent Government" of the Confederate States . . . That 22d of February was a day of pouring rain, and the concourse of umbrellas in the square beneath us had the effect of an immense mushroom-bed. As the bishop and the President-elect came upon the stand there was an almost painful hush in the crowd. All seemed to feel the gravity of the trust our chosen leader was assuming. When he kissed the Book a shout went up; but there was no elation visible as the people slowly dispersed.
—*A Virginia Girl in the First Year of the War*, 1885.

4   And it was thought ominous afterwards [of Jefferson Davis's inauguration], when the story was repeated, that, as Mrs. Davis, who had a Virginia negro for coachman, was driven to the inauguration, she observed the carriage went at a snail's pace and was escorted by four negro men in black clothes, wearing white cotton gloves and walking solemnly, two on either side of the equipage; she asked the coachman what such a spectacle could mean, and was answered, "Well, ma"m, you tole me to arrange everything as it should be; and this is the way we do in Richmon' at funerals and sichlike." Mrs. Davis promptly ordered the outwalkers away, and with them departed all the pomp and circumstance the occasion admitted of. In the mind of a negro, everything of dignified ceremonial is always associated with a funeral!
—*A Virginia Girl in the First Year of the War*, 1885.

5   The gathering of many troops around the town [Richmond] filled the streets with a continually moving panorama of war, and we spent our time in greeting, cheering, choking with sudden emotion, and quivering in anticipation of what was yet to follow.
—*A Virginia Girl in the First Year of the War*, 1885.

In face of recent reverses, we in Richmond had begun to feel like the prisoner of the   1
Inquisition in Poe's story, cast into a dungeon with slowly contracting walls.
   —*A Virginia Girl in the First Year of the War*, 1885.

★ This was on May 31, 1862.

Early next morning [after the battle of Seven Pines] the whole town [Richmond] was   2
on the street. Ambulances, litters, carts, every vehicle that the city could produce,
went and came with a ghastly burden; those who could walk limped painfully home,
in some cases so black with gunpowder they passed unrecognized. Women with pallid faces flitted bareheaded through the streets, searching for their dead or wounded.
The churches were thrown open, many people visiting them for a sad communion-
service or brief time of prayer; the lecture-rooms of various places of worship were
crowded with ladies volunteering to sew, as fast as fingers and machines could fly,
the rough beds called for by the surgeons. Men too old or infirm to fight went on
horseback or afoot to meet the returning ambulances, and in some cases served as
escort to their own dying sons. By afternoon of the day following the battle, the streets
were one vast hospital.
   —*A Virginia Girl in the First Year of the War*, 1885.

The constant activity our work entailed was as relief from the strained excitement of   3
life after the battle of Seven Pines. When the first flurry of distress was over, the residents of those pretty houses standing back in gardens full of roses set their cooks to
work, or better still went themselves into the kitchen, to compound delicious messes
for the wounded, after the appetizing old Virginia recipes. Flitting about the streets
in the direction of the hospitals were smiling white-jacketed negroes, carrying silver
trays with dishes of fine porcelain under napkins of thick white damask, containing
soups, creams, jellies, thin biscuit, eggs a la creme, broiled chicken, etc., surmounted
by clusters of freshly gathered flowers. A year later we had cause to pine after these
culinary glories, when it came to measuring out, with sinking hearts, the meager portions of milk and food we could afford to give our charges.
   —*A Virginia Girl in the First Year of the War*, 1885.

From our patients [after the battle of Seven Pines], when they could syllable the tale,   4
we had accounts of the fury of the fight, which were made none the less horrible by
such assistance as imagination could give to the facts. . . . It was at the end of one of
these narrations that a piping voice came from a pallet in the corner: "They fit
[fought] right smart, them Yanks did, I tell *you!*" and not to laugh was as much of an
effort as it had just been not to cry.
   —*A Virginia Girl in the First Year of the War*, 1885.

Day by day we were called to our windows [in Richmond] by the wailing dirge of a   5
military band preceding a soldier's funeral. One could not number those sad pag-
eants: the coffin crowned with cap and sword and gloves, the riderless horse following with empty boots fixed in the stirrups of an army saddle; such soldiers as could
be spared from the front marching after with arms reversed and crape-enfolded banners; the passers-by standing with bare, bent heads.
   —*A Virginia Girl in the First Year of the War*, 1885.

1   During all this time President Davis was a familiar and picturesque figure on the street [of Richmond], walking through the Capitol square from his residence to the executive office in the morning, not to return until late in the afternoon, or riding just before nightfall to visit one or another of the encampments near the city. He was tall, erect, slender, and of a dignified and soldierly bearing, with clear-cut and high-bred features, and of a demeanor of stately courtesy to all. He was clad always in Confederate gray cloth, and wore a soft felt hat with wide brim. Afoot, his step was brisk and firm; in the saddle he rode admirably and with a martial aspect.
—*A Virginia Girl in the First Year of the War*, 1885.

2   When on the 27th of June [1862] the Seven Days' strife began, there was none of the excitement attending the battle of Seven Pines. People had shaken themselves down, as it were, to the grim reality of a fight that must be fought. "Let the war bleed, and let the mighty fall," was the spirit of their cry.
—*A Virginia Girl in the First Year of the War*, 1885.

3   Another incident of note, in personal experience during the autumn of '61, was that to two of my cousins and to me was intrusted the making of the first three battle-flags of the Confederacy, directly after Congress had decided upon a design for them. They were jaunty squares of scarlet crossed with dark blue, the cross bearing stars to indicate the number of the seceding States. We set our best stitches upon them, edged them with golden fringes, and when they were finished dispatched one to [General Albert] Johnston, another to [General Pierre G. T.] Beauregard, and the third to [General] Early Van Dorn,—the latter afterwards a dashing cavalry leader, but then commanding infantry at Manassas.
—*A Virginia Girl in the First Year of the War*, 1885.

Hawthorne, Nathaniel (1806–1864)

WRITER

4   Unquestionably, Western man though he be, and Kentuckian by birth, President Lincoln is the essential representative of all Yankees, and the veritable specimen, physically, of what the world seems determined to regard as our characteristic qualities.
—"Chiefly About War Matters" in *Atlantic Monthly*, July 1862.

★ Hawthorne wrote this after visiting Washington, D.C., and the battlefields of northern Virginia.

5   [Lincoln] is evidently a man of keen faculties, and what is still more to the purpose, of powerful character.
—*Atlantic Monthly*, July 1862.

6   The whole physiognomy [of Lincoln] is as coarse a one as you would meet anywhere in the length and breadth of the states; but, withal, it is redeemed, illuminated, softened, and brightened by a kindly though serious look out of his eyes and an expression of homely sagacity that seems weighted with rich results of village experience.
—*Tales, Sketches and Other Papers*, 1883.

Haydon, Charles B.

US LIEUTENANT

I have great faith in General McClellan, still . . . I do not believe Napoleon would **1** have spent so much time in preparation. Indeed everyone knows he would not and knows equally well he would have succeeded. We all know that as a rule delay means defeat to the invader and victory to the invaded.
   —diary quoted by Stephen W. Sears in *For Country Cause and Leader*, 1993.

★ Lincoln eventually relieved McClellan of his command of the Army of the Potomac because of his delaying tactics. Haydon was a member of the 2nd Michigan Infantry.

Hays, Alexander

US MAJOR GENERAL

We are tired of scientific leaders and regard strategy as it is called—a humbug. Next **2** thing to cowardice. What we want is a leader who will go ahead.
   —letter to John B McFadden, July 18, 1865.

Hays, Gilbert Adams

US CAPTAIN

The peculiarity of the rebel yell is worthy of mention, but none of the old soldiers **3** who heard it once will ever forget it. Instead of the deep-chested manly cheer of the Union men, the rebel yell was a falsetto yelp which, when heard at a distance, reminded one of a lot of school boys at play. It was a peculiar affair for a battle yell, but though we made fun of it at first, we grew to respect it before the war was over. The yell might sound effeminate, but those who uttered it were not effeminate by any means. When the Union men charged, it was heads erect, shoulders squared and thrown back, and with a firm stride, but when the Johnnies charged, it was with a jog trot in a half-bent position, and although they might be met with heavy and blight-ing volleys, they came on with the pertinacity of bulldogs, filling up the gaps and trotting on with their never-ceasing "ki-yi" until we found them face to face.
   —*Under the Red Patch: Story of the Sixty Third Regiment, Pennsylvania Volunteers, 1861–1864*, 1908.

Fathers, mothers, wives, children, brothers, sisters and other friends were lined up **4** on each side to bid the last farewell to their loved ones. . . . Many a hearty cheer, and many a God speed were wafted to the boys, and the sad and weeping friends moved off to their homes, feeling that there was a vacant chair at the fireside that perhaps would never again be filled by the absent one.
   —*Under the Red Patch: Story of the Sixty Third Regiment, Pennsylvania Volunteers, 1861–1864*, 1908.

Heintzelman, Samuel P. (1805–1880)

US BRIGADIER GENERAL

1   Such a rout I never witnessed before. No efforts could induce a single regiment to form after the retreat had commenced.
    —quoted by Alfred H. Guernsey and Henry M. Alden in *Harper's Pictorial History of the Great Rebellion in the United States*, 1866.

    ★ He was referring to Union troops at the first battle of Bull Run (first Manassas).

Helper, Hinton Rowan

2   What are you [slaveholders] going to do about it? Something dreadful, of course. Perhaps you will dissolve the Union again. Do it, if you dare. Our motto, and we would have you understand it, is "The abolition of slavery and the perpetuation of the American Union." If, by any means, you do succeed in your treasonable attempts to take the South out of the Union today, we will bring her back tomorrow; if she goes away with you, she will return without you.
    —*The Impending Crisis in the South: How to Meet It*, 1857.

Henderson, G. F. R.

BRITISH LIEUTENANT COLONEL

3   The men of the Stonewall Brigade had a saying that Jackson always marched at dawn, except when he started the night before, and it was perhaps this habit, which his enemies found so unreasonable, that led him to lay so much stress on early rising.
    —*Stonewall Jackson and the American Civil War*, vol. 1, 1898.

4   Lee's strategy was indeed remarkable. He knew McClellan and he knew Lincoln. He knew that the former was over-cautious; he knew that the latter was over-anxious.
    —*Stonewall Jackson and the American Civil War*, vol. 1, 1898.

5   Seven miles in peace are very short. In war, in the neighborhood of the enemy, they are very long. In peace, roads are easy to find. In war, it is the exception that they are found, even when messengers are provided with good maps and the country is thickly populated; and it is from war that the soldier's trade is to be learned.
    —*Stonewall Jackson and the American Civil War*, vol. 2, 1898.

Hicks, Thomas H. (1798–1865)

MARYLAND GOVERNOR

6   A collision between the citizens and the Northern troops has taken place in Baltimore, and the excitement is fearful. Send no more troops here.
    —letter with Baltimore mayor George W. Brown to Lincoln, April 19, 1861.

    ★ This "collision" was a riot that killed three Massachusetts soldiers and eight civilians on this day. The troops were marching to defend Washington, D.C.

I feel it my duty most respectfully to advise you that no more troops be ordered or   **1**
allowed to pass through Maryland, and that the troops now off Annapolis be sent
elsewhere.
    —letter to Lincoln, April 22, 1861.

Higgins, Edward (1821–1875)

CS LIEUTENANT COLONEL

Better go to cover, boys; our cake is all dough!   **2**
    —quoted by US commander David D. Porter in *Battles and Leaders of the Civil
    War*, vol. 2, 1888.

★ Higgins, in charge of Fort Jackson guarding the lower Mississippi River, was viewing
the large Union ships passing by on April 24, 1862. "Cake is all dough" was an expression meaning that hopes or chances were defeated.

Hill, Adams S. (1833–1910)

NEW YORK TRIBUNE REPORTER

Mr. Sumner called upon the President twice on July 4th, to urge the reconsecration   **3**
of the day by a decree of emancipation. . . . Mr. Lincoln seemed not disinclined to do
it for Eastern Virginia; objected to a general decree, as being "too big a lick."
    —letter to Sydney Howard Gay, July 9, 1862.

★ Gay was managing editor of the *New York Tribune*, and Charles Sumner was as a
senator from Massachusetts.

Are we going, as all Republics have gone?—to the military devil?   **4**
    —letter to Sydney Howard Gay, September 7, 1862.

★ This comment came during rumors of a Confederate invasion of Washington, D.C.

Abraham Lincoln has killed himself this week.   **5**
    —letter to Sydney Howard Gay, September 7, 1862.

★ This referred to Lincoln's appointment of Major General George B. McClellan to
command the defenses of Washington, D.C.

Hill, Ambrose P. (1825–1865)

CS BRIGADIER GENERAL

Poor Kearny! He deserved a better death than this.   **6**
    —quoted by CS captain James H. Haynes in *Battles and Leaders of the Civil War*,
    vol. 2, 1888.

★ Philip Kearny had happened upon Confederate troops in the rain and growing darkness and was shot while trying to ride away.

1   Face the fire and go in where it is hottest.
      —quoted by Randall Bedwell in *Brink of Destruction*, 1999.

    ★ This order came during the inconclusive battle of the Wilderness in Virginia that ended May 7, 1864. Hill was then a lieutenant general.

2   The straggler is generally a thief, and always a coward, lost to all sense of shame: he can only be kept in the ranks by a strict and sanguinary discipline.
      —quoted by William Swinton in *Campaigns of the Army of the Potomac*, 1866.

Hill, Benjamin H. (1823–1882)

CS SENATOR

3   Every citizen with his gun, and every negro with his spade and axe, can do the work of a soldier. You can destroy the enemy by retarding his march. Georgians, be firm! Act promptly, and fear not!
      —proclamation to the people of Georgia, November 18, 1864.

    ★ He was referring to Major General William T. Sherman's march through his state. Hill became a US congressman and senator after the war.

4   [Lee] possessed every virtue of the great commanders, without their vices. He was a foe without hate; a friend without treachery; a private citizen without wrong; a neighbor without reproach; a Christian without hypocrisy, and a man without guilt. He was a Caesar without his ambition; a Frederick without his tyranny; a Napoleon without his selfishness; and a Washington without his reward. He was obedient to authority as a servant, and loyal in authority as a true king. He was gentle as a woman in life; modest and pure as a virgin in thought; watchful as a Roman vestal in duty; submissive to law as Socrates, and grand in battle as Achilles.
      —speech in Atlanta to the Georgia branch of the Southern Historical Society, February 18, 1874.

Hill, Daniel H. (1821–1889)

CS MAJOR GENERAL

5   I have yet to see a dead man with spurs on.
      —quoted by CS brigadier general Gilbert Moxley Sorrel in *Recollections of a Confederate Staff Officer*, 1905.

    ★ This was said to ridicule cavalrymen.

6   When our independence is won, the most trifling soldier in the ranks will be more respected, as he is now more respectable, than an army of these skulking exempts.
      —quoted by John D. Wright in *The Language of the Civil War*, 2001.

    ★ "Exempts" were persons exempted from military service, as well as members of the home guard.

Every battle-field of the Civil War beheld the deadly conflict of former friends with   1
each other. . . . If we had to be beaten it was better to be beaten by former friends.
Every true soldier loves to have "a foeman worthy of his steel." Every true man likes
to attribute high qualities to those who were only friends, though now alienated for
a time. The temporary estrangement cannot obliterate the recollection of noble
traits of character.
   —quoted in *Battles and Leaders of the Civil War*, vol. 2, 1888.

The sons of the South struck her many heavy blows. Farragut, of Tennessee, rose, as   2
a reward of merit, to the highest rank in the Federal navy. A large number of his
associates were from the South. . . . Moreover, the South had three hundred thousand of her sons in the Federal army in subordinate capacities. Her armies surrendered when a Southern-born President and a Southern-born Vice-President were at
the head of the United States Government. That the wounds of defeat and humiliation have been so soon healed has been owing largely to this balm to mortified pride.
   —quoted in *Battles and Leaders of the Civil War*, vol. 2, 1888.

The late Civil War was relieved of very much of its sectional character by the pres-   3
ence of so many Southerners in the Union armies. Therefore, it will be in the United
States as in all the unsectional civil wars of the world's history in which race and religion were not involved,—the waves of oblivion will roll over the bitter recollections
of the strife. But we trust that fragrant forever will be the memory of deeds of heroism, patience, fortitude, self-denial, and constancy to principle, whether those deeds
were performed by the wearers of the blue or of the gray.
   —quoted in *Battles and Leaders of the Civil War*, vol. 2, 1888.

A line of dismounted staff-officers, couriers, teamsters, and cooks was formed behind   4
the guns to give the appearance of battery supports. I do not remember ever to have
experienced a feeling of greater *loneliness*. It seemed as though we were deserted by
"all the world and the rest of mankind."
   —quoted in *Battles and Leaders of the Civil War*, vol. 2, 1888.

★ Three of Hill's brigades had not arrived after one had been defeated at the battle of
South Mountain, Maryland, on September 14, 1862.

The muscles of [Jackson] would twitch convulsively when a battle was about to open,   5
and his hand would tremble so that he could not write. The men often noticed the
working of his face, and would say, "Old Jack is making mouths at the Yankees." But
all this only indicated weak nerves, and not timidity. I think that he loved danger for
its own sake, and, though his nervous system was weak, he gloried in battle, and
never shrank from its dangers or its responsibilities.
   —*Century Magazine*, February 1894.

★ Hill was Jackson's brother-in-law.

[Jackson] used neither tobacco, nor coffee, nor spirits; he would go all winter with-   6
out cloak or overcoat in the mountains of Virginia, giving no other reason than that
he "did not wish to give way to cold." These peculiarities were laughed at, and he was
regarded as a marvel of eccentricity. But there was nothing erratic in it. This self-

denial and self-control explain his wonderful success. He had conquered himself, and was thus made fit to be a conqueror.
—*Century Magazine*, February 1894.

1   No self-indulgent man was every truly great, however lavishly nature may have showered upon him her bounties. How many splendid opportunities have been lost through the wine-bibbing or pleasure-seeking of some officer of rank!
—*Century Magazine*, February 1894.

2   [Jackson] had not the grace and suavity of Marlborough, the easy fascination of Napoleon, the imposing dignity of Washington. His bearing was awkward, his address unprepossessing, his conversational powers limited save when warmed up, his manner cold and ungenial to strangers. Success threw a halo of glory around all this, and endeared even his ungainly qualities to his men. The successful general is always popular.
—*Century Magazine*, February 1894.

3   Jackson's men loved him, then, for his victories, and not for his piety and purity of character. It is true that this love was mingled with a good deal of awe, because of his communings with Heaven; but his prayers, unaccompanied by heavy and telling blows, would have been looked upon as tokens of weakness.
—*Century Magazine*, February 1894.

4   I think it was Jackson's reticence more than anything else that gave offense. His next in command knew no more than the private soldier what he intended to do.
—*Century Magazine*, February 1894.

5   Jackson's genius never shone when he was under the command of another. It seemed then to be shrouded or paralyzed.
—quoted by Lieutenant Colonel G. F. R. Henderson in *Stonewall Jackson and the American Civil War*, vol. 2, 1898.

6   We were very lavish of blood in those days.
—quoted by James M. McPherson in *The Battle Cry of Freedom: The Civil War Era*, 1989.

★ He was recalling the Confederate charges against batteries during the battle of Gaines's Mill, Virginia, on June 27, 1862.

Hindman, Thomas C. (1828–1868)

CS MAJOR GENERAL

7   Remember that the enemy you engage has no feeling of mercy or kindness toward you. His ranks are made up of Pin Indians, free negroes, Southern tories, Kansas jayhawkers, and hired Dutch cut-throats. These bloody ruffians have invaded your country; stolen and destroyed your property; murdered your neighbors; outraged

your women; driven your children from their homes, and defiled the graves of your kindred.

—speech to his troops, December 4, 1862.

★ A "pin Indian" was one who had been converted by ministers and denounced slavery, for which they were given a pin or badge to wear. They were thus loyal to the Union cause.

Hoke, Jacob (1837–1912)

PENNSYLVANIA RESIDENT

All along the route by which this [wagon] train made its way, broken wagons and   1
dead and dying soldiers were strewed. The bottom of the wagons was smeared with blood. . . . The vastness of the train, and the aggregate of human agony it contained, has never been understood.

—quoted by William C. Davis in *Brothers in Arms*, 1995.

Holmes, Oliver Wendell, Jr. (1841–1935)

US CAPTAIN

★ Holmes later became an associate justice of the US Supreme Court and a great judicial figure in US history.

The first gun that spat its iron insult at Fort Sumter smote every loyal American full   2
in the face.

—speech in Boston, July 4, 1863, quoted by Richard B. Harwell in *The Civil War Reader*, 1958.

Get down, you damn fool, before you get shot!   3

—quoted by Shelby Foote in *The Civil War*, 1958.

★ Holmes was yelling at Lincoln, whom he failed to recognize as the president, as Lincoln stood on the parapet of Fort Stevens in Washington, D.C., on July 12, 1864. Confederate snipers had just felled an officer three feet away. Lincoln was bemused by the profane order but quickly obeyed.

War is an organized bore.   4

—quoted by Geoffrey C. Ward in *The Civil War: An Illustrated History*, 1990.

Hood, John B. (1831–1879)

CS GENERAL

. . . permit me to say that the unprecedented measure you propose transcends, in   5
studied and ingenious cruelty, all acts ever brought to my attention in the dark history of war. In the name of God and country, I protest, believing you will find that

you are expelling from their homes and fireside the wives and children of a brave people.
   —letter to Major General William T. Sherman, September 8, 1864.

★ Hood was protesting Sherman's order forcing civilians to leave occupied Atlanta.

1   You came into our country with your army, avowedly for the purpose of subjugating free white men, women, and children, and not only intend to rule over them, but you make negroes your allies, and desire to place over us an inferior race, which we have raised from barbarism to its present position, which is the highest ever attained by that race, in any country, in all time.
   —letter to Major General William T. Sherman, September 12, 1864.

2   You say we insulted your flag. The truth is, we fired upon it, and those who fought under it, when you came to our doors upon the mission of subjugation.
   —letter to Major General William T. Sherman, September 12, 1864.

3   When our troops were in the greatest confusion [at the battle of Nashville], a young lady of Tennessee, Miss Mary Bradford, rushed in their midst regardless of the storm of bullets, and, in the name of God and of our country, implored them to re-form and face the enemy. Her name deserves to be enrolled among the heroes of the war, and it is with pride that I bear testimony to her bravery and patriotism.
   —*Advance and Retreat*, 1880.

Hooker, Joseph (1814–1879)

US MAJOR GENERAL

4   We retreated like a parcel of sheep, and a few shots from the rebels would have panic-stricken the whole command.
   —quoted by Lieutenant Colonel G. F. R. Henderson in *Stonewall Jackson and the American Civil War*, vol. 2, 1898.

★ This was at the battle of Malvern Hill, Virginia, on July 1, 1862.

5   We are through for to-night, gentlemen, but to-morrow we fight the battle that will decide the fate of the republic.
   —edited by Frank Moore in *The Rebellion Record: A Diary of American Events, with Documents, Narratives, Illustrative Incidents, Poetry, Etc.*, vol. 5, 1862.

★ This was said to his officers on September 16, 1862. The next day, the battle of Antietam (Sharpsburg), was the bloodiest day of the war.

6   It was never my fortune to witness a more bloody, dismal battle-field.
   —quoted in *Battles and Leaders of the Civil War*, vol. 2, 1888.

★ Hooker was referring to the Antietam (Sharpsburg) battlefield.

Finding that I had lost as many men as my orders required me to lose, I suspended **1**
the attack.
>—quoted by William Swinton in *Campaigns of the Army of the Potomac*, 1866.

★ This caustic comment was made at the battle of Fredericksburg on December 13,
1862. Hooker was then a brigadier general.

The enemy is in my power, and God Almighty can not deprive me of them. **2**
>—quoted by Nathaniel W. Stephenson in *Lincoln: An Account of His Personal
>Life, Especially of Its Springs of Action as Revealed and Deepened by the Ordeal
>of War*, 1922.

★ Hooker was a brigadier general at that time.

My plans are perfect, and when I start to carry them out, may God have mercy on **3**
Bobby Lee, for I shall have none.
>—quoted by Shelby Foote in *The Civil War*, vol. 2, 1958.

★ This was on April 12, 1863, before Lee, with some 60,000 men, defeated Hooker's
force of 130,000 at Chancellorsville.

Gentlemen, if I can plant my army there, God Almighty can't drive me out. **4**
>—quoted by Alexander Hunter in *Johnny Reb and Billy Yank*, 1905.

★ In late April 1863, Hooker had placed his finger on a map at Chancellorsville, whose
battle he soon lost.

It is with heartfelt satisfaction that the commanding general announces to the army **5**
that the operations of the last three days have determined that our enemy must
either ingloriously fly, or come out from behind his defenses and give us battle on
our own ground, where certain destruction awaits him.
>—General Order No. 47, April 30, 1863.

★ This was announced at Chancellorsville before Brigadier General Hooker's defeat
there on May 4.

The rebel army is now the legitimate property of the Army of the Potomac. They **6**
may as well pack up their haversacks and make for Richmond.
>—quoted by William Swinton in *Campaigns of the Army of the Potomac*, 1866.

★ Hooker made this boast before his defeat at the battle of Chancellorsville on May 4,
1863.

Doubleday, I was not hurt by a shell, and I was not drunk. For once I lost confidence **7**
in Joe Hooker, and that is all there is to it.
>—quoted by John Bigelow Jr., in *The Campaign of Chancellorsville: A Strategic
>and Tactical Study*, 1910.

★ Major General Abner Doubleday had questioned Brigadier General Hooker, known
as a drinker, about his strange behavior during the battle.

1   Profoundly loyal, and conscious of its strength, the Army of the Potomac will give or decline battle, whenever its interest or honor may demand. It will also be the guardian of its own history and its own fame.
      —General Order No. 49, May 6, 1863.

      ★ This was made two days after Hooker's defeat at Chancellorsville.

2   I don't know whether I'm standing on my head or feet.
      —quoted by Randall Bedwell in *Brink of Destruction*, 1999.

      ★ Brigadier General Hooker had recently been relieved as commander of the Army of the Potomac.

3   Our artillery had always been superior to that of the rebels, as was also our infantry, except in discipline; and that, for reasons not necessary to mention, never did equal Lee's army. With a rank and file vastly inferior to our own, intellectually and physically, that army had, by discipline alone, acquired a character for steadiness and efficiency unsurpassed, in my judgment, in ancient or modern times. We have not been able to rival it, nor has there been any approximation to it in the other rebel armies.
      —quoted in *Annals of the War*, 1879.

Hosmer, James Kendall (1834–1927)

US NURSE

4   God pity the world if it has sights in it more melancholy than a military hospital!
      —quoted by John D. Wright in *The Language of the Civil War*, 2001.

Hotze, Henry (1833–1887)

CS COMMERCIAL AGENT IN LONDON

5   It is marvellous with what wild-fire rapidity this tune of "Dixie" has spread over the whole South. Considered as an intolerable nuisance when first the streets re-echoed it from the repertoire of wandering minstrels, it now bids fair to become the musical symbol of a new nationality, and we shall be fortunate if it does not impose its very name on our country.
      —*Index*, 1862.

      ★ Hotze began and edited the *Index* newspaper in London. This article appeared in the spring of 1862.

Houston, Sam (1793–1863)

TEXAS GOVERNOR

6   Let me tell you what is coming. . . . Your fathers and husbands, your sons and brothers, will be herded at the point of the bayonet. . . . You may, after the sacrifice of countless millions of treasure and hundreds of thousands of lives, as a bare possibility, win Southern independence. . . . But I doubt it. I tell you that, while I believe

with you in the doctrine of States Rights, the North is determined to preserve this Union. They are not a fiery, impulsive people as you are, for they live in colder climates. But when they begin to move in a given direction . . . they move with a steady momentum and perseverance of a mighty avalanche.
    —quoted by Geoffrey C. Ward in *The Civil War*, 1990.

★ Houston, who gave this warning in 1861, was deposed after refusing to swear allegiance to the Confederacy.

I am for the Union without any "if."   1
    —quoted by Kenneth C. Davis in *Don't Know Much about the Civil War*, 1996.

Howard, Oliver O. (1830–1909)

US MAJOR GENERAL

★ Howard later founded Howard University for Negroes in Washington, D.C.

Stonewall Jackson was victorious. Even his enemies praise him; but, providentially   2
for us, [Chancellorville] was the last battle he waged against the American Union.
    —quoted by Lieutenant Colonel G. F. R. Henderson in *Stonewall Jackson and the American Civil War*, vol. 2, 1898.

Our countrymen—large numbers of them—combined and fought us hard for a   3
cause. They failed and we succeeded; so that, in an honest desire for reconcilement, I would be the more careful, even in the use of terms, to convey no hatred or reproach for the past.
    —*Autobiography of General O. O. Howard*, vol. 1, 1907.

Hereafter we buy our gloves together.   4
    —quoted by Carl Sandburg in *Abraham Lincoln: The War Years*, 1939.

★ Brigadier General Howard, whose right arm was shattered, was greeting Brigadier General Philip Kearny, who had lost his left arm.

Howe, Julia Ward (1819–1910)

WRITER

Mine eyes have seen the glory of the coming of the Lord: He is trampling out the   5
vintage where the grapes of wrath are stored; He hath loosed the fateful lightning of his terrible swift sword: His truth is marching on.
    —*Battle Hymn of the Republic*, 1862.

As He died to make men holy, let us die to make men free.   6
    —*Battle Hymn of the Republic*, 1862.

Hughes, John (1797–1864)

New York archbishop

1   We, Catholics, and a vast majority of our brave troops in the field, have not the slightest idea of carrying on a war that costs so much blood and treasure just to gratify a clique of Abolitionists in the North.
    —quoted by John R. G. Hassard in *Life of the Most Reverend John Hughes, First Archbishop of New York, with Extracts from his Private Correspondence*, 1866.

Humphreys, Benjamin G. (1808–1882)

Mississippi governor

2   The South having ventured all upon the arbitrament of the sword, has lost all save her honor, and now accepts the result in good faith.
    —inaugural address, October 16, 1865.

    ★ Humphreys was Mississippi's first governor after the war.

3   The Negro is free, whether we like it or not; we must realize that fact now and forever. To be free, however, does not make him a citizen or entitle him to social or political equality with the white man. But the constitution and justice do entitle him to protection and security in his person and property, both real and personal.
    —speech to the Mississippi legislature, November 20, 1865.

4   Four years of cruel war, conducted on principles of vandalism disgraceful to the civilization of the age, were scarcely more blighting and destructive to the homes of the white man, and impoverishing and degrading to the Negro, than has resulted in the last six or eight months from the administration of this black incubus.
    —speech to the Mississippi legislature, November 20, 1865.

    ★ Humphreys was attacking the Freedmen's Bureau that had jurisdiction over freed slaves.

Hunter, Alexander

CS private

5   How the Yankees did enjoy smoking the Rebel tobacco! At the North they sold the soldiers a vile compound made of chickory, cabbage and sumac leaves ground together and christened tobacco. It burned the tongue, parched the throat, and almost salivated the consumer.
    —*Johnny Reb and Billy Yank*, 1905.

6   Reckon up the killed, and you would have a mighty host. Collect the tears that have been shed over soldiers slain in battle, and you would have an ocean.
    —*Johnny Reb and Billy Yank*, 1905.

Dirty! Well, we were! Not clean dirt either, or a mild type of dirt, but dirt absolute   **1**
and invincible, dirt which had accumulated, hardened and stuck fast, had almost
become scales; dirt which cracked at intervals like varnish on furniture. No wonder
the Northern papers described Lee's army as composed of the lowest type of humanity, certainly they had that appearance.
    —*Johnny Reb and Billy Yank*, 1905.

At this time the privates of the rank and file had not much belief in Grant's general-   **2**
ship. His mad charges in which he lost thousands, his repeated attacks and repulses,
until the vicinity of Spottsylvania resembled a great abattoir, where, instead of cattle
being slaughtered, precious humanity gave up their lives, was not their idea of a master of the art of war.
    —*Johnny Reb and Billy Yank*, 1905.

Every girl in Virginia had her share of nursing to do, and it was too common to excite   **3**
remark to see some wounded soldier, who had been carried into the farmer's house
dirty, unkempt, and literally in rags, emerge therefrom spick, span and clean, with
underclothing made from the garments of the girls, who had sacrificed their own
comfort for the man who could pull a trigger.
    —*Johnny Reb and Billy Yank*, 1905.

If the South had run mad, the North was demented; neither side considered the over-   **4**
whelming proportions, the fearful, far-reaching consequences of the impending struggle. In such wise both parties boasted and raved before closing in deadly combat.
    —*Johnny Reb and Billy Yank*, 1905.

The soldier's first battle-field is marked by a variety of sensations; trembling fear,   **5**
curiosity, and an insane desire to get up and leave, a half-feeling of awe, a strange
nervousness, doubt as to his fate, all mingle together, making his heart beat fast and
his pulse thrill with nameless horror; his breathing becomes thick and his face deadly
pale; no matter what may be the temperament of the man, the first battle causes him
more agony of mind than all other conflicts combined.
    —*Johnny Reb and Billy Yank*, 1905.

Send a soldier on picket duty and give him sufficiency of food if you wish to make   **6**
him happy. The fact that he is close to an enemy exhilarates his spirits, and the danger of sudden attack keeps him in good humor. It has all the charm of novelty to be
isolated, as it were, from the thousands who form the army. To be only with chosen
comrades and boon companions—this is of itself enough to change the dull, mechanical soldier into a bright, sentient, hopeful being.
    —*Johnny Reb and Billy Yank*, 1905.

Pick out of any thronged thoroughfare ten Irishmen, and you will find at least six   **7**
honest men. They are the bone and sinew of our land. They rear our stately struc-
tures, build our great industrial works, develop our mines, and join heart and soul in
our battles. What a happy, devil-me-care, laughter-loving fellow he is withal! In all
the troops of the Confederates, there were none truer or braver.
    —*Johnny Reb and Billy Yank*, 1905.

1   Every soldier in the [Confederate] army owes a personal debt of gratitude to the women of Virginia, for sooner or later they were ministered to with the tenderest care when sick or wounded. In all the four years of the war no one ever heard of a woman being insulted in the street of Virginia's Capital.
  —*Johnny Reb and Billy Yank*, 1905.

2   The freedman has absorbed every element of those old Southern slaves, and if advanced to the dignity of voter and citizenship—our legislators and rules withal— they yet have lost all their light-heartedness, the happy-go-lucky carelessness that made of them the jolliest race in the world.
  —*Johnny Reb and Billy Yank*, 1905.

3   Many a bullet after it has done its deadly work has stricken friends as well as foe; many a ball that sped from Southern ranks has rebounded into Southern homes; many a Northern missile has found its after-mark in Northern hearts. A mother had a son who wore the blue and another who wore the gray. Father and son have fought on either side.
  —*Johnny Reb and Billy Yank*, 1905.

4   The commandment from the Mount, "love one's enemy," finds strange translation in bursting shells and tearing shot, and screaming bullets and gaping wounds, and holo- causts of precious lives, and bleeding hearts, and broken homes and fiercest hatred. However, to the end of time "there shall be wars and rumors of war!" But in all the range of Creation . . . has there ever existed, or ever shall exist, aught so ruthlessly, utterly, hopelessly cruel as civil and internecine war?
  —*Johnny Reb and Billy Yank*, 1905.

5   There is something rascally low and mean about a shell—it never goes straight, it is never reliable; it always starts so high and ends so low; and then again it is a born spy. If there chances to be a dark wood a half mile away, a shell is sent there to try to find out whether or not anybody is lurking within.
  —*Johnny Reb and Billy Yank*, 1905.

6   I have heard of soldiers whose "bowels yearned" for a fight, but such "bowels" were not inside of my anatomy.
  —quoted by John D. Wright in *The Language of the Civil War*, 2001.

Hunter, David (1802–1886)

US MAJOR GENERAL

7   The three States of Georgia, Florida and South Carolina, comprising the military department of the south, having deliberately declared themselves no longer under the protection of the United States of America, and having taken up arms against the said United States, it becomes a military necessity to declare them under martial law. This was accordingly done on the 25th day of April, 1862. Slavery and martial law in a free country are altogether incompatible; the persons in these three States—

Georgia, Florida and South Carolina—heretofore held as slaves, are therefore declared forever free.

    —General Orders No. 11, May 9, 1862.

★ Ten days later, Lincoln annulled this order by Hunter, who commanded the Department of the South.

Illinois Legislature

Resolved: That the emancipation proclamation of the President of the United States **1** is as unwarranted in military as in civil law; a gigantic usurpation, at once converting the war, professedly commenced by the administration for the vindication of the authority of the constitution, into the crusade for the sudden, unconditional, and violent liberation of 3,000,000 negro slaves; a result which would not only be a total subversion of the Federal Union, but a revolution in the social organization of the Southern States, the immediate and remote, the present and far-reaching consequences of which to both races cannot be contemplated without the most dismal foreboding of horror and dismay. The proclamation invites servile insurrection as an element in this emancipation crusade—a means of warfare, the inhumanity and diabolism of which are without example in civilized warfare, and which we denounce, and which the civilized world will denounce, as an uneffaceable disgrace to the American people.

    —resolution quoted in the *Illinois State Register*, January 7, 1863.

★ This was Lincoln's home state.

Jackman, John S.

CS PRIVATE

I met a fellow dressed in a suit of "butter-nut" jeans, who was limping [away from the **2** battle of Shiloh], but I don't believe was scratched. He asked me, in that whining way: "Has you'ns been in the fight yet?" I thought he meant some general, and asked my "brown" interrogator what troops General "Youens" commanded. He seemed astounded, and at last made me understand him. I told him "no," and went on. I afterwards got quite familiar with the "youens" and "weens" vernacular of "Brown Jeans."

    —edited by William C. Davis in *Diary of a Confederate Soldier: John S. Jackman of the Orphan Brigade*, 1990.

★ This diary entry was written on April 16, 1862. Jackman was a member of the 1st Kentucky Brigade known as the "Orphan Brigade" because that state stayed in the Union; "butternut" refers to the brownish-gray color of Confederate uniforms.

All day long the ambulances continued to discharge their loads of wounded [Con- **3** federates from the battle of Shiloh]. At last night set in, and the musketry ceased; but the Federal gunboats continued shelling awhile after dark. Nearly midnight when we got through with the wounded. A heavy rain set in. I was tired, sick and all covered with blood. But I was in far better fix than many that were there. I sat on a medicine chest in the surgeon's tent, and "nodded" the long night through.

—edited by William C. Davis in *Diary of a Confederate Soldier: John S. Jackman of the Orphan Brigade*, 1990.

★ This diary entry was written on April 16, 1862.

1   Four miles brought us to Monterey, and just beyond, we met some of the wounded on foot with their arms and heads bound up in bloody bandages, & I felt then that I was getting in the vicinity of the "warfare." Soon we met ambulances and wagons loaded with wounded, and I could hear the poor fellows groaning and shrieking, as they were being jolted over the rough road. Met a man on horseback with a stand of captured colors. We were not in proximity of the fighting, and we met crowds of men; some crippling along, wounded in the legs or about the body; others, no blood could be seen about their persons—yet all seemed bent on getting away.

—edited by William C. Davis in *Diary of a Confederate Soldier: John S. Jackman of the Orphan Brigade*, 1990.

★ This diary entry was written on April 16, 1862, and refers to Confederate troops at the battle of Shiloh.

2   The brigade was actively engaged with the enemy when the sad news was received on the 29th day of April, 1865, near Statesburg, S.C. that both Lee and Johnston had surrendered, that the Confederate Government was overthrown, and its flag, embalmed in the tears of the South, was furled forever.

—quoted in the *Louisville Courier-Journal*, September 5, 1894.

★ The town's name is actually Stateburg.

Jackson, Claiborne F. (1806–1862)

MISSOURI GOVERNOR

3   Your dispatch of the 15th instant, making a call on Missouri for four regiments of men for immediate service, has been received. There can be, I apprehend, no doubt but the men are intended to form a part of the President's army to make war on the people of the seceded States. Your requisition, in my judgment, is illegal, unconstitutional, and revolutionary in its object, inhuman and diabolical, and cannot be complied with. Not one man will the State of Missouri furnish to carry on any such unholy crusade.

—quoted by Philip Katcher in *Great Gambles of the Civil War*, 1996.

★ This was a letter sent by Jackson on April 17, 1861, to Secretary of War Simon Cameron.

4   Missouri, you know, is yet under the tyranny of Lincoln's Government, so far, at least, as forms go. We are woefully deficient here in arms, and cannot furnish them at present; but so far as men are concerned, we have plenty of them, ready, willing, and anxious to march at any moment to the defense of the South.

—letter to CS secretary of war Leroy P. Walker, May 5, 1861.

★ Walker had asked for Missouri troops.

Jackson, Thomas J. "Stonewall" (1824–1863)

CS LIEUTENANT GENERAL

If the general government should persist in the measures now threatened, there **1**
must be *war*. It is painful to discover with what unconcern they speak of war, and
threaten it. They do not know its horrors. I have seen enough of it to make me look
upon it as the sum of all evils.
    —letter to Reverend William White, December 19, 1860.

★ Jackson, who gained the nickname "Stonewall" early in the war, was then teaching at
Virginia Military Institute.

Should the step be taken which is now threatened [by the general government], we **2**
shall have no other alternative: we must fight. But do you not think that all Christian
people of the land could be induced to unite in a concert of prayer, to avert so great
an evil? It seems to me that if they would unite thus in prayer, war might be prevented and peace preserved.
    —letter to Reverend William White, December 19, 1860.

Why should Christians be disturbed about the dissolution of the Union? It can come **3**
only by God's permission, and will only be permitted if for His people's good; for
does He not say, "All things work together for good to them that love God?" I cannot
see how we should be distressed about such things, whatever be their consequences.
    —quoted by Mary Anna Jackson in *Life and Letters of General Thomas J. Jackson*,
    1892.

★ This was said in 1860 to the Reverend J. B. Ramsey when Jackson taught at the
Virginia Military Institute and was a major in the Virginia Militia. Mary Anna was
Jackson's wife.

The time for war has not yet come, but it will come, and that soon; and when it does **4**
come, my advice is to draw the sword and throw away the scabbard.
    —speech to cadets at the Virginia Military Institute, April 13, 1861.

It is better for the South to fight for her rights in the Union than out of it. **5**
    —quoted by Lieutenant Colonel G. F. R. Henderson in *Stonewall Jackson and the*
    American Civil War, vol. 1, 1898.

★ This was said before the war.

It is painful enough to discover with what unconcern they speak of war and threaten **6**
it. I have seen enough of it to make me look upon it as the sum of all evils.
    —quoted by Lieutenant Colonel G. F. R. Henderson in *Stonewall Jackson and the*
    American Civil War, vol. 1, 1898.

★ This was before Jackson earned his "Stonewall" nickname.

1   One of my greatest desires for advancement is the gratification it will give my darling, and of serving my country more efficiently.
  —letter to his wife, Mary Anna, July 3, 1861.

  ★ He had been made a brigadier general on June 17.

2   Nothing justifies profanity.
  —quoted in *Battles and Leaders of the Civil War*, vol. 1, 1887.

  ★ A wounded Jackson said this to Captain John Imboden on July 24, 1861, three days after the first battle of Bull Run (first Manassas).

3   Captain, my religious belief teaches me to feel as safe in battle as in bed. God has fixed the time for my death. I do not concern myself about *that*, but to be always ready, no matter when it may overtake me. Captain, that is the way all men should live, and then all would be equally brave.
  —quoted in *Battles and Leaders of the Civil War*, vol. 1, 1887.

  ★ A wounded Jackson said this to Captain John Imboden on July 24, 1861, three days after the first battle of Bull Run. Imboden had asked how he had appeared "so utterly insensible to danger in such a storm of shell and bullets" after his hand was hit.

4   If you think so, sir, you had better not say anything about it.
  —quoted by Lieutenant Colonel G. F. R. Henderson in *Stonewall Jackson and the American Civil War*, vol. 1, 1898.

  ★ This was said at the first battle of Bull Run (first Manassas) after an officer had told Jackson the day was going against them. Henderson was a British officer.

5   Give me 10,000 fresh troops and I would be in Washington tomorrow.
  —quoted by Lieutenant Colonel G. F. R. Henderson in *Stonewall Jackson and the American Civil War*, vol. 1, 1898.

  ★ This was said just after the first battle of Bull Run (first Manassas).

6   And so you think the papers ought to say more about your husband [after the first battle of Bull Run (first Manassas)]. My brigade is not a brigade of newspaper correspondents. . . . You must not be concerned at seeing other parts of the army lauded, and my brigade not mentioned. Truth is mighty and will prevail.
  —letter to his wife, Mary Anna, August 5, 1861.

7   I can't be absent [from camp] as my attention is necessary in preparing my troops for hard fighting, should it be required; and as my officers and soldiers are not permitted to visit their wives and families, I ought not to see mine. It might make the troops feel that they are badly treated, and that I consult my own comfort, regardless of theirs.
  —quoted by Lieutenant Colonel G. F. R. Henderson in *Stonewall Jackson and the American Civil War*, vol. 1, 1898.

  ★ This was written to his wife, Mary Anna, in the summer of 1861.

I am very thankful to that God who withholds no good thing from me (though I am **1** so utterly unworthy and ungrateful) for making me a Major General.
—letter to his wife, Mary Anna, October 7, 1861.

★ This was written on the day he was promoted.

We ought to invade their country now, and not wait for them to make the necessary **2** preparations to invade ours. If the President [Jefferson Davis] would reinforce this army by taking troops from other points not threatened and let us make an active campaign of invasion before winter sets in, McClellan's raw recruits could not stand against us in the field.
—quoted by Lieutenant Colonel G. F. R. Henderson in *Stonewall Jackson and the American Civil War*, vol. 1, 1898.

★ This was said to Major General G. W. Smith in October 1861.

In the Army of the Shenandoah you were the First Brigade! In the Army of the **3** Potomac you were the First Brigade! In the Second Corps of the army you are the First Brigade! You are the First Brigade in the affections of your general, and I hope by your future deeds and bearing, you will be handed down to posterity as the First Brigade in this our second War of Independence. Farewell!
—quoted by Lieutenant Colonel G. F. R. Henderson in *Stonewall Jackson and the American Civil War*, vol. 1, 1898.

★ Jackson was saying good-bye to his beloved "Stonewall Brigade" after being reassigned on November 4, 1861, to command of the Shenandoah Valley District. The brigade, however, was soon sent to rejoin him.

I never found anything impossible with this brigade. **4**
—quoted by Lieutenant Colonel G. F. R. Henderson in *Stonewall Jackson and the American Civil War*, vol. 1, 1898.

★ This was said on January 1, 1862, to Brigadier General Robert S. Garnett, who had said it was impossible for the brigade to march without cooking their rations.

I do not feel at liberty to close this report without alluding to the conduct of the **5** reprobate Federal commanders, who, in Hampshire County, have not only burned valuable mill property, but also many private houses. The track from Romney to Hanging Rock, a distance of fifteen miles, was one of desolation. The number of dead animals lying along the roadside, where they had been shot by the enemy, exemplified the spirit of the Northern army.
—quoted by Mary Anna Jackson in *Life and Letters of General Thomas J. Jackson*, 1892.

★ He wrote this in an official report of January 7, 1862. Mary Anna was Jackson's wife.

With such interference in my command I cannot expect to be of much service in **6** the field, and, accordingly, respectfully request to be ordered to report for duty to the Superintendent of the Virginia Military Institute at Lexington, as has been done in the case of other professors. Should this application not be granted, I respect-

fully request that the President [Jefferson Davis] will accept my resignation from the army.
—letter to CS secretary of war Judah P. Benjamin, January 31, 1862.

★ Benjamin had ordered Major General Jackson to order Brigadier General William W. Loring's army back to Winchester, Virginia, from Romney in western Virginia after Loring had appealed directly to Benjamin. After Jackson's threat to resign, the Confederate government became more diplomatic with its generals.

1   Sacrifices! Have I not made them? What is my life here but a daily sacrifice? Nor shall I ever withhold sacrifices for my country, where they will avail anything. I intend to serve here, anywhere, in any way I can, even if it be as a private soldier. But if this method of making war is to prevail, the country is ruined.
—quoted by Lieutenant Colonel G. F. R. Henderson in *Stonewall Jackson and the American Civil War*, vol. 1, 1898.

★ He was replying to a letter from General Joseph E. Johnston asking him to withdraw his threat of resignation of January 31, 1862, and appealing to his patriotism.

2   This army stays here until the last man is removed. Before I leave them to the enemy I will lose many men more.
—quoted by Lieutenant Colonel G. F. R. Henderson in *Stonewall Jackson and the American Civil War*, vol. 1, 1898.

★ This was said to Dr. Hunter Holmes McGuire about the men wounded at the battle of Kernstown, Virginia, on March 23, 1862.

3   This is the last council of war I will ever hold!
—quoted by Lieutenant Colonel G. F. R. Henderson in *Stonewall Jackson and the American Civil War*, vol. 1, 1898.

★ His council of war had just gone against his desire to defend Winchester, Virginia, in March 1862.

4   Our gallant little army is increasing in numbers, and my prayer is that it may be an army of the living God as well as of its country.
—letter to his wife, Mary Anna, April 7, 1862, quoted by Lieutenant Colonel G. F. R. Henderson in *Stonewall Jackson and the American Civil War*, vol. 1, 1898.

5   Under Divine blessing we must rely upon the bayonet when firearms cannot be furnished.
—quoted by Lieutenant Colonel G. F. R. Henderson in *Stonewall Jackson and the American Civil War*, vol. 1, 1898.

★ Jackson had ordered 1,000 bayonets from Richmond on April 9, 1862, because guns were scarce.

6   I do hope that the war will soon be over, and that I shall never again be called upon to take the field.
—letter to his wife, Mary Anna, April 11, 1862.

★ He was then a major general.

You appear much concerned at my attacking *on Sunday*. I was greatly concerned,   1
too; but I felt it my duty to do it, in consideration of the ruinous effects that might
result from postponing the battle until morning. So far as I can see, my course was a
wise one; the best that I could do under the circumstances, though very distasteful
to my feelings; and I hope and pray to our Heavenly Father that I may never again
be circumstanced as on that day.
    —letter to his wife, Mary Anna, April 11, 1862.

★ Sunday attacks were considered to be bad luck, and Jackson was especially religious.

Stragglers cover the country, and Richmond is no doubt filled with the absent with-   2
out leave. . . . The men are full of spirit when near the enemy, but at other times to
avoid restraint leave their regiments in crowds.
    —quoted by Lieutenant Colonel G. F. R. Henderson in *Stonewall Jackson and the
    American Civil War*, vol. 1, 1898.

★ This was said to General Robert E. Lee on May 9, 1862.

You must not expect long letters from me in such busy times as these, but always   3
believe your husband never forgets his little darling.
    —letter to his wife, Mary Anna, June 2, 1862.

★ Jackson had escaped a Union trap the day before, during his Shenandoah Valley
Campaign.

[Ashby's] daring was proverbial, his powers of endurance almost incredible, his char-   4
acter heroic, and his sagacity almost intuitive in divining the purposes and movements of the enemy.
    —quoted by Lieutenant Colonel G. F. R. Henderson in *Stonewall Jackson and the
    American Civil War*, vol. 1, 1898.

★ Jackson made this statement shortly after Brigadier General Turner Ashby was killed
in battle on June 6, 1862.

The country is full of spies, and our plans are immediately carried to the enemy.   5
    —letter to General Robert E. Lee, June 17, 1862.

From me you have a friend's sympathy, and I wish the suffering condition of our coun-   6
try permitted me to show it. But we must think of the living and of those who are to
come after us, and see that, with God's blessing, we transmit to them the freedom we
have enjoyed. What is life without honor? Degradation is worse than death. It is necessary that you should be at your post immediately. Join me tomorrow morning.
    —letter to one of his majors, August 2, 1862.

★ The major had been on a furlough because of a family death and then requested an
extension because of another family illness.

[General Nathaniel] Banks is in front of me, and he is always ready to fight. And he   7
generally gets whipped.
    —quoted by Hunter Holmes McGuire in the *Richmond Dispatch*, July 19, 1891.

★ This was before Jackson's success at the battle of Cedar Mountain, Virginia, on
August 9, 1862.

1   Don't shout, boys, the Yankees will hear us.
>   —quoted by Lieutenant Colonel G. F. R. Henderson in *Stonewall Jackson and the American Civil War*, vol. 2, 1898.

★ His soldiers had cheered as he passed along their marching line on August 26, 1862. After his warning, they swung their caps silently in his honor.

2   No, sir, we have won this day by the blessing of Almighty God.
>   —quoted by Hunter Holmes McGuire in the *Richmond Dispatch*, July 19, 1891.

★ McGuire, Jackson's brigade doctor, had just told him at the second battle of Bull Run (second Manassas), "We have only won this day by hard fighting."

3   The Confederate army should at once leave the malarious district round Richmond and moving northwards, carry the horrors of invasion across the border.
>   —quoted by CS major Robert Lewis Dabney in *The Life and Campaigns of Lieut.-General Thomas J. Jackson*, vol. 2, 1865.

★ This was said in the summer of 1862, when Jackson was a major general.

4   Give my compliments to General Hill, and tell him the Yankee ammunition is as wet as his—stay where he is.
>   —quoted by Hunter Holmes McGuire in the *Richmond Dispatch*, July 19, 1891.

★ An aide-de-camp had arrived during the battle of Chantilly, Virginia, to tell Jackson, "General A. P. Hill asks permission to retire; his ammunition is wet."

5   We will evidently have no friends in this town.
>   —quoted by Lieutenant Colonel G. F. R. Henderson in *Stonewall Jackson and the American Civil War*, vol. 2, 1898.

★ They were passing through Middletown, Maryland, on September 10, 1862, and two girls ran out with US flags to wave them at him. The general bowed, raised his hat, and smiled at his staff.

6   Let the work be done thoroughly.
>   —quoted by CS colonel Henry Kyd Douglas in *Battles and Leaders of the Civil War*, vol. 2, 1888.

★ This was said to CS major general Lafayette McLaws for the attack on Harper's Ferry, Virginia, which was captured on September 15, 1862.

7   God has been very kind to us this day.
>   —quoted by Lieutenant Colonel G. F. R. Henderson in *Stonewall Jackson and the American Civil War*, vol. 2, 1898.

★ This was said on September 17, 1862, during the battle of Antietam (Sharpsburg).

8   We'll drive McClellan into the Potomac.
>   —quoted by CS major general John G. Walker in *Battles and Leaders of the Civil War*, vol. 2, 1888.

★ This was during the battle of Antietam (Sharpsburg). Told later that the Potomac was closer than he thought, preventing a planned rear attack on Federal troops, Jackson said, "It is a great pity,—we should have driven McClellan into the Potomac."

I want a yard of bandaging to put on the arm of every soldier in this night's attack, so   **1**
that the men may know each other from the enemy.
> —quoted by Lieutenant Colonel G. F. R. Henderson in *Stonewall Jackson and the
> American Civil War*, vol. 2, 1898.

★ Jackson said this during the battle of Fredericksburg to his brigade doctor, Hunter
Holmes McGuire, but not enough bandaging was available. The doctor suggested shirt
tails, but half the men did not even have shirts. The attack never happened because
General Robert E. Lee thought it was too dangerous.

Kill them, sir! Kill every man!   **2**
> —quoted by Lieutenant Colonel G. F. R. Henderson in *Stonewall Jackson and the
> American Civil War*, vol. 2, 1898.

★ Jackson was responding to Hunter Holmes McGuire, his brigade doctor, who asked
how they could cope with the overwhelming numbers of the enemy at the battle of
Fredericksburg. Jackson was distraught, having just witnessed the death of Brigadier
General Maxcy Gregg.

We shall very soon see whether I shall not frighten them.   **3**
> —quoted by Lieutenant Colonel G. F. R. Henderson in *Stonewall Jackson and the
> American Civil War*, vol. 2, 1898.

★ This was Jackson's reply on December 13, 1862, during the battle of Fredericksburg,
to Major General James Longstreet, who asked, "General, do not all of those multi-
tudes of Federals frighten you?"

Mr. Smith, had you not better go to the rear? They might shoot you.   **4**
> —quoted by Lieutenant Colonel G. F. R. Henderson in *Stonewall Jackson and the
> American Civil War*, vol. 2, 1898.

★ He was warning his aide-de-camp, Lieutenant James P. Smith, just after a sniper's
bullet had whistled between their heads during the battle of Fredericksburg.

We must do more than defeat their armies. We must destroy them.   **5**
> —quoted by Hunter Holmes McGuire in a speech dedicating Jackson Memorial
> Hall in Lexington, Virginia, June 23, 1897.

★ This was said after the battle of Fredericksburg in December 1862; McGuire had
been Jackson's brigade doctor.

But what a cruel thing is war; to separate and destroy families and friends, and mar   **6**
the purest joys and happiness God has granted us in this world; to fill our hearts with
hatred instead of love for our neighbors, and to devastate the fair face of this beautiful world.
> —letter to his wife, Mary Anna, December 25, 1862.

I pray that, on this day when only peace and good-will are preached to mankind, bet-   **7**
ter thoughts may fill the hearts of our enemies and turn them to peace.
> —letter to his wife, Mary Anna, December 25, 1862.

I do not want to make an appointment on my staff except of such as are early risers.   **8**
> —letter to his wife, 1862.

1   My health is essentially good, but I do not think I shall be able in future to stand
     what I have already stood.
     —quoted by Lieutenant Colonel G. F. R. Henderson in *Stonewall Jackson and the
     American Civil War*, vol. 2, 1898.

     ★ This was written to his wife, Mary Anna, in January 1863.

2   Mystery, mystery, is the secret of success.
     —quoted by John Esten Cooke in *The Life of Stonewall Jackson*, 1863.

3   You must hold your ground, General Pender; you must hold out to the last, sir.
     —quoted by Lieutenant Colonel G. F. R. Henderson in *Stonewall Jackson and the
     American Civil War*, vol. 2, 1898.

     ★ Jackson gave this order to Brigadier General William D. Pender as he lay mortally
     wounded on May 2, 1863, at the battle of Chancellorsville. Pender was wounded three
     times during this battle but never left the field. Henderson gives the name incorrectly
     as "Fender."

4   I think I am [hurt], and all my wounds are from my own men.
     —quoted by Lieutenant Colonel G. F. R. Henderson in *Stonewall Jackson and the
     American Civil War*, vol. 2, 1898.

     ★ This was on May 2, 1863, at the battle of Chancellorsville, when his own men mor-
     tally wounded him by accident in the darkness.

5   Wild fire, that, sir; wild fire.
     —quoted by John D. Wright in *The Language of the Civil War*, 2001.

     ★ He said this to the first officer on the scene after Jackson's own men had mortally
     wounded him by accident.

6   General Lee is very kind; but he should give the glory to God!
     —quoted by Edward Lee Childe in *Life and Campaigns of General Lee*, 1875.

     ★ The mortally wounded Jackson had just received a note from Lee praising him for
     driving back the Union forces during the battle of Chancellorsville.

7   Better that ten Jacksons should fall than one Lee.
     —quoted by Captain Robert E. Lee in *Recollections and Letters of General
     Robert E. Lee*, 1904.

     ★ Mortally wounded, Jackson said this on being read General Robert E. Lee's regret
     that he was not wounded instead of Jackson.

8   I consider these wounds a blessing; they were given me for some good and wise pur-
     pose, and I would not part with them if I could.
     —quoted by John Esten Cooke in *The Life of Stonewall Jackson*, vol. 1, 1863.

     ★ Jackson said this as he lay dying, days after being accidentally shot by his own men
     on May 2, 1863, at the battle of Chancellorsville.

Our movement [at Chancellorsville] was a great success; I think the most successful 1
military movement of my life. But I expect to receive far more credit for it than I
deserve.
>   —quoted by Lieutenant Colonel G. F. R. Henderson in *Stonewall Jackson and the*
>   *American Civil War*, vol. 2, 1898.

★ He said this on his deathbed.

No, no. Let us pass over the river and rest under the shade of the trees. 2
>   —quoted by Rod Graff in *Civil War Quiz and Fact Book*, 1985.

★ These were Jackson's last words before dying on May 10, 1863.

No, let the poor fellows sleep; I will guard the camp myself. 3
>   —quoted by CS major Robert Lewis Dabney in *The Life and Campaigns of Lieut.-*
>   *General Thomas J. Jackson*, 1865.

★ After an especially tiring march, an officer told Jackson that soldiers should be awakened to stand sentry, but the general himself stayed awake on guard all night to give
them rest.

Always mystify, mislead, and surprise the enemy, if possible; and when you strike and 4
overcome him, never let up in the pursuit so long as your men have strength to follow; for an army routed, if hotly pursued, becomes panic-stricken, and can then be
destroyed by half their number. The other rule is, never fight against heavy odds, if
by any possible maneuvering you can hurl your own force on only a part, and that the
weakest part, of your enemy and crush it. Such tactics will win every time, and a
small army may thus destroy a large one in detail, and repeated victory will make it
invincible.
>   —quoted by CS brigadier general John D. Imboden in *Battles and Leaders of the*
>   *Civil War*, vol. 2, 1888.

I would rather let them all die than have one of my men shot intentionally under the 5
yellow flag when trying to save their wounded.
>   —quoted by CS brigadier general John D. Imboden in *Battles and Leaders of the*
>   *Civil War*, vol. 2, 1888.

★ Jackson, who said this to Imboden, had sent out soldiers under the hospital yellow flag
to recover the wounded, but the enemy had fired at them. The Confederate wounded
were brought back, but Jackson called off a recovery of Union soldiers because of
the fire.

A man rests all over when he lies down. 6
>   —quoted by CS brigadier general John D. Imboden in *Battles and Leaders of the*
>   *Civil War*, vol. 2, 1888.

★ He said this to explain why he encouraged his men to lie flat on the ground during
breaks in marching.

1   I like [whiskey], and that's the reason I don't drink.
    —quoted by Hunter Holmes McGuire in the *Richmond Dispatch*, July 19, 1891.

    ★ McGuire, Jackson's brigade doctor, had just given him a drink during a cold night on the Potomac River. He swallowed it with a "wry face."

2   Do? Thrash them!
    —quoted by Hunter Holmes McGuire in the *Richmond Dispatch*, July 19, 1891.

    ★ McGuire, Jackson's brigade doctor, had asked the general what they should do about the northern invasion.

3   How horrible is war!
    —quoted by Hunter Holmes McGuire in the *Richmond Dispatch*, July 19, 1891.

    ★ This was said to McGuire, Jackson's brigade doctor.

4   Drive them into the river.
    —quoted by Hunter Holmes McGuire in the *Richmond Dispatch*, July 19, 1891.

    ★ Jackson had fallen asleep during a council of war with Generals Robert E. Lee and James Longstreet. He uttered these words while dimly conscious after hearing someone ask for his opinion.

5   [Brigadier General Turner] Ashby never had his equal in a charge; but he never had his men in hand, and some of his most brilliant exploits were performed by himself and a handful of followers. He was too kind-hearted to be a good disciplinarian.
    —quoted by CS major general Daniel H. Hill in *Century Magazine*, February 1894.

    ★ Hill was Jackson's brother-in-law.

6   "Jeb" Stuart is my ideal of a cavalry leader; prompt, vigilant, and fearless.
    —quoted by CS major general Daniel H. Hill in *Century Magazine*, February 1894.

7   The manner in which the press, the army, and the people seem to lean upon certain persons is positively frightful. They are forgetting God in the instruments he has chosen. It fills me with alarm.
    —quoted by CS major general Daniel H. Hill in *Century Magazine*, February 1894.

    ★ This was said to Hill.

8   What do you want with military news? Don't you know that it is unmilitary and unlike an officer to write news respecting one's post? You couldn't wish your husband to do an unofficer-like thing, could you?
    —quoted by Lieutenant Colonel G. F. R. Henderson in *Stonewall Jackson and the American Civil War*, vol. 1, 1898.

9   The service cannot afford to keep a man who does not succeed.
    —quoted by Lieutenant Colonel G. F. R. Henderson *Stonewall Jackson and the American Civil War*, 1898.

I rather think that fire by file is best on the whole, for it gives the enemy an idea that   **1**
the fire is heavier than if it was by company or battalion.
> —quoted by Lieutenant Colonel G. F. R. Henderson in *Stonewall Jackson and the American Civil War*, vol. 1, 1898.

Wait until they come within fifty yards and then give them the bayonet.   **2**
> —quoted by Lieutenant Colonel G. F. R. Henderson in *Stonewall Jackson and the American Civil War*, vol. 1, 1898.

Thoughtless fellows for serious work.   **3**
> —quoted by Lieutenant Colonel G. F. R. Henderson in *Stonewall Jackson and the American Civil War*, vol. 1, 1898.

★ Jackson was observing a Creole band playing a waltz in camp.

Let the Federals get very close before your infantry fire; they won't stand long.   **4**
> —quoted by Lieutenant Colonel G. F. R. Henderson in *Stonewall Jackson and the American Civil War*, vol. 1, 1898.

★ This was said to Major General Richard S. Ewell.

The only true rule of cavalry is to follow as long as the enemy retreats.   **5**
> —quoted by Lieutenant Colonel G. F. R. Henderson in *Stonewall Jackson and the American Civil War*, vol. 1, 1898.

To move swiftly, strike vigorously, and secure all the fruits of victory, is the secret of   **6**
successful war.
> —quoted by Lieutenant Colonel G. F. R. Henderson in *Stonewall Jackson and the American Civil War*, vol. 1, 1898.

The hardships of forced marches are often more painful than the dangers of battle.   **7**
> —quoted by Lieutenant Colonel G. F. R. Henderson in *Stonewall Jackson and the American Civil War*, vol. 1, 1898.

I had rather lose one man in marching than five in fighting.   **8**
> —quoted by Lieutenant Colonel G. F. R. Henderson in *Stonewall Jackson and the American Civil War*, vol. 1, 1898.

If I can deceive my own friends I can make certain of deceiving the enemy.   **9**
> —quoted by Lieutenant Colonel G. F. R. Henderson in *Stonewall Jackson and the American Civil War*, vol. 1, 1898.

★ He was referring to withholding military plans from his officers.

Who could fail to win battles with such men as these?   **10**
> —quoted by Lieutenant Colonel G. F. R. Henderson in *Stonewall Jackson and the American Civil War*, vol. 2, 1898.

1   We must make this campaign an exceedingly active one. Only thus can a weaker country cope with a stronger; it will make up in activity what it lacks in strength.
    —quoted by Lieutenant Colonel G. F. R. Henderson in *Stonewall Jackson and the American Civil War*, vol. 2, 1898.

2   Some day the men of that brigade will be proud to say to their children, "I was one of the Stonewall Brigade."
    —quoted by Lieutenant Colonel G. F. R. Henderson in *Stonewall Jackson and the American Civil War*, vol. 2, 1898.

    ★ Jackson considered that the name "Stonewall" belonged to the brigade and not personally to himself.

3   My men sometimes fail to drive the enemy from a position, but they always fail to drive us away.
    —quoted by Lieutenant Colonel G. F. R. Henderson in *Stonewall Jackson and the American Civil War*, vol. 2, 1898.

4   That was the sweetest music I ever heard.
    —quoted by Lieutenant Colonel G. F. R. Henderson in *Stonewall Jackson and the American Civil War*, vol. 2, 1898.

    ★ He had just listened to the rebel yell reverberating throughout his camp.

5   I can do whatever I will to do.
    —quoted by Lieutenant Colonel G. F. R. Henderson in *Stonewall Jackson and the American Civil War*, vol. 2, 1898.

6   The War of Secession may be the precursor of a fiercer and a mightier struggle, and the volunteers of the Confederacy, enduring all things and sacrificing all things, the prototype and model of a new army, in which North and South shall march to battle side by side.
    —quoted by Lieutenant Colonel G. F. R. Henderson in *Stonewall Jackson and the American Civil War*, vol. 2, 1898.

7   My idea is that the best mode of fighting is to reserve your fire till the enemy get— or you get them—to close quarters. Then deliver one deadly, deliberate fire—and charge!
    —quoted by Lieutenant Colonel G. F. R. Henderson in *Stonewall Jackson and the American Civil War*, vol. 1, 1898.

8   Lee is a phenomenon. He is the only man whom I would follow blindfold.
    —quoted by Captain Robert E. Lee in *Recollections and Letters of General Robert E. Lee*, 1904.

    ★ Captain Lee was the general's son.

9   The patriot volunteer, fighting for his country and his rights, makes the most reliable soldier on earth.
    —quoted by Lieutenant Colonel F. G. R. Henderson in *Stonewall Jackson and the American Civil War*, 1898.

Duty is ours; consequences are God's.   1
    —quoted by Frank E. Vandiver in *Mighty Stonewall*, 1995.

★ John Quincy Adams had previously said this.

Arms is a profession that, if its principles are adhered to for success, requires an offi-   2
cer do what he fears may be wrong, and yet, according to military experience, must
be done, if success is to be attained.
    —letter to his wife, Mary Anna.

Johnson, Andrew (1808–1875)

US VICE PRESIDENT

. . . rather than see this Union divided into thirty-three petty governments, with a lit-   3
tle prince in one, a potentate in another, a little aristocracy in a third, a little democracy in a fourth, and a republic somewhere else—a citizen not being permitted to
pass from one State to another without a passport or a commission from his government—with quarreling and warring among the petty powers, which would result in
anarchy—I would rather see this government today—I proclaim it here in my place—
converted into a consolidated government.
    —quoted in *Harper's Weekly*, May 13, 1865.

★ Johnson, then a senator from Tennessee, said this in a speech on December 19, 1860.

Show me those who make war on the Government and fire on its vessels, and I will   4
show you a traitor. If I were President of the United States I would have all such
arrested, and, if convicted, by the Eternal God I would have them hung.
    —quoted in *Harper's Weekly*, May 13, 1865.

★ US senator Johnson made this statement in a speech on March 2, 1861. After becoming president on Lincoln's assassination, he backed away from harsh punishments of
Southerners.

When you ask me what I would do [to Confederate leaders], my reply is—I would   5
arrest them, I would try them, I would convict them, and I would hang them.
    —speech to a Republican rally in Washington, D.C., April 4, 1865.

★ Johnson was vice president at the time.

Johnson, Bradley T.

CS COLONEL

The men fought until their ammunition was exhausted and then threw stones.   6
    —quoted in *Battles and Leaders of the Civil War*, vol. 2, 1888.

★ This occurred during the second battle of Bull Run (second Manassas) on August 30,
1862. Johnson later became a brigadier general.

Johnson, Hannah

1   They tell me some of you will take back the [Emancipation] Proclamation; don't do it. When you are dead and in Heaven, in a thousand years that action of yours will make the Angels sing your praises, I know it.
—letter to Lincoln, July 31, 1863.

★ The writer had a son in the 54th Massachusetts.

Johnson, Herschel V. (1812–1880)

GEORGIA GOVERNOR

2   Yield to the Federal authorities—to vassalage and subjugation! The bleaching of the bones of one hundred thousand gallant soldiers slain in battle would be clothed in tongues of fire to curse to everlasting infamy the man who whispers *yield*.
—speech at Milledgeville, Georgia, November 24, 1863.

Johnston, Albert S. (1803–1862)

CS GENERAL

3   I have put you in motion to offer battle to the invaders of your country. With the resolution and disciplined valor becoming men fighting, as you are, for all worth living or dying for, you can but march to a decisive victory over agrarian mercenaries, sent to subjugate and despoil you of your liberties, property, and honor. Remember the precious stake involved. Remember the dependence of your mothers, your wives, your sisters, and our children on the result. Remember the fair, broad, abounding land, the happy homes, and ties that will be desolated by your defeat. The eyes and hopes of 8,000,000 of people rest upon you. You are expected to show yourself worthy of your valor and lineage; worthy of the women of the South, whose noble devotion in this war has never been exceeded in any time. With such incentives to brave deeds and with the trust that God is with us your generals will lead you confidently to the combat, assured of success.
—proclamation to the soldiers of the Army of the Mississippi, April 3, 1862.

★ This was three days before his army made a surprise attack on General Grant's troops to begin the battle of Shiloh, during which Johnston was killed.

4   I would fight them if they were a million.
—quoted by Shelby Foote in *The Civil War*, vol. 1, 1958.

★ Johnston was killed that same day, April 6, 1862, at the battle of Shiloh.

Johnston, Joseph E. (1807–1891)

CS GENERAL

5   How can I eat, sleep, or rest in peace without you upon the outpost?
—quoted by Lieutenant Colonel G. F. R. Henderson in *Stonewall Jackson and the American Civil War*, vol. 1, 1898.

★ This was written to Captain J. E. B. Stuart, who had just been transferred to the west. Henderson was a British officer.

Comrades, our brothers who have fallen have earned undying renown upon earth, **1** and their blood, shed in our holy cause, is a precious and acceptable sacrifice to the Father of Truth and of Right. Their graves are beside the tomb of Washington; their spirits have joined with his in eternal communion. . . . We drop one tear on their laurels and move forward to avenge them. Soldiers, we congratulate you on a glorious, triumphant and complete victory, and we thank you for doing your whole duty in the service of your country.
> —proclamation, with Brigadier General Pierre G. T. Beauregard, to the soldiers of
> the Confederate States, July 25, 1861.

★ The victory was the first battle of Bull Run (first Manassas).

It is with the profoundest emotions of gratitude to an overruling God, whose hand is **2** manifest in protecting our homes and our liberties, that we, your generals commanding, are enabled, in the name of our whole country, to thank you for that patriotic courage, that heroic gallantry, that devoted daring exhibited by you in the actions of the 18th and 21st, by which the hosts of the enemy were scattered and a signal and glorious victory obtained.
> —proclamation, with Brigadier General Pierre G. T. Beauregard, to the soldiers of
> the Confederate States, July 25, 1861.

★ The victory was the first battle of Bull Run (first Manassas).

Soldiers! we congratulate you on an event which ensures the liberty of our country. **3** We congratulate every man of you, whose glorious privilege it was to participate in this triumph of courage and of truth—to fight in the battle of Manassas [Bull Run]. You have created an epoch in the history of liberty and unborn nations will rise up and call you "blessed."
> —speech with Brigadier General Pierre G. T. Beauregard to their soldiers,
> July 28, 1861.

No one but McClellan could have hesitated to attack. **4**
> —letter to General Robert E. Lee, April 22, 1862.

★ Both sides were aware of McClellan's slowness to engage, this time at Yorktown, Virginia.

I consider saving Vicksburg hopeless. **5**
> —letter to CS secretary of war James A. Seddon, June 15, 1863.

We may confidently trust that the Almighty Father will still reward the patriot's toil. **6**
> —speech to his troops, May 19, 1864.

Our army was more disorganized by victory than that of the United States by defeat. **7**
> —quoted by Lieutenant Colonel G. F. R. Henderson in *Stonewall Jackson and the*
> *American Civil War*, vol. 1, 1898.

★ He said this about the first battle of Bull Run (first Manassas).

1   Had an attack been made in force [at the first battle of Bull Run (first Manassas)], with double line of battle such as any major-general in the United States service would now make, we could not have held for half an hour, for they would have enveloped us on both flanks.
    —quoted by Lieutenant Colonel G. F. R. Henderson in *Stonewall Jackson and the American Civil War*, vol. 1, 1898.

Jones, J. William (1836–1909)

CS CHAPLAIN

2   The large proportion of the soldiers were wicked and many were reckless. For more than a year very few manifested any desire to become Christians save the sick or wounded.
    —quoted by William C. Davis in *Brothers in Arms*, 1995.

Jones, John B. (?–1896)

CS BUREAU OF WAR CLERK

3   Oh, the extortioners! Meats of all kinds are selling at fifty cents per pound; butter, seventy-five cents; coffee, a dollar and half; tea, ten dollars; boots, thirty dollars per pair; shoes, eighteen dollars; ladies' shoes, fifteen dollars; shirts, six dollars each. Houses that rented for five hundred dollars last year are a thousand dollars now. Boarding, from thirty to forty dollars per month. General Winder has issued an order fixing the maximum prices of certain articles of marketing, which has only the effect of keeping a great many things out of market. The farmers have to pay . . . extortionate prices and complain very justly of the partiality of the general. It does more harm than good.
    —*A Rebel War Clerk's Diary at the Confederate States Capital*, 1866.

★ This diary entry was written on May 23, 1862.

4   God speed the day of peace! Our patriotism is mainly in the army and among the ladies of the South. The avarice and cupidity of the men at home could only be excelled by the ravenous wolves; and most of our sufferings are fully deserved.
    —*A Rebel War Clerk's Diary at the Confederate States Capital*, 1866.

★ This diary entry was written on December 1, 1863.

5   A portion of the people look like vagabonds. We see men and women and children in the streets in dingy and dilapidated clothes; and some seem gaunt and pale with hunger—the speculators and thieving quartermasters and commissaries only looking sleek and comfortable. If this state of things continues a year or so longer, they will have their reward. There will be governmental bankruptcy, and all their gains will turn to dust and ashes!
    —*A Rebel War Clerk's Diary at the Confederate States Capital*, 1866.

★ This diary entry was written on December 1, 1863.

A few squads of local troops and reserves-guards may be seen marching here and 1
there. Perhaps they are to burn the tobacco, cotton, etc., if indeed anything is to be
burned. . . . The negroes stand about mostly silent, as if wondering what will be their
fate. They make no demonstrations of joy.
    —*A Rebel War Clerk's Diary at the Confederate States Capital*, 1866.

★ This diary entry was written on April 2, 1865. Union troops would occupy the city the
following day.

A street rumor says there was bloody fighting yesterday a little beyond Petersburg, 2
near the South Side Road, in which Gen. Pickett's division met with fearful loss,
being engaged with superior numbers. . . . I hear nothing of all this at the [Con-
federate war] department; but the absence of dispatches there is now interpreted
as bad news! Certain it is, the marching of veteran troops from the defenses of
Richmond, and replacing them hurriedly with militia, can only indicate an emergency of alarming importance.
    —*A Rebel War Clerk's Diary at the Confederate States Capital*, 1866.

★ This diary entry was written on April 2, 1865. Union troops would occupy the city the
following day.

[A Union] officer told me, 3 P.M., that a white brigade will picket the city to-night, 3
and he assured the ladies standing near that there would not be a particle of danger
of molestation. After 9 P.M., all will be required to remain in their houses. Soldiers
or citizens, after that hour, will be arrested. He said we had done ourselves great
injury by the fire, the lower part of the city being in ashes, and declared that the
United States troops had no hand in it. I acquitted them of the deed, and told him
that the fire had spread from the tobacco warehouses and military depots, fired by
our troops as a military necessity.
    —*A Rebel War Clerk's Diary at the Confederate States Capital*, 1866.

★ This diary entry was written on April 3, 1865.

Four P.M. Thirty-four guns announced the arrival of President Lincoln. He flitted 4
through the mass of human beings in Capital Square, his carriage drawn by four
horses, preceded by out-riders, motioning the people, etc. out of the way, and followed by a mounted guard of thirty. The cortege passed rapidly, precisely as I had
seen royal parties ride in Europe.
    —*A Rebel War Clerk's Diary at the Confederate States Capital*, 1866.

★ This diary entry was written on April 3, 1865.

At 7 A.M. Committees appointed by the city government visited the liquor shops 5
and had the spirits (such as they could find) destroyed. The streets ran with liquor;
and women and boys, black and White, were seen filling pitchers and buckets from
the gutters.
    —*A Rebel War Clerk's Diary at the Confederate States Capital*, 1866.

★ This diary entry was written on April 3, 1865. Liquor was destroyed to prevent it
from falling into the hands of Union troops about to occupy the city.

1   The Square is nearly vacated by the negroes. An officer told me they intended to put them in the army in a few days, and that the Northern people did not really like negro equality any better than we did.
      —*A Rebel War Clerk's Diary at the Confederate States Capital*, 1866.

      ★ This diary entry was written on April 5, 1865, with Richmond occupied by Federal troops.

2   The burnt district includes all the banks, money-changers, and principal speculators and extortioners. This seems like a decree from above!
      —*A Rebel War Clerk's Diary at the Confederate States Capital*, 1866.

      ★ This diary entry was written on April 5, 1865. The city district was burned mostly by retreating Confederate troops.

3   The cheers that greeted President Lincoln were mostly from the negroes and Federals comprising the great mass of humanity. The white citizens felt annoyed that the city should be held mostly by negro troops. If this measure were not unavoidable, it was impolitic if conciliation be the purpose.
      —*A Rebel War Clerk's Diary at the Confederate States Capital*, 1866.

      ★ This diary entry was written on April 5, 1865.

4   Negotiations are in progress by the clergymen, who are directed to open the churches on Sunday, and it was intimated to the Episcopalians that they should pray for the President of the United States. To this they demur, being ordered by the Convention to pray for the President of the Confederate States. They are willing to omit the prayer altogether, and await the decision of the military authority on that proposition.
      —*A Rebel War Clerk's Diary at the Confederate States Capital*, 1866.

      ★ This diary entry was written on April 7, 1865. The occupying military authority ruled that a prayer must be said for the US president.

5   Rev. Dr. Minnegerode, and others, leading clergymen, consider the cause at an end. . . . The clergy also seem to favor a convention, and the resumption by Virginia of her old position in the Union—minus slavery. . . . We shall now have no more interference in Caesar's affairs by the clergy—may they attend to God's hereafter!
      —*A Rebel War Clerk's Diary at the Confederate States Capital*, 1866.

      ★ This diary entry was written on April 9, 1865. Charles Minnegerode was the minister at St. Paul's Episcopal Church in Richmond.

6   All hope of peace with independence is extinct and valor alone is relied upon now for our salvation. Everyone thinks the Confederacy will at once gather up its material strength and strike such blows as will astonish the world.
      —*A Rebel War Clerk's Diary at the Confederate States Capital*, 1866.

      ★ This diary entry was written on April 10, 1865.

It is true! Yesterday Gen. Lee surrendered the "Army of Northern Virginia." . . . If **1**
Mr. Davis had been present, he never would have consented to it; and I doubt if he
will ever forgive Gen. Lee.
  —*A Rebel War Clerk's Diary at the Confederate States Capital*, 1866.

★ This diary entry was written on April 10, 1865.

Gen. Weitzel publishes an order to-day, requiring all ministers who have prayed for **2**
the President of the Confederate States to pray hereafter for the President of the
United States. He will not allow them to omit the prayer.
  —*A Rebel War Clerk's Diary at the Confederate States Capital*, 1866.

★ This diary entry was written on April 12, 1865.

Confederate money is valueless, and we have no Federal money. To such extremity **3**
are some of the best and wealthiest families reduced, that the ladies are daily engaged
making pies and cakes for the Yankee soldiers of all colors, that they may obtain
enough greenbacks to purchase such articles as are daily required in their house-
keeping.
  —*A Rebel War Clerk's Diary at the Confederate States Capital*, 1866.

★ This diary entry was written on April 13, 1865.

Owing to recent events [Lee's surrender], the permission for the reassembling of the **4**
gentlemen recently acting as the Legislature of Virginia is rescinded. Should any of
the gentlemen come to the city under the notice of reassembling, already published,
they will be furnished passports to return to their homes.
  —*A Rebel War Clerk's Diary at the Confederate States Capital*, 1866.

★ This diary entry was written on April 14, 1865.

It was whispered, yesterday, that President Lincoln had been assassinated! I met **5**
Gen. Duff Green[e], in the afternoon, who assured me there could be no doubt of
it. Still, supposing it might be an April hoax, I inquired at the headquarters of Gen.
Ord, and was told it was true. I cautioned those I met to manifest no feeling, as the
occurrence might be a calamity for the South; and possibly the Federal soldiers, supposing the deed to have been done by a Southern man, might become uncontrollable and perpetrate deeds of horror on the unarmed people.
  —*A Rebel War Clerk's Diary at the Confederate States Capital*, 1866.

★ This diary entry was written on April 17, 1865.

President Lincoln was killed by Booth (Jno. Wilkes), an actor. I suppose his purpose **6**
is to live in history as the slayer of a tyrant; thinking to make the leading character in
a tragedy, and have his performance acted by others on the stage. I see no grief on
the faces of either officers or men of the Federal army.
  —*A Rebel War Clerk's Diary at the Confederate States Capital*, 1866.

★ This diary entry was written on April 17, 1865.

Julian, George W. (1817–1899)

US CONGRESSMAN FROM INDIANA

1   It is not alone a fight between the North and the South; it is a fight between freedom and slavery; between God and the devil; between heaven and hell.
        —speech, October 21, 1856.

    ★ Julian later was elected five times to Congress.

2   When I say that this rebellion has its source and life in slavery, I only repeat a simple truism.
        —speech to the House of Representatives, January 14, 1862.

3   As for Jeff Davis, I would indict him, I would convict him and hang him in the name of God. As for Robert E. Lee, unmolested in Virginia, hang him too. And stop there? Not at all. I would hang liberally while I had my hand in.
        —quoted by Shelby Foote in *The Civil War*, vol. 3, 1958.

Kean, Robert G. H.

CS COLONEL AND BUREAU OF WAR CHIEF

4   Prying, indirection, vindictiveness, and insincerity are the repulsive traits which mark [General Braxton] Bragg's character.
        —*Inside the Confederate Government: The Diary of Robert Garlick Hill Kean*, 1957.

Kearny, Philip (1814–1862)

US MAJOR GENERAL

5   I, Philip Kearny, an old soldier, enter my solemn protest against this order for retreat. We ought instead of retreating to follow up the enemy and take Richmond. And in full view of the responsibility of such a declaration, I say to you all, such an order can only be prompted by cowardice or treason.
        —quoted by Shelby Foote in *The Civil War*, vol. 1, 1958.

    ★ This was said to his staff after Major General George B. McClellan failed to follow up after the battle of Malvern Hill, Virginia, on July 1, 1862. Kearny's comment may have helped Lincoln relieve McClellan of his command.

6   I can make men follow me to hell.
        —quoted by Rod Graff in *Civil War Quiz and Fact Book*, 1985.

7   Don't flinch, boys! They're shooting at me, not at you!
        —quoted by Geoffrey C. Ward in *The Civil War: An Illustrated History*, 1990.

    ★ This was in Williamsburg on May 5, 1862. He was then a brigadier general.

War is horrible because it strangles youth.   **1**
> —quoted by Randall Bedwell in *Brink of Destruction*, 1999.

Keeler, William F. (1821–1886)

US LIEUTENANT

I experienced a peculiar sensation; I do not think it was fear, but it was different from   **2**
anything I ever knew before. We were enclosed in what we supposed to be an
impenetrable armor—we knew that a powerful foe was about to meet us—ours was
an untried experiment and our enemy's fire might make a coffin for us all.
> —quoted by Harold Holzer in *Witness to War: The Civil War, 1861–1865*, 1996.

★ Keeler was on the ironclad USS *Monitor*, about to face the Confederacy's ironclad
Virginia (the renamed *Merrimack*) on March 9, 1862.

Keiley, Anthony M.

A Yankee inspects each [prisoner], taking away his extra blanket, if he has one, and   **3**
appropriating any other superfluity he may chance to possess, and this accomplished,
he visits the tents and seizes everything therein that under the convenient nomen-
clature of the Federals, is catalogued as "contraband,"—blankets, boots, hats, anything. The only way to avoid this, is by a judicious use of greenbacks,—and a trifle
will suffice—it being true, with a few honorable exceptions, of course, that Yankee
soldiers are very much like ships: to move them, you must "slush the ways."
> —*In Vinculis, or The Prisoner of War*, 1866.

★ Keiley, a prominent citizen of Petersburg, Virginia, was a prisoner at the Union's
infamous Point Lookout prison in Maryland.

Keitt, Lawrence

US CONGRESSMAN FROM SOUTH CAROLINA

Thank God! Thank God! . . . South Carolina has seceded. I feel like a boy let out of   **4**
school.
> —quoted by Hudson Strode in *Jefferson Davis: American Patriot*, 1955.

★ This enthusiasm occurred at a party attended by President James Buchanan on
December 20, 1860.

Kelly, Amie

I heard before that some of the Reg. were lousy. Is it the case? Do try to keep them   **5**
off you. I would hate it so bad for you to get lousy.
> —quoted by John D. Wright in *The Language of the Civil War*, 2001.

★ Mrs. Kelly was writing to her husband, who was serving with the Army of Northern
Virginia. "Lousy" means full of lice.

Kemper, James L.

CS BRIGADIER GENERAL

1   Longstreet rode slowly and alone immediately in front of our entire line [at Gettysburg]. He sat his large charger with a magnificent grace and composure I never before beheld. His bearing was to me the grandest moral spectacle of the war. I expected to see him fall every instant. Still he moved on, slowly and majestically, with a confidence, composure, self-possession and repressed power in every movement and look, that fascinated me.
     —quoted by Larry Tagg in *The Generals of Gettysburg: The Leaders of America's Greatest Battle*, 1998.

     ★ Kemper became governor of Virginia after the war.

Kennedy, Robert

CS CAPTAIN

2   Gentlemen, this is judicial murder.
     —quoted by Ernest A. McKay in *The Civil War and New York City*, 1990.

     ★ Kennedy said this on the gallows before being executed, March 25, 1865, for setting fires in New York City.

Kentucky Delegates

3   Let these hostile armies meet on our soil, and it will matter but little to us which may succeed, for destruction to us will be the inevitable result. Our fields will be laid waste, our houses and cities will be burned, our people will be slain, and this goodly land be rebaptized "the land of blood;" and even the institution, to preserve and control which this wretched war was undertaken, will be exterminated in the general ruin. Such is the evil that others will bring upon us, no matter which side we take, if this is to be the battle-field.
     —proclamation to the people of Kentucky, May 27, 1861.

     ★ They were delegates to the "Convention of border slave states and such other slave states as have not passed Ordinances of Secession." Only Kentucky and Missouri were represented at this convention.

4   [Kentucky] refuses allegiance with any who would destroy the Union. All she asks is permission to keep out of this unnatural strife.
     —proclamation to the people of Kentucky, May 27, 1861.

5   It is a proud and grand thing for Kentucky to stand up and say, as she can, truthfully, in the face of the world, "We had no hand in this thing; our skirts are clear." And, in looking at the *terrorism* that prevails elsewhere—beholding freedom of speech denied to American citizens, their homesteads subjected to lawless visitation, their property confiscated, and their persons liable to incarceration and search—how grandly does she not loom up, as she proclaims to the oppressed and miserable, We offer you a refuge!
     —proclamation to the people of Kentucky, May 27, 1861.

Kerr, William Schomberg Robert, 8th Marquess of Lothian

Why did the South secede? She had suffered enough from the Union to have learned, **1**
that whatever its advantages might be for the North, it was of no advantage to her;
and every session proved that the chance of equal legislation was growing less and
less, for the majority had neither mercy nor good faith. . . . The South clung from
sentimental motives to the Union; and she persisted in hoping against hope that things
would grow better.
　—quoted by Hudson Strode in *Jefferson Davis: American Patriot*, 1955.

★ The marquess was one of numerous British nobles supporting the South during
the war.

Keyes, Erasmus D. (1810–1895)

US BRIGADIER GENERAL

If ever there was a diamond in the rough, or good fruit enclosed in shabby husk, it **2**
was Abraham Lincoln.
　—*Fifty Years' Observation of Men and Events, Civil and Military*, 1884.

King, Charles (1789–1867)

NEW YORK CITY COLLEGE PRESIDENT

Against the most beneficial Government, the most equal laws, and a system carrying **3**
within itself a recognized and peaceful mode of adjusting every real or imaginary
wrong or hardship, a portion of the people of the United States—the least civilized,
the least educated, the least industrious, without a single wrong specified on the part
of the National Government—have risen in rebellion against it, robbing its treasur-
ies, and even its hospitals; firing upon and treading under foot the flag of our country; menacing its Capital with armed hordes, led by the double-dyed traitors, who,
educated at the cost of the nation, and sworn to defend its laws, have deserted in the
hour of need and turned their arms against their nursing mother; and appealed to all
the scoundrels of the world to come and take service under the Rebel flag, against
the commerce of the United States.
　—speech to the Columbia College graduating class, June 26, 1861.

Kinsley, Rufus

US CORPORAL

Slavery must die, and if the South insists on being buried in the same grave I shall **4**
see in it nothing but the retributive hand of God.
　—edited by David C. Rankin in *Diary of a Christian Soldier: Rufus Kinsley and
　the Civil War*, 2004.

★ Kinsley was with the 8th Vermont Regiment and later became a lieutenant with the
Corps d'Afrique made up of Negro soldiers.

Kirby Smith, Edmund (1824–1893)

CS MAJOR GENERAL

1   Let no one make you believe we come as invaders, to coerce your will or to exercise control over your soil. . . . We come to test the truth of what we believe to be a foul aspersion, that Kentuckians willingly join the attempt to subjugate us and to deprive us of our prosperity, our liberty, and our dearest rights.
    —proclamation to the people of Kentucky, August 1862.

2   The Kentuckians are slow and backward in rallying to our standard. Their hearts are evidently with us, but their blue-grass and fat cattle are against us.
    —letter to General Braxton Bragg, September 1862.

    ★ Kirby Smith, part of the Confederate invasion of Kentucky in August 1862, was upset that only a few Kentuckians wished to join the Southern cause.

3   Why should I stay with my handful of brave Southern men to fight for cowards who skulked about in the dark to say to us, "We are with you. Only whip these fellows out of our country and let us see you can protect us, and we will join you."
    —letter to his wife, October 12, 1862.

    ★ Kirby Smith was writing from Kentucky, frustrated by the lack of locals wanting to join the Confederate army.

4   The crisis of our revolution is at hand. Great disasters have overtaken us. The Army of Northern Virginia and our Commander-in-Chief are prisoners of war. With you rest the hopes of our nation, and upon your action depends the fate of our people. I appeal to you in the name of the cause you have so heroically maintained—and in the name of your fire-sides and families so dear to you—in the name of your bleeding country whose future is in your hands. Show that you are worthy of your position in history. Prove to the world that your hearts have not failed in the hour of disaster, and that at the last moment you will sustain the holy cause which has been so gloriously battled for, by your brethren east of the Mississippi.
    —message to his troops, April 21, 1865.

    ★ Smith commanded all Confederate forces west of the Mississippi, an area that became known as "Kirby Smithdom." He surrendered this last Confederate army on May 26, 1865.

Klem, Johnny

US PRIVATE

5   I did not like to stand and be shot at without shooting back.
    —quoted by Bell Irvin Wiley in *The Life of Billy Yank*, 1952.

    ★ Klem, a twelve-year-old drummer with the 22nd Massachusetts Regiment, was explaining why he had forsaken the drum at the battle of Chickamauga and shot dead a Confederate colonel who attempted to capture him. Klem, already known as "the Drummer Boy of Shiloh," then also was called "the Drummer Boy of Chickamauga."

Knox

In this section of Tennessee a large majority of the people are still true to the Union, 1 and many pant for the opportunity to take up arms against the oppressors. But they have no standard to rally around—no Government to throw its protecting shield over them.
    —letter to *Harper's Weekly*, June 1, 1861.

★ The letter writer lived in eastern Tennessee.

This war is no war of the North against the South—no war of sections. It is a war of 2 the whole Government against an insurrection and usurpation in certain States. It is a war not to "subjugate the South" or the Southern States but to liberate the citizens of those States from that military subjugation under which they are placed by usurpation and intimidation.
    —letter to *Harper's Weekly*, June 1, 1861.

Knox, Thomas W. (1835–1896)

NEW YORK HERALD CORRESPONDENT

I have no feeling against you personally, but you are regarded as the enemy of our set 3 and we must in self-defense write you down.
    —quoted by John D. Wright in *The Language of the Civil War*, 2001.

★ Knox said this to Major General William T. Sherman, who had just arrested him. "Write you down" meant to write a negative article about someone.

Kollock, Augusta J.

The whole city [Savannah] has been wild with excitement ever since Sumter was 4 taken, & has just begun to get a little quiet, but I suppose we must prepare for hot times now, that is if the Federal Government persists in the insane policy of coercion. It is the most absurd thing I ever heard of, & I rather think if they attempt it, they will find to their cost, that it is not quite so easy to subdue us as they fancied. They will be obliged to exterminate us.
    —letter to her brother, George, January 22, 1861.

★ She wrote her return address as "Republic of Georgia."

Lamon, Ward Hill (1828–1893)

US MARSHAL

Plums delivered nicely. 5
    —quoted by Colonel Alexander K. McClure in *Lincoln's Yarns and Stories*, 1904.

★ This was the code wired by Lamon, Lincoln's friend and protector, to announce the newly elected president's arrival in Washington, D.C.

1   Promise me that you will not go out after night while I'm gone, particularly to the theater.
     —quoted by Colonel Alexander K. McClure in *Lincoln's Yarns and Stories*, 1904.

     ★ Lamon said this to Lincoln the day that Lincoln was assassinated in Ford's Theater.

Law, Evander

CS BRIGADIER GENERAL

2   It was not war; it was murder.
     —quoted by Geoffrey C. Ward in *The Civil War: An Illustrated History*, 1990.

     ★ Law was referring to the battle of Cold Harbor, Virginia, on June 3, 1864. The same words had been said by CS major general Daniel H. Hill after the battle of Malvern Hill, Virginia, on July 1, 1862.

Lawler, Michael K.

US BRIGADIER GENERAL

3   If you see a head, hit it.
     —quoted by John D. Wright in *The Language of the Civil War*, 2001.

     ★ Lawler often said this on the battlefield.

Lawley, Francis

TIMES (LONDON) CORRESPONDENT

4   There is only one opinion with regard to the discipline of the Southern troops, and that is that it is perfect. The men march calmly and steadily forward, looking neither right nor left, with the solemnity and immobility of marble statues. There is among them none of the thoughtlessness and levity of the Northern troops, none of that craving for newspapers which has always been so conspicuous in the Federals.
     —article, *Times* (London), September 12, 1862.

     ★ Although he had previously written for New York magazines, this British journalist and former member of Parliament wrote pro-Southern reports for the *Times*.

5   It is absurd to talk of such a word as earnestness being applicable to the coloured race, but to the fullest extent of their powers detestation of the Yankee is expressed by the negroes. . . . Women and children without one adult white male have constantly lived in the voiceless solitudes of the South surrounded by negroes; in no instance known to me has anything but the greatest loyalty and affection been evinced.
     —article, *Times* (London), December 1, 1862.

6   In the annals of civilized warfare such harmony in support of a war has never been approached.
     —article, *Times* (London), December 1, 1862.

     ★ Lawley was observing the Southern support for the war.

Such a sight has rarely been seen by man. It is doubtful whether any living pen could **1**
do justice to its horrors; but it is certain that it would be easy to write more than any
ordinary reader would care to read.
—article, *Times* (London), January 23, 1863.

★ Lawley was describing bodies strewn over the battlefield at Fredericksburg; this dispatch was published more than a month after Lawley wrote it.

No man had so magnificent prospect before him as General Jackson. Whether he **2**
desired it or not, he could not have escaped being Governor of Virginia, and also, in
the opinion of competent judges, sooner or later President of the Confederacy.
—article, *Times* (London), June 11, 1863.

As I sheltered myself in a little farmhouse on the plank road the brigades of Anderson's **3**
division came splashing though the mud, in wild tumultuous spirits, singing, shouting,
jesting, heedless of soaking rags, drenched to the skin, and burning again to mingle
in the mad revelry of battle
—article, *Times* (London), June 16, 1863.

★ This was at the battle of Chancellorsville.

The thundering roar of all the accumulated battles ever fought upon earth rolled into **4**
one volume could hardly have rent the skies with fiercer or more unearthly resonance and din.
—article, *Times* (London), August 18, 1863.

★ The London newspaper published this report of the battle of Gettysburg more than
six weeks after Lawley completed it.

The sufferings of the men [of General Lee] from the pangs of hunger have not been **5**
approached in the military annals of the last fifty years. But the sufferings of the
mules and horses must have been even keener; for the men assuaged their craving
by plucking the buds and twigs of trees just shooting in the early spring, whereas the
grass had not yet started from its winter sleep and food for the unhappy quadrupeds
there was none.
—quoted by Stanley F. Horn in *The Robert E. Lee Reader*, 1949.

★ Lawley was with Lee's forces a few days before their surrender at Appomattox Court
House.

Lawton, Alexander R.

CS BRIGADIER GENERAL

I think there is a popular delusion about the amount of praying Jackson did. He cer- **6**
tainly preferred a fight on Sunday to a sermon.
—quoted by Mary Boykin Chesnut in *A Diary from Dixie*, 1905.

★ This diary entry was written on December 5, 1863.

LeComte, Ferdinand (1826–1899)

SWISS OBSERVER ASSIGNED TO THE STAFF OF MAJOR GENERAL GEORGE B. McCLELLAN

1   Upon the whole, the navy of the United States, whether it be by its creations or by its operations, has acquired, and is acquiring still, the greatest honor in this war. It may well console her for the disappointments which the land army has experienced.
    —quoted by Richard B. Harwell in *The Civil War Reader*, 1958.

2   The old wooden navy, those colossi of 120 guns, which made the pride of England and of France, are now only decayed powers in the presence of the heavy calibres and the armored vessels created by the Americans.
    —quoted by Richard B. Harwell in *The Civil War Reader*, 1958.

Lee, Fitzhugh (1835–1905)

CS MAJOR GENERAL AND NEPHEW OF ROBERT E. LEE

3   [Lee said] that he was controlled too far by the great confidence he felt in the fighting qualities of his people, and by assurances of most of his higher officers.
    —quoted by Lieutenant General James Longstreet in *From Manassas to Appomattox: Memoirs of the Civil War in America*, 1896.

    ★ This referred to Pickett's charge at Gettysburg on July 3, 1863.

4   Over the splendid scene of human courage and human sacrifice at Gettysburg there arises in the South an apparition, like Banquo's ghost at Macbeth's banquet, which says the battle was lost to the Confederates because someone blundered.
    —quoted by Lieutenant General James Longstreet in *From Manassas to Appomattox: Memoirs of the Civil War in America*, 1896.

Lee, Mary Custis (1807–1873)

5   General Lee is not the Confederacy.
    —quoted by Judith Brockenbrough McGuire in *Diary of a Southern Refugee during the War, by a Lady of Virginia*, 1867.

    ★ This entry by General Lee's wife was dated April 16, 1865, a week after Lee's surrender. Earlier, when Richmond was evacuated, Mrs. Lee had said, "Richmond is not the Confederacy."

6   They have achieved by *starvation* what they never could win by their valor; nor have they taken a *single town* in the South, except Vicksburg, that we have not *evacuated*.
    —letter to Mary Meade, April 23, 1865.

    ★ This letter from General Lee's wife was written to her cousin two weeks after her husband's surrender.

Lee, Robert E. (1807–1870)

CS GENERAL

In this enlightened age there are few, I believe, but will acknowledge that slavery as   **1**
an institution is a moral and political evil in any country. It is useless to expatiate on
its disadvantages. I think it, however, a greater evil to the white than to the black
race, and while my feelings are strongly interested in behalf of the latter, my sympathies are stronger for the former.
    —letter to his wife, Mary, December 27, 1856.

★ Lee was then a US lieutenant colonel.

The blacks are immeasurably better off here than in Africa, morally, socially and phys-   **2**
ically. The painful discipline they are undergoing is necessary for their instruction as
a race and, I hope, will prepare and lead them to better things. How long their sub-
jection may be necessary is known and ordered by a wise and merciful Providence.
Their emancipation will sooner result from a mild and melting influence than the
storms and contests of fiery controversy. This influence, though slow, is sure.
    —letter to his wife, Mary, December 27, 1856.

★ Lee was then a US lieutenant colonel.

While we see the course of the final abolition of slavery is onward, and we give it the   **3**
aid of our prayers and all justifiable means in our power, we must leave the progress
as well as the result in His hands who sees the end and who chooses to work by slow
things, and with whom a thousand years are but as a single day, although the abolitionist must know this, and must see that he has neither the right nor the power of
operating except by moral means and suasion; and if he means well to the slave he
must not create angry feelings in the master.
    —letter to his wife, Mary, December 27, 1856.

★ Lee was then a US lieutenant colonel.

[John Brown] avows that his object was the liberation of the slaves of Virginia, and of   **4**
the whole South; and acknowledges that he has been disappointed in the expectation
of aid from the blacks as well as white population, both in the Southern and Northern
states. . . . The result proves that the plan was the attempt of a fanatic or madman,
which could only end in failure.
    —official report to Adjutant General Samuel Cooper, October 19, 1859.

★ Lieutenant Colonel Lee was in charge of the US Marines, who two days earlier had
stormed Harper's Ferry, Virginia, and captured the abolitionist John Brown.

Secession is nothing but revolution.   **5**
    —quoted by Lloyd Lewis in *Sherman, Fighting Prophet*, 1932.

★ Lieutenant Colonel Lee wrote this to his son in 1860, when he was serving at a frontier post in Texas just over a year before the war began.

1   I only see that a fearful calamity is upon us, & fear that the country will have to pass through for its sins a fiery ordeal.
        —letter to Martha Custis Williams, January 22, 1861.

    ★ She was Lee's first cousin.

2   I am unable to realize that our people will destroy a government inaugurated by the blood & wisdom of our patriot fathers, that has given us peace & prosperity at home, power & security abroad, & under which we have acquired a colossal strength unequalled in the history of mankind. I wish to live under no other government, & there is no sacrifice I am not ready to make for the preservation of the Union save that of honour. If a disruption takes place, I shall go back in sorrow to my people & share the misery of my native state, & save in her defence there will be one soldier less in the world than now. I wish for no other flag than the "Star Spangled banner," & no other air than "Hail Columbia." I still hope that the wisdom & patriotism of the nation will yet save it.
        —letter to Martha Custis Williams, January 22, 1861.

3   I believe that the South justly complains of the aggressions of the North, & I have believed that the North would cheerfully redress the grievances complained of. I see no cause of disunion, strife & civil war & I pray it may be averted.
        —letter to Martha Custis Williams, January 22, 1861.

4   We must all endeavour to do our whole duty however far we know we fall short of it.
        —letter to Martha Custis Williams, January 22, 1861.

5   As an American citizen, I take great pride in my country, her prosperity and institutions, and would defend any State if her rights were invaded. But I can anticipate no greater calamity for the country than a dissolution of the Union. It would be an accumulation of all the evils we complain of, and I am willing to sacrifice everything but honor for its preservation.
        —letter to his son Custis, January 23, 1861.

6   Still, a Union that can only be maintained by swords and bayonets, and in which strife and civil war are to take the place of brotherly love and kindness, has no charm for me. I shall mourn for my country and for the welfare and progress of mankind.
        —letter to his son Custis, January 23, 1861.

7   If the Union is dissolved, and the Government disrupted, I shall return to my native State and share the miseries of my people; and save in defense will draw my sword on none.
        —letter to his son Custis, January 23, 1861.

8   It is idle to talk of secession.
        —letter to his son Custis, January 23, 1861.

As an American citizen, I take great pride in my country, her prosperity and institu-   1
tions, and would defend any State if her rights were invaded. But I can anticipate no
greater calamity for the country than a dissolution of the Union.
   —letter to his son Custis, January 23, 1861.

The framers of our Constitution never exhausted so much labor, wisdom, and for-   2
bearance in its formation, if it was intended to be broken up by every member of the
[Union] at will.
   —quoted by James M. McPherson in *The Battle Cry of Freedom: The Civil War
   Era*, 1989.

★ This was said by the future Confederate general in January 1861.

I hope we have seen the last of secession.   3
   —quoted by CS colonel John S. Mosby in *The Memoirs of Colonel John S. Mosby*,
   1917.

★ This was said in the rotunda of the Virginia capitol while looking at a statue of George
Washington, before delegates to the secession convention voted on leaving the Union.

I must say that I am one of those dull creatures that cannot see the good of secession.   4
   —quoted by CS colonel John S. Mosby in *The Memoirs of Colonel John S. Mosby*,
   1917.

★ A shopkeeper in Alexandria, Virginia, said that Lee made the comment as he paid a
bill on April 19, 1861. This was two days after the Virginia Convention had submitted
an Ordinance of Secession for a referendum vote.

With all my devotion to the Union and the feeling of loyalty and duty of an American   5
citizen, I have not been able to make up my mind to raise my hand against my relatives, my children, my home.
   —letter to his sister, Mrs. Anne Marshall, April 20, 1861.

I therefore tender my resignation, which I request you will recommend for accep-   6
tance. It would have been presented at once but for the struggle it has cost me to
separate myself from a service to which I have devoted the best years of my life, and
all the ability I possessed.
   —letter to General Winfield Scott, April 20, 1861.

★ This was Lee's official resignation from the US Army.

I shall carry with me to the grave the most grateful recollections of your kind con-   7
sideration, & your name & fame will always be dear to me.
   —letter to General Winfield Scott, April 20, 1861.

Save in defense of my native state, I never desire again to draw my sword.   8
   —letter to General Winfield Scott, April 20, 1861.

1   Mr. Blair, I look upon secession as anarchy. If I owned the four millions of slaves in the South, I would sacrifice all for the Union but how can I draw my sword upon Virginia?
  —quoted in the *National Intelligencer*, August 9, 1866.

  ★ This conversation with Francis P. Blair Sr. occurred in April 1861.

2   Make your plans for a long war.
  —quoted by Stanley F. Horn in *The Robert E. Lee Reader*, 1949.

  ★ This was written in early May 1861; Lee was commissioned a brigadier general in the Confederate army on May 14.

3   [Newspapers] do not contribute to our self respect, or to a solution of the troubles of the country.
  —letter to his wife, Mary, July 2, 1861.

4   Our poor sick, I know, suffer much. They bring it on themselves by not doing what they are told. They are worse than children, for the latter can be forced.
  —letter to his wife, Mary, September 17, 1861.

5   I am sorry, as you say, that the movements of the armies cannot keep pace with the expectations of the editors of papers. I know they can regulate matters satisfactorily to themselves on paper. I wish they could do so in the field.
  —letter to his wife, Mary, October 7, 1861.

6   I hope our enemy will be polite enough to wait for us.
  —letter to his daughters, November 22, 1861.

  ★ Lee was in Savannah, Georgia, repairing its defenses.

7   Our people are opposed to work. Our troops, officers, community and press all ridicule and resist it. . . . There is nothing so military as labor, and nothing so important to an army as to save the lives of its soldiers.
  —letter to Confederate president Jefferson Davis, June 5, 1862.

8   Your recent successes have been the cause of the liveliest joy in this army as well as in the country. The admiration excited by your skill and boldness has been constantly mingled with solicitude for your situation.
  —letter to Major General Thomas J. "Stonewall" Jackson, June 11, 1862.

9   We mourn the loss of our gallant dead in every conflict, yet our gratitude to Almighty God for his mercies rises higher and higher each day. To Him and to the valor of our troops a nation's gratitude is due.
  —letter to Confederate president Jefferson Davis, September 1, 1862.

  ★ This was just after his victory at the second battle of Bull Run (second Manassas).

The body of General Philip Kearny was brought from the field last night, and he was **1**
reported dead. I send it forward under a flag of truce, thinking the possession of his
remains may be a consolation to his family.
>   —note to US general John Pope, September 2, 1862.

★ Kearny was killed at Chantilly, Virginia.

The army is not properly equipped for an invasion of an enemy's territory. It lacks **2**
much of the material of war, is feeble in transportation, the animals being much
reduced, and the men are poorly provided with clothes, and in thousands of instances
are destitute of shoes. Still we cannot afford to be idle, and though weaker than our
opponents in men and military equipments, must endeavor to harass them if we cannot destroy them.
>   —letter to Confederate president Jefferson Davis, September 3, 1862.

★ Lee was explaining his upcoming campaign into Maryland.

The people of the Confederate States have long watched with the deepest sympathy **3**
the wrongs and outrages that have been inflicted upon the citizens of a Commonwealth allied to the states of the South by the strongest social, political and commercial ties. They have seen, with profound indignation, their sister state deprived of
every right, and reduced to the condition of a conquered province. . . . Believing
that the people of Maryland possessed a spirit too lofty to submit to such a government, the people of the South have long wished to aid you in throwing off this foreign yoke, to enable you again to enjoy the inalienable rights of freemen, and restore
independence and sovereignty to your state. In obedience to this wish, our army has
come among you and is prepared to assist you with the power of its arms in regain-
ing the rights of which you have been despoiled.
>   —proclamation to the people of Maryland, September 8, 1862.

Great God! Where is the splendid division you had this morning? **4**
>   —quoted by Lieutenant Colonel G. F. R. Henderson in *Stonewall Jackson and the
>   American Civil War*, vol. 2, 1898.

★ Lee said this at the battle of Antietam (Sharpsburg) on September 17, 1862, to Major
General John B. Hood, whose reply was, "They are lying on the field, where you sent
them, for few have straggled. My division has been almost wiped out."

History records few examples of greater fortitude and endurance than this army has **5**
exhibited, and I am commissioned by the President to thank you in the name of the
Confederate States for the undying fame you have won for their arms.
>   —quoted by Stanley F. Horn in *The Robert E. Lee Reader*, 1949.

★ Lee gave this congratulatory order just after the battle of Antietam (Sharpsburg).

A few days rest at Hagerstown will be of great service to our men. Hundreds of them **6**
are barefooted, and nearly all of them are ragged. I hope to get shoes and clothing
for the most needy.
>   —quoted by Stanley F. Horn in *The Robert E. Lee Reader*, 1949.

★ This was said to Brigadier General John G. Walker during the Confederate push into
Maryland in September 1862.

1   My opinion of General Jackson has been greatly enhanced during this expedition. He is true, honest, and brave; has a single eye to the good of the service, and spares no exertion to accomplish his object.
    —letter to Confederate president Jefferson Davis, October 2, 1862.

2   The enemy apparently is so strong in numbers that I think it preferable to baffle his designs by manoeuvring, rather than resist his advance by main force. To accomplish the latter without too great a risk and loss would require more than double our present numbers.
    —letter to CS secretary of war James A. Seddon, November 10, 1862.

    ★ This was during the Fredericksburg campaign.

3   [McClellan] is a very able general but a very cautious one. His enemies among his own people think him too much so. His army is in a very chaotic condition.
    —quoted by CS major general John G. Walker in *Battles and Leaders of the Civil War*, vol. 2, 1888.

4   I hate to see McClellan go. He and I had grown to understand each other so well.
    —quoted by Stanley F. Horn in *The Robert E. Lee Reader*, 1949.

    ★ Lee wrote this letter to his wife, Mary, after Major General George B. McClellan was removed from his command. The two generals were both engineers, but this comment was in jest because of McClellan's famous habit of inaction.

5   We always understood each other so well. I fear they may continue to make those changes till they find someone whom I don't understand.
    —quoted by Lieutenant General James Longstreet in *Battles and Leaders of the Civil War*, 1888.

    ★ Lee was regretting on November 10, 1862, the dismissal three days earlier of the hesitant Major General George B. McClellan as head of the Army of the Potomac.

6   It is well that war is so terrible! We should grow too fond of it!
    —quoted by Stanley F. Horn in *The Robert E. Lee Reader*, 1949.

    ★ Lee's comment came on December 13, 1862, after Union troops were repulsed by Lieutenant General Thomas J. "Stonewall" Jackson's men during the battle of Fredericksburg, Virginia.

7   They went as they came—in the night. They suffered heavily as far as the battle went, but it did not go far enough to satisfy me.
    —letter to his wife, Mary, December 15, 1862.

    ★ This was two days after the battle of Fredericksburg.

8   . . . what a cruel thing war is. To separate & destroy families & friends & mar the purest joys and happiness God has granted us in this world. To fill our hearts with hatred instead of love for our neighbours & devastate the fair face of this beautiful world.
    —letter to his wife, Mary, December 25, 1862.

If only I am permitted to finish the work I have on hand, I would be content to live   **1**
on bread and beef for the rest of my life.
    —quoted by Francis Lawley in the *Times* (London), December 30, 1862.

The success with which our efforts have been crowned, under the blessing of God,   **2**
should not betray our people into the dangerous delusion that the armies now in the
field are sufficient to bring this war to a successful termination.
    —letter to CS secretary of war James A. Seddon, January 10, 1863.

While the spirit of the soldiers is unabated, their ranks have been greatly thinned by   **3**
the casualties of battle and the diseases of the camp. Losses in battle are rendered
much heavier by reason of our being compelled to encounter the enemy with inferior numbers, so that every man who remains out of service increases the dangers to
which the brave men, who have so well borne the burden of the war, are exposed.
The great increase of the enemy's forces will augment the disparity of numbers to
such a degree that victory, if attained, can only be achieved by a terrible expenditure
of the most precious blood of the country.
    —letter to CS secretary of war James A. Seddon, January 10, 1863.

[General Joseph Hooker] is playing the Chinese game, trying what frightening will   **4**
do. He runs out his guns, starts wagons and troops up and down the river, and cre-
ates an excitement generally. Our men look on in wonder, give a cheer, and all again
subsides in statu quo ante bellum.
    —letter to his daughter Agnes, February 6, 1863.

★ The "Chinese game" was one of creating great military noise and activity just to
frighten the enemy.

. . . I read yesterday, my precious daughter, your letter, and grieved very much when   **5**
late in Richmond at not seeing you. My movements are so uncertain that I cannot be
relied on for anything. The only place I am to be found is in camp, and I am so cross
now that I am not worth seeing anywhere.
    —letter to his daughter Agnes, February 6, 1863.

Our horses and mules suffer the most. They have to bear the cold and rain, tug   **6**
through the mud, and suffer all the time with hunger.
    —letter to his daughter Agnes, February 6, 1863.

I fear our short rations for man and horse will have to be curtailed.   **7**
    —letter to his wife, Mary, February 23, 1863.

The cars have arrived and brought me a young French officer, full of vivacity, and   **8**
ardent for service with me. I think the appearance of things will cool him. If they do
not, the night will, for he brought no blankets.
    —letter to his wife, Mary, February 23, 1863.

1   I shall feel very much obliged to [the Confederate congress] if they will pass a law relieving me from all duty and legislating some one in my place, better able to do it.
        —letter to his son Custis, February 1863.

    ★ Lee was frustrated by the politicians giving little attention to his soldiers' needs and spending too much time on appointments for favorites.

2   The greatest difficulty I find is in causing orders and regulations to be obeyed. This arises not from a spirit of disobedience, but from ignorance.
        —letter to Confederate president Jefferson Davis, March 21, 1863.

3   From the condition of our horses and the amount of our supplies I am unable even to act on the defensive as vigorously as circumstances might require.
        —message to Confederate president Jefferson Davis, April 27, 1863.

4   Well, I heard firing, and I was beginning to think it was time some of you lazy young fellows were coming to tell me what it was all about. Say to General Jackson that he knows just as well what to do with the enemy as I do.
        —quoted by Captain Robert E. Lee in *Recollections and Letters of General Robert E. Lee*, 1904.

    ★ Lee had just been told on April 29, 1863, that Union forces were crossing the Rappahannock River. Captain Lee was his son.

5   General: I have just received your note, informing me that you were wounded. I can not express my regret at the occurrence. Could I have directed events, I should have chosen, for the good of the country, to have been disabled in your stead.
        —note to Lieutenant General Thomas J. "Stonewall" Jackson, May 2, 1863.

6   You are better off than I am, for while you have lost your left, I have lost my right arm.
        —letter to Lieutenant General Thomas J. "Stonewall" Jackson, May 4, 1863.

    ★ Jackson's arm had been amputated when he was wounded. He died six days after this was written.

7   Tell him I am praying for him as I believe I have never prayed for myself.
        —quoted by Captain Robert E. Lee in *Recollections and Letters of General Robert E. Lee*, 1904.

    ★ He sent his message to the mortally wounded Lieutenant General Thomas J. "Stonewall" Jackson. Captain Lee was the general's son.

8   Surely General Jackson must recover! God will not take him from us, now that we need him so much. Surely he will be spared to us, in answer to the many prayers which are offered for him!
        —quoted by Edward Lee Childe in *Life and Campaigns of General Lee*, 1875.

    ★ Lieutenant General Thomas J. "Stonewall" Jackson was dying from wounds he received at the battle of Chancellorsville.

9   The daring, skill and energy of this great and good soldier [Jackson], by the decree of an All Wise Providence, are now lost to us. But while we mourn his death we feel that his spirit still lives and will inspire the whole army with his indomitable courage and unshaken confidence in God as our hope and strength. Let his name be a watchword to his corps, who have followed him to victory on so many fields. Let his officers and soldiers emulate his invincible determination to do everything in the defence of our beloved country.

    —General Order No. 61, May 11, 1863.

In addition to the deaths of officers and friends consequent upon the late battles, **1** you will see that we have to mourn the loss of the great and good Jackson. Any victory would be dear at such a price. His remains go to Richmond to-day. I know not how to replace him.

    —letter to his wife, Mary, May 11, 1863.

I agree with you in believing that our army would be invincible if it could be prop- **2** erly organized and officered. There were never such men in an army before. They will go anywhere and do anything if properly led.

    —letter to Major General John B. Hood, May 21, 1863.

There is always hazard in military movements, but we must decide between the pos- **3** sible loss of inaction and the risk of action.

    —letter to CS secretary of war James A. Seddon, June 8, 1863.

I reviewed the cavalry in this section yesterday. It was a splendid sight. The men and **4** horses looked well. They have recuperated since last fall. Stuart was in all his glory. Your sons and nephews were well and flourishing.

    —letter to his wife, Mary, June 8, 1863.

★ Lee had reviewed his entire cavalry corps the previous day near Brandy Station in Culpeper, Virginia.

The country here looks very green and pretty, notwithstanding the ravages of war. **5** What a beautiful world God, in His loving kindness to His creatures, has given us! What a shame that men endowed with reason and knowledge of right should mar His gifts.

    —letter to his wife, Mary, June 8, 1863.

★ Lee was near Culpeper, Virginia.

Conceding to our enemies the superiority claimed by them in numbers, resources **6** and all the means and appliance for carrying on the war, we have no right to look for exemption from the military consequences of a vigorous use of these advantages, except by such deliverance as the mercy of Heaven may accord to the courage of our soldiers, the justice of our cause and the constancy and prayers of our people.

    —letter to Confederate president Jefferson Davis, June 10, 1863.

When peace is proposed to us it will be time enough to discuss its terms, and it is not **7** the part of prudence to spurn the proposition in advance merely because those who wish to make it believe, or affect to believe, that it will result in bringing us back to the Union. We entertain no such apprehension, nor doubt that the desire of our

people for a distinct and independent national existence will prove as steadfast under the influence of peaceful measures as it has shown itself in the midst of war.
    —letter to Confederate president Jefferson Davis, June 10, 1863.

★ Lee was reacting to calls in the North for peace talks.

1   I cannot hope that Heaven will prosper our cause when we are violating its laws. I shall, therefore, carry on the war in Pennsylvania without offending the sanctions of high civilization and of Christianity.
    —quoted by Douglas Southall Freeman in *R. E. Lee: A Biography*, vol. 3, 1934.

★ This was a letter to Major General Isaac R. Trimble as Lee's push into Pennsylvania was beginning.

2   I shall throw an overwhelming force on their advance, crush it, follow up the success, drive one corps back on another, and by successive repulses and surprises, before they can concentrate, create a panic and virtually destroy the army.
    —quoted by Douglas Southall Freeman in *R. E. Lee: A Biography*, vol. 3, 1934.

★ This was said to Major General Isaac R. Trimble concerning Lee's push into Pennsylvania.

3   It must be remembered that we make war only against armed men. The Commanding General, therefore, earnestly exhorts the troops to abstain, with most scrupulous care, from unnecessary or wanton injury to private property, and he enjoins upon all officers to arrest and bring to summary punishment all who shall in any way offend against the orders on this subject.
    —General Order No. 73, June 27, 1863.

★ This was issued as Lee's troops entered Pennsylvania, four days before the beginning of the battle of Gettysburg.

4   The commanding general considers that no greater disgrace could befall the army, and through it our whole people, than the perpetration of the barbarous outrages upon the unarmed and defenseless and the wanton destruction of private property that have marked the course of the enemy in our own country.
    —General Orders No. 73, June 27, 1863.

★ Lee's forces were in Pennsylvania.

5   It must be remembered that we make war only upon armed men, and that we cannot take vengeance for the wrongs our people have suffered without lowering ourselves in the eyes of all whose abhorrence has been excited by the atrocities of our enemy, and offending against Him to whom vengeance belongeth, and without whose favor and support our efforts must all prove in vain.
    —speech to his troops, June 27, 1863.

★ This was during his invasion of Pennsylvania.

6   General Meade will commit no blunder on my front, and if I make one he will make haste to take advantage of it.
    —quoted by Shelby Foote in *The Civil War*, vol. 2, 1958.

★ Major General George G. Meade had just taken over as commander of the Army of the Potomac.

Hereabouts we shall probably meet the enemy and fight a great battle, and if God **1** gives us the victory, the war will be over and we shall achieve the recognition of our independence.
　　—quoted by Douglas Southall Freeman in *R. E. Lee: A Biography*, vol. 3, 1934.

★ Lee, at his camp in Pennsylvania, was pointing out Gettysburg on a map to Major General Isaac R. Trimble.

Ah, General, the enemy is a long time finding us; if he does not succeed soon, we **2** must go in search of him.
　　—quoted by Douglas Southall Freeman in *R. E. Lee: A Biography*, vol. 3, 1934.

★ This was said to Major General John B. Hood on June 29, 1863, two days before the battle of Gettysburg.

Tomorrow, gentlemen, we will not move to Harrisburg, as we expected, but will go **3** over to Gettysburg and see what General Meade is after.
　　—quoted by Douglas Southall Freeman in *R. E. Lee: A Biography*, vol. 3, 1934.

★ Lee's reference to Major General George Meade was made to his officers on June 29, 1863, two days before the battle of Gettysburg.

If the enemy is there, we must attack him.   **4**
　　—quoted by Douglas Southall Freeman in *R. E. Lee: A Biography*, vol. 3, 1934.

★ This was said to Lieutenant General James Longstreet on July 1, 1863, the first day of the battle of Gettysburg.

Longstreet is a very good fighter when he gets in position and gets everything ready, **5** but he is so slow.
　　—quoted by Douglas Southall Freeman in *R. E. Lee: A Biography*, vol. 3, 1934.

★ He said this to his officers on July 1, 1863, the first day of the battle of Gettysburg.

I cannot think what has become of Stuart. I ought to have heard from him long **6** before now. He may have met with disaster, but I hope not. In absence of reports from him, I am ignorant as to what we have in front of us here. It may be the whole Federal army, it may be only a detachment.
　　—quoted by Douglas Southall Freeman in *R. E. Lee: A Biography*, vol. 3, 1934.

★ This was said to Major General Richard H. Anderson on July 1, 1863, the first day of the battle of Gettysburg. Stuart did not return from his reconnaissance raid until the next day.

If we do not gain a victory, those defiles and gorges which we passed this morning **7** will shelter us from disaster.
　　—quoted by Douglas Southall Freeman in *R. E. Lee: A Biography*, vol. 3, 1934.

★ This was said to Major General Richard H. Anderson on July 1, 1863, the first day of the battle of Gettysburg.

1   The whole affair was disjoined. There was an utter absence of accord in the movements of several commands.
     —quoted by Douglas Southall Freeman in *R. E. Lee: A Biography*, vol. 3, 1934.

     ★ He was describing the Confederate forces at the second day of the battle of Gettysburg on July 2, 1863. Walker was the chief of artillery of the 3rd Corps.

2   The enemy is here and if we do not whip him, he will whip us.
     —quoted by Douglas Southall Freeman in *R. E. Lee: A Biography*, vol. 3, 1934.

     ★ This was said to Lieutenant General James Longstreet on July 2, 1863, during the second day of the battle of Gettysburg.

3   I do not approve of young officers needlessly exposing themselves; their place is with their batteries.
     —quoted by Douglas Southall Freeman in *R. E. Lee: A Biography*, vol. 3, 1934.

     ★ Lee had just observed CS major James Dearing on a ridge within range of Union fire at the battle of Gettysburg on July 3, 1863, the third day of the battle.

4   The enemy is there, General Longstreet, and I'm going to strike him.
     —quoted by Major General George E. Pickett in a letter to his future wife, Sally, July 3, 1863.

     ★ Major General James Longstreet had pointed out the difficulty of crossing the open ground to steep hills held by Union forces at Gettysburg. This was earlier in the day of Pickett's disastrous charge over this terrain.

5   All this will come right in the end, we'll talk it over afterwards; but in the mean time all good men must rally. We want all good and true men just now.
     —quoted by British lieutenant colonel Arthur James Lyon Fremantle in *Three Months in the Southern States: April–June 1863*, 1863.

     ★ Lee gave this encouragement after Pickett's charge failed, on the third day of the battle of Gettysburg. Fremantle was an observer with the Confederate army.

6   All will come right in the end.
     —quoted by Douglas Southall Freeman in *R. E. Lee: A Biography*, vol. 3, 1934.

     ★ Lee gave this encouragement while riding past his retreating forces at the battle of Gettysburg on July 3, 1863. He used the same words when he offered his resignation to Confederate president Jefferson Davis on August 8.

7   My son, I hope that you will soon be well.
     —quoted by Douglas Southall Freeman in *R. E. Lee: A Biography*, vol. 3, 1934.

     ★ Lee extended his hand and said this to a wounded Union prisoner who had just yelled, "Hurrah for the Union!" This was as Lee's troops were in retreat at the battle of Gettysburg.

8   Don't whip him, Captain; don't whip him. I've got such another foolish horse, myself, and whipping does no good.
     —quoted by Douglas Southall Freeman in *R. E. Lee: A Biography*, vol. 3, 1934.

★ This was said to Lieutenant F. M. Colston, who was hitting his horse with a stick during the Confederate retreat at Gettysburg on July 3, 1863. Lee had a very protective attitude toward animals.

General Pickett, place your division in the rear of this hill, and be ready to repel the   **1**
advance of the enemy should they follow up their advantage.
    —quoted by Douglas Southall Freeman in *R. E. Lee: A Biography*, vol. 3, 1934.

★ Lee said this to Major General George E. Pickett as Lee's forces were retreating at the battle of Gettysburg on July 3, 1863. This was one of the few times Lee called the Union forces "the enemy" instead of "those people."

Come, General Pickett, this has been my fight and upon my shoulders rests the blame.   **2**
The men and officers of your command have written the name of Virginia as high today as it has ever been written before. . . . Your men have done all that men could do; the fault is entirely my own.
    —quoted by Douglas Southall Freeman in *R. E. Lee: A Biography*, vol. 3, 1934.

★ He was consoling Major General George E. Pickett after his disastrous charge at Gettysburg on July 3, 1863.

It is my fault, I take it all—get together, men, we shall yet beat them.   **3**
    —quoted by CS brigadier general Gilbert Moxley Sorrel in *Recollections of a
    Confederate Staff Officer*, 1905.

★ This was said at the battle of Gettysburg after Pickett's charge had failed.

This has been a sad day for us, Colonel—a sad day; but we cannot expect always to   **4**
gain victories.
    —quoted by British lieutenant colonel Arthur James Lyon Fremantle in *Three
    Months in the Southern States: April–June 1863*, 1863.

★ Lee said this to Fremantle, an observer with the Confederate army, on the last day of the battle of Gettysburg.

Never mind, General, all this has been my fault—it is I that have lost this fight, and   **5**
you must help me out of it the best way you can.
    —quoted by Douglas Southall Freeman in *R. E. Lee: A Biography*, vol. 3, 1934.

★ Lee said this to Brigadier General Cadmus M. Wilcox at the battle of Gettysburg after Pickett's charge had failed.

I never saw troops behave more magnificently than Pickett's division of Virginians   **6**
did to-day in that grand charge upon the enemy. And if they had been supported as they were to have been—but, for some reason not yet explained to me, were not—we would have held the position and the day would have been ours.
    —quoted by CS brigadier general John D. Imboden in *Battles and Leaders of the
    Civil War*, vol. 3, 1888.

★ Lee made this assessment to Imboden on July 3, 1863, after the defeat at Gettysburg.

1   It is believed that the enemy suffered severely in these operations, but our own loss has not been light.
       —letter to Confederate president Jefferson Davis, July 4, 1863.

       ★ This was written as he retreated from the battle of Gettysburg.

2   No one grieves more than I do at the loss suffered by your noble division in the recent conflict, or honors it more for its bravery and gallantry. It will afford me hereafter satisfaction, when an opportunity occurs, to do all in my power to recruit its diminished ranks, and to recognize it in the most efficient manner.
       —letter to Major General George E. Pickett, July 9, 1863.

       ★ This was in regard to their action at Gettysburg, especially Pickett's disastrous charge.

3   Oh, general, had I but followed your advice, instead of pursuing the course that I did, how different all would have been.
       —quoted by Lieutenant General James Longstreet in *From Manassas to Appomattox: Memoirs of the Civil War in America*, 1896.

       ★ This was in a letter to Longstreet, who had advised against attacking Cemetery Ridge at the battle of Gettysburg.

4   You will, however, learn before this reaches you that our success at Gettysburg was not so great as reported—in fact, that we failed to drive the enemy from his position, and that our army withdrew to the Potomac.
       —letter to his wife, Mary, July 12, 1863.

5   I can appreciate your distress at Fitzhugh's situation. I deeply sympathise with it, and in the lone hours of the night, I groan in sorrow at his captivity and separation from you. But we must bear it, exercise all our patience, and do nothing to aggravate the evil. This, besides injuring ourselves, would rejoice our enemies and be sinful in the eyes of God.
       —letter to Charlotte, the wife of his son, W. H. Fitzhugh Lee, July 12, 1863.

       ★ Fitzhugh had been wounded and then captured on June 26; he was imprisoned until March 1864, but Charlotte died three months before that. (General Lee also had a nephew, Fitzhugh Lee, nicknamed "Fitz.")

6   The consequences of war are horrid enough at best, surrounded by all the ameliorations of civilisation and Christianity.
       —letter to his wife, Mary, July 12, 1863.

7   The men are in good health and spirits, but want shoes and clothing badly. . . . As soon as these necessary articles are obtained, we shall be prepared to resume operations.
       —letter to Confederate president Jefferson Davis, July 16, 1863.

8   It had not been intended to fight a general battle at such a distance from our base, unless attacked by the enemy.
       —quoted by CS lieutenant Randolph H. McKim in *A Soldier's Recollections: Leaves from the Diary of a Young Confederate*, 1910.

★ This was part of Lee's report of July 31, 1863, on the battle of Gettysburg.

The general remedy for the want of success in a military commander is his removal. **1**
This is natural, and in many instances proper. For no matter what may be the ability
of the officer, if he loses the confidence of his troops disaster must sooner or later
ensue.
    —letter tendering his resignation to Confederate president Jefferson Davis a
    month after Gettysburg, August 8, 1863.

I cannot even accomplish what I myself desire. How can I fulfil the expectations of **2**
others? In addition, I sensibly feel the growing failure of my bodily strength. . . . I
am becoming more and more incapable of exertion, and am thus prevented from
making the personal supervision of the operations in the field which I feel to be necessary. I am so dull that in making use of the eyes of others I am frequently misled.
    —letter tendering his resignation to Confederate president Jefferson Davis a
    month after Gettysburg, August 8, 1863.

I have no complaints to make of any one but myself. **3**
    —letter tendering his resignation to Confederate president Jefferson Davis a
    month after Gettysburg, August 8, 1863.

We must expect reverses, even defeats. They are sent to teach us wisdom and pru- **4**
dence, to call forth greater energies, and to prevent our falling into greater disasters.
Our people have only to be true and united, to bear manfully the misfortunes incident to the war, and all will come right in the end.
    —letter tending his resignation to Confederate president Jefferson Davis a month
    after Gettysburg, August 8, 1863.

★ He had used the same words, "All will come right in the end," to his defeated soldiers
at Gettysburg.

Soldiers! we have sinned against Almighty God. We have forgotten his signal mer- **5**
cies, and have cultivated a revengeful, haughty and boastful spirit. . . . Let us confess
our many sins, and beseech him to give us a higher courage, a purer patriotism and
more determined will: that he will convert the hearts of our enemies: that he will
hasten the time when war, with its sorrows and sufferings, shall cease, and that he
will give us a name and place among the nations of the earth.
    —General Orders No. 83, August 13, 1863.

I regret exceedingly the jealousies, heart-burnings, and other evil consequences **6**
resulting from the crude misstatements of newspaper correspondents, who have
necessarily a very limited acquaintance with the facts about which they write, and
who magnify the deeds of troops from their own States at the expense of others. But
I can see no remedy for this.
    —letter to CS secretary of war James A. Seddon, September 9, 1863.

Nothing prevented my continuing in [General Meade's] front but the destitute con- **7**
dition of the men, thousands of whom are barefooted, a greater number partially
shod, and nearly all without overcoats, blankets or warm clothing. I think the sub-

limest sight of the war was the cheerfulness and alacrity exhibited by this army in the pursuit of the enemy under all the trials and privations to which it was exposed.
—letter to CS secretary of war James A. Seddon, October 19, 1863.

1   I am glad you have some socks for the army. Send them to me. They will come safely. Tell the girls to send all they can. I wish they could make some shoes too. We have thousands of barefooted men. . . . General Meade, I believe, is repairing the railroad, and I presume will come on again. If I could only get some shoes and clothes for the men I would save him the trouble.
—letter to his wife, Mary, October 25, 1863.

2   I am too old to command this army.
—quoted in *War of the Rebellion: A Compilation of the Official Records of the Union and Confederate Armies*, 1880.

★ Lee was discouraged after letting the Army of the Potomac escape on December 2, 1863, from its aborted Mine Run campaign in Virginia.

3   If Grant could be driven back and Mississippi and Tennessee recovered, it would do more to relieve the country and inspirit our people than the mere capture of Washington.
—letter to Lieutenant General James Longstreet, January 10, 1864.

4   Soldiers! You tread with no unequal step the road by which your fathers marched through suffering, privations and blood, to independence. Continue to imitate in the future, as you have in the past, their valor in arms, their patient endurance of hardships, their high resolve to be free, which no trial could shake, no bribe seduce, no danger appal; and be assured that the just God who rewarded their efforts with success will in His own good time send down His blessing upon yours.
—General Order No. 70, January 22, 1864.

5   I can scarcely think of him without weeping.
—quoted by John Esten Cooke in *A Life of General Robert E. Lee*, 1875.

★ Lee was referring to Major General J. E. B. Stuart after he was killed at the battle of Yellow Tavern, Virginia, on May 12, 1864. Cooke was a captain in Stuart's cavalry.

6   If I can get one more pull at [Grant], I will defeat him.
—quoted by Douglas Southall Freeman in *R. E. Lee: A Biography*, vol. 4, 1934.

★ This was said on May 25, 1864.

7   My dear, my boys need to be heartened up when they get their furloughs. Go on, look your prettiest, and be just as nice to them as ever you can be.
—quoted by Hudson Strode in *Jefferson Davis: Tragic Hero*, 1964.

★ This was a reply to a young Virginia lady who asked Lee, in early 1864, if he approved of the soldiers' partying.

I think it is clear that the railroads are not working energetically and unless some   **1**
improvement is made, I do not know what will become of us.
    —letter to Confederate president Jefferson Davis, June 16, 1864.

I have understood that most of the garrison there [at Point Lookout, Maryland] was   **2**
composed of negroes. I should suppose that the commander of such troops would be
poor and feeble.
    —letter to Confederate president Jefferson Davis, June 26, 1864.

Your country was born almost a hundred years ago.   **3**
    —quoted by Major General George E. Pickett in a letter to his wife, Sally,
    July 14, 1864.

★ Lee was turning down Pickett's request for leave to see his son, who had been born
that morning.

Grant will get every man he can. Unless we can obtain a reasonable approximation   **4**
to his force, I fear a great calamity will befall us.
    —letter to Confederate president Jefferson Davis, November 2, 1864.

The General Commanding has heard with pain and mortification that outrages and   **5**
depredations amounting in some cases to flagrant robbery, have been perpetrated
upon citizens living within the lines, and near the camps of the army. Poor and helpless persons have been stripped of the means of subsistence and suffered violence by
the hands of those upon whom they had a right to rely for protection. In one instance
an atrocious murder was perpetrated upon a child by a band of ruffians whose supposed object was plunder. The General Commanding is well aware that the great
body of the army which so unselfishly devotes itself to the defence of the country,
regards these crimes with abhorrence; and that they are committed by a few miscreants unworthy of the name of soldiers. But he feels that we cannot escape the disgrace that attends these evildoers, except by the most strenuous exertions on our
part to restrain their wickedness and bring upon them the just punishment of their
offences.
    —General Order No. 71, December 12, 1864.

I have been up to see the [Confederate] Congress and they do not seem to be able   **6**
to do anything except to eat peanuts and chew tobacco, while my army is starving.
    —quoted by Carl Sandburg in *Abraham Lincoln: The War Years*, 1939.

★ This was said to his son Custis while General William T. Sherman was marching
through Georgia toward the end of 1864.

Mr. Custis, when this war began I was opposed to it, bitterly opposed to it, and I told   **7**
these people that unless every man should do his whole duty, they would repent it,
and now—they will repent.
    —quoted by Carl Sandburg in *Abraham Lincoln: The War Years*, 1939.

★ He said this in late 1864 to his son Custis because the Confederate congress seemed unable to feed his troops or draft new ones.

1   The reasons that induce me to recommend the employment of negro troops at all render the effect of the measures I have suggested upon slavery immaterial, and in my opinion the best means of securing the efficiency and fidelity of this auxiliary force would be to accompany the measure with a well-digested plan of gradual and general emancipation.
    —letter to Virginia state senator Andrew Hunter, January 11, 1865.

2   [Brave men] cannot barter manhood for peace, nor the right of self-government for life or property.
    —amnesty proclamation, February 11, 1865.

    ★ Lee was offering amnesty to all soldiers absent without leave if they would report for duty within twenty days.

3   This is a bad business, colonel.
    —quoted by John Esten Cooke in *A Life of General Robert E. Lee*, 1875.

    ★ Lee's comment to a staff member came as Union troops broke his lines, forcing the evacuation from Petersburg and Richmond on April 3, 1865.

4   Is that man [General George Pickett] still with this army?
    —quoted by CS colonel John S. Mosby in *The Memoirs of Colonel John S. Mosby*, 1917.

    ★ Lee made this comment to his personal aide, Lieutenant Colonel Charles S. Venable, after Pickett passed them during their retreat from the Appomattox campaign in April 1865. Venable later taught at Washington College while Lee was president there.

5   My God! Has the army been dissolved?
    —quoted by Shelby Foote in *The Civil War*, vol. 3, 1958.

    ★ Lee was watching his troops retreat at Sayler's Creek on April 6, 1865, three days before surrendering at Appomattox Court House.

6   That is right, men; that is all I want you to do. Just keep *those people* back awhile. I do not wish you to expose yourselves to unnecessary danger.
    —quoted by CS private Carlton McCarthy in *Detailed Minutiae of Soldier Life in the Army of Northern Virginia, 1861–1865*, 1882.

    ★ This was two days before he surrendered. Lee often referred to the enemy as "those people."

7   Keep your command together and in good spirits, general. Don't let them think of surrender. I will get you out of this.
    —quoted by John Esten Cooke in *A Life of General Robert E. Lee*, 1875.

    ★ Lee was addressing his son General W. H. F. "Rooney" Lee on April 7, 1865, two days before the surrender at Appomattox Court House.

8   General: I have received your note of this date. Though not entertaining the opinion you express of the hopelessness of further resistance on the part of the Army of

Northern Virginia, I reciprocate your desire to avoid useless effusion of blood, and therefore, before considering your proposition, ask the terms you will offer on condition of its surrender.
> —letter to General Ulysses S. Grant, April 7, 1865.

★ The surrender occurred two days later.

I trust it has not come to [surrender]! We certainly have too many brave men to think 1 of laying down our arms. They still fight with great spirit, whereas the enemy does not. And, besides, if I were to intimate to General Grant that I would listen to terms, he would at once regard it as such an evidence of weakness that he would demand an unconditional surrender and sooner than that I am resolved to die. Indeed we must all determine to die at our posts.
> —quoted by Douglas Southall Freeman in *R. E. Lee: A Biography*, vol. 4, 1934.

★ Lee was responding to General Pendleton, who brought word on April 8, 1865, that several officers felt it was useless to continue fighting. Lee's reply was summarized by other writers as: "Surrender? I have too many good fighting men for that!" He surrendered the next day.

There is nothing left but to go to General Grant; and I would rather die a thousand 2 deaths.
> —quoted by Edward Lee Childe in *Life and Campaigns of General Lee*, 1875.

★ This was said on April 8, 1865, a day before Lee surrendered.

Yes, yes, [posterity] will not understand our situation; but that is not the question. 3 The question is, whether it is right; and if it is right, I take the responsibility.
> —quoted by Edward Lee Childe in *Life and Campaigns of General Lee*, 1875.

★ In the early hours of April 9, 1865, the day he surrendered, Lee was told by a staff officer that posterity would not understand why he did not escape.

How easily I could get rid of all this and be at rest! I have only to ride along the lines 4 and all will be over! But it is our duty to live. What will become of the women and children of the South, if we are not here to protect them?
> —quoted by Edward Lee Childe in *Life and Campaigns of General Lee*, 1875.

★ This was said to his staff in the early hours of April 9, 1865, the day he surrendered.

We have fought this fight as long as, and as well as, we know how. We have been 5 defeated. For us, as a Christian people, there is now but one course to pursue. We must accept the situation. These men must go home and plant a crop, and we must proceed to build up our country on a new basis.
> —quoted by Charles Francis Adams in *Lee at Appomattox*, 1902.

★ Lee, on the morning he surrendered, was turning down a suggestion by Brigadier General Edward P. Alexander to disperse the troops to fight on in smaller groups.

I received your letter of this date containing the terms of the surrender of the Army 6 of Virginia proposed by you. As they are substantially the same as those expressed in

your letter of the 8th instant, they are accepted. I will proceed to designate the proper officers to carry the stipulations into effect.
  —letter of surrender to General Ulysses S. Grant, April 9, 1865.

★ This was handed to Grant in the McLean house at Appomattox Court House, Virginia.

1   I could always rely on my army for *fighting*; but its discipline was poor.
      —quoted by William Swinton in *Campaigns of the Army of the Potomac*, 1866.

  ★ Lee said this during the surrender at Appomattox Court House, Virginia.

2   Men, we have fought through the war together. I have done the best I could for you. My heart is too full to say more.
      —quoted by CS lieutenant William Miller Owen in *In Camp and Battle with the Washington Artillery*, 1885.

  ★ These were Lee's words as he returned to his troops following his surrender at Appomattox Court House.

3   After four years of arduous service, marked by unsurpassed courage and fortitude, the Army of Northern Virginia has been compelled to yield to overwhelming numbers and resources. I need not tell the survivors of so many hard-fought battles, who have remained steadfast to the last, that I have consented to this result from no distrust of them; but, feeling that valor and devotion could accomplish nothing that could compensate for the loss that would have attended the continuation of the contest, I have determined to avoid the useless sacrifice of those whose past services have endeared them to their countrymen. By the terms of the agreement, officers and men can return to their homes and remain until exchanged. You will take with you the satisfaction that proceeds from the consciousness of duty faithfully performed, and I earnestly pray that a merciful God will extend to you His blessing and protection. With an increasing admiration of your constancy and devotion to your country, and a grateful remembrance of your kind and generous consideration of myself, I bid you an affectionate farewell.
      —quoted by A. L. Long in *Memoirs of Robert E. Lee, His Military and Personal History*, 1886.

  ★ This was Lee's General Order No. 9, his farewell to his army, read to the soldiers by Colonel Charles Marshall on April 10, 1865, at Appomattox Court House, Virginia, the day after the surrender.

4   Mr President: It is with pain that I announce to your excellency the surrender of the Army of Northern Virginia.
      —letter to Confederate president Jefferson Davis, April 12, 1865.

  ★ This was written from Appomattox Court House.

5   The enemy was more than five times our numbers. If we could have forced our way one day longer, it would have been at a great sacrifice of life, and at its end I did not see how a surrender could have been avoided. We had no subsistence for man or horse and it could not be gathered in the country. The supplies ordered to Pamplin's

Station from Lynchburg could not reach us and the men, deprived of food and sleep for many days, were worn out and exhausted.
> —letter to Confederate president Jefferson Davis, April 12, 1865.

★ This was written from Appomattox Court House

We must be resigned to necessity, & commit ourselves in adversity to the will of a **1** merciful God as cheerfully as in prosperity. All is done for our good & our faith must continue unshaken.
> —letter to Martha Custis Williams, May 2, 1865.

★ Lee had surrendered the previous month. Williams was Lee's first cousin.

I shall avoid no prosecution the Govt thinks proper to institute. I am aware of hav- **2** ing done nothing wrong & cannot flee.
> —letter to Martha Custis Williams, June 20, 1865.

★ Lee was indicted for treason, but the charge was quashed by General Ulysses S. Grant.

Praise I never deserve, & the censure of others is so much lighter than what I inflict **3** upon myself, that it fails in its object.
> —letter to Martha Custis Williams, June 24, 1865.

All should unite in honest efforts to obliterate the effects of the war, and to restore **4** the blessings of peace. They should remain, if possible, in the country; promote harmony and good feeling; qualify themselves to vote; and elect to the state and general Legislatures wise and patriotic men, who will devote their abilities to the interests of the country, and the healing of all dissensions. I have invariably recommended this course since the cessation of hostilities, and have endeavored to practice it myself.
> —letter to John Letcher, former governor of Virginia, August 25, 1865, quoted by J. William Jones in *Personal Reminiscences, Anecdotes, and Letters of Gen. Robert E. Lee*, 1874.

I am now considered such a monster, that I hesitate to darken with my shadow, the **5** doors of those I love, lest I should bring upon them misfortune.
> —quoted by Rod Graff in *Civil War Quiz and Fact Book*, 1985.

★ This was said a few months after his surrender at Appomattox Court House.

The war being at an end, the Southern states having laid down their arms and the **6** questions at issue between them and the Northern states having been decided, I believe it to be the duty of every one to unite in the restoration of the country and the reestablishment of peace and harmony.
> —letter to Josiah Tattnall, September 7, 1865.

★ Tattnall was a former captain in the Confederate navy.

It appears to me that the allayment of passion, the dissipation of prejudice, and the **7** restoration of reason will alone enable the people of the country to acquire a true knowledge and form a correct judgment of the events of the past four years.
> —letter to Josiah Tattnall, September 7, 1865.

1   It will, I think, be admitted that Mr. Davis has done nothing more than all the citizens of the Southern states and should not be held accountable for acts performed by them in the exercise of what had been considered by them unquestionably right.
—letter to Josiah Tattnall, September 7, 1865.

2   After the surrender of the Southern armies in April, the revolution in the opinions and feelings of the people seemed so complete and the return of the Southern States into the Union of all the states so inevitable, that it became in my opinion the duty of every citizen, the contest being virtually ended, to cease opposition and place himself in a position to serve the country.
—letter to General Pierre G. T. Beauregard, October 3, 1865.

3   I need not tell you that true patriotism sometimes requires of men to act exactly contrary at one period to that which it does at another, and the motive that impels them—the desire to do right—is precisely the same. The circumstances which govern their actions change and their conduct must conform to the new order of things.
—letter to General Pierre G. T. Beauregard, October 3, 1865.

4   I am not writing a history of the war. I am endeavoring to repair as far as possible the loss of my papers, records, reports, orders &c, & desire if not prevented, to write the history of the Campaigns in Virginia.
—letter to Martha Custis Williams, December 20, 1865.

★ This history was never written.

5   I had, while in Richmond, a great many inquiries after you [Longstreet], and learned that you intended commencing business in New Orleans. If you become as good a merchant as you were a soldier, I shall be content.
—letter to Lieutenant General James Longstreet, January 19, 1866.

★ Lee was then president of Washington College in Lexington, Virginia.

6   I have thought, from the time of the cessation of hostilities, that silence and patience on the part of the South was the true course; and I think so still. Controversy of all kinds will, in my opinion, only serve to continue excitement and passion, and will prevent the public mind from the acknowledgment and acceptance of the truth. These considerations have kept me from replying to accusations made against myself, and induced me to recommend the same to others.
—letter to Varina Davis, February 23, 1866.

★ Davis was the wife of former Confederate president Jefferson Davis.

7   As regards the treatment of the Andersonville prisoners, to which you allude, I know nothing and can say nothing of my own knowledge. I never had anything to do with any prisoners, except to send those taken on the fields, where I was engaged, to the Provost Marshal General at Richmond.
—letter to Varina Davis, February 23, 1866.

8   I have felt most keenly the sufferings and imprisonment of your husband, and have earnestly consulted with friends as to any possible mode of affording him relief and consolation. He enjoys the sympathy and respect of all good men; and if, as you state,

his trial is now near, the exhibition of the whole truth in his case will, I trust, prove his defense and justification.
—letter to Varina Davis, February 23, 1866.

★ Jefferson Davis was never brought to trial, being released after two years in prison at Fort Monroe, Virginia.

It will be difficult to get the world to understand the odds against which we fought.   1
—letter to CS major general Jubal A. Early, March 15, 1866.

I hope in time peace will be restored to the country and that the South may enjoy   2
some measure of prosperity. I fear, however, much suffering is still in store for her and that her people must be prepared to exercise fortitude and forbearance.
—letter to CS major general Jubal A. Early, March 15, 1866.

I have been pained to see the attempts made to cast odium upon Mr. Davis, but do   3
not think they will be successful with the reflecting or reformed portion of the country. The accusations against myself I have not thought proper to notice, or even to correct misrepresentations of my words and acts. We shall have to be patient and suffer for a while at least; and all controversy, I think, will only serve to provoke angry and bitter feelings and postpone the period when reason and charity may resume their sway. At present the public mind is not prepared to receive the truth.
—letter to CS major general Jubal A. Early, March 15, 1866.

My own grief at one subject referred to, is as poignant now as on the day of its occur-   4
rence, & my blood boils at the thought of the atrocious outrage, against every manly & christian sentiment which the Great God alone is able to forgive. I cannot trust my pen or tongue to utter my feelings. He alone can give us resignation.
—letter to Martha Custis Williams, December 1, 1866.

★ Lee was referring to the wartime execution by Union forces of Orton Williams as a spy. He was the brother of Martha Custis Williams, and both were Lee's first cousins.

I believe I may say, looking into my own heart, and speaking as in the presence of   5
God, that I have never known one moment of bitterness or resentment. When you go home, I want you to take a message to your young friends. Tell them from me that it is unworthy of them as women, and especially as Christian women, to cherish feelings of resentment against the North. Tell them that it grieves me inexpressibly to know that such a state of things exists, and that I implore them to do their part to heal our country's wounds.
—quoted by Stanley F. Horn in *The Robert E. Lee Reader*, 1949.

★ This was said to a Maryland lady at a social event in 1867.

As to the battle of Gettysburg, I must again refer you to the official accounts. Its loss   6
was occasioned by a combination of circumstances. It was commenced in the absence of correct intelligence. It was continued in the effort to overcome the difficulties by which we were surrounded, and it would have been gained could one determined and united blow have been delivered by our whole line. As it was, victory trembled in the balance for three days, and the battle resulted in the infliction

of as great an amount of injury as was received and in frustrating the Federal campaign for the season.
—quoted by Captain Robert E. Lee, the general's son, in *Recollections and Letters of General Robert E. Lee*, 1904.

★ This was part of a letter written in 1868 to Major William M. McDonald of Berryville, Virginia, who intended to write a history.

1   Tell Hill he must come up. Strike the tent.
—quoted by Stanley F. Horn in *The Robert E. Lee Reader*, 1949.

★ These were Lee's final words before he died, on October 12, 1870.

★ Hill was CS general Ambrose P. Hill.

2   No one knows how *brittle* an army is.
—quoted by CS Inspector General John Esten Cooke in *A Life of General Robert E. Lee*, 1875.

3   Men must be habituated to obey or they cannot be controlled in battle, and the neglect of the least important order impairs the proper influence of the officer.
—quoted by A. L. Long in *Memoirs of Robert E. Lee, His Military and Personal History*, 1886.

★ Long was a Confederate brigadier general.

4   The spirit which animates our soldiers and the natural courage with which they are so liberally endowed, have led to a reliance upon those good qualities, to the neglect of measures which would increase their efficiency and contribute to their safety.
—quoted by A. L. Long in *Memoirs of Robert E. Lee, His Military and Personal History*, 1886.

5   Those who oppose our purposes are not always to be regarded as our enemies. We usually think and act from our local surroundings. The better rule is to judge our adversaries from their standpoint, not from our own.
—quoted by A. L. Long in *Memoirs of Robert E. Lee, His Military and Personal History*, 1886.

★ These sentiments were found on Lee's desk in Washington College after he died.

6   God disposes. This ought to satisfy us.
—quoted by A. L. Long in *Memoirs of Robert E. Lee, His Military and Personal History*, 1886.

★ These sentiments were found on Lee's desk at Washington College after he died. Long was a Confederate brigadier general.

7   These newspapers with their trumpery praise make me ashamed.
—quoted by CS major general Daniel H. Hill in *Century Magazine*, February 1894.

Longstreet is the hardest man to move in my army.   **1**
>—quoted by Lieutenant General James Longstreet in *From Manassas to Appomattox: Memoirs of the Civil War in America*, 1896.

There is no better way of defending a long line than by moving into the enemy's   **2**
territory.
>—quoted by Lieutenant Colonel G. F. R. Henderson in *Stonewall Jackson and the American Civil War*, vol. 2, 1898.

Such an executive officer [Jackson] the sun never shone on. I have but to show him   **3**
my design and I know that if it can be done it will be done. No need for me to send
or watch him. Straight as the needle to the pole he advances to the execution of my
purpose.
>—quoted by Lieutenant Colonel G. F. R. Henderson in *Stonewall Jackson and the American Civil War*, vol. 2, 1898.

You ought not to mind that; they will stick by you the longer.   **4**
>—quoted by Captain Robert E. Lee in *Recollections and Letters of General Robert E. Lee*, 1904.

★ General Lee was amused by a younger officer complaining about tough biscuits.
Captain Lee was the general's son.

I had such implicit confidence in [Jackson's skill and energy that I never troubled   **5**
myself to give him detailed instructions. The most general suggestions were all that
he needed.
>—quoted by Captain Robert E. Lee in *Recollections and Letters of General Robert E. Lee*, 1904.

★ He said this to one of his officers after Jackson's death. Captain Lee was his son.

General Hooker has been very daring this past week, and quite active. He has not   **6**
said what he intends to do, but is giving out by his movements that he designs crossing the Rappahannock. I hope we may be able to frustrate his plans, in part, if not in
whole.
>—quoted by Captain Robert E. Lee in *Recollections and Letters of General Robert E. Lee*, 1904.

★ Captain Lee was his son.

If I had had Stonewall Jackson at Gettysburg I would have won that fight and a com-   **7**
plete victory which would have given us Washington and Baltimore, if not Philadelphia, and would have established the independence of the Confederacy.
>—quoted by Alexander Hunter in *Johnny Reb and Billy Yank*, 1905.

★ Hunter was repeating a quotation reported by one of Lee's intimate friends, the
Reverend J. William Jones.

If it comes to a conflict of arms, the war will last at least four year. Northern politi-   **8**
cians do not appreciate the determination and pluck of the South, and Southern
politicians do not appreciate the numbers, resources, and patient perseverance of

the North. Both sides forget that we are all Americans, and that it must be a terrible struggle if it comes to war.
—quoted by J. William Jones in *Life and Letters of Robert Edward Lee: Soldier and Man*, 1906.

1   I have fought against the people of the North because I believed they were seeking to wrest from the South its dearest rights. But I have never cherished toward them bitter or vindictive feelings, and I have never seen the day when I did not pray for them.
—quoted by J. William Jones in *Life and Letters of Robert Edward Lee, Soldier and Man*, 1906.

2   I hope that you may be more fortunate than I.
—quoted by Gamaliel Bradford in *Lee, the American*, 1912.

★ Lee, president of Washington College after the war, was responding to a sophomore student who reminded the general that he had failed.

3   It is a moral, social and political evil.
—quoted by CS colonel John S. Mosby in *The Memoirs of Colonel John S. Mosby*, 1917.

★ This was one of Lee's many condemnations of slavery.

4   My interference in battle would do more harm than good. I have then to rely on my brigade and division commanders. I think and work with all my power to bring the troops to the right place at the right time; then I have done my duty. As soon as I order them forward into battle, I leave my duty in the hands of God.
—quoted by CS major general Sir Frederick Maurice in *Robert E. Lee, the Soldier*, 1925.

5   Come on, General, this man needs this food more than we do.
—quoted by CS major general Sir Frederick Maurice in *An Aide-de-Camp of Lee*, 1927.

★ A tired, hungry soldier had accidentally entered a house where Lee and Major General Wade Hampton were eating. Lee immediately stood and gave his place to the private.

6   However long you live and whatever you accomplish, you will find that the time you spent in the Confederate army was the most profitably spent portion of your life. Never again speak of having lost time in the army!
—quoted by Douglas Southall Freeman in *R. E. Lee: A Biography*, vol. 4, 1934.

7   The gentleman does not needlessly and unnecessarily remind an offender of a wrong he may have committed against him. He can not only forgive, he can forget; and he strives for that nobleness of self and mildness of character which imparts sufficient strength to let the past be but the past.
—quoted by Douglas Southall Freeman in *R. E. Lee: A Biography*, vol. 4, 1934.

★ Lee wrote this during the war on a scrap of paper that was not discovered until after his death.

Teach him he must deny himself. 1
> —quoted by Douglas Southall Freeman in *R. E. Lee: A Biography*, vol. 4, 1934.

★ He said this in his last days to a mother who brought her baby to receive his blessing.

Our country demands all our strength, all our energies. To resist the powerful com- 2
bination now forming against us will require every man at his place. If victorious, we
have everything to hope for in the future. If defeated, nothing will be left for us to
live for.
> —quoted by Stanley F. Horn in *The Robert E. Lee Reader*, 1949.

[Grant's] talent and strategy consists in accumulating overwhelming numbers. 3
> —quoted by Shelby Foote in *The Civil War*, vol. 3, 1958.

I don't believe we can have an army without music.
> —quoted by Geoffrey C. Ward in *The Civil War: An Illustrated History*, 1990.

The greatest mistake in my life was taking a military education. 4
> —quoted by Geoffrey C. Ward in *The Civil War: An Illustrated History*, 1990.

★ This was said after the war.

LeGrand, Julia (1829–1881)

This is a cruel war. These people are treated with the greatest haughtiness by the 5
upper classes and rudeness by the lower.
> —*The Journal of Julia LeGrand, New Orleans, 1862–1863.*

★ This entry of May 9, 1862, refers to reactions to Union troops occupying New
Orleans.

Leon, Louis

CS PRIVATE

★ Leon was a member of the 53rd North Carolina Regiment.

The battle [of Gettysburg] is over, and although we did not succeed in pushing the 6
enemy out of their strong position, I am sure they have not any thing to boast about.
They have lost at least as many in killed and wounded as we have. We have taken
more prisoners from them than they have from us. If that is not the case, why did
they lay still all to-day and see our army going to the rear? An army that has gained
a great victory follows it up while the enemy is badly crippled; but Meade, their commander, knows he has had as much as he gave, at least, if not more.
> —*Diary of a Tar Heel Confederate Soldier*, 1913.

Limbarker, William E.

US PRIVATE

I pray God that I may be one of the men who will pull the rope to hang Jeff Davis 7
and that the Spirits of Washington, Jefferson and Jackson and Adams may look over

the Batalments of Heaven down upon the Bleaching Carcuss as the flesh Drops from the Bones and Listen to the Winds Whistleing Hail Columbia and Yankee doodle through the Decaying ribs which once enclosed his corrupt and Traitirous heart—for causing this war and Still Caring on this Wicked and Cruell War and Keeping W. E. Limbarker from his Dear Wife and Daughter.
—diary, January 16, 1862.

Lincoln, Abraham (1809–1865)

US PRESIDENT

1   At what point shall we expect the approach of danger? By what means shall we fortify against it? Shall we expect some transatlantic military giant, to step the Ocean, and crush us at a blow? Never! . . . If destruction be our lot, we must ourselves be its author and finisher. As a nation of freemen, we must live through all time, or die by suicide.
—speech at the Young Men's Lyceum of Springfield, Illinois, January 27, 1838, quoted by Geoffrey C. Ward in *The Civil War: An Illustrated History*, 1990.

2   The probability that we may fall in the struggle ought not to deter us from the support of a cause we believe to be just; it shall not deter me.
—speech in the Illinois House of Representatives, December 26, 1839.

3   Many free countries have lost their liberty and ours may lose hers; but if she shall, be it my proudest plume, not that I was last to desert, but that I *never* deserted her.
—quoted by Colonel Alexander K. McClure in *Lincoln's Yarns and Stories*, 1904.

★ This was said in a speech in 1840.

4   Any people anywhere, being inclined and having the power, have the right to rise up and shake off the existing government, and form a new one that suits them better. This is a most valuable and most sacred right. A right which we hope and believe is to liberate the world. Nor is this right confined to cases in which the whole people of an existing government may choose to exercise it. Any portion of such people that can, may revolutionize, putting down a minority intermingled with or near about them who oppose their movements. Such a minority was precisely the case of the Tories of the Revolution. It is a quality of revolutions not to go by old lines or old laws, but to break up both and make new ones.
—speech to the House of Representatives, January 12, 1848.

★ Lincoln served from 1847 to 1849 as a Whig member of the House from Illinois.

5   If as the friends of colonization hope, the present and coming generations of our countrymen shall by any means, succeed in freeing our land from the dangerous presence of slavery; and at the same time, in restoring a captive people to their long-lost father-land, with bright prospects for the future; and this too, so gradually, that

neither races nor individuals shall have suffered by the change, it will indeed be a glorious consummation.
　　—eulogy for Henry Clay, July 6, 1852.

★ This was an early indication of Lincoln's proposal during the war to send blacks to other countries.

Slavery is founded in the selfishness of man's nature—opposition to it in his love of 1
justice. These principles are an eternal antagonism; and when brought into collision so fiercely, as slavery extension brings them, shocks, and throes, and convulsions must ceaselessly follow.
　　—speech in Peoria, Illinois, October 16, 1854.

★ Two weeks earlier, Lincoln had spoken in Springfield, Illinois, and acknowledged the rights of Southerners and the idea of gradual emancipation.

Repeal the Missouri Compromise—repeal all compromises—repeal the Declara- 2
tion of Independence—repeal all past history, you still can not repeal human nature. It still will be the abundance of man's heart, that slavery extension is wrong; and out of the abundance of his heart, his mouth will continue to speak.
　　—speech in Peoria, Illinois, October 16, 1854.

We know that some southern men do free their slaves, go north, and become tip-top 3
abolitionists; while some northern ones go south, and become most cruel slave-masters.
　　—speech in Peoria, Illinois, October 16, 1854.

When southern people tell us they are no more responsible for the origin of slavery, 4
than we; I acknowledge the fact. When it is said that the institution exists; and that it is very difficult to get rid of it, in any satisfactory way, I can understand and appreci-ate the saying. I surely will not blame them for not doing what I should not know how to do myself. If all earthly power were given me, I should not know what to do, as to the existing institution.
　　—speech in Peoria, Illinois, October 16, 1854.

When the white man governs himself that is self-government; but when he governs 5
himself, and also governs *another* man, that is *more* than self-government—that is despotism. If the negro is a *man*, why then my ancient faith teaches me that "all men are created equal;" and that there can be no moral right in connection with one man's making a slave of another.
　　—speech in Peoria, Illinois, October 16, 1854.

How common is the remark now in the slave States—"If we were only clear of our 6
slaves, how much better it would be for us." They are actually deprived of the privi-lege of governing themselves as they would, by the action of a very few, in the begin-ning. The same thing was true of the whole nation at the time our constitution was formed.
　　—speech in Peoria, Illinois, October 16, 1854.

1   Near eighty years ago we began by declaring that all men are created equal; but now from that beginning we have run down to the other declaration, that for some men to enslave others is a "sacred right of self-government." These principles cannot stand together.
    —speech in Peoria, Illinois, October 16, 1854.

2   Free [the slaves], and make them politically and socially, our equals? My own feelings will not admit of this; and if mine would, we well know that those of the great mass of white people will not.
    —speech in Peoria, Illinois, October 16, 1854.

3   [Southern people] are just what we would be in their situation. If slavery did not now exist amongst them, they would not introduce it. If it did now exist amongst us, we should not instantly give it up. This I believe of the masses north and south.
    —speech in Peoria, Illinois, October 16, 1854.

4   I hate [slavery] because it deprives the republican example of its just influence in the world—enables the enemies of free institutions, with plausibility, to taunt us as hypocrites—causes the real friends of freedom to doubt our sincerity, and especially because it forces so many really good men amongst ourselves into an open war with the very fundamental principles of civil liberty.
    —speech in Peoria, Illinois, October 16, 1854.

5   My first impulse would be to free all the slaves, and send them to Liberia,—to their own native land. But a moment's reflection would convince me, that whatever of high hope, (as I think there is) there may be in this, in the long run, its sudden execution is impossible.
    —speech in Peoria, Illinois, October 16, 1854.

6   I suppose my opposition to the principle of slavery is as strong as that of any member of the Republican party.
    —letter to Ichabod Codding, November 27, 1854.

7   On the question of liberty, as a principle, we are not what we have been. When we were the political slaves of King George, and wanted to be free, we called the maxim that "all men are created equal" a self-evident truth; but now when we have grown fat, and have lost all dread of being slaves ourselves, we have become so greedy to be *masters* that we call the same maxim "a self-evident lie." The fourth of July has not quite dwindled away; it is still a great day—*for burning firecrackers*!!!
    —letter to Judge George Robertson, August 15, 1855.

    ★ Robertson, of Lexington, Kentucky, had once represented Lincoln in family matters.

8   Our political problem now is "Can we, as a nation, continue together *permanently—forever*—half slave, and half free?" The problem is too mighty for me. May God, in his mercy, superintend the solution."
    —letter to Judge George Robertson, August 15, 1855.

The Autocrat of all the Russias will resign his crown, and proclaim his subjects free **1**
republicans sooner than will our American masters voluntarily give up their slaves.
    —letter to Judge George Robertson, August 15, 1855.

You know I dislike slavery; and you fully admit the abstract wrong of it.   **2**
    —letter to Joshua Speed, August 24, 1855.

The slave-breeders and slave-traders, are a small, odious and detested class, among **3**
you; and yet in politics, they dictate the course of all of you, and are as completely
your masters, as you are the master of your own negroes.
    —letter to Joshua Speed, August 24, 1855.

I also acknowledge your rights and my obligations, under the constitution, in regard **4**
to your slaves. I confess I hate to see the poor creatures hunted down, and caught,
and carried back to their stripes, and unrewarded toils; but I bite my lip and keep
quiet.
    —letter to Joshua Speed, August 24, 1855.

It is hardly fair to you to assume, that I have no interest in a thing [slavery] which has, **5**
and continually exercises, the power of making me miserable. You ought rather to
appreciate how much the great body of the Northern people do crucify their feelings, in order to maintain their loyalty to the constitution and the Union.
    —letter to Joshua Speed, August 24, 1855.

As a nation, we began by declaring that "all men are created equal." We now practi- **6**
cally read it "all men are created equal, except Negroes." When the Know-Nothings
get control, it will read "all men are created equal, except Negroes and foreigners
and Catholics." When it comes to this, I shall prefer emigrating to some country
where they make no pretense of loving liberty—to Russia, for instance, where despotism can be taken pure and without the base alloy of hypocrisy.
    —letter to Joshua Speed, August 24, 1855.

All this talk about the dissolution of the Union is humbug—nothing but folly. We **7**
won't dissolve the union, and you *shan't*.
    —speech in Galena, Illinois, July 23, 1856.

★ He was addressing this remark to the Democrats and other opponents of the Republican Party.

Don't interfere with anything in the Constitution. That must be maintained, for it is **8**
the only safeguard of our liberties.
    —speech in Kalamazoo, Michigan, August 27, 1856.

Our government rests in public opinion. Whoever can change public opinion, can **9**
change the government, practically just so much.
    —speech in Chicago, December 10, 1856.

1   We shall never be able to declare that "all States as States are equal," nor yet that "all citizens are equal," but to renew the broader, better description, including both these and much more, that "all men are created equal."
     —speech at a Republican banquet in Chicago, December 10, 1856.

2   There is a natural disgust in the minds of nearly all white people, to the idea of an indiscriminate amalgamation of the white and black races.
     —speech in Springfield, Illinois, June 26, 1857.

3   To give victory to the right, not bloody bullets, but peaceful ballots only, are necessary.
     —speech, May 18, 1858.

     ★ This is normally reworded as "The ballot is stronger than the bullet."

4   A house divided against itself cannot stand. I believe this government cannot endure permanently, half-slave and half-free. I do not expect the Union to be dissolved—I do not expect the house to fall—but I do expect it will cease to be divided. It will become *all* one thing, or *all* the other.
     —opening statement in a debate with Stephen A. Douglas, June 16, 1858.

     ★ Lincoln emphasized the slavery problem in his famous debates with Douglas, a Democrat who won reelection to the Senate.

5   I leave you, hoping that the lamp of liberty will burn in your bosoms until there shall no longer be a doubt that all men are created free and equal.
     —speech in Chicago, July 10, 1858.

6   I have always hated slavery, I think as much as any Abolitionist. . . . I always believe that everybody was against it, and that it was in course of ultimate extinction.
     —speech in Chicago, July 10, 1858.

7   I have said a hundred times, and I have now no inclination to take it back, that I believe there is no right, and ought to be no inclination in the people of the free States to enter into the slave States, and interfere with the question of slavery at all.
     —speech in Chicago, July 10, 1858.

8   All I ask for the negro is that if you do not like him, let him alone. If God gave him but little, that little let him enjoy.
     —speech in Springfield, Illinois, July 17, 1858.

9   In their enlightened belief, nothing stamped with the Divine image and likeness was sent into the world to be trodden on, and degraded, and imbruted by its fellows.
     —speech in Lewistown, Illinois, August 17, 1858.

     ★ He meant the belief of the Founding Fathers.

10   I have no purpose to introduce political and social equality between the white and black races. There is a physical difference between the two which, in my judgment, will probably for ever forbid their living together upon the footing of perfect equal-

ity; and inasmuch as it becomes a necessity that there must be a difference, I . . . am in favor of the race to which I belong having the superior position.
—speech in Charleston, Illinois, August 21, 1858.

Public sentiment is everything. With public sentiment, nothing can fail; without it **1** nothing can succeed.
—debate with Stephen A. Douglas in Ottawa, Illinois, August 21, 1858.

I do not stand today pledged to the abolition of slavery in the District of Columbia. **2**
—speech in Freeport, Illinois, August 27, 1858.

★ This was the second Lincoln-Douglas debate.

When . . . you have succeeded in dehumanizing the Negro, when you have put him **3** down and made it forever impossible for him to be but as the beasts of the field; when you have extinguished his soul and placed him where the ray of hope is blown out in darkness like that which broods over the spirits of the damned, are you quite sure that the demon you have roused will not turn and rend you?
—speech in Edwardsville, Illinois, September 11, 1858.

I will not allege that the Democratic party consider slavery morally, socially and polit- **4** ically *right*; though their tendency to that view has, in my opinion, been constant and unmistakable for the past five years.
—speech in Edwardsville, Illinois, September 11, 1858.

What constitutes the bulwark of our own liberty and independence? It is not our **5** frowning battlements, our bristling sea coasts, the guns of our war steamers, or the strength of our gallant and disciplined army. These are not the reliance against the resumption of tyranny in our fair land. All of them may be turned against our liberties without making us stronger or weaker for the struggle. Our reliance is in the *love of liberty* which God has planted in our bosoms. Our defense is the preservation of the spirit which prizes liberty as the heritage of all men, in all lands, every where.
—speech in Edwardsville, Illinois, September 11, 1858.

I will say then that I am not, nor ever have been in favor of bringing about in any way **6** the social and political equality of the white and black races,—that I am not nor ever have been in favor of making voters or jurors of negroes, nor of qualifying them to hold office, nor to intermarry with white people; and I will say in addition to this that there is a physical difference between the white and black races which I believe will for ever forbid the two races living together on terms of social and political equality. And inasmuch as they cannot so live, while they do remain together there must be the position of superior and inferior, and I as much as any other man am in favor of having the superior position assigned to the white race. . . . I will add to this that I have never seen to my knowledge a man, woman or child who was in favor of producing a perfect equality, social and political, between negroes and white men.
—speech in Charleston, Illinois, September 18, 1858.

★ This was the fourth Lincoln-Douglas debate.

1   Judge Douglas, and whoever like him teaches that the negro has no share, humble though it may be, in the Declaration of Independence, is going back to the era of our liberty and independence, and so far as in him lies, muzzling the cannon that thunders its annual joyous return; that he is blowing out the moral lights around us; when he contends that whoever wants slaves has a right to hold them; that he is penetrating, so far as lies in his power, the human soul, and eradicating the light of reason and the love of liberty, when he is in every possible way preparing the public mind, by his vast influence, for making the institution of slavery, perpetual and national.
—debate with Stephen A. Douglas in Galesburg, Illinois, October 7, 1858.

2   Now I confess myself as belonging to that class in the country who contemplate slavery as a moral, social and political evil.
—debate with Stephen A. Douglas in Galesburg, Illinois, October 7, 1858.

3   When Judge Douglas says that whoever, or whatever community, wants slaves, they have a right to have them, he is perfectly logical if there is nothing wrong in the institution; but if you admit that it is wrong, he cannot logically say that anybody has a right to do wrong.
—debate with Stephen A. Douglas in Quincy, Illinois, October 13, 1858.

4   That is the issue that will continue in this country when these poor tongues of Judge Douglas and myself shall be silent. It is the eternal struggle between these two principles—right and wrong—throughout the world. They are the two principles that have stood face to face from the beginning of time, and will ever continue to struggle. The one is the common rights of humanity, the other the divine right of kings.
—debate with Stephen A. Douglas in Alton, Illinois, October 15, 1858.

5   I believe the declaration that "all men are created equal" is the great fundamental principle upon which our free institutions rest; that negro slavery is violative of that principle; but that, by our frame of government, that principle has not been made one of legal obligation; that by our frame of government, the States which have slavery are to retain it, or surrender it at their own pleasure; and that all others—individuals, free-states and national government—are constitutionally bound to leave them alone about it.
—letter to James N. Brown, October 18, 1858.

★ Brown was a former state representative in Illinois.

6   I do not perceive how I can express myself, more plainly, than I have done in the foregoing extracts. In four of them I have expressly disclaimed all intention to bring about social and political equality between the white and black races, and, in all the rest, I have done the same thing by clear implication. I have made it equally plain that I think the negro is included in the word "men" used in the Declaration of Independence [in "all men are created equal"].
—letter to James N. Brown, October 18, 1858.

7   I believe our government was thus framed [of slave and free states] because of the necessity springing from the actual presence of slavery, when it was framed. That such necessity does not exist in the teritories, where slavery is not present. . . . It

does not follow that social and political equality between whites and blacks, must be incorporated, because slavery must not.
　—letter to James N. Brown, October 18, 1858.

To the best of my judgment I have labored *for*, and not *against*, the Union.   **1**
　—speech in Springfield, Illinois, October 29, 1858.

I am glad I made the late race [for the US Senate]. It gave me a hearing on the great   **2**
and durable questions of the age, which I could have had in no other way; and though I now sink out of view, and shall be forgotten, I believe I have made some marks which will tell for the cause of civil liberty long after I am gone.
　—letter to Anson G. Henry, November 19, 1858.

The fight must go on. The cause of civil liberty must not be surrendered at the end   **3**
of one, or even one hundred defeats. Douglas had the ingenuity to be supported in the late contest both as the best means to break down, and to uphold the Slave interest. No ingenuity can keep those antagonistic elements in harmony long. Another explosion will soon come.
　—letter to Henry Asbury, November 19, 1858.

★ This followed Lincoln's defeat by Stephen A. Douglas in the race for the US Senate.

I think we have fairly entered upon a durable struggle as to whether this nation is to   **4**
ultimately become all slave or all free, and though I fall early in the contest, it is nothing if I shall have contributed, in the least degree, to the final rightful result.
　—letter to H. D. Sharpe, December 8, 1858.

★ He means he fell early by losing the recent race for the US Senate.

Although we may not bring ourselves to the idea that it is to our interest to have   **5**
slaves in this Northern country, we shall soon bring ourselves to admit that, while we may not want them, if any one else does he has the moral right to have them.
　—speech in Chicago, March 1, 1859.

I suppose [slavery] may long exist, and perhaps the best way for it to come to an end   **6**
peaceably is for it to exist for a length of time. But I say that the spread and strengthening and perpetuation of it is an entirely different proposition. There we should in every way resist it as a wrong, treating it as a wrong, with the fixed idea that it must and will come to an end.
　—speech in Chicago, March 1, 1859.

Those who deny freedom to others, deserve it not for themselves; and, under a just   **7**
God, can not long retain it.
　—letter to Henry L. Pierce and others, April 6, 1859.

This is a world of compensations; and he who would be no slave, must consent to   **8**
have no slave.
　—letter to Henry L. Pierce and others, April 6, 1859.

1   Understanding the spirit of our institutions to aim at the *elevation* of men, I am opposed to whatever tends to *degrade* them.
    —letter to Theodore Canisius, May 17, 1859.

    ★ Canisius was a German American newspaper owner whose *Illinois Staats-Anzeiger* strongly supported Lincoln.

2   Now what is Judge [Stephen A.] Douglas' Popular Sovereignty? It is, as a principle, no other than that, if one man chooses to make a slave of another man, neither that other man nor anybody else has a right to object.
    —speech in Columbus, Ohio, September 16, 1859.

3   I believe we have no power, under the Constitution of the United States; or rather under the form of government under which we live, to interfere with the institution of Slavery, or any other of the institutions of our sister States, be they Free or Slave States.
    —speech in Cincinnati, Ohio, September 17, 1859.

4   Will you [slave supporters] make war upon us and kill us all? Why, gentlemen, I think you are as gallant and as brave men as live; that you can fight as bravely in a good cause, man for man, as any other people living; that you have shown yourselves capable of this upon various occasions; but, man for man, you are not better than we are, and there are not so many of you as there are of us.
    —speech in Cincinnati, Ohio, Sept, 17, 1859.

5   We believe that the spreading out and perpetuity of the institution of slavery impairs the general welfare. We believe—nay, we know, that is the only thing that has ever threatened the perpetuity of the Union itself. The only thing which has ever menaced the destruction of the government under which we live, is this very thing. To repress this thing, we think is providing for the general welfare.
    —speech in Cincinnati, Ohio, September 17, 1859.

6   You may examine the debates under the Confederation, in the convention that framed the Constitution and in the first session of Congress and you will not find a single man saying that slavery is a good thing. They all believed it was an evil.
    —speech in Elwood, Kansas, December 1, 1859.

7   I was losing interest in politics, when the repeal of the Missouri Compromise aroused me again.
    —autobiography sheet, December 20, 1859.

    ★ The Missouri Compromise had made Missouri a slave state and Maine a free one and outlawed slavery in the north; the Kansas-Nebraska bill of 1854 explicitly permitted slavery in those northern territories, repealing the Missouri Compromise.

8   Seriously, I do not think I am fit for the Presidency.
    —quoted by Colonel Alexander K. McClure in *Lincoln's Yarns and Stories*, 1904.

    ★ This was said at the beginning of 1860, when Lincoln had been proposed as a candidate.

The fact that we get no votes in your [Southern] section, is a fact of your making, and **1** not of ours. And if there be fault in that fact, that fault is primarily yours, and remains until you show that we repel you by some wrong principle or practice.
    —speech at the Cooper Union, New York City, February 27, 1860.

★ This is considered one of America's best political speeches and made Lincoln the prime Republican candidate for president.

John Brown's effort was peculiar. It was not a slave insurrection. It was an attempt by **2** white men to get up a revolt among slaves, in which the slave refused to participate. In fact, it was so absurd that the slaves, with all their ignorance, saw plainly enough it could not succeed.
    —speech at the Cooper Union, New York City, February 27, 1860.

An inspection of the Constitution will show that the right of property in a slave is not **3** "*distinctly* and *expressly* affirmed" in it.
    —speech at the Cooper Union, New York City, February 27, 1860.

Neither let us be slandered from our duty by false accusations against us, nor fright- **4** ened from it by menaces of destruction to the Government nor of dungeons to ourselves.
    —speech at the Cooper Union, New York City, February 27, 1860.

Let us have faith that right makes might, and in that faith let us, to the end, dare to **5** do our duty as we understand it.
    —speech at the Cooper Union, New York City, February 27, 1860.

I know there is a God, and that He hates injustice and slavery. I see the storm com- **6** ing, and I know that His hand is in it. If He has a place and work for me, and I think He has, I believe I'm ready. I am nothing, but Truth is everything.
    —quoted by Colonel Alexander K. McClure in *Lincoln's Yarns and Stories*, 1904.

★ Lincoln said this to Newton Bateman, superintendent of public instruction for Illinois, during his first campaign for the presidency.

It seems as if God had borne with this thing [slavery] until the teachers of religion **7** have come to defend it from the Bible, and to claim for it a divine character and sanction; and now the cup of iniquity is full, and the vials of wrath will be poured out.
    —quoted by Colonel Alexander K. McClure in *Lincoln's Yarns and Stories*, 1904.

★ Lincoln said this to Newton Bateman, superintendent of public instruction for Illinois, during his first campaign for the presidency.

May the Almighty grant that the cause of truth, justice, and humanity, shall in no **8** wise suffer at my hands.
    —letter to Joshua Giddings, May 21, 1860.

Well, boys, your troubles are over now; mine have just begun.   **9**
    —comments to journalists in Springfield, Illinois, November 7, 1860.

★ He had been elected president the previous day.

1   I am not at liberty to shift ground—that is out of the question. If I thought a *repetition* would do any good I would make it. But my judgment is it would do positive harm. The secessionists, *per se* believing they had alarmed me, would clamor all the louder.
        —letter to Nathaniel Paschall, November 16, 1860.

    ★ Paschall was editor of the *Missouri Republican.*

2   Let us at all times remember that all American citizens are brothers of a common country, and should dwell together in the bonds of fraternal feeling.
        —comments at Springfield, Illinois, November 20, 1860.

3   Let there be no compromise on the question of extending slavery. If there is, all our labor is lost, and, ere long, must be done again.
        —letter to US senator Lyman Trumbull, December 10, 1860.

    ★ Trumbull, of Illinois, later wrote the Thirteenth Amendment, abolishing slavery.

4   The dangerous ground—that into which some of our friends have a hankering to run—is Popular Sovereignty. Have none of it.
        —letter to US senator Lyman Trumbull, December 10, 1860.

5   I believe you can pretend to find but little, if any thing, in my speeches, about secession; but my opinion is that no state can, in any way lawfully, get out of the Union, without the consent of the others; and that it is the duty of the President, and other government functionaries to run the machine as it is.
        —letter to Thurlow Weed of New York, December 17, 1860.

6   Do the people of the South really entertain fears that a Republican administration would, *directly*, or *indirectly*, interfere with their slaves, or with them, about their slaves? If they do, I wish to assure you, as once a friend, and still, I hope, not an enemy, that there is no cause for such fears.
        —letter to Alexander H. Stephens, December 22, 1860.

    ★ Lincoln had been elected president the previous month. Stephens was a US congressman from Georgia who was opposed to secession but later became vice president of the Confederacy.

7   You think slavery is right and should be extended; while we think slavery is wrong and ought to be restricted. That I suppose is the rub. It certainly is the only substantial difference between us.
        —letter to Alexander H. Stephens, December 22, 1860.

8   I fully appreciate the present peril the country is in, and the weight of responsibility on me.
        —letter to Alexander H. Stephens, December 22, 1860.

9   [Lincoln] entered my studio on Sunday morning, remarking that a friend at the hotel had invited him to attend church, "but," said Mr. Lincoln, "I thought I'd rather come and sit for the bust. The fact is," he continued, "I don't like to hear cut and dried ser-

mons. No—when I hear a man preach, I like to see him act as if he were fighting bees!"

   —quoted by Leonard Volk in *Century Magazine*, December 1881.

★ Lincoln posed in 1860 for Volk, the Chicago sculptor who made the president's life mask and the bronze statue standing today in the Illinois Capitol Building. Volk was the brother-in-law of Stephen A. Douglas.

I say now, however, as I have all the while said, that on the territorial question—that **1** is, the question of extending slavery under the national auspices,—I am inflexible. I am for no compromise which *assists* or *permits* the extension of the institution on soil owned by the nation.

   —letter to Secretary of State William H. Seward, February 1, 1861.

I have read on my knees the story of Gethsemane, when the Son of God prayed in **2** vain that the cup of bitterness might pass from him. I am in the Garden of Gethsemane now and my cup of bitterness is full and overflowing now.

   —quoted by Nathaniel W. Stephenson in *Lincoln: An Account of His Personal Life, Especially of Its Springs of Action as Revealed and Deepened by the Ordeal of War*, 1922.

★ Lincoln said this to William Herndon, his law partner in Springfield, Illinois, before leaving for Washington as the president-elect.

If I live, I am coming back some time, and then we'll go right on practising law as if **3** nothing had happened.

   —quoted by Nathaniel W. Stephenson in *Lincoln: An Account of His Personal Life, Especially of Its Springs of Action as Revealed and Deepened by the Ordeal of War*, 1922.

★ Lincoln said this to William Herndon, his law partner in Springfield, Illinois, before leaving for Washington as the president-elect.

I only wish I could have got there to lock the door before the horse was stolen. But **4** when I get to the spot, I can find the tracks.

   —quoted by Colonel Alexander K. McClure in *Lincoln's Yarns and Stories*, 1904.

★ Lincoln said this to William Herndon, his law partner in Springfield, Illinois, before leaving for Washington as the president-elect.

I now leave, not knowing when, or whether ever, I may return, with a task before me **5** greater than that which rested upon Washington. Without the assistance of that Divine Being who every attended him, I cannot succeed. With that assistance I cannot fail.

   —speech on leaving Springfield, Illinois, February 11, 1861.

I appeal to you again to constantly bear in mind that not with politicians, not with **6** Presidents, not with office-seekers, but with you, is the question, Shall the Union and shall the liberties of this country be preserved to the latest generations?

   —speech in Indianapolis, February 11, 1861.

1   In all the trying positions in which I shall be placed, and doubtless I shall be placed in many trying ones, my reliance will be placed upon you and the people of the United States—and I wish you to remember now and forever, that it is your business, and not mine; that if the union of these States, and the liberties of this people, shall be lost, it is but little to any one man of fifty-two years of age, but a great deal to the thirty millions of people who inhabit these United States, and to their posterity in all coming time. It is your business to rise up and preserve the Union and liberty, for yourselves, and not for me.
  —speech in Indianapolis, February 11, 1861.

2   When the people rise in masses in behalf of the Union and the liberties of their country, truly may it be said, "The gates of hell shall not prevail against them."
  —comments in Indianapolis to Indiana governor Oliver P. Morton and citizens, February 11, 1861.

3   I am rather inclined to silence, and whether that be wise or not, it is at least more unusual nowadays to find a man who can hold his tongue than to find one who cannot.
  —"Remarks at Monongahela House," Pittsburgh, February 14, 1861.

4   There is really no crisis except an artificial one. . . . If the great American people will only keep their temper, on both sides of the line, the troubles will come to an end.
  —speech in Pittsburgh, February 15, 1861.

5   If all do not now join to save the good old ship of the Union on this voyage, nobody will have a change to pilot her on another voyage.
  —speech in Cleveland, Ohio, February 15, 1861.

6   It is true that while I hold myself without mock modesty the humblest of all individuals that have ever been elevated to the Presidency, I have a more difficult task to perform than any one of them.
  —speech to the New York State legislature, February 18, 1861.

7   The man does not live who is more devoted to peace than I am. None who would do more to preserve it. But it may be necessary to put the foot down firmly.
  —speech to the New Jersey General Assembly, February 21, 1861.

8   I am exceedingly anxious that this Union, the Constitution, and the liberties of the people shall be perpetuated in accordance with the original idea for which that struggle was made, and I shall be most happy indeed if I shall be an humble instrument in the hands of the Almighty, and of this, his almost chosen people, for perpetuating the object of that great struggle.
  —speech to the New Jersey Senate, February 21, 1861.

9   I have never had a feeling politically that did not spring from the sentiments embodied in the Declaration of Independence.
  —speech at Independence Hall, Philadelphia, February 22, 1861.

This [idea that all men are created equal] is the sentiment embodied in the Declar-   **1**
ation of Independence. Now, my friends, can this country be saved upon that basis?
If it can I will consider myself one of the happiest men in the world, if I can help save
it. If it cannot be saved upon that principle, it will be truly awful. But if this country
cannot be saved without giving up that principle, I was about to say I would rather
be assassinated on this spot, than surrender it.
   —speech at Independence Hall, Philadelphia, February 22, 1861.

As the country has placed me at the helm of the ship, I'll try to steer her through.   **2**
   —quoted by Colonel Alexander K. McClure in *Lincoln's Yarns and Stories*, 1904.

★ He said this on arriving in Washington, D.C., on February 23, 1861.

I hold, that in contemplation of universal law, and of the Constitution, the Union of   **3**
these States is perpetual.
   —first inaugural address, March 4, 1861.

The Union is much older than the Constitution. It was formed in fact, by the Articles   **4**
of Association in 1774. It was matured and continued by the Declaration of Independence in 1776.
   —first inaugural address, March 4, 1861.

I do but quote from one of those speeches when I declare that "I have no purpose,   **5**
directly or indirectly, to interfere with the institution of slavery in the states where it
exists. I believe I have no lawful right to do so, and I have no inclination to do so."
Those who nominated and elected me did so with full knowledge that I had made
this and many similar declarations, and had never recanted them.
   —first inaugural address, March 4, 1861.

In *your hands*, my dissatisfied fellow countrymen, and not in *mine* is the momentous   **6**
issue of civil war. The government will not assail *you*. You can have no conflict without being yourselves the aggressors. *You* have no oath registered in Heaven to destroy
the government, while *I* shall have the most solemn one to "preserve, protect and
defend" it.
   —first inaugural address, March 4, 1861.

We are not enemies, but friends. We must not be enemies. Though passion may   **7**
have strained, it must not break our bonds of affection. The mystic chords of memory, stretching from every battle-field, and patriot grave, to every living heart and
hearthstone, all over this broad land, will yet swell the chorus of the Union, when
again touched, as surely they will be, by the better angels of our nature.
   —first inaugural address, March 4, 1861.

Physically speaking, we cannot separate. We cannot remove our respective sections   **8**
from each other, nor build an impassable wall between them. A husband and wife
may be divorced, and go out of the presence and beyond the reach of each other; but
the different parts of our country cannot do this.
   —first inaugural address, March 4, 1861.

1   While the people retain their virtue and vigilance, no administration, by any extreme of wickedness or folly, can very seriously injure the government in the short space of four years.
    —first inaugural address, March 4, 1861.

2   The power confided in me will be used to hold, occupy, and possess the property and places belonging to the government.
    —first inaugural address, March 4, 1861.

3   It follows . . . that no State, upon its own mere motion, can lawfully get out of the Union; that resolves and ordinances to that effect are legally void; and that acts of violence, with any State or States, against the authority of the United States, are insurrectionary or revolutionary, according to circumstances. I, therefore, consider that, in view of the Constitution and the laws, the Union is unbroken.
    —first inaugural address, March 4, 1861.

4   It is safe to assert that no government proper, ever had a provision in its organic law for its own termination.
    —first inaugural address, March 4, 1861.

5   Plainly, the central idea of secession is the essence of anarchy. . . . The rule of a minority, as a permanent arrangement, is wholly inadmissible; so that, rejecting the majority principle, anarchy or despotism in some form is all that is left.
    —first inaugural address, March 4, 1861.

6   Intelligence, patriotism, Christianity, and a firm reliance on Him, who has never yet forsaken this favored land, are still competent to adjust, in the best way, all our present difficulty.
    —first inaugural address, March 4, 1861.

7   This country, with its institutions, belongs to the people who inhabit it. Whenever they shall grow weary of the existing government, they can exercise their constitutional right of amending it, or their revolutionary right to dismember or overthrow it.
    —first inaugural address, March 4, 1861.

8   I hope to be man enough not to know one citizen of the United States from another, nor one section from another.
    —speech to a Massachusetts delegation, March 5, 1861.

    ★ This was the day after his inauguration.

9   If you can't bring back any good news, bring a palmetto.
    —quoted by Colonel Alexander K. McClure in *Lincoln's Yarns and Stories*, 1904.

    ★ This was said to Ward Hill Lamon, whom Lincoln sent to South Carolina on an information-gathering trip before the war. Lamon brought back a palmetto branch.

10   Oh, well, I guess we'll manage to keep house.
    —quoted by Lloyd Lewis in *Sherman, Fighting Prophet*, 1932.

★ Lincoln was responding in March 1861 to civilian William T. Sherman's news that the South was preparing for war. During the meeting in the White House, Lincoln turned down Sherman's offer to serve the army and said soldiers were not needed to handle the crisis.

I feel like a man letting lodgings at one end of his house while the other end is on fire.

    —quoted by Colonel Alexander K. McClure in *Lincoln's Yarns and Stories*, 1904.

★ He was referring to the many office-seekers besieging him while war was breaking out.

If war is to be the result, I perceive no reason why it may not best be begun in consequence of military resistance to the efforts of the Administration to sustain troops of the Union, stationed under authority of the government in a fort of the Union, in the ordinary course of service.

    —comments to his cabinet, March 29, 1861.

I think the necessity of being *ready* increases. Look to it.

    —letter to Pennsylvania governor Andrew Curtin, April 8, 1861.

★ These two sentences were the complete letter.

I have desired as sincerely as any man—I sometimes think more than any other man—that our present difficulties might be settled without the shedding of blood.

    —speech to the Frontier Guard, April 26, 1861.

★ The Frontier Guard was made up mostly of Kansas men.

You and I both anticipated that the cause of the country would be advanced by making the attempt to provision Fort Sumter, even if it should fail; and it is no small consolation now to feel that our anticipation is justified by the result.

    —letter to Gustavus V. Fox, May 1, 1861.

★ Fox was a retired naval captain assigned to resupply Fort Sumter. This failed, but Lincoln's words indicate that the plan was to provoke the Confederate forces into firing on the fort.

Whereas, existing exigencies demand immediate and adequate measure for the protection of the national Constitution and the preservation of the national Union by the suppression of the insurrectionary combinations now existing in several states for opposing the laws of the Union and obstructing the execution thereof, to which end a military force, in addition to that called forth by my proclamation of the fifteenth day of April in the present year, appears to be indispensably necessary; now, therefore, I, Abraham Lincoln, President of the United States, and Commander-in-Chief of the Army and Navy thereof, and of the militia of the several states when called into actual service, do hereby call into the service of the United States forty-two thousand and thirty-four volunteers, to serve for a period of three years, unless sooner discharged, and to be mustered into service as infantry and cavalry.

    —proclamation, May 3, 1861.

1   For my own part, I consider the first necessity that is upon us, is of proving that popular government is not an absurdity. We must settle this question now—whether in a free government the minority have the right to break it up whenever they choose. If we fail, it will go far to prove the incapability of the people to govern themselves.
    —quoted by Carl Sandburg in *Abraham Lincoln: The War Years*, 1939.

    ★ Lincoln said this to his young secretary John Hay in May 1861.

2   The London *Times* is one of the greatest powers in the world. In fact, I don't know anything which has much more power, except perhaps the Mississippi.
    —quoted by John D. Wright in *The Language of the Civil War*, 2001.

    ★ Lincoln said this during his first meeting with William Howard Russell, the famous war correspondent for that newspaper. Russell eventually had to leave the United States after his description of the Confederate victory at the first battle of Bull Run (first Manassas) infuriated the North. He was labeled "Dr. Bull Run Russell."

3   You are green, it is true; but they are green also. You are all green alike.
    —quoted by Carl Sandburg in *Abraham Lincoln, the Prairie Years and the War Years*, 1954.

    ★ This was said at a cabinet meeting on June 29, 1861, when Brigadier General Irvin McDowell requested more time before engaging the Confederates at Bull Run.

4   My policy is to have no policy.
    —quoted by Carl Sandburg in *Abraham Lincoln: The War Years*, 1939.

    ★ Lincoln revealed this to his secretary John Hay in the spring of 1861.

5   I have never had a policy. I have simply tried to do what seemed best each day, as each day came.
    —quoted by Colonel Alexander K. McClure in *Lincoln's Yarns and Stories*, 1904.

6   It might seem, at first thought, to be of little difference whether the present movement at the South be called "secession" or "rebellion." The movers, however, well understand the difference. At the beginning, they knew they could never raise their treason to any respectable magnitude, by any name which implies *violation* of law.
    —message to the special session of Congress, July 4, 1861.

7   In this act [of bombing Fort Sumter], discarding all else, they have forced upon the country, the distinct issue: "Immediate dissolution, or blood." And this issue embraces more than the fate of these United States. It presents to the whole family of man, the question, whether a constitutional republic, or a democracy—a government of the people, by the same people—can, or cannot, maintain its territorial integrity, against its own domestic foes.
    —message to the special session of Congress, July 4, 1861.

8   It is worthy to note that while in this, the Government's hour of trial, large numbers of those in the army and navy who have been favored with offices, have resigned and

proved false to the hand which had pampered them, not one common soldier or common sailor is known to have deserted his flag. . . . This is the patriotic instinct of a plain people.
—message to the special session of Congress, July 4, 1861.

The states have their status in the Union, and they have no other legal status. If they 1 break from this, they can only do so against law and by revolution. The Union, and not themselves separately, procured their independence and their liberty. By conquest or purchase the Union gave each of them whatever of independence and liberty it has. The Union is older than any of the states, and, in fact, it created them as states. Originally, some dependent colonies made the Union; and, in turn, the Union threw off their old dependence, for them, and made them States, such as they are.
—message to the special session of Congress, July 4, 1861.

This is essentially a people's contest. On the side of the Union it is a struggle for 2 maintaining in the world that form and substance of government whose leading objective is to elevate the condition of men; to lift artificial weights from all shoulders; to clear the paths of laudable pursuit for all; to afford all an unfettered start and a fair chance in the race of life.
—message to the special session of Congress, July 4, 1861.

Our popular government has often been called an experiment. Two points in it our 3 people have already settled—the successful *establishing* and the successful *administering* of it. One still remains: its successful *maintenance* against a formidable internal attempt to overthrow it.
—message to the special session of Congress, July 4, 1861

It may well be questioned whether there is, today, a majority of the legally qualified 4 voters of any State, except perhaps South Carolina, in favor of disunion. There is much reason to believe that the Union men are the majority in many, if not in every other one, of the so-called seceded States.
—message to the special session of Congress, July 4, 1861.

Our adversaries have adopted some Declarations of Independence; in which, unlike 5 the good old one, penned by Jefferson, they omit the words "all men are created equal." Why? They have adopted a temporary national constitution, in the preamble of which, unlike our good old one, signed by Washington, they omit "We, the People," and substitute "We, the deputies of the sovereign and independent States." Why? Why this deliberate pressing out of view, the rights of men, and the authority of the people?
—message to the special session of Congress, July 4, 1861.

Is there, in all republics, this inherent and fatal weakness? Must a government, of 6 necessity, be too strong for the liberties of its own people, or too weak to maintain its own existence?
—message to the special session of Congress, July 4, 1861.

1   The principle [of secession] itself is one of disintegration, and upon which no government can possibly endure.
    —message to the special session of Congress, July 4, 1861.

2   Such will be a great lesson of peace; teaching men that what they cannot take by an election neither can they take by a war; teaching all the folly of being the beginners of a war.
    —message to the special session of Congress, July 4, 1861.

3   And having thus chosen our course, without guile, and with pure purpose, let us renew our trust in God, and go forward without fear, and with manly hearts.
    —message to the special session of Congress, July 4, 1861.

4   The provision of the Constitution that "The privilege of the writ of habeas corpus, shall not be suspended unless when, in cases of rebellion or invasion, the public safety may require it," is equivalent to a provision—is a provision—that such privilege may be suspended when, in cases of rebellion, or invasion, the public safety does require it. It was decided that we have a case of rebellion, and that the public safety does require the qualified suspension of the privilege of the writ which was authorized to be made.
    —message to the special session of Congress, July 4, 1861.

5   So it is your notion that we whipped the rebels and then ran away from them.
    —quoted by Colonel Alexander K. McClure in *Lincoln's Yarns and Stories*, 1904.

    ★ He was summarizing the opinions of some people who had witnessed the Union's rout at the first battle of Bull Run (first Manassas).

6   I think to lose Kentucky is nearly the same as to lose the whole game. Kentucky gone, we can not hold Missouri, nor, as I think, Maryland. These all against us, and the job on our hands is too large for us. We would as well consent to separation at once, including the surrender of this capitol.
    —letter to US senator Orville H. Browning of Illinois, September 22, 1861.

7   One war at a time.
    —quoted by John D. Wright in *The Language of the Civil War*, 2001.

    ★ Lincoln was replying to Secretary of State William H. Seward, who suggested that war with Great Britain might force the South's return to the Union. Seward's idea came during the "Trent affair" when a Union ship fired at a British one and seized two Confederate envoys on board. Britain deployed 8,000 troops to Canada and put its fleet on alert.

8   I had to exercise all the rude tact I have to avoid quarreling with her.
    —quoted by Colonel Alexander K. McClure in *Lincoln's Yarns and Stories*, 1904.

    ★ Lincoln was referring to Jessie Benton Fremont, the wife of Major General John C. Fremont, who had come to the White House to argue for her husband's career. The president later relieved Fremont of his command, on November 2, 1861. Fremont ran against Lincoln in 1864 as the presidential candidate of the new Radical Democracy Party.

The Mississippi is the backbone of the Rebellion; it is the key to the whole situation.   **1**
While the confederates hold it they can obtain supplies of all kinds, and it is a barrier
against our forces.
> —quoted in *Battles and Leaders of the Civil War*, vol. 2, 1888.

★ This was said on November 12, 1861, to Commander David D. Porter.

It has been said that one bad general is better than two good ones; and the saying is   **2**
true, if taken to mean no more than that an army is better directed by a single mind,
though inferior, than by two superior ones, at variance, and cross-purposes with each
other.
> —annual message to Congress, December 31, 1861.

In a storm at sea, no one on board can wish the ship to sink; and yet, not unfrequently,   **3**
all go down together, because too many will direct, and no single mind can be allowed
to control.
> —annual message to Congress, December 31, 1861.

He who does something at the head of one Regiment, will eclipse him who does noth-   **4**
ing at the head of a hundred.
> —letter to Major General David Hunter, December 31, 1861.

If [McClellan] can't fight himself, he excels in making others ready to fight.   **5**
> —quoted by Nathaniel W. Stephenson in *Lincoln: An Account of His Personal
> Life, Especially of Its Springs of Action as Revealed and Deepened by the Ordeal
> of War*, 1922.

Does not your plan involve a larger expenditure of *time* and *money* than mine?   **6**
Wherein is a victory more certain by your plan than mine? Wherein is a victory *more
valuable* by your plan than mine?
> —letter to Major General George B. McClellan, February 3, 1862.

★ Lincoln was arguing for an overland invasion into Virginia and against McClellan's
plan for a peninsula campaign.

My dear McClellan: If you don't want to use the Army I should like to borrow it for   **7**
a while. Yours respectfully, A. Lincoln
> —unsent letter of 1862 quoted in *The Annals of America*, vol. 9, 1968.

★ The president was complaining about Major General George B. McClellan's reluctance to engage the enemy.

It seems to me that McClellan has been wandering around and has sort of got lost.   **8**
He's been hollering for help ever since he went South—wants somebody to come to
his deliverance and get him out of the place he's got into.
> —quoted by Colonel Alexander K. McClure in *Lincoln's Yarns and Stories*, 1904.

Sending men to that army is like shoveling fleas across a barnyard—half of them never   **9**
get there.
> —quoted by Colonel Alexander K. McClure in *Lincoln's Yarns and Stories*, 1904.

★ Lincoln was referring to the discrepancy between the number of troops sent to Major General George B. McClellan and the number that McClellan said he had.

1 If I gave McClellan all the men he asks for, they couldn't find room to lie down. They'd have to sleep standing up.
—quoted by Colonel Alexander K. McClure in *Lincoln's Yarns and Stories*, 1904.

2 Little Mac has got the slows.
—quoted by John D. Wright in *The Language of the Civil War*, 2001.

★ Lincoln was complaining that Major General George B. McClellan was not attacking with his Army of the Potomac.

3 [McClellan] is an admirable engineer, but he seems to have a special talent for a stationary engine.
—quoted by Colonel Alexander K. McClure in *Lincoln's Yarns and Stories*, 1904.

★ This is one of Lincoln's complaints about Major General George B. McClellan's reluctance to pursue the enemy.

4 If McClellan can't fish, he ought at least to be cutting bait at a time like this.
—quoted by Colonel Alexander K. McClure in *Lincoln's Yarns and Stories*, 1904.

★ This was one of Lincoln's complaints about Major General George B. McClellan's reluctance to pursue the enemy.

5 Perhaps he is intrenching.
—quoted by Colonel Alexander K. McClure in *Lincoln's Yarns and Stories*, 1904.

★ This was one of Lincoln's complaints against Major General George B. McClellan's reluctance to pursue the enemy.

6 I will hold McClellan's horse if he will only bring us success.
—quoted by Shelby Foote in *The Civil War*, vol. 1, 1958.

7 You can not, if you would, be blind to the signs of the time. . . . The change [that emancipation] contemplates would come gently as the dews of heaven, not rending or wrecking anything.
—quoted by Nathaniel W. Stephenson in *Lincoln: An Account of His Personal Life, Especially of Its Springs of Action as Revealed and Deepened by the Ordeal of War*, 1922.

★ He was asking the slave-holding border states to accept compensated emancipation.

8 A practical reacknowledgement of the national authority would render the war unnecessary, and it would at once cease. If, however, resistance continues, the war must also continue; and it is impossible to foresee all the incidents, which may attend and all the ruin which may follow it.
—message to Congress, March 6, 1862.

Resolved, That the United States ought to co-operate with any State which may adopt   **1**
a gradual abolishment of slavery, giving to such State pecuniary aid, to be used by
such State in its discretion to compensate for the inconveniences, public and private,
produced by such change of system.
    —resolution presented to Congress, March 6, 1862.

★ The Senate and House of Representatives approved the resolution by large majorities.

Have you noticed the facts that less than one-half day's cost of this war would pay for   **2**
all the slaves in Delaware, at four hundred dollars per head?
    —letter to Henry Raymond, March 9, 1862.

★ Raymond was editor of the *New York Times*.

Engaged, as I am, in a great war, I fear it will be difficult for the world to understand   **3**
how fully I appreciate the principles of peace, inculcated in this letter, and everywhere, by the Society of Friends.
    —letter to Samuel B. Tobey, March 19, 1862.

I am a little uneasy about the abolishment of slavery in this District [of Columbia],   **4**
not but I would be glad to see it abolished, but as to the time and manner of doing it.
    —letter to Horace Greeley, March 24, 1862.

★ Lincoln wanted a more gradual abolition. Greeley founded and edited the *New York
Tribune*.

I can't spare this man—he fights!   **5**
    —quoted by Carl Sandburg in *Abraham Lincoln: The War Years*, 1939.

★ Lincoln was rebuffing Republican calls to relieve General Ulysses S. Grant of his
command after the battle of Shiloh.

Your dispatches complaining that you are not properly sustained, while they do not   **6**
offend me, pain me very much.
    —telegram to Major General George B. McClellan, April 9, 1862.

By delay, the enemy will readily gain on you; that is, he will gain faster by fortifica-   **7**
tions and re-enforcements than you can by re-enforcements alone. And once more
let me tell you, it is indispensable to you that you strike a blow. . . . The country will
not fail to note—is noting now—that the present hesitation to move upon an intrenched enemy is but the story of Manassas [Bull Run] repeated.
    —telegram to Major General George B. McClellan, April 9, 1862.

I think the time is near when you must either attack Richmond or give up the job   **8**
and come to the defense of Washington.
    —telegram to Major General George B. McClellan, April 25, 1862.

1   Your call for Parrott guns from Washington alarms me, chiefly because it argues indefinite procrastination. Is anything to be done?
     —telegram to Major General George B. McClellan, May 1, 1862.

2   Ordered: By virtue of the authority vested by act of Congress, the President takes military possession of all the railroads in the United States from and after this date until further order, and directs that the respective railroad companies, their officers and servants, shall hold themselves in readiness for the transportation of such troops and munitions of war as may be ordered by the military authorities, to the exclusion of all other business.
     —order, May 25, 1862.

3   You say General [John] Geary's scouts report that they find no enemy this side of the Blue Ridge. Neither do I.
     —telegram to Major General Irvin McDowell, May 28, 1862.

4   Stand well on your guard, hold all your ground, or yield any only inch by inch and in good order.
     —telegram to Major General George B. McClellan, May 31, 1862.

5   By proper scout lookouts, and beacons of smoke by day and fires by night you can always have timely notice of the enemy's approach. I know not as to you, but by some this has been too much neglected.
     —telegram to Major General John C. Fremont, June 13, 1862.

6   We have no definite power of sending reinforcements; so that we are compelled rather to consider the proper disposal of the forces we have than of those we could wish to have. We may be able to send you some dribs by degrees, but I do not believe we can do more.
     —telegram to Major General John C. Fremont, June 15, 1862.

7   As you alone beat Jackson last Sunday, I argue that you are stronger than he is to-day, unless he has been reinforced; and that he cannot have been materially reinforced, because such reinforcement could only have come from Richmond, and he is much more like to go to Richmond than Richmond is to come to him. Neither is very likely.
     —telegram to Major General John C. Fremont, June 15, 1862.

     ★ Lincoln was referring to the battle of Cross Keys, Virginia, but Fremont had not actually defeated Jackson.

8   I think Jackson's game—his assigned work-now is to magnify the accounts of his numbers and reports of his movements, and thus by constant alarms keep three or four times as many of our troops away from Richmond as his own force amounts to. Thus he helps his friends at Richmond three or four times as much as if he were there. Our game is not to allow this.
     —telegram to Major General John C. Fremont, June 15, 1862.

The Secretary of War, you know, holds a pretty tight rein on the press, so that they shall not tell more than they ought to; and I'm afraid that if I blab too much, he might draw a tight rein on me.
  —speech at Jersey City, New Jersey, June 24, 1862.

I expect to maintain this contest until successful, or till I die, or am conquered, or my term expires, or Congress or the country forsakes me.
  —letter to Secretary of State William H. Seward, June 28, 1862.

Save your army, at all events. Will send reinforcements as fast as we can. Of course they cannot reach you to-day, to-morrow, or next day. I have not said you were ungenerous for saying you needed reinforcements. I thought you were ungenerous in assuming that I did not send them as fast as I could.
  —telegram to Major General George B. McClellan, June 28, 1862.

If you have had a drawn battle, or a repulse, it is the price we pay for the enemy not being in Washington. We protected Washington, and the enemy concentrated on you. Had we stripped Washington, he would have been upon us before the troops could have gotten to you.
  —telegram to Major General George B. McClellan, June 28, 1862.

To take and hold the railroad at or east of Cleveland, in east Tennessee, is, I think, fully as important as the taking and holding of Richmond.
  —telegram to Major General Henry W. Halleck, June 30, 1862.

★ Lincoln was emphasizing the importance of the expedition against Chattanooga.

It is impossible to reinforce you for your present emergency. If we had a million of men, we could not get them to you in time. We have not the men to send. If you are not strong enough to face the enemy, you must find a place of security, and wait, rest, and repair. Maintain your guard if you can, but save the army at all events.
  —telegram to Major General George B. McClellan, July 1, 1862.

If, in your frequent mention of responsibility, you have the impression that I blame you for not doing more than you can, please be relieved of such impression. I only beg that in like manner you will not ask impossibilities of me.
  —telegram to Major General George B. McClellan, July 2, 1862.

★ McClellan had asked for much more than 100,000 additional troops.

If at any time you feel able to take the offensive, you are not restrained from doing so.
  —message to Major General George B. McClellan, July 4, 1862.

I do not speak of emancipation *at once*, but of a *decision* at once to emancipate *gradually*. Room in South America for colonization, can be obtained cheaply, and in abundance; and when numbers shall be large enough to be company and encouragement for one another, the freed people will not be so reluctant to go.
  —quoted by Brooks D. Simpson in *Think Anew, Act Anew*, 1998.

★ Lincoln was speaking on July 12, 1862, to representatives of the border states.

1   Our common country is in great peril, demanding the loftiest views, and the boldest action to bring it speedy relief. Once relieved, its form of government is saved to the world; its beloved history, and cherished memories, are vindicated; and its happy future fully assured, and rendered inconceivably grand.
—quoted by Brooks D. Simpson in *Think Anew, Act Anew*, 1998.

★ Lincoln was speaking on July 12, 1862, to representatives of the border states.

2   Our country is in great peril, demanding the loftiest views and boldest action to bring it speedy relief.
—speech to senators and representatives from slave-holding border states, July 12, 1862.

3   Let the States that are in rebellion see definitely and certainly that in no event will the States you represent ever join the proposed Confederacy, and they can not much longer maintain the contest. But you can not divest them of their hope to ultimately have you with them so long as you show a determination to perpetuate the institution within your own States.
—speech to senators and representatives from slave-holding border states, July 12, 1862.

4   If the war continues long, as it must if the object be not sooner attained, the institution in your States will be extinguished by mere friction and abrasion—by the mere incidents of war.
—speech to senators and representatives from slave-holding border states, July 12, 1862.

5   Room in South America for colonization, can be obtained cheaply, and in abundance; and when numbers shall be large enough to be company and encouragement for one another, the freed people will not be so reluctant to go.
—speech to senators and representatives from slave-holding border states, July 12, 1862.

★ This involved Lincoln's early plan to have freed slaves voluntarily removed to other countries.

6   We must free the slaves or be ourselves subdued. The slaves were undeniably an element of strength to those who had their service, and we must decide whether that element should be with us or against us.
—quoted by James M. McPherson in *The Battle Cry of Freedom: The Civil War Era*, 1989.

★ This was said to Secretary of the Navy Gideon Welles on July 13, 1862.

7   Things had gone on from bad to worse, until I felt that we had reached the end of our rope on the plan of operations we had been pursuing; that we had about played our last card, and must change our tactics, or lose the game. I now determined upon the adoption of the emancipation policy; and without consultation with, or the knowl-

edge of, the Cabinet, I prepared the original draft of the proclamation, and after much anxious thought, called a Cabinet meeting upon the subject.
　—edited by Arthur Brooks Lapsley in *The Writings of Abraham Lincoln*, vol. 7, 1906.

★ The meeting was on July 22, 1862. A preliminary version of the proclamation was released on September 22, 1862, and became effective on January 1, 1863.

I am a patient man—always willing to forgive on the Christian terms of repentance; 1 and also to give ample *time* for repentance. Still I must save this government if possible. What I *cannot* do, of course I *will* not do; but it may as well be understood, once for all, that I shall not surrender this game leaving any available card unplayed.
　—letter to Reverdy Johnson, July 26, 1862.

★ Johnson was a member of the Maryland House of Representatives. He had previously been the attorney general under President Zachary Taylor and later in the war became a US senator.

The people of Louisiana—all intelligent people everywhere—know full well, that I 2 never had a wish to touch the foundations of their society, or any right of theirs. With perfect knowledge of this, they forced a necessity upon me to send armies among them, and it is their own fault, not mine, that they are annoyed by the presence of General Phelps.
　—letter to Brigadier General George F. Shepley, July 26, 1862.

★ Brigadier General John W. Phelps, occupying New Orleans, was protecting refugee slaves. Shepley was the military governor of occupied Louisiana.

This government cannot much longer play a game in which it stakes all, and its ene- 3 mies stake nothing. Those enemies must understand that they cannot experiment for ten years trying to destroy the government, and if they fail still come back into the Union unhurt.
　—letter to August Belmont, July 26, 1862.

★ Belmont was a Democratic adviser.

You are ready to say I apply to friends what is due only to enemies. I distrust the wis- 4 dom if not the sincerity of friends who would hold my hands while my enemies stab me. This appeal of professed friends has paralyzed me more in this struggle than any other one thing.
　—letter to Reverdy Johnson, July 26, 1862.

★ Johnson was a member of the Maryland House of Representatives. He was previously the attorney general under President Zachary Taylor and later in the war became a US senator.

I am in no boastful mood. I shall not do *more* than I can, and I shall do *all* I can to 5 save the government, which is my sworn duty as well as my personal inclination. I shall do nothing in malice. What I deal with is too vast for malicious dealing.
　—letter to Cuthbert Bullitt, July 28, 1862.

★ Bullitt was a merchant.

1   Broken eggs cannot be mended; but Louisiana has nothing to do now but to take her place in the Union as it was, barring the already broken eggs.
        —letter to August Belmont, July 31, 1862.

    ★ The US Navy had captured New Orleans three months earlier.

2   General McClellan has sometimes asked for things that the Secretary of War did not give him. General McClellan is not to blame for asking for what he wanted and needed, and the Secretary of War is not to blame for not giving when he had none to give.
        —speech at war meeting in Washington, D.C., August 6, 1862.

3   Your despatch saying "I can't get those regiments off because I can't get quick work out of the V.S. [Volunteer Service] disbursing officer and the paymaster" is received. Please say to these gentlemen that if they do not work quickly I will make quick work with them. In the name of all that is reasonable, how long does it take to pay a couple of regiments? We were never more in need of the arrival of regiments than now—even to-day.
        —telegram to Massachusetts governor John A. Andrew, August 12, 1862.

4   If there be those who would not save the Union unless they could at the same time *save* slavery, I do not agree with them. If there be those who would not save the Union unless they could at the same time *destroy* slavery, I do not agree with them. My paramount object in this struggle *is* to save the Union, and is *not* either to save or destroy slavery.
        —letter to Horace Greeley, founder and editor of the *New York Tribune*, August 22, 1862.

    ★ Lincoln was replying to Greeley's editorial of August 19, 1862, which accused him of not making slavery the main issue of the war.

5   If I could save the Union without freeing any slave, I would do it—If I could save it by freeing all the slaves, I would do it—and if I could do it by freeing some and leaving others alone, I would also do that.
        —letter to Horace Greeley, August 22, 1862.

    ★ Greeley was an advocate for emancipation but opposed war when the southern states seceded.

6   What I do about slavery and the colored race, I do because I believe it helps to save the Union; and what I forbear, I forbear because I do not believe it would help to save the Union.
        —letter to Horace Greeley, August 22, 1862.

7   I have here stated my purpose according to my view of official duty; and I intend no modification of my oft-expressed personal wish that all men everywhere could be free.
        —letter to Horace Greeley, August 22, 1862.

I would save the Union. I would save it the shortest way under the Constitution. The **1** sooner the national authority can be restored; the nearer the Union will be "the Union as it was."

   —letter to Horace Greeley, August 22, 1862.

At break-neck speed we reached a haven of safety. Meanwhile, I was left in doubt **2** whether death was more desirable from being thrown from a runaway Federal horse, or as the tragic result of a rifle ball fired by a disloyal bushwhacker in the middle of the night.

   —quoted by Nathaniel W. Stephenson in *Lincoln: An Account of His Personal Life, Especially of Its Springs of Action as Revealed and Deepened by the Ordeal of War*, 1922.

★ Someone had fired a rifle at Lincoln when he was riding in Washington, D.C., at 11 o'clock on a night in August 1862. The shot missed but frightened his horse, which started and made the president lose his eight-dollar plug hat.

I am approached with the most opposite opinions and advice, and that by religious **3** men, who are equally certain that they represent the Divine will. I am sure that either the one or the other class is mistaken in that belief, and perhaps in some respects both. I hope it will not be irreverent for me to say that if it is probable that God would reveal his will to others, on a point so connected with my duty, it might be supposed he would reveal it directly to me . . . These are not, however, the days of miracles, and I suppose it will be granted that I am not to expect a direct revelation.

   —reply to a committee from the religious denominations of Chicago, September 13, 1862.

★ Lincoln was replying to a Christian committee that presented him with a written memorial supporting emancipation; their memorial had been passed on September 7, 1862, at the group's meeting in Chicago. Nine days later, however, the president announced his preliminary emancipation proclamation.

General [Benjamin] Butler wrote me a few days since that he was issuing more rations **4** to the slaves who have rushed to him than to all the white troops under his command [in New Orleans]. They eat, and that is all; though it is true General Butler is feeding the whites also by the thousand; for it nearly amounts to a famine there.

   —reply to a committee from the religious denominations of Chicago, September 13, 1862.

Now, then, tell me, if you please, what possible result of good would follow the issu- **5** ing of such a proclamation [of emancipation] as you desire?

   —reply to a committee from the religious denominations of Chicago, September 13, 1862.

I admit that slavery is the root of the rebellion, or at least its sine qua non. The ambi- **6** tion of politicians may have instigated them to act, but they would have been impotent without slavery as their instrument.

   —reply to a committee from the religious denominations of Chicago, September 13, 1862.

1   Would my word free the slaves, when I cannot even enforce the Constitution in the rebel states?
> — reply to a committee from the religious denominations of Chicago, September 13, 1862.

2   What *good* would a proclamation of emancipation from me do, especially as we are now situated? I do not want to issue a document that the whole world will see must necessarily be inoperative, like the Pope's bull against the comet! Would *my word* free the slave, when I cannot even enforce the Constitution in the rebel States? Is there a single court, or magistrate, or individual that would be influenced by it there? . . . And suppose [slaves] could be induced by a proclamation of freedom from me to throw themselves upon us, *what should we do with them*? How can we feed and care for such a multitude?
> —quoted in the *Chicago Tribune*, September 13, 1862.

3   I view the matter [of issuing an emancipation proclamation] as a practical war measure, to be decided upon according to the advantages or disadvantages it may offer to the suppression of the rebellion.
> —quoted in the *Chicago Tribune*, September 13, 1862.

4   Why, the rebel soldiers are praying with a great deal more earnestness, I fear, than our own troops, and expecting God to favor their side.
> —quoted in the *Chicago Tribune*, September 13, 1862.

5   God bless you and all with you. Destroy the rebel army, if possible.
> —telegram to Major General George B. McClellan, September 15, 1862.

6   The fact is the people haven't yet made up their minds that we are at war with the South. They haven't buckled down to the determination to fight this war through; for they have got the idea into their heads that we are going to get out of this fix, somehow, by strategy!
> —quoted by Mary A. Livermore in *My Story of the War*, 1887.

★ Lincoln's frustration came shortly after the battle of Antietam (Sharpsburg) on September 17, 1862, when McClellan failed to renew the attack.

7   Is it not odd that the only channel [God] could send it was that roundabout route by the awfully wicked city of Chicago?
> —quoted by Nathaniel W. Stephenson in *Lincoln: An Account of His Personal Life, Especially of Its Springs of Action as Revealed and Deepened by the Ordeal of War*, 1922.

★ Lincoln was joking with one of a group of Chicago clergyman who visited in mid-September 1862. The man had said that Lincoln should heed their message about abolition as if it came directly from the Almighty.

8   When the rebel army was at Frederick, I determined, as soon as it should be driven out of Maryland, to issue a proclamation of emancipation, such as I thought most

likely to be useful. I said nothing to anyone; but I made the promise to myself and to my Maker. The rebel army is now driven out, and I am going to fulfill that promise.
—comments to his cabinet, September 22, 1862.

The original [emancipation] proclamation has no . . . legal justification, except as a 1 military measure.
—quoted by Walter E. Williams in Thomas J. DiLorenzo's book *The Real Lincoln: A New Look at Abraham Lincoln, His Agenda, and an Unnecessary War*, 2002.

★ This was written to Secretary of the Treasury Salmon P. Chase.

From time to time I added or changed a line [of the Emancipation Proclamation], 2 anxiously watching the process of events. Well, the next news we had was of [General John] Pope's disaster at Bull Run. Things looked darker than ever. Finally came the week of the battle of Antietam [Sharpsburg]. I determined to wait no longer. The news came, I think, on Wednesday [September 17, 1862], that the advantage was on our side. I was then staying at the Soldiers' Home. Here I finished writing the second draft of the preliminary proclamation; came up on Saturday; called the Cabinet together to hear it, and it was published on the following Monday.
—edited by Arthur Brooks Lapsley in *The Writings of Abraham Lincoln*, vol. 7, 1906.

★ The proclamation became effective on January 1, 1863.

On the first day of January in the year of our Lord, one thousand eight hundred and 3 sixty-three, all persons held as slaves within any state, or designated part of a state, the people whereof shall then be in rebellion against the United States, shall be then, thenceforward, and forever free.
—preliminary emancipation proclamation, September 22, 1862.

★ The pronouncement thus retained slavery in the Union's loyal states.

What I did, I did after very full deliberation, and under a heavy and solemn sense of 4 responsibility. I can only trust in God that I have made no mistake.
—response to a serenade, September 24, 1862.

★ He was referring to the preliminary emancipation proclamation issued two days before.

It is known to some that, while I hope something from the [emancipation] procla- 5 mation, my expectations are not as sanguine as are those of some friends. . . . It is six days old, and, while commendation in newspapers and by distinguished individuals is all that a vain man could wish, the stocks have declined, and troops come forward more slowly than ever. This, looked soberly in the face, is not very satisfactory. We have fewer troops in the field at the end of the six days than we had at the beginning—the attrition among the old outnumbering the addition by the new. The North responds to the proclamation sufficiently in breath; but breath alone kills no rebels.
—letter to Vice President Hannibal Hamlin, September 28, 1862.

1   I sincerely wish war was a pleasanter and easier business than it is, but it does not admit of holidays.
    —quoted by Colonel Alexander K. McClure in *Lincoln's Yarns and Stories*, 1904.

★ This was in a letter written October 2, 1862.

2   May our children and our children's children to a thousand generations, continue to enjoy the benefits conferred upon us by a united country, and have cause yet to rejoice under those glorious institutions bequeathed us by Washington and his compeers.
    —speech in Frederick, Maryland, October 4, 1862.

3   You remember my speaking to you of what I called your over-cautiousness. Are you not over-cautious when you assume that you cannot do what the enemy is constantly doing? Should you not claim to be at least his equal in prowess, and act upon the claim?
    —telegram to Major General George B. McClellan, October 13, 1862.

4   Again, one of the standard maxims of war, as you know, is "to operate upon the enemy's communications as much as possible, without exposing your own." You seem to act as if this applies against you, but cannot apply in your favor.
    —telegram to Major General George B. McClellan, October 13, 1862.

5   I have just read your despatch about sore tongued and fatigued horses. Will you pardon me for asking what the horses of your army have done since the battle of Antietam [Sharpsburg] that fatigue anything?
    —message to Major General George B. McClellan, October 24, 1862.

★ This was after McClellan had won the battle of Antietam (Sharpsburg) but failed to pursue Lee's retreating troops.

6   Three times round and out is the rule in baseball. Stuart has been round twice around McClellan. The third time, by the rules of the game, he must surrender.
    —quoted by Don E. Fehrenbacher and Virginia Fehrenbacher in *Recollected Words of Abraham Lincoln*, 1996.

★ This was said to the *New York Tribune* correspondent Adams S. Hill in October 1862. Major General J. E. B. Stuart had just taken his cavalry safely around Major General George B. McClellan's army for the second time, an embarrassment to both McClellan and Lincoln.

7   If I had had my way, this war would never have been commenced; If I had been allowed my way this war would have ended before this, but we find it still continues; and we must believe that He permits it for some wise purpose of his own, mysterious and unknown to us; and though with our limited understandings we may not be able to comprehend it, yet we cannot but believe, that he who made the world still governs it.
    —letter to Eliza Gurney, October 26, 1862.

8   To be told, after more than five weeks' total inaction of the army, and during which period we have sent to the army every fresh horse we possibly could, amounting in

the whole to 7918, that the cavalry horses were too much fatigued to move, presents a cheerless, almost hopeless, prospect for the future, and it may have forced something of impatience in my despatch. If not recruited and rested then, when could they ever be?
    —telegram to Major General George B. McClellan, October 27, 1862.

It doesn't seem worth while to secure divorces and then marry the Army and McClellan to others, for they won't get along any better than they do now, and there'll only be a new set of heartaches started. I think we'd better wait; perhaps a real fighting general will come along some of these days, and then we'll all be happy. If you go to mixing in a mixup, you only make the muddle worse.   **1**
    —quoted by Colonel Alexander K. McClure in *Lincoln's Yarns and Stories*, 1904.

★ This decision, to allow McClellan to continue to command the Army of the Potomac, was soon reversed.

I said I would remove him if he let Lee's army get away from him, and I must do so.   **2**
He has got the "slows," Mr. Blair.
    —letter to Brigadier General Francis P. Blair, November 7, 1862.

★ Lincoln was referring to Major General George B. McClellan and his failure to pursue General Robert E. Lee after the battle of Antietam (Sharpsburg). On this same day, McClellan received orders relieving him of his command of the Army of the Potomac.

The President, Commander-in-Chief of the Army and Navy, desires and enjoins the   **3**
orderly observance of the Sabbath by the officers and men in the military and naval service. The importance for man and beast of the prescribed weekly rest, the sacred rights of Christian soldiers and sailors, a becoming deference to the best sentiment of a Christian people, and a due regard for the Divine will, demand that Sunday labor in the Army and Navy be reduced to the measure of strict necessity.
    —Order for Sabbath Observance, November 15, 1862.

I certainly know that if the war fails the administration fails, and that I will be blamed   **4**
for it, whether I deserve it or not. And I ought to be blamed if I could do better. You think I could do better; therefore you blame me already. I think I could not do better; therefore I blame you for blaming me.
    —telegram to Brigadier General Carl Schurz, November 24, 1862.

★ Schurz later made many campaign speeches for Lincoln.

I wish to disparage no one certainly not those who sympathize with me; but I must   **5**
say I need success more than I need sympathy, and that I have not seen the so much greater evidence of getting success from my sympathizers than from those who are denounced as the contrary.
    —telegram to Brigadier General Carl Schurz, November 24, 1862.

Is it true, then, that colored people can displace any more white labor, by being free,   **6**
than by remaining slaves? If they stay in their old places, they jostle no white laborers; if they leave their old places, they leave them open to white laborers. Logically, there is neither more nor less of it.
    —second annual message to Congress, December 1, 1862.

1   In giving freedom to the slave, we assure freedom to the free—honorable alike in what we give and what we preserve. We shall nobly save, or meanly lose, the last, best hope of earth.
     —second annual message to Congress, December 1, 1862.

2   The dogmas of the quiet past, are inadequate to the stormy present. The occasion is piled high with difficulty, and we must rise with the occasion. As our case is new, so we must think anew, and act anew. We must disenthrall ourselves, and then we shall save our country.
     —second annual message to Congress, December 1, 1862.

3   I cannot make it better known than it already is that I strongly favor colonization.
     —second annual message to Congress, December 1, 1862.

     ★ This referred to sending freed slaves to other countries.

4   Without slavery the rebellion could never have existed; without slavery it could not continue.
     —second annual message to Congress, December 1, 1862.

5   Fellow citizens, we cannot escape history. We of this Congress and this administration, will be remembered in spite of ourselves. No personal significance or insignificance can spare one or another of us. The fiery trial through which we pass will light us down in honor or dishonor to the last generation.
     —second annual message to Congress, December 1, 1862.

6   In times like the present, men should utter nothing for which they would not willingly be responsible through time and eternity.
     —second annual message to Congress, December 1, 1862.

7   It is easy to see that, under the sharp discipline of civil war, the nation is beginning a new life.
     —second annual message to Congress, December 1, 1862.

8   If there is a worse place than Hell, I am in it.
     —quoted by Randall Bedwell in *Brink of Destruction*, 1999.

     ★ Lincoln had just heard of the Union defeat at Fredericksburg on December 13, 1862.

9   N. W. Watkins, of Jackson, Mo., (who is half brother to Henry Clay), writes me that a colonel of ours has driven him from his home at Jackson. Will you please look into the case and restore the old man to his home if public interest will admit?
     —telegram to Major General Samuel R. Curtis, December 16, 1862.

10   I have just read your general's report of the battle of Fredericksburg. Although you were not successful, the attempt was not an error, nor the failure other than accident. The courage with which you, in an open field, maintained the contest against an intrenched foe, and the consummate skill and success with which you crossed and

recrossed the river in the face of the enemy, show that you possess all the qualities of a great army, which will yet give victory to the cause of the country and of popular government.

—message to the Army of the Potomac, December 22, 1862.

It is with deep regret that I learn of the death of your kind and brave father, and **1** especially that it is affecting your young heart beyond what is common in such cases. In this sad world of ours sorrow comes to all, and to the young it comes with bitterest agony because it takes them unawares. The older have learned ever to expect it. I am anxious to afford some alleviation of your present distress. Perfect relief is not possible, except with time. You cannot now realize that you will ever feel better. Is not this so? And yet it is a mistake. You are sure to be happy again. To know this, which is certainly true, will make you some less miserable now. I have had experience enough to know what I say, and you need only to believe it, to feel better at once. The memory of your dear father, instead of an agony, will yet be a sad, sweet feeling in your heart, of a purer and holier sort than you have known before.

—letter to Miss Fanny McCullough, December 23, 1862.

I told them in September, if they did not return to their allegiance, and cease murdering our soldiers, I would strike at this pillar of their strength [slavery]. And now **2** the promise shall be kept [with the Emancipation Proclamation], and not one word of it will I ever recall.

—quoted by Colonel Alexander K. McClure in *Lincoln's Yarns and Stories*, 1904.

★ This was said on December 31, 1862.

I would be very happy to oblige you, if my passes were respected. But the fact is, sir, **3** I have, within the last two years, given passes to two hundred and fifty thousand men to go to Richmond, and not one has got there yet.

—quoted in *The Annals of America*, vol. 9, 1968.

★ Lincoln was replying in 1863 to a man seeking a "safe conduct" to Richmond.

I never in my life felt more certain that I was doing right than I do in signing this **4** paper.

—quoted by John Hope Franklin in *The Emancipation Proclamation*, 1963.

★ He said this just before signing the Emancipation Proclamation on January 1, 1863.

And by virtue of the power, and for the purpose aforesaid, I do order and declare **5** that all persons held as slaves within said designated States, and parts of States, are, and henceforward shall be free; and that the Executive government of the United States, including the military and naval authorities thereof, will recognize and maintain the freedom of said persons.

—Emancipation Proclamation, January 1, 1863.

1   We are like whalers who have been on a long chase. We have at last got the harpoon into the monster, but we must look now how we steer, or with one flop of his tail he will send us all into eternity.
      —quoted by Henry J. Raymond in *The Life, Public Services, and State Papers of Abraham Lincoln*, 1865.

      ★ This was said after Lincoln announced his Emancipation Proclamation.

2   After the commencement of hostilities I struggled nearly a year and a half to get along without touching the "institution" [of slavery]; and when finally I conditionally determined to touch it, I gave a hundred days fair notice of my purpose, to all the States and people, within which time they could have turned it wholly aside, by simply again becoming good citizens of the United States. They chose to disregard it, and I made the peremptory [emancipation] proclamation on what appeared to me to be a military necessity. And being made, it must stand.
      —letter to Major General John A. McClernand, January 8, 1863.

3   Still, to use a coarse, but an expressive figure, broken eggs can not be mended. I have issued the emancipation proclamation, and I can not retract it.
      —letter to Major General John A. McClernand, January 8, 1863

4   As to any dread of my having a "purpose to enslave, or exterminate, the whites of the South," I can scarcely believe that such dread exists. It is too absurd. I believe you can be my personal witness that no man is less to be dreaded for undue severity, in any case.
      —letter to Major General John A. McClernand, January 8, 1863.

5   I have understood well that duty of self-preservation rests solely with the American people. But I have at the same time been aware that favor or disfavor of foreign nations might have a material influence in enlarging and prolonging the struggle with disloyal men in which the country is engaged.
      —letter to the workingmen of Manchester, England, January 19, 1863.

      ★ Lincoln was replying to their congratulations, sent December 31, 1862, concerning the Emancipation Proclamation.

6   I much fear that the spirit which you have aided to infuse into the army, of criticizing their commander and withholding confidence from him, will now turn upon you. I shall assist you as far as I can to put it down. Neither you, nor Napoleon if he were alive again, could get any good out of an army while such a spirit prevails in it.
      —letter to Brigadier General Joseph Hooker, January 26, 1863.

      ★ This letter was, despite these words, appointing Hooker to the command of the Army of the Potomac. Lincoln invited the ambitious Hooker to his office and handed him the letter.

7   You are ambitious, which, within reasonable bounds, does good rather than harm; but I think that during General Burnside's command of the army, you have taken counsel of your ambition, and thwarted him as much as you could, in which you

did a great wrong to the country and to a most meritorious and honorable brother officer.

> —letter to Brigadier General Joseph Hooker, appointing him to the command of the Army of the Potomac, January 26, 1863.

Beware of rashness, but with energy and sleepless vigilance go forward and give us 1 victories.

> —letter to Brigadier General Joseph Hooker, appointing him to the command of the Army of the Potomac, January 26, 1863.

Only those generals who gain success can set up dictators. What I ask of you is mili- 2 tary success, and I will risk the dictatorship.

> —letter to Brigadier General Joseph Hooker, appointing him to the command of the Army of the Potomac, January 26, 1863.

For [horses being stolen] I am sorry, for I can make brigadier generals but I can't 3 make horses.

> —quoted by Geoffrey C. Ward in *The Civil War: An Illustrated History*, 1990.

★ Lincoln was reacting to news that CS lieutenant John Singleton Mosby's troops on March 9, 1863, had captured Brigadier General Edwin H. Stoughton, two more officers, 30 privates, and 58 horses.

I am told you have at least thought of raising a negro military force. In my opinion 4 the country now needs no specific thing so much as some man of your ability and position to go to this work. When I speak of your position, I mean that of an eminent citizen of a slave State and himself a slaveholder. The colored population is the great available and yet unavailed of force for restoring the Union. The bare sight of fifty thousand armed and drilled black soldiers upon the banks of the Mississippi would end the rebellion at once; and who doubts that we can present that sight if we but take hold in earnest?

> —letter to Andrew Johnson, March 26, 1863.

★ Johnson was then the military governor of Tennessee and succeeded Lincoln as president.

We have been preserved, these many years, in peace and prosperity. We have grown 5 in numbers, wealth, and power as no other nation has ever grown; but we have forgotten God.

> —proclamation, March 30, 1863.

I am glad to see the accounts of your colored force at Jacksonville, Florida. I see the 6 enemy are driving at them fiercely, as is to be expected. It is important to the enemy that such a force shall not take shape and grow and thrive in the South, and in precisely the same proportion it is important to us that it shall. Hence the utmost caution and vigilance is necessary on our part. The enemy will make extra efforts to destroy them, and we should do the same to preserve and increase them.

> —message to Major General David Hunter, April 1, 1863.

★ Colored troops were part of Union forces that occupied Jacksonville from March 23 to March 31.

1   The hen is the wisest of all the animal creation, because she never cackles until *after* the egg is laid.
       —quoted by Geoffrey C. Ward in *The Civil War: An Illustrated History*, 1990.

     ★ The president was hesitant to join Union officers in predicting a victory before the battle of Chancellorsville, which took place in April 1863.

2   My God! My God! What will the country say?
       —quoted by Geoffrey C. Ward in *The Civil War: An Illustrated History*, 1990.

     ★ The president uttered this lament after the Union defeat at Chancellorsville on May 4, 1863.

3   I frequently make mistakes myself, in the many things I am compelled to do hastily.
       —letter to Major General William S. Rosecrans, May 20, 1863.

4   Let your military measures be strong enough to repel the invader and keep the peace, and not so strong as to unnecessarily harass and persecute the people.
       —message to Major General John M. Schofield, May 27, 1863.

5   The proportions of this rebellion were not for a long time understood. I saw that it involved the greatest difficulties, and would call forth all the powers of the whole country.
       —reply to members of the Presbyterian General Assembly, June 2, 1863.

6   See what a lot of land these fellows hold, of which Vicksburg is the key. . . . The war can never be brought to a close until that key is in our pocket.
       —quoted by Carl Sandburg in *Abraham Lincoln: The War Years*, 1939.

     ★ Lincoln was pointing out the area on a map to Rear Admiral David D. Porter, who would be at the surrender of Vicksburg.

7   In a word, I would not take any risk of being entangled upon the river, like an ox jumped half over a fence, and liable to be torn by dogs, front and rear, without a fair chance to gore one way or kick the other.
       —message to Brigadier General Joseph Hooker, June 5, 1863.

     ★ Hooker had wanted to cross the Rappahannock to threaten Richmond.

8   I think Lee's Army, and not Richmond, is your true objective point. . . . If he stays where he is, fret him, and fret him.
       —telegram to Brigadier General Joseph Hooker, June 10, 1863.

     ★ Lee had begun to move his troops north from Fredericksburg the previous week, and Hooker thought this would be an apt time to take Richmond.

9   Must I shoot a simpleminded soldier boy who deserts, while I must not touch a hair of a wily agitator who induces him to desert? I think that, in such a case, to silence the agitator and save the boy is not only constitutional but withal a great mercy.
       —letter to Erastus Corning and other Democrats of Albany, New York, June 12, 1863.

★ Lincoln's letter to Corning, a New York Democrat, was a response to resolutions passed on May 16, 1863, by the Albany Democratic Convention. These denounced Lincoln for allowing the arrest for treason of Clement Vallandigham, an Ohio congressman and lawyer who opposed the war.

The Rebellion thus begun soon ran into the present Civil War; and, in certain respects, **1** it began on very unequal terms between the parties. The insurgents had been preparing for it for more than thirty years, while the Government had taken no steps to resist them.
  —letter to Erastus Corning and other Democrats of Albany, New York,
  June 12, 1863.

If the head of Lee's army is at Martinsburg and the tail of it on the plank road between **2** Fredericksburg and Chancellorsville, the animal must be very slim somewhere. Could you not break him?
  —letter to Brigadier General Joseph Hooker, June 14, 1863.

★ Hooker, defeated at Chancellorsville the month before, was unable to break Lee's forces. He was relieved of his command on June 28.

I have very earnestly urged the slave-states to adopt emancipation; and it ought to **3** be, and is an object with me not to overthrow, or thwart what any of them may in good faith do, to that end.
  —letter to Major General John M. Schofield, June 23, 1863.

★ This letter particularly concerned Missouri.

We cannot help beating them, if we have the man. How much depends in military **4** matters on one master mind!
  —quoted in *Diary of Secretary of the Navy Gideon Welles*, 1911.

★ This comment came on June 26, 1863, two days before Lincoln relieved Brigadier General Joseph Hooker as commander of the Army of the Potomac.

"Drive the *invaders* from our soil." My God! Is that all? **5**
  —quoted by Carl Sandburg in *Abraham Lincoln: The War Years*, 1939.

★ The president had just read Major General George G. Meade's message thanking his troops for the Gettysburg victory and adding that he looked to the army for "greater efforts to drive from our soil every vestige of the presence of the invader."

We had them in our grasp. We had only to stretch forth our hands and they were **6** ours. And nothing I could say or do could make the army move.
  —edited by Tyler Dennett in *Lincoln and the Civil War in the Diaries and Letters
  of John Hay*, 1939.

★ Hay was Lincoln's secretary. This comment to him on July 14, 1863, referred to General Robert E. Lee's escape from Union forces in the aftermath of the battle of Gettysburg.

1   Our army held the war in the hollow of their hand, and they would not close it. We had gone through all the labor of tilling and planting an enormous crop, and when it was ripe we did not harvest it.
    —edited by Tyler Dennett in *Lincoln and the Civil War in the Diaries and Letters of John Hay*, 1939.

    ★ Hay was Lincoln's secretary. This comment to him on July 19, 1863, referred to General Robert E. Lee's escape from Union forces in the aftermath of the battle of Gettysburg.

2   I am profoundly grateful down to the bottom of my boots for what [General George Meade] did at Gettysburg, but I think that if I had been General Meade I would have fought another battle.
    —quoted by Colonel Alexander K. McClure in *Lincoln's Yarns and Stories*, 1904.

    ★ Lincoln greatly regretted that General Lee's troops were allowed to retreat peacefully after Gettysburg without further engagements.

3   I was deeply mortified by the escape of Lee across the Potomac, because the substantial destruction of his army would have ended the war.
    —letter to Oliver O. Howard, July 21, 1863.

    ★ He was referring to the Confederate retreat after the battle of Gettysburg.

4   The government of the United States will give the same protection to all its soldiers, and if the enemy shall sell or enslave anyone because of his color, the offense shall be punished by retaliation upon the enemy's prisoners in our possession. It is therefore ordered that for every soldier of the United States killed in violation of the laws of war, a rebel soldier shall be executed; and for every one enslaved by the enemy or sold into slavery, a rebel soldier shall be placed at hard labor on the public works and continued at such labor until the other shall be released and receive the treatment due to a prisoner of war.
    —Order of Retaliation, July 30, 1863.

5   Those who shall have tasted actual freedom I believe can never be slaves, or quasi slaves again.
    —letter to Stephen A. Hurlburt, July 31, 1863.

6   With us every soldier is a man of character, and must be treated with more consideration than is customary in Europe.
    —letter to Count A. de Gasparin, August 4, 1863.

    ★ Agénor Étienne de Gasparin was a French politician who was living in Switzerland as a result of his dislike for Louis Napoléon.

7   Be not alarmed if you shall learn that we shall have resorted to a draft for part of this [manpower]. It seems strange even to me, but it is true, that the government is now pressed to this course by a popular demand.
    —letter to Count A. de Gasparin, August 4, 1863.

8   You are quite right as to the importance to us, for its bearing upon Europe, that we should achieve military successes, and the same is true for us at home as well as

abroad. Yet it seems unreasonable that a series of successes, extending through half a year, and clearing more than 100,000 square miles of country, should help us so little, while a single half-defeat should hurt us so much. But let us be patient.
—letter to Count A. de Gasparin, August 4, 1863.

My purpose is to be, in my action, just and constitutional; and yet practical, in performing the important duty, with which I am charged, of maintaining the unity, and the free principles of our common country. **1**
—letter to New York governor Horatio Seymour, August 7, 1863.

We are contending with an enemy who, as I understand, drives every able-bodied man he can reach into his ranks, very much as a butcher drives bullocks into a slaughter-pen. No time is wasted, no argument is used. This produces an army which will soon turn upon our now victorious soldiers already in the field, if they shall not be sustained by recruits. **2**
—letter to New York governor Horatio Seymour, August 7, 1863.

★ Lincoln was explaining the need for the draft, which Seymour wished to suspend until the Supreme Court ruled on its legality.

We never should, and I am sure, never shall be niggard of gratitude and benefaction to the soldiers who have endured toil, privations and wounds, that the nation may live. **3**
—letter to Mrs. Hunter and others, August 10, 1863.

The Father of Waters again goes unvexed to the sea. **4**
—letter to James C. Conkling, August 26, 1863.

★ Conkling was an Illinois political associate of Lincoln's. Lincoln was referring to the fall of Vicksburg on July 4, 1863, freeing passage along the Mississippi. Lincoln asked that this letter be read at a Republican rally on September 3, 1863, in Springfield, Illinois.

Peace does not appear so distant as it did. I hope it will come soon, and come to stay; and so come as to be worth the keeping in all future time. It will then have been proved that among freemen there can be no successful appeal from the ballot to the bullet; and that they who take such appeal are sure to lose their case and pay the cost. **5**
—letter to James C. Conkling, August 26, 1863.

I think the Constitution invests its commander in chief with the law of war in time of war. **6**
—letter to James C. Conkling, August 26, 1863.

Negroes, like other people, act upon motives. Why should they do anything for us, if we will do nothing for them? If they stake their lives for us, they must be prompted by the strongest motive—even the promise of freedom. And the promise must be kept. **7**
—letter to James C. Conkling, August 26, 1863.

You say you will not fight to free negroes. Some of them seem willing to fight for you; but, no matter. Fight you, then, exclusively to save the Union. I issued the [emancipation] proclamation on purpose to aid you in saving the Union. Whenever you shall **8**

have conquered all resistance to the Union, if I shall urge you to continue fighting, it will be an apt time, then, for you to declare you will not fight to free negroes.
—letter to James C. Conkling, August 26, 1863.

1   You dislike the emancipation proclamation; and, perhaps, would have it retracted. . . . But the proclamation, as law, either is valid, or is not valid. If it is not valid, it needs no retraction. If it valid, it can not be retracted, any more than the dead can be brought to life.
—letter to James C. Conkling, August 26, 1863.

2   Let the reconstruction be the work of such men only as can be trusted for the Union. Exclude all others, and trust that your [Tennessee] government so organized will be recognized here as being the one of republican form to be guaranteed to the state, and to be protected against invasion and domestic violence. It is something on the question of time to remember that it cannot be known who is next to occupy the position I now hold, nor what he will do.
—letter to Andrew Johnson, September 11, 1863.

★ Johnson was the military governor of Union-occupied Tennessee and, ironically, "the next to occupy the position."

3   I do therefore invite my fellow citizens in every part of the United States, and also those who are at sea and those who are sojourning in foreign lands, to set apart and observe the last Thursday on November next, as a day of Thanksgiving and Praise to our beneficent Father who dwelleth in the Heavens.
—proclamation of Thanksgiving, October 3, 1863.

★ This was the first time this date was set as a national Thanksgiving holiday.

4   We are in civil war. In such cases there always is a main question; but in this case that question is a perplexing compound—Union and Slavery. It thus becomes a question not of two sides merely, but of at least four sides, even among those who are for the Union, saying nothing of those who are against it.
—letter to Charles Drake and others, October 5, 1863.

5   I'll be hanged if I could think of anything else than an old woman trying to shoo her geese across the creek.
—quoted by Shelby Foote in *The Civil War*, vol. 2, 1958.

★ This was Lincoln's description of Major General George G. Meade's attitude in letting General Robert E. Lee escape across the Potomac River after the battle of Gettysburg. The President made this comment to Meade on October 23, 1863.

6   [Rosecrans] is confused and stunned, like a duck hit on the head, ever since Chickamauga.
—quoted by Shelby Foote in *The Civil War*, vol. 2, 1958.

★ Lincoln said this to John Hay, his young secretary, on October 24, 1863, five days after relieving General William Rosecrans of his command.

Nevertheless, amid the greatest difficulties of my Administration, when I could not   **1**
see any other resort, I would place my whole reliance on God, knowing that all
would go well, and that He would decide for the right.
  —remarks to the Baltimore Presbyterian Synod, October 24, 1863.

I have endured a great deal of ridicule without much malice, and I have received a   **2**
great deal of kindness not quite free from ridicule. I am used to it.
  —letter to James H. Hackett, November 2, 1863.

★ Hackett was a prominent actor.

Samuel Wellers, private in Company B, Forty-ninth Pennsylvania Volunteers, writes   **3**
that he is to be shot for desertion on the 6th instant. His own story is rather a bad
one, and yet he tells it so frankly, that I am somewhat interested in him. Has he been
a good soldier except the desertion? About how old is he?
  —telegram to Major General George G. Meade, November 3, 1863.

★ Lincoln suspended the execution two days later.

Fourscore and seven years ago our fathers brought forth, upon this continent, a new   **4**
nation, conceived in liberty and dedicated to the proposition that all men are created
equal.
  Now we are engaged in a great civil war, testing whether that nation, or any nation
so conceived and so dedicated, can long endure. We are met on a great battlefield of
that war. We have come to dedicate a portion of that field, as a final resting place for
those who here gave their lives that a nation might live. It is altogether fitting and
proper that we should do this.
  But, in a larger sense, we cannot dedicate—we cannot consecrate—we cannot
hallow—this ground. The brave men, living and dead, who struggled here have consecrated it far above our power to add or detract. The world will little note, nor long
remember, what we say here, but it can never forget what they did here. It is rather
for us to be here dedicated to the great task remaining before us; that from these
honored dead we take increased devotion to that cause for which they gave the last
full measure of devotion; that we here highly resolve that these dead shall not have
died in vain; that this nation, under God, shall have a new birth of freedom; and that
government of the people, by the people, for the people, shall not perish from the
earth.
  —speech at the Dedication of the National Cemetery at Gettysburg, Pennsylvania
  (the Gettysburg Address), November 19, 1863.

Lamon, that speech won't scour. It is a flat failure and the people are disappointed.   **5**
  —quoted by Shelby Foote in *The Civil War*, vol. 2, 1958.

★ Sitting down after making his short Gettysburg Address, Lincoln made the comment
to Ward Hill Lamon, who had introduced him. "Scour" meant to clean by polishing or
rubbing, and Lincoln's image was of a plow that did not scour while turning up wet soil.

I am proud to be the countryman of the men who assailed those heights.   **6**
  —quoted by Confederate president Jefferson Davis in *The Rise and Fall of the
  Confederate Government*, 1881.

★ Lincoln was praising the brave Confederate attackers as he visited the hills defended by Union troops in Gettysburg.

1   Honor to the Soldier, and Sailor everywhere, who bravely bears his country's cause. Honor also to the citizen who cares for his brother in the field, and serves, as he best can, the same cause—honor to him, only less than to him, who braves, for the common good, the storms of heaven and the storms of battle.
    —letter to New York mayor George Opdyke and others, December 2, 1863.

2   Of those who were slaves at the beginning of the rebellion, full one hundred thousand are now in the United States military service, about one-half of which number actually bear arms in the ranks; thus giving the double advantage of taking so much labor from the insurgent cause, and supplying the places which otherwise must be filled with so many white men. So far as tested, it is difficult to say they are not as good soldiers as any.
    —third annual message to Congress, December 8, 1863.

3   In the midst of other cares, however important, we must not lose sight of the fact that the war power is still our main reliance. To that power alone can we look, yet for a time, to give confidence to the people in the contested regions, that the insurgent power will not again overrun them. Until that confidence shall be established, little can be done anywhere for what is called reconstruction.
    —third annual message to Congress, December 8, 1863.

4   According to our political system, as a matter of civil administration, the general government had no lawful power to effect emancipation in any state, and for a long time it had been hoped that the rebellion could be suppressed without resorting to it as a military measure. . . . It came, and, as was anticipated, it was followed by dark and doubtful days.
    —third annual message to Congress, December 8, 1863.

5   I may add at this point, that while I remain in my present position I shall not attempt to retract or modify the Emancipation Proclamation; nor shall I return to slavery any person who is free by the terms of that proclamation or by any of the acts of Congress.
    —third annual message to Congress, December 8, 1863.

6   I, _____, do solemnly swear, in presence of Almighty God, that I will henceforth faithfully support, protect, and defend the Constitution of the United States and the Union of the states thereunder; and that I will in like manner abide by and faithfully support all acts of Congress passed during the existing rebellion with reference to slaves, so long and so far as not repealed, modified, or held void by Congress or by decision of the Supreme Court; and that I will in like manner abide by and faithfully support all proclamations of the President made during the existing rebellion having reference to slaves, so long and so far as not modified or declared void by decisions of the Supreme Court. So help me God.
    —third annual message to Congress, December 8, 1863.

★ Lincoln's proclamation of amnesty and reconstruction to Congress presented this oath of allegiance required for rebellious Southerners to receive a full pardon.

I understand you have under sentence of death, a tall old man, by the name of Henry **1** F. Luckett. I personally know him, and did not think him a bad man. Please do not let him be executed unless upon further order from me, and in the meantime send me a transcript of the record.
   —telegram to Major General Stephen A. Hurlbut, December 17, 1863.

On principle I dislike an oath which requires a man to swear he *has* not done wrong. **2** It rejects the Christian principle of forgiveness on terms of repentance. I think it is enough if the man does no wrong *hereafter*.
   —message to Secretary of War Edwin M. Stanton, February 5, 1864.

I dislike making changes in office so long as they can be avoided. It multiplies my **3** embarrassments immensely.
   —letter to W. Jayne, February 26, 1864.

The President directs that the sentences of all deserters who have been condemned **4** by court-martial to death, and that have not been otherwise acted upon by him, be mitigated to imprisonment during the war at the Dry Tortugas, Florida, where they will be sent under suitable guards by orders from army commanders.
   —General Order No. 76, February 26, 1864.

Mr. General, there are already too many weeping widows in the United States. For **5** God's sake, don't ask me to add to the number, for I won't do it.
   —quoted by Colonel Alexander K. McClure in *Lincoln's Yarns and Stories*, 1904.

★ He was responding to a complaint that he would not sign warrants for the execution of deserters.

I neither ask nor desire to know anything of your plans. Take the responsibility and **6** act, and call on me for assistance.
   —quoted by Lieutenant Colonel G. F. R. Henderson in *Stonewall Jackson and the American Civil War*, vol. 1, 1898.

★ This was said when Lincoln appointed Grant to the command of all the Union armies on March 12, 1864.

I feel better, for now I'm like the man who was blown up in a steamboat explosion **7** and said, on coming down, "It makes no difference to me—I'm only a passenger."
   —quoted by Carl Sandburg in *Abraham Lincoln: The War Years*, 1939.

★ Lieutenant General Ulysses S. Grant had recently been given overall command of the Union armies.

Allow me to suggest that if you wish to remain in the military service, it is very dan- **8** gerous for you to get temporarily out of it; because, with a major-general once out, it is next to impossible for even the President to get him in again.
   —letter to Major General Carl Schurz, March 13, 1864.

1   I congratulate you on having fixed your name in history as the first free-state governor of Louisiana. Now, you are about to have a convention, which among other things will probably define the elective franchise. I barely suggest for your private consideration, whether some of the colored people may not be let in—as, for instance, the very intelligent, and especially those who have fought gallantly in our ranks. They would probably help, in some trying time to come, to keep the jewel of liberty within the family of freedom. But this is only a suggestion,—not to the public, but to you alone.
   —letter to Governor Michael Hahn, March 13, 1864.

2   This extraordinary war in which we are engaged falls heavily upon all classes of people but the most heavily upon the soldier. For it has been said, "All that a man hath will he give for his life;" and while all contribute of their substance, the soldier puts his life at stake, and often yields it up in his country's cause. The highest merit, then, is due to the soldier.
   —speech at a fair in the Patent Office for the relief of soldiers, March 16, 1864.

3   In this extraordinary war, extraordinary developments have manifested themselves, such as have not been seen in former wars; and among these manifestations nothing has been more remarkable than these fairs for the relief of suffering soldiers and their families. And the chief agents of these fairs are the women of America.
   —speech at a fair in the Patent Office for the relief of soldiers, March 16, 1864.

4   I am not accustomed to the use of language of eulogy: I have never studied the art of paying compliments to women; but I must say, that if all that has been said by orators and poets since the creation of the world in praise of women were applied to the women of America, it would not do them justice for their conduct during this war. I will close by saying, God bless the women of America.
   —speech at a fair in the Patent Office for the relief of soldiers, March 16, 1864.

5   I never knew a man who wished himself to be a slave. Consider if you know any good thing that no man desires for himself.
   —inscription in an album at a Sanitary Commission Fair, March 18, 1864.

   ★ A Sanitary Commission Fair, or Sanitary Fair, was a regular event held in the North during the war to raise money for the Sanitary Commission, a private relief organization for the Union army. Lincoln inscribed this book at a fair held in Washington, D.C.

6   While we must, by all available means, prevent the overthrow of the government, we should avoid planting and cultivating too many thorns in the bosom of society.
   —letter to Secretary of War Edwin M. Stanton, March 18, 1864.

7   Was it possible to lose the nation, and yet preserve the constitution? By general law life *and* limb must be protected; yet often a limb must be amputated to save a life; but a life is never wisely given to save a limb. I felt that measures, otherwise unconstitutional, might become lawful, by becoming indispensable to the preservation of the constitution, through the preservation of the nation
   —letter to Albert G. Hodges, editor of the *Frankfort* (Kentucky) *Commonwealth*, April 4, 1864.

I am naturally anti-slavery. If slavery is not wrong, nothing is wrong.   **1**
   —letter to Albert G. Hodges, editor of the *Frankfort* (Kentucky) *Commonwealth,*
   April 4, 1864.

I claim not to have controlled events, but confess plainly that events have controlled   **2**
me. Now, at the end of three years struggle the nation's condition is not what either
party, or any man devised, or expected. God alone can claim it.
   —letter to Albert G. Hodges, editor of the *Frankfort* (Kentucky) *Commonwealth,*
   April 4, 1864.

If God now wills the removal of a great wrong, and wills also that we of the North as   **3**
well as you of the South, shall pay fairly for our complicity in that wrong, impartial
history will find therein new cause to attest and revere the justice and goodness of
God.
   —letter to Albert G. Hodges, editor of the *Frankfort* (Kentucky) *Commonwealth,*
   April 4, 1864.

★ Slavery was the "great wrong."

The petition of persons under eighteen, praying that I would free all slave children,   **4**
and the heading of which petition it appears you wrote, was handed me a few days
since by Senator [Charles] Sumner. Please tell these little people I am very glad their
young hearts are so full of just and generous sympathy, and that, while I have not the
power to grant all they ask, I trust they will remember that God has, and that, as it
seems, he wills to do it.
   —letter to Mrs. Horace Mann, April 5, 1864.

To take the life of one of their prisoners on the assumption that they murder ours,   **5**
when it is short of certainty that they do murder ours, might be too serious, too cruel
a mistake.
   —quoted by Nathaniel W. Stephenson in *Lincoln: An Account of His Personal
   Life, Especially of Its Springs of Action as Revealed and Deepened by the Ordeal
   of War,* 1922.

★ He was reflecting on revenge for the Fort Pillow massacre on April 12, 1864, when
Union prisoners, many of them black, were reportedly shot.

When the war began, three years ago, neither party, nor any man, expected it would   **6**
last till now. Each looked for the end, in some way, long ere today. Neither did any
anticipate that domestic slavery would be much affected by the war. But here we are;
the war has not ended, and slavery has been much affected—how much needs not
now to be recounted. So true is it that man proposes, and God disposes.
   —remarks at the opening of the Sanitary Commission Fair in Baltimore,
   Maryland, April 18, 1864.

The world has never had a good definition of the word liberty, and the American   **7**
people, just now, are much in want of one. We all declare for liberty; but in using the
same *word* we do not all mean the same *thing*. With some the word liberty may
mean for each man to do as he pleases with himself, and the product of his labor;

while with others the same word may mean for some men to do as the please with other men, and the product of other men's labor.

—remarks at the opening of the Sanitary Commission Fair in Baltimore, Maryland, April 18, 1864, quoted by Brooks D. Simpson in *Abraham Lincoln on Slavery, Freedom, and Union*, 1998.

1   The shepherd drives the wolf from the sheep's throat, for which the sheep thanks the shepherd as a *liberator*, while the wolf denounces him for the same act as the destroyer of liberty, especially as the sheep was a black one. Plainly the sheep and the wolf are not agreed upon a definition of the word liberty; and precisely the same difference prevails today among us human creatures, even in the North, and all professing to love liberty. Hence we behold the processes by which thousands are daily passing from under the yoke of bondage, hailed by some as the advance of liberty, and bewailed by others as the destruction of all liberty.

—remarks at the opening of the Sanitary Commission Fair in Baltimore, Maryland, April 18, 1864.

2   Tell Tad the goats and father are very well—especially the goats.

—telegram to his wife, Mary, April 28, 1864.

★ Tad was Lincoln's nickname for his youngest son, Thomas, who was almost eleven when this was written.

3   You are vigilant and self-reliant; and, pleased with this, I wish not to obtrude any constraints or restraints upon you. While I am very anxious that any great disaster or capture of our men in great numbers shall be avoided, I know these points are less likely to escape your attention than they would be mine.

—letter to General Ulysses S. Grant, April 30, 1864.

4   There is enough yet before us requiring all loyal men and patriots to perform their share of the labor and follow the example of the modest General [Grant] at the head of our armies, and sink all personal consideration for the sake of the country. I commend you to keep yourselves in the same tranquil mood that is characteristic of that brave and loyal man.

—response to a serenade, May 9, 1864.

5   Nobly sustained, as the Government has been, by all the churches, I would utter nothing which might in the least appear invidious against any. Yet without this, it may fairly be said, that the Methodist Episcopal Church, not less devoted than the best, is by its greatest numbers the most important of all. It is no fault in others that the Methodist Church sends more soldiers to the field, more nurses to the hospitals, and more prayers to Heaven than any other.

—edited by Arthur Brooks Lapsley in *The Writings of Abraham Lincoln*, vol. 7, 1906.

★ This was written on May 14, 1864, in response to a Methodist delegation.

When my wife had her first baby, the doctor from time to time reported to me that 1
everything was going on as well as could be expected under the circumstances. That
satisfied me *he* was doing his best, but still I felt anxious to hear the first squall. It
came at last, and I felt mightily relieved. I feel very much so about our army operations at this moment.
    —quoted by James R. Gilmore in a letter to Sydney Howard Gay, May 18, 1864.

★ Gilmore was reporting Lincoln's reaction on May 16 after the battle of the
Wilderness on May 5–7. Gilmore was an intermediary between the *New York Tribune*
and the White House, and Gay was managing editor of the newspaper.

Mr. J. C. Swift wishes a pass from me to follow your army to pick up rags and cast- 2
off clothing. I will give it to him if you say so, otherwise not.
    —telegram to Major General George G. Meade, May 25, 1864.

★ Lincoln was the type of president to deal with a ragpicker's request.

To read in the Bible, as the word of God himself, that "In the sweat of *thy* face shalt 3
thou eat bread," and to preach therefrom that, "In the sweat of *other mans* faces
shalt thou eat bread," to my mind can scarcely be reconciled with honest sincerity.
    —letter to George Ide and others, May 30, 1864.

★ This was a response to the preamble and resolutions of the American Baptist Home
Missionary Society.

Complaint is made to me that in the vicinity of Henderson [Kentucky], our militia is 4
seizing negroes and carrying them off without their own consent, and according to
no rules whatever, except those of absolute violence. I wish you would look into this
and inform me, and see that the making soldiers of negroes is done according to the
rules you are acting upon, so that unnecessary provocation and irritation be avoided.
    —telegram to Brigadier General Lorenzo Thomas, June 13, 1864.

We accepted this war for an object, a worthy object, and the war will end when that 5
object is attained. Under God, I hope it never will until that time.
    —speech at the Sanitary Fair in Philadelphia, June 16, 1864.

War at the best is terrible, and this of ours in its magnitude and duration is one of the 6
most terrible the world has ever known. It has deranged business totally in many
places, and perhaps in all. It has destroyed property, destroyed life, and ruined
homes. It has produced a national debt and a degree of taxation unprecedented in
the history of this country. It has caused mourning among us until the heavens may
almost be said to be hung in black. And yet it continues.
    —speech at the Sanitary Fair in Philadelphia, June 16, 1864.

1   From the fair and tender hand of women is much, very much, done for the soldier, continually reminding him of the care and thought for him at home. The knowledge that he is not forgotten is grateful to his heart.
—speech at the Sanitary Fair in Philadelphia, June 16, 1864.

2   It is a pertinent question, When is this war to end? I do not wish to name the day when it will end, lest the end should not come at the given time. We accepted this war, and did not begin it. We accepted it for an object, and when that object is accomplished the war will end, and I hope to God that it will never end until that object is accomplished. We are going through with our task, so far as I am concerned, if it takes us three years longer.
—speech at the Sanitary Fair in Philadelphia, June 16, 1864.

★ It took less than ten months.

3   When we wanted every able-bodied man who could be spared to go to the front, and my opposers kept objecting to the negroes, I used to tell them that at such times it was just as well to be a little color-blind.
—quoted by Horace Porter in *Campaigning with Grant*, 1897.

★ Lincoln was reviewing black troops who had fought well at Petersburg in 1864.

4   I don't expect I can do any good, and in fact I'm afraid I may do harm, but I'll just put myself under your orders and if you find me doing anything wrong just send me right away.
—quoted by Shelby Foote in *The Civil War*, vol. 3, 1958.

★ Lincoln was paying a surprise visit to General Ulysses S. Grant's headquarters at City Point, near Petersburg, Virginia, on June 21, 1864.

5   You mean Confederates!
—quoted by Colonel Alexander K. McClure in *Lincoln's Yarns and Stories*, 1904.

★ Lincoln was cutting short Dr. Jerome Walker who, while showing him through the hospital at City Point near Petersburg, Virginia, stopped before a ward and said, "Mr. President, you won't want to go in there; they are only rebels." Lincoln went in to say kind words to the wounded prisoners.

6   Dr. Worster wishes to visit you with a view of getting your permission to introduce into the army "Harmon's Scandal Socks." Shall I give him a pass for that object?
—telegram to General Ulysses S. Grant, June 29, 1864.

7   Let us be vigilant, but keep cool. I hope neither Baltimore or Washington will be sacked.
—telegram to Thomas Swan and others, July 10, 1864.

★ Rumors were about that Washington was to be invaded by Confederate troops.

8   In your dispatch of yesterday to General Sherman, I find the following, to wit: "I shall make a desperate effort to get a position here, which will hold the enemy without the necessity of so many men." Pressed as we are by lapse of time I am glad to

hear you say this; and yet I do hope you may find a way that the effort shall not be desperate in the sense of great loss of life.
    —telegram to General Ulysses S. Grant, July 17, 1864.

I have seen your dispatches objecting to agents of Northern States opening recruit- 1
ing stations near your camps. An act of Congress authorizes this, giving the appointment of agents to the States, and not to the Executive Government. . . . Many of the
States were very anxious for it, and I hoped that, with their State bounties, and active
exertions, they would get out substantial additions to our colored forces, which
unlike white recruits, help us where they come from, as well as where they go to. . . .
May I ask, therefore, that you will give your hearty co-operation.
    —telegram to Major General William T. Sherman, July 18, 1864.

Any proposition which embraces the restoration of peace, the integrity of the whole 2
Union, and the abandonment of slavery, and which comes by and with an authority
that can control the armies now at War against the United States, will be received
and considered by the Executive Government of the United States, and will be met
by liberal terms on other substantial and collateral points, and the bearer or bearers
thereof shall have safe-conduct both ways.
    —open letter "To Whom It May Concern," July 18, 1864.

The plaid you sent me is just now placed in my hands. I thank you for that pretty and 3
useful present, but still more for those good wishes for myself and our country,
which prompted you to present it.
    —letter to Mrs. Anne Williamson, July 29, 1864.

Hold on with a bulldog grip, and chew and choke as much as possible.   4
    —telegram to General Ulysses S. Grant, August 7, 1864.

★ Grant's troops were pressuring those of General Lee along the James River.

The Secretary of War and I concur that you had better confer with General Lee, and 5
stipulate for a mutual discontinuance of house-burning and other destruction of private property.
    —telegram to General Ulysses S. Grant, August 14, 1864.

I do not think it is personal vanity or ambition, though I am not free from these infir- 6
mities, but I cannot but feel that the weal or woe of this great nation will be decided
in November. There is no program offered by any wing of the Democratic party but
that must result in the permanent destruction of the Union.
    —interview with John T. Mills, August 15?, 1864.

There are now in the service of the United States nearly one hundred and fifty thou- 7
sand able-bodied colored men, most of them under arms, defending and acquiring
Union territory. The Democratic [Party] strategy demands that these forces be disbanded, and that the masters be conciliated by restoring them to slavery. The black
men who now assist Union prisoners to escape are to be converted into our enemies,

in the vain hope of gaining the good-will of their masters. We shall have to fight two nations instead of one.
    —interview with John T. Mills, August 15?, 1864.

1   There have been men base enough to propose to me to return to slavery the black warriors of Port Hudson [Louisiana] and Olustee [Florida], and thus win the respect of the masters they fought. Should I do so, I should deserve to be damned in time and eternity. Come what will, I will keep my faith with friend and foe.
    —interview with John T. Mills, August 15?, 1864.

    ★ He refers to Union black soldiers who took part in those battles (May 27, 1863, and February 20, 1864, respectively).

2   My enemies pretend I am now carrying on this war for the sole purpose of abolition. So long as I am President, it shall be carried on for the sole purpose of restoring the Union.
    —interview with John T. Mills, August 15?, 1864.

3   Let my enemies prove to the country that the destruction of slavery is not necessary to a restoration of the Union. I will abide the issue.
    —interview with John T. Mills, August 15?, 1864.

4   I cannot fly from my thoughts—my solicitude for this great country follows me wherever I go.
    —interview with John T. Mills, August 15?, 1864.

5   We have, as all will agree, a free Government, where every man has a right to be equal with every other man. In this great struggle, this form of Government and every form of human right is endangered if our enemies succeed.
    —speech to the 164th Ohio Regiment, August 18, 1864.

6   In this great struggle, this form of government and every form of human right is endangered if our enemies succeed. There is more involved in this contest than is realized by every one. There is involved in this struggle, the question whether your children and my children shall enjoy the privileges we have enjoyed. I say this, in order to impress upon you, if you are not already so impressed, that no small matter should divert us from our great purpose.
    —speech to the 164th Ohio Regiment, August 18, 1864.

7   When you return to your homes, rise up to the height of a generation of men worthy of a free government, and we will carry out the great work we have commenced.
    —speech to the 164th Ohio Regiment, August 18, 1864.

8   I almost always feel inclined, when I happen to say anything to soldiers, to impress upon them in a few brief remarks the importance of success in this contest. It is not merely for to-day, but for all time to come that we should perpetuate for our children's children this great and free government, which we have enjoyed all our lives.
    —speech to the 166th Ohio Regiment, August 22, 1864.

I happen, temporarily, to occupy this big White House. I am a living witness that any   1
one of your children may look to come here as my father's child has. It is in order that
each one of you may have, through this free government which we have enjoyed, an
open field, and a fair chance for your industry, enterprise, and intelligence; that you
may all have equal privileges in the race of life with all its desirable human aspirations—it is for this that the struggle should be maintained, that we may not lose our
birthrights—not only for one, but for two or three years, if necessary. The nation is
worth fighting for, to secure such an inestimable jewel.
   —speech to the 166th Ohio Regiment, August 22, 1864.

This morning, as for some time past, it seems exceedingly probable that this adminis-   2
tration will not be re-elected. Then it will be my duty to so co-operate with the President elect, as to save the Union between the election and the inauguration; as he will
have secured his election on such ground that he can not possibly save it afterwards.
   —blind memorandum to his cabinet members, August 23, 1864.

Again I admonish you not to be turned from your stern purpose of defending your   3
beloved country and its free institutions by any arguments urged by ambitious and
designing men, but stand fast to the Union and the old flag.
   —speech to the 148th Ohio Regiment, August 31, 1864.

Nowhere in the world is presented a government of so much liberty and equality. To   4
the humblest and poorest amongst us are held out the highest privileges and positions. The present moment finds me at the White House, yet there is as good a
chance for your children as there was for my father's.
   —speech to the 148th Ohio Regiment, August 31, 1864.

The marches, battles, sieges, and other military operations, that have signalized the   5
[Atlanta] campaign, must render it famous in the annals of war, and have entitled
those who have participated therein the applause and thanks of the nation.
   —letter to Major General William T. Sherman, September 3, 1864.

We hoped for a happy termination of this terrible war long before this; but God   6
knows Your people—the Friends—have had, and are having, a very great trial. On
principle, and faith, opposed to both war and oppression, they can only practically
oppose oppression by war. For those appealing to me on conscientious grounds, I
have done, and shall do, the best I could and can, in my own conscience, under my
oath to the law.
   —letter to Eliza P. Gurney, September 4, 1864.

★ She was a Quaker who had visited Lincoln with others of that religious group two
years before.

We hoped for a happy termination of this terrible war long before this, but God   7
knows best, and has ruled otherwise. . . . Surely He intends some great good to follow this mighty convulsion, which no mortal could make, and no mortal could stay.
   —letter to Eliza P. Gurney, September 4, 1864.

1   In regard to this Great Book, I have but to say, it is the best gift God has given to man. All the good the Savior gave to the world was communicated through this book.
    —speech in Baltimore, September 7, 1864.
    ★ He was responding to receiving the gift of a Bible from "loyal colored people."

2   Much is being said about peace; and no man desires peace more ardently than I. Still I am yet unprepared to give up the Union for a peace which, so achieved, could not be of much duration.
    —letter to Isaac Schermerhorn, September 12, 1864.

3   You have generously said to me, more than once, that whenever your resignation could be a relief to me, it was at my disposal. The time has come.
    —letter to Postmaster General Montgomery Blair, September 23, 1864.
    ★ This was done to keep the peace among cabinet members. Before and after the war, Blair supported the opposition Democratic Party.

4   I wish all men to be free. I wish the material prosperity of the already free which I feel sure the extinction of slavery would bring. I wish to see, in process of disappearing, that only thing which ever could bring this nation to civil war.
    —letter to Henry W. Hoffman, October 10, 1864.
    ★ Hoffman was chairman of the Maryland Unconditional Union Central Committee.

5   I, Abraham Lincoln, President of the United States, do hereby appoint and set apart the last Thursday in November next as a day which I desire to be observed by all my fellow-citizens, wherever they may be then, as a day of thanksgiving and praise to Almighty God, the beneficent Creator and Ruler of the Universe. And I do further recommend to my fellow-citizens aforesaid, that on that occasion they do reverently humble themselves in the dust, and from thence offer up penitent and fervent prayers and supplications to the great Disposer of events for a return of the inestimable blessings of peace, union, and harmony throughout the land which it has pleased him to assign as a dwelling-place for ourselves and for our posterity throughout all generations.
    —proclamation, October 20, 1864.
    ★ Lincoln had officially established Thanksgiving as a national day the previous year.

6   I do not suppose that [the delegates] have concluded to decide that I am either the greatest or best man in America, but rather they have concluded it is not best to swap horses while crossing the river, and have further concluded that I am not so poor a horse that they might not make a botch of it in trying to swap.
    —quoted by Shelby Foote in *The Civil War*, vol. 3, 1958.
    ★ This referred to his renomination in 1864 as the Republican candidate for president.

7   As to my re-election it matters not [to call up more men]. We must have the men. If I go down, I intend to go, like the Cumberland, with my colors flying.
    —quoted by Colonel Alexander K. McClure in *Lincoln's Yarns and Stories*, 1904.
    ★ The USS *Cumberland* had been sunk by the CSS *Virginia* (formerly USS *Merrimack*) on March 8, 1862, at the battle of Hampton Roads.

I have no reason to believe that Grant prefers my election to that of McClellan.   **1**
   —quoted by Colonel Alexander K. McClure in *Lincoln's Yarns and Stories*, 1904.
★ This was said to McClure before the 1864 election.

I feel certain that, if I live, I am going to be re-elected. Whether I deserve to be or   **2**
not, it is not for me to say; but on the score of even remunerative chances of specu-
lative service, I am now inspired with the hope that our disturbed country further
requires the valuable services of your humble servant.
   —quoted by Colonel Alexander K. McClure in *Lincoln's Yarns and Stories*, 1904.
★ This was said before the 1864 election.

I have seen enough to satisfy me that I am a failure, not only in the opinion of the   **3**
people in rebellion, but of many distinguished politicians of my own party. But time
will show whether I am right or they are right and I am content to abide its decision.
   —quoted by Colonel Alexander K. McClure in *Lincoln's Yarns and Stories*, 1904.
★ This was said before the 1864 election.

I have enough to look after without giving much of my time to the consideration of   **4**
the subject of who shall be my successor in office. The position is not an easy one;
and the occupant, whoever he may be, for the next four years, will have little leisure
to pluck a thorn or plant a rose in his own pathway.
   —quoted by Colonel Alexander K. McClure in *Lincoln's Yarns and Stories*, 1904.
★ This was his depressing thought before his second election.

I hope, however, that I may never have another four years of such anxiety, tribulation   **5**
and abuse. My only ambition is and has been to put down the rebellion and restore
peace, after which I want to resign my office, go abroad, take some rest, study foreign governments, see something of foreign life, and in my old age die in peace with
all of the good of God's creatures.
   —quoted by Colonel Alexander K. McClure in *Lincoln's Yarns and Stories*, 1904.

I do not impugn the motives of any one opposed to me. It is no pleasure to me to tri-   **6**
umph over anyone, but I give thanks to the Almighty for this evidence of the people's
resolution to stand by free government and the rights of humanity.
   —speech to supporters after being reelected president, November 8, 1864.

I am thankful to God for this approval of the people. But while deeply grateful for   **7**
this mark of their confidence in me, if I know my heart, my gratitude is free from any
taint of personal triumph.
   —response to a serenade on the White House lawn, November 8, 1864.
★ He had won reelection on this day.

While I am deeply sensible to the high compliment of a re-election; and duly grate-   **8**
ful, as I trust, to Almighty God for having directed my countrymen to a right conclusion, as I think, for their own good, it adds nothing to my satisfaction that any
other man may be disappointed or pained by the result.
   —response to a serenade on the White House lawn, November 10, 1864.

1   We cannot have free government without elections; and if the rebellion could force us to forego or postpone a national election, it might fairly claim to have already conquered and ruined us . . . [This event] has demonstrated that a people's government can sustain a national election in the midst of a great civil war. Until now, it has not been known to the world that this was a possibility. It shows, also, how sound and how strong we still are.
        —response to a serenade on the White House lawn, November 10, 1864.

2   So long as I have been here I have not willingly planted a thorn in any man's bosom.
        —response to a serenade on the White House lawn, November 10, 1864.

3   Human nature will not change. In any future great national trial, compared with the men of this, we shall have as weak and as strong; as silly and as wise; as bad and as good.
        —response to a serenade on the White House lawn, November 10, 1864.

4   It has long been a grave question whether any government, not *too* strong for the liberties of its people, can be strong *enough* to maintain its own existence, in great emergencies. On this point the present rebellion brought our republic to a severe test.
        —response to a serenade on the White House lawn, November 10, 1864, quoted
        by Brooks D. Simpson in *Abraham Lincoln on Slavery, Freedom, and Union*, 1998.

5   Every advocate of slavery naturally desires to see blasted, and crushed, the liberty promised the black man by the new constitution.
        —letter to Major General Stephen A. Hurlbut, November 14, 1864.

6   No candidate for any office, high or low, has ventured to seek votes on the avowal that he was for giving up the Union.
        —quoted by Nathaniel W. Stephenson in *Lincoln: An Account of His Personal Life, Especially of Its Springs of Action as Revealed and Deepened by the Ordeal of War*, 1922.
        ★ This was said after his reelection in 1864.

7   You say your husband is a religious man; tell him when you meet him, that I say I am not much of a judge of religion, but that, in my opinion, the religion that sets men to rebel and fight against their own government, because, as they think, that government does not sufficiently help some men to eat their bread in the sweat of other men's faces, is not the sort of religion upon which people can get to heaven.
        —memorandum, December 3, 1864.
        ★ In this memorandum, Lincoln was quoting his own words to two ladies from Tennessee who visited three times to ask for the release of their Confederate husbands, who were being held as prisoners of war. After making this statement to the women, Lincoln released the prisoners.

8   Maryland is secure to Liberty and Union for all the future. The genius of rebellion will no more claim Maryland. Like another foul spirit, being driven out, it may seek to tear her, but it will woo her no more.
        —fourth annual message to Congress, December 6, 1864.

9   In a great national crisis, like ours, unanimity of action among those seeking a common end is very desirable—almost indispensable. And yet no approach to such una-

nimity is attainable, unless some deference shall be paid to the will of the majority, simply because it is the will of the majority.
—fourth annual message to Congress, December 6, 1864.

While it is melancholy to reflect that the war has filled so many graves, and carried   1
mourning to so many hearts, it is some relief to know that, compared with the surviving, the fallen have been so few. While corps, and divisions, and brigades, and regiments have formed, and fought, and dwindled, and gone out of existence, a great majority of the men who composed them are still living. The same is true of the naval service.
—fourth annual message to Congress, December 6, 1864.

The important fact remains demonstrated, that we have *more* men *now* than we had   2
when the war *began*; that we are not exhausted, nor in process of exhaustion; that we are *gaining* strength, and may, if need be, maintain the contest indefinitely.
—message to Congress, December 6, 1864.

In stating a single condition of peace, I mean simply to say that the war will cease on   3
the part of the government, whenever it shall have ceased on the part of those who began it.
—fourth annual message to Congress, December 6, 1864.

I believe I shall never be old enough to speak without embarrassment when I have   4
nothing to talk about. I have no good news to tell you, and yet I have no bad news to tell.
—response to a serenade, December 6, 1864.

The most interesting news we have is from Sherman. We all know where he went in   5
at, but I can't tell where he will come out at.
—response to a serenade, December 6, 1864.

★ Major General William T. Sherman was on his march through Georgia.

Excuse me for not noticing you. I was thinking of a man down South.   6
—quoted by Colonel Alexander K. McClure in *Lincoln's Yarns and Stories*, 1904.

★ The man was Major General William T. Sherman on his march through Georgia.
This was said to someone at a levee (reception).

I have long determined to make public the origin of the greenback and tell the world   7
that it is Dick Taylor's creation. . . . Said you, "Why, issue Treasury notes bearing no interest, printed on the best banking paper. Issue enough to pay off the Army expenses and declare it legal tender." . . . It is due to you, the father of the present greenback, that the people should know it, and I take great pleasure in making it known.
—letter to Colonel B. D. Taylor, December 16?, 1864.

★ Lincoln had introduced the "greenback" in 1862, standardizing the look of paper currency and creating the first US notes not redeemable upon demand to the holder.

1   How many times have I laughed at you telling me plainly that I was too lazy to be anything but a lawyer.
    —letter to Colonel B. D. Taylor, December 16?, 1864.

2   Grant has the bear by the hind leg while Sherman takes off its hide.
    —quoted by Geoffrey C. Ward in *The Civil War: An Illustrated History*, 1990.

    ★ This was Lincoln's reaction to Major General William T. Sherman's capture of Savannah, Georgia, on December 21, 1864.

3   When you were about leaving Atlanta for the Atlantic coast, I was anxious, if not fearful; but feeling that you were the better judge, and remembering "nothing risked, nothing gained," I did not interfere. Now, the undertaking being a success, the honor is all yours; for I believe none of us went further than to acquiesce.
    —telegram to Major General William T. Sherman, December 26, 1864.

4   Many, many thanks for your Christmas gift, the capture of Savannah.
    —telegram to Major General William T. Sherman, December 26, 1864.

    ★ Sherman had telegraphed Lincoln on December 22 to offer him the city as a Christmas gift.

5   Thoughtful men must feel that the fate of civilization upon this continent is involved in the issue of our contest.
    —letter to Dr. John Maclean, December 27, 1864.

    ★ Maclean was president of the College of New Jersey (now Princeton University), which had awarded Lincoln an honorary degree of Doctor of Laws in 1864 shortly after he was reelected.

6   Gentlemen, after Boston, Chicago has been the chief instrument in bringing war on this country. The Northwest has opposed the South as New England has opposed the South. It is you who are largely responsible for making blood flow as it has. You called for war until we had it.
    —quoted by Colonel Alexander K. McClure in *Lincoln's Yarns and Stories*, 1904.

    ★ He was complaining to Joseph Medill, editor of the *Chicago Tribune*, and others, after Chicago resisted Lincoln's call for extra troops in 1864.

7   Please read and answer this letter as though I was not President, but only a friend. My son, now in his twenty-second year, having graduated at Harvard, wishes to see something of the war before it ends. I do not wish to put him in the ranks, nor yet to give him a commission, to which those who have already served long are better entitled and better qualified to hold. Could he, without embarrassment to you, or detriment to the service, go into your military family with some nominal rank, I, and not the public, furnishing his necessary means? If no, say so without the least hesitation, because I am anxious and as deeply interested that you shall not be encumbered as you can be yourself.
    —letter to General Ulysses S. Grant, January 19, 1865.

    ★ Lincoln's son, Robert Todd Lincoln, served on Grant's staff for the rest of the war and later became secretary of war for presidents James Garfield and Chester Arthur.

The true rule for the Military is to seize such property as is needed for Military uses **1** and reasons, and let the rest alone.
> —letter to Joseph J. Reynolds, January 20, 1865.

[Jefferson Davis] can not voluntarily reaccept the Union; we can not voluntarily **2** yield it.
> —quoted by Nathaniel W. Stephenson in *Lincoln: An Account of His Personal Life, Especially of Its Springs of Action as Revealed and Deepened by the Ordeal of War*, 1922.

★ This referred to possible peace talks.

Let nothing which is transpiring, change, hinder, or delay your military movements, **3** or plans.
> —telegram to General Ulysses S. Grant, February 1, 1865.

★ Lincoln was referring to the Hampton Roads Peace Conference with representatives of the Confederate government.

While I cannot order as within requested, allow me to say that it is my wish for you **4** to relieve the people from all burdens, harassments, and oppressions, so far as is possible consistently with your military necessities; that the object of the war being to restore and maintain the blessings of peace and good government, I desire you to help, and not hinder, every advance in that direction.
> —message to military officers commanding in West Tennessee, February 13, 1865.

You are all against me. **5**
> —quoted by Nathaniel W. Stephenson in *Lincoln: An Account of His Personal Life, Especially of Its Springs of Action as Revealed and Deepened by the Ordeal of War*, 1922.

★ This was said to his cabinet in February 1865 after they rejected his proposal to offer $400 million to the Confederate states to end the war and accept the authority of the US government.

Well, didn't you think it was the biggest shuck and the littlest ear that ever you did see? **6**
> —quoted by General Ulysses S. Grant in *Personal Memoirs of U. S. Grant*, vol. 2, 1886.

★ Lincoln made this humorous query to Grant in February 1865 shortly after they had seen the small Confederate vice president Alexander H. Stephens remove his very large overcoat.

We must make it easy for them [the Democrats] because we can't live through the **7** case without them.
> —quoted by Nathaniel W. Stephenson in *Lincoln: An Account of His Personal Life, Especially of Its Springs of Action as Revealed and Deepened by the Ordeal of War*, 1922.

★ He said this before his second inauguration, meaning that the Democrats should be given some face-saving encouragement to join the war effort. Lincoln, the lawyer, here uses "the case" to mean the war.

1   Both parties deprecated war; but one of them would make war rather than let the nation survive; and the other would accept war rather than let it perish. And the war came.
     —second inaugural address, March 4, 1865.

2   One eighth of the whole population were colored slaves, not distributed generally over the Union, but localized in the Southern part of it. These slaves constituted a peculiar and powerful interest. All knew that this interest was, somehow, the cause of the war.
     —second inaugural address, March 4, 1865.

3   Neither party expected for the war, the magnitude, or the duration, which it has already attained. Neither anticipated that the cause of the conflict might cease with, or even before, the conflict itself should cease. Each looked for an easier triumph, and a result less fundamental and astounding.
     —second inaugural address, March 4, 1865.

4   Both sides read the same Bible, and pray to the same God; and each invokes his aid against the other. It may seem strange that any men should dare to ask a just God's assistance in wringing their bread from the sweat of other men's faces; but let us judge not that we be not judged.
     —second inaugural address, March 4, 1865.

5   Fondly do we hope, fervently do we pray, that this mighty scourge of war may speedily pass away. Yet, if God wills that it continue until all the wealth piled by the bondman's two hundred and fifty years of unrequited toil shall be sunk, and until every drop of blood drawn with the lash shall be paid by another drawn with the sword, as was said three thousand years ago, so still it must be said, "The judgments of the Lord are true and righteous altogether."
     —second inaugural address, March 4, 1865.

6   With malice towards none, with charity for all; with firmness in the right as God gives us to see the right, let us strive to finish the work we are in; to bind up the nation's wounds, to care for him who shall have borne the battle and for his widow, and his orphan—to do all which may achieve and cherish a just and lasting peace among ourselves, and with all nations.
     —second inaugural address, March 4, 1865.

7   I am a tired man. Sometimes I think I am the tiredest man on earth.
     —quoted by Geoffrey C. Ward in *The Civil War: An Illustrated History*, 1990.

     ★ The president made this comment after his second inaugural address on March 4, 1865.

8   I expect the [second inaugural address] to wear as well as—perhaps better than—anything I have produced, but I believe it is not immediately popular.
     —letter to Thurlow Weed of New York, March 15, 1865.

     ★ He had made the address on March 4.

Whenever I hear anyone arguing for slavery, I feel a strong impulse to see it tried on 1
him personally.
    —speech to the 140th Indiana Regiment, March 17, 1865.

I have in my lifetime heard many arguments why the negroes ought to be slaves; but 2
if they fight for those who would keep them in slavery it will be a better argument
than any I have yet heard. He who will fight for that ought to be a slave.
    —speech to the 140th Indiana Regiment, March 17, 1865.

I want no one punished. Treat them liberally all around. We want those people to 3
return to their allegiance to the Union and submit to the laws.
    —messages to General Ulysses S. Grant, General William T. Sherman, and
    Admiral David D. Porter, March 28, 1865.

★ Lincoln dispatched these instructions twelve days before General Robert E. Lee's
surrender.

My poor friends, you are free—free as air. You can cast off the name of slave and 4
trample upon it. It will come to you no more. Liberty is your birthright. God gave it
to you as He gave it to others, and it is a sin that you have been deprived of it for so
many years. But you must try to deserve the priceless boon. Let the world see that
you merit it, and are able to maintain it by your good work. Don't let your joy carry
you into excesses; learn the laws and obey them. Obey God's commandments, and
thank Him for giving you liberty, for to Him you owe all things.
    —quoted by Colonel Alexander K. McClure in *Lincoln's Yarns and Stories*, 1904.

★ Lincoln was speaking to blacks during his visit to captured Richmond on April 4,
1865.

If I were in your place I'd let 'em up easy; let 'em up easy. 5
    —quoted by Shelby Foote in *The Civil War*, vol. 3, 1958.

★ Lincoln was responding to Brigadier General Godfrey Weitzel, who conducted the
president on a tour of captured Richmond on April 4, 1865, and asked how the conquered people should be treated.

Why, if any one else had been President and had gone to Richmond, I would have 6
been alarmed; but I was not scared about myself a bit.
    —quoted by Colonel Alexander K. McClure in *Lincoln's Yarns and Stories*, 1904.

★ Union forces entered Richmond on April 3, 1865, and Lincoln and his son, Tad, visited there on April 4 and 5.

Tell your father, the rascal, that I forgive him for the sake of that kiss and those 7
bright eyes.
    —edited by La Salle Corbell Pickett in *The Heart of a Soldier*, 1913.

★ Lincoln said this to the infant son of CS major general George E. Pickett. While visiting the captured Richmond, the president stopped in to speak with Pickett's wife,
Sally (La Salle). Before the war, Pickett had been friends with Lincoln, who got him the
appointment to West Point.

1   Thank God that I have lived to see this! It seems to me that I have been dreaming a horrid dream for four years, and now the nightmare is gone. I wish to see Richmond.
—quoted by Colonel Alexander K. McClure in *Lincoln's Yarns and Stories*, 1904.

★ He said this to Rear Admiral David D. Porter on the flagship USS *Malvern* in front of Richmond, which he was visiting on April 4 and 5, 1865.

2   Let the *thing* be pressed.
—note to General Ulysses S. Grant, April 7, 1865.

★ Grant had sent Lincoln a message from Major General Philip H. Sheridan, who said "If the thing is pressed, I think Lee will surrender." Lee surrendered two days later.

3   Tad wants some flags—can he be accommodated?
—note to Secretary of War Edwin M. Stanton, April 10, 1865.

★ Tad was Lincoln's nickname for his youngest son, Thomas, who was eleven.

4   I have always thought "Dixie" one of the best tunes I ever heard. Our adversaries over the way attempted to appropriate it, but I insisted yesterday that we fairly captured it. I presented the question to the Attorney General and he gave it as his legal opinion that it is now our lawful prize.
—quoted by Shelby Foote in *The Civil War*, vol. 3, 1958.

★ The president made the remarks on April 11, 1865, from the White House balcony to some 3,000 people celebrating the end of the war. He then requested the band to play "Dixie." Lincoln had used the tune with different words for his 1860 presidential campaign: "At Chicago they selected, Lincoln who will be elected, Abraham, Abraham, Abraham, Abraham."

5   We meet this evening not in sorrow, but in gladness of heart. The evacuation of Petersburg and Richmond, and the surrender of the principal insurgent army, give hope of a righteous and speedy peace, whose joyous expression cannot be restrained. In the midst of this, however, He from whom blessings flow must not be forgotten.
—speech from the White House balcony, April 11, 1865.

★ This was Lincoln's last public speech, given to a crowd on the White House lawn.

6   [Reconstruction] is fraught with great difficulty. Unlike the case of a war between independent nations, there is no authorized organ for us to treat with. No one man has authority to give up the rebellion for any other man. We simply must begin with, and mould from, disorganized and discordant elements. Nor is it a small additional embarrassment that we, the loyal people, differ among ourselves as to the mode, manner, and means of reconstruction.
—speech from the White House balcony, April 11, 1865.

7   We all agree that the seceded states, so called, are out of their proper practical relation with the Union, and that the sole object of the government, civil and military, in regard to those states is to again get them into that proper practical relation. I believe that it is not only possible but in fact easier to do this without deciding or even considering whether those states have ever been out of the Union than with it.

Finding themselves safely at home, it would be utterly immaterial whether they had been abroad.
>—speech from the White House balcony, April 11, 1865.

Bad promises are better broken than kept.   1
>—speech from the White House balcony, April 11, 1865.

★ This referred to Lincoln's promised support of the provisional Louisiana government that was formed after the war.

Concede that the new government of Louisiana is only to what it should be as the   2
egg is to the fowl, we shall sooner have the fowl by hatching the egg than by smashing it.
>—speech from the White House balcony, April 11, 1865.

As a general rule, I abstain from reading the reports of attacks upon myself, wishing   3
not to be provoked by that to which I cannot properly offer an answer.
>—speech from the White House balcony, April 11, 1865.

In the present situation, as the phrase goes, it may be my duty to make some new   4
announcement to the people of the South. I am considering and shall not fail to act when satisfied that action will be proper.
>—quoted by Nathaniel W. Stephenson in *Lincoln: An Account of His Personal
>Life, Especially of Its Springs of Action as Revealed and Deepened by the Ordeal
>of War*, 1922.

★ Lincoln's future announcement remains a mystery, although some believed it would be an offer of reimbursement for the end of slavery.

What does any one want to assassinate me for? If any one wants to do so, he can do   5
it any day or night if he is ready to give his life for mine. It is nonsense.
>—quoted by Colonel Alexander K. McClure in *Lincoln's Yarns and Stories*, 1904.

★ Lincoln said this to Secretary of the Interior John P. Usher and Marshal Ward Hill Lamon, his friend and bodyguard, on the day he was assassinated.

Well, I think the boy can do us more good above ground than under ground.   6
>—quoted by Colonel Alexander K. McClure in *Lincoln's Yarns and Stories*, 1904.

★ He was pardoning, on the day he was assassinated, a soldier sentenced to be shot for desertion.

Some of our generals complain that I impair discipline and subordination in the   7
army by my pardons and respites, but it makes me rested, after a hard day's work, if I can find some good excuse for saving a man's life, and I go to bed happy as I think how joyous the signing of my name will make him and his family and his friends.
>—quoted by Colonel Alexander K. McClure in *Lincoln's Yarns and Stories*, 1904.

★ This was said to Schuyler Colfax, speaker of the House, as Lincoln pardoned a soldier to be shot for desertion.

During the war, when we were adding a couple of millions of dollars every day to our   8
national debt, I did not care about encouraging the increase in volume of our pre-

cious metals. We had the country to save first. But now that the rebellion is over-thrown, and we know pretty nearly the amount of our national debt, the more gold and silver we mine, we make the payment of that debt so much the easier.
    —interview with Congressman Schuyler Colfax, April 14, 1865.

★ Lincoln was assassinated that evening. Colfax was speaker of the House and later became Grant's vice president.

1   We shall have hundreds of thousands of disbanded soldiers, and many have feared that their return home in such great numbers might paralyze industry, by furnishing, suddenly, a greater supply of labor than there will be demand for. I am going to try to attract them to the hidden wealth of our mountain ranges, where there is room enough for all.
    —interview with Congressman Schuyler Colfax, April 14, 1865.

2   It has been advertised that we will be there, and I cannot disappoint the people. Otherwise I would not go. I do not want to go.
    —quoted by Shelby Foote in *The Civil War*, vol. 3, 1958.

★ This was said on the afternoon of April 14, 1965, the day Lincoln was assassinated at Ford's Theater.

3   It's a good face [that Lee has]. I am glad the war is over.
    —quoted by Shelby Foote in *The Civil War*, vol. 3, 1958.

★ Lincoln's son, Robert, had just presented him with a photograph of Lee on April 14, 1865.

4   I hope there will be no persecution [of Confederate leaders], no bloody work after the war is over. No one need expect me to take any part in hanging or killing these men, even the worst of them.
    —quoted by Shelby Foote in *The Civil War*, vol. 3, 1958.

★ Lincoln said this on April 14, 1865, the day of his assassination.

5   The war is over. It has been a tough time, but we have lived it out. Or some of us have.
    —quoted by Shelby Foote in *The Civil War*, vol. 3, 1958.

★ Lincoln said this to Senator John Creswell of Maryland on April 14, 1864, the day he was assassinated.

6   I thank you for the assurance you give me that I shall be supported by conservative men like yourself, in the efforts I may make to restore the Union, so as to make it, to use your language, a Union of hearts and hands as well as States.
    —letter to Brigadier General James H. Van Alen, April 14, 1865.

★ Lincoln was assassinated that evening.

7   Broken by [slave power] I too may be; bow to it I never will.
    —quoted by Reverend Matthew Simpson in his speech at Lincoln's funeral, May 4, 1865.

★ The funeral was in Springfield, Illinois. Reverend Simpson was a bishop of the Methodist Episcopal Church.

I never shall live out the four years of my term. When the rebellion is crushed my   **1**
work is done.
 —quoted by Reverend Matthew Simpson in his speech at Lincoln's funeral,
 May 4, 1865.

If I were to try to read, much less answer, all the attacks made on me, this shop might   **2**
as well be closed for any other business.
 —quoted by Francis B. Carpenter in *The Inner Life of Abraham Lincoln: Six
 Months at the White House*, 1866.

I do the very best I know how—the very best I can; and I mean to keep doing so until   **3**
the end. If the end brings me out all right, what is said against me won't amount to
anything. If the end brings me out wrong, ten angels swearing I was right would
make no difference.
 —quoted by Francis B. Carpenter in *The Inner Life of Abraham Lincoln: Six
 Months at the White House*, 1866.

Whoever saw a dead cavalry man?   **4**
 —quoted by General Philip H. Sheridan in *Personal Memoirs of P. H. Sheridan,
 General United States Army*, vol. 1, 1888.

★ This was said to Sheridan in the White House, and he always wondered if the president was joking or criticizing.

What I want, and what the people want, is generals who will fight battles and win vic-   **5**
tories. Grant has done this, and I propose to stand by him.
 —quoted by Clifton M. Nichols in *Life of Abraham Lincoln*, 1896.

★ Lincoln said this to Brigadier General John Thayer when Grant's popularity had dipped.

There are three persons of the South who can never receive amnesty: Mr. Davis,   **6**
General Lee, and yourself. You have given the Union cause too much trouble.
 —quoted by former CS lieutenant general James Longstreet in *From Manassas to
 Appomattox: Memoirs of the Civil War in America*, 1896.

★ Lincoln told Longstreet this when Longstreet visited him in the White House with the request. However, Lee and Longstreet soon received amnesty with the help of Grant.

It is true that you may fool all the people some of the time; you can even fool some   **7**
of the people all the time; but you can't fool all of the people all the time.
 —quoted by Colonel Alexander K. McClure in *Lincoln's Yarns and Stories*, 1904.

★ This was said to a caller at the White House, but the quotation has also been attributed to the showman Phineas T. Barnum.

1   When Grant gets possession of a place, he holds on to it as if he had inherited it.
  —quoted by Horace Porter in *Campaigning with Grant*, 1897.

  ★ The comment was made to Major General Benjamin Butler.

2   Sir, I have the best possible reason for knowing the number [of Confederate soldiers] to be one million of men, for whenever one of our generals engages a rebel army he reports that he has encountered a force twice his strength. Now I know we have half a million soldiers, so I am bound to believe that the rebels have twice that number.
  —quoted by Lieutenant Colonel G. F. R. Henderson in *Stonewall Jackson and the American Civil War*, vol. 2, 1898.

  ★ This tongue-in-cheek answer came after someone asked the president if he knew how many armed rebels they were fighting.

3   I have a white elephant on my hands—one hard to manage. With a fire in my front and rear to contend with, the jealousies of the military commanders and not receiving that cordial co-operative support from Congress that could reasonably be expected with an active and formidable enemy in the field threatening the very life-blood of the Government, my position is anything but a bed of roses.
  —quoted by Colonel Alexander K. McClure in *Lincoln's Yarns and Stories*, 1904.

  ★ This was said to a friend from Springfield, Illinois.

4   Mother [Mrs. Lincoln] has got a notion into her head that I shall be assassinated, and to please her I take a cane when I go over to the War Department at night—when I don't forget it.
  —quoted by Colonel Alexander K. McClure in *Lincoln's Yarns and Stories*, 1904.

5   The fact is, General [Sickles], in the stress and pinch of the campaign there, I went to my room, and got down on my knees and prayed God Almighty for victory at Gettysburg. I told Him that this was His country, and the war was His war, but that we really couldn't stand another Fredericksburg or Chancellorsville. And then and there I made a solemn vow with my Maker that if He would stand by you boys at Gettysburg I would stand by Him. And He did, and I will! And after this I felt that God Almighty had taken the whole thing into His hands.
  —quoted by Colonel Alexander K. McClure in *Lincoln's Yarns and Stories*, 1904.

6   Some of these generals experiment so long and so much with newfangled, fancy notions that when they are finally brought to a head they are useless.
  —quoted by Colonel Alexander K. McClure in *Lincoln's Yarns and Stories*, 1904.

7   I wish there was a stronger disposition manifested on the part of our civilian warriors to unite in suppressing the rebellion, and a little less noise as to how and by whom the chief executive office shall be administered.
  —quoted by Colonel Alexander K. McClure in *Lincoln's Yarns and Stories*, 1904.

8   [Alexander Schimmelpfennig] may be deaf and dumb for all I know, but whatever language he speaks, if any, we can furnish troops who will understand what he says.

That name of his will make up for any differences in religion, politics or under-standing, and I'll take the risk of his coming out all right.
   —quoted by Colonel Alexander K. McClure in *Lincoln's Yarns and Stories*, 1904.

★ Lincoln, who wanted to appoint a German as a brigadier general to satisfy German Americans, said this to Secretary of War Edwin M. Stanton.

I could as easily bail out the Potomac River with a teaspoon as attend to all the   1
details of the army.
   —quoted by Colonel Alexander K. McClure in *Lincoln's Yarns and Stories*, 1904.

We must have troops, and as they can neither crawl under Maryland nor fly over it,   2
they must come across it.
   —quoted by Colonel Alexander K. McClure in *Lincoln's Yarns and Stories*, 1904.

★ He was answering early appeals from the Maryland government to avoid moving Union troops south over Maryland.

If you once forfeit the confidence of your fellow-citizens, you can never regain their   3
respect and esteem.
   —quoted by Colonel Alexander K. McClure in *Lincoln's Yarns and Stories*, 1904.

Some of my generals are so slow that molasses in the coldest days of winter is a race   4
horse compared with them. They're brave enough, but somehow or other they get fastened in a fence corner, and can't figure their way out.
   —quoted by Colonel Alexander K. McClure in *Lincoln's Yarns and Stories*, 1904.

The fact is I have got more pegs than I have holes to put them in.   5
   —quoted by Colonel Alexander K. McClure in *Lincoln's Yarns and Stories*, 1904.

★ He was answering appeals to give commands to certain generals.

General Grant is a copious worker and fighter, but a meagre writer or telegrapher.   6
   —quoted by Colonel Alexander K. McClure in *Lincoln's Yarns and Stories*, 1904.

True patriotism is better than the wrong kind of piety.   7
   —quoted by Colonel Alexander K. McClure in *Lincoln's Yarns and Stories*, 1904.

I would rather have Democrats whom I know than Republicans I don't know.   8
   —quoted by Colonel Alexander K. McClure in *Lincoln's Yarns and Stories*, 1904.

★ Someone had complained that the president was appointing Democrats to his cabinet.

Get out of the way, Swett; to-morrow is butcher-day, and I must go through these   9
papers and see if I cannot find some excuse to let these poor fellows off.
   —quoted by Colonel Alexander K. McClure in *Lincoln's Yarns and Stories*, 1904.

★ He was referring to courts-martial of men to be executed the next day. Leonard Swett was Lincoln's close friend from Illinois.

1   If the unworthy ambition of politicians and the jealousy that exists in the army could be repressed, and all unite in a common aim and a common endeavor, the rebellion would soon be crushed.
>   —quoted by Colonel Alexander K. McClure in *Lincoln's Yarns and Stories*, 1904.

2   If [the Confederates] can get subsistence they have everything else, except a just cause.
>   —quoted by Colonel Alexander K. McClure in *Lincoln's Yarns and Stories*, 1904.

3   You can't carry on war without blood-letting.
>   —quoted by Colonel Alexander K. McClure in *Lincoln's Yarns and Stories*, 1904.

4   You know better than any man living that from my boyhood up my ambition was to be President. I am President of one part of this divided country at least; but, look at me! Oh, I wish I had never been born!
>   —quoted by Colonel Alexander K. McClure in *Lincoln's Yarns and Stories*, 1904.

★ This was said to a friend from Springfield, Illinois.

5   Oh, there is no alternative but to keep "pegging" away.
>   —quoted by Colonel Alexander K. McClure in *Lincoln's Yarns and Stories*, 1904.

★ He had been asked what would happen if the war lasted three or four years.

6   How willingly would I exchange places to-day with the solider who sleeps on the ground in the Army of the Potomac.
>   —quoted by Colonel Alexander K. McClure in *Lincoln's Yarns and Stories*, 1904.

★ He said this to Schuyler Colfax, speaker of the House, after receiving bad news from the field.

7   If a man had more than one life, I think a little hanging would not hurt this one; but after he is once dead we cannot bring him back, no matter how sorry we may be; so the boy should be pardoned.
>   —quoted by Colonel Alexander K. McClure in *Lincoln's Yarns and Stories*, 1904.

★ This regarded a Confederate soldier who had deserted to return to his home in Kentucky and was then arrested as a spy.

8   I cannot always be sure that permits given by me ought to be granted. There is an understanding between myself and [Secretary of War Edwin] Stanton that when I send a request to him which cannot consistently be granted, he is to refuse to honor it. This he sometimes does.
>   —quoted by Colonel Alexander K. McClure in *Lincoln's Yarns and Stories*, 1904.

★ He was referring to passes through the lines.

9   Yes, it is a heavy hog to hold.
>   —quoted by Colonel Alexander K. McClure in *Lincoln's Yarns and Stories*, 1904.

★ He had been asked if the war was a great care to him.

. . . as the Scriptures say that in the shedding of blood is the remission of sins, I guess 1
we'll have to let him off this time.
  —quoted by Colonel Alexander K. McClure in *Lincoln's Yarns and Stories*, 1904.

★ He was pardoning a death sentence given a brave soldier who had been severely
wounded and then deserted.

I shall never be glad any more. 2
  —quoted by Colonel Alexander K. McClure in *Lincoln's Yarns and Stories*, 1904.

★ He was responding to a woman who said if he granted her petition for new hospitals,
"You will be glad as long as you live."

I begin to believe that there is no North. 3
  —quoted by Colonel Alexander K. McClure in *Lincoln's Yarns and Stories*, 1904.

★ Fearing an attack on Washington, Lincoln wondered why requested Union troops
had not arrived. (They soon came.)

I could not think of going into eternity with the blood of the poor young man on my 4
skirts. It is not to be wondered at that a boy, raised on a farm, probably in the habit
of going to bed at dark, should, when required to watch, fall asleep; and I cannot
consent to shoot him for such an act.
  —quoted by Colonel Alexander K. McClure in *Lincoln's Yarns and Stories*, 1904.

We must let the other nations know that we propose to settle our family row in our 5
own way, and "teach these brats [seceding states] their places" if we have to "lick the
hide off" of each and every one of them.
  —quoted by Colonel Alexander K. McClure in *Lincoln's Yarns and Stories*, 1904.

★ This was said during a cabinet meeting.

Congress has taken the responsibility and left the women to howl all about me. 6
  —quoted by Colonel Alexander K. McClure in *Lincoln's Yarns and Stories*, 1904.

★ He was responding to Brigadier General Robert O. Tyler's saying that Congress
assumed responsibility for the war. Lincoln was referring to the grieving mothers of soldiers.

I have often inquired of myself what great principle or idea it was that kept this 7
Confederacy [the United States] so long together. It was not the mere matter of the
separation of the colonies from the motherland, but that sentiment in the Declaration of Independence which gave liberty not alone to the people of the country but
hope to all the world for all future time.
  —quoted by Nathaniel W. Stephenson in *Lincoln: An Account of His Personal
  Life, Especially of Its Springs of Action as Revealed and Deepened by the Ordeal
  of War*, 1922.

1   . . . the crucial idea pervading this struggle is the necessity that is upon us to prove that popular government is not an absurdity.
—quoted by Nathaniel W. Stephenson in *Lincoln: An Account of His Personal Life, Especially of Its Springs of Action as Revealed and Deepened by the Ordeal of War*, 1922.

★ This was said to his secretary, John Hay.

2   In considering the policy to be adopted in suppressing the insurrection, I have been anxious and careful that the inevitable conflict for this purpose shall not degenerate into a violent and remorseless revolutionary struggle.
—quoted by Nathaniel W. Stephenson in *Lincoln: An Account of His Personal Life, Especially of Its Springs of Action as Revealed and Deepened by the Ordeal of War*, 1922.

★ Stephenson notes that Lincoln persisted in regarding the war as an insurrection of a "disloyal portion of the American people" rather than a struggle between the North and the South.

3   We are civilians, we should justly be held responsible for any disaster if we set up our opinions against those of experienced military men in the practical management of a campaign.
—quoted by Nathaniel W. Stephenson in *Lincoln: An Account of His Personal Life, Especially of Its Springs of Action as Revealed and Deepened by the Ordeal of War*, 1922.

4   I hope I am a Christian.
—quoted by Nathaniel W. Stephenson in *Lincoln: An Account of His Personal Life, Especially of Its Springs of Action as Revealed and Deepened by the Ordeal of War*, 1922.

5   You are all the time exercised about somebody taking my life; murdering me; and now you have discovered a new danger; now you think the people of this great government are likely to turn me out of office. I do not fear this from the people any more than I fear assassination from an individual.
—quoted by Nathaniel W. Stephenson in *Lincoln: An Account of His Personal Life, Especially of Its Springs of Action as Revealed and Deepened by the Ordeal of War*, 1922.

★ Lincoln said this to Marshal Ward Hill Lamon, his friend and bodyguard, who had warned about a plot to depose Lincoln and appoint a military dictator.

6   They don't want much; they get but little, and I must see them.
—quoted by Nathaniel W. Stephenson in *Lincoln: An Account of His Personal Life, Especially of Its Springs of Action as Revealed and Deepened by the Ordeal of War*, 1922.

★ This referred to the great variety of people visiting him with requests.

7   I call these receptions my public opinion baths; for I have but little time to read the papers, and gather public opinion that way; and though they may not be pleasant in

all their particulars, the effect as a whole, is renovating and invigorating to my perceptions of responsibility and duty.
   —quoted by Nathaniel W. Stephenson in *Lincoln: An Account of His Personal Life, Especially of Its Springs of Action as Revealed and Deepened by the Ordeal of War*, 1922.

I'll have nothing to do with this business, nor with any man who comes to me with **1** such degrading propositions. What! Do you take the President of the United States to be a commission broker? You have come to the wrong place, and for you and for every one who comes for the same purpose, there is the door.
   —quoted by Nathaniel W. Stephenson in *Lincoln: An Account of His Personal Life, Especially of Its Springs of Action as Revealed and Deepened by the Ordeal of War*, 1922.

★ He was rebuking a "gentlemanly profiteer."

Call me Lincoln. Mr. President is entirely too formal for us.   **2**
   —quoted by Nathaniel W. Stephenson in *Lincoln: An Account of His Personal Life, Especially of Its Springs of Action as Revealed and Deepened by the Ordeal of War*, 1922.

★ Lincoln often said this to friends and close associates.

It would never do for a president to have guards with drawn sabers at his door, as if **3** he fancied he were, or were trying to be, or were assuming to be, an emperor.
   —quoted by Nathaniel W. Stephenson in *Lincoln: An Account of His Personal Life, Especially of Its Springs of Action as Revealed and Deepened by the Ordeal of War*, 1922.

★ This was said after he had accepted his friends' idea of stationing a cavalry guard at the gates of the White House, and then reversed his decision.

When the Peninsula Campaign terminated suddenly at Harrison's Landing, I was as **4** near inconsolable as I could be and live.
   —quoted by Nathaniel W. Stephenson in *Lincoln: An Account of His Personal Life, Especially of Its Springs of Action as Revealed and Deepened by the Ordeal of War*, 1922.

What is the Presidency worth to me if I have no country?   **5**
   —quoted by Nathaniel W. Stephenson in *Lincoln: An Account of His Personal Life, Especially of Its Springs of Action as Revealed and Deepened by the Ordeal of War*, 1922.

Judge not that ye be not judged.   **6**
   —quoted by Nathaniel W. Stephenson in *Lincoln: An Account of His Personal Life, Especially of Its Springs of Action as Revealed and Deepened by the Ordeal of War*, 1922.

★ Lincoln replied with this biblical quotation when someone suggested that the Confederate president Jefferson Davis be hanged.

1   Men moving only in an official circle are apt to become merely official—not to say arbitrary—in their ideas, and are apter and apter with each passing day to forget that they only hold power in a representative capacity.
    —quoted by Nathaniel W. Stephenson in *Lincoln: An Account of His Personal Life, Especially of Its Springs of Action as Revealed and Deepened by the Ordeal of War*, 1922.

2   As to the crazy folks, Major, why I must only take my chances—the most crazy people at present, I fear, being some of my own too zealous adherents.
    —quoted by Nathaniel W. Stephenson in *Lincoln: An Account of His Personal Life, Especially of Its Springs of Action as Revealed and Deepened by the Ordeal of War*, 1922.

3   All I have to say [about the ironclad USS *Monitor*] is what the girl said when she put her foot into the stocking. It strikes me there's something in it.
    —quoted by Carl Sandburg in *Abraham Lincoln: The War Years*, 1939.

4   I am Halleck's friend because he has no others.
    —quoted by Carl Sandburg in *Abraham Lincoln: The War Years*, 1939.

    ★ Major General Henry W. Halleck was Lincoln's very unpopular general in chief in Washington.

5   I pass my life preventing the storm from blowing down the tent, and I drive in the pegs as fast as they are pulled up.
    —quoted by Carl Sandburg in *Abraham Lincoln: The War Years*, 1939.

6   When you have an elephant by the hind leg, and he's trying to run away, it's best to let him run.
    —quoted by Carl Sandburg in *Abraham Lincoln: The War Years*, 1939.

    ★ Lincoln was replying just after the war ended to a War Department message asking if Jacob Thompson should be arrested. Thompson was a Confederate commissioner in Canada and a former US secretary of the interior (1857–1861), and he was about to escape.

7   What, madam? Do I not destroy them when I make them my friends?
    —quoted by Carl Sandburg in *Abraham Lincoln: The War Years*, 1939.

    ★ Lincoln was replying to a woman who said he should destroy his enemies rather than speak kindly about them.

8   In the present civil war it is quite possible that God's purpose is something different from the purpose of either party; and yet the human instrumentalities, working just as they do, are of the best adaptation to effect his purpose.
    —edited by Roy P. Basler in *The Collected Works of Abraham Lincoln*, 1953.

    ★ This was a written fragment found by Lincoln's secretary, John Hay.

9   By his mere great power on the minds of the now contestants, [God] could have either saved or destroyed the Union without a human contest. Yet the contest began.

And, having begun, he could give the final victory to either side any day. Yet the contest proceeds.
  —edited by Roy P. Basler in *The Collected Works of Abraham Lincoln*, 1953.

★ This was a written fragment found by Lincoln's secretary, John Hay.

As I would not be a slave, so I would not be a master. This expresses my idea 1
of democracy. Whatever differs from this, to the extent of the difference, is no democracy.
  —edited by Roy P. Basler in *The Collected Works of Abraham Lincoln*, 1953.

Too many pigs for the tits. 2
  —quoted by Shelby Foote in *The Civil War*, vol. 3, 1958.

★ Lincoln was referring to office seekers.

General, there are too many weeping widows in the United States now. For God's 3
sake don't ask me to add to the number; for I tell you plainly that I won't do it.
  —quoted by Paul Dickson in *War Slang*, 1994.

★ A general had asked the president to sign a death warrant for a Union soldier.

I have been driven many times upon my knees by the overwhelming conviction that 4
I had nowhere else to go. My own wisdom and that of all about me seemed insufficient for that day.
  —edited by Michael Burlingame in *Lincoln Observed: The Civil War Dispatches
  of Noah Brooks*, 1998.

You and we are different races. We have between us a broader difference than exists 5
between almost any other two races. Whether it is right or wrong I need not discuss,
but this physical difference is a great disadvantage to us both, as I think your race
suffer very greatly, many of them by living among us, while ours suffer from your
presence. In a word we suffer on each side. If this is admitted, it affords a reason at
least why we should be separated.
  —quoted by Brooks D. Simpson in *Think Anew, Act Anew*, 1998.

★ Lincoln was speaking to five free Negro leaders invited to the White House to hear
his plan for the voluntary removal of black people to another country.

Your race are suffering, in my judgment, the greatest wrong inflicted on any people. 6
But even when you cease to be slaves, you are yet far removed from being placed on
an equality with the white race. You are cut off from many of the advantages which
the other race enjoy. The aspiration of men is to enjoy equality with the best when
free, but on this broad continent, not a single man of your race is made the equal of
a single man of ours.
  —quoted by Brooks D. Simpson in *Think Anew, Act Anew*, 1998.

★ Lincoln was speaking to five free Negro leaders invited to the White House to hear
his plan for the voluntary removal of black people to another country.

I need not recount to you the effects upon white men, growing out of the institution 7
of Slavery. I believe in its general evil effects on the white race. See our present

condition—the country engaged in war!—our white men cutting one another's throats. . . . But for your race among us there could not be war, although many men engaged on either side do not care for you one way or the other. Nevertheless, I repeat, without the institution of Slavery and the colored race as a basis, the war could not have an existence.
—quoted by Brooks D. Simpson in *Think Anew, Act Anew*, 1998.

★ Lincoln was speaking to five free Negro leaders invited to the White House to hear his plan for the voluntary removal of black people to another country.

1   There is an unwillingness on the part of our people, harsh as it may be, for you free colored people to remain with us. . . . The place I am thinking about having for a colony is in Central America.
—quoted by Brooks D. Simpson in *Think Anew, Act Anew*, 1998.

★ Lincoln was speaking to five free Negro leaders invited to the White House to hear his plan for the voluntary removal of black people to another country.

2   If there is a hell, I am in it.
—quoted by John D. Wright in *The Language of the Civil War*, 2001.

★ This was said when Lincoln was exasperated with the demands by radical Republicans.

3   To fill up the army is like undertaking to shovel fleas. You take up a shovelful, but before you can dump them anywhere they are gone.
—quoted by John D. Wright in *The Language of the Civil War*, 2001.

★ Lincoln was lamenting that deserters and furloughed soldiers outnumbered recruits.

4   And then, there will be some black men who can remember that, with silent tongue, and clenched teeth, and steady eye, and well-poised bayonet, they have helped mankind on to this great consummation.
—letter to James C. Conkling.

★ Conkling was an Illinois political associate of Lincoln's.

5   I freely acknowledge myself the servant of the people, according to the bond of service—the United States Constitution; and that, as such, I am responsible to them.
—letter to James C. Conkling.

6   Complaint has been made to me that you are forcing negroes into the military service, and even torturing them—riding them on rails and the like to extort their consent. I hope this may be a mistake. The like must not be done by you, or any one under you. You must not force negroes any more than white men.
—telegram to Lieutenant Colonel John Glenn.

★ Glenn was commanding the 120th Colored Infantry at Henderson, Kentucky.

Lincoln, Mary Todd (1818–1882)

WIFE OF ABRAHAM LINCOLN

Grant is a butcher and not fit to be at the head of an army. He loses two men to the **1**
enemy's one. He has no *management*, no regard for life. . . . I could fight an army as
well myself.
>   —quoted by Geoffrey C. Ward in *The Civil War: An Illustrated History*, 1990.

He has killed the President! **2**
>   —quoted by Colonel Alexander K. McClure in *Lincoln's Yarns and Stories*, 1904.

★ She yelled this leaning from her box at Ford's Theater and pointing at the assassin,
John Wilkes Booth, who was escaping from the stage.

His dream was prophetic! **3**
>   —quoted by Colonel Alexander K. McClure in *Lincoln's Yarns and Stories*, 1904.

★ She said this the night of April 14, 1865, when the president was shot, recalling a
dream he had had a few days before, in which he had seen his corpse lying in state in
the White House.

Lincoln, Sally Bush

STEPMOTHER OF ABRAHAM LINCOLN

I knowed when he went away he wasn't ever coming back. **4**
>   —quoted by Shelby Foote in *The Civil War*, vol. 3, 1958.

★ She said this when Lincoln was first elected president and again when he was assassinated. She lived in Coles County, Illinois.

Lincoln, Thomas "Tad"

YOUNGEST SON OF ABRAHAM LINCOLN

I am not a President's son now. I won't have many presents anymore. **5**
>   —quoted by John D. Wright in *The Language of the Civil War*, 2001.

★ Tad said this to a servant days after his father was assassinated. (Lincoln was shot ten
days after Tad's twelfth birthday).

Livermore, Mary A. (1820–1905)

SOCIAL REFORMER WITH THE SANITARY COMMISSION

For the soldier, he had his comrades about him, shoulder to shoulder. He had excite- **6**
ment. He had praise, if he did well. He had honorable mention, and pitying tears, if
he fell nobly striving. But alas for his wife!
>   —*My Story of the War*, 1888.

1   This silent army of heroines [soldiers' wives] was too often forgotten. They were martyrs who died and made no sign. The shouts of far-off victories drowned their feeble wailings, and the horrors of hospitals over-shadowed deeply their unobtruded miseries.
—*My Story of the War*, 1888.

2   Women are here [in the Midwest] in the field everywhere, driving the reapers, binding and shocking, and loading grain. . . . So I said to myself, "They are worthy women, and deserve praise: their husbands are probably too poor to hire help, and, like the 'helpmeets' God designed them to be, they have girt themselves to this work—and they are doing it superbly. Good wives! Good women!"
—*My Story of the War*, 1888.

3   This proclamation [of Lincoln's for troops] was like the first peal of a surcharged thunder-cloud, clearing the murky air. The South received it as a declaration of war, the North as a confession that civil war had begun; and the whole North arose as one man. . . . I had never seen anything like this before. I had never dreamed that New England, slow to wrath, could be fired with so warlike a spirit. Never before had the national flag signified anything to me. But as I saw it now [in Boston], kissing the skies, all that it symbolized as representative of government and emblematic of national majesty became clear to my mental vision.
—*The Story of My Life*, 1890.

Long, A. L.

CS BRIGADIER GENERAL

4   A deathlike stillness then reigned over the field [at Gettysburg], and each army remained in breathless expectation of something yet to come still more dreadful.
—*Memoirs of Robert E. Lee, His Military and Personal History*, 1886.

★ Long, a colonel during the battle, was describing the quiet just before Pickett's charge.

Longstreet, James (1821–1904)

CS LIEUTENANT GENERAL

5   [General Irvin] McDowell's first mistake [at the first battle of Bull Run (first Manassas)] was his display, and march for a grand military picnic.
—*From Manassas to Appomattox: Memoirs of the Civil War in America*, 1896.

6   The mistake of supposing [General E.] Kirby Smith's and [General Arnold] Elzey's approaching troops to be Union reinforcements for [General Irvin] McDowell's right was caused by the resemblance, at a distance, of the original Confederate flag to the colors of Federal regiments. This mishap caused the Confederates to cast about for a new ensign, brought out our battle-flag, led to its adoption by General

[Pierre G. T.] Beauregard, and afterwards by high authority as the union shield of the Confederate national flag.
—*From Manassas to Appomattox: Memoirs of the Civil War in America*, 1896.

The best [shot I ever saw] was at Yorktown. There a Federal officer came out in front **1** of our line, and sitting down to his little platting table began to make a map. One of our officers carefully sighted a gun, touched it off, and dropped a shell into the hands of the man at the little table.
—quoted in *Battles and Leaders of the Civil War*, vol. 2, 1888.

★ The victim was Lieutenant Orlando G. Wagner, a topographical engineer, who was fatally wounded by the shot and died on April 21, 1862.

I don't fear McClellan or any one in Yankeedom.   **2**
—letter to CS major general Gustavus W. Smith, May 8, 1862.

★ Longstreet was then a major general.

Oh, that I had ten thousand men more!   **3**
—letter to CS major general Gustavus W. Smith, June 1, 1862.

★ This was at the battle of Seven Pines, Virginia, when he was a major general.

This was one of the most graceful and daring rides known to military history.   **4**
—*From Manassas to Appomattox: Memoirs of the Civil War in America*, 1896.

★ He meant the raid of Brigadier General J. E. B. Stuart around the Union army on June 12, 1862.

Keep cool, obey orders and aim low.   **5**
—edited by Frank Moore in *The Rebellion Record: A Diary of American Events, with Documents, Narratives, Illustrative Incidents, Poetry, Etc.*, vol. 5, 1862.

★ This advice to his troops was given on June 17, 1862.

It may have been fortunate for the Confederates that he was not instructed to fight **6** like Jackson.
—quoted by Lieutenant Colonel G. F. R. Henderson in *Stonewall Jackson and the American Civil War*, vol. 2, 1898.

★ This referred to Major General Henry W. Halleck urging Major General John Pope to "fight like the devil" in August 1862.

. . . the field lying along the Antietam and including in its scope the little town of **7** Sharpsville—was destined to pass into history as the scene of the bloodiest single day of fighting of the war, and the 17th of September was to become memorable as the day of greatest carnage in the campaigns between North and South . . . And this tremendous tumult of carnage was entirely compassed in the brief hours from dawn to four o'clock in the afternoon.
—*From Manassas to Appomattox: Memoirs of the Civil War in America*, 1896.

And in this great tumult of sound, which shook the air and seemed to shatter the **8** cliffs and ledges above the Antietam, bodies of the facing foes were pushed forward to closer work, and soon added the clash of steel to the thunderous crash of cannon shots.

—*From Manassas to Appomattox: Memoirs of the Civil War in America*, 1896.

1   Confederate affairs were not encouraging [at the battle of Antietam (Sharpsburg)]. Our men were all leg-weary and heavy to handle, while McClellan, with his tens of thousands, whom he had marched in healthful exercise the past two weeks, was finding and pounding us from left to right under converging fire of his batteries, east and west, of the Antietam.

—*From Manassas to Appomattox: Memoirs of the Civil War in America*, 1896.

2   General [Lee], if you put every man now on the other side of the Potomac in that field to approach me over that same line, and give me plenty of ammunition, I will kill them all before they reach my line.

—quoted in *Battles and Leaders of the Civil War*, vol. 3, 1888.

★ This was said at Marye's Heights during the battle of Fredericksburg.

3   [Lee] was assured, however, that the war was virtually over, and that we need not harass our troops by marches and other hardships.

—quoted by Lieutenant Colonel G. F. R. Henderson in *Stonewall Jackson and the American Civil War*, vol. 2, 1898.

★ This was after the battle of Fredericksburg.

4   If [the enemy] is there, it will be because he is anxious that we should attack him— a good reason, in my judgment, for not doing so.

—quoted by Douglas Southall Freeman in *R. E. Lee: A Biography*, vol. 3, 1934.

★ Longstreet was opposing Lee's comment, "If the enemy is there, we must attack him," but was overruled on this first day of the battle of Gettysburg.

5   When they attack, we shall beat them, as we proposed to do before we left Fredericksburg, and the probabilities are that the fruits of our success will be great.

—quoted by Douglas Southall Freeman in *R. E. Lee: A Biography*, vol. 3, 1934.

★ This was said to General Robert E. Lee on July 1, 1863, the first day of the battle of Gettysburg.

6   The General [Lee] is a little nervous this morning; he wishes me to attack; I do not wish to do so without Pickett. I never like to go into battle with one boot off.

—quoted by Douglas Southall Freeman in *R. E. Lee: A Biography*, vol. 3, 1934.

★ He said this to Major General John B. Hood on July 2, 1863, the second day of the battle of Gettysburg.

7   [Lee] lost the matchless equipoise that usually characterized him.

—quoted by Douglas Southall Freeman in *R. E. Lee: A Biography*, vol. 3, 1934.

★ Longstreet was observing Lee on the second day of the battle of Gettysburg, July 2, 1863.

Never was I so depressed as upon that day.   **1**
    —quoted by Douglas Southall Freeman in *R. E. Lee: A Biography*, vol. 3, 1934.

★ General Robert E. Lee had overruled him on the crucial day at the battle of Gettysburg, July 3, 1863. Longstreet had wanted to maneuver to lure a Union attack, but Lee decided to attack instead.

[Lee] knew that I did not believe that success was possible; that care and time should   **2**
be taken to give the troops the benefit of positions and the grounds; and he should
have put an officer in charge who had more confidence in his plan.
    —quoted by Douglas Southall Freeman in *R. E. Lee: A Biography*, vol. 3, 1934.

★ Lee had put Longstreet in general command of the disastrous assault on the third day of the battle of Gettysburg, July 3, 1863.

I do not want to make this charge. I do not see how it can succeed. I would not make   **3**
it now but that General Lee has ordered it and is expecting it.
    —quoted by Douglas Southall Freeman in *R. E. Lee: A Biography*, vol. 3, 1934.

★ Longstreet was in command of the fatal Pickett's charge at the battle of Gettysburg on July 3, 1863.

I could see the desperate and hopeless nature of the charge and the hopeless slaugh-   **4**
ter it would cause.
    —quoted by James M. McPherson in *The Battle Cry of Freedom: The Civil War
    Era*, 1989.

★ This referred to Pickett's charge at the battle of Gettysburg on July 3, 1863.

If the artillery fire does not have the effect to drive off the enemy or greatly demor-   **5**
alize him, so as to make our effort pretty certain, I would prefer that you should not
advise Pickett to make the charge.
    —quoted by Douglas Southall Freeman in *R. E. Lee: A Biography*, vol. 3, 1934.

★ He gave this order to the artillerist, Colonel E. P. Alexander, at the battle of Gettysburg on July 3, 1863. The Confederate fire was fierce and the charge was made, but Alexander's message that Longstreet was virtually out of ammunition to support the charge never reached General Robert E. Lee.

Pickett, I am being crucified at the thought of the sacrifice of life which this attack   **6**
will make.
    —quoted by Major General George E. Pickett in a letter to his future wife, Sally,
    July 4, 1863.

★ Pickett was quoting Longstreet's words the previous day, just before Pickett's disastrous charge at Gettysburg.

General Pickett, finding the battle broken while the enemy was still reinforcing,   **7**
called the troops off. There was no indication of panic. The broken files marched
back in steady step. The effort was nobly made and failed from the blows that could
not be fended.
    —*From Manassas to Appomattox: Memoirs of the Civil War in America*, 1896.

★ This described the failure of Pickett's charge at the battle of Gettysburg.

1   Our most precious blood is now flowing in streams from the Atlantic to the Rocky Mountains and may yet be exhausted before we have succeeded. Then goes honor, treasure, and independence.
       —letter to CS secretary of war James A. Seddon, September 26, 1863.

2   To express my conviction in a few words, our chief [General Braxton Bragg] has done but one thing that he ought to have done since I joined his army. . . . All other things that he has done he ought not to have done. I am convinced that nothing but the hand of God can save us and help us as long as we have our present commander. Now to our wants. Can't you send us General Lee?
       —letter to CS secretary of war James A. Seddon, September 26, 1863.

3   I recognized the authority of [Jefferson Davis's] high position, but called to his mind that neither his words nor his manner were so impressive as the dissolving scenes that foreshadowed the dreadful end.
       —*From Manassas to Appomattox: Memoirs of the Civil War in America*, 1896.

       ★ He said this on October 10, 1863, to Davis, who was visiting the army during the Chattanooga campaign.

4   [Jefferson Davis] referred to his worry and troubles with politicians and non-combatants. In that connection, I suggested that all that the people asked for was success; with that the talk of politicians would be as spiders' webs before him.
       —*From Manassas to Appomattox: Memoirs of the Civil War in America*, 1896.

       ★ He said this on October 10, 1863, to Davis, who was visiting the army during the Chattanooga campaign.

5   The President [Jefferson Davis] left the army more despondent than he found it.
       —*From Manassas to Appomattox: Memoirs of the Civil War in America*, 1896.

       ★ This referred to a visit the Confederate president made to the army during the Chattanooga campaign.

6   That man [Grant] will fight us every day and every hour till the end of the war.
       —quoted by Geoffrey C. Ward in *The Civil War: An Illustrated History*, 1990.

       ★ Longstreet was responding to Grant's promotion to lieutenant general and general in chief in March 1864.

7   Hit hard when you start, but don't start until you have everything ready.
       —quoted by Shelby Foote in *The Civil War*, vol. 3, 1958.

       ★ This was said to his chief of staff, Lieutenant Colonel Gilbert Moxley Sorrel, during the battle of the Wilderness on May 6, 1864.

8   If General Lee doesn't know when to surrender until I tell him, he will never know.
       —*From Manassas to Appomattox: Memoirs of the Civil War in America*, 1896.

       ★ He said this on April 8, 1865, to Brigadier General William N. Pendleton, who had met with other officers and wanted Longstreet to convince Lee to surrender, as Lee did the next day.

General, unless he offers us honorable terms, come back and let us fight it out! **1**
   —quoted by Rod Graff in *Civil War Quiz and Fact Book*, 1985.

★ He said this to General Robert E. Lee as he rode off to surrender to Lieutenant General Ulysses S. Grant.

The next time we met was at Appomattox, and the first thing that General Grant said **2**
to me when we stepped inside, placing his hand in mine, was, "Pete, let us have another game of brag, to recall the days that were so pleasant." Great God! I thought to myself, how my heart swells out to such magnanimous touch of humanity. Why do men fight who were born to be brothers.
   —quoted in the *New York Times*, July 24, 1885.

★ This comment was made the day after Grant died. "Pete" was Longstreet's nickname.

Without a doubt the greatest man of rebellion times, the one matchless among forty **3**
millions for the peculiar difficulties of the period, was Abraham Lincoln.
   —quoted in *Battles and Leaders of the Civil War*, vol. 2, 1888.

In glancing backward over the period of the war, and the tremendous and terrible **4**
events with which it was fraught, the reflection irresistibly arises, that it might perhaps have been avoided and without dishonor. The flag and the fame of the nation could have suffered no reproach had General Scott's advice, before the outbreak, been followed,—"Wayward sisters, depart in peace." The Southern States would have found their way back to the Union without war far earlier than they did by war. . . . But the inflexible fiat of fate seemingly went forth for war; and so for four long years the history of this great nation was written in the blood of its strong men.
   —*From Manassas to Appomattox: Memoirs of the Civil War in America*, 1896.

The assignment of General Lee to command the army of Northern Virginia was far **5**
from reconciling the troops to the loss of our beloved chief, Joseph E. Johnston, with whom the army had been closely connected since its earliest active life. General Lee's experience in active field work was limited to his West Virginia campaign against General Rosecrans, which was not successful . . . There were, therefore, some misgivings as to the power and skill for field service of the new commander.
   —*From Manassas to Appomattox: Memoirs of the Civil War in America*, 1896.

During [Lee's] first week of his authority he called his general officers to meet him **6**
on the Nine Miles road for a general talk. This novelty was not reassuring, as experience had told that secrecy in war was an essential element of success; that public discussion and secrecy were incompatible. As he disclosed nothing, those of serious thought became hopeful, and followed his wise example.
   —*From Manassas to Appomattox: Memoirs of the Civil War in America*, 1896.

The leading proverb impressed upon the minds of young soldiers of the line by old **7**
commanders is, "Never despise your enemy."
   —*From Manassas to Appomattox: Memoirs of the Civil War in America*, 1896.

1   Gettysburg was the greatest battle of the war, but it was for three days, and its total of casualties on either side, terrible as it was, should be one-third larger to make the average per diem equal to the losses at Sharpsburg [Antietam].
    —*From Manassas to Appomattox: Memoirs of the Civil War in America*, 1896.

2   As the world continues to look and study the grand combinations and strategy of General Grant, the higher will be his award as a great soldier. Confederates should be foremost in crediting him with all that his admirers so justly claim, and ask at the same time that his great adversary be measured by the same high standards.
    —*From Manassas to Appomattox: Memoirs of the Civil War in America*, 1896.

3   On the 12th of April [1865] the Army of Northern Virginia marched to the field in front of Appomattox Court House, and by divisions and parts of divisions deployed into line, stacked their arms, folded their colors, and walked empty-handed to find their distant, blighted homes.
    —*From Manassas to Appomattox: Memoirs of the Civil War in America*, 1896.

4   It is well known that after driving off attacking forces, if immediate pursuit can be made, so that the victors can go along with the retreating forces, pell-mell, it is well enough to do so; but the attack should be immediate.
    —quoted by Lieutenant Colonel G. F. R. Henderson in *Stonewall Jackson and the American Civil War*, vol. 2, 1898.

Lovie, Henri

Frank Leslie's Illustrated Newspaper artist

5   I am deranged about the stomach, ragged, unkempt and unshorn, and need the co-joined skill and services of the apothecary, the tailor and the barber, and above all the attentions of home.
    —*Frank Leslie's Illustrated Newspaper*, May 17, 1862.

Lowell, James Russell (1819–1891)

Atlantic Monthly editor

6   Rebellion smells no sweeter because it is called "secession," nor does "order" lose its divine precedence in human affairs because a knave may nickname it "coercion."
    —"E Pluribus Unum," *Atlantic Monthly*, February 1861.

7   A danger is always great so long as we are afraid of it.
    —"E Pluribus Unum," *Atlantic Monthly*, February 1861.

    ★ Lowell was urging military action against South Carolina, which had seceded weeks before, on December 20.

8   We cannot bring ourselves to think that Mr. Lincoln has done anything that would furnish a precedent dangerous to our liberties, or in any way overstepped the just

limits of his constitutional discretion. If his course has been unusual, it was because the danger was equally so.

—*North American Review*, January 1864.

We've a war, an' a debt, an' a flag; an' ef this Ain't to be inderpendunt, why, wut on **1** airth is?

—*The Biglow Papers*, 2nd ser., no. 4, "A Message of Jeff. Davis in Secret Session," 1867.

Lowry, Robert (1829?–1910)

CS BRIGADIER GENERAL AND MISSISSIPPI GOVERNOR

The people of the Southern States were subjected by the victors to a species of **2** tyranny and oppression, that to-day can scarcely be realized, even by those sought to be humiliated.

—with William H. McCardle, *A History of Mississippi*, 1891.

★ McCardle was editor of the *Vicksburg Times*.

Instead of a separate nationality, as was intended by Confederate contention, based **3** upon the great principle that the people have a right to choose their own form of government, and to be sustained in that choice by the fundamental law of the land, we have a united country, the executive administration of which is confided to one section.

—with William H. McCardle, *A History of Mississippi*, 1891.

Whatever has been written, and now alleged to the contrary, fidelity to the constitu- **4** tion of the fathers has been the test of loyalty with Southern men, and for this, as understood by them, they followed the stars and bars for four long and eventful years, against overwhelming odds, to see it at last buried in a military defeat.

—with William H. McCardle, *A History of Mississippi*, 1891.

Lyman, Theodore

US COLONEL

These rebels are not half starved. A more sinewy, tawny, formidable-looking set of **5** men could not be. In education they are certainly inferior to our native-born people, but they are usually very quick-witted, and they know enough to handle weapons with terrible effect. Their great characteristic is their stoical manliness. They never beg or whimper or complain, but look you straight in the face with as little animosity as if they had never heard a gun fired.

—letter to his family, May 18, 1864.

★ This observation was made of General Robert E. Lee's troops during the battle of Spotsylvania.

1   The wagoners and train rabble and stragglers have committed great outrages in the rear of this army. . . . All this proceeds from one thing—the uncertainty of the death penalty through the false merciful policy of the President.
—*Meade's Headquarters, 1863–1865: The Life and Letters of Colonel Theodore Lyman*, 1922.

2   People must learn that war is a thing of life or death: if a man won't go to the front he must be shot; but our people can't make up their minds to it; it is repulsive to the forms of thought, even of most of the officers who willingly expose their own lives, but will shrink from shooting down a skulker.
—*Meade's Headquarters, 1863–1865: The Life and Letters of Colonel Theodore Lyman*, 1922.

Mackay, Charles (1812–1889)

TIMES (LONDON) WAR CORRESPONDENT

3   The whole moral atmosphere is warlike. The people have eaten of the insane root of military glory that takes the reason captive, and clamours for large doses of the stimulant.
—article, *Times* (London), April 17, 1862.

★ McKay was describing the atmosphere in New York City.

4   The [Emancipation Proclamation] document is what it is the fashion to call "a step in advance"; but it has the fatal demerit of being insufficient to please the ultra-abolitionists, and of being more than enough to offend the Southern slave-owners, the Northern Pro-slavery party, the advocates of State rights, and all that large class of persons, American as well as Irish, who have a social, a political, and an economic objection to the negro, and who, though refusing to enslave him, would absolutely expel and banish him from their territories, as in Illinois and Wisconsin, and who would deny him all social status, as in New York and Pennsylvania.
—article, *Times* (London), October 7, 1862.

5   The Proclamation is as cruel and illogical as the war of which it is the climax. It only declares slaves to be free in States where the President has no more power either to make them free or white than the Imaum of Muscat has, while it retains them in bondage in every place in which his armies could give effect to his words, and convert his theories into facts.
—article, *Times* (London), January 15, 1863.

★ Mackay gave this analysis of Lincoln's Emancipation Proclamation.

6   Raw lads of 18 and 20 form the bulk of the army that defends Washington against the imminent aggression of General Lee. These youths revel and riot in their premature

manhood, and exhibit their exuberant strength and insolence in drunken and other orgies that seem to have no limits but their purses.

—article, *Times* (London), February 28, 1863.

Hitherto the march of Grant—though, if it be ultimately successful, it will be considered heroic—is the advance of a piece of mechanism. He sees no obstacles, and goes blindly and ruthlessly on. He trusts to nothing but superior numbers and hard fighting. The lives of his men are of no value. He throws them away by thousands, to gain half a mile of jungle. . . . At every step he fights at a disadvantage, on ground of the enemy's choosing. But he fights on.

—article, *Times* (London), May 27, 1864.

Magoffin, Beriah

KENTUCKY GOVERNOR

Your dispatch has been received. In answer, I say emphatically that Kentucky will furnish no troops for the wicked purpose of subduing her sister Southern States.

—message to Secretary of War Simon Cameron, April 15, 1861.

★ Although he proclaimed Kentucky's neutrality, Union troops moved into the state and Magoffin resigned in August 1862.

Malet, William Wyndham

Never did I see a happier set than these negroes. For six months had this lady been left with them alone. Her husband's regiment had been ordered to the Mississippi, about 1000 miles west. . . . Not only women, but the men wept: they said they would never leave him—they loved their "massa and missis:" and not one of them has left.

—*An Errand to the South in the Summer of 1862*, 1863.

★ Malet, an Englishman, was writing about a plantation in Horry County, South Carolina.

Maryland Legislature

Whereas the war against the Confederate States is unconstitutional and repugnant to civilization, and will result in a bloody and shameful overthrow of our institutions; and while recognizing the obligations of Maryland to the Union, we sympathize with the South in the struggle for their rights—for the sake of humanity, we are for peace and reconciliation, and solemnly protest against this war, and will take no part in it; *Resolved*, That Maryland implores the President, in the name of God, to cease this unholy war, at least until Congress assembles; that Maryland desires and consents to the recognition of the independence of the Confederate States.

—resolution, May 10, 1861.

Mason, James M. (1798–1871)

CS COMMISSIONER

1   The [British] public mind is very much disturbed by the prospect for the winter, and I am not without hope that it will produce its effects on the councils of the government.
>   —quoted by Nathaniel W. Stephenson in *The Day of the Confederacy: A Chronicle of the Embattled South*, 1919.

★ Mason, the Confederate diplomat in Great Britain, had this hope in November 1862 that Britain would support the Confederacy because the Union blockade was causing Britain's cotton mills to shut down, creating unemployment.

Maury, Betty Herndon (1835–1903)

2   Not a gun was heard this morning. I hope our old National holidays will not be dropped by the Southern Confederacy.
>   —quoted by John D. Wright in *The Language of the Civil War*, 2001.

★ This diary entry was written on July 4, 1861, in Fredericksburg, Virginia.

3   The town is intensely Yankee and looks as though it never had been anything else. Yankee ice carts go about selling Yankee ice. Yankee newsboys cry Yankee papers along the streets. Yankee citizens and Yankee Dutchmen have opened all the stores on Main Street. Some of them have brought their families and look as if they had been born and bred here and intended to stay here until they died. One man has built him a house!
>   —*Diary of Betty Herndon Maury, 1861–1863.*

★ This entry of June 12, 1862, referred to the Union occupation of Fredericksburg, Virginia.

4   Hurrah for domestic manufactures, and a fig for the Yankees. We can do without them.
>   —quoted by John D. Wright in *The Language of the Civil War*, 2001.

★ This diary entry was written on August 18, 1862, while Union forces were occupying her city of Fredericksburg, Virginia, where she was making clothes at home. "Fig" is something worthless.

McCabe, James D.

5   In this hour of darkness the country turned to General Lee, as its last hope. During the entire period between June 1862 and April 1865, he was the only public man whose wisdom was believed in throughout the country, and whose integrity was never impeached; and now men came to the conclusion that if the cause was not already lost, General Lee was the only person capable of saving it.
>   —*Life and Campaigns of General Robert E. Lee*, 1870.

McCardle, William H.

Vicksburg Times editor

★ [See also quotations at Robert Lowry.]

For all physical purposes we are powerless, but brave men can always make them- **1** selves respected, even in the hour of their direst misery. There is a dignity in misfortune, when bravely borne, which commands admiration.
    —letter to the members of the Mississippi State Convention, August 17, 1865.

McCarthy, Carlton

CS private

At Gettysburg, when the artillery fire was at its height, a brawny fellow, who seemed **2** happy at the prospect for a hot time, broke out singing:—"Backward, roll backward, O Time in thy flight: Make me a child again, just for this *fight!*" Another fellow near him replied, "Yes; and a *gal* child at that."
    —*Detailed Minutiae of Soldier Life in the Army of Northern Virginia, 1861–1865,* 1882.

It was not the flag of the Confederacy, but simply the banner, the battle-flag, of the **3** Confederate soldier. As such it should not share in the condemnation which our *cause* received, or suffer from its downfall. The whole world can unite in a chorus of praise to the gallantry of the men who followed where this banner led.
    —*Detailed Minutiae of Soldier Life in the Army of Northern Virginia, 1861–1865,* 1882.

★ This refers to the familiar Confederate flag, not the virtually unknown national one.

No man can exactly define the cause for which the Confederate soldier fought. He **4** was above human reason and above human law, secure in his own rectitude of purpose, accountable to God only, having assumed for himself a "nationality," which he was minded to defend with his life and his property, and thereto pledged his sacred honor.
    —*Detailed Minutiae of Soldier Life in the Army of Northern Virginia, 1861–1865,* 1882.

The romance of war charmed [the Confederate soldier], and he hurried from the **5** embrace of his mother to the embrace of death.
    —*Detailed Minutiae of Soldier Life in the Army of Northern Virginia, 1861–1865,* 1882.

The Confederate soldier fought a host of ills occasioned by the deprivation of chlo- **6** roform and morphia, which were excluded from the Confederacy, by the blockade, as contraband of war.
    —*Detailed Minutiae of Soldier Life in the Army of Northern Virginia, 1861–1865,* 1882.

1   If the peace of this country can only be preserved by forgetting the Confederate soldier's deeds and his claims upon the South, the blessing is too dearly bought. We have sworn to be grateful to him.
      —*Detailed Minutiae of Soldier Life in the Army of Northern Virginia, 1861–1865,* 1882.

2   Everybody remembers how we used to talk about "one Confederate whipping a dozen Yankees." Literally true sometimes, but, generally speaking, two to one made hard work for the boys.
      —*Detailed Minutiae of Soldier Life in the Army of Northern Virginia, 1861–1865,* 1882.

3   Wounds were in great demand after the first wounded hero made his appearance. His wound was the envy of thousands of unfortunates who had not so much as a scratch to boast, and who felt "small" and of little consequence before the man with a bloody bandage. . . . After awhile the wound was regarded as a practical benefit. It secured a furlough of indefinite length, good eating, the attention and admiration of the fair, and, if permanently disabling, a discharge.
      —*Detailed Minutiae of Soldier Life in the Army of Northern Virginia, 1861–1865,* 1882.

4   The newspaper men delighted in telling the soldiers that the Yankees were a diminutive race, of feeble constitution, timid as hares, with no enthusiasm, and that they would perish in short order under the glow of our southern sun.
      —*Detailed Minutiae of Soldier Life in the Army of Northern Virginia, 1861–1865,* 1882.

5   Only the wisest men, those who had seen war before, imagined that the war would last more than a few months. The young volunteers thought one good battle would settle the whole matter; and, indeed, after "first Manassas [Bull Run]" many thought they might as well go home! The whole North was frightened, and no more armies would dare assail the soil of Old Virginia.
      —*Detailed Minutiae of Soldier Life in the Army of Northern Virginia, 1861–1865,* 1882.

6   The Confederate soldier was peculiar in that he was ever ready to fight, but never ready to submit to the routine duty and discipline of the camp or the march. The soldiers were determined to be soldiers after their own notions, and do their duty, for the love of it, as they thought best.
      —*Detailed Minutiae of Soldier Life in the Army of Northern Virginia, 1861–1865,* 1882.

7   But a real good hearty war like that dies hard. No country likes to part with a good earnest war. It likes to talk about the war, write its history, fight its battles over and over again, and build monument after monument to commemorate its glories. A

long time after a war, people begin to find out, as they read, that the deadly struggle **1**
marked a grand period in their history!
> —*Detailed Minutiae of Soldier Life in the Army of Northern Virginia, 1861–1865,*
> 1882.

The soldier may forget the long, weary march, with its dust, heat, and thirst, and he **2**
may forget the horrors and blood of the battlefield, or he may recall them sadly, as
he thinks of the loved dead; but the cheerful, happy scenes of the camp-fire he will
never forget.
> —*Detailed Minutiae of Soldier Life in the Army of Northern Virginia, 1861–1865,*
> 1882.

The "Boys in Blue" generally preferred to camp in the open fields. The Confeds took **3**
to the woods, and so the Confederate camp was not as orderly or as systematically
arranged, but the most picturesque of the two.
> —*Detailed Minutiae of Soldier Life in the Army of Northern Virginia, 1861–1865,*
> 1882.

If there were any true men in the South, any brave, any noble, they were in the army. **4**
> —*Detailed Minutiae of Soldier Life in the Army of Northern Virginia, 1861–1865,*
> 1882.

The very intensity of their sufferings became a source of merriment. Instead of **5**
growling, and deserting, they laughed at their own bare feet, ragged clothes, and
pinched faces; and weak, hungry, cold, wet and dirty, with no hope of reward or rest,
they marched cheerfully to meet the warmly clad and well-fed hosts of the enemy.
> —*Detailed Minutiae of Soldier Life in the Army of Northern Virginia, 1861–1865,*
> 1882.

The more experienced troops knew better when to give up than green ones, and **6**
never fought well after they were satisfied that they could not accomplish their purpose. Consequently it often happened that the best troops failed where the raw ones
did well.
> —*Detailed Minutiae of Soldier Life in the Army of Northern Virginia, 1861–1865,*
> 1882.

The Confederate soldier knows the elements of his success—courage, endurance, **7**
and devotion. He knows also by whom he was defeated—sickness, starvation, death.
He fought not men only, but food, raiment, pay, glory, fame, and fanaticism. He
endured privation, toil, and contempt. He won, and despite the cold indifference of
all and the hearty hatred of some, he will have for all time, in all places where gen-
erosity is, a fame untarnished.
> —*Detailed Minutiae of Soldier Life in the Army of Northern Virginia, 1861–1865,*
> 1882.

Many of the men were sobbing and crying like children recovering from convulsions **8**
of grief after a severe whipping. They were sorely grieved, mortified, and humili-

ated. . . . Other men fairly raved with indignation and declared their desire to escape or die in the attempt; but not a man was heard to blame General Lee. On the contrary, all expressed the greatest sympathy for him and declared their willingness to submit at once or fight to the last man, as he ordered. At no period of the war was he held in higher veneration or regarded with more sincere affection than on that sad and tearful day.
>   —*Detailed Minutiae of Soldier Life in the Army of Northern Virginia, 1861–1865*, 1882.

>   ★ McCarthy was describing the Confederate scene after the surrender at Appomattox Court House, Virginia.

McClellan, George B. (1826–1885)

US MAJOR GENERAL

1   I almost think that were I to win some small success now I could become Dictator or anything else that might please me—but nothing of that kind would please me.
>   —letter to his wife, Ellen, July 27, 1861.

>   ★ McClellan had just assumed command of the Division of the Potomac defending Washington, D.C., after the Union defeat at the first battle of Bull Run (first Manassas) on July 21, 1861.

2   By some strange operation of magic I seem to have become the power of the land.
>   —letter to his wife, Ellen, July 27, 1861.

3   I found no army to command; a mere collection of regiments, cowering on the banks of the Potomac, some perfectly raw, others dispirited by the recent defeat. . . . The city [of Washington, D.C.] was almost in a condition to have been taken by a dash of cavalry.
>   —quoted by Alfred H. Guernsey and Henry M. Alden in *Harper's Pictorial History of the Great Rebellion in the United States*, 1866.

>   ★ This was on July 27, 1861, six days after the Union defeat at the first battle of Bull Run (first Manassas). McClellan was assuming command of the Division of the Potomac.

4   I shall carry this thing on "en grand" and crush the rebels in one campaign.
>   —letter to his wife, Ellen, August 2, 1861.

5   We have had our last retreat. We have seen our last defeat. You stand by me, and I will stand by you, and henceforth victory will crown our efforts.
>   —speech to Pennsylvania soldiers, September 10, 1861.

>   ★ Lincoln and his cabinet were also there.

6   Averell, if any army can save this country, it will be the Army of the Potomac, and it must be saved for that purpose.
>   —quoted by Major General William W. Averell in *Battles and Leaders of the Civil War*, vol. 2, 1888.

★ McClellan was turning down Averell's suggestion that they march on Richmond during the Peninsular campaign.

Soldiers of the Army of the Potomac! For a long time I have kept you inactive, but   1
not without a purpose; you were to be disciplined, armed and instructed; the formidable artillery you now have, had to be created; other armies were to move and accomplish certain results. I have held you back that you might give the death-blow to the rebellion that has distracted our once happy country.
  —speech to troops, March 14, 1862.

★ McClellan's hesitancy continued, and Lincoln relieved him of his command in November.

I am to watch over you as a parent over his children; and you know that your general   2
loves you from the depths of his heart.
  —speech to his troops, March 1862.

It shall be my care, as it ever has been, to gain success with the least possible loss;   3
but I know that, if necessary, you will willingly follow me to our graves for our righteous cause.
  —speech to his troops, March 1862.

The President very coolly telegraphed me yesterday that he thought I had better   4
break the enemy's lines at once. I was tempted to reply that he had better come and do it himself.
  —letter to his wife, Ellen, April 8, 1862.

I am tired of the sickening sight of the battlefield, with its mangled corpses & poor   5
suffering wounded! Victory has no charms for me when purchased at such cost.
  —letter to his wife, Ellen, June 2, 1862.

Soldiers! I will be with you in this battle, and share its dangers with you. Our confi-   6
dence in each other is now founded upon the past. Let us strike the blow which is to restore peace and union to this distracted land.
  —speech to his troops, June 3, 1862.

After to-morrow we shall fight the rebel army as soon as Providence will permit. We   7
shall await only a favorable condition of the earth and sky and the completion of some necessary preliminaries.
  —telegram to Secretary of War Edwin M. Stanton, June 18, 1862.

★ Lincoln was fuming about McClellan's delaying tactics, and the general's many promises were never fulfilled.

I shall do my best to save the army. Send more gunboats.   8
  —quoted by Rod Graff in *Civil War Quiz and Fact Book*, 1985.

★ McClellan appealed to Washington while in retreat during the Seven Days' battles in 1862.

1   I have lost this battle [Gaines's Mill] because my force is too small. The Government must not and cannot hold me responsible for the result. . . . If I save this army now, I tell you plainly that I owe no thanks to you or to any other persons in Washington. You have done your best to sacrifice this army.
      —telegram to Secretary of War Edwin M. Stanton, June 28, 1862.

      ★ McClellan's 34,214 troops engaged 57,018 Confederate ones.

2   If I save the army now, I tell you plainly that I owe no thanks to you or any other persons in Washington.
      —letter to Secretary of War Edwin M. Stanton, June 28, 1862.

      ★ This was written nine days before McClellan sent Lincoln a letter instructing him on how to run the war.

3   On this our Nation's Birthday we declare to our foes, who are rebels against the best interests of mankind, that this Army shall enter the Capital of their so-called Confederacy; that our National Constitution shall prevail; and that the Union which can alone insure internal peace and external security to each State must and shall by preserved, cost what it may in time, treasure and blood.
      —speech to the Army of the Potomac, July 4, 1862.

4   This rebellion has assumed the character of a war; as such it should be regarded, and it should be conducted upon the highest principles known to Christian civilization. It should not be a war looking to the subjugation of the people of any state, in any event. It should not be at all a war upon population but against armed forces and political organizations. Neither confiscation of property, political executions of persons, territorial organization of states, or forcible abolition of slavery should be contemplated for a moment.
      —letter to Lincoln, July 7, 1862.

5   Unless the principles governing the future conduct of our struggle shall be made known and approved, the effort to obtain requisite forces will be almost hopeless. A declaration of radical views, especially upon slavery, will rapidly disintegrate our present armies.
      —letter to Lincoln, July 7, 1862.

6   The national forces should not be dispersed in expeditions, posts of occupation, and numerous armies, but should be mainly collected into masses and brought to bear upon the armies of the Confederate States. Those armies thoroughly defeated, the political structure which they support would soon cease to exist.
      —letter to Lincoln, July 7, 1862.

7   I am tired of serving fools. God help my country! He alone can save it.
      —letter to his wife, Ellen, July 20, 1862.

8   I don't like Jackson's movements—he will suddenly appear when least expected.
      —telegram to Major General Henry W. Halleck, August 14, 1862.

★ This worry about "Stonewall" Jackson was expressed during the second Bull Run campaign.

Please say a kind word to my army that I can repeat to them in general orders . . . No 1 one has ever said anything to cheer them but myself. Say nothing about me. Merely give my men and officers credit for what they have done. It will do you much good, and will strengthen you much with them, if you issue a handsome order to them in regard to what they have accomplished. They deserve it.
    —message to Major General Henry W. Halleck, August 18, 1862.

★ Halleck was general in chief, an administrative post in Washington, D.C., at the time.

I cannot express to you the pain and mortification I have experienced to-day in lis- 2 tening to the distant sound of the firing of my men. As I can be of no further use here [at his camp near Alexander, Virginia], I respectfully ask that if there is a possibility of the conflict being renewed to-morrow, I may be permitted to go to the scene of battle with my staff, merely to be with my own men, if nothing more; they will fight none the worse for my being with them. If it is not deemed best to intrust me with the command even of my own army, I simply ask to be permitted to share their fate on the field of battle.
    —telegram to Major General Henry W. Halleck, August 30, 1862.

★ McClellan had been relieved of his command of the Army of the Potomac, and this request was not approved. Two days later he was put in charge of troops defending Washington, D.C.

[Lincoln] then said that he regarded Washington as lost, and asked me if I would, 3 under the circumstances, consent to accept command of all the forces. Without one moment's hesitation and without making any conditions whatever, I at once said that I would accept the command and would stake my life that I would save the city. Both the President and [General Henry] Halleck again asserted that it was impossible to save the city, and I repeated my firm conviction that I could and would save it. They then left, the President verbally placing me in entire command of the city and of the troops falling back upon it from the front.
    —quoted in *Battles and Leaders of the Civil War*, vol. 2, 1888.

★ This happened on September 1, 1862.

Again I have been called upon to save the country.   4
    —letter to his wife, Ellen, September 5, 1862.

★ He had been replaced as commander in chief of the army by Major General John Pope but then reinstated. McClellan was again relieved of his command this same month.

Should an able-bodied man leave ranks without orders and become a straggler, he 5 will be tried by a drum-head court martial and shot.
    —order to his troops, September 10, 1862.

★ This warning was printed on handbills distributed to his troops.

1   Here is a paper with which if I cannot whip Bobby Lee I will be willing to go home.
　　　—quoted by John Gibbon in *Personal Recollections of the Civil War*, 1928.

　　　★ McClellan made this comment to Brigadier General John Gibbon after he had been handed, on September 13, 1862, the "lost dispatch" of General Robert E. Lee, detailing Lee's military plans in Maryland. After the horrific battle of Antietam (Sharpsburg) four days later, Lee withdrew from Maryland (but it was McClellan who soon lost his command).

2   If I don't crush Lee now, you may call me whatever you please.
　　　—quoted by CS lieutenant William Miller Owen in *In Camp and Battle with the Washington Artillery*, 1885.

　　　★ On September 13, 1862, McClellan had been handed a discovered Special Order No. 191 (the "lost dispatch") of General Robert E. Lee, detailing Lee's military plans in Maryland.

3   By George, this is a magnificent field, and if we win this fight it will cover all our errors and misfortunes forever.
　　　—quoted by Kenneth C. Davis in *Don't Know Much about the Civil War*, 1996.

　　　★ This was said at the battle of Antietam (Sharpsburg).

4   Our victory [at Antietam (Sharpsburg)] was complete, and the disorganized rebel army has rapidly returned to Virginia, its dreams of "invading Pennsylvania" dissipated for ever. I feel some little pride in having, with a beaten and demoralized army, defeated Lee so utterly and saved the North so completely.
　　　—letter to his wife, Ellen, September 20, 1862.

　　　★ He was soon relieved of his command for not pursuing Lee's army.

5   You should see my soldiers now! You never saw anything like their enthusiasm. It surpasses anything you ever imagined.
　　　—letter to his wife, Ellen, September 20, 1862.

　　　★ This was written after the battle of Antietam (Sharpsburg).

6   The army is not now in a condition to undertake another campaign nor to bring on another battle, unless some great advantages are offered by some mistake of the enemy, or pressing military exigencies render it necessary.
　　　—quoted by Lieutenant Colonel G. F. R. Henderson in *Stonewall Jackson and the American Civil War*, vol. 2, 1898.

　　　★ This message to Washington was on September 27, 1862.

7   One battle lost and almost all would have been lost. Lee's army might have marched as it pleased on Washington, Baltimore, Philadelphia, or New York. It could have levied its supplies from a fertile and undevastated country, extorted tribute from wealthy and populous cities, and nowhere east of the Alleghanies was there another organized force to avert its march.
　　　—quoted by Lieutenant Colonel G. F. R. Henderson in *Stonewall Jackson and the American Civil War*, vol. 2, 1898.

★ McClellan was explaining his failure to pursue Lee after the battle of Antietam (Sharpsburg).

The States of the North are flooded with deserters and absentees. One corps of this **1** army has 18,000 men present and 15,000 absent; of this 15,000, 8,000 probably are at work at home.
   —quoted by Lieutenant Colonel G. F. R. Henderson in *Stonewall Jackson and the American Civil War*, vol. 2, 1898.

★ This was in September 1862.

That I must have made many mistakes I cannot deny. I do not see any great blun- **2** ders—but no one can judge of himself. Our consolation must be that we have tried to do what was right; if we have failed, it was not our fault.
   —letter to his wife, Ellen, November 7, 1862.

★ He had received orders that day relieving him of his command of the Army of the Potomac.

In parting from you I cannot express the love and gratitude I bear to you. As an army **3** you have grown up under my care. In you I have never found doubt or coldness. The battles you have fought under my command will proudly live in our nation's history.
   —farewell speech to the Army of the Potomac, November 7, 1862.

★ He had been relieved of his command for failing to pursue General Robert E. Lee after the battle of Antietam (Sharpsburg).

The glory you have achieved, our mutual perils and fatigues, the graves of our com- **4** rades fallen in battle and by disease, the broken forms of those whom wounds and sickness have disabled—the strongest associations which can exist among men,—unite us still by an indissoluble tie.
   —farewell speech to the Army of the Potomac, November 7, 1862.

Stand by General Burnside as you have stood by me and all will be well.   **5**
   —farewell speech to the Army of the Potomac, November 7, 1862.

★ Major General Ambrose E. Burnside replaced McClellan as commander of the Army of the Potomac.

Burnside is the best and honestest of men. He is no Mr. Pope. He will do a great deal **6** better than you expect.
   —quoted in *Harper's Weekly*, November 29, 1862.

★ General Ambrose Burnside had been given command of the Army of the Potomac in September 1862. General John Pope had failed in that position.

As a general rule, officers (and, of course, the non-commissioned officers) of volun- **7** teer regiments were entirely ignorant of their duties, and many were unfitted, from

their education, moral character, or mental deficiencies, for ever acquiring the requisite efficiency.
—*McClellan's Own Story*, 1887.

1   Many of these raw civilians, who were men of pride, intelligence, and education, soon became excellent officers; though these very men most keenly regretted their lack of a good military education in early life.
—*McClellan's Own Story*, 1887.

2   Among the Northern men there was little difficulty in establishing discipline when the officers were intelligent gentlemen; but, in the early part of the war particularly, it occurred that the officers were sometimes inferior in intelligence and education to the soldiers, and in these cases the establishment of discipline presented far greater difficulties.
—*McClellan's Own Story*, 1887.

3   The Army of the Potomac was mainly composed of good men, who took up arms from the noblest of motives; and I doubt whether any troops ever did so little needless damage in hostile country. But at best a large army leaves a wide swath in its rear, and cannot move without leaving the marks of its passage.
—*McClellan's Own Story*, 1887.

4   An incompetent division commander could not often jeopardize the safety of an army; while an unfit corps commander could easily lose a battle and frustrate the best-conceived plan of campaign.
—quoted in *Battles and Leaders of the Civil War*, vol. 2, 1888.

5   General Lee and I knew each other well. In the days before the war we served together in Mexico, and we had commanded against each other in the Peninsula. I had the highest respect for his ability as a commander, and knew that he was a general not to be trifled with or carelessly afforded an opportunity of striking a fatal blow. Each of us naturally regarded his own army as the better, but each entertained the highest respect for the endurance, courage, and fighting qualities of the opposing army; and this feeling extended to the officers and men.
—quoted in *Battles and Leaders of the Civil War*, vol. 2, 1888.

6   Perhaps there is no doubt that he [Pickett] was the best infantry soldier developed on either side during the Civil War.
—edited by La Salle Corbell Pickett in *The Heart of a Soldier*, 1913.

★ Although on opposing sides, McClellan and Major General George E. Pickett were close friends.

7   Action, action is what we want and what we must have.
—quoted by Randall Bedwell in *Brink of Destruction*, 1999.

★ This was an ironic declaration from the hesitant McClellan.

McDowell, Irvin (1818–1885)

US BRIGADIER GENERAL

It is with the deepest mortification that the commanding general finds it necessary **1**
to reiterate his orders for the preservation of the property of the inhabitants of the
district occupied by the troops under his command. It is again ordered that no one
shall arrest or attempt to arrest any citizen not in arms at the time, or search, or
attempt to search any house, or even to enter the same, without permission. The
troops must behave themselves with as much forbearance and propriety as if they
were at their own homes. They are here to fight the enemies of the country, not to
judge and punish the unarmed and defenseless, however guilty they may be.
    —quoted by Alfred H. Guernsey and Henry M. Alden in *Harper's Pictorial
    History of the Great Rebellion in the United States*, 1866.

★ This order was given before the first battle of Bull Run (first Manassas). A few of
McDowell's soldiers had sacked and burned houses.

This is not an army. It will take a long time to make an army. **2**
    —quoted by Nathaniel W. Stephenson in *Lincoln: An Account of His Personal
    Life, Especially of Its Springs of Action as Revealed and Deepened by the Ordeal
    of War*, 1922.

★ McDowell said this as commander of those Union troops about to lose the first battle of Bull Run (first Manassas).

I wanted very much a little time—all of us wanted it. We did not have a bit of it. **3**
    —quoted by William Swinton in *Campaigns of the Army of the Potomac*, 1866.

★ McDowell was lamenting about having to rush green Union soldiers into their defeat
at the first battle of Bull Run (first Manassas).

The retreat soon became a rout, and this soon degenerated still farther into a panic. **4**
    —quoted by Alfred H. Guernsey and Henry M. Alden in *Harper's Pictorial
    History of the Great Rebellion in the United States*, 1866.

★ He was describing the Union defeat at the first battle of Bull Run (first Manassas).

McGuire, Hunter Holmes (1835–1900)

CS BRIGADE DOCTOR

General Jackson demanded of his subordinates implicit, blind obedience. He gave **5**
orders in his own peculiar, terse, rapid way, and he did not permit them to be questioned. He obeyed his own superiors in the same fashion.
    —quoted by Lieutenant Colonel G. F. R. Henderson in *Stonewall Jackson and the
    American Civil War*, vol. 2, 1898.

★ McGuire was Jackson's doctor.

There is no measuring the intensity with which the very soul of Jackson burned in **6**
battle. Out of it he was very gentle. Indeed, as I look back on the two years that I was

daily, indeed hourly, with him, his gentleness as a man, his tenderness to those in trouble or affliction—the tenderness of a woman—impress me more than his wonderful prowess as a warrior.

—quoted by Lieutenant Colonel G. F. R. Henderson in *Stonewall Jackson and the American Civil War*, vol. 1, 1898.

McGuire, Judith Brockenbrough

1 The fires of our enthusiasm and patriotism were burning all the while to a degree which might have been consuming, but that our tongues served as safety-valves.

—*Diary of a Southern Refugee during the War, by a Lady of Virginia*, 1867.

★ This entry of May 10, 1861, described a gathering of ladies sewing for Confederate soldiers.

2 "Thank God," said a man with his leg amputated, "that it was not my right arm, for then I could never have fought again; as soon as this stump is well I shall join Stuart's cavalry; I can ride with a wooden leg as well as a real one.

—*Diary of a Southern Refuge during the War, by A Lady of Virginia*, 1867.

★ This entry was written on June 9, 1862.

3 General Johnston surrendered on the 26th of April. "My native land, good-night!"

—*Diary of a Southern Refugee during the War, by a Lady of Virginia*, 1867.

★ This entry, dated May 4, 1865, was the final one.

McKim, Randolph H.

CS Lieutenant

★ McKim, a member of the Army of Northern Virginia, was from Baltimore. He became a clergyman after the war.

4 Do not, my precious mother, be too much alarmed and too anxious about me. I trust and hope that God will protect me from "the terror by night" and "the destruction that wasteth at noon-day."

—letter to his mother, July 20, 1861.

5 Well, I *may* get used to standing up and being shot at, but this kind of food will kill me in a week. I had expected a baptism of fire, and looked forward to it with some nervousness, but, instead I had had a baptism of soup which threatened an untimely end to my military career.

—*A Soldier's Recollections: Leaves from the Diary of a Young Confederate*, 1910.

★ This comment was made before the first battle of Bull Run (first Manassas).

6 Somehow I was especially moved by the sight of the battery horses on Henry Hill, so frightfully torn by shot and shell. The sufferings of the poor brutes, not in their own battle or by their own fault, but for man's sake, appealed to me in a peculiar way.

—*A Soldier's Recollections: Leaves from the Diary of a Young Confederate*, 1910.

★ This was at the first battle of Bull Run (first Manassas).

It so happened that the same Massachusetts regiment which was so roughly handled **1** by the people of Baltimore on the 19th of April was in our front on the 21st of July [at the first battle of Bull Run (first Manassas)], and prisoners afterwards told us that when we charged the Massachusetts men said, "Here come those d—d Baltimore men! It's time for us to git up and git!"
    —*A Soldier's Recollections: Leaves from the Diary of a Young Confederate*, 1910.

★ He is referring to secessionist sympathizers attacking Massachusetts troops when they passed through Baltimore.

The people in this neighborhood [of Fairfax County, Virginia] said that when they **2** saw the [Union] army pass here they thought we would never return again, but that the Southern army would be certainly crushed. How different the result.
    —*A Soldier's Recollections: Leaves from the Diary of a Young Confederate*, 1910.

★ He was referring to the first battle of Bull Run (first Manassas).

Nearly seven months have flown by in my soldier's life, and they have been months **3** of external activity, but activity of the body only. It has been a period of mental slumber—nay, sloth—for the mind has not even *dreamed*, it has stagnated.
    —*A Soldier's Recollections: Leaves from the Diary of a Young Confederate*, 1910.

★ This diary entry was written on January 24, 1862.

Our affairs look dark, but not hopeless. The war may be a long one, but it *can* have **4** but one termination—our independence. We are stimulated to new exertion, our people are roused to action, and there exists a deep-seated resolve in the heart of the nation, to choose extermination before subjugation.
    —letter to his mother, March 10, 1862.

Go it boys! Maryland whip Maryland! **5**
    —*A Soldier's Recollections: Leaves from the Diary of a Young Confederate*, 1910.

★ McKim was describing "a lovely girl of about fifteen" who ran into the street at Fort Royal, Maryland, from her house waving a Confederate flag while bullets whistled around her. McKim and his rebel Maryland soldiers were battling loyal ones. This diary entry was written on May 23, 1862.

We are all brothers and sisters now in the South. I always feel sure wherever I am **6** that I will be a welcomed guest on account of the proud title I bear, "a soldier of the South."
    —letter to his mother, June 24, 1862.

Again and again in this Pennsylvania campaign the citizens told us that we treated **7** them far better than their own soldiers did. I can truly say I didn't see a fence rail burned between Hagerstown and Gettysburg.
    —*A Soldier's Recollections: Leaves from the Diary of a Young Confederate*, 1910.

Let me tell you not to believe the stories in the Northern papers about the rout and **8** demoralization of our army. We remained in Maryland ten days after the battle [of Gettysburg], and yet our enemy dared not attack us, though we lay in line of battle

three days within half a mile of him. Our loss was not as heavy as theirs according to their own account, either in killed or prisoners. The men are in good discipline and spirits, and ready to teach our foes a lesson when they meet them again.
    —letter to his mother, July 15, 1863.

1   It is a great mistake to suppose that the army of Lee was at all shaken or demoralized by the battle [of Gettysburg]. It was on the contrary as full of fight as ever—as ready to obey the commands of its idolized chief.
    —*A Soldier's Recollections: Leaves from the Diary of a Young Confederate*, 1910.

2   I never felt so miserable in my life—the possibility of defeat, the slaughter of the men, the retreat from the breastworks, and the consequent confusion, and the almost certain expectation of being killed or wounded, and the vivid foresight of the grief of my poor wife—all made me feel more miserable than I have ever been before.
    —*A Soldier's Recollections: Leaves from the Diary of a Young Confederate*, 1910.

3   I hope I may be among those who before long shall march into Baltimore and deliver her from her oppressors. Poor Baltimore! My heart bleeds for her.
    —*A Soldier's Recollections: Leaves from the Diary of a Young Confederate*, 1910.

4   During those ten days [in October 1861] I had frequent opportunity of seeing that superb soldier and strategist, Gen. Joseph E. Johnston, whose removal in 1864 from the command of the southwestern army sealed, or at any rate hastened, the doom of the Confederacy.
    —*A Soldier's Recollections: Leaves from the Diary of a Young Confederate*, 1910.

5   I may also mention that the present eminent professor of oriental languages in Harvard University, Dr. Crawford H. Toy, was a private in a Virginia regiment. He was found by a friend in an interval of the battle of Cold Harbor in June, 1864, lying on his oil-cloth immersed in the study of Arabic.
    —*A Soldier's Recollections: Leaves from the Diary of a Young Confederate*, 1910.

6   The Southern soldier was fighting to repel invasion. He was regarded as the defender of the homes and firesides of the people. The common perils, the common hardships, the common sacrifices of the war, welded the Southern people together as if they were all of the same blood, all of one family. In fact, there was, independently of the war, a homogeneity in the South that the North knew nothing of. But when the war came, this was greatly intensified.
    —*A Soldier's Recollections: Leaves from the Diary of a Young Confederate*, 1910.

7   Had [Jefferson Davis] been quite ignorant of military matters, he would have been a more successful President. In that case it is likely Robert E. Lee would have been made commander-in-chief in 1862, instead of in 1865, when it was too late.
    —*A Soldier's Recollections: Leaves from the Diary of a Young Confederate*, 1910.

[Jackson's] figure was bad, his riding was ungraceful (he rode, as I remember him, **1** with short stirrups and with one shoulder higher than the other), and his uniform usually rusty, with scarce anything to mark him out as a general.
　—*A Soldier's Recollections: Leaves from the Diary of a Young Confederate*, 1910.

The fact is we were soldier boys, and sometimes the "boy" was more in evidence **2** than the "soldier."
　—*A Soldier's Recollections: Leaves from the Diary of a Young Confederate*, 1910.

★ McKim was writing about camp life.

The valley of Virginia was for four years a constant battle ground. Up and down, all **3** the way from Staunton to Shepherdstown the two armies swept, till at the end it was reduced to a scene of desolation.
　—*A Soldier's Recollections: Leaves from the Diary of a Young Confederate*, 1910.

We loved Maryland. We were proud of her history, of her traditions. We felt that she **4** was in bondage against her will, and we burned with desire to have part in liberating her. She had not seceded. There was no star in the Confederate flag to represent Maryland. But we believed, in spite of the division of sentiment in the State, that if she had been free to speak, her voice would have been for the South.
　—*A Soldier's Recollections: Leaves from the Diary of a Young Confederate*, 1910.

Believing as we did that the war was a war of subjugation, and that it meant, if suc- **5** cessful, the destruction of our liberties, the issue in our minds was clear drawn . . . The Union without Liberty, or Liberty without the Union.
　—*A Soldier's Recollections: Leaves from the Diary of a Young Confederate*, 1910.

★ This was a popular Confederate slogan.

Everyone who was conversant with the opinions of the soldiers of the Southern **6** Army, knows that they did not wage that tremendous conflict for slavery. That was a subject very little in their thoughts or on their lips. Not one in twenty of the grim veterans, who were so terrible on the battlefield, had any financial interest in slavery. No, they were fighting for liberty, for the right of self-government. They believed the Federal authorities were assailing that right. . . . They may have been right, or they may have been wrong, but that was the issue they made. On that they stood. For that they died.
　—*The Soul of Lee*, 1918.

Meade, George G. (1815–1872)

US GENERAL

I am tired of this playing war without risks. We must encounter risks if we fight, and **7** we cannot carry on the war without fighting.
　—letter to his wife, January 2, 1863.

1   There is now no doubt that [McClellan] allowed three distinct occasions to take Richmond slip through his hands for want of nerve to run what he considered risks. Such a general will never command success, though he may avoid disaster.
      —letter to his wife, January 2, 1863.

2   From the time I took command till today, I . . . have not had a regular night's rest, and many nights not a wink of sleep, and for several days did not even wash my face and hands, no regular food, and all the time in a state of mental anxiety. Indeed, I think I have lived as much in this time as in the last thirty years.
      —letter to his wife, July 7, 1863.

3   If you have any orders to give me I am prepared to receive and obey them, but I must insist on being spared the infliction of such truisms in the guise of opinions as you have recently honored me with, particularly as they were not asked for.
      —telegram to Major General Henry W. Halleck, October 18, 1863.

4   Not years, but General Lee himself has made me gray.
      —quoted by CS major general John B. Gordon in *Reminiscences of the Civil War*, 1904.

      ★ This was his retort when Lee, after surrendering, teased him about looking older. Before the war, they had served together in the US Army.

5   My God, what misery this dreadful war has produced, and how it comes home to the doors of almost every one!
      —letter to his wife, April 13, 1865.

Medill, Joseph (1823–1899)

Chicago Tribune editor

6   Lincoln has some very weak and foolish traits of character.
      —letter to E. B. Washburne, April 12, 1864.

Meehan, John

US private

      ★ Meehan was a member of the 118th Pennsylvania Regiment.

7   As this was my first time actually under enemy fire, I was greatly excited. My feelings are hard to describe. When walking across the open field, with the artillery firing overhead and the rebels firing at us, I felt afraid. My heart beat tumultuously. I thought I might be killed, and had no wish to die. I longed to live, and thought myself a fool for voluntarily placing myself in the army. Yet I had no idea at all of turning back.
      —*History of the Corn Exchange Regiment*, 1888.

Melville, Herman (1819–1891)

Writer

All wars are boyish and are fought by boys.   **1**
 —*Battle-Pieces*, 1866.

Miles, Nelson A. (1839–1925)

US lieutenant general

We never knew whether [Jackson] would descend upon us on the right flank, or the   **2**
left, or out of the clouds. He was the very embodiment of the genius of war, and, had
he lived, in my opinion, the South must certainly have succeeded.
 —quoted by CS lieutenant Randolph H. McKim in *A Soldier's Recollections:
Leaves from the Diary of a Young Confederate*, 1910.

Miller, William B. (1840–1864)

US private

 ★ Miller was a member of the 75th Indian Infantry.

The arsenal contained some small-arms and about four thousand pikes and sabers   **3**
for cutting up Yankees and now we are here for the sacrifice and the butchers are not
at home.
 —diary quoted by Philip Katcher in *Great Gambles of the Civil War*, 1996.

 ★ Miller helped raid the arsenal in Atlanta.

I seen one old Reb lying along the road (quite an old man) that had a saber stroke   **4**
across his back and he was not dead yet but mortally wounded and under other circumstances his gray hairs would have appealed to my heart for sympathy, but we are
not here to sympathize with men who brought it on themselves.
 —diary quoted by Philip Katcher in *Great Gambles of the Civil War*, 1996.

 ★ Miller was encountering Confederate soldiers in Georgia.

Mitchel, Ormsby M. (1809–1862)

US major general

When [the rebels] come to their senses, we will receive them with open arms; but till   **5**
that time, while they are trailing our glorious banner in the dust, when they scorn it,
condemn it, curse it, and trample it under foot, then I must smite. In God's name I
will smite, and as long as I have strength I will do it.
 —speech at the Union Meeting in Union Square, New York City, April 20, 1861.

 ★ Mitchel, a native of Kentucky, was at this time superintendent of the Dudley Obser-
vatory in Albany, New York.

1 Let every man put his life in his hand, and say, "There is the altar of my country; there I will sacrifice my life." I, for one, will lay my life down. It is not mine any longer. Lead me to the conflict.

—speech at the Union Meeting in Union Square, New York City, April 20, 1861.

2 I owe allegiance to no particular State, and never did, and, God helping me, I never will. I owe allegiance to the Government of the United States.

—speech at the Union Meeting in Union Square, New York City, April 20, 1861.

3 I shall soon have watchful guards among the slaves on the plantations from Bridgeport to Florence [both in Alabama], and all who communicate to me valuable information I have promised the protection of my government.

—telegram to Secretary of War Edwin M. Stanton, May 4, 1862.

★ Mitchel was a major general at this time. He died in the war of yellow fever.

4 The most terrible outrages—robberies, rapes, arsons, and plunderings—are being committed by lawless brigands and vagabonds connected with the army.

—quoted by Major General Don Carlos Buell in *Battles and Leaders of the Civil War*, vol. 2, 1888.

★ This was a telegram to Secretary of War Edwin M. Stanton reporting on Mitchel's occupation of north Alabama.

Mitchell, J. B. (1833–1916)

CS LIEUTENANT

5 There was a great deal of pilfering performed on the dead bodies of the Yankees by our men. Some of them were left as naked as they were born, everything in the world they had being taken from them. I ordered my men to take their fine guns and canteens if they wished, but nothing else.

—quoted in *Civil War Times Illustrated*, November 1977.

Mitchell, Mary Bedinger

6 There are always stragglers, of course, but never before or after did I see anything comparable to the demoralized state of the Confederates at this time. Never were want and exhaustion more visibly put before my eyes, and that they could march or fight at all seemed incredible.

—"In the Wake of Battle (A Woman's Recollections of Shepherdstown during Antietam Week)," *Century Magazine*, July 1886.

★ This was on September 13, 1862, four days before the battle of Antietam (Sharpsburg). Shepherdstown was in western Virginia (now West Virginia).

It is curious how much louder guns sound when they are pointed at you than when **1**
turned the other way!
> —"In the Wake of Battle (A Woman's Recollections of Shepherdstown during
> Antietam Week)," *Century Magazine*, July 1886.

★ Union forces were shelling her town.

What we feared were the stragglers and hangers-on and nondescripts that circle **2**
round an army like the great buzzards we shuddered to see wheeling silently over us.
> —"In the Wake of Battle (A Woman's Recollections of Shepherdstown during
> Antietam Week)," *Century Magazine*, July 1886.

We presently passed into debatable land, when we were in the Confederacy in the **3**
morning, in the Union after dinner, and on neutral ground at night.
> —"In the Wake of Battle (A Woman's Recollections of Shepherdstown during
> Antietam Week)," *Century Magazine*, July 1886.

★ This was because the townspeople did not know which side would control Shepherdstown next.

A Federal soldier once said to me, "I was always sorry for your wounded; they never **4**
seemed to get any care." The remark was extreme, but there was much justice in it.
We were fond of calling them Spartans, and they were but too truly called upon to
endure a Spartan system of neglect and privation. They were generally ill-fed and ill-
cared for.
> —"In the Wake of Battle (A Woman's Recollections of Shepherdstown during
> Antietam Week)," *Century Magazine*, July 1886.

★ This was on September 13, 1862, four days before the battle of Antietam (Sharpsburg).

Then there was the hunt for bandages. Every housekeeper ransacked her stores and **5**
brought forth things new and old. I saw one girl, in despair for a strip of cloth, look
about helplessly, and then rip off the hem of her white petticoat.
> —"In the Wake of Battle (A Woman's Recollections of Shepherdstown during
> Antietam Week)," *Century Magazine*, July 1886.

★ This was on September 13, 1862, four days before the battle of Antietam (Sharpsburg).

The road [out of Shepherdstown] was thronged, the streets blocked; men were **6**
vociferating, women crying, children screaming; wagons, ambulances, guns, cais-
sons, horsemen, footmen, all mingled—nay, even wedged and jammed together—in
one struggling, shouting mass. The negroes were the worst, and with faces of a
ghastly ash-color, and staring eyes, they swarmed into the fields, carrying their
babies, their clothes, their pots and kettles, fleeing from the wrath behind them.
> —"In the Wake of Battle (A Woman's Recollections of Shepherdstown during
> Antietam Week)," *Century Magazine*, July 1886.

★ Shepherdstown was being shelled by Union troops.

1   An ever present sense of anguish, dread, pity, and, I fear, hatred—these are my recollections of Antietam.
> —"In the Wake of Battle (A Woman's Recollections of Shepherdstown during Antietam Week)," *Century Magazine*, July 1886.

Monroe, John T. (1823–1871)

New Orleans mayor

2   We yield to physical force alone, and maintain our allegiance to the Government of the Confederate States. Beyond this a due respect for our dignity, our rights, and the flag of our country does not, I think, permit us to go.
> —message to the city council, April 25, 1862.

★ Three days later, Monroe surrendered the city to Captain David G. Farragut.

3   Come and take the city; we are powerless.
> —quoted by US Navy captain Albert Kautz in *Battles and Leaders of the Civil War*, vol. 2, 1888.

★ Monroe was replying to Kautz, then a lieutenant, who had been sent ashore by Captain David G. Farragut to demand the surrender of the city.

Morse, Samuel F. B. (1791–1872)

Inventor of the telegraph

4   There is something so unnatural and abhorrent in this outcry of arms in one great family that I cannot believe it will come to a decision of the sword. Such counsels are in the court of passion, not of reason. Imagine such a conflict, imagine a victory, no matter by which side. Can the victors rejoice in the blood of brethren shed in a family brawl?
> —quoted by Edward L. Morse in *Samuel F. B. Morse: His Letters and Journals*, 1973.

★ After this prewar statement by Morse, his invention of the telegraph made an immense wartime contribution to armies, governments, and newspapers.

5   Everybody south of a certain geographic line is an enemy; you live south of that line, ergo you are an enemy; I send you my love, you being the enemy; this gives you *comfort*; ergo I have given comfort to the enemy; ergo I am a traitor, ergo I must be hanged.
> —letter to his brother-in-law, A. B. Griswold, July 13, 1861.

★ Morse was highlighting what he considered the nonsense of the country's split to Griswold, who lived in New Orleans.

6   I see no hope of union. If there was a corner of the world where I could hide myself, and I could consult the welfare of my family, I would sacrifice all my interests here

and go at once. I have no heart to write or do anything. Without a country: Without 1
a country!
   —quoted by Edward L. Morse in *Samuel F. B. Morse: His Letters and Journals*,
   1973.

★ Morse wrote this in New York City in July 1861.

Mosby, John S. (1833–1916)

CS COLONEL

Well, it made you immortal.   2
   —*The Memoirs of Colonel John S. Mosby*, 1917.

★ He said this after the war to Major General George E. Pickett, whose fatal charge led
to the Confederate defeat at Gettysburg.

I had strong personal reasons for being friendly with General Grant. If he had not 3
thrown his shield over me, I should have been outlawed and driven into exile. . . .
General Grant, who was then all powerful, interposed, and sent me an offer of the
same parole that he had given General Lee. Such a service I could never forget.
When the opportunity came, I remembered what he had done for me, and I did all
I could for him.
   —*The Memoirs of Colonel John S. Mosby*, 1917.

★ After the war, Mosby supported Grant for president.

One of the most effective ways of impeding the march of an army is by cutting off its 4
supplies; and this is just as legitimate as to attack in the line of battle.
   —*Mosby's War Reminiscences*, 1887.

The line that connects an army with its base of supplies is the Heel of Achilles—its 5
most vital and vulnerable spot.
   —*Mosby's War Reminiscences*, 1887.

My success had been so uninterrupted that the men thought that victory was 6
chained to my standard. Men who go into a fight under the influence of such feelings are next to invincible, and generally are the victors before it begins.
   —*Mosby's War Reminiscences*, 1887.

It is just as legitimate to fight an enemy in the rear as in the front. The only differ- 7
ence is the danger.
   —*Mosby's War Reminiscences*, 1887.

I never admired and did not imitate the example of the commander who declined 8
the advantage of the first fire.
   —*Mosby's War Reminiscences*, 1887.

1   I fought for success and not for display. There was no man in the Confederate army who had less of the spirit of knight-errantry in him, or took a more practical view of war than I did.
        —*Mosby's War Reminiscences*, 1887.

Mower, Joseph A. (1827–1870)

US COLONEL

2   Yes, General, but if they had reported me for being "shot in the neck" to-day instead of yesterday, it would have been correct.
        —quoted by Major General William S. Rosecrans in *Century Magazine*, October, 1886.

    ★ Mower had just been shot in the neck during the battle of Corinth, Mississippi, and was referring to the day before when he had been incorrectly reported as being drunk.

Nelson, William (1824–1862)

US MAJOR GENERAL

3   Send for a clergyman, I wish to be baptised. I have been basely murdered.
        —quoted by Rod Graff in *Civil War Quiz and Fact Book*, 1985.

    ★ US general Jefferson C. Davis fatally shot Nelson, his commanding officer, after they argued in a Louisville, Kentucky, hotel lobby on September 29, 1862. Davis was never disciplined.

Norton, Oliver W. (1839–1920)

US PRIVATE
    ★ Norton was a member of the 83rd Pennsylvania Regiment.

4   The first thing in the morning is drill, then drill, then drill again. Then drill, drill, a little more drill. Then drill, and lastly drill. Between drills, we drill and sometimes stop to eat a little and have a roll-call.
        —letter to a friend, October 9, 1861.

Oates, William C.

CS COLONEL
    ★ Oates was a member of the 15th Alabama Regiment.

5   I thought [Lee] at that moment the grandest specimen of manhood I ever beheld. He looked as though he ought to have been, and was, the monarch of the world.
        —*The War between the Union and the Confederacy*, 1905.

    ★ Oates observed Lee on May 4, 1864, at the battle of the Wilderness.

Ochiltree, Tom P. (1839–1902)

CS ASSISTANT ADJUTANT GENERAL

★ Ochiltree was a member of the Army of New Mexico.

The Confederate flag flies over Santa Fe and Albuquerque. At the latter place, the 1
flag was made of a captured United States flag, raised upon a United States flag-
staff—the salute fired by a captured United States battery, and Dixie played by a
captured United States band.
    —report to Confederate president Jefferson Davis, April 27, 1862.

★ This glowing report was sent on March 27 before the Confederate forces had to
retreat when their supplies were destroyed at the battle of Glorieta Pass, or Pigeon's
Ranch, in the Territory of New Mexico.

Oldham, Williamson Simpson (1813–1868)

CS SENATOR FROM TEXAS

Sherman's march from Atlanta was actually a retreat; he could neither stay there nor 2
return by the way he came. He availed himself of the only road of escape, on which
there was no army to oppose him and on which he could with impunity forage upon
a country filled with supplies for the support of his army.
    —speech, January 30, 1865.

All is not lost; honor is not lost; liberty and independence are not lost, while we have 3
the spirit to defend them. [The enemy] have not as yet touched the vital point of the
Confederacy. It has no vital point, but is vital in every part and can but by annihila-
tion die.
    —speech, January 30, 1865.

Why should any man doubt our final success? Sum up the results of the last cam- 4
paign and it will be found that the loss of the enemy was five to our one. We beat
them in ten battles to where we lost one. . . . Our enemy can never conquer us.
    —speech, January 30, 1865.

★ General Lee surrendered ten weeks later.

Opdyke, George (1805–1880)

NEW YORK CITY MAYOR

The importance of this city to the nation demands that it should not be left at the 5
mercy of the rebel navy.
    —letter to Major General John E. Wool, July 3, 1863.

★ The mayor feared an attack by the Confederate navy because General Robert E. Lee
had invaded Pennsylvania (although the battle of Gettysburg was taking place on this
day). Wool commanded the Department of the East.

Osborn, Thomas Ward (1833–1898)

US MAJOR

1   We have torn up and destroyed about 200 miles of railroad, burned all bridges and cleaned up the country generally of almost everything upon which the people could live. The Army in this movement covered a strip of country about forty miles wide. We burned all cotton, took all provisions, forage, wagons, mules, horses, cattle, hogs and poultry and the many other things which a country furnishes and which may be made available for the support of an army. In fact, as we have left the country I do not see how the people can live for the next two years
   —edited by Richard Harwell and Philip Racine in *The Fiery Trail*, 1986.

   ★ Osborne, chief of General William T. Sherman's artillery, was describing the march through Georgia in his letter home written December 17, 1864.

Otis, L. B.

CHRISTIAN MEN OF CHICAGO CHAIRMAN

2   The slave oligarchy has organized the most unnatural, perfidious and formidable rebellion known to history.
   —with other delegates, letter to Lincoln, September 7, 1862.

   ★ A delegation from the Christian Men of Chicago carried this letter to Lincoln, calling for a proclamation of national emancipation. Otis was chairman of the organization's meeting in Chicago. The president gave a negative reply, but on September 22 issued his preliminary emancipation proclamation.

3   We urge you, therefore, as the head of this Christian nation, from considerations of moral principle, and, as the only means of preserving the Union, to proclaim, without delay, NATIONAL EMANCIPATION.
   —with other delegates, letter to Lincoln, September 7, 1862.

4   We cannot expect God to save a nation that clings to its sin [of slavery]. This is too fearful an hour to insult God, or to deceive ourselves. National existence is in peril: our sons and brothers are falling by tens of thousands on the battle-field: the war becomes daily more determined and destructive. While we speak the enemy thunders at the gates of the capital. Our acknowledged superiority of resources has thus far availed little or nothing in the conflict. As Christian patriots we dare not conceal the truth, that these judgments mean what the divine judgments meant in Egypt. They are God's stern command—"LET MY PEOPLE GO!"
   —with other delegates, letter to Lincoln, September 7, 1862.

Parker, William H. (1826–1896)

CS CAPTAIN

5   On one occasion two of our boats were returning from City Point [near Petersburg, Virginia], fortunately with no passengers, when one of them struck a torpedo and immediately went down. A boat went from the other steamer and found the captain

struggling in the water, with a Webster's *Unabridged Dictionary* in his arms. As he was pulled into the boat he said: "I did not have time to get it on." He thought he had seized a life-preserver!
    —*Recollections of a Naval Officer, 1841–1865.*

★ Torpedoes were underwater mines.

Parsons, H. C.

US CAPTAIN

Every man felt, as he tightened his saber belt, that he was summoned to a ride to death.
    —quoted by Shelby Foote in *The Civil War*, vol. 2, 1958.

★ This referred to a cavalry charge at the battle of Gettysburg.

Patterson, Edmund D.

CS PRIVATE

When a fellow's time comes, down he goes. Every bullet has its billet.
    —diary entry of April 4, 1862, quoted by Bell Irvin Wiley in *The Life of Johnny Reb*, 1943.

Peck, Hiram T.

US PRIVATE

★ Peck was a member of the 10th Connecticut Regiment.

An inspiring feature of the first evening of our occupation in the city was the music of our military bands, discoursing such patriotic airs as "Yankee Doodle," "Hail Columbia," "The Star Spangled Banner" etc.—airs that must have fallen rather oddly on the ears of the citizens, after having listened four years to the music of treason.
    —quoted in the *National Tribune*, September 27, 1900.

★ Peck's regiment was one of the first to enter the captured Confederate capital of Richmond.

The scene of Richmond in flames was both terrible and sublime, and one never to be forgotten by those who witnessed it so long as life shall last.
    —quoted in the *National Tribune*, September 27, 1900.

Stores were boldly broken into by the mob of straggling soldiers and civilians, and plunder was the order of the hour.
    —quoted in the *National Tribune*, September 27, 1900.

We were at last in Richmond—the city that had cost so many thousands of loyal lives, through many fruitless attempts to capture, during the preceding four years of terrible conflict, and which had cost so many thousands of other lives in its defense.
    —quoted in the *National Tribune*, September 27, 1900.

Pemberton, John C. (1814–1881)

CS LIEUTENANT GENERAL

1   I will endeavor to hold out as long as we have anything to eat.
    —letter to General Joseph E. Johnston, May 25, 1863.

    ★ He sent this from Vicksburg under the siege. Confederate soldiers there eventually had to eat mule meat and surrendered on July 4.

2   Two days having elapsed since your dead and wounded have been lying in our front, and as yet no disposition on your part of a desire to remove them being exhibited, in the name of humanity I have the honor to propose a cessation of hostilities for two hours and a half, that you may be enabled to remove your dead and dying. If you cannot do this, on notification from you that hostilities will be suspended on your part for the time specified, I will endeavor to have the dead buried and the wounded cared for.
    —letter to Major General Ulysses S. Grant, May 25, 1863.

    ★ Grant accepted the cessation the same day and had his troops collect their dead and wounded.

3   Unless the siege of Vicksburg is raised, or supplies are thrown in, it will become necessary very shortly to evacuate the place. I see no prospect of the former, and there are many great, if not insuperable obstacles in the way of the latter.
    —letter to four Confederate generals: John S. Bowen, John H. Forney, Martin Luther Smith, and Carter L. Stevenson, July 1, 1863.

    ★ Pemberton, commanding the trapped Confederates at Vicksburg, surrendered three days later.

4   You have heard that I was incompetent and a traitor; and that it was my intention to sell Vicksburg. Follow me and you will see the cost at which I will sell Vicksburg. When the last pound of beef, bacon and flour, the last grain of corn, the last cow and hog and horse and dog shall have been consumed, and the last man shall have perished in the trenches, then, and only them, will I sell Vicksburg.
    —quoted by Carl Sandburg in *Abraham Lincoln: The War Years*, 1939.

    ★ In this speech to his troops, the "traitor" comment involved Pemberton's being a native of Pennsylvania.

Pendleton, George (1825–1889)

US SENATOR FROM OHIO

5   . . . if it be necessary to violate the Constitution in order to carry on the war, the war ought instantly to be stopped.

—quoted by Nathaniel W. Stephenson in *Lincoln: An Account of His Personal Life, Especially of Its Springs of Action as Revealed and Deepened by the Ordeal of War*, 1922.

Pendleton, William N. (1808–1883)

CS COLONEL

Lord preserve the soul while I destroy the body.   **1**
—quoted by Bell Irvin Wiley in *The Life of Johnny Reb*, 1943.

★ Pendleton, an Episcopal minister, said this during the first battle of Bull Run (first Manassas), where he was chief of artillery for General Joseph E. Johnston's troops. He later became a brigadier general and chief of artillery for General Robert E. Lee.

Perrin, Albert

CS BRIGADIER GENERAL

I shall come out of this fight a live major general or a dead brigadier.   **2**
—quoted by Rod Graff in *Civil War Quiz and Fact Book*, 1985.

★ He said this before the battle of Spotsylvania, in which he was killed on May 12, 1864.

Petigru, James L. (1789–1863)

SOUTH CAROLINA JUDGE

My friend, look around you; the whole State is one vast insane asylum.   **3**
—quoted by W. F. G. Peck in "Four Years under Fire at Charleston," *Harper's New Monthly Magazine*, August 1865.

★ Petigru was responding to a stranger who stopped him on a street in Columbia, South Carolina, to ask directions to the insane asylum. This was when secession fever was at its height.

They have this day set a blazing torch to the temple of constitutional liberty and, **4** please God, we shall have no more peace forever.
—quoted by Bruce Catton in *The Coming Fury*, 1972.

★ Petigru, who opposed secession, said this on December 20, 1860, the day that South Carolina left the Union.

South Carolina is too small for a republic and too large for an insane asylum.   **5**
—quoted by Earl S. Miers in *The Great Rebellion*, 1958.

★ Petigru was responding in the Christmas week of 1860 to a secessionist leader and former US congressman, Robert Barnwell Rhett, who had asked if he was with them.

Pettit, Frederick (1842–1863)

US PRIVATE

1   We think Burnside did all he could do and cannot understand why he was relieved of the command. Burnside appeared much like Washington to the troops that knew him best.
        —*Infantryman Pettit*, 1990.

    ★ General Ambrose Burnside had just been replaced as commander of the Army of the Potomac after his disastrous "Mud March" that began on January 20, 1863.

Phelan, James

CS SENATOR FROM MISSISSIPPI

2   The spirit of enlistment is thrice dead. Enthusiasm has expired to a cold pile of damp ashes. Defeats, retreats, sufferings, dangers, magnified by spiritless helplessness and an unchangeable conviction that our army is in the hands of ignorant and feeble commanders, are rapidly producing a sense of settled despair.
        —letter to Confederate president Jefferson Davis, December? 1862.

Phelps, John W.

US BRIGADIER GENERAL

3   Carr, that's not picket shooting. It is your men shooting p-e-e-g-s.
        —quoted by Major General Joseph B. Carr in *Battles and Leaders of the Civil War*, vol. 2, 1888.

    ★ Phelps, disregarding shooting and commotion in his camp, was correct that it involved pigs.

Phillips, Wendell (1811–1884)

BOSTON ABOLITIONIST

4   This war means one of two things—emancipation or disunion.
        —speech in Boston, April 21, 1861.

5   The abolition enterprise was started in 1831. Until 1846 we thought it was possible to kill slavery and save the Union. We then said, over the ruins of the American Church and the Union is the only way to freedom. From '46 to '61 we preached that doctrine.
        —speech in Boston, July 6, 1862.

    ★ Phillips was stating the view that the Union would have to be abolished to defeat slavery.

[Lincoln] may be honest—nobody cares whether the tortoise is honest or not. He **1** has neither insight, nor prevision, nor decision.
  —quoted by Shelby Foote in *The Civil War*, vol. 1, 1958.

★ Phillips said this in a speech during the summer of 1862.

The war can be ended only by annihilating that Oligarchy which formed and rules **2** the South and makes the war—by annihilating a state of society.
  —quoted by James M. McPherson in *The Battle Cry of Freedom: The Civil War Era*, 1989.

★ Phillips wrote this on January 23, 1863.

Pickens, Francis (1807–1869)

SOUTH CAROLINA GOVERNOR

Governor Pickens, after stating the position of South Carolina toward the United **3** States, says that any attempt to send United States troops into Charleston Harbor, to re-enforce the forts, would be regarded as an act of hostility.
  —letter to Major Robert Anderson, January 9, 1861.

★ Earlier in the day, Charleston's batteries had fired on a ship bringing two hundred soldiers to reinforce Fort Sumter, commanded by Major Anderson.

We have defeated their twenty millions, and we have made the proud flag of the **4** stars and stripes, that never was lowered before to any nation on their earth, we have lowered it in humility before the palmetto and the confederate flags. . . . We have humbled the flag of the United States. . . . It has triumphed for seventy years; but to-day, on the thirteenth day of April, it has been humbled, and humbled before the glorious little state of South Carolina.
  —speech in Charleston, April 13, 1861.

★ This was the day that Fort Sumter was evacuated, after surrendering the previous day.

Pickett, Eli K.

US SERGEANT

I have never been in favor of the abolition of slavery until since this war has detir- **5** mend me in the conviction that it is a greater sin than our Government is able to stand . . . It is opposed to the Spirit of the age—and in my opinion this Rebelion is but the death struggle of the overgrown monster.
  —letter to his wife, March 27, 1863.

Pickett, George E. (1825–1875)

CS MAJOR GENERAL

[McClellan] was, he is and he will always be, even were his pistol pointed at my **6** heart, my dear, loved friend. May God bless him and spare his life.
  —letter to his future wife, Sally, January 1, 1862.

1   The enemy is our enemy because he neither knows nor understands us, and yet will not let us part in peace and be neighbors, but insists on fighting us to make us one with him, forgetting that both slavery and secession were his own institutions.
    —letter to his future wife, Sally, May? 1862.

2   The tin cup is clear and shining; but the corn-bread is greasy and smoked. And the bacon—that is greasy, too but it is good and tastes all right, if it will only hold out till our Stars and Bars wave over the land of the free and the home of the brave, and we have our own home.
    —letter to his future wife, Sally, May? 1862.

3   How I wish I could say [the battle of Seven Pines] ended all battles and that the last shot that will ever be heard was fired on June first, 1862.
    —letter to his future wife, Sally, June 1, 1862.

    ★ Pickett was a brigadier general at this time.

4   This war was never really contemplated in earnest. I believe if either the North or the South had expected that their differences would result in this obstinate struggle, the cold-blooded Puritan and the cock hatted Huguenot and Cavalier would have made a compromise.
    —letter to his future wife, Sally, June 27, 1862.

5   Never, never did men, since the world began, fight like ours [at Gaines's Mill]. The Duke of Somerset, who seemingly laughed when he saw our ragged, dirty, bare-footed soldiers—"Mostly beardless boys," as he said—took off his hat in reverence when he saw them fight.
    —letter to his future wife, Sally, July 15, 1862.

6   As poor a marksman as the Yankee was who shot me, I wish he had been poorer still, aiming, as he must have been, either at my head or my heart and breaking my wing.
    —letter to his future wife, Sally, July 15, 1862.

    ★ He had been severely wounded in the shoulder on June 27 during the battle of Gaines's Mill.

7   The seventeenth . . . is recorded in letters of blood for both armies [at Antietam (Sharpsburg)], and in its wake came Lincoln's great political victory, proving the might of the pen, in his Emancipation Proclamation—winning with it the greatest victory yet for the North.
    —letter to his future wife, Sally, September 25, 1862.

8   [Jackson] places no value on human life, caring for nothing so much as fighting, unless it be praying.
    —letter to his future wife, Sally, October 11, 1862.

    ★ Pickett became a major general in October 1862.

If General Lee had Grant's resources he would soon end the war; but Old Jack 1
[Jackson] can do it without resources.
　　—letter to his future wife, Sally, October 11, 1862.

If war, my darling, is a necessity—I suppose it is—it is a very cruel one.   2
　　—letter to his future wife, Sally, December 14, 1862.

I can't help feeling sorry for Old Burnside—proud, plucky, hard-headed old dog. I 3
always liked him, but I loved little Mac [McClellan], and it was a godsend to the
Confederacy that he was relieved.
　　—letter to his future wife, Sally, December 14, 1862.

★ Major General Ambrose E. Burnside had replaced McClellan as commander of the
Army of the Potomac after McClellan failed to pursue General Robert E. Lee after the
battle of Antietam (Sharpsburg).

Old Peter [Longstreet], our far-seeing, slow by sure, indefatigable, plodding old war- 4
horse, has planned to secure these sorely needed supplies for our poor, half fed
army—and there never was such an army, such an uncomplaining, plucky body of
men—never.
　　—letter to his future wife, Sally, February? 1863.

You would hardly recognize these ragged, barefoot soldiers as the trim, tidy boys of 5
two years ago in their handsome gray uniforms, with shining equipment and full
haversacks and knapsacks.
　　—letter to his future wife, Sally, February? 1863.

Why, my darling, during these continuous ten days' march, the ground snowy and 6
sleety, the feet of many of these soldiers covered only with improvised moccasins of
raw beef hide, and hundreds of them without shoes or blankets or overcoats, they
have not uttered one word of complaint, nor one murmuring tone; but cheerily,
singing and telling stories, they have tramped-tramped-tramped.
　　—letter to his future wife, Sally, February? 1863.

If "the battle is not to the strong" then we may win; but when all our ports are closed 7
and the world is against us, when for us a man killed is a man lost, while Grant may
have twenty-five of every nation to replace one of his, it seems that the battle is to
the strong.
　　—letter to his future wife, Sally, April 15, 1863.

Oh, the desolate homes—the widows and orphans and the heartbroken mothers that 8
this campaign [into Pennsylvania] will make!
　　—letter to his future wife, Sally, June 18, 1863.

I never could quite enjoy being a "Conquering Hero." . . . I can fight for a cause I 9
know to be just, can risk my own life and the lives of those in my keep, without a
thought of the consequences; but when we've conquered, when we've downed the

enemy and won the victory, I don't want to hurrah. I want to go off all by myself and be sorry for them.
 —letter to his future wife, Sally, June 24, 1863.

★ This was written from Greencastle, Pennsylvania.

1   The object of this great march [into Pennsylvania] is, of course, unknown to us. Its purpose and our destination are known at present only to the Commanding General and his Chief Lieutenants. The men generally believe that the intention is to entirely surround the Army of the Potomac and place Washington and Baltimore within our grasp.
 —letter to his future wife, Sally, June 27, 1863.

2   Think of it, my darling—an army of sixty thousand men marching through the enemy's country without the least opposition!
 —letter to his future wife, Sally, June 27, 1863.

★ The Confederates were marching through Pennsylvania, with the battle of Gettysburg only four days away.

3   The Yanks have taken into the mountains and across the Susquehanna all the supplies they could, and we pay liberally for those which we are compelled to take, paying for them in money which is paid to us, our own Confederate script.
 —letter to his future wife, Sally, June 29, 1863.

★ This was during their invasion of Pennsylvania.

4   I wish, my darling, you could see this wonderfully rich and prosperous country, abounding in plenty, with its great, strong, vigorous horses and oxen, its cows and crops and verdantly thriving vegetation—none of the ravages of war, no signs of devastation—all in woeful contrast to the land where we lay dreaming.
 —letter to his future wife, Sally, June 29, 1863.

★ This referred to Pennsylvania during their invasion.

5   Oh, the responsibility for the lives of such men as these! Well, my darling, their fate and that of our beloved Southland will be settled ere your glorious brown eyes rest on these scraps of penciled paper—your soldier's last letter, perhaps.
 —letter to his future wife, Sally, July 3, 1863.

★ This was just before Pickett's disastrous charge at Gettysburg on this day.

6   Well, it is over now. The battle [of Gettysburg] is lost, and many of us are prisoners, many are dead, many wounded, bleeding and dying. Your Soldier lives and mourns and but for you, my darling, he would rather, a million times rather, be back there with his dead, to sleep for all time in an unknown grave.
 —letter to his future wife, Sally, July 4, 1863.

7   Over on Cemetery Ridge, the Federals beheld a scene never before witnessed on this continent,—a scene which has never previously been enacted and can never take place again—an army forming in line of battle in full view, under their very eyes—charging across a space nearly a mile in length over fields of waving grain and

anon of stubble and then a smooth expanse—moving with the steadiness of a dress parade, the pride and glory soon to be crushed by an overwhelming heartbreak.
  —letter to his future wife, Sally, July 4, 1863.

★ He was referring to the previous day's disaster, Pickett's charge at Gettysburg.

My brave boys were full of hope and confidence of victory as I led them forth, form- 1
ing them in column of attack, and though officers and men alike knew what was before them,—knew the odds against them,—they eagerly offered up their lives on the altar of duty, having absolute faith in their ultimate success.
  —letter to his future wife, Sally, July 4, 1863.

★ He was referring to the previous day's disaster, Pickett's charge at Gettysburg.

Even now I can hear them cheering as I gave the order. "Forward"! I can feel their 2
faith and trust in me and their love for our cause. I can feel the thrill of their joyous voices as they called out all along the line, "We'll follow you, Marse George. We'll follow you, we'll follow you." Oh, how faithfully they kept their word, following me on, on to their death, and I, believing in the promised support, led them on, on, on. Oh, God!
  —letter to his future wife, Sally, July 6, 1863.

★ He was referring to Pickett's charge at Gettysburg on July 3, 1863.

No words can picture the anguish of that roll-call—the breathless waits between 3
responses.
  —letter to his future wife, Sally, July 6, 1863.

★ This roll call was held after the battle of Gettysburg.

The moans of my wounded boys, the sight of the dead, upturned faces, flood my soul 4
with grief—and here am I whom they trusted, whom they followed, leaving them on that field of carnage [at Gettysburg]—and guarding four thousand prisoners across the river back to Winchester [Virginia].
  —letter to his future wife, Sally, July 6, 1863.

The sacrifice of life on that blood-soaked field [of Gettysburg] on the fatal third [of 5
July] was too awful for the heralding of victory, even for our victorious foe, who, I think, believe as we do, that it decided the fate of our cause.
  —letter to his future wife, Sally, July 6, 1863.

Not all the glory in the world, General Lee, could atone for the widows and orphans 6
this day has made.
  —edited by La Salle Corbell Pickett in *The Heart of a Soldier*, 1913.

★ After his disastrous charge at Gettysburg, Pickett was replying to General Robert E. Lee, who had said, "General Pickett, you and your men have covered yourself with glory."

My noble division lies there.   7
  —edited by La Salle Corbell Pickett in *The Heart of a Soldier*, 1913.

★ Pickett was pointing to the valley at Gettysburg after his men's tragic charge.

1   General, I have no division.
    —quoted by John D. Wright in *The Language of the Civil War*, 2001.

    ★ Pickett was replying to General Robert E. Lee's order to prepare his division for a counterattack at the battle of Gettysburg, but it had been decimated during Pickett's charge.

2   [Jefferson Davis] believed that England and, in fact, all foreign powers were like the woman who saw her husband fighting a bear—she didn't care a continental which was whipped, but she'd be the best pleased if both were.
    —letter to his wife, Sally, January 25, 1864.

3   The Wilderness, alas, is one vast graveyard where sleep thousands of Grant's soldiers; but Grant, like our Stonewall [Jackson], is "fighting not to save lives, but country."
    —letter to his wife, Sally, June 3, 1864.

4   This morning Grant made an assault along the entire six miles of our line, and our guns opened a counter attack, followed by advance skirmishes of my division. The whole Confederate line poured a stream of fire, and thousands of Grant's soldiers have gone to re-enforce the army of the dead.
    —letter to his wife, Sally, June 3, 1864.

    ★ This was written from Cold Harbor, Virginia.

5   [Our home] was burned by [General Benjamin] Butler at a great expense to the Government and in revenge for having been outgeneraled by a little handful of my men at Petersburg and for Grant's telegram to Mr. Lincoln, saying, "Pickett has bottled up Butler at Petersburg."
    —letter to his wife, Sally, June? 1864.

6   Now, heaven help us, it will be war to the knife, with the knife no longer keen, the thrust of the arm no longer strong, the certainty that when peace comes it will follow the tread of the conqueror.
    —letter to his wife, Sally, January 28, 1865.

7   May God pity those who wait at home for the soldier who has reported to the Great Commander!
    —letter to his wife, Sally, April 2, 1865.

8   Ah, my Sally, the triumphs of might are transient, but the sufferings and crucifixions for the right can never be forgotten. The sorrow and song of my glory-crowned division nears its doxology.
    —letter to his wife, Sally, April 2, 1865.

9   The horrors of the march from Five Forks to Amelia Court House and thence to Sailor's Creek beggars all description. For forty-eight hours the man or officer who had a handful of parched corn in his pocket was most fortunate.
    —letter to his wife, Sally, April? 1865.

    ★ All locations are in Virginia.

The cloud of despair settled over all on the third [of April], when the tidings came to   1
us of the evacuation of Richmond and its partial loss by fire. The homes and families
of many of my men were there, and all knew too well that with the fall of our Capital
the last hope of success was over.
—letter to his wife, Sally, April? 1865.

It is finished! Ah, my beloved division! Thousands of them have gone to their eter-   2
nal home, having given up their lives for the cause they knew to be just. The others,
alas, heartbroken, crushed in spirit, are left to mourn its loss. Well, it is practically all
over now. We have poured out our blood, and suffered untold hardships and privations, all in vain. And now, well—*I* must not forget, either, that God reigns.
—letter to his wife, Sally, April 8, 1865.

★ This was dated "Appomattox—Midnight—the night of the 8th and the dawn of the
9th" (the day Lee surrendered).

After to-night you will be my whole command—staff, field officers, men—all.   3
—letter to his wife, Sally, April? 1865.

★ This was Pickett's romantic way of describing his return at the war's end.

Well, I think the Yankees had a little something to do with it.   4
—quoted by La Salle Corbell Pickett in *The Heart of a Soldier*, 1913.

★ He had just been asked by the governor general of Canada why the Confederates lost
the battle of Gettysburg.

That old man [Lee] had my division massacred.   5
—quoted by John D. Wright in *The Language of the Civil War*, 2001.

★ This was said years after the war, referring to Pickett's charge at the battle of
Gettysburg.

Pinto, Facundo

The enemy is Texas and the Texans. With their hostile armed regiments, rebels to   6
the Government of the United States, to whose protection and flag, our good faith,
our duties, our confidence, interests and hopes turn and belong, they have come
upon us [in New Mexico], in violation of every principle of right, of justice and
friendship. . . . They strive to cover the iniquity of their marauding inroad, under the
pretence, that they are under the authority of a new arrangement they call a Confederacy, but in truth is a rebel organization.
—with J. M. Gallegos, speech to the Legislative Assembly of New Mexico,
January 9, 1862, quoted by Richard B. Harwell in *The Civil War Reader*, 1958.

★ This followed an invasion of Texas soldiers into the territory of New Mexico.

Pius IX (1792–1878)

It is particularly agreeable to us to see that you, illustrious and honorable President,   7
and your people, are animated with the same desires of peace and tranquillity which
we have in our letters inculcated upon our venerable brothers. May it please God at

the same time to make the other peoples of America and their rulers, reflecting seriously how terrible is civil war and what calamities it engenders, listen to the inspirations of a calmer spirit, and adopt resolutely the art of peace. . . . We, at the same time, beseech the God of pity to shed abroad upon you the light of His grace, and attach you to us by a perfect friendship.
    —letter to Confederate president Jefferson Davis, December 3, 1863.

★ This was a reply to Davis's letter of September 23 praising Pope Pius's peace messages to the archbishops of New Orleans and New York. This reply, which was a de facto recognition of the Confederacy, was especially welcomed by Davis.

Pleasonton, Alfred (1824–1897)

US MAJOR GENERAL

1   Fire! Fire, you damned asses!
    —quoted by Shelby Foote in *The Civil War*, vol. 3, 1958.

★ Pleasonton shouted at his troops, who were watching the enemy retreat at the battle of the Big Blue River in Missouri on October 22, 1864.

Polk, Leonidas (1806–1864)

CS MAJOR GENERAL

2   "Skirmish"! hell and damnation! I'd like to know what he calls a *battle*.
    —edited by Frank Moore in *The Rebellion Record: A Diary of American Events, with Documents, Narratives, Illustrative Incidents, Poetry, Etc.*, vol. 3, 1862.

★ This was his reaction to a message from Brigadier General Ulysses S. Grant referring to their "skirmish" on November 7, 1861, at Belmont, Missouri. At that time he was a major general. Despite the language, Polk was an Episcopal bishop.

3   Give them what General Cheatham says, boys! Give them what General Cheatham says!
    —quoted by Shelby Foote in *The Civil War*, vol. 2, 1958.

★ Polk, holding back curses, was advising his troops to follow Cheatham's cry of "Give 'em hell, boys!"

Pollard, Edward A. (1831–1872)

RICHMOND EXAMINER EDITOR

4   The most distressing abuses were visible in the ill-regulated hygiene of our camps.
    —*The First Year of the War*, 1862.

The estimation of General Lee . . . was with reference to his unfortunate campaign   **1**
in western Virginia. It was founded on the events of that campaign, in which there is
no doubt General Lee blundered and showed an absurd misconception of mountain
warfare.
  —quoted by Stanley F. Horn in *The Robert E. Lee Reader*, 1949.

★ This referred to Lee's first campaign of the war, a minor defeat at Cheat Mountain in
what is now West Virginia, on September 15, 1861. Pollard was trying to explain his
previous criticism of Lee since this was written after Lee's success during the Seven
Days' battle in the summer of 1862.

As long as the intelligent of this world are persuaded of the opinion that a great   **2**
General is he who accomplishes his purpose with small, but admirably drilled
armies; who defeats large armies with small ones; who accomplishes great military
results by strategy, more than by fighting; who makes of war an intellectual exercise
rather than a match of brute force, that title will be given to Robert E. Lee above all
men in America, and the Confederate commander will be declared to have been
much greater in defeat than Grant in his boasted victory.
  —*The Lost Cause*, 1866.

It was simply the consummation of the disgrace of this commander [Grant]—that he   **3**
should have taken eleven months to capture a position [Richmond] at no time held
by more than one third of his forces, having lost in the enterprise in killed and
wounded more than double the numbers actually in arms against him!
  —*The Lost Cause*, 1866.

It would be immeasurably the worst consequence of defeat in this war that the South   **4**
should lose its moral and intellectual distinctiveness as a people, and cease to assert
its well-known superiority in civilization, in political scholarship, and in all the standards of individual character over the people of the North. That superiority has been
recognized by every foreign observer, and by the intelligent everywhere; for it is the
South that in the past produced four-fifths of the political literature of America, and
presented in its public men that list of American names best known in the Christian
world.
  —*The Lost Cause*, 1866.

There are certain coarse advisers who tell the Southern people that the great ends of   **5**
their lives now are to repair their stock of national wealth; to bring in Northern capital and labour; to build mills and factories and hotels and gilded caravansaries; and
to make themselves rivals in the clattering and garish enterprise of the North. This
advice has its proper place. But there are higher objects than the Yankee *magna
bona* of money and display, and loftier aspirations than the civilization of material
things.
  —*The Lost Cause*, 1866.

Pope, John (1822–1892)

US MAJOR GENERAL

1   Success and glory are in the advance, disaster and shame lurk in the rear.
　　—speech to soldiers of the Army of Virginia, July 14, 1862.

★ Pope had just taken command, replacing the hesitant Major General George B. McClellan.

2   I hear constantly of taking "strong positions and holding them," or "lines of retreat" and of "bases of supplies." Let us discard such ideas. The strongest position a soldier should desire to occupy is one from which he can most easily advance against the enemy.
　　—speech to soldiers of the Army of Virginia, July 14, 1862.

3   Soldiers were called into the field to do battle against the enemy, and it is not expected that their force and energy shall be wasted in protecting private property of those most hostile to the Government.
　　—general order, July 23, 1862.

★ Pope's order gave tacit approval of plundering by his soldiers.

4   If you will march promptly and rapidly at the earliest dawn upon Manassas Junction, we shall bag the whole crowd.
　　—order to Major General Irvin McDowell, August 27, 1862.

★ Pope's optimism failed two days later at the second battle of Bull Run (second Manassas).

Porter, Andrew (1820–1872)

US BRIGADIER GENERAL

5   The words, gestures, and threats of our officers were thrown away upon men who had lost all presence of mind, and only longed for absence of body.
　　—quoted by Alfred H. Guernsey and Henry M. Alden in *Harper's Pictorial History of the Great Rebellion in the United States*, 1866.

★ Porter was describing the Union retreat at the first battle of Bull Run (first Manassas).

Porter, David D. (1813–1891)

US ADMIRAL

6   This is sharp practice, but if *you* can stand the explosion when it comes, we can.
　　—quoted in *Battles and Leaders of the Civil War*, vol. 2, 1888.

★ Porter said this on April 28, 1862, when he was a commander, to Confederate officers aboard his ship *Harriet Lane* to surrender forts protecting the lower Mississippi River. He was referring to the ironclad *Louisiana* set on fire by the Confederate navy to drift into Porter's ship. The *Louisiana*, however, exploded before reaching them.

The Confederates were a wide-awake set of adversaries, full of energy and courage, **1** and not lacking in resources. They were working with all their souls to attain an object which they considered conducive to their happiness, and they did not care whom they hurt, so long as they could succeed.

> —*Incidents and Anecdotes of the Civil War*, 1885.

A man of ordinary intellect could see the end which would be the downfall of the **2** Southern Confederacy. It was as plain as the writing on the wall at the feast of Belshazzar.

> —*Incidents and Anecdotes of the Civil War*, 1885.

The Southerners were fighting with the energy of despair, hoping that some un- **3** toward event might spring up to help them. At all events, they were determined to command the enemy's respect for their courage and ability, and I don't think any brave sailor or soldier ever withheld it.

> —*Incidents and Anecdotes of the Civil War*, 1885.

Porter, Horace (1837–1921)

US BRIGADIER GENERAL

The charges were now withdrawn from the guns, the campfires were left to smolder **4** in their ashes, the flags were tenderly furled—those historic banners, battle-stained, bullet-riddled, many of them but remnants of their former selves, with scarcely enough left of them on which to imprint the names of the battles they had seen— and the Army of the Union and the Army of Northern Virginia turned their backs upon each other for the first time in four long, bloody years.

> —quoted in *Battles and Leaders of the Civil War*, vol. 4, 1888.

★ Porter, the aide-de-camp to General Ulysses S. Grant, was describing the scene at Appomattox Court House, Virginia, on April 10, 1865, the day after Lee's surrender.

Powell, William H.

US CAPTAIN

It was Sunday [August 31, 1862]. The morning was cold and rainy; everything bore **5** a look of sadness in unison with our feelings. All about were the *disjecta membra* of a shattered army; here were stragglers plodding though the mud, inquiring for their regiments; little squads, just issuing from their shelterless bivouac on the wet ground; wagons wrecked and forlorn; half-formed regiments, part of the men with guns and part without; wanderers driven in by the patrols; while every one you met had an unwashed, sleepy, downcast aspect, and looked as if he would like to hide his head somewhere from all the world.

> —letter to *Century Magazine*, March 12, 1885.

★ This recalled the aftermath of the second battle of Bull Run (second Manassas).

1   We were gloomy, despondent, and about "tired out"; we had not had a change of clothing from the 14th to the 31st of August [1862], and had been living, in the words of the men, on "salt horse," "hard-tack," and "chicory juice."
     —letter to *Century Magazine*, March 12, 1885.

     ★ This recalled the aftermath of the second battle of Bull Run (second Manassas).

Price, Sterling (1809–1867)

CS MAJOR GENERAL

2   Well, Mr. President [Jefferson Davis], if you will not let me serve *you*, I will nevertheless serve my *country*. You cannot prevent me from doing that. I will send you my resignation, and go back to Missouri and raise another army there without your assistance, and fight again under the flag of Missouri, and win new victories for the South in spite of the Government.
     —quoted by CS colonel Thomas L. Snead in *Battles and Leaders of the Civil War*, vol. 2, 1888.

     ★ Price had asked Davis for permission to take his army to Arkansas to prepare an invasion of his own state of Missouri. Davis refused, disliking Price because he had not been educated at West Point and because his army had been compared to a mob. After these words, however, Davis relented and gave permission.

Pryor, Roger A. (1828–1919)

CS BRIGADIER GENERAL

3   I could not fire the first gun of the war.
     —quoted by Carl Sandburg in *Abraham Lincoln: The War Years*, 1939.

     ★ Pryor, a former US congressman from Virginia, turned down the offer from the battery commander, CS captain George S. James, to fire the first shot. The first shot at Fort Sumter was then given to Edmund Ruffin, sixty-seven, a Virginia farmer. Pryor became a Confederate congressman, resigning to be commissioned a CS colonel; he was promoted to brigadier general in 1862.

Pryor, Sara Agnes (Mrs. Roger A.)

4   This [secession of South Carolina] was the tremendous event which was to change all our lives—to give us poverty for riches, mutilation and wounds for strength and health, obscurity and degradation for honor and distinction, exile and loneliness for inherited homes and friends, pain and death for happiness and life.
     —*Reminiscences of Peace and War*, 1908.

Pryor, Shepard G.

CS CAPTAIN

     ★ Pryor was a member of the 12th Georgia Regiment.

Oh Dear it is impossible for me to express my feelings when the fight was over and 1 I saw what was done the tears came then free oh that I never could behold such a sight again to think of it among civilized people killing one another like beasts one would think that the supreme ruler would put a stop to it but we sinned as a nation and must suffer in the flesh as well as spiritually those things we can't account for.
> —letter to his wife, Penelope, May 18, 1862.

Quintard, Charles Todd (1824–1898)

CS PHYSICIAN AND CHAPLAIN

After half past five in the morning of the ninth, I dropped—I could do no more. I 2 went out by myself and leaning against a fence, I wept like a child. And all that day I was so unnerved that if anyone asked me about the regiment, I could make no reply without tears. Having taken off my shirt to make bandages, I took a severe cold.
> —edited by the Reverend Arthur Howard Noll in *Doctor Quintard, Chaplain C.S.A., and Second Bishop of Tennessee, Being His History of the War (1861–65),* 1905.

★ Dr. Quintard was physician and chaplain of the 1st Tennessee Regiment. He was describing his mental state after working through the night after the battle of Perryville, Kentucky, on October 8, 1862.

Randall, James M.

US CAPTAIN

★ Randall was with the 14th Wisconsin Volunteer Infantry.

I think [Murfreesboro's] people regarded themselves as belonging to the very elect— 3 that is they were very aristocratic, and the fact that the most of them fled to the southward upon our arrival, leads me to conclude that their sympathies were strongly in that direction. But now the town is torn from center to circumference. Fences have entirely disappeared and many houses have been torn down. Fine shade trees have been laid low, and the once beautiful lawns have been trodden into quagmire. Thus we see the havoc of war.
> —letter to a friend, May 1, 1863.

You ask if I think the Emancipation Proclamation will serve to bring the war to a 4 more speedy close. I answer candidly that I don't believe it will yet I am heartily in favor of the measure, because I am convinced that its tendency will be to give us a more permanent peace in the end.
> —letter to a friend, June 10, 1863.

I have no sympathy with those people of the North that would favor peace upon dis- 5 honorable terms. Every soldier in the field knows that there can be no peace until our armed foe are conquered. I think that the opposition given by so many in the north to every war measure, has tendency to encourage our foe and prolong the war. And this leads me to say that the most despicable man in our land today is the northern copperhead. The man in arms against us is wrong, decidedly wrong, but he is

honest, and he has the courage to fight for his convictions. The people of the south are building their hopes upon a divided north, and you can be assured that anything which seems to strengthen this hope is looked upon with dread by our soldiers in the field.
>   —letter to a friend, June 10, 1863.

Ransom, John L. (1843–1919)

US QUARTERMASTER

★ Ransom was a member of the 9th Michigan Cavalry.

1   Over 150 dying per day now, and 26,000 in camp. Guards shoot now very often. Boys, as guards, are the most cruel. It is said that if they kill a Yankee they are given a thirty-day furlough.
>   —*Andersonville Diary: Life Inside the Civil War's Most Infamous Prison*, 1881.

★ Ransom became a prisoner in Andersonville in 1863.

Rawlins, John A. (1831–1869)

US LIEUTENANT COLONEL

2   The great solicitude I feel for the safety of this army leads me to mention what I hoped never again to do—the subject of your drinking. . . . and tonight when you [Grant] should, because of the condition of your health if nothing else, have been in bed, I find you where the wine bottle has just been emptied, in company with those who drink and urge you to do likewise, and the lack of your usual promptness of decision and clearness in expressing yourself in writing tended to confirm my suspicions.
>   —letter to General Ulysses S. Grant, June 6, 1863.

★ Rawlins was Grant's chief aide.

Raymond, Henry J. (1820–1869)

NEW YORK TIMES EDITOR AND REPUBLICAN PARTY CHAIRMAN

3   I am in active correspondence with your staunchest friends in every state, and from them all I hear but one report. The tide is setting strongly against us.
>   —letter to Lincoln, August 23, 1864.

★ Raymond was giving his pessimistic—and incorrect—estimate about Lincoln's chances of being reelected.

4   I fear that the desire for peace, aided by the impression or suspicion even that Mr. Lincoln is fighting not for the Union but for the abolition of slavery, and by the draft, the tax, the lack of victories, the discontent with the Cabinet and the other influ-

ences that are swelling the tide of hostility to the Administration will overbear it and give control of everything to the Opposition.
—quoted by Francis Brown in *Raymond of the Times*, 1951.

★ This letter to former Secretary of War Simon Cameron was written before the election of 1864.

Reagan, John H. (1818–1905)

US CONGRESSMAN FROM TEXAS

Suppose these slaves were liberated: suppose the people of the South would today **1** voluntarily consent to surrender $3,000,000,000 of slave property, and send their slaves at their expense into the free States, would you accept them as freemen and citizens in your States? You dare not answer me that you would.
—speech to the House of Representatives, January 15, 1861.

★ Reagan was later the Confederate postmaster general. He returned to the US Congress after the war.

Wisdom requires us to accept the decision of battle upon the issues involved and to **2** be thankful that no more has been demanded by the conquerors, and to unite frankly and as cheerfully as we can with the government in carrying out the policy it has propounded.
—open letter to Texans, quoted by Walter F. McCaleb, editor of *Memoirs with Special Reference to Secession and the Civil War*, 1906.

★ Reagan wrote this while a prisoner in Fort Warren at Boston Harbor. He was Confederate postmaster general at the time but returned to the US Congress after the war.

Reed, H. B.

US COLONEL

The immense number of wounded [at Shiloh] required an army of surgeons. Many **3** young doctors, among others, were sent from home to help care for them, and, with the best intentions, their want of practical knowledge left much to wish for.
—*The 44th Indiana Voluntary Infantry, History of Its Services in the War of the Rebellion and a Personal Record of Its Members*, 1880.

A day or two after the battle [at Shiloh], I went on board a steamer filled with **4** wounded men. Very many of them were wandering aimlessly about over the boat, presenting a most ghastly appearance, their wounds having been tied up hurriedly, the blood and grime of battle being left to be removed at a more convenient season.
—*The 44th Indiana Voluntary Infantry, History of Its Services in The War of the Rebellion and a Personal Record of Its Members*, 1880.

Reilly, Frank W.

CINCINNATI TIMES REPORTER

1   I hope my eyes may never again look upon such sights. Men with their entrails protruding, others with bullets in their breasts or shoulders, and one poor wretch I found whose eyes had been shot entirely away. . . . On either side the battle was fought with a desperation which I could not have believed to exist in the minds of men.

—article, *New York Times*, April 13, 1862.

★ Reilly was reporting on the battle of Shiloh, Tennessee, during which he was shot in the leg.

Reynolds, Belle

US NURSE

2   At night I lived over the horrors of the field hospital and the amputating table. If I but closed my eyes, I saw such horrible sights that I would spring from my bed; and not until fairly awakened could I be convinced of my remoteness from the sickening scene. Those groans were in my ears! I saw again the quivering limbs, the spouting arteries, and the pinched and ghastly faces of the sufferers.

—quoted by Kenneth C. Davis in *Don't Know Much about the Civil War*, 1996.

★ Reynolds was a Union nurse known as "Mrs. Major" Reynolds.

Richards, Caroline

DIARIST

★ Richards lived in Canandaigua, New York.

3   "Whether I am in the body, or out of the body, I know not, but I one thing I know," Lee has surrendered! and all the people seem crazy in consequence. The bells are ringing, boys and girls, men and women are running though the streets wild with excitement; the flags are all flying, one from the top of our church, and such a "hurrah boys" generally, I never dreamed of.

—*Village Life in America 1852–1872*, 1913.

★ This diary entry was for April 10, 1865. The quotation at the beginning is from the *Pilgrimage of Etheria*, a fourth-century Christian account of a nun's travels.

4   Oh, how horrible it is! I went down town shortly after I heard the news [of Lincoln's assassination], and it was wonderful to see the effect of the intelligence upon everybody, small and great, rich or poor. Every one was talking low, with sad and anxious looks.

—*Village Life in America 1852–1872*, 1913.

★ This diary entry was for April 15, 1865.

Richardson, Israel B. (1815–1862)

US COLONEL

Why the change [in troop dispositions] was made, I do not know; but I have no con- 1
fidence in Colonel Miles, for he is drunk.
> —quoted by Alfred H. Guernsey and Henry M. Alden in *Harper's Pictorial
> History of the Great Rebellion in the United States*, 1866.

★ This happened at the first battle of Bull Run (first Manassas). A court of inquiry
found that Miles had been drunk but said that a court-martial would be too inconve-
nient to hold at that time.

Rock, John S. (1825–1866)

BOSTON PHYSICIAN AND LAWYER

★ Rock was the first black lawyer admitted to the bar of the Supreme Court.

I do not deny that there is a deep and cruel prejudice lurking in the bosoms of the 2
white people of this country. It is much more abundant in the North than in the
South.
> —speech to the Massachusetts Anti-Slavery Society, January 23, 1862, quoted in
> *The Liberator*, February 14, 1862.

It is true the government is but little more antislavery now than it was at the com- 3
mencement of the war; but while fighting for its own existence, it has been obliged
to take slavery by the throat and, sooner or later, *must* choke her to death.
> —speech to the Massachusetts Anti-Slavery Society, January 23, 1862, quoted in
> *The Liberator*, February 14, 1862.

Let me tell you, my friends, *the slaveholders are not the men we dread*! They do not 4
desire to have us removed. The Northern pro-slavery men have done the free people
of color tenfold more injury than the Southern slaveholders.
> —speech to the Massachusetts Anti-Slavery Society, January 23, 1862, quoted in
> *The Liberator*, February 14, 1862.

Roebling, Washington (1837–1926)

US MAJOR

The demand down here for killing purposes is far ahead of the supply. Thank God, 5
however, for the consolation that when the last man is killed, the war will be over.
This war . . . differs from all previous wars in having no object to fight for; it can't be
finished until all the men on either the one side or the other are killed; both sides are
trying to do that as fast as they can because it would be a pity to spin this affair out
for two or three years longer.
> —quoted by Geoffrey C. Ward in *The Civil War: An Illustrated History*, 1990.

★ This was written June 23, 1864, during the Petersburg campaign. After the war,
Roebling, a civil engineer, was in charge of building the Brooklyn Bridge.

Rogers, J. C.

CS MAJOR

1   Compliments, hell! Who wants compliments in such a damned place as this? Go back and ask General Law if he expects me to hold the world in check with the 5th regiment!
　　　—quoted by Shelby Foote in *The Civil War*, vol. 2, 1958.

　　★ Rogers was replying to a messenger from Major General Evander M. Law, who congratulated him on his Texas regiment's fighting during the battle of Gettysburg on July 2, 1863.

Rosecrans, Sylvester (1827–1878)

ROMAN CATHOLIC BISHOP

2   While the General [Rosecrans] is wielding the sword of the flesh, I trust that I am using the sword of the Spirit. He is fighting the rebels, and I am fighting the spirits of darkness. There is this difference: he is fighting with Price, while I am fighting without price.
　　　—quoted by Frank Moore in *Anecdotes, Poetry and Incidents of the War: North and South, 1860–1865*, 1867.

　　★ The bishop was comparing his battles with those of his military brother, who was then facing CS major general Sterling Price in Mississippi. His brother, General William Rosecrans, had converted him to Roman Catholicism. See next entry.

Rosecrans, William S. (1819–1898)

US MAJOR GENERAL

3   Feel them, but don't get into their fingers.
　　　—*Century Magazine*, October, 1886.

　　★ He was asking Colonel Joseph A. Mower to feel out the Confederate forces at the battle of Corinth, Mississippi, on October 4, 1862.

4   I need no other stimulus to make me do my duty than the knowledge of what it is. To threats of removal or the like I must be permitted to say that I am insensible.
　　　—telegram to Major General Henry W. Halleck, December 4, 1862.

　　★ Halleck had warned Rosecrans that he could lose his command if he kept his troops in Nashville another week.

5   Be cool—I need not ask you to be brave. Keep ranks, do not throw away your fire; fire slowly, deliberately—above all, fire low, and be always sure of your aim. Close readily in upon the enemy, and when you get within charging distance, rush upon him with the bayonet. Do this and victory will certainly be yours.
　　　—orders to his troops, December 31, 1862.

　　★ These orders were for that day's battle of Stone's River at Murfreesboro, Tennessee.

6   Never mind! Brave men must die in battle. We must seek results.
　　　—edited by Frank Moore in *The Rebellion Record: A Diary of American Events, with Documents, Narratives, Illustrative Incidents, Poetry, Etc.*, vol. 6, 1864.

★ Rosecrans had just been told during the battle of Stone's River at Murfreesboro, Tennessee, on December 31, 1862, that General Joshua W. Sill had been killed. (Sill's division commander during this battle was Major General Philip H. Sheridan, who later named Fort Sill, Oklahoma, for him.)

Bragg's a good dog, but Hold Fast's a better.   **1**
   —quoted by Mark Boatner III in *The Civil War Dictionary*, 1988.

★ Rosecrans, who nicknamed himself "Hold Fast," supposedly said this after repulsing General Braxton Bragg's attacks at the battle of Stone's River at Murfreesboro, Tennessee, on December 31, 1862.

Ross, Fitzgerald

AUSTRIAN CAPTAIN AND OBSERVER IN THE CONFEDERATE ARMY

★ Ross, born in England, had joined the Imperial Austrian Army and was an observer in the Confederate army.

A month after the battle of Chickamauga, we rode over the field of battle, which is   **2**
seven or eight miles to the rear of our camp. The Yankee dead are still unburied, which is a great shame. . . . If there be one good feeling to be found in the North, it is the respect they show to their dead; and doubtless, if these poor fellows had been identified and properly buried, very many of them would have been brought to their homes after the war, and their bones laid amongst their own kindred. Now the pigs are fattening on them—a disgusting sight to behold.
   —quoted by Richard B. Harwell in *The Civil War Reader*, 1958.

Were it not for the friendly neutrality of the British Government towards the North,   **3**
the Confederates would have had a fleet, and the war in consequence would have been over long ago.
   —quoted by Richard B. Harwell in *The Civil War Reader*, 1958.

Ruffin, Edmund (1794–1865)

The murderer and robber and fire-raiser [John Brown] so notorious for these crimes   **4**
in his Kansas career, and now the attempter of the thousand-fold horrors in Virginia is, for these reasons, the present popular idol of the north.
   —quoted by Randall Bedwell in *Brink of Destruction*, 1999.

★ Ruffin made this comment on November 27, 1859. He supposedly fired the first shot at Fort Sumter and after the war committed suicide to avoid living under a US government.

I here declare my unmitigated hatred to Yankee rule to all political, social & business   **5**
connection with Yankees & to the Yankee race. Would that I could impress these sentiments, in their full force, on every living southerner, & bequeath them to every one yet to be born! May such sentiments be held universally in the outraged & downtrodden South, though in silence & stillness, until the now far distant day shall arrive for just retribution for Yankee usurpation, oppression, & atrocious outrages & for deliverance & vengeance for the now ruined, subjugated, & enslaved Southern States! May the maledictions of every victim to their malignity, press with full weight on the perfidious Yankee people & their perjured rulers & especially on those of the

invading forces who perpetrated, & their leaders & higher authorities who encouraged, directed, or permitted, the unprecedented & generally extended outrages of robbery, rapine & destruction, & house burning, all committed contrary to the laws of war on noncombatant residents, & still worse on aged men & helpless women!
—quoted in *The Civil War and Reconstruction: A Documentary Collection*, edited by William E. Gienapp, 2001.

★ Ruffin wrote this in his diary just before shooting himself on June 17, 1865.

Russell, John, 1st Earl Russell (1792–1878)

BRITISH FOREIGN MINISTER

1   I agree with you that the time is come for offering mediation to the United States Government, with a view to recognition of the independence of the Confederates. I agree further that, in case of failure, we ought ourselves to recognize the Southern States as an independent State.
—message to the prime minister, Lord Palmerston, September 17, 1862.

★ This idea was dropped the following year, after the battle of Gettysburg.

Russell, William Howard (1820–1907)

TIMES (LONDON) CORRESPONDENT

2   Secession is the fashion here [in Charleston]. Young ladies sing for it; old ladies pray for it; young men are dying to fight for it; old men are ready to demonstrate it.
—quoted by Carl Sandburg in *Abraham Lincoln: The War Years*, 1939.

3   Soon afterwards there entered, with a shambling, loose, irregular, almost unsteady gait, a tall, lank, lean man, considerably over six feet in height, with stooping shoulders, long pendulous arms, terminating in hands of extraordinary dimensions, which, however, were far exceeded in proportion by his feet. He was dressed in an ill-fitting, wrinkled suit of black, which put one in mind of an undertaker's uniform at a funeral; round his neck a rope of black silk was knotted in a large bulb, with flying ends projecting beyond the collar of his coat; his turned-down shirt-collar disclosed a sinewy muscular yellow neck, and above that, nestling in a great black mass of hair, bristling and compact like a ruff of mourning pins, rose the strange quaint face and head, covered with its thatch of wild, republican hair, of President Lincoln.
—*My Diary North and South*, 1863.

★ This diary entry was written on March 27, 1861.

4   A person who met Mr. Lincoln in the street would not take him to be what—according to the usages of European society—is called a "gentleman;" and, indeed, since I came to the United States, I have heard more disparaging allusions made by Americans to him on that account than I could have expected among simple republicans, where all should be equals.
—*My Diary North and South*, 1863.

★ This diary entry was written on March 27, 1861.

Where men bred in courts, accustomed to the world, or versed in diplomacy, would 1
use some subterfuge, or would make a polite speech, or give a shrug of the shoulders
as the means of getting out of an embarrassing position, Mr. Lincoln raises a laugh
by some bold west-country anecdote, and moves off in the cloud of merriment produced by his joke.
    —*My Diary North and South*, 1863.

★ This diary entry was written on March 28, 1861.

The Georgians are by no means as keen as the Carolinians on their border—nay, 2
they are not so belligerent today as they were a week ago.
    —quoted in *Harper's Weekly*, June 22, 1861.

★ This quoted a report written by Russell on May 2, 1861.

The New Englander must have something to persecute, and as he has hunted down 3
all his Indians, burnt all his witches, and persecuted all his opponents to death, he
invented Abolitionism as the sole resource left to him for the gratification of his
favoured passion. Next to this motive principle is his desire to make money dishon-
estly, trickily, meanly, and shabbily. He has acted on it in all his relations with the
South, and has cheated and plundered her in all his dealings by villainous tariffs.
    —article, *Times* (London), May 28, 1861.

This poor President [Lincoln]! He is to be pitied; . . . trying with all his might to 4
understand strategy, naval warfare, big guns, the movements of troops, military
maps, reconnaissances, occupations, interior and exterior lines, and all the technical
details of the art of slaying. He runs from one house to another, armed with plans,
papers, reports, recommendations, sometimes good humoured, never angry, occasionally dejected, and always a little fussy.
    —*My Diary North and South*, 1863.

★ This diary entry was written on October 9, 1861.

But for all that, there have been many more courtly presidents who, in a similar cri- 5
sis, would have displayed less capacity, honesty, and plain dealing than Abraham
Lincoln.
    —*My Diary North and South*, 1863.

★ This diary entry was written on October 9, 1861.

The impression produced by the size of [Lincoln's] extremities, and by his flapping 6
and wide projecting ears, may be removed by the appearance of kindliness, sagacity,
and the awkward bonhommie of his face.
    —*My Diary North and South*, 1863.

On my way to dinner at the Legation I met the President crossing Pennsylvania 7
Avenue, striding like a crane in a bulrush swamp among the great blocks of marble,
dressed in an oddly cut suit of gray, with a felt hat on the back of his head, wiping his
face with a red pocket-handkerchief.
    —*My Diary North and South*, 1863.

1   Conversation ensued for some minutes, which the President [Lincoln] enlivened by two or three peculiar little sallies, and I left agreeably impressed with his shrewdness, humor, and natural sagacity.
     —*My Diary North and South*, 1863.

Sanderson, James M.

US CAPTAIN

2   Remember that beans, badly boiled, kill more than bullets; and fat is more fatal than powder. In cooking, more than anything else in this world, always make haste slowly. One hour too much is vastly better than five minutes too little, with rare exceptions. A big fire scorches your soup, burns your face, and crisps your temper. Skim, simmer, and scour, are the true secrets of good cooking.
     —*Camp Fires and Camp Cooking, or Culinary Hints for the Soldier*, 1862.

Satterlee, Alfred

3   If S.C. would only go *alone* out of the Union it would be a good riddance.
     —diary, 1990.

     ★ This diary entry was written on November 9, 1860, and South Carolina seceded on December 20.

Saxton, Rufus

US BRIGADIER GENERAL

4   Should it ever be [the colored regiment's] good fortune to get into action, I have no fear but it will win its way to the confidence of those who are willing to recognize courage and manhood, and vindicate the wise policy of the Administration, in putting these men into the field and giving them a chance to strike a blow for the country and their own liberty.
     —letter to Secretary of War Edwin M. Stanton, January 25, 1863.

     ★ This was the 1st South Carolina Volunteer Infantry, composed of colored troops.

Schaff, Morris

US LIEUTENANT GENERAL

5   A real adept skulker or coffee boiler is a most interesting specimen, and how well I remember the coolness with which he and his companion "for they go in pairs" would rise from their little fires upon being discovered, and ask innocently, "Lieutenant, can you tell us where the Umpteenth Regiment is?" And the answer, I am sorry to say, was too often: "Yes, right up there at the front, you damned rascal, as you well know!" Of course, they would make a show of moving, but were back at their little fires as soon as you were out of sight.
     —*The Battle of the Wilderness*, 1910.

Scheibert, Justus

PRUSSIAN CAPTAIN

[Lee] was not at his ease, but was riding to and fro, frequently changing his position, **1** making anxious inquiries here and there, and looking careworn.
—quoted by Douglas Southall Freeman in *R. E. Lee: A Biography*, vol. 3, 1934.

★ Scheibert, a Prussian observer, was describing Lee's behavior on the second day of the battle of Gettysburg, July 2, 1863.

Schneider, Anna

I am taking my pen in hand to tell you about the terrible situation I have to endure. **2** I am writing and telling you that I am left alone with my four children in the woods because my husband has gone to War for one year, as of today, September 25 . . . This is the third time that they drafted, but the first two times, one was free if one would pay $300. Nearly everyone would have paid it if he could scrape it together, but in this draft they could not, else they would not be able to get enough men. First they took the money, but now they take the men. Now you can see the racket they have here in America.
—letter to her mother and sisters, September 25, 1865.

★ She was writing from her home in Minnesota to her family in Bavaria, Germany. General Robert E. Lee had already surrendered in May, and Anna's husband, Engelbert, returned to civilian life a few days after this letter was written.

Schofield, John M. (1831–1906)

US MAJOR GENERAL

The veteran American soldier fights very much as he has been accustomed to work **3** his farm or run his sawmill. He wants to see a fair prospect that it is going to pay.
—quoted by Shelby Foote in *The Civil War*, vol. 3, 1958.

To mass troops against the fire of a covered line is simply to devote them to destruc- **4** tion. The greater the mass, the greater the loss—that is all.
—quoted by William C. Davis in *Brothers in Arms*, 1995.

Scott, Julian A.

US PRIVATE

★ Scott was a member of the 9th New York Regiment.

So now I am minus a leg! But never mind, dear parents, I suffer but little pain, and **5** will [be] home in a few weeks, I think.
—letter to his parents, April 16, 1862.

★ The fifteen-year-old Scott was wounded at South Mills, Virginia.

Scott, Winfield (1786–1866)

US GENERAL IN CHIEF

1   With an army faithful to its allegiance, and the navy probably equally so, and with a federal executive, for the next twelve months, of firmness and moderation, which the country has a right to expect,—*moderation* being an element of power not less than *firmness*—there is good reason to hope that the danger of secession may be made to pass away without one conflict of arms, one execution, or one arrest for treason.
        —memorandum to President James Buchanan and Secretary of War John B. Floyd, October 29, 1860.

    ★ Scott did not support Lincoln but knew that he had been elected.

2   Lee, you have made the greatest mistake of your life, but I feared it would be so.
        —quoted by James M. McPherson in *The Battle Cry of Freedom: The Civil War Era*, 1989.

    ★ Scott said this to Robert E. Lee after he turned down the offer to command all US troops against the Confederacy.

3   Say to the seceded states, "Wayward sisters, depart in peace."
        —letter to Secretary of State William H. Seward, March 3, 1861.

    ★ Scott was supreme commander of the US Army from 1841 to 1861.

4   Major General McClellan has propagated in high quarters the idea expressed in the letter before me, that Washington was not only "insecure," but in "imminent danger." Relying on our numbers, our forts, and the Potomac River, I am confident in the opposite opinion; and considering the stream of new regiments that is pouring in upon us (before this alarm could have reached their homes), I have not the slightest apprehension for the safety of the Government here.
        —letter to Lincoln, August 9, 1861.

5   Having now been long unable to mount a horse, or to walk more than a few paces at a time, and consequently being unable to review troops, much less to direct them in battle,—in short, being broken down by many particular hurts, besides the general infirmities of age,—I feel that I have become an incumbrance to the army as well as to myself, and that I ought, giving way to a younger commander, to seek the palliatives of physical pain and exhaustion.
        —letter to Lincoln, August 9, 1861.

    ★ Scott, seventy-five, was replaced in November by Major General George B. McClellan.

6   The original offense given to me by Major-General McClellan . . . seems to have been the result of deliberation between him and some of the members of the Cabinet, by whom all the greater war questions are to be settled, without resort to or consultation with me, the nominal General-in-Chief of the army. . . . That freedom of

access and consultation have, very naturally, deluded the junior general into a feeling of indifference toward his senior.
>   —letter to Secretary of War Simon Cameron, August 12, 1861.

★ Scott was explaining his reasons for retiring.

Scurry, William R.

CS LIEUTENANT COLONEL

Soldiers—I am proud of you. Go on as you have commenced, and it will not be long **1** until not a single soldier of the United States will be left upon the soil of New Mexico. The Territory, relieved of the burden imposed on it by its late oppressors, will once more, throughout its beautiful valleys, "blossom as the rose," beneath the plastic hand of peaceful industry.
>   —General Order No. 4, March 29, 1862.

★ He was commending his men's efforts on March 27 at the battle of Glorieta Pass, or Pigeon's Ranch, in the Territory of New Mexico.

Seddon, James A. (1815–1880)

CS SECRETARY OF WAR

Rely on it, the eyes and hopes of the whole Confederacy are upon you [Johnston] **2** with the full confidence that you will act, and with the sentiment that it were better to fail nobly daring than, through prudence even, to be inactive.
>   —letter to General Joseph E. Johnston, June 21, 1863.

★ This referred to the possibility of saving Vicksburg, Mississippi, because Johnston had informed Seddon six days earlier that the rescue was hopeless. Johnston never attempted it.

If the present system be continued, prices, already many hundred percent above **3** true values, must be indefinitely enhanced, the credit of the government must be wrecked utterly, and no alternative left for the continuance of our patriotic struggle and the preservation of our lives and liberties but grinding taxation and the systematized seizure, without present compensation, of all supplies needed for the employees as well as the armies of the Confederacy.
>   —letter to Confederate president Jefferson Davis, November 26, 1863.

★ Seddon was warning about the problems of supplying the army.

If our [Confederacy] had had one million more people, which would have put one **4** hundred thousand more men at my disposal, the Federal armies would have got the lesson they so justly deserve a long time ago. Unfortunately, in almost all our engagements, we have fought one against two, and, many times, one against three.
>   —quoted by Charles Girard in *A Visit to the Confederate States of America in 1863*, 1864.

★ This quotation comes from an interview of Seddon by Girard, a French military supplier to the Confederacy.

Sedgwick, John (1813–1864)

US MAJOR GENERAL

1   Stuart is the best cavalry officer ever *foaled* in North America.
    —quoted by John Esten Cooke in *A Life of General Robert E. Lee*, 1875.

2   Don't duck; they couldn't hit an elephant at this distance.
    —quoted by Carl Sandburg in *Abraham Lincoln: The War Years*, 1939.

    ★ A couple of minutes later, Sedgwick was killed by a sharpshooter (May 9, 1864, during the battle of Spotsylvania).

Semmes, Raphael (1809–1877)

CS COMMANDER

3   When will the demonlike passions of the North be stilled?
    —journal, December 15, 1863.

    ★ Semmes commanded the *Alabama*, which captured sixty-five Union merchant ships around the world. This question was penned as the ship sailed the China Sea.

4   Confound them; they've been fighting twenty minutes, and they're as cool as posts.
    —quoted by Frederick M. Edge in *Englishman's View of the Battle between the "Alabama" and the "Kearsarge": An Account of the Naval engagement in the British Channel on Sunday, June 19th, 1864*, 1864.

    ★ Semmes was reacting to the efficiency of the Union sailors before they sank his ship.

5   A noble Roman once stabbed his daughter, rather than she should be polluted by the foul embrace of a tyrant. It was with a similar feeling that [Lieutenant John] Kell and I saw the *Alabama* go down. We had buried her as we had christened her, and she was safe from the polluting touch of the hated Yankee!
    —quoted by Shelby Foote in *The Civil War*, vol. 3, 1958.

    ★ Semmes was describing the sinking of his ship by the USS *Kearsarge* in the English Channel on June 19, 1864.

6   It will never do in this nineteenth century for us to go down and the decks covered with our gallant wounded.
    —quoted by Charles M. Robinson III in *Shark of the Confederacy*, 1995.

    ★ Semmes was describing the sinking of his ship by the USS *Kearsarge* in the English Channel on June 19, 1864.

7   Civil war is a terrible crucible through which to pass character; the dross drops away from the pure metal at the first touch of the fire.
    —*Memoirs of Service Afloat*, 1868.

Seward, William H. (1801–1872)

US SENATOR FROM NEW YORK AND SECRETARY OF STATE

Shall I tell you what this collision means? They who think that it is accidental, unnec- **1**
essary, the work of interested or fanatical agitators, and therefore ephemeral, mistake
the case altogether. It is an irrepressible conflict between opposing and enduring
forces, and it means the United States must and will, sooner or later, become either
entirely a slave-holding nation or entirely a free-labor nation. . . . I know, and you
know, that a revolution has begun.
   —speech in Rochester, New York, October 25, 1858.

Sixty days' more suns will give you a much brighter and more cheerful atmosphere. **2**
   —speech in New York City, December 22, 1860.

★ South Carolina had seceded two days before, and the North estimated that secession
or war would last about two months.

I do not know what the Union would be worth if saved by the use of the sword.   **3**
   —speech to the Senate, January 12, 1861.

My system is built upon this idea as a ruling one, namely, that we must CHANGE **4**
THE QUESTION BEFORE THE PUBLIC FROM ONE UPON SLAVERY, OR
ABOUT SLAVERY, for a question upon UNION OR DISUNION.
   —written suggestion to Lincoln, April 1, 1861.

★ This was the last of four suggestions by Seward on formulating the war policy.

We from that hour shall cease to be friends and become once more, as we have twice **5**
before been forced to be, enemies of Great Britain.
   —letter to Charles Francis Adams, May 21, 1861.

★ "That hour" would come if Britain recognized the Confederacy. Adams was the
newly appointed minister to that country.

Tell no one, but the battle is lost. The army is in full retreat.   **6**
   —quoted by Nathaniel W. Stephenson in *Lincoln: An Account of His Personal
   Life, Especially of Its Springs of Action as Revealed and Deepened by the Ordeal
   of War*, 1922.

★ Seward said this to the White House secretaries after the first battle of Bull Run
(first Manassas) in July 1861.

If the [Emancipation] Proclamation were issued now, it would be received and con- **7**
sidered as a despairing cry—a shriek from and for the Administration, rather than
for freedom. The government stretching forth its hands to Ethiopia, instead of
Ethiopia stretching forth her hands to the government.
   —comments at a cabinet meeting, July 22, 1862.

★ This was after Lincoln read the preliminary draft of the document. The official
announcement was delayed until after the victory at the battle of Antietam (Sharpsburg) two months later. "Ethiopian" was a nickname for a black.

1   We show our sympathy with slavery by emancipating slaves where we cannot reach them and holding them in bondage where we can set them free.
    —quoted by Walter E. Williams in Thomas J. DiLorenzo's book *The Real Lincoln: A New Look at Abraham Lincoln, His Agenda, and an Unnecessary War*, 2002.

    ★ Seward was referring to the Emancipation Proclamation.

2   Executive force and vigor are rare qualities. The President is the best of us.
    —quoted by Colonel Alexander K. McClure in *Lincoln's Yarns and Stories*, 1904.

3   They tell us that we are to encounter opposition. Why, bless my soul, did anybody ever expect to reach a fortune, or fame, or happiness on earth or a crown in heaven, without encountering resistance and opposition? What are we made men for but to encounter and overcome opposition arrayed against us in the line of our duty?
    —quoted by Nathaniel W. Stephenson in *Lincoln: An Account of His Personal Life, Especially of Its Springs of Action as Revealed and Deepened by the Ordeal of War*, 1922.

4   A fundamental principle of politics is always to be on the side of your country in a war. It kills any party to oppose a war.
    —quoted by Nathaniel W. Stephenson in *Lincoln: An Account of His Personal Life, Especially of Its Springs of Action as Revealed and Deepened by the Ordeal of War*, 1922.

5   The agitators for war in time of peace, and for peace in time of war, are not necessarily, or perhaps ordinarily, unpatriotic in their purposes or motives. Results alone determine whether they are wise or unwise.
    —letter to US ambassador Charles Francis Adams in London, February 7, 1865.

    ★ Seward was reporting on the unsuccessful meeting that he and Lincoln had four days earlier with a Confederate delegation to discuss peace terms.

Seymour, Horatio (1810–1886)

NEW YORK GOVERNOR

6   Mr. Lincoln values many things above the Union; we put it first of all. He thinks a proclamation worth more than peace; we think the blood of our people more precious than the edicts of the President.
    —speech to the Democratic National Convention in Chicago, August 29, 1864.

Shaw, Robert G. (1837–1863)

US COLONEL

7   The eyes of thousands will look on what you do tonight.
    —quoted by John D. Wright in *The Language of the Civil War*, 2001.

★ Shaw commanded the Union's first black unit, the 54th Massachusetts Regiment. He was encouraging his six hundred men before their attack on Battery Wagner in Charleston harbor, July 18, 1863. It failed, resulting in 272 deaths, as well as Shaw's own.

Sheahan, John P.

US LIEUTENANT

I felt a joyous exaltation, a perfect indifference to circumstances through the whole   1
of that three days fight, and have seldom enjoyed three days more in my life.
   —letter to his father, July 10, 1863.

★ Sheahan, an artilleryman with the 31st Maine Regiment, was referring to the battle of Gettysburg.

Sheridan, Philip H. (1831–1888)

US MAJOR GENERAL

. . . our advent was so unexpected by the people of the region through which we   2
passed that supposing us to be Confederate cavalry, they often gave us all they had, the women and servants contributing most freely from their reserve stores.
   —*Personal Memoirs of P. H. Sheridan, General United States Army*, vol. 1, 1888.

★ This was in Mississippi in May 1862.

They [soldiers of the Second Division of the Union Army of the Cumberland] had   3
never given me any trouble, nor done anything that could bring aught but honor to themselves. I had confidence in them, and I believe they had in me. They were ever steady, whether in victory or in misfortune, and as I tried always to be with them, to put them in the hottest fire if good could be gained, or save them from unnecessary loss, as occasion required, they amply repaid all my care and anxiety, courageously and readily meeting all demands in every emergency that arose.
   —*Personal Memoirs of P. H. Sheridan, General United States Army*, vol. 1, 1888.

★ He was leaving to take command of the Cavalry Corps of the Army of the Potomac in March 1864.

[Sigel] will do nothing but run. He never did anything else.   4
   —quoted by Rod Graff in *Civil War Quiz and Fact Book*, 1985.

★ Major General Franz Sigel had just been defeated at New Market, Virginia, on May 15, 1864. Four days later, he was relieved of his command.

Where all the colored people came from and what started them was inexplicable, but   5
they began joining us just before we reached Trevillian [Virginia]—men, women, and children with bundles of all sorts containing their few worldly goods, and the number increased from day to day until they arrived at West Point [Virginia]. Probably not one of the poor things had the remotest idea when he set off, as to where he

would finally land, but to a man they followed the Yankees in full faith that they would lead to freedom, no matter what road they took.
>   —*Personal Memoirs of P. H. Sheridan, General United States Army*, vol. 1, 1888.

★ This was in June 1864.

1   If I had been with you this morning this disaster would not have happened. We must face the other way, we will go back and recover our camp.
>   —*Personal Memoirs of P. H. Sheridan, General United States Army*, vol. 2, 1888.

★ He said this to his retreating soldiers on October 19, 1864. Confederates had attacked Sheridan's camp on the bank of Cedar Creek, Virginia, while he was away. He rallied his men and retook the camp.

2   A crow would have had to carry its rations if it had flown across the valley.
>   —quoted by Rod Graff in *Civil War Quiz and Fact Book*, 1985.

★ Sheridan destroyed the Shenandoah Valley, burning crops and homes, during a campaign from August 7, 1864, to March 2, 1865.

3   The proper strategy consists, in the first place, in inflicting as telling blows as possible upon the enemy's army, and then in causing the inhabitants so much suffering that they must long for peace, and force their government to demand it. The people must be left nothing but their eyes to weep with over the war.
>   —quoted by CS lieutenant Randolph H. McKim in *A Soldier's Recollections: Leaves from the Diary of a Young Confederate*, 1910.

★ Sheridan gave this advice to Otto von Bismarck on September 8, 1870, the year before Bismarck became Germany's first chancellor.

4   Indeed, it may be said that till General Grant was matched against him, [Lee] never met an opponent he did not vanquish, for while it is true that defeat was inflicted on the Confederates at Antietam [Sharpsburg] and Gettysburg, yet the fruits of these victories were not gathered for after each of these battles Lee was left unmolested till he had a chance to recuperate.
>   —*Personal Memoirs of P. H. Sheridan, General United States Army*, vol. 2, 1888.

5   From the moment [Grant] set our armies in motion simultaneously, in the spring of 1864, it could be seen that we should be victorious ultimately, for though on different lines we were checked now and then, yet we were harassing the Confederacy at so many vital points that plainly it must yield to our blows.
>   —*Personal Memoirs of P. H. Sheridan, General United States Army*, vol. 2, 1888.

6   The assignment of General Grant to the command of the Union armies in the winter of 1863–64 gave presage of success from the start, for his eminent abilities had already been proved, and besides, he was a tower of strength to the Government, because he had the confidence of the people.
>   —*Personal Memoirs of P. H. Sheridan, General United States Army*, vol. 2, 1888.

While this parting salute of deadly projectiles was going on a little daughter of 1
Colonel William J. Landram, whose home was in Danville [Kentucky], came running
out from his house and planted a small national flag on one of [Captain Henry]
Hescock's guns. The patriotic act was so brave and touching that it thrilled all who
witnessed the scene; and until the close of the war, when peace separated the surviving officers and men of the battery, that little flag was protected and cherished as
a memento of the Perryville campaign.
   —*Personal Memoirs of P. H. Sheridan, General United States Army*, vol. 1, 1888.

The intense loyalty of this part of Tennessee [the Knoxville area] exceeded that of 2
any other section I was in during the war. The people could not do too much to aid
the Union cause, and brought us an abundance of everything needful. The women
were especially loyal, and as many of their sons and husbands, who had been compelled to "refugee" on account of their loyal sentiments, returned with us, numbers
of the women went into ecstasies of joy when this part of the Union army appeared
among them.
   —*Personal Memoirs of P. H. Sheridan, General United States Army*, vol. 1, 1888.

Many jealousies and much ill-feeling, the outgrowth of former campaigns, existed 3
among officers of high grade in the Army of the Potomac in the winter of 1864
[when Grant was made general-in-chief of all Union armies], and several general
officers were to be sent elsewhere in consequence.
   —*Personal Memoirs of P. H. Sheridan, General United States Army*, vol. 1, 1888.

. . . there was little chance for mounted fighting in eastern Virginia, the dense woods, 4
the armament of both parties, and the practice of barricading, making it impractica-
ble to use the sabre with anything like a large force; and so with the exception of
Yellow Tavern the dismounted method prevailed in almost every engagement.
   —*Personal Memoirs of P. H. Sheridan, General United States Army*, vol. 1, 1888.

I do not hold war to mean simply that lines of men shall engage each other in battle, 5
and material interests be ignored. This is but a duel, in which one combatant seeks
the other's life; war means much more, and is far worse than this.
   —*Personal Memoirs of P. H. Sheridan, General United States Army*, vol. 1, 1888.

I deemed it necessary to be very cautious; and the fact that the Presidential election 6
[of 1864] was impending made me doubly so, the authorities at Washington having
impressed upon me that the defeat of my army might be followed by the overthrow
of the party in power, which event, it was believed, would at least retard the progress
of the war, if, indeed, it did not lead to the complete abandonment of all coercive
measures.
   —*Personal Memoirs of P. H. Sheridan, General United States Army*, vol. 1, 1888.

General Grant was never impulsive, and always met his officers in an unceremoni- 7
ous way, with a quiet "How are you" soon putting one at his ease, since the pleasant
tone in which he spoke gave assurance of welcome, although his manner was other-

wise impassive. When the ordinary greeting was over, he usually waited for his visitor to open the conversation.
—*Personal Memoirs of P. H. Sheridan, General United States Army*, vol. 2, 1888.

1   Men who march, scout, and fight, and suffer all the hardships that fall to the lot of soldiers in the field, in order to do vigorous work must have the best bodily sustenance, and every comfort that can be provided.
—*Personal Memoirs of P. H. Sheridan, General United States Army*, vol. 1, 1888.

2   Soldiers are averse to seeing their comrades killed without compensating results, and none realize more quickly than they the blundering that often takes place on the field of battle.
—*Personal Memoirs of P. H. Sheridan, General United States Army*, vol. 1, 1888.

3   My regiment had lost very few men since coming under my command, but it seemed, in my eyes of all who belonged to it, that casualties to the enemy and some slight successes for us had repaid every sacrifice, and in consequence I had gained not only their confidence as soldiers but also their esteem and love as men, and to a degree far beyond what I then realized.
—*Personal Memoirs of P. H. Sheridan, General United States Army*, vol. 1, 1888.

4   General Halleck did not know much about taking care of himself in the field. His camp arrangements were wholly inadequate, and in consequence he and all the officers about him were subjected to much unnecessary discomfort and annoyance.
—*Personal Memoirs of P. H. Sheridan, General United States Army*, vol. 1, 1888.

5   I have never in my life taken a command into battle, and had the slightest desire to come out alive unless I won.
—quoted by Horace Porter in *Campaigning with Grant*, 1897.

6   The trouble with the commanders of the Army of the Potomac was that they never marched out to "lick" anybody; all they thought of was to escape being "licked" themselves.
—quoted by Lieutenant Colonel G. F. R. Henderson in *Stonewall Jackson and the American Civil War*, vol. 2, 1898.

7   Death is popularly considered the maximum punishment of war, but it is not; reduction to poverty brings prayers of peace more quickly than does the destruction of human life, as the selfishness of man has demonstrated in more than one conflict.
—*Personal Memoirs of P. H. Sheridan, General United States Army*, 1888.

8   Smash 'em up! Smash 'em up!
—quoted by John D. Wright in *The Language of the Civil War*, 2001.

★ Sheridan often fired up his men with this catchphrase.

Sherman, John (1823–1900)

US SENATOR FROM OHIO AND BROTHER OF WILLIAM T. SHERMAN

All this difficulty has been brought about by men who, because they could not rule, **1**
are determined to ruin.
> —comment in the Senate, July 25, 1861.

The result of the contest will not depend upon the first blow or the first year, but **2**
blood shed in civil war will yield its baleful fruits for generations.
> —letter to a particular body of Philadelphians, December 22, 1861.

★ Sherman wrote this on the day the Crittenden Compromise on slavery was defeated
in Congress, two days after South Carolina seceded.

The truth is, the close of the war with our resources unimpaired gives an elevation, **3**
a scope to the ideas of leading capitalists far higher than anything ever undertaken in
this country before.
> —letter to his brother, Major General William T. Sherman, November 10, 1865.

Sherman, William Tecumseh (1801–1872)

US BRIGADIER GENERAL

I would not if I could abolish or modify slavery. I don't know that I would materially **4**
change the actual political relation of master and slave. Negroes in the great numbers that exist here must of necessity be slaves.
> —letter to Thomas Ewing Jr., December 23, 1859.

★ Sherman was at that time superintendent of the Louisiana State Seminary of
Learning and Military Academy near Alexandria. His friend Ewing was a Kansas lawyer
who became chief justice of that state. Ewing resigned the position in 1862 to lead the
11th Kansas Volunteers and became a major general.

The South are right in guarding against insidious enemies or against any enemies **5**
whatever, and I would aid her in so doing. All I would object to is the laying of plans
designed to result in secession and Civil War.
> —letter to Thomas Ewing Jr., December 23, 1859.

Three years? It will take a hundred.
> —quoted by Lloyd Lewis in *Sherman, Fighting Prophet*, 1932.

★ Sherman, still a civilian, was responding to advice to become a colonel because the
war might last three years.

You are rushing into war with one of the most powerful, ingeniously mechanical and **6**
determined people on earth—right at your doors.
> —quoted by Shelby Foote in *The Civil War*, vol. 1, 1958.

★ Sherman said this on December 24, 1860, to Professor David F. Boyd of Virginia.

You people of the South don't know what you are doing. This country will be **7**
drenched in blood, and God only knows how it will end. It is all folly, madness, a

crime against civilization! You people speak so lightly of war; you don't know what you're talking about. War is a terrible thing!
—quoted by Shelby Foote in *The Civil War*, vol. 1, 1958.

★ Sherman said this on December 24, 1860, to Professor David F. Boyd of Virginia.

1   I have seen enough of war not to be caught by its first glittering bait, and when I engage in this it must be with a full consciousness of its real character.
—letter to Thomas Ewing Jr., January 23, 1861.

2   As to abolishing slavery in the South or turning loose 4,000,000 slaves, I would have no hand in it.
—letter to his brother, US senator John Sherman of Ohio, April 18, 1861.

★ Sherman was still a civilian.

3   If the North design to conquer the South, we must begin at Kentucky and reconquer the country from there as we did from the Indians.
—quoted by Shelby Foote in *The Civil War*, vol. 3, 1958.

4   A fatal mistake in war is to underrate the strength, feeling and resources of an enemy.
—letter to Thomas Ewing Jr., May 23, 1861.

5   Nobody, no man can save the country.
—quoted by Lloyd Lewis in *Sherman, Fighting Prophet*, 1932.

★ Sherman was writing in despair to his wife, Ellen, in July 1861 after his troops fought in the first battle of Bull Run (first Manassas).

6   The [Kentucky] state board is impressed with the necessity of energy in the organization of volunteers, but we are still embarrassed for want of clothing and arms. Promises are a poor substitute for them, but are all we have.
—letter to General George H. Thomas, October 25, 1861.

★ Sherman was commanding the Department of the Cumberland.

7   We don't want the truth told about things here—that's what we *don't* want! Truth, eh? No, sir! We don't want the enemy any better informed than he is!
—quoted by Louis M. Starr in *Reporting the Civil War*, 1962.

★ Sherman was ranting at Florus B. Plimpton, a reporter for the *Cincinnati Commercial*, in October 1861.

8   To the People of South Carolina: The civilized world stands appalled at the course you are pursuing!—Appalled at the crime you are committing against your own mother; the best, the most enlightened, and heretofore the most prosperous of nations. You are in a state of active rebellion against the laws of your country.
—proclamation, November 8, 1861.

★ Brigadier General Sherman had just captured Port Royal in that state.

I suppose I have been morose and cross and could I now hide myself in some **1** obscure corner I would do so, for my conviction is that our Government is destroyed and no human power can restore it.

>—letter to his brother, US senator John Sherman of Ohio, November 21, 1861.

You fellows make the best paid spies that can be bought. Jeff Davis owes more to you **2** newspaper men than to his army.

>—quoted in *Frank Leslie's Illustrated Newspaper*, December 7, 1861.

★ Sherman was addressing an artist from the newspaper.

I have no doubt that nothing will occur to-day more than some picket firing. The **3** enemy is saucy, but got the worst of it yesterday, and will not press our pickets far. I will not be drawn out far, unless with the certainty of advantage, and I do not apprehend anything like an attack upon our position.

>—telegram to Brigadier General Ulysses S. Grant, April 5, 1862.

★ The battle of Shiloh began the next day.

The scenes on this field would have cured anybody of war. Mangled bodies, dead, **4** dying in every conceivable shape, without heads, legs; and horses!

>—letter to his wife, Ellen, April 11, 1862.

★ He was describing the aftermath of the battle of Shiloh.

Stealing, robbery and pillage have become so common in this army that it is a disgrace **5** to any civilized people. This demoralizing and disgraceful practice of pillage must cease, else the country will rise on us and justly shoot us down like dogs and wild beasts.

>—order to troops, July 7, 1862.

I deplore the war as much as ever, but if the thing has to be done, let the means be **6** adequate. Don't expect to overrun such a country or subdue such a people in two or five years. It is the task of a century.

>—letter to his brother, US senator John Sherman of Ohio, August 13, 1862.

Whereas many families of known rebels and of Confederates in arms against us have **7** been permitted to reside in peace and comfort in Memphis, and whereas the Confederate authorities either sanction or permit the firing on unarmed boats carrying passengers and goods for the use and benefit of the inhabitants of Memphis, it is ordered that for every boat fired on, ten families must be expelled from Memphis.

>—Special Order No. 254, September 27, 1862.

★ Sherman never enforced this order.

We cannot change the hearts of those people of the South, but we can make war so **8** terrible that they will realize the fact that however brave and gallant and devoted to their country, still they are mortal and should exhaust all peaceful remedies before they fly to war.

>—letter to Brigadier General Ulysses S. Grant, October 4, 1862.

★ This was written during the battle of Corinth.

1   Thousands will perish by the bullet or sickness; but war must go on—it can't be stopped. The North must rule or submit to degradation and insult forevermore.
    —letter to his brother, US senator John Sherman of Ohio, November 24, 1862.

2   We have been to Vicksburg, and it was too much for us, and we have backed out.
    —letter to his wife, Ellen, January 4, 1863.

    ★ Vicksburg fell exactly six months later, on July 4.

3   Indeed I wish I had been killed long since. Better that than struggle with the curses and maledictions of every woman that has a son or brother to die in any army with which I chance to be associated.
    —letter to his wife, Ellen, January 28, 1863.

4   I see no end, or even the beginning of the end [of the war].
    —letter to his brother, Senator John Sherman of Ohio, January? 1863.

5   Two years have passed and the rebel flag still haunts our nation's capital. Our armies enter the best rebel territory and the wave closes in behind. The utmost we can claim is that our enemy respects our power to do them physical harm more than they did at first; but as to loving us any more, it were idle even to claim it.
    —letter to his brother, Senator John Sherman of Ohio, January? 1863.

6   I am going to have the correspondent of the New York Herald tried by a court martial as a spy, not that I want the fellow shot, but because I want to establish the principle that such people cannot attend our armies, in violation of orders, and defy us, publishing their garbled statements and defaming officers who are doing their best.
    —quoted by Louis M. Starr in *Reporting the Civil War*, 1962.

    ★ This was said on February 4, 1863, to Rear Admiral David D. Porter.

7   We have reproached the South for arbitrary conduct in coercing their people; at last we find we must imitate their example. We have denounced their tyranny in filling their armies with conscripts, and now we must follow her example. We have denounced their tyranny in suppressing freedom of speech and the press, and here, too, in time, we must follow their example. The longer it is deferred the worse it becomes.
    —letter to his brother, Senator John Sherman of Ohio, February 18, 1863.

8   I say with the press unfettered as now we are defeated to the end of time. 'Tis folly to say the people must have news.
    —letter to his brother, Senator John Sherman of Ohio, February 18, 1863.

9   Of course devastation marked the whole path of the army, and I know all the principal officers detest the infamous practice as much as I do. Of course I expect and do take corn, bacon, ham, mules and everything to support an army, and don't object much to the using of fences for firewood. But [a straggler's] universal burning and wanton destruction of private property is not justified in war.
    —letter to his wife, Ellen, May 6, 1863.

This is a success if we never take the town.   **1**
 —quoted by General Ulysses S. Grant in *Personal Memoirs of U. S. Grant*, vol. 1,
 1885.

★ This was said on May 17, 1863, and referred to Vicksburg, which fell on July 4.

Grant is now deservedly the hero . . . belabored with praise by those who a month   **2**
ago accused him of all the sins in the calendar, and who next will turn against him if
so blows the popular breeze. *Vox populi, vox humbug.*
 —letter to his wife, Ellen, June 2, 1863.

I doubt if history affords a parallel to the deep and bitter enmity of the women of the   **3**
South. No one who sees them and hears them but must feel the intensity of their
hate.
 —letter to his wife, Ellen, June 27, 1863.

Surely I will not punish any soldier for being "unco happy" this most glorious anni-   **4**
versary of the birth of a nation.
 —letter to General Ulysses S. Grant, July 4, 1863.

★ This was the day their troops had captured Vicksburg, Mississippi. "Unco" meant
"very" and was derived from the Scottish language.

This is a day of jubilee, a day of rejoicing to the faithful. . . . Already are my orders   **5**
out to give one big huzza and sling the knapsack for new fields.
 —letter to General Ulysses S. Grant, July 4, 1863.

★ This was the day Vicksburg surrendered.

We have made fine progress today in the work of destruction. The enemy burned   **6**
the greater part of Jackson [Mississippi] and we have done some in that line; the
place is ruined.
 —letter to General Ulysses S. Grant, July 17, 1863.

A government resting immediately on the caprice of a people is too unstable to last.   **7**
The will of the people is the ultimate appeal, but the Constitution, laws of Congress,
and regulations of the executive departments subject to the decisions of the Supreme
Court are the laws which all must obey without stopping to inquire why. All *must*
obey.
 —letter to his brother, Senator John Sherman of Ohio, August 3, 1863.

There are about 6 million men in this country, all thinking themselves sovereign and   **8**
qualified to govern, some 34 governors of states who feel like petty kings, and about
10,000 editors who presume to dictate to generals, presidents, and cabinets.
 —letter to his brother, Senator John Sherman of Ohio, August 3, 1863.

As to the press of America, it is a shame and a reproach to a civilized people. . . . I   **9**
begin to feel a high opinion of myself that I am their butt; I shall begin to suspect
myself of being in a decline when a compliment appears in type.
 —letter to his brother, Senator John Sherman of Ohio, August 3, 1863.

1   I say that our government, judged by its conduct as a whole, paved the way for rebellion. The South that lived on slavery saw the United States yield to Abolition pressure at the North, to pro-slavery pressure at the South, to the miners of California, the rowdies of Baltimore, and to the people everywhere. They paved the way to this rebellion.
   —letter to his brother, Senator John Sherman of Ohio, August 3, 1863.

2   Obedience to law, absolute—yea, even abject—is the lesson that this war, under Providence, will teach the free and enlightened American citizen. As a nation, we shall be the better for it.
   —letter to Major General Henry W. Halleck, September 17, 1863.

3   I would make this war as severe as possible, and show no symptoms of tiring till the South begs for mercy.
   —letter to Brigadier General John A. Rawlins, September 17, 1863.

   ★ Rawlins was Grant's chief aide.

4   To secure the safety of the navigation of the Mississippi River, I would slay millions.
   —letter to Major General John A. Logan, December 21, 1863.

5   If [Southerners] want eternal war, well and good; we accept the issue, and will dispossess them and put our friends in their places.
   —letter to Major Roswell M. Sawyer, January 31, 1864.

6   Next year their lands will be taken; for in war we can take them, and rightfully, too, and in another year they may beg in vain for their lives.
   —letter to Major Roswell M. Sawyer, January 31, 1864.

7   The chief characteristic in your nature is the simple faith in success you have always manifested, which I can liken to nothing else than the faith a Christian has in his Savior.
   —letter to General Ulysses S. Grant, March 10, 1864.

8   I knew wherever I was that you thought of me, and if I got in a tight place you would come—if alive.
   —letter to General Ulysses S. Grant, March 10, 1864.

9   No amount of poverty or adversity seems to shake their faith: niggers gone, wealth and luxury gone, money worthless, starvation in view within a period of two or three years, and causes enough to make the bravest tremble. Yet I see no signs of let up— some few deserters, plenty tired of war, but the masses determined to fight it out.
   —letter to his wife, Ellen, March 12, 1864.

10   Georgia has a million of inhabitants. If they can live, we should not starve.
   —letter to General Ulysses S. Grant, April 10, 1864.

   ★ He was beginning his march through Georgia.

All Southerners, old and young, rich and poor, educated and ignorant, united in this, **1**
that they will kill as vipers the whites who attempt to free their slaves, and also "the
ungrateful slaves" who attempt to change their character from slave to free.
    —letter to Brigadier General Lorenzo Thomas, April 12, 1864.

★ Thomas was in charge of organizing US black troops.

To make war we must and will harden our hearts.   **2**
    —letter to Assistant Secretary of War Charles Dana, April 21, 1864.

In peace there is a beautiful harmony in all the departments of life—they all fit **3**
together like a Chinese puzzle, but in war all is ajar. Nothing fits, and it is the struggle between the stronger and weaker, and the latter, however much it may appeal to
the better feelings of our nature, must kick the beam.
    —letter to Assistant Secretary of War Charles Dana, April 21, 1864.

War, like the thunderbolt, follows its laws and turns not aside even if the beautiful, **4**
the virtuous and charitable stand in its path.
    —letter to Assistant Secretary of War Charles Dana, April 21, 1864.

If you don't have my army supplied, and keep it supplied, we'll eat your mules up, sir. **5**
    —quoted by Rod Graff in *Civil War Quiz and Fact Book*, 1985.

★ This warning was given to his quartermaster at Chattanooga before Sherman's troops
moved toward Atlanta in May 1864.

The men loitered around the trenches carelessly, or busied themselves in construct- **6**
ing ingenious huts out of the abundant timber, and seemed as snug, comfortable,
and happy as though they were at home.
    —*Memoirs of General W. T. Sherman*, revised edition, vol. 2, 1886.

★ This was in May 1864 during the siege of Atlanta.

There never will be peace in Tennessee till [General Nathan Bedford] Forrest is **7**
dead.
    —letter to Secretary of War Edwin Stanton, June 5, 1864.

The press caused the war, the press gives it point and bitterness, and as long as the **8**
press, both North and South, is allowed to fan the flames of discord and hostility, so
long must the war last.
    —letter to his wife, Ellen, June 9, 1864.

The whole country is one vast fort.   **9**
    —letter to Major General Henry W. Halleck, June 23, 1864.

★ Sherman was describing northern Georgia.

I begin to regard the death and mangling of a couple of thousand men as a small **10**
affair, a kind of morning dash—and it may be well that we become so hardened.
    —letter to his wife, Ellen, June 29, 1864.

1   I would not subjugate the South . . . but I would make every citizen of the land obey the common law, submit to the same that we do—no more, no less—our equals and not our superiors.
      —letter to Mrs. Annie Gilman Bower, June 30, 1864.

      ★ Mrs. Bower, now living in Baltimore, had welcomed Sherman into her home in Charleston before the war.

2   I want to make a raid that will make the South feel the terrible character of our people.
      —quoted by Lee Kennett in *Marching through Georgia*, 1995.

3   If the rear be the post of honor than we had better all change front on Washington.
      —letter to Inspector General James A. Hardie, July 25, 1864.

      ★ Sherman was upset because two generals had been promoted after being moved to the rear of the action while no promotions were given to his serving officers.

4   We keep hammering away all the time, and there is no peace, inside or outside of Atlanta.
      —telegram to Major General Henry W. Halleck, August 7, 1864.

5   One thing is certain, whether we get inside of Atlanta or not, it will be a used-up community when we are done with it.
      —telegram to Major General Henry W. Halleck, August 7, 1864.

6   Let us destroy Atlanta and make it a desolation.
      —message to Major General Oliver O. Howard, August 10, 1864.

7   I pledge my honor when the South ceases its strife, sends its members to Congress and appeals to the courts for its remedy and not to "horrid war," I will be the open advocate of mercy and a restoration to home, and peace, and happiness of all who have lost them by my acts.
      —letter to Leslie Coombes, August 11, 1864.

      ★ Coombes was a friend in Kentucky who protested against the destruction caused by Sherman's troops in Georgia.

8   War is the remedy our *enemies* have chosen, and I say let us give them all they want.
      —letter to James Guthrie, August 14, 1864.

      ★ Guthrie was president of the Louisville & Nashville Railroad.

9   The only principle in this war is which party can whip. It is as simple as a schoolboy's fight and when one or the other party gives in, we will be the better friends.
      —letter to James Guthrie, August 14, 1864.

10   Atlanta is ours and fairly won.
      —telegram to Lincoln, September 1, 1864.

I have had the question put to me often: "Is not a negro as good as a White man to   1
stop a bullet?" Yes, and a sand-bag is better.
  —letter to Major General Henry W. Halleck, September 4, 1864.

If the people raise a howl against my barbarity and cruelty, I will answer that war is   2
war, and not popularity-seeking. If they want peace, they and their relatives must
stop the war.
  —letter to Major General Henry W. Halleck, September 4, 1864.

★ He was referring to his order that all civilians leave Atlanta.

If we must be enemies, let us be men and fight it out as we propose to do, and not   3
deal in such hypocritical appeals to God and humanity.
  —letter to CS general John B. Hood, September 10, 1864.

★ Hood had complained about Sherman ordering the residents of occupied Atlanta to
leave the city and had protested "in the name of God and humanity."

You cannot qualify war in harsher terms than I will. War is cruelty and you cannot   4
refine it; and those who brought war into our country deserve all the curses and
maledictions a people can pour out.
  —letter to Atlanta mayor James M. Calhoun, September 12, 1864.

We don't want your negroes or your horses, or your houses or your land, or anything   5
you have; but we do want and will have a just obedience to the laws of the United
States.
  —letter to Atlanta mayor James M. Calhoun, September 12, 1864.

★ The mayor had complained to Sherman about Sherman's order that all civilians leave
Atlanta. During Sherman's march through Georgia, his men did want and take some of
the above mentioned.

You might as well appeal against the thunderstorm as against the terrible hardships   6
of war.
  —letter to Atlanta mayor James M. Calhoun, September 12, 1864.

If the United States submits to a division now, it will not stop, but will go on until we   7
reap the fate of Mexico, which is eternal war.
  —letter to Atlanta mayor James M. Calhoun, September 12, 1864.

I was not bound by the laws of war to give notice of the shelling of Atlanta, a "forti-   8
fied town, with magazines, arsenals, foundries, and public stores;" you were bound
to take notice. See the books.
  —letter to CS general John B. Hood, September 14, 1864.

If you can whip Lee and I can march to the Atlantic, I think Uncle Abe will give us   9
a twenty days' leave of absence to see the young folks.
  —message to General Ulysses S. Grant, September 20, 1864.

1   Atlanta is a fortified town, was stubbornly defended, and fairly captured. As captors, we have a right to it.
   —telegram to Major General Henry W. Halleck, September 20, 1864.

   ★ He was justifying his order expelling the civilians from the town.

2   You can beat us in fighting, madam, but we can out-maneuver you; your generals do not work half enough; we work day and night, and spare no labor, nor pains, to carry out our plans.
   —quoted by the *Macon* (Georgia) *Telegraph*, November 23, 1864.

   ★ Sherman was speaking to an Atlanta lady who was questioning his order to evacuate the occupied city. MacDonell, at Turnwold Plantation near Eatonton, Georgia, was a friend of the lady. Sherman reportedly told her that he regarded the Southern soldiers as the bravest in the world because they had fought against four or five times their number.

3   Behind us lay Atlanta, smoldering and in ruins, the black smoke rising high in air, and hanging like a pall over the ruined city.
   —*Memoirs of W. T. Sherman, vol. 2*, 1875.

   ★ Sherman was telling of leaving the conquered city on November 16, 1864, to begin his march through Georgia.

4   We ought to ask our country for the largest possible armies that can be raised as so important a thing as the self-existence of a great nation should not be left to the fickle chances of war.
   —message to General Ulysses S. Grant, September 20, 1864.

5   Sherman is moving in force. Hold out.
   —lag signal to Major General John M. Corse.

   ★ This was soon followed by another wigwag signal saying "General Sherman says hold fast. We are coming." These messages during the battle of Allatoona Pass, Georgia, on October 5, 1864, were misquoted as "Hold the fort, for I am coming."

6   Until we can repopulate Georgia, it is useless to occupy it, but the utter destruction of its roads, houses and people will cripple their military resources. . . . I can make the march and make Georgia howl!
   —letter to General Ulysses S. Grant, October 9, 1864.

7   I propose to abandon Atlanta and the railroad back to Chattanooga, to sally forth to ruin Georgia and bring up on the seashore.
   —telegram to Amos Beckworth, October 19, 1864.

   ★ Beckworth was Sherman's chief commissary in Atlanta and acting chief quartermaster.

8   If we can march a well-appointed army right through [Jefferson Davis's] territory, it is a demonstration to the world, foreign and domestic, that we have a power which Davis cannot resist. This may not be war but rather statesmanship, nevertheless it is overwhelming to my mind that there are thousands of people abroad and in the

South who reason thus: If the North can march an army right through the South, it is proof positive that the North can prevail.
  —letter to General Ulysses S. Grant, November 6, 1864.

In revolutions men fall and rise. Long before this war is over, much as you hear me   1
praised now, you may hear me cursed and insulted. . . . Grant, Sheridan and I are
now the popular favorites, but neither of us will survive this war. Some other must
rise greater than either of us, and he has not yet manifested himself.
  —quoted by Lloyd Lewis in *Sherman, Fighting Prophet*, 1932.

★ Sherman was writing to his wife, Ellen, before beginning his march through Georgia
in November 1864.

In districts and neighborhoods where the army is unmolested, no destruction of such   2
property should be permitted; but should the inhabitants burn bridges, obstruct
roads, or otherwise manifest local hostility, then army commanders should order and
enforce a devastation more or less relentless, according to the measure of such hostility.
  —order to his troops, November 9, 1864.

★ This was issued during Sherman's march through Georgia.

Like one who has walked a narrow plank, I look back and wonder if I really did it.   3
  —quoted by Lloyd Lewis in *Sherman, Fighting Prophet*, 1932.

★ He was writing to his wife, Ellen, about his march through Georgia.

I don't believe I will draw anything for them but salt.   4
  —quoted by John D. Wright in *The Language of the Civil War*, 2001.

★ Sherman was saying he would only supply his troops with salt because they were so
good at stealing during their march through Georgia.

I estimate the damage done to the State of Georgia at one hundred million dollars,   5
at least twenty millions of which inured to our benefit, and the remainder was simply waste and destruction.
  —quoted by CS lieutenant Randolph H. McKim in *A Soldier's Recollections:
  Leaves from the Diary of a Young Confederate*, 1910.

My first duty will be to clear the army of surplus negroes, mules, and horses.   6
  —telegram to Secretary of War Edwin M. Stanton, December 13, 1864.

★ This was after Sherman had captured Fort McAllister near Savannah, Georgia, on
December 13, 1864.

This nigger will have no sleep tonight.   7
  —*Memoirs of General W. T. Sherman*, revised edition, vol. 2, 1886.

★ He said this on December 13, 1864, after capturing Fort McAllister near Savannah,
Georgia, repeating the earlier words of a Georgia slave who had stayed awake from his
excitement about the approaching Union troops.

1   I do sincerely believe that the whole United States, North and South, would rejoice
     to have this army turned loose on South Carolina, to devastate that state in the man-
     ner we have done in Georgia.
       —message to General Ulysses S. Grant, December 18, 1864.

2   When I go through South Carolina, it will be one of the most horrible things in the
     history of the world. The devil himself couldn't restrain my men in that state.
       —quoted by Geoffrey C. Ward in *The Civil War: An Illustrated History*, 1990.

3   The truth is the whole army is burning with an insatiable desire to wreak vengeance
     upon South Carolina. I almost tremble for her fate, but feel that she deserves all that
     seems in store for her.
       —quoted by Shelby Foote in *The Civil War*, vol. 3, 1958.

4   . . . I beg to present to you, as a Christmas gift, the city of Savannah, with one hun-
     dred and fifty heavy guns and plenty of ammunition; and also about twenty-five
     thousand (25,000) bales of cotton.
       —telegram to Lincoln, December 22, 1864.

5   I can chuckle over Jeff. Davis's disappointment in not turning my Atlanta campaign
     into a "Moscow disaster."
       —telegram to Major General Henry W. Halleck, December 24, 1864.

     ★ His reference is to Napoleon's Moscow campaign, which was defeated by guerrilla
     attacks in the vast land of Russia.

6   I think the time has come now when we should attempt the boldest moves, and my
     experience is, that they are easier of execution than more timid ones, because the
     enemy is disconcerted by them—as, for instance, my recent [Georgia] campaign.
       —telegram to Major General Henry W. Halleck, December 24, 1864.

7   I attach more importance to these deep incisions into the enemy's country, because
     this war differs from European wars in this particular: we are not only fighting hos-
     tile armies, but a hostile people, and must make old and young, rich and poor, feel
     the hard hand of war, as well as their organized armies.
       —telegram to Major General Henry W. Halleck, December 24, 1864.

8   I look upon Columbia as quite as bad as Charleston, and I doubt if we shall spare the
     public buildings there as we did at Milledgeville [Georgia].
       —telegram to Major General Henry W. Halleck, December 24, 1864.

9   The whole army is burning with an insatiable desire to wreck vengeance upon South
     Carolina. I almost tremble at her fate, but feel that she deserves all that seems in
     store for her.
       —letter to Major General Henry W. Halleck, December 26, 1864.

10   They regard us just as the Romans did the Goths and the parallel is not unjust.
       —letter to his wife, Ellen, December 27, 1864.

     ★ This was written just after his march through Georgia.

I will accept no commission that would tend to create a rivalry with Grant. I want **1** him to hold what he has earned and got. I have all the rank I want.
>—letter to his brother, Senator John Sherman of Ohio, 1865.

Mr. Barclay, former [British] consul at New York . . . called on me with reference to **2** cotton claimed by English subjects. He seemed amazed when I told him . . . that in no event would I treat an English subject with more favor than one of our own deluded citizens, and that for my part I was unwilling to fight for cotton for the benefit of Englishmen openly engaged in smuggling arms and instruments of war to kill us; that, on the contrary, it would afford me great satisfaction to conduct my army to Nassau, and wipe out that nest of pirates.
>—letter to Secretary of War Edwin M. Stanton, January 2, 1865.

We quietly and deliberately destroyed Atlanta. **3**
>—Special Field Order No. 6, January 8, 1865.

But the nigger? Why, in God's name, can't sensible men let him alone. . . . The South **4** deserves all she has got for her injustice to the negro, but that is no reason why we should go to the other extreme.
>—letter to Major General Henry W. Halleck, January 12, 1865.

I never saw a more confident army. The soldiers think I know everything and that **5** they can do anything.
>—letter to his wife, Ellen, January 17, 1865.

I will take infinitely more delight in curing the wounds made by war than in inflict- **6** ing them.
>—letter to Mrs. Caroline Carson, January 20, 1865.

★ This was written as his troops entered South Carolina. Mrs. Carson of Baltimore had considered him as "one of her standard beaux" when they were friends on Sullivan's Island, South Carolina, before the war.

I suspect Jeff. Davis will move heaven and earth to catch me, for success to this col- **7** umn is fatal to his dream of empire.
>—telegram to General Ulysses S. Grant, January 29, 1865.

I think that the "poor white trash" of the South are falling out of their ranks by sick- **8** ness, desertion, and every available means; but there is a large class of vindictive Southerners who will fight to the last.
>—telegram to General Ulysses S. Grant, January 29, 1865.

The people of South Carolina, instead of feeding Lee's army, will now call on Lee to **9** feed them.
>—telegram to Secretary of War Edwin M. Stanton, March 12, 1865.

1   I take it for granted the United States will never again trust North Carolina with an arsenal to appropriate at her pleasure.
    —telegram to Secretary of War Edwin M. Stanton, March 12, 1865.

    ★ Sherman was destroying the arsenal at Fayetteville, North Carolina.

2   I think I see pretty clearly how, in one more move, we can check-mate Lee, forcing him to unite [General Joseph] Johnston with him in the defense of Richmond, or to abandon the cause. I feel certain, if he leaves Richmond, Virginia leaves the Confederacy.
    —telegram to General Ulysses S. Grant, March 24, 1865.

3   As to Jeff. Davis, [Lincoln] was hardly at liberty to speak his mind fully, but intimated that he ought to clear out, "escape the country," only it would not do for him to say so openly.
    —*Memoirs of General W. T. Sherman*, revised edition, vol. 2, 1886.

    ★ Sherman was recalling a conference that he and General Ulysses S. Grant had with Lincoln on March 28, 1865, at City Point near Petersburg, Virginia.

4   It is a general truth that men exposed to the elements don't "catch cold," and I have not heard a man cough or sneeze for three months, but were these same men to go into houses in a month the doctor would have half of them. Now the doctors have no employment.
    —letter to his wife, Ellen, April 5, 1865.

5   I know that all men of substance [in the] South want peace, and I do not believe they will resort to war again during this century. I have no doubt that they will, in the future, be perfectly subordinate to the laws of the United States.
    —letter to General Ulysses S. Grant, April 18, 1865.

6   The news of Mr. Lincoln's death produced a most intense effect on our troops. At first I feared it would lead to excesses; but now it has softened down, and can easily be guided. None evinced more feeling than General [Joseph] Johnston, who admitted that the act was calculated to stain his cause with a dark hue; and he contended that the loss was most serious to the South, who had begun to realize that Mr. Lincoln was the best friend they had.
    —telegram to Major General Henry W. Halleck, April 18, 1865.

7   The mass of the people south will never trouble us again. They have suffered terrifically, and I now feel disposed to befriend them—of course not the leaders and lawyers, but the armies who have fought and manifested their sincerity though misled by risking their persons. But the rascals who by falsehood and misrepresentation kept up the war, they are infamous.
    —letter to his wife, Ellen, April 28, 1865.

8   I perceive the politicians are determined to drive the confederates into guerilla bands, a thing more to be feared than open organized war. They may fight it out. I won't.
    —letter to his wife, Ellen, April 28, 1865.

We should not drive a people into anarchy, and it is simply impossible for our mili- **1** tary power to reach all the masses of their unhappy country.
     —telegram to General Ulysses S. Grant, April 28, 1865.

★ He was referring to there being at that time no official plan for reconstruction and to the destruction of the Southerners' armies and civil authorities.

The South is broken and ruined and appeals to our pity. To ride the people down with **2** persecutions and military exactions would be like slashing away at the crew of a sinking ship.
     —letter to Major General John A. Rawlins, April 29, 1865.

I have never heard a negro ask for [the vote], and I think it would be his ruin. . . . **3** Besides it is not the province even of our Congress, much less the Executive, to impose conditions on the voters in "organized States." That is clearly reserved to them.
     —letter to Major General John Schofield, May 28, 1865.

Your general now bids you farewell, with the full belief that, as in war you have been **4** good soldiers, so in peace you will make good citizens; and if, unfortunately, new war should arise in our country, "Sherman's army" will be the first to buckle on its old armor, and come forth to defend and maintain the Government of our inheritance.
     —Special Field Order No. 76, May 30, 1865.

★ This was Sherman's official farewell to his troops.

The legitimate object of war is a more perfect peace.   **5**
     —speech in St. Louis, July 20, 1865.

Every attempt to make war easy and safe will result in humiliation and disaster.   **6**
     —*Memoirs of General W. T. Sherman*, vol. 2, 1875.

The regiment is the family. The colonel, as the father, should have a personal acquain- **7** tance with every officer and man, and should instill a feeling of pride and affection for himself, so that his officers and men naturally look to him for personal advice and instruction.
     —*Memoirs of General W. T. Sherman*, vol. 2, 1875.

In war the regiment should never be subdivided, but should always be maintained **8** entire. In peace this is impossible.
     —*Memoirs of General W. T. Sherman*, vol. 2, 1875.

Insult to a soldier does not justify pillage, but it takes from the officer the disposition **9** he would otherwise feel to follow up the inquiry and punish the wrong-doers.
     —*Memoirs of General W. T. Sherman*, vol. 1, 1875.

A bulky staff implies a division of responsibility, slowness of action, and indecision, **10** whereas a small staff implies activity and concentration of purpose. The smallness of Grant's staff throughout the civil war forms the best model for future generations.
     —*Memoirs of General W. T. Sherman*, vol. 2, 1875.

1   Soldiers are very quick to catch the general drift and purpose of a campaign, and are always sensible when they are well commanded or well cared for. Once impressed with this fact, and that they are making progress, they bear cheerfully any amount of labor and privation.
    —*Memoirs of General W. T. Sherman*, vol. 2, 1875.

2   I believe that five hundred new men added to an old and experienced regiment were more valuable than a thousand men in the form of a new regiment, for the former by association with good, experienced captains, lieutenants, and non-commissioned officers, soon became veterans, whereas the latter were generally unavailable for a year.
    —*Memoirs of General W. T. Sherman*, vol. 2, 1875.

3   I feel kindly toward all Southern Generals. I think people of the West and North cherish no bad feelings except toward Jeff. Davis. He did no worse than anybody else but people seem bound to have somebody to hate. For instance the Southern people hate [General Benjamin] Butler.
    —quoted in the *New York Herald*, March 8, 1876.

4   War is at best barbarism. . . . Its glory is all moonshine. It is only those who have neither fired a shot, nor heard the shrieks and groans of the wounded, who cry aloud for blood, more vengeance, more desolation. War is hell.
    —speech at the Michigan Military Academy, June 19, 1879.

5   There is many a boy here today who looks on war as all glory, but, boys, it is all hell. You can bear this warning voice to generations yet to come.
    —quoted in *Ohio State Journal*, August 12, 1880.

    ★ This was in an article about his speech on the previous day to veterans and civilians in Columbus, Ohio.

6   No doubt [General Nathan B.] Forrest's men acted like a set of barbarians, shooting down the helpless negro garrison [at Fort Pillow, Tennessee] after the fort was in their possession; but I am told that Forrest personally disclaims any active participation in the assault, and that he stopped the firing as soon as he could. He had a desperate set of fellows under him.
    —*Memoirs of General W. T. Sherman*, revised edition, vol. 2, 1886.

7   I always estimated my force at about double [General Joseph Johnston's], and could afford to lose two to one without disturbing our relative proportion, but I also reckoned that, in the natural strength of the country, in the abundance of mountains, streams, and forests, he had a fair offset to our numerical superiority, and therefore endeavored to act with reasonable caution while moving on the vigorous "offensive."
    —*Memoirs of General W. T. Sherman*, revised edition, vol. 2, 1886.

The weather has a wonderful effect on troops: in action and on the march, rain is favorable; but in the woods, where all is blind and uncertain, it seems almost impossible for an army covering ten miles of front to act in concert during wet and stormy weather. **1**
—*Memoirs of General W. T. Sherman*, revised edition, vol. 2, 1886.

General [Joseph] Hooker had come from the East with great fame as a "fighter," and at Chattanooga he was glorified by the "battle above the clouds," which I fear turned **2** his head. He seemed jealous of all the army commanders, because in years, former rank, and experience, he thought he was our superior.
—*Memoirs of General W. T. Sherman*, revised edition, vol. 2, 1886.

I regarded both Generals [John] Logan and [Francis] Blair as "volunteers," that looked to personal fame and glory as auxiliary and secondary to their political ambi- **3** tion, and not as professional soldiers.
—*Memoirs of General W. T. Sherman*, revised edition, vol. 2, 1886.

Atlanta was known as the "Gate-City of the South," was full of foundries, arsenals, and machine-shops, and I knew that its capture would be the death-knell of the **4** Southern Confederacy.
—*Memoirs of General W. T. Sherman*, revised edition, vol. 2, 1886.

. . . we filled up many deep [railroad] cuts with trees, brush, and earth, and commingled with them loaded shells, so arranged that they would explode on an attempt **5** to haul out the bushes. The explosion of one such shell would have demoralized a gang of negroes, and thus would have prevented even the attempt to clear the [rail]road.
—*Memoirs of General W. T. Sherman*, revised edition, vol. 2, 1886.

★ This was during his march through Georgia.

The news [of Atlanta's fall] seemed to [Brigadier General George H. Thomas] too good to be true. He snapped his fingers, whistled, and almost danced, and, as the **6** news spread to the army, the shouts that arose from our men, the wild hallooing and glorious laughter, were to us a full recompense for the labor and toils and hardships through which we had passed in the previous three months.
—*Memoirs of General W. T. Sherman*, revised edition, vol. 2, 1886.

I was resolved to make Atlanta a pure military garrison or depot, with no civil population to influence military measures. **7**
—*Memoirs of General W. T. Sherman*, revised edition, vol. 2, 1886.

★ He was explaining why he ordered Atlanta's residents to leave the town.

I knew that the people of the South would read in this measure [ordering civilians **8** out of occupied Atlanta] two important conclusions: one, that we were in earnest, and the other, if they were sincere in their common and popular clamor "to die in the last ditch," that the opportunity would soon come.
—*Memoirs of General W. T. Sherman*, revised edition, vol. 2, 1886.

1   Then we turned our horses' heads to the east; Atlanta was soon lost behind the screen of trees, and became a thing of the past. Around it clings many a thought of desperate battle, of hope and fear, that now seem like the memory of a dream, and I have never seen the place since.
—*Memoirs of General W. T. Sherman*, revised edition, vol. 2, 1886.

2   There was a "devil-may-care" feeling pervading officers and men, that made me feel the full load of responsibility, for success would be accepted as a matter of course, whereas, should we fail, this "march" would be adjudged the wild adventure of a crazy fool.
—*Memoirs of General W. T. Sherman*, revised edition, vol. 2, 1886.

★ Sherman is describing the beginning of his famous march through Georgia.

3   Whenever [the Negroes] heard my name, they clustered about my horse, shouted and prayed in their peculiar style, which had a natural eloquence that would have moved a stone.
—*Memoirs of General W. T. Sherman*, revised edition, vol. 2, 1886.

★ His troops were passing through Covington, Georgia.

4   No doubt, many acts of pillage, robbery, and violence, were committed by these parties of foragers, usually called "bummers;" for I have since heard of jewelry taken from women, and the plunder of articles that never reached the commissary, but these acts were exceptional and incidental.
—*Memoirs of General W. T. Sherman*, revised edition, vol. 2, 1886.

★ He was recalling his march through Georgia.

5   Never do I recall a more agreeable sensation than the sight of our camps by night, lit up by the fires of fragrant pine-knots.
—*Memoirs of General W. T. Sherman*, revised edition, vol. 2, 1886.

6   Were I to express my measure of relative importance of the march to the sea, and of that from Savannah northward, I would place the former at one, and the latter at ten, or the maximum.
—*Memoirs of General W. T. Sherman*, revised edition, vol. 2, 1886.

7   The negro question was beginning to loom up among the political eventualities of the day, and many foresaw that not only would the slaves secure their freedom, but that they would also have votes. I did not dream of such a result then [January 1863], but knew that slavery, as such, was dead forever, and did not suppose that the former slaves would be suddenly, without preparation, manufactured into voters, equal to all others, politically and socially.
—*Memoirs of General W. T. Sherman*, revised edition, vol. 2, 1886.

8   My aim then [after capturing Savannah] was, to whip the rebels, to humble their pride, to follow them to their inmost recesses, and make them fear and dread us. "Fear of the Lord is the beginning of wisdom."
—*Memoirs of General W. T. Sherman*, revised edition, vol. 2, 1886.

In my official report of this conflagration [in Columbia, South Carolina], I distinctly 1
charged it to General Wade Hampton, and confess I did so pointedly, to shake the
faith of his people in him, for he was in my opinion boastful, and professed to be the
special champion of South Carolina.
  —*Memoirs of General W. T. Sherman*, revised edition, vol. 2, 1886.

Of all the men I every met, [Lincoln] seemed to possess more of the elements of 2
greatness, combined with goodness, than any other.
  —*Memoirs of General W. T. Sherman*, revised edition, vol. 2, 1886.

I have never in my life questioned or disobeyed an order, though many and many a 3
time have I risked my life, health, and reputation, in obeying orders, or even hints to
execute plans and purposes, not to my liking.
  —*Memoirs of General W. T. Sherman*, revised edition, vol. 2, 1886.

The greatest mistake made in our Civil War was in the mode of recruitment and pro- 4
motion. When a regiment became reduced by the necessary wear and tear of service, instead of being filled up at the bottom, and the vacancies among the officers
filled from the best noncommissioned officers and men, the habit was to raise new
regiments, with new colonels, captains, and men, leaving the old experienced battalions to dwindle away into mere skeleton organizations.
  —*Memoirs of General W. T. Sherman*, revised edition, vol. 2, 1886.

Wounds which, in 1861, would have sent a man to the hospital for months, in 1865 5
were regarded as mere scratches, rather the subject of a joke than of sorrow.
  —*Memoirs of General W. T. Sherman*, revised edition, vol. 2, 1886.

To new soldiers the sight of blood and death always has a sickening effect, but soon 6
men become accustomed to it, and I have heard them exclaim on seeing a dead comrade borne to the rear, "Well, Bill has turned up his toes to the daisies."
  —*Memoirs of General W. T. Sherman*, revised edition, vol. 2, 1886.

Europeans frequently criticised our war, because we did not always take full advan- 7
tage of a victory; the true reason was, that habitually the woods served as a screen,
and we did not realize the fact that our enemy had retreated till he was already miles
away and was again entrenched, having left a mere skirmish-line to cover the movement, in turn to fall back to the new position.
  —*Memoirs of General W. T. Sherman*, revised edition, vol. 2, 1886.

I would prefer to have this a white man's war and provide for the negroes after the 8
time has passed, but we are in revolution and I must not pretend to judge. With my
opinions of negroes and my experience, yea, prejudice, I cannot trust them yet.
  —quoted by Lloyd Lewis in *Sherman, Fighting Prophet*, 1932.

★ This alluded the enlistment of black soldiers.

1   Fighting is the least part of a general's work, the battle will fight itself.
        —quoted by Lloyd Lewis in *Sherman, Fighting Prophet*, 1932.

2   Wilson, I'm a damned sight smarter man than Grant; I know more about organiza-
        tion, supply and administration and about everything else than he does; but I'll tell
        you where he beats me and where he beats the world. He don't care a damn for what
        the enemy does out of his sight but it scares me like hell. I'm more nervous than he
        is. I am much more likely to change my orders or to countermarch my command
        than he is.
        —quoted by Lloyd Lewis in *Sherman, Fighting Prophet*, 1932.

        ★ This was said to Major General James H. Wilson.

3   The true way to be popular with troops is not to be free and familiar with them, but
        to make them believe you know more than they do. My men believe I know every-
        thing; they are much mistaken but it gives them confidence in me.
        —quoted by Lloyd Lewis in *Sherman, Fighting Prophet*, 1932.

4   Pierce the shell of the Confederacy and it's all hollow inside.
        —quoted by Lloyd Lewis in *Sherman, Fighting Prophet*, 1932.

5   Grant is a great general. I know him well. He stood by me when I was crazy and I
        stood by him when he was drunk. And now, sir, we stand by each other always.
        —quoted by Shelby Foote in *The Civil War*, vol. 3, 1958.

6   This is a death struggle and will be terrible.
        —quoted by Randall Bedwell in *Brink of Destruction*, 1999.

7   Now I am in high feather.
        —quoted by John D. Wright in *The Language of the Civil War*, 2001.

        ★ Sherman said this to General Grant after the battle of Shiloh, Virginia. "High
        feather," meaning "high spirits," was one of Sherman's favorite sayings.

8   I think we understand what military fame is—to be killed on the field of battle and
        have our names spelled wrong in the newspapers.
        —quoted by Lloyd Lewis in *Sherman, Fighting Prophet*, 1932.

Ship, Scott

CS LIEUTENANT COLONEL

9   The cadets did their duty, as the long list of casualties will attest. . . . Wet, hungry,
        and many of them shoeless—for they had lost their shoes and socks in the deep mud
        through which it was necessary to march—they bore their hardships with that un-
        complaining resignation, which characterizes the true soldier.
        —report to Major General F. H. Smith, July 4, 1864.

        ★ The cadets, from Virginia Military Institute, won a battle at New Market, Virginia, on
        May 15, 1864.

Simpson, Matthew (1811–1884)

Methodist Episcopal Church bishop

★ Simpson spoke at Lincoln's funeral, which was held in Springfield, Illinois.

Standing, as, we do to-day, by his coffin and his sepulcher, let us resolve to carry for- 1
ward the policy which he so nobly began. Let us do right to all men.
  —speech at Lincoln's funeral, May 4, 1865.

There was a Cabinet meeting that day, said to have been the most cheerful and 2
happy of any held since the beginning of the rebellion. After this meeting [Lincoln]
talked with his friends, and spoke of the four years of tempest, of the storm being
over, and of the four years of pleasure and joy now awaiting him, as the weight of
care and anxiety would be taken from his mind, and he could have happy days with
his family again. In the midst of these anticipations he left his house never to return
alive.
  —speech at Lincoln's Funeral, May 4, 1865.

But never was there in the history of man such mourning as that which has accom- 3
panied this funeral procession [of Lincoln's]. . . . Tears filled the eyes of manly, sun-
burnt faces. Strong men as they clasped the hands of their friends, were not able in
words to find vent for their grief. Women and little children caught up the tidings as
they ran through the land, and were melted into tears. The nation stood still. Men
left their plows in the fields and asked what the end should be. The hum of manufactories ceased, and the sound of the hammer was not heard. Busy merchants
closed their doors, and in the exchange gold passed no more from hand to hand.
Though three weeks have elapsed, the nation has scarcely breathed easily yet. A
mournful silence is abroad upon the land; nor is this mourning confined to any class
or to any district of country.
  —speech at Lincoln's funeral, May 4, 1865.

More persons have gazed on the face of the departed [Lincoln] than ever looked 4
upon the face of any other departed man. More have looked on the procession for
sixteen hundred miles, by night and by day, by sunlight, dawn, twilight, and by torch-
light, than ever before watched the progress of a procession.
  —speech at Lincoln's funeral, May 4, 1865.

Then the tidings came that Richmond was evacuated, and that Lee had surren- 5
dered. . . . Just in the midst of this wildest joy, in one hour, nay, in one moment, the
tidings thrilled throughout the land that Abraham Lincoln, the best of presidents,
had perished by the hands of an assassin. Then all the feelings which had been gathering for four years in forms of excitement, grief, horror, and joy, turned into one
wail of woe, a sadness inexpressible, an anguish unutterable.
  —speech at Lincoln's funeral, May 4, 1865.

If you ask me on what mental characteristic [Lincoln's] greatness rested, I answer, 6
On a quick and ready perception of facts; on a memory, unusually tenacious and

retentive; and on a logical turn of mind, which followed sternly and unwaveringly every link in the chain of thought on every subject which he was called to investigate.
—speech at Lincoln's funeral, May 4, 1865.

1   The evening [of Lincoln's assassination] was Good Friday, the saddest day in the whole calendar for the Christian Church, henceforth in this country to be made sadder, if possible by the memory of our nation's loss.
—speech at Lincoln's funeral, May 4, 1865.

2   Who that has read [Lincoln's] messages fails to perceive the directness and the simplicity of his style? And this very trait, which was scoffed at and decried by opponents, is now recognized as one of the strong points of that mighty mind which has so powerfully influenced the destiny of this nation, and which shall, for ages to come, influence the destiny of humanity.
—speech at Lincoln's funeral, May 4, 1865.

3   Money, or a desire for fame, collected those [European] armies, or they were rallied to sustain favorite thrones or dynasties; but the armies [Lincoln] called into being fought for liberty, for the Union, and for the right of self-government; and many of them felt that the battles they won were for humanity everywhere, and for all time; for I believe that God has not suffered this terrible rebellion to come upon our land merely for a chastisement to us, or as a lesson to our age.
—speech at Lincoln's funeral, May 4, 1865.

4   But the great act of [Lincoln] the mighty chieftain, on which his fame shall rest long after his frame shall moulder away, is that of giving freedom to a race.
—speech at Lincoln's funeral, May 4, 1865.

5   Look over all [Lincoln's] speeches; listen to his utterances. He never spoke unkindly of any man. Even the rebels received no word of anger from him.
—speech at Lincoln's funeral, May 4, 1865.

6   Let us vow, in the sight of Heaven, to eradicate every vestige of human slavery; to give every human being his true position before God and man; to crush every form of rebellion, and to stand by the flag which God has given us. How joyful that it floated over parts of every state before Mr. Lincoln's career was ended! How singular that, to the fact of the assassin's heels being caught in the folds of the flag, we are probably indebted for his capture. The flag and the traitor must ever be enemies.
—speech at Lincoln's funeral, May 4, 1865.

7   A republic was declared by monarchists too weak to endure a civil war; yet we have crushed the most gigantic rebellion in history, and have grown in strength and population every year of the struggle. We have passed through the ordeal of a popular election while swords and bayonets were in the field, and have come out unharmed. . . . The world will learn that republics are the strongest governments on earth.
—speech at Lincoln's funeral, May 4, 1865.

Chieftain, farewell! The nation mourns thee. Mothers shall teach thy name to their **1** lisping children. The youth of our land shall emulate thy virtues. Statesmen shall study thy record and learn lessons of wisdom. Mute though thy lips be, yet they still speak. Hushed is thy voice, but its echoes of liberty are ringing through the world, and the sons of bondage listen with joy.
    —speech at Lincoln's funeral, May 4, 1865.

Sims, Leora

We do not feel afraid of the Yankees but we must be ready for anything. "Booty & **2** Beauty" for their watch word, the women may expect no quarter, and if I ever fall into their hands, I earnestly pray I may be enabled to give them one "fire eater" to deal with.
    —letter to Mary Elizabeth Bellamy, November 14, 1861.

Skinner, Frederick

CS COLONEL

The enemy won't see that part of them. **3**
    —quoted by Brigadier General Gilbert Moxley Sorrel in *Recollections of a Confederate Staff Officer*, 1905.

★ This referred to the torn pants seats of the 1st Virginia Infantry as they passed in review. Skinner made the observation to Prince Jerome Napoleon, the nephew of Napoleon Bonaparte, who was visiting.

Slidell, John (1793–1871)

US SENATOR AND DIPLOMAT AND CS DIPLOMAT

This is a rascally world, and it is most hard to say who can be trusted. **4**
    —quoted by Rod Graff in *Civil War Quiz and Fact Book*, 1985.

★ This was said after Slidell, who had been sent to France, failed to get that country's official recognition of the Confederacy.

Slocum, Henry W. (1826–1894)

US MAJOR GENERAL

During the night of February 17th [1865] the greater portion of the city of Columbia **5** was burned. The lurid flames could easily be seen from my camp, many miles distant. Nearly all the public buildings, several churches, an orphan asylum, and many of the residences were destroyed. The city was filled with helpless women and children and invalids, many whom were rendered houseless and homeless in a single night. No sadder scene was presented during the war. The suffering of so many helpless and innocent persons could not but move the hardest heart.
    —quoted in *Battles and Leaders of the Civil War*, vol. 4, 1888.

1   A drunken soldier with a musket in one hand and a match in the other is not a pleasant visitor to have about the house on a dark, windy night, particularly when for a series of years you have urged him to come, so that you might have an opportunity of performing a surgical operation on him.
  —quoted in *Battles and Leaders of the Civil War*, vol. 4, 1888.

  ★ Slocum was expressing his belief that drunken Union soldiers had burned Columbia, South Carolina, on February 17, 1865.

Smalley, George W.

NEW YORK TRIBUNE CORRESPONDENT

2   It is the greatest fight since Waterloo.
  —telegram to the *New York Tribune*, September 17, 1862.

  ★ Smalley was reporting on the battle of Antietam (Sharpsburg) in Maryland.

Smith, William (1797–1887)

VIRGINIA GOVERNOR

3   Even if the result were to emancipate our slaves, there is not a man who would not cheerfully put the negro into the Army rather than become a slave himself to our hated and vindictive foe.
  —quoted by Nathaniel W. Stephenson in *The Day of the Confederacy: A Chronicle of the Embattled South*, 1919.

  ★ Smith was addressing the state legislature in March 1865.

Sneed, Sebron (1848–?)

CS PRIVATE

  ★ Sneed served in the Texas Infantry.

4   In this army one hole in the seat of the breeches indicates a captain, two holes a lieutenant, and the seat of the pants all out indicates that the individual is a private.
  —quoted by William C. Davis in *Brothers in Arms*, 1995.

Sorrel, Gilbert Moxley (1838–1901)

CS BRIGADIER GENERAL

5   [Mott's] black servant in the rear immediately took a horse and went to the firing line for his master's body. I met the two coming out of the fire and smoke. The devoted negro had straddled the stiffened limbs of his master on the saddle before him, covered his face with a handkerchief, and thus rescued his beloved master's body for interment with his fathers on the old Mississippi estate.
  —*Recollections of a Confederate Staff Officer*, 1905.

  ★ Colonel Christopher H. Mott was killed at Williamsburg on May 5, 1862.

Alas! The butcher's bill is always to be paid after these grand operations, and at [second] Manassas [Bull Run] especially there were some splendid young lives laid down for our cause and our homes.   **1**
   —*Recollections of a Confederate Staff Officer*, 1905.

 Pickett's charge at Gettysburg stirs every heart that beats for great deeds, and will forever live in song and story.   **2**
   —*Recollections of a Confederate Staff Officer*, 1905.

[Lee's] eyes—sad eyes!—the saddest it seems to me of all men's—beaming the highest intelligence and with unvarying kindliness, yet with command so firmly set that all knew him for the unquestioned chief.   **3**
   —*Recollections of a Confederate Staff Officer*, 1905.

Lee was an aggressive general, a fighter. To succeed, he knew battles were to be won, and battles cost blood, and blood he did not mind in his General's work. Although always considerate and sparing of his soldiers, he would pour out their blood when necessary or when strategically advisable.   **4**
   —*Recollections of a Confederate Staff Officer*, 1905.

The soldiers were fond of chanting hymns and quaint old plantation airs, and at times they were touching with the recollections of home. Homesickness was often very prevalent, and the awful nostalgia came near crippling us.   **5**
   —*Recollections of a Confederate Staff Officer*, 1905.

★ Sorrel was adjutant general on the staff of Lieutenant General James Longstreet.

We were at no loss to understand Grant's intention. The Northern papers, as well as himself, had boldly and brutally announced the purpose of "attrition"—that is, the Federals could stand the loss of four or five men to the Confederates' one, and threw nice strategy into the background.   **6**
   —*Recollections of a Confederate Staff Officer*, 1905.

General Grant's conduct toward our leader in the closing scenes at Appomattox and his vigorous defense of Lee when threatened by unprincipled and powerful Northern politicians are not likely to be forgotten by the Southern people.   **7**
   —*Recollections of a Confederate Staff Officer*, 1905.

For my part, when the time comes to cross the river like the others, I shall be found asking at the gates above, "Where is the Army of Northern Virginia? For there I make my camp.   **8**
   —*Recollections of a Confederate Staff Officer*, 1905.

South Carolina Commissioners

By your course you have probably rendered civil war inevitable. Be it so.   **9**
   —letter to President James Buchanan, January 1, 1861.

★ This followed Buchanan's refusal to order the withdrawal of Union troops from Fort Sumter.

Spratt, L. W.

CHARLESTON MERCURY EDITOR

1   Slavery cannot share a government with democracy—it cannot bear a brand upon it; thence another revolution. It may be painful, but we must make it.
　　—letter to John Perkins, February 13, 1861.

★ Spratt believed that a democratic Confederacy would abolish slavery. John Perkins was one of the writers of the Confederate constitution.

2   The South is now in the formation of a *Slave* Republic. This, perhaps, is not admitted generally.
　　—letter to John Perkins, February 13, 1861.

3   The contest is not between the North and South as geographical sections, for between such sections merely there can be no contest; nor between the people of the North and the people of the South, for our relations have been pleasant, and on neutral grounds there is still nothing to estrange us. . . . But the real contest is between *two forms of society* which have become established, the one at the North and the other at the South. . . . The one is a society composed of one race, the other of two races.
　　—letter to John Perkins, February 13, 1861.

4   The principle that races are unequal and that among unequals inequality is right, would have been destructive to the form of pure democracy at the North. The principle that all men are equal and equally right, would have been destructive of slavery at the South.
　　—letter to John Perkins, February 13, 1861.

5   If the foreign slave trade had never been suppressed, slave society must have triumphed [in the North]. It extended to the limits of New England. . . . But, the slave trade suppressed, democratic society has triumphed.
　　—letter to John Perkins, February 13, 1861.

6   That the Republic of the South shall sustain her independence there is little question. . . . But in the independence of the South is there surely the emancipation of domestic slavery? That is greatly to be doubted.
　　—letter to John Perkins, February 13, 1861.

7   If, in short, you shall own slavery as the source of your authority, and act for it, and erect, as you are commissioned to erect, not only a Southern, but a Slave Republic, the work will be accomplished. Those States intending to espouse and perpetuate the institution will enter your Confederacy; those that do not, will not. Your Republic will not require the pruning process of another revolution; but, poised upon its institutions, will move on to a career of greatness and of glory unapproached by any other nation in the world.
　　—letter to John Perkins, February 13, 1861.

It is assumed that the negro is unfit for mechanical employments, when he exhibits **1** an imitative power of manipulation unsurpassed by any other creature in the world; and when, as a matter of fact, we see him daily in the successful prosecution of the trades, and are forced to know that he is not more generally employed for reason of the high prices offered for him by our fields of cotton.

 —letter to John Perkins, February 13, 1861.

We are erecting a nationality upon a union of races, where other nations have but **2** one. We cannot dodge the issue; we cannot disguise the issue; we cannot safely change our front in the face of a vigilant adversary.

 —letter to John Perkins, February 13, 1861.

Stanley, Henry M. (1841–1904)

CS SOLDIER

   ★ Stanley served with the 6th Arkansas Infantry.

It was the first Field of Glory I had seen in my May of life, and the first time that **3** Glory sickened me with its repulsive aspect, and made me suspect it was all a glittering lie.

 —edited by Henry Steele Commager in *The Blue and the Gray*, 1950.

   ★ Stanley, born in Wales, was describing the battle of Shiloh. Fighting for the South, he was captured and later served for one month in the Union army. In 1871 he went to Africa to find Dr. David Livingstone and utter the famous words, "Dr. Livingstone, I presume."

I marvelled, as I heard the unintermitting patter, snip, thud, and hum of the bullets, **4** how anyone could live under this raining death.

 —quoted by Randall Bedwell in *Brink of Destruction*, 1999.

Stanton, Edwin M. (1814–1869)

US SECRETARY OF WAR

Now we two will save the country.   **5**

 —quoted by Major General George B. McClellan in *Battles and Leaders of the Civil War*, vol. 2, 1888.

   ★ He said this to McClellan, who had just approved of his appointment.

If [McClellan] had a million men he would swear the enemy has two millions, and **6** then he would sit down in the mud and yell for three.

 —quoted by James M. McPherson in *The Battle Cry of Freedom: The Civil War Era*, 1989.

   ★ This reflected the government's frustration over Major General George B. McClellan's reluctance to attack Confederate forces.

1   There is no doubt that the enemy in great force are marching on Washington.
   —quoted by Lieutenant Colonel G. F. R. Henderson in *Stonewall Jackson and the American Civil War*, vol. 1, 1898.

   ★ Stanton wrote this fearful prediction to Governor John A. Andrew of Massachusetts after the battle of Winchester, Virginia, fought on May 25, 1862.

2   The President directs me to say to you that there can be nothing to justify a panic at Fredericksburg. He expects you to maintain your position there as becomes a soldier and a general.
   —telegram to Brigadier General George A. McCall, May 31, 1862.

   ★ McCall was soon afterward captured and sent to Libby Prison.

3   Lee's army overthrown; Grant victorious. You and your noble army now have the chance to give the finishing blow to the rebellion. Will you neglect the chance?
   —letter to Major General William Rosecrans, July 7, 1863.

   ★ Stanton was referring to General Robert E. Lee's defeat at Gettysburg and to General Ulysses S. Grant's taking of Vicksburg, both on July 4, 1863. Rosecrans lost the battle of Chickamauga on September 19, 1863, and was relieved of his command.

4   The President directs me to say to you that he wishes you to have no conference with General Lee unless it be for the capitulation of General Lee's army; or on some minor or purely military matter. He instructs me to say that you are not to decide, discuss, or confer upon any political question.
   —telegram to General Ulysses S. Grant, March 3, 1865.

5   Now he belongs to the ages.
   —quoted by I. M. Tarbell in *Life of Abraham Lincoln*, 1900.

   ★ Stanton said this after the president's death on April 15, 1865.

Stephens, Alexander H. (1812–1883)

US CONGRESSMAN AND CS VICE PRESIDENT

6   I look upon this country, with our institutions, as the Eden of the world, the paradise of the universe. It may be that out of it we may become greater and more prosperous, but I am candid and sincere in telling you that I fear, if we rashly evince passion, and, without sufficient cause, shall take that step, that instead of becoming greater or more peaceful, prosperous, and happy—instead of becoming gods, we will become demons, and at no distant day commence cutting one another's throats.
   —speech to the Georgia House of Representatives, November 14, 1860.

7   The first question that presents itself is, Shall the people of the South secede from the Union in consequence of the election of Mr. Lincoln to the presidency of the United States? My countrymen, I tell you frankly, candidly, and earnestly that I do not think that they ought. In my judgment, the election of no man, constitutionally chosen to that high office, is sufficient cause for any state to separate from the Union. It ought to stand by and aid still in maintaining the Constitution of the coun-

try. To make a point of resistance to the government, to withdraw from it because a man has been constitutionally elected puts us in the wrong.
   —speech to the Georgia House of Representatives, November 14, 1860.

The President of the United States is no emperor, no dictator; he is clothed with no **1** absolute power.
   —speech to the Georgia House of Representatives, November 14, 1860.

I will never consent myself, as much as I admire this Union for the glories of the **2** past, or the blessings of the present, as much as it has done for the people of all these states, as much as it has done for civilization, as much as the hopes of the world hang upon it, I would never submit to aggression upon my rights to maintain it longer; and if they can not be maintained in the Union . . . I would be in favor of disrupting every tie which binds the states together.
   —speech to the Georgia House of Representatives, November 14, 1860.

The greatest curse that can befall a free people is civil war.   **3**
   —speech to the Georgia House of Representatives, November 14, 1860.

We and our posterity shall see our lovely South desolated by the demon of war.   **4**
   —edited by Frank Moore in *The Rebellion Record: A Diary of American Events, with Documents, Narratives, Illustrative Incidents, Poetry, Etc.*, vol. 1, 1861.

★ Stephens said this on January 18, 1861, a day before his state of Georgia seceded.

I have ever believed, and do now believe, that it is to the interest of all the states to **5** be and remain united under the Constitution of the United States, with a faithful performance by each of all its constitutional obligations; if the Union could be maintained on this basis, and on these principles, I think it would be the best for the security, the liberty, happiness, and common prosperity of all.
   —speech, January 18, 1861.

★ Georgia seceded the next day.

The cause of Georgia, whether for weal or woe, must and will be the cause of us all. **6** Her safety, rights, interests, and honor, whatever fortunes await her, must and will be cherished in all our hearts, and defended, if need be, by all our hands.
   —speech, January 18, 1861.

I have looked, and do look, upon our present government as the best in the world. **7** This, with me, is a strong conviction. I have acted upon it as a great truth. But another great truth also presents itself to my mind, and that is, that no government is a good one for any people who do not so consider it. The wisdom of all governments consists mainly in their adaptation to the habits, the tastes, the feelings, wants, and affection of the people.
   —speech, January 18, 1861.

The new constitution has put at rest, *forever*, all the agitating questions relating to **8** our peculiar institution—African slavery as it exists amongst us—the proper *status* of

the negro in our form of civilization. This was the immediate cause of the late rupture and present revolution.
—speech in Savannah, Georgia, March 21, 1861.

★ Stephens became vice president of the Confederate States on February 18, 1861.

1   The prevailing ideas entertained by [Thomas Jefferson] and most of the leading statesmen at the time of the formation of the old constitution, were that the enslavement of the African was in violation of the laws of nature; that it was wrong in *principle*, socially, morally, and politically. . . . Our new government is founded upon exactly the opposite idea; its foundations are laid, its cornerstone rests upon the great truth, that the negro is not equal to the white man; that slavery—subordination to the superior race—is his natural and normal condition.
—speech in Savannah, Georgia, March 21, 1861.

★ This is popularly known as Stephens's "Cornerstone Speech."

2   Have we the means and ability to maintain nationality among the powers of the earth? On this point I would barely say, that as anxiously as we all have been, and are, for the border States, with institutions similar to ours, to join us, still we are abundantly able to maintain our position, even if they should ultimately make up their minds not to cast their destiny with us. That they ultimately will join us—be compelled to do it—is my confident belief; but we can get on very well without them, even if they should not.
—speech in Savannah, Georgia, March 21, 1861.

3   [Northerners] assume that the negro is equal, and hence conclude that he is entitled to equal privileges and rights with the white man. If their premises were correct, their conclusions would be logical and just—but their premise being wrong, their whole argument fails.
—speech in Savannah, Georgia, March 21, 1861.

4   We are in the midst of one of the greatest epochs in our history. The last ninety days will mark one of the most memorable eras in the history of modern civilization. . . . Seven states have within the last three months thrown off an old government and formed a new. This revolution has been signally marked, up to this time, by the fact of its having been accomplished without the loss of a single drop of blood.
—speech in Savannah, Georgia, March 21, 1861.

5   In the new constitution, provision has been made by which our heads of departments can speak for themselves and the administration, in behalf of its entire policy, without resorting to the indirect and highly objectionable medium of a newspaper. It is to be greatly hoped that under our system we shall never have what is known as a government organ.
—speech in Savannah, Georgia, March 21, 1861.

6   In the new constitution [the president's tenure] is six years instead of four, and the President rendered ineligible for a re-election. This is certainly a decidedly conser-

vative change. It will remove from the incumbent all temptation to use his office or exert the powers confided to him for any objects of personal ambition.
—speech in Savannah, Georgia, March 21, 1861.

Many governments have been founded upon the principle of the subordination and   1
serfdom of certain classes of the same race; such were and are in violation of the laws of nature. Our system commits no such violation of nature's laws. With us, all of the white race, however high or low, rich or poor, are equal in the eye of the law. Not so with the negro. Subordination is his place. He, by nature, or by the curse against Canaan, is fitted for that condition which he occupies in our system.
—speech in Savannah, Georgia, March 21, 1861.

The idea has been given out at the North, and even in the border States, that we are   2
too small and too weak to maintain a separate nationality. This is a great mistake. In extent of territory we embrace five hundred and sixty-four thousand square miles and upward. This is upward of two hundred thousand square miles more than was included within the limits of the original thirteen States.
—speech in Savannah, Georgia, March 21, 1861.

★ His figures involved only the first seven states to secede.

Of the men I met in the Congress at Montgomery, I may be pardoned for saying this,   3
an abler, wiser, a more conservative, deliberate, determined, resolute, and patriotic body of men, I never met in my life.
—speech in Savannah, Georgia, March 21, 1861.

We are a young republic, just entering upon the arena of nations; we will be the   4
architects of our own fortunes. Our destiny, under Providence, is in our own hands.
—speech in Savannah, Georgia, March 21, 1861.

The process of disintegration in the old Union may be expected to go on with almost   5
absolute certainty is we pursue the right course. We are now the nucleus of a growing power which, if we are true to ourselves, our destiny, and high mission, will become the controlling power on this continent.
—speech in Savannah, Georgia, March 21, 1861.

Our object is *peace*, not only with the North, but with the world. All matters relating   6
to the public property, public liabilities of the union when we were members of it, we are ready and willing to adjust and settle upon the principles of right, equity, and good faith. War can be of no more benefit to the North than to us.
—speech in Savannah, Georgia, March 21, 1861.

Whether the intention of evacuating Fort Sumter is to be received as an evidence of   7
a desire for a peaceful solution of our difficulties with the United States, or the result of necessity, I will not undertake to say. I would fain hope the former. Rumors are afloat, however, that it is the result of necessity. All I can say to you, therefore, on that point is, keep your armor bright and your powder dry.
—speech in Savannah, Georgia, March 21, 1861.

★ Lincoln, however, had no intention of evacuating the fort.

1   Why cannot the whole question be settled, if the north desire peace, simply by the Congress, in both branches, with the concurrence of the President, giving their consent to the separation, and a recognition of our independence?
    —speech in Savannah, Georgia, March 21, 1861.

    ★ This was said less than a month before the bombardment of Fort Sumter.

2   The principles and position of the present administration of the United States—the republican party—present some puzzling questions. While it is a fixed principle with them never to allow the increase of a foot of slave territory, they seem to be equally determined not to part with an inch "of the accursed soil." . . . Why is this? How can this strange paradox be accounted for? There seems to be but one rational solution—and that is, notwithstanding their professions of humanity, they are disinclined to give up the benefits they derive from slave labor.
    —speech in Savannah, Georgia, March 21, 1861.

3   If we are true to ourselves, true to our cause, true to our destiny, true to our high mission, in presenting to the world the highest type of civilization ever exhibited by man—there will be found in our lexicon no such word as fail.
    —speech in Savannah, Georgia, March 21, 1861.

4   Lincoln may bring his 75,000 troops against us. We fight for our homes, our fathers and mothers, our wives, brothers, sisters, sons, and daughters!
    —speech in Richmond, April 22, 1861.

5   While I do not and never have regarded [Jefferson Davis] as a great man or statesman on a large scale, or a man of any marked genius, yet I have regarded him as a man of good intentions, weak and vacillating, timid, petulant, peevish, obstinate, but not firm. Am now beginning to doubt his good intentions. . . . His whole policy on the organization and discipline of the army is perfectly consistent with the hypothesis that he is aiming at absolute power.
    —quoted by Nathaniel W. Stephenson in *The Day of the Confederacy: A Chronicle of the Embattled South*, 1919.

    ★ This was in a letter sent in early 1864 to Herschel V. Johnson, a Georgia senator in the Confederate congress.

6   Liberty once lost will never be recovered without blood.
    —quoted by Randall Bedwell in *Brink of Destruction*, 1999.

    ★ Stephens was referring to the Confederate cause on March 12, 1864.

7   Liberty and life together. Not independence first and liberty later!
    —speech to the Georgia legislature, March 16, 1864.

    ★ Stephens was strongly against Jefferson Davis's conscription act and his suspension of habeas corpus.

Tell me not to put confidence in the president [Jefferson Davis]! That he will never   1
abuse the power attempted to be lodged in his hands!
   —speech to the Georgia legislature, April 14, 1864.

Stevens, Isaac I. (1818–1862)

US BRIGADIER GENERAL

Damn it, sir, there isn't any plan. You will fire when you get a chance, and be careful   2
not to hit any of our own men.
   —quoted by Philip Katcher in *Great Gambles of the Civil War*, 1996.

★ One of Stevens's officers had asked what the plan of battle was to capture an uncompleted fort on James Island near Charleston, South Carolina. The no-plan attack on
June 16, 1862 (the battle of Secessionville) failed.

Stevens, Thaddeus (1792–1868)

US CONGRESSMAN FROM PENNSYLVANIA

If the South is ever to be made a safe republic, let her lands be cultivated by the toil   3
of the owners or the free labor of intelligent citizens. This must be done even though
it drive her nobility into exile. If they go, all the better.
   —speech in Lancaster, Pennsylvania, September 6, 1865, quoted in the *New York
   Herald*, December 13, 1865.

★ Stevens was a radical Republican who advocated severe punishment of the South,
which he called a "conquered province."

While I hear it said everywhere that slavery is dead, I cannot learn who killed it. No   4
thoughtful man has pretended that Lincoln's proclamation, so noble in sentiment,
liberated a single slave. It expressly excluded from its operation all those within our
lines.
   —speech in Lancaster, Pennsylvania, September 6, 1865, quoted in the *New York
   Herald*, December 13, 1865.

If a majority of Congress can be found wise and firm enough to declare the Con-   5
federate States a conquered enemy, reconstruction will be easy and legitimate; and
the friends of freedom will long rule in the councils of the nation.
   —speech in Lancaster, Pennsylvania, September 6, 1865, quoted in the *New York
   Herald*, December 13, 1865.

Stewart, Charles (1778–1869)

US COMMODORE

You in the South and Southwest are decidedly the aristocratic portion of this Union;   6
you are so in holding persons in perpetuity in slavery; you are so in every domestic

quality; so in every habit in your lives, living, and actions; so in habits, customs, intercourse, and manners; you neither work with your hands, heads, nor any machinery, but live and have your living, not in accordance with the will of your Creator, but by the sweat of slavery, and yet you assume all the attributes, professions, and advantages of democracy.

—letter to G. W. Childs of Philadelphia, May 4, 1861.

★ Stewart was quoting his remarks to US congressman John C. Calhoun of South Carolina in December 1812.

Stiles, Robert

1   Surely it was not for slavery they fought. The great majority of them had never owned a slave and had little or no interest in the institution. My own father, for example, had freed his slaves long years before; that is, all save one, who would not be "emancipated," our dear "Mammy," who clung to us when we moved to the North and never recognized any change in her condition or her relations to us. The great war will never be properly comprehended by the man who looks upon it as a war for the preservation of slavery.

—*Four Years under Marse Robert*, 1903.

2   Virginia . . . did not favor the exercise of the right of secession. Up to President Lincoln's call for troops she refused to secede. She changed her position under the distinct threat of *invasion*.

—*Four Years under Marse Robert*, 1903.

3   Here, then, we have the essential, the distinctive spirit of the Southern volunteer. As he hastened to the front in the spring of '61, he felt: "With me is Right, before me is Duty, *behind me is Home*."

—*Four Years under Marse Robert*, 1903.

4   I have known the burial of a tame crow . . . to be dignified not only by salvos of artillery, but also by an English speech, a Latin oration, and a Greek ode, which would have done honor to any literary or memorial occasion at old Yale.

—*Four Years under Marse Robert*, 1903.

★ Stiles had recently graduated from Yale.

Stillson, Jerome B. (1841–1880)

New York World CORRESPONDENT

5   Headquarters tonight is wildly exciting. Scores of officers are here, talking the battle over. General Custer arrived about 9 o'clock. The first thing he did was to hug General Sheridan with all his might, lifting him in the air, whirling him around and around with the shout, "By J——s, we've cleaned them out and got the guns!

—article, *New York World*, October 22, 1864.

★ This was after Major General Philip H. Sheridan's troops had recaptured artillery pieces taken by Confederates led by Major General John B. Gordon.

The shadows of evening fall; the sounds of battle cease; a hundred thousand yellow **1**
camp-fires mock the stars. Not all their light combined is bright enough to show the
watchful eyes of Lee what fate is gathering round him. . . . He does not know, in fact,
that while the night speeds on his army is surrounded!
   —article, *New York World*, April 12, 1865.

★ Stillson was reporting on the final days before General Robert E. Lee's surrender at
Appomattox Court House, Virginia.

The campaign has made General Grant what he never was before—a great general **2**
in the estimation of the whole army. It has elevated every corps commander into the
pride of his command; it has given the Army of the Potomac that decisive victory for
which it has heretofore striven in vain through four years of almost constant fighting;
it has given the union a fresh and final assurance that "it must and shall be preserved."
   —article, *New York World*, April 12, 1865.

★ This was written three days after General Robert E. Lee's surrender at Appomattox
Court House, Virginia.

Stone, Kate

In proportion as we have been a race of haughty, indolent, and waited-on people, so **3**
now are we ready to do away with all forms and work and wait on ourselves.
   —edited by John Q. Anderson in *Brokenburn: The Diary of Kate Stone,*
   1861–1868, 1955.

★ This diary entry was written on May 22, 1862. Brokenburn was a large plantation in
Madison Parish, Louisiana.

A year ago we would have considered it impossible to get on for a day without the **4**
things that we have been doing without for months.
   —edited by John Q. Anderson in *Brokenburn: The Diary of Kate Stone,*
   1861–1868, 1955.

★ This diary entry was written on May 22, 1862.

Stone, Roy (1836–1905)

US COLONEL

We have come to stay. **5**
   —quoted by William Swinton in *Campaigns of the Army of the Potomac*, 1866.

★ Stone made this confident statement to his 149th Pennsylvania brigade as they settled into a dangerous post under heavy artillery fire at the battle of Gettysburg. The
saying became a watchword for his men, many of whom were killed on this spot.

Storrow, Samuel

US CORPORAL

★ Storrow was a member of the 44th Massachusetts Infantry.

1   If our country and our nationality is to perish, better that we should all perish with it.
—letter to his father, October 12, 1862.

Stowe, Harriet Beecher (1811–1896)

WRITER AND ABOLITIONIST

★ Stowe was the author of *Uncle Tom's Cabin*.

2   We have sealed our devotion by desolate hearth and darkened homestead,—by the blood of sons, husbands, and brothers. In many of our dwellings the very light of our lives has gone out; and yet we accept the lifelong darkness as our own part in the great and awful expiation, by which the bonds of wickedness shall be loosed, and abiding peace established on the foundation of righteousness.
—*Atlantic Monthly*, January 1863.

★ This reprinted the novelist's reply of November 27, 1862, to a petition signed by more than 500,000 British women and given to Stowe during her visit to that country on May 7, 1853. The petition had called on American women to support the antislavery cause.

3   If we succeed, the children of these very men who are now fighting us will rise up to call us blessed. Just as surely as there is a God who governs the world, so surely all the laws of national prosperity follow in the train of equity; and if we succeed, we shall have delivered the children's children of our misguided brethren from the wages of sin, which is always and everywhere death.
—*Atlantic Monthly*, January 1863.

4   In a recent battle fell a secession colonel, the last remaining son of his mother, and she a widow. That mother had sold eleven children of an old slave mother, her servant. That servant went to her and said, "Missis, we even now. You sold all my children. God took all yourn. Not one to bury either of us. Now I forgive you."
—*Atlantic Monthly*, January 1863.

5   Better a generation should die on the battlefield, that their children may grow up in liberty and justice.
—*Atlantic Monthly*, January 1863.

6   Remember, then, that wishing success to this slavery-establishing effort is only wishing to the sons and daughters of the South all the curses that God has written against oppression.
—*Atlantic Monthly*, January 1863.

Slavery will be sent out by this agony. We are only in the throes and ravings of the 1 exorcism. The roots of the cancer have gone everywhere, but they must die—and will.

    —quoted by Randall Bedwell in *Brink of Destruction*, 1999.

Strong, George Templeton (1820–1875)

SANITARY COMMISSION FOUNDER

We have never been a nation; we are only an aggregate of communities, ready to fall 2 apart at the first serious shock.

    —quoted by Geoffrey C. Ward in *The Civil War: An Illustrated History*, 1990.

Today will be known as BLACK MONDAY. We are utterly and disgracefully routed, 3 beaten, whipped by secessionists.

    —edited by Allan Nevins in *Diary of the Civil War, 1860–1865: George Templeton Strong*, 1962.

★ This entry was written on July 22, 1861, the day after the first battle of Bull Run (first Manassas).

The rebels are hunted out of the North, their best army is routed, and the charm of 4 Robert Lee's invincibility is broken.

    —edited by Allan Nevins in *Diary of the Civil War, 1860–1865: George Templeton Strong*, 1962.

★ This entry was written on July 6, 1863, and referred to the battle of Gettysburg.

Death has suddenly opened the eyes of the people. A hero has been holding a high 5 place among them. But this hero has been despised and rejected by a third of this community [New York City], and only tolerated by the other two-thirds.

    —edited by Allan Nevins in *Diary of the Civil War, 1860–1865: George Templeton Strong*, 1962.

★ Lincoln was the hero referred to in this diary entry written after his assassination. Strong had founded the Sanitary Commission as a relief organization for the Union army.

Strong, Robert H. (1843–?)

US PRIVATE

★ Strong was a member of the 105th Illinois Infantry.

I remember two things in particular after I got home for good. It was hard for me to 6 sit in a chair or sleep in a bed. In the army, only captains and up had chairs. I hadn't sat in a chair in three years or about that. As for beds, they were too soft to sleep in. For a long time, I preferred to sleep and to sit on the floor.

    —diary edited by Ashley Halsey in *A Yankee Private's Civil War*, 1961.

Strother, David H. (1816–1888)

US LIEUTENANT

1   I have observed in this war that the fire of infantry is our main dependence in battle. There has been no bayonet charge from either side that amounted to anything. The opposing forces have never crossed bayonet to my knowledge.
      —diaries edited by Cecil D. Eby Jr. in *A Virginia Yankee in the Civil War*, 1961.

      ★ Strother served in the 3rd West Virginia Cavalry and later became a brigadier general.

Stuart, J. E. B. (1833–1864)

CS MAJOR GENERAL

2   Our loss was not a scratch to man or horse.
      —report of the engagement at Lewinsville, Virginia, September 11, 1861.

3   Gentlemen, in ten minutes every man must be in his saddle!
      —quoted by E. B. Long in *The Civil War Day by Day: An Almanac, 1861–1865*, 1971.

      ★ This order on June 12, 1862, began Stuart's cavalry's risky reconnaissance mission around Major General George B. McClellan's army.

4   General Consternation.
      —quoted by former CS lieutenant general James Longstreet in *From Manassas to Appomattox: Memoirs of the Civil War in America*, 1896.

      ★ This was the humorous name given by Stuart after he told fellow officers he had left a general behind during his raid around the Union army on June 12, 1862.

5   Jine [join] the cavalry.
      —quoted by former CS lieutenant general James Longstreet in *Battles and Leaders of the Civil War*, vol. 2, 1888.

      ★ Stuart was singing this loudly as he rode among Confederate soldiers at the second battle of Bull Run (second Manassas) in August 1862.

6   Our Southern ideals of patriotism provided us with the concepts of chivalry. I tried to excel in these virtues, but others provided a truer interpretation of gallant conduct. A devoted champion of the South was one who possessed a heart intrepid, a spirit invincible, a patriotism too lofty to admit a selfish thought and a conscience that scorned to do a mean act. His legacy would be to leave a shining example of heroism and patriotism to those who survive.
      —letter to R. H. Chilton, December 3, 1862.

7   Old Joe Hooker, will you come out of the Wilderness!
      —quoted by John Esten Cooke in *A Life of General Robert E. Lee*, 1875.

      ★ Stuart sang this on May 3, 1863, as his men charged at the battle of Chancellorsville.

Charge! And remember Jackson!   **1**
  —quoted by John Esten Cooke in *A Life of General Robert E. Lee*, 1875.

★ Lieutenant General Thomas J. "Stonewall" Jackson had been mortally wounded the day before, and Stuart was temporarily leading his brigade at the battle of Chancellorsville.

Indeed in this war more truly than in any other the spirit of lovely woman points the   **2** dart, hurls the javelin, ignites the mine, pulls the trigger, draws the lanyard and gives a fiercer truer temper to the blade in a far more literal sense than the mere muscular aggressions of man.
  —letter to his cousin, Nannie, November 13, 1863.

Dance away, young ladies; half of these young men will be dead or wounded next   **3** week.
  —quoted by Alexander Hunter in *Johnny Reb and Billy Yank*, 1905.

★ Stuart was speaking to a group of young women who had held an all-night dance.

I am going fast now. I am resigned; God's will be done.   **4**
  —quoted by Rod Graff in *Civil War Quiz and Fact Book*, 1985.

★ These were his last words before dying on May 12, 1864, after being wounded the previous day at the battle of Yellow Tavern, Virginia.

If we oppose force to force we cannot win, for their resources are greater than ours.   **5** We must substitute *esprit* for numbers. Therefore I strive to inculcate in my men the spirit of the chase.
  —quoted by Shelby Foote in *The Civil War*, vol. 1, 1958.

Sturgis, Samuel D. (1822–1889)

US GENERAL

I don't care for John Pope one pinch of owl dung.   **6**
  —quoted by Bruce Catton in *The Army of the Potomac: Mr. Lincoln's Army*, 1962.

★ This criticism of Major General Pope was said to Colonel Herman Haupt, superintendent of military railroads, when he told Sturgis his troops would have to wait for transportation because others were first being moved to support Pope's army at the second battle of Bull Run (second Manassas) in August 1862.

For God's sake, if Mr. Forrest will let me alone, I will let him alone!   **7**
  —quoted by Shelby Foote in *The Civil War*, vol. 3, 1958.

★ Sturgis was hoping CS major general Nathan Bedford Forrest would relent his attack at Brice's Crossroads, Mississippi, on June 10, 1864. Forrest, however, routed the Union troops, who numbered more than double those of the Confederates.

Sumner, Charles (1811–1874)

US SENATOR FROM MASSACHUSETTS

1   Our President is now dictator, imperator—what you will; but how vain to have the power of a god and not to use it godlike!
    —quoted by Carl Sandburg in *Abraham Lincoln: The War Years*, 1939.

    ★ This was said after the Union's defeat at the first battle of Bull Run (first Manassas). Sumner was a radical Republican.

2   Abolition is not to be the object of the war, but simply one of its agencies.
    —quoted by Randall Bedwell in *Brink of Destruction*, 1999.

    ★ This was said in November 1861.

3   Where Slavery is, there Liberty cannot be; and where Liberty is, there Slavery cannot be.
    —speech at Cooper Institute in New York City, November 5, 1864.

Sumner, Edwin V. (1797–1863)

US MAJOR

4   Under cover of the houses of your city, shots have been fired upon the troops of my command. Your mills and manufactories are furnishing provisions and the material for clothing for armed bodies in rebellion against the Government of the United States. Your railroads and other means of transportation are removing supplies to the depots of such troops. This condition of things must terminate, and by direction of General Burnside I accordingly demand the surrender of your city into my hands, as the representative of the Government of the United States, at or before 5 o'clock this afternoon. Failing in an affirmative reply to this demand by the hour indicated, sixteen hours will be permitted to elapse for the removal from the city of women and children, the sick and wounded and aged, etc., which period having expired I shall proceed to shell the town.
    —proclamation to the mayor and common council of Fredericksburg, November 21, 1862.

    ★ This preceded the battle of Fredericksburg on December 13, a Confederate victory.

5   It is difficult to describe the state of the (Union) army in other way than by saying there is a great deal too much croaking—there is not sufficient confidence.
    —quoted by William Swinton in *Campaigns of the Army of the Potomac*, 1866.

    ★ Sumner made this comment after the battle of Fredericksburg on December 13, 1862.

6   I never leave a victorious field.
    —quoted by Major General William B. Franklin in *Battles and Leaders of the Civil War*, vol. 2, 1888.

    ★ He meant that he would not soon leave a field after a victory.

Swinton, William

NEW YORK TIMES CORRESPONDENT

The ground had gone from bad to worse, and now showed such a spectacle as might **1**
be presented by the elemental wrecks of another deluge. An indescribable chaos of
pontoons, vehicles, and artillery encumbered all the roads—supply wagons upset by
the roadside, guns stalled in the mud, ammunition trains ruined by the way, and
hundreds of horses and mules buried in the liquid mud. The army, in fact, was
embargoed: it was no longer a question of how to go forward—it was a question of
how to get back. . . . Next morning the army floundered and staggered back to the
old camps; and so ended a movement that will always live in the recollection of the
army as "the mud march."
    —*Campaigns of the Army of the Potomac*, 1866.

★ This describes the disastrous march of the Army of the Potomac beginning January 20, 1863, as Major General Ambrose E. Burnside tried to outflank the Confederates at Fredericksburg. On January 26, Burnside was relieved of his command.

Bearing on its bayonets the fate of the Confederacy, the Army of Northern Virginia **2**
stood erect and defiant, defending Richmond—threatening Washington.
    —*Campaigns of the Army of the Potomac*, 1866.

★ This described the situation after Gettysburg.

That an army that had moved so far from its base, as that of Lee; that had crossed the **3**
frontier; that had been defeated [at Gettysburg] in a great battle of three days duration, in which it suffered immense loss; that then sought safety in flight only to find
itself barred at the frontier by the rise of the Potomac (as though Providence fought
with the Union Army), should have been either destroyed or hopelessly crippled,
appears indisputable.
    —*Campaigns of the Army of the Potomac*, 1866.

★ Swinton was questioning Major General George G. Meade's decision to not pursue
Lee's retreating forces.

[Jackson] was essentially an executive officer, and in that sphere he was incompara- **4**
ble; but he was devoid of high mental parts, and destitute of that power of planning
and combination, and of that calm, broad, military intelligence which distinguished
General Lee.
    —*Campaigns of the Army of the Potomac*, 1866.

The very relentlessness with which General Grant dealt his blows, and sacrificed **5**
lives to deal these blows, assumed at length to the enemy the aspect of a remorseless
fate; taught him that there was a hand at his throat that never would unloose its
grasp, and shook him in advance with anticipated doom.
    —*Campaigns of the Army of the Potomac*, 1866.

★ This described Grant's advance on Richmond at the end of the war.

Taylor, Richard (1826–1879)

CS LIEUTENANT GENERAL

1   Sheep would have made as much resistance as we met.
     —*Destruction and Reconstruction: Personal Experiences of the Late War*, 1879.

     ★ He was referring to the German troops of Brigadier General Louis Blenker in fighting near Cedar Creek on June 1, 1862.

2   Long will the accursed race remember the great river of Texas and Louisiana. The characteristic hue of its turbid waters has a darker tinge from the liberal admixture of Yankee blood. The cruel alligator and the ravenous garfish wax fat on rich food, and our native vulture holds high revelry over many a festering corpse.
     —order to his troops, May 23, 1864.

3   The difficulty of converting raw men into soldiers is enhanced manifold when they are mounted. Both man and horse require training, and facilities for rambling, with temptation to do so, are increased.
     —*Destruction and Reconstruction: Personal Experiences of the Late War*, 1879.

4   In retreat, Jackson would fight for a wheelbarrow.
     —*Destruction and Reconstruction: Personal Experiences of the Late War*, 1879.

     ★ That is, Jackson would leave nothing behind.

5   Where Jackson got his lemons "No fellow could ever find out," but he was rarely without one. To have lived twelve miles from that fruit would have disturbed him.
     —quoted by Lieutenant Colonel G. F. R. Henderson in *Stonewall Jackson and the American Civil War*, vol. 1, 1898.

     ★ One of Jackson's several eccentricities was the habit of sucking lemons.

Taylor, Walter H.

CS MAJOR

6   With God's help we expect to take a step or two toward an honorable peace.
     —quoted by Douglas Southall Freeman in *R. E. Lee: A Biography*, vol. 3, 1934.

     ★ Taylor, who was General Robert E. Lee's adjutant general, wrote this on June 29, 1863, two days before the battle of Gettysburg.

Taylor, William B.

CS COLONEL

7   Our army is ruined, I fear.
     —letter to his mother, April 5, 1865.

     ★ This was written four days after the battle of Five Forks, Virginia.

Thedford, Mrs.

Hold on, Mister Officer! Those are my potatoes and my boys. Let 'em take 'em.   **1**
—quoted by John D. Wright in *The Language of the Civil War*, 2001.

★ Mrs. Thedford of Thedford's Ford, Tennessee, called to a Confederate officer who was stopping his soldiers from taking her potatoes. This occurred on September 18, 1863, the night before the battle of Chickamauga. She opened her home as a hospital after the battle and became known as the "Mother of Chickamauga."

Thomas, George H. (1816–1870)

US BRIGADIER GENERAL

If you advance as soon as possible on them in front, while I attack them in flank, I   **2**
think we can use them up.
—message to Major General John M. Palmer.

★ This was at the battle of Chickamauga on September 19, 1863. Although the Union lost, Thomas became known as "the Rock of Chickamauga" for holding off the enemy until the Union troops could retreat to Chattanooga.

I am well aware that extreme outposts are always exposed, and for that reason they   **3**
should be sleeplessly vigilant. If we do not run risks we never shall know anything of the enemy.
—message to Major General Absalom Baird, April 24, 1864.

Thompson, David L.

US PRIVATE

★ Thompson was a member of the 9th New York Volunteers.

We came up at the close of the fight at Frederick [Maryland], and, forming line of   **4**
battle, went at double-quick through cornfields, potato patches, gardens, and back-yards—the German washer-woman of the 103d New York regiment going in with us on the run.
—quoted in *Battles and Leaders of the Civil War*, vol. 2, 1888.

★ This was on September 13, 1862.

It was in this charge that I first heard the "rebel yell"; not the deep-breasted Northern   **5**
cheer, given in unison and after a struggle, to signify an advantage gained, but a high shrill yelp, uttered without concert, and kept up continually when the fighting was approaching a climax, as an incentive to further effort.
—quoted in *Battles and Leaders of the Civil War*, vol. 2, 1888.

★ This happened during the battle of South Mountain, Maryland, on September 14, 1862.

1   As the range grew better, the firing became more rapid, the situation desperate and exasperating to the last degree. Human nature was on the rack, and there burst forth from it the most vehement, terrible swearing I have ever heard. Certainly the joy of conflict was not ours that day.
    —quoted in *Battles and Leaders of the Civil War*, vol. 2, 1888.

    ★ Thompson was describing the battle of Antietam (Sharpsburg) on September 17, 1862.

2   In a second the air was full of the hiss of bullets and the hurtle of grape-shot. The mental strain was so great that I saw at that moment the singular effect mentioned, I think in the life of Goethe on a similar occasion—the whole landscape for an instant turned slightly red.
    —quoted in *Battles and Leaders of the Civil War*, vol. 2, 1888.

    ★ Thompson was describing the battle of Antietam (Sharpsburg) on September 17, 1862.

3   All around lay the Confederate dead. . . . As I looked down on the poor, pinched faces, worn with marching and scant fare, all enmity died out. There was no "secession" in those rigid forms, nor in those fixed eyes staring blankly at the sky. Clearly it was not "their war."
    —quoted in *Battles and Leaders of the Civil War*, vol. 2, 1888.

    ★ Thompson was referring to the battle of Antietam (Sharpsburg) on September 17, 1862.

4   Drawing our blankets over us, we went to sleep, lying upon our arms in line as we had stood, living Yankee and dead Confederate side by side, and indistinguishable.
    —quoted in *Battles and Leaders of the Civil War*, vol. 2, 1888.

    ★ Thompson was referring to the battle of Antietam (Sharpsburg) on September 17, 1862.

5   We were hungry [at Antietam (Sharpsburg)], of course, but, as no fires were allowed, we could only mix our ground coffee and sugar in our hands and eat them dry. I think we were the more easily inclined to this crude disposal of our rations from a feeling that for many of us the need of drawing them would cease forever with the following day.
    —quoted in *Battles and Leaders of the Civil War*, vol. 2, 1888.

6   A silence fell on every one at once [at Antietam (Sharpsburg)], for each felt that the momentous "now" had come. Just as we started I saw, with a little shock, a line-officer take out his watch to note the hour, as though the affair beyond the creek were a business appointment which he was going to keep.
    —quoted in *Battles and Leaders of the Civil War*, vol. 2, 1888.

7   If the march has just begun, you hear the sound of voices everywhere, with roars of laughter in spots, marking the place of the company wag—generally some Irishman,

the action of whose tongue bears out his calling. Later on, when the weight of knapsack and musket begins to tell, these sounds die out; a sense of weariness and labor rises from the toiling masses streaming by, voiced only by the shuffle of a multitude of feet, the rubbing and straining of innumerable straps, and the flop of full canteens.
—quoted in *Battles and Leaders of the Civil War*, vol. 2, 1888.

Catch up a handful of snow and throw it, it flies to fluff; pack it, it strikes like stone. **1**
Here is the secret of organization—the aim and crown of drill, to make the units one, that when the crisis comes, the missile may be thoroughly compacted.
—quoted in *Battles and Leaders of the Civil War*, vol. 2, 1888.

No remark was oftener on the lips of officers during the war than this: "Obey orders! **2**
I do your thinking for you." But that soldier is the best whose good sense tells him when to be merely a part of a machine and when not.
—quoted in *Battles and Leaders of the Civil War*, vol. 2, 1888.

It is astonishing how soon, and by what slight causes, regularity of formation and **3**
movement are lost in actual battle. Disintegration begins with the first shot. To the book-soldier all order seems destroyed, months of drill apparently going for nothing in a few minutes.
—quoted in *Battles and Leaders of the Civil War*, vol. 2, 1888.

We heard all through the war that the army "was eager to be led against the enemy." **4**
It must have been so, for truthful correspondents said so, and editors confirmed it. But when you came to hunt for this particular itch, it was always the next regiment that had it. The truth is, when bullets are whacking against tree-trunks and solid shot are cracking skulls like egg-shells, the consuming passion in the breast of the average man is to get out of the way. Between the physical fear of going forward and the moral fear of turning back, there is a predicament of exceptional awkwardness from which a hidden hole in the ground would be a wonderfully welcome outlet.
—quoted in *Battles and Leaders of the Civil War*, vol. 2, 1888.

Thompson, Edwin Porter

North Carolina has claimed, through the public press, the honor of having made the **5**
last fight east of the Mississippi, but we think that the facts will bear us out in the assertion that Colonel Thompson and his Fourth Regiment won that distinction for their own old Kentucky. He was engaged with the rear guard of Potter's Division, April 29, 1865, when General [Joseph] Lewis received the order announcing surrender, or truce, and dispatched last to him to recall these old veterans from their familiar work, and led them to Washington, to part with their "friends," as they called their trusty rifles, when looking wistfully at them for the last time.
—*History of the First Kentucky Brigade*, 1868.

Thompson, M. Jeff (1826–1876)

CS BRIGADIER GENERAL

1   I hope, and have reasonable expectations now, that Missouri will soon wheel into line with her Southern sisters, in which case I and my men will be needed here at home.
　　—letter to Confederate president Jefferson Davis, May 6, 1861.

　　★ Thompson, a colonel at this time, was inspector of the 4th Military District of the Missouri Volunteer Militia.

2   Patriots of Washington, Jefferson, Ste. Genevieve, St. Francois, and Iron Counties [of Missouri]! I have thrown myself into your midst to offer you an opportunity to cast off the yoke you have unwillingly worn so long. Come to me and I will assist you, and drive the invaders from your soil or die with you among your native hills. Soldiers from Iowa, Nebraska, and Illinois, go home! We want you not here, and we thirst not for your blood.
　　—proclamation, October 14, 1861.

　　★ This was issued in Missouri, where his troops were known as the "Swamp Rats."

Thoreau, Henry David (1817–1862)

WRITER

3   No man has yet appeared in America who loved his fellow man so well, and treated them so well. For him he took up his life; for him he will lay it down. This event [of John Brown's raid on Harper's Ferry] advertises us that there is such a thing as death. There has been before no death in America, because there has been no life. Men have only rotted and sloughed along. The best only run down as a clock. They say they will die. I defy them; they cannot do it; they only deliquesce, and leave a hundred eulogists mopping the spot where they left off. These men at Harper's Ferry, in teaching us how to die, have taught us how to live. Their deed is the best news America has ever heard.
　　—speech in Worcester, Massachusetts, November 3, 1859, quoted in the *Worcester Daily Spy*, November 4, 1859.

4   I hear many condemn these men because they were so few. When were the good and the brave ever in a majority?
　　—*A Plea for Captain John Brown*, 1859.

5   He is not Old Brown any longer; he is an angel of light.
　　—*A Plea for Captain John Brown*, 1859.

Thornwell, James Henley (1812–1862)

PRESBYTERIAN MINISTER

Slavery is no new thing. It has not only existed for ages in the world but it has existed, **1**
under every dispensation of the covenant of grace, in the Church of God.
> —*Minutes of the General Assembly of the Presbyterian Church in the Confederate States of America*, vol. 1, 1861.

★ Thornwell, from South Carolina, was attempting to justify church support of slavery in this speech on December 4, 1861, to the General Assembly of the Presbyterian Church in the Confederate States of America, meeting in Augusta, Georgia.

Toombs, Robert A. (1810–1885)

US SENATOR AND CS SECRETARY OF STATE AND BRIGADIER GENERAL

Secession by the 4th day of March should be thundered from the ballot-box by the **2**
unanimous vote of Georgia on the 2nd day of January next. Such a voice will be your best guarantee for liberty, security, tranquillity, and glory.
> —speech to the people of Georgia, December 24, 1860.

★ Toombs, who issued this call from Washington, D.C., would briefly become Confederate secretary of state and then a CS brigadier general.

Mr. President [Jefferson Davis], at this time it is suicide, murder, and you will lose us **3**
every friend at the North [by attacking Fort Sumter]. You will wantonly strike a hornet's nest which extends from mountains to ocean; legions, not quiet, will swarm out and sting us to death. It is unnecessary; it puts us in the wrong; it is fatal.
> —quoted by Carl Sandburg in *Abraham Lincoln: The War Years*, 1939.

Townsend, E. D.

US BRIGADIER GENERAL

Before on their way to the field, their new and fresh-looking banners were borne **4**
with the air of men determined to stand by them to the last. Now, they were brought back torn in shreds by bullets, and dingy with the smoke of war, vastly more prized than ever, and sending to the hearts of spectators a strange thrill of admiration for those men who had fulfilled their silent pledge, and brought back what was left of their colors, enveloped in glorious histories.
> —*Anecdotes of the Civil War in the United States*, 1884.

★ During the war, Townsend was a colonel and acting adjutant general of the US Army.

Tracy, Prescott

US PRIVATE

For a man to find, on waking, that his comrade by his side was dead, was an occur- **5**
rence too common to be noted. I have seen death in almost all the forms of the hos-

pital and battlefield, but the daily scenes in Camp Sumter exceeded in the extremity of misery all my previous experience.
　　—quoted in *Narrative of the Privations and Sufferings of United States Officers and Privates while Prisoners of War in the Hands of Rebel Authorities*, 1864.

★ Camp Sumter was the official name of the notorious Confederate prison at Andersonville, Georgia. Tracy, a member of the 82nd New York Regiment, was a prisoner there for less than two months in 1864.

Trescot, William H. (1822–1898)

1　If there be any truth in protests of our Northern brethren—if slavery be a burden to their consciences, why interfere against an Exodus which would carry with it the plague—why not let the South and slavery go together?
　　—*The Position and Course of the South*, 1850.

2　It is the truth of history, untouched by an exception, that no nation has ever yet matured its political growth without the stern and scarring experience of civil war.
　　—*The Position and Course of the South*, 1850.

Trimble, Isaac R. (1802–1888)

CS BRIGADIER GENERAL

3　By God, General Jackson, I will be a major general or a corpse before this war is over.
　　—quoted by Hunter Holmes McGuire in the *Richmond Dispatch*, July 19, 1891.

★ This was said on August 26, 1862, to Major General Thomas J. "Stonewall" Jackson after Trimble had been passed over for promotion. He was made a major general on April 23, 1863, at the age of sixty.

Trollope, Anthony (1815–1882)

ENGLISH WRITER

4　The Northerners say that they have given no offence to the Southerners, and that therefore the South is wrong to raise a revolution. The very fact that the North is the North is an offence to the South.
　　—*North America*, 1862.

★ Trollope visited America during the war.

5　The days of my visit to Milwaukee were days of civil war and national trouble, but in spite of civil war and national trouble Milwaukee looked healthy.
　　—*North America*, 1862.

Trumbull, H. Clay

CHAPLAIN

★ Trumbull was with the 10th Connecticut Regiment.

I speak of what came under my own observation, when I say that substitutes enlisted **1** and deserted three, five, and seven times over; that in single regiments one-fourth and again one-half, and yet again a larger proportion, of all the men assigned under the new call of the President for five hundred thousand more volunteers, deserted within a few weeks of being started to the front.
— *War Memories of an Army Chaplain*, 1898.

★ Trumbull was writing about recruits joining for a bounty payment as a substitute for others but then deserting and enlisting again as a substitute for another payment.

Trumbull, Lyman

US SENATOR

We immediately mounted our horses and galloped to the road, by which time it was **2** crowded, hundreds being in advance on the way to Centerville and two guns of Sherman's battery having already passed in full retreat. . . . I am dreadfully disappointed and mortified.
— letter to his wife, July 22, 1861.

★ This referred to the Union panic after the first battle of Bull Run (first Manassas) the previous day. Trumbull, of Illinois, later wrote the Thirteenth Amendment, abolishing slavery.

Tubman, Harriet (c. 1820–1913)

FORMER SLAVE

There's two things I've got a right to . . . death or liberty." **3**
— quoted by Sarah H. Bradford in *Harriet, the Moses of Her People*, 1886.

★ An escaped slave, Tubman led more than three hundred slaves to freedom via the Underground Railroad.

Tucker, Gideon J.

LAWYER, EDITOR, AND FORMER NEW YORK SECRETARY OF STATE

As one of those who through the long and dreadful Civil War, always opposed Coer- **4** cion and deplored bloodshed, who believed that the cause of representative government was cruelly damnified by the people of my section, I cannot refrain from congratulating you at this moment upon the consistency and dignity of your course. I trust your life may yet be prolonged sufficiently to see some returning reason come to the people of the North, and lead them to consider what a spectacle they represented to the world from 1861 to 1865, when, under the name of freedom, they fought for dominion.

—letter to Confederate ex-president Jefferson Davis, May 10, 1886.

Turchin, John B.

US COLONEL

1   I shut mine eyes for one hour.

—quoted by Rod Graff in *Civil War Quiz and Fact Book*, 1985.

★ Turchin did so to allow his troops, the 8th Brigade of the Army of Ohio, to burn Athens, Alabama, as revenge for guerrilla attacks.

Tyler, John (1790–1862)

FORMER US PRESIDENT

2   Well, my dearest one, Virginia has severed her connection with the Northern hive of abolitionists, and takes her stand as a sovereign and independent State.

—letter to his wife, Julia, April 17, 1861.

★ Tyler, a Virginian, was seventy-one at this time.

US House of Representatives

3   That the policy of emancipation as indicated in that Proclamation is an assumption of powers dangerous to the rights of citizens and to the perpetuity of a free people.

—proposed resolution by Democratic members of the US House of Representatives quoted by Nathaniel W. Stephenson in *Lincoln: An Account of His Personal Life, Especially of Its Springs of Action as Revealed and Deepened by the Ordeal of War*, 1922.

★ This resolution failed.

Upson, Theodore

US PRIVATE

★ Upson was with the 100th Indiana Regiment.

4   Father and I were husking out some corn . . . when William Cory came across the field . . . and said, "Johnathan, the Rebs have fired upon and taken Fort Sumter." Father got white and couldn't say a word. . . . William said, "The President will soon fix them. He has called for 75,000 men and is going to blockade their ports, and just as soon as those fellas find out that the North means business, they will get down off their high horse." . . . Father looked ten years older.

—edited by Oscar O. Winthur in *With Sherman to the Sea: The Civil War Letters, Diaries and Reminiscences of Theodore Upson*, 1943.

Upton, Emory (1839–1881)

US COLONEL

I am disgusted with the generalship displayed. Our men have, in many instances, **1** been foolishly and wantonly sacrificed.
—letter to his sister, June 4, 1864.

★ He was reflecting on the battle of Cold Harbor, Virginia, the previous day.

Urban, John W.

US PRIVATE

★ Urban was a member of the 1st Pennsylvania Infantry.

As we marched through the gate [of Andersonville prison camp] I could hardly **2** believe it to be possible that this horrible place was to contain us even for a few days, and my blood froze with horror as I looked around and saw men who but a short time before enjoyed health and strength, worn down by suffering and disease, until they hardly looked like human beings.
—*My Experiences mid Shot and Shell and in Rebel Den*, 1882.

Vallandigham, Clement L.

US CONGRESSMAN FROM OHIO

Now, sir, I repeat it and defy contradiction, that not a soldier enlisted, out of the first **3** 900,000, for any other purpose than the restoration of the Union and the maintenance of the Constitution.
—*Speeches, Arguments, Addresses, and Letters of Clement L. Vallandigham*, 1864.

★ Vallandigham made this speech on March 7, 1863, to the Democratic Union Association in New York City, advocating that the North end the war. He was later arrested for treason and banished to the Confederacy.

Van Brunt, G. J.

US CAPTAIN

Never before was anything like it dreamed of by the greatest enthusiast in maritime **4** warfare.
—report, March 8, 1862.

★ On the USS *Minnesota*, Van Brunt had watched his ship's shells bounce off the Confederacy's ironclad *Virginia* (the renamed *Merrimack*).

Van Buren, John (1810–1866)

LAWYER AND SON OF PRESIDENT MARTIN VAN BUREN

1　I am for destroying the usurped Government that has been set up over the Southern States, and this thing that calls itself a Confederate Government; and until that is done I hold that all propositions for peace are entirely preposterous and absurd.
　　—speech at the Cooper Institute, New York City, March 6, 1863.

Vance, Zebulon B. (1830–1894)

GOVERNOR OF NORTH CAROLINA

2　It is mortifying to find entire brigades of North Carolina soldiers commanded by strangers, and in many cases our own brave and war-torn colonels are made to give place to colonels from distant states.
　　—quoted by Nathaniel W. Stephenson in *The Day of the Confederacy: A Chronicle of the Embattled South*, 1919.

　　★ This was said to his legislators in late 1862.

3　If God Almighty had yet in store another plague for the Egyptians worse than all others, I am sure it must have been a regiment or so of half-armed, half-disciplined confederate cavalry.
　　—letter to CS secretary of war James A. Seddon, December 1, 1863.

　　★ Vance was a Confederate colonel and after the war was elected to the Senate.

4　Thank God, the Confederacy does not consist in brick and mortar, or particular spots of ground, however valuable they may be in a military point of view. Our nationality consists in our people.
　　—official statement, February 14, 1865.

Van Horne, Thomas B.

CHAPLAIN

　　★ Van Horne was with the 13th Ohio Regiment.

5　[Shiloh] was a victory because it was not a crushing defeat.
　　—*Army of the Cumberland*, 1875.

6　Battle-fields become a part of history equally with the story of the conflicts enacted upon them. . . . Not alone do the topographical features which suggest plans of battle and dominate tactical combinations become historic, but those also of mere grandeur and beauty, whenever the hosts of war commingle in deadly strife, where nature has been lavish of her gifts. . . . And in all that is grandly concomitant with grandest battle, Chattanooga is pre-eminent.
　　—*Army of the Cumberland*, 1875.

War's visage, despite the glory of heroism and victory, and all the gentle courtesies   1
which enemies may extend at all times, except when the rage of battle brooks no
restraint, is grim and forbidding; but when the ordinary usages of civilized and
Christian nations in the conduct of war are ignored, then are its features forbidding
in the extreme.
   —*Army of the Cumberland*, 1875.

Andersonville and other prisons, where starvation and want of room for captives   2
entailed the intensest suffering and fearful mortality, and Chickamauga, with its
hundreds of unburied dead, give proof of the most revolting inhumanity.
   —*Army of the Cumberland*, 1875.

The last campaigns had inflicted upon the South losses of a magnitude transcending   3
approximate estimation and a desolated country, wasted resources and the traditions
of a lost cause (but a cause which, during the bloody trial of its existence and
supremacy, had commanded the persistent efforts and strongest aspirations of millions) were now the sad inheritance of a proud people.
   —*Army of the Cumberland*, 1875.

In expression of the value of each citizen who fell in the war, the body of each was   4
placed in a separate grave. And so thorough was the search for the dead upon every
battlefield and over the whole country, that their friends may be assured that,
whether identified or not, all rest in grounds consecrated for their abode forever.
   —*Army of the Cumberland*, 1875.

The ruling cause [of the Confederacy's defeat] was that the war on the part of the   5
South was the expression of an insurrection and not a true revolution; and the inherent vices of a false revolution may be traced from the very beginning of the despotic
measures of the government. All true revolutions of popular expression have their
foundation and force in the sentiments of the masses engaged in them, and will be
maintained to the direst extremity. No insurrection that is impressed upon a people
by a few leaders or by an influential or powerful minority, can command the perpetual support of the masses.
   —*Army of the Cumberland*, 1875.

Wade, Benjamin F. (1800–1878)

US SENATOR FROM OHIO

You are the father of every military blunder that has been made during the war. You   6
are on the road to hell, sir, with this government, by your obstinacy, and you are not
a mile off this minute.
   —quoted by Colonel Alexander K. McClure in *Lincoln's Yarns and Stories*, 1904.

★ Wade, a radical Republican, said this to Lincoln. Concerning the mentioned mile,
the president replied: "Senator, that is just about from here to the Capitol, is it not?"

1   . . . if the President of the United States operating through his major generals can initiate a State government, and can bring it here [to the Senate] and force us, compel us, to receive on this floor these mere mockeries, these men of straw who represent no body, your Republic is at an end.

   —quoted by Nathaniel W. Stephenson in *Lincoln: An Account of His Personal Life, Especially of Its Springs of Action as Revealed and Deepened by the Ordeal of War*, 1922.

   ★ Wade, a radical Republican from Ohio, was referring to the establishment of the new government in occupied Louisiana.

2   Boys, we'll stop this damned runaway.

   —quoted by Nathaniel W. Stephenson in *Lincoln: An Account of His Personal Life, Especially of Its Springs of Action as Revealed and Deepened by the Ordeal of War*, 1922.

   ★ During the Union panic retreat after the first battle of Bull Run (first Manassas), Wade, of Ohio, blocked a road with his carriage and other ones a mile from Fairfax Court House and successfully ended that avenue of retreat.

Walker, Alexander

CONFEDERATE JOURNALIST

3   The wives and families of our citizens are frequently ejected from their houses to make way for coarse Federal officers and the Negro women whom they appropriate as their wives and concubines.

   —letter to Jefferson Davis, September 13, 1862.

   ★ Walker, who was in a Federal prison in New Orleans, was complaining about the "crimes" of Major General Benjamin Butler and his troops occupying that city.

Walker, R. Lindsay

CS COLONEL

4   As we rode together, General Lee manifested more impatience than I ever saw him exhibit on any other occasion; seemed very disappointed and worried that the attack had not opened earlier, and very anxious for Longstreet to attack at the earliest possible moment. He even, for a little while, placed himself at the head of one of the brigades to hurry the column forward.

   —quoted by Douglas Southall Freeman in *R. E. Lee: A Biography*, vol. 3, 1934.

   ★ This occurred on the second day of the battle of Gettysburg, July 2, 1863. Walker was the chief of artillery of the 3rd Corps.

Walker, Robert J. (1801–1869)

FORMER US SENATOR FROM MISSISSIPPI

The world looks on with scorn and derision. We have, it is said, no government—a **1**
mere voluntary association of independent states—a debating society, or a moot
court, without any real power to uphold the laws or maintain the Constitution. We
have no country, no flag, no Union; but each state at its pleasure, upon its own mere
whim or caprice, with or without cause, may secede and dissolve the Union. Secession, we are told, is a constitutional right of each state, and the Constitution has
inscribed its own death-warrant upon its face. If this be so, we have indeed no government, and Europe may well speak of us with contempt and derision.
     —speech at the Union Meeting in Union Square, New York City, April 20, 1861.

The recognition of such a doctrine [of secession] is fatal to the existence of any gov- **2**
ernment of the Union: it is death—it is national suicide.
     —speech at the Union Meeting in Union Square, New York City, April 20, 1861.

I see, in the permanent overthrow of the Union, the utter ruin of the South and the **3**
complete prostration of all their interests.
     —speech at the Union Meeting in Union Square, New York City, April 20, 1861.

And now let me say that this Union must, will, and shall be perpetuated; that not a **4**
star shall be dimmed or a stripe erased from our banner; that the integrity of the government shall be preserved, and that, from the Atlantic to the Pacific, from the
Lakes of the North to the Gulf of Mexico, never shall be surrendered a single acre
or our soil or a drop of its waters.
     —speech at the Union Meeting in Union Square, New York City, April 20, 1861.

You are fighting the last great decisive battle for the liberties of our country and of **5**
mankind; faint not, falter not, but move onward in one great column for the maintenance of the Constitution and the Union.
     —speech at the Union Meeting in Union Square, New York City, April 20, 1861.

Our responsibilities are fearful. We have a solemn duty to perform—we are this day **6**
making history. We are writing a book whose pages can never be erased—it is the
destiny of our country and of mankind.
     —speech at the Union Meeting in Union Square, New York City, April 20, 1861.

Walker, W. A.

US CAPTAIN

The darkeys make good soldiers enough, but the attempt to mix them up with white **7**
soldiers and people is productive of mischief, they are very arrogant and insolent,
presuming altogether too much on their social position. Republican as I am, keep
me clear of the darkey in any relation. My repugnance to them increases with the

acquaintance, they have their place and their work, but the time is not yet, in my judgement, when they can strike hands with the whites.
   —letter to "James," January 16, 1864.

Wallace, Lewis (1827–1905)

US BRIGADIER GENERAL

1   You have been wanting a fight; you have got it. Hell's before you!
   —quoted by Shelby Foote in *The Civil War*, vol. 1, 1958.

   ★ This was on February 14, 1862, two days before their attack on Fort Donelson, Tennessee.

Warren, Fritz Henry (1816–1878)

2   On to Richmond, then is the voice of the people. . . . Again, we repeat, On to Richmond! . . . To Richmond! To Richmond!
   —quoted in the *New York Tribune*, May 27, 1861.

3   Our soldiers have been requested to fire blank cartridges in all engagements with Southern forces.
   —quoted in the *New York Tribune*, June 21, 1861.

   ★ This erroneous story appeared a month before the first battle of Bull Run.

4   Shall I tell you, frankly and honestly, what I hear all around me and abroad? It is, that there is no intention to press this suppression of the rebellion—that the patience of the people is to be worn out by delay—that the soldier is to have his spirit wasted in the torpor and inaction of the camp, and when, at length, the nation are disgusted and outraged to a proper point, then we are to run after the old harlot of a compromise.
   —quoted in the *New York Tribune*, June 22, 1861.

Warren, G. K. (1830–1882)

US GENERAL

5   Bobby Lee was always getting people into trouble.
   —quoted by General Philip H. Sheridan in *Personal Memoirs of P. H. Sheridan, General United States Army*, vol. 2, 1888.

Washington, Edward L.

US PRIVATE

   ★ Washington was a member of the 54th Massachusetts Regiment of colored soldiers.

6   Now it seems strange to me that we [black soldiers] do not receive the same pay and rations as the white soldiers. Do we not fill the same ranks? Do we not cover the same space of ground? Do we not take up the same length of ground in a grave-yard

that others do? The ball does not miss the black man and strike the white, nor the white and strike the black.
—letter, March 13, 1864.

Watkins, Sam R.

CS PRIVATE

★ Watkins was a member of the 1st Tennessee Regiment.

Not a single soldier in the whole army ever loved or respected [General Braxton 1
Bragg].
—*Co. Aytch*, 1881.

[The Confederacy's conscription act] gave us the blues; we wanted twenty negroes. 2
Negro property suddenly became very valuable, and there was raised the howl of "rich man's war, poor man's fight."
—*Co. Aytch*, 1881.

★ The Conscription Act said that any person who owned twenty slaves was exempt from being drafted.

A private is but an automator, a machine that works by the command of a good, bad, 3
or indifferent engineer, and is presumed to know nothing of all these great events.
—*Co. Aytch*, 1881.

Is it true that I have seen all these things? that they are real incidents in my life's his- 4
tory? Did I see those brave and noble countrymen of mine laid low in death and wel-
tering in their blood? Did I see our country laid waste and in ruins? Did I see
soldiers marching, the earth trembling and jarring beneath their measured tread?
Did I see the ruins of smouldering cities and deserted homes? Did I see my comrades buried and see the violet and wild flowers bloom over their graves? Did I see
the flag of my country, that I had followed so long, furled to be no more unfurled forever? Surely they are but the vagaries of mine own imagination.
—*Co. Aytch*, 1882.

I always shot at privates. It was they that did the shooting and killing, and if I could 5
kill or wound a private, why, my chances were so much the better. I always looked
upon officers as harmless personages.
—*Co. Aytch*, 1882.

Dying on the field of battle and glory is about the easiest duty a soldier has to 6
undergo.
—*Co. Aytch*, 1882.

The Federal army was advancing all along the line. They expected to march right 7
into the heart of the South, set the negroes free, take our property, and whip the
rebels back into the Union. But they soon found that secession was a bigger mouth-
ful than they could swallow at one gobble.
—*Co. Aytch*, 1882.

1   We shed a tear over their flower-strewn graves. We live after them. We love their memory yet. But one generation passes away and another generation follows. We know our loved and brave soldiers. We love them yet. But when we pass away, the impartial historian will render a true verdict, and a history will then be written in justification and vindication of those brave and noble boys who gave their all in fighting the battles of their homes, their country, and their God. "The United States has no North, no South, no East, no West." "*We are one and undivided.*"
     —*Co. Aytch*, 1882.

2   The South is our country, the North is the country of those who live there. We are an agricultural people; they are a manufacturing people. They are the descendants of the good old Puritan Plymouth Rock stock, and we of the South from the proud and aristocratic stock of Cavaliers. We believe in the doctrine of State rights, they in the doctrine of centralization.
     —*Co. Aytch*, 1882.

3   One evening, General Robert E. Lee came to our camp. . . . He had a calm and collected air about him, his voice was kind and tender, and his eye was as gentle as a dove's. His whole make-up of form and person, looks and manner had a kind of gentle and soothing magnetism about it that drew every one to him and made them love, respect, and honor him. I fell in love with the old gentleman and felt like going home with him. I know I have never seen a finer looking man, nor one with more kind and gentle features and manners.
     —*Co. Aytch*, 1882.

4   The fire opened—bang, bang, bang, a rattle de bang, bang, bang, a boom, de bang, bang, bang, boom, bang, boom, bang, boom, bang, boom, bang, boom, whirr-siz-siz-siz—a rippling, roaring boom, bang!
     —*Co. Aytch*, 1882.

     ★ Watkins was describing the battle of Shiloh on April 6, 1862.

5   A law was passed by the Confederate States Congress called the conscript act. A soldier had no right to volunteer and to choose the branch of service he preferred. He was conscripted. From this time on till the end of the war, a soldier was simply a machine, a conscript. It was mighty rough on rebels. We cursed the war, we cursed [General Braxton] Bragg, we cursed the Southern Confederacy. All our pride and valor had gone, and we were sick of war and the Southern Confederacy.
     —*Co. Aytch*, 1882.

     ★ Confederate conscription began on April 16, 1862. Watkins's unit was part of Bragg's Army of Tennessee.

6   The dead are heroes, the living are but men compelled to do the drudgery and suffer the privations incident to the thing called "glorious war."
     —*Co. Aytch*, 1882.

7   The private loses his life, the general his country.
     —*Co. Aytch*, 1882.

An halo ever surrounds the soldier's life, because he is ever willing to die for his   1
country.
　　—*Co. Aytch*, 1882.

As long as I was in action, fighting for my country, there was no chance for promo-   2
tion, but as soon as I fell out of ranks and picked up a forsaken and deserted flag, I
was promoted for it. . . . And had I only known that picking up flags entitled me to
promotion and that every flag picked up would raise me one notch higher, I would
have quit fighting and gone to picking up flags, and by that means I would have soon
been President of the Confederate States of America.
　　—*Co. Aytch*, 1882.

We were inured to privations and hardships; had been upon every march, in every   3
battle, in every skirmish, in every advance, in every retreat, in every victory, in every
defeat. We had laid under the burning heat of a tropical sun; had made the cold,
frozen earth our bed, with no covering save the blue canopy of heaven; had braved
dangers, had breasted floods; had seen our comrades slain upon our right and our
left hand; had heard guns that carried death in their missiles; had heard the shouts
of the charge; had seen the enemy in full retreat and flying in every direction; had
heard the shrieks and groans of the wounded and dying; had seen the blood of our
countrymen dyeing the earth and enriching the soil; had been hungry when there
was nothing to eat; had been in rags and tatters. We had marked the frozen earth
with bloody and unshod feet; had been elated with victory and crushed by defeat;
had seen and felt the pleasure of the life of a soldier, and had drank the cup to its
dregs. Yes, we had seen it all, and had shared in its hopes and its fears; its love and
its hate; its good and its bad; its virtue and its vice; its glories and its shame. We had
followed the successes and reverses of the flag of the Lost Cause through all these
years of blood and strife.
　　—*Co. Aytch*, 1882.

The death angel was there to gather its last harvest. It was the grand coronation of   4
death.
　　—*Co. Aytch*, 1882.

★ Watkins was referring to the battle of Franklin, Tennessee, on November 30, 1864.

As a soldier [General John B. Hood] was brave, good, noble, and gallant, and fought   5
with the ferociousness of the wounded tiger, and with the everlasting grit of the bulldog; but as a general he was a failure in every particular.
　　—*Co. Aytch*, 1882.

Our cause was lost from the beginning. Our greatest victories—Chickamauga and   6
Franklin—were our greatest defeats. Our people were divided upon the question of
Union and secession. Our generals were scrambling for "*Who ranked.*" The private
soldier fought and starved and died for naught.
　　—*Co. Aytch*, 1882.

I see broken homes and broken hearts. I see war in all of its desolation. I see a coun-   7
try ruined and impoverished. I see a nation disfranchised and maltreated. I see a

commonwealth forced to pay dishonest and fraudulent bonds that were issued to crush that people. I see sycophants licking the boots of the country's oppressor. I see other and many wrongs perpetrated upon a conquered people.
    —*Co. Aytch*, 1882.

Waud, A. R. (1828–1891)

ILLUSTRATOR

1   The murderous traitors, without remorse, shot down all who approached. Men with children dependent on them—men whose wives trembled for them—men who had been little children, and whose mothers would have feared to have a cold wind blow on them—there they lay.
    —article, *Harper's Weekly*, January 10, 1863.

    ★ Waud was describing the battle of Fredericksburg.

Weed, Stephen H.

US BRIGADIER GENERAL

2   I'm as dead a man as Julius Caesar.
    —quoted by Randall Bedwell in *Brink of Destruction*, 1999.

    ★ Weed said this after being mortally wounded during the battle of Gettysburg.

Weitzel, Godfrey

US LIEUTENANT

3   Fort Jackson was subjected to a torrent of 13-inch and 11-inch shells during 140 hours. To an inexperienced eye it seems as if this work were badly cut up. It is as strong to-day as when the first shell was fired at it
    —quoted by William T. Meredith in *Battles and Leaders of the Civil War*, vol. 2, 1888.

    ★ Weitzel was reporting on the amazing survival of the Confederate fort protecting the lower Mississippi River in May 1862. Meredith was his secretary.

Welles, Gideon (1802–1878)

US SECRETARY OF THE NAVY

4   [McClellan] is an intelligent engineer and officer, but not a commander to lead a great army in the field. To attack or advance with energy and power is not in him; to fight is not his forte.
    —quoted by Henry Steele Commager in *The Blue and the Gray: The Story of the Civil War as Told by Participants*, 1950.

[McClellan] likes show, parade, and power. Wishes to outgeneral the Rebels, but not   1
to kill and destroy them.
    —quoted by Henry Steele Commager in *The Blue and the Gray: The Story of the
    Civil War as Told by Participants*, 1950.

[Lincoln] remarked that he had made a vow, a covenant, that if God gave us the vic-   2
tory in the approaching battle, he would consider it an indication of Divine will, and
that it was his duty to move forward in the cause of emancipation.
    —*Diary of Gideon Welles*, 1911.

★ This diary entry was written on September 22, 1862, the day Lincoln issued the preliminary emancipation proclamation.

At the meeting to-day, the President read the draft of his Emancipation Proclama-   3
tion, invited criticism, and finally directed that copies should be furnished to each. It
is a good and well-prepared paper.
    —*Diary of Gideon Welles*, 1911.

★ This diary entry was written on December 29, 1862.

In the absence of news the President strives to feel encouraged and to inspire oth-   4
ers, but I can perceive he has doubts and misgivings, though he does not express
them.
    —*Diary of Gideon Welles*, 1911.

★ This diary entry was written on May 5, 1863, the day after the Union's defeat at the
battle of Chancellorsville.

The President read to-day a paper which he had prepared in reply to Erastus Corn-   5
ing and others. It has vigor and ability and with some corrections will be a strong
paper.
    —*Diary of Gideon Welles*, 1911.

★ This diary entry was written on June 5, 1863. Lincoln's letter was sent June 12 to
Corning, a New York Democrat, responding to resolutions passed on May 16, 1863, by
the Albany Democratic Convention. These denounced Lincoln for allowing the arrest
for treason of Clement Vallandigham, an Ohio congressman and lawyer who opposed
the war.

God bless the Russians.   6
    —quoted by Charles M. Robinson III in *Shark of the Confederacy*, 1995.

★ The Russian fleet made a goodwill visit to the United States in 1863 at a time when
the US government was feeling isolated from other world powers.

Both the President and [Secretary of State William H.] Seward consider Clay and   7
Webster to have been hard and selfish leaders, whose private personal ambition had
contributed to the ruin of their [Whig] party.
    —*Diary of Gideon Welles*, 1911.

★ This diary entry was written on January 8, 1864.

The President has great regard for [Secretary of the Treasury Salmon] Chase's abili-   8
ties, but is glad to be relieved of him, for C. has been a load of late,—is a little dis-

appointed and dissatisfied, has been captious, and uncertain, favored the faultfinders, and, in a way, encouraged opposition to the President.
        —*Diary of Gideon Welles*, 1911.

★ This diary entry was written on July 1, 1864. Chase became Chief Justice of the Supreme Court that October.

1   No one can claim that the blacks, in the slave states especially, can exercise the elective franchise intelligently. In most of the free states they are not permitted to vote.
        —*Diary of Gideon Welles*, 1911.

★ This diary entry was written on May 9, 1865, less than a month after Lincoln's assassination.

Wheat, Chatham Roberdeau

CS MAJOR

2   I don't feel like dying yet.
        —quoted by John D. Wright in *The Language of the Civil War*, 2001.

★ Wheat led the 1st Special Battalion of the Louisiana Infantry, the "Tiger Rifles." He said this when told that he would die after being wounded in both lungs on July 21, 1861, at the first battle of Bull Run (first Manassas). He recovered and fought until he was killed on June 27, 1862, at the battle of Gaines's Mill in Virginia.

Wheeler, Joseph (1836–1906)

CS MAJOR GENERAL

3   Come boys, mount. The War Child rides tonight.
        —quoted by CS brigadier general Gilbert Moxley Sorrel in *Recollections of a Confederate Staff Officer*, 1905.

★ This was heard in November 1863 as Confederate forces moved on Union ones at Knoxville. Wheeler's men had nicknamed him "the War Child."

4   During Sherman's march through Georgia you retarded his advance and defeated his cavalry daily, preventing his spreading over and devastating the country. During the last five months you have traveled nearly three thousand miles, fighting nearly every day, and always with success.
        —speech to his troops, December 31, 1864.

★ This is an example of Wheeler describing a lost situation as a victory.

Whitaker, Edward W.

US CORPORAL

★ Whitaker served in the 1st Connecticut Cavalry.

5   This country [near Alexandria, Virginia] is so beautiful I wish I had been born here.
        —letter to his sister, June 24, 1861.

Whiting, William H. C.

CS BRIGADIER GENERAL

> I believe [Jackson] has no more sense than my horse.   **1**
> —quoted by Lieutenant Colonel G. F. R. Henderson in *Stonewall Jackson and the American Civil War*, vol. 1, 1898.

★ Jackson had just refused to tell him his military plans.

> Great God! Won't some ranking officer come, and save us from this fool!   **2**
> —quoted by CS lieutenant Randolph H. McKim in *A Soldier's Recollections: Leaves from the Diary of a Young Confederate*, 1910.

★ Whiting was referring to Major General Thomas J. "Stonewall" Jackson, who had just ordered a charge at the battle of Malvern Hill on July 1, 1862.

Whitman, Walt (1819–1892)

POET

★ Whitman worked as a volunteer hospital visitor and correspondent for the *New York Times* during the war.

> [Lincoln] looked with curiosity upon that immense sea of faces, and the sea of faces   **3**
> return'd the look with similar curiosity.
> —quoted by Justin Kaplan in *Walt Whitman, A Life*, 1980.

★ The poet was observing the president-elect on Broadway during Lincoln's visit to New York City on February 19, 1861.

> Where are the vaunts and the proud boasts with which you went forth?   **4**
> —quoted by John D. Wright in *The Language of the Civil War*, 2001.

★ Whitman asked this question after Union troops were defeated at the first battle of Bull Run (first Manassas) in July 1861. A "vaunt" is a vain display.

> The soldier's hospital! How many sleepless nights, how many woman's tears, how   **5**
> many long and aching hours and days of suspense, from every one of the Middle, Eastern and Western States have concentrated here!
> —article, *New York Times*, February 26, 1863.

> He is one of the thousands of our unknown American young men in the ranks about   **6**
> whom there is no record or fame, no fuss made about their dying so unknown, but I find in them the real precious & royal ones of this land, giving themselves up, aye even their young & precious lives, in their country's cause.
> —letter to the parents of Erastus Haskell, August 10, 1863.

★ Whitman was then a nurse in the Armory Square Hospital in Washington, D.C. Haskell, a musician from Breesport, New York, for the 141st New York Volunteers, had died eight days before.

1   The fighting has been hard enough, but the papers make lots of additional items, and a good deal they just entirely make up.
  —quoted by Louis S. Starr in *Reporting the Civil War*, 1962.

  ★ Whitman was writing his mother during the battle of the Wilderness of May 5–7, 1864.

2   Outdoors, at the foot of a tree, within ten yards of the front of the house, I noted a heap of amputated feet, legs, arms, hands, &c, about a load for a one horse cart. Several dead bodies lie near, each covered with its brown woolen blanket.
  —article, *New York Times*, December 11, 1864.

3   A wanderer like me about Washington pauses on some high land which commands the sweep of the city (one never tires of the noble and simple views presented here, in the generally fine, soft, peculiar air and light,) and has his eyes stirred by these white clusters of barracks in almost every direction.
  —article, *New York Times*, December 11, 1864.

4   The actual soldier of 1861–65, North and South, with all his ways, his incredible dauntlessness, habits, practices, tastes, language, his fierce friendship, his appetite, rankness, his superb strength and animality, lawless gait, and a hundred unnamed lights and shades of camp, I say, will never be written.
  —*Specimen Days*, 1882.

5   Such was the war. It was not a quadrille in a ball-room. Its interior history will not only never be written—its practicality, minutiae of deeds and passions, will never even be suggested.
  —*Specimen Days*, 1882.

Wilkeson, Frank

US PRIVATE

6   Volunteers vehemently asserted that the bounty-paid recruits really deserted [Grant] during action to seek safety in Confederate prison pens.
  —*Recollections of a Private in the Army of the Potomac*, 1887.

  ★ This happened during Grant's Petersburg campaign in June 1864.

7   Almost every death on the battlefield is different. And the manner of the death depends on the wound and on the man, whether he is cowardly or brave, whether his vitality is large or small, whether he is a man of active imagination or is dull of intellect, whether he is of nervous or lymphatic temperament.
  —*Recollections of a Private Soldier in the Army of the Potomac*, 1887.

8   Sometimes the dead smile, again they stare with glassy eyes, and lolling tongues, and dreadfully distorted visages at you. It goes for nothing. One death was as painless as the other.
  —*Recollections of a Private Soldier in the Army of the Potomac*, 1887.

Long before the campaign was over, I concluded that dying soldiers seldom called   1
on those who were dearest to them, seldom conjured their Northern or Southern
homes, until they became delirious. Then, when their minds wandered and fluttered
at the approach of freedom, they babbled of their homes. Some were boys again and
were fishing in Northern trout streams. Some were generals leading their men to
victory. Some were with their wives and children. Some wandered over their family's
homestead; but all, with rare exceptions, were delirious.

   —*Recollections of a Private Soldier in the Army of the Potomac*, 1887.

The enlisted men were exceedingly accurate judges of the probable result which   2
would ensue from any wound they saw. They had seen hundreds of soldiers
wounded, and they had noticed that certain wounds always resulted fatally. They
knew when they were fatally wounded, and after the shock of discovery had passed,
they generally braced themselves and died in a manly manner. It was seldom that an
American or Irish volunteer flunked in the presence of death.

   —*Recollections of a Private Soldier in the Army of the Potomac*, 1887.

Williamson, Alice

DIARIST

★ Alice was a sixteen-year-old schoolgirl in Gallatin, Tennessee, which was occupied by
the Union troops of General Paine.

I have been studying all the morning and talking all the evening seeking & sighing   3
for rebels. Our king [Brigadier General Eleazer A. Paine] has just passed. I suppose
he has killed every rebel in twenty miles of Gallatin and burned every town. Poor fellow! You had better be praying old Sinner!

   —diary, February 19, 1864.

Gen. Payne [Eleazer Paine] rode out this evening to look at the stock, in his last trip   4
he killed only one man (citizen, he always kills citizens when he cant find soldiers)
swears he will kill every man in Gallatin and Hartsville if bush whacking isn't stopped
shortly

   —diary, March 3, 1864.

Another soldier was shot yesterday. The yankees went to jail and brought him while   5
a citizen was standing near. He said the soldier was very poorly clad but his countenance was that of a gentleman. When the guard brought his horse to him (a broken
down one from the camp) he asked what they were going to do with them. On being
told to "Mount that horse and say no more . . ." he did so remarking that he supposed they were going to shoot him. . . . When they carry them out to shoot them
they given them a worn out horse and tell them if they can escape they may: they say
they "have fine fun chasing the boy with fresh horses."

   —diary, April 7, 1864.

★ The next day's entry said the soldier was shot "while the yankees taunted him with
such remarks as 'I will have his boots.'"

1   Today a Yankee officer made his appearance in the school room accompanied by a Northern being whom I supposed to be a man, as he was not a gentleman; he came to look at the church saying that he was president of a school and that six of his assistants had just arrived and was going to teach the "freedmen." He says he will have 3 or 400 scholars and will need the largest house in town. What a learned city—or rather yankee nest—this will be. I suppose some of us citizens will get a situation as assistant teacher in the "Freedmens university."
        —diary, April 26, 1864.

2   Sis has just come home from Mrs. Lanes: while there she visited the grave of the stranger soldier who was shot Friday. The yankees took his coat and boots off and put him in the grave without coffin or wrappings of any kind.
        —diary, April 27, 1864.

3   Weather pleasant, yankees behaving very well.
        —diary, May 12, 1864.

4   Mrs. Cage [the teacher] has gone to Nashville. The scholars went to school this morning expecting her up on the train. Before the train come the President of the contraband school came over with twenty negro men and took every bench in the school house except one that was greasy; the girls told him to take that, it was good enough for negroes: but no, he said it would "soil the ladies dresses." The girls took that and threw it into the street. Mag King took the broom and threatened to break his head if he came up the step again: he seen she was determined and left.
        —diary, May 16, 1864.

5   The country is overrun with Yanks: they are camped in the woods in front of us and have already paid us several visits killed sheep, goats and chickens. Our new yankees are very neighborly. They come over to see us every few minutes in the day. Some came today and demanded their dinner at two o'clock but did not get it. They went off cursing us for being d—n rebels.
        —diary, June, 10, 1864.

6   In all the doings of the Yanks their fiendish acts today will ballance them all. They brought a man in today and hung him up by the thumbs to make him tell where he came from: he told them but they would not believe him. He fainted three times. They took him down at three o'clock to shoot him. I have not heard whether they did so or not. They would neither give him food or water though he begged for the latter often.
        —diary, June 15, 1864.

        ★ The next day's entry said the man was "shot today without any charge."

Yankees all ran in the fortifications today and carried with them all the citizens they **1**
could find. They are going to shell the town [of Gallatin] if [Major General Joseph]
Wheeler comes . . . Wheeler has not come yet. Yanks still frightened.
  —diary, August 30, 1864.

Williamson, George (1829–1890)

LOUISIANA STATE COMMISSIONER

With the social balance wheel of slavery to regulate its machinery, we may fondly **2**
indulge the hope that our Southern government will be perpetual.
  —speech to the Texas Secession Convention on March 9, 1861, quoted by
  E. W. Winkler in the *Journal of the Secession Convention of Texas*, 1861.

Louisiana looks to the formation of a Southern confederacy to preserve the blessings **3**
of African slavery, and of the free institutions of the founders of the Federal Union,
bequeathed to their posterity.
  —speech to the Texas Secession Convention on March 9, 1861, quoted by
  E. W. Winkler in the *Journal of the Secession Convention of Texas*, 1861.

Wills, Charles W.

US CAPTAIN

★ Wills was a member of the 103rd Illinois Infantry.

I sat down by a fire [in Scottsboro, Alabama] in company with three young women, **4**
all cleanly dressed, and powdered to death. Their ages were from 18 to 24. Each of
them had a quid of tobacco in her cheek about the size of my stone inkstand, and if
they didn't make the extract fly worse than I ever saw in any country grocery, shoot
me. These women here have so disgusted me with the use of tobacco that I have
determined to abandon it.
  —*Army Life of an Illinois Soldier*, 1906.

Wilson, James H. (1837–1925)

US GENERAL

Let's crush the head and heart of the rebellion, and the tail can then be ground to **5**
dust or allowed to die when the sun goes down.
  —letter to Assistant Secretary of War Charles A. Dana, January 15, 1864.

Our hair is badly entangled in [Confederate] fingers and our nose firmly inserted in **6**
his mouth. We shall, therefore, hold on here till something breaks.
  —quoted by Shelby Foote in *The Civil War*, vol. 3, 1958.

★ Wilson was replying to Major General Philip H. Sheridan's order to hold his position
during Sheridan's Richmond raid in May 1864.

1   One hundred thousand dollars reward in gold, will be paid to any person or persons who will apprehend and deliver Jefferson Davis to any of the military authorities of the United States. Several million of specie, reported to be with him, will become the property of the captors.
　　—poster, May 6, 1865.

★ A detachment of Wilson's forces captured the fleeing Confederate president Jefferson Davis four days later in Georgia.

Wilson, William

US COLONEL

2   Boys! You want to come with me, eh? Well, if you do, three-fourths of you will be in your graves in three weeks!
　　—quoted in *Harper's Weekly*, May 11, 1861.

★ Wilson, who founded the "Wilson Zouaves" of New York City, was talking to thirty young volunteers.

Wirz, Henry (1823–1865)

CS COMMANDANT OF ANDERSONVILLE PRISON

3   When these lines reach you, the hand which wrote them will be stiff and cold. In a few hours from now I will be dead. O, if I could express myself as I wish! If I could tell you what I have suffered when I thought about you and the children! I must leave you without the means to live, to the mercies of a cold, cruel world. Lize, do not grieve, do not despair; we will meet again in a better world; console yourself; think as I do, that I die innocent.
　　—letter to his wife and children, November 10, 1865.

★ Wirz was executed for the conditions at Andersonville. He signed the letter, "Your unfortunate husband and father, H. Wirz." He was offered his life if he implicated Confederate president Jefferson Davis but refused, having never met or communicated with Davis.

4   Please help my poor family, my dear wife and children. War, cruel war, has swept everything from me, and to-day my wife and children are beggars. My life is demanded as an atonement. I am willing to give it, and I hope after a while I will be judged differently from what I am now. If any one ought to come to the relief of my family, it is the people of the South, for whose sake I have sacrificed all.
　　—letter to the *New Orleans Daily True Delta*, November 10, 1865.

★ The newspaper printed Wirz's letter on November 17.

Wise, Henry A., Jr.

CS GENERAL

Wanted—A few more Young Men, of good moral character, to fill up the Corps of **1** Cadets, at the Virginia Military Institute. Applicants must be between the ages of eighteen and twenty-five years of age. This is a good chance for young men who wish to avoid the Conscript Act.
  —*Southern Illustrated News*, November 1, 1862.

★ This was a Richmond publication.

Country be damned. There is no country. There has been no country, General, for a **2** year or more. You are the country to these men. They have fought for you . . . there are thousands left who will die for you.
  —quoted by Randall Bedwell in *Brink of Destruction*, 1999.

★ Wise's comments were to General Robert E. Lee before his surrender at Appomattox Court House on April 9, 1865.

I would rather have embraced the tabernacle of death. **3**
  —quoted by CS private Carlton McCarthy in *Detailed Minutiae of Soldier Life in the Army of Northern Virginia, 1861–1865*, 1882.

★ Wise was speaking to a group of Confederate soldiers after the surrender at Appomattox Court House.

Wise, John S.

CS LIEUTENANT

I saw a government go by on wheels. **4**
  —quoted by Hudson Strode in *Jefferson Davis: Tragic Hero*, 1964.

★ Wise was describing the evacuation of the Confederate government from Richmond. He had watched several special trains filled with government officials (including Jefferson Davis) pass Clover Station, Virginia, on April 3, 1865.

Wolseley, Garnet

BRITISH COLONEL

Old General Scott was correct in saying that when Lee joined the Southern cause it **5** was worth as much as the accession of 20,000 men to the "rebels."
  —"A Month's Visit to the Confederate Headquarters," *Edinburgh Magazine*, January 1863.

Wood, Benjamin

New York Daily News editor

1   One out of about two and a half of our citizens are destined to be brought over into Messrs. Lincoln and Company's charnel house.
—article, *New York Daily News*, July 13, 1863.

★ Wood was responding to the new Conscription Act of March 3, 1863, that initiated the draft on July 11, 1863.

Wood, Fernando (1812–1881)

New York City mayor

2   With our aggrieved brethren of the slave states we have friendly relations and a common sympathy. . . . Why should not New York City, instead of supporting by her contributions in revenue two-thirds of the expenses of the United States, become also equally independent? As a free city, with but nominal duty on imports, her local government could be supported without taxation upon her people. Thus we could live free from taxes and have cheap goods nearly duty free. In this she would have the whole and united support of the Southern states, as well as all the other states to whose interest and rights under the Constitution she has always been true.
—speech to the Common Council of New York City, January 7, 1861.

★ Wood suggested that New York City also secede, but after the attack on Fort Sumter, he dropped the idea and supported the war. The Common Council was the city's legislative body.

3   We have not participated in warfare upon [the South's] constitutional rights or upon their domestic institutions.
—speech to the Common Council of New York City, January 7, 1861.

★ This was included in Wood's proposal that New York City should also secede from the Union.

4   We fear that if the Union dies, the present supremacy of New York may perish with it.
—speech in New York's City Hall, February 20, 1861.

★ Wood and his Common Council were meeting with president-elect Lincoln during his visit to New York.

5   In times of great peril great sacrifices are required.
—speech at the Union Meeting in Union Square, New York City, April 20, 1861.

6   In behalf of you I am prepared to say here, and, through the press, to our friends of the South, that before that [Confederate] flag shall float over the national Capitol, every man, woman, and child would enlist for the war.
—speech at the Union Meeting in Union Square, New York City, April 20, 1861.

We know no party now. We are for maintaining the integrity of the national Union 1
intact. We are for exhausting every power at our command in this great, high, and
patriotic struggle.
> —speech at the Union Meeting in Union Square, New York City, April 20, 1861.

[Republicans] are in favor of war as long as slavery exists on this continent and they 2
will prosecute it as long as a drop of southern blood is to be shed and so long as they
themselves are removed from the scene of danger.
> —quoted by Samuel A. Pleasants in *Fernando Wood of New York*, 1948.

★ He said this while running unsuccessfully for reelection in December 1861.

Wool, John E. (1784–1869)

US BRIGADIER GENERAL

★ Wool commanded the US Army's Department of the East.

A separation of the states will bring with it the desolation of the cotton states, which 3
are unprepared for war. Their weakness will be found in the number of their slaves,
with but few of the essentials to carry on war, while the free states will have all the
elements and materials for war, and to a greater extent than any other people on the
face of the globe.
> —letter to Secretary of State Lewis Cass, December 6, 1860.

Peaceable secession is not to be thought of. Even if it should take place, in three 4
months we would have a bloody war on our hands.
> —letter to Secretary of State Lewis Cass, December 6, 1860.

If a separation [of the South] should take place, you may rest assured blood would 5
flow in torrents, followed by pestilence, famine, and desolation.
> —letter to Secretary of State Lewis Cass, December 6, 1860.

So long as the United States keeps possession of this fort [Sumter], the indepen- 6
dence of South Carolina will only be in name, and not in fact. If, however, it should
be surrendered to South Carolina, which I do not apprehend, the smothered indignation of the free States would be roused beyond control.
> —quoted in *Harper's Weekly*, January 12, 1861.

Woolsey, Abby Howland

The more troops who can be sent off to Washington, the less chance for fighting. 7
The immensity of our preparations may overawe the South. Last night we had rather
jolly times, joking and telling war anecdotes, and worked ourselves up into a very
merry cheerful spirit. It is well that we can sometimes seize on the comic points of
the affair or we should be overwhelmed by the dreadful probabilities.
> —letter to her sister, Eliza, April 14, 1861.

★ She had just read about the shelling of Fort Sumter.

1   What awful times we have fallen upon! The sound last night of the newsboys crying till after midnight with hoarse voice, "Bombardment of Fort Sumter," was appalling. . . . The city [New York] is like a foreign one now; the flag floats from every
public building and nearly every shop displays some patriotic emblem.
        —letter to her sister, Eliza, April 14, 1861.

Woolsey, Jane Stuart

2   New York, at any rate, is all on one side now [about the war]—all ready to forget
lesser differences, like the household into which grief has entered. . . . It seems certainly like a miracle, this fresh and universal inspiration of patriotism surmounting
the sorrow, like a fire kindled by God's own hand from His own altar—and this alone
ought to inspire us with hope of the future.
        —quoted by Sylvia G. L. Dannett in *Noble Women of the North*, 1959.

    ★ This was written in April 1861.

Workingmen of Manchester, England

3   Heartily do we congratulate you and your country on this humane and righteous
course. We assume that you cannot now stop short of a complete uprooting of slavery.
        —open declaration to Abraham Lincoln, December 31, 1862.

    ★ This was a reaction to Lincoln's Emancipation Proclamation.

Worsham, John H. (1839–1920)

CS SERGEANT

    ★ Worsham was with the 21st Virginia Infantry.

4   There was something about Jackson that always attracted his men. He was the idol
of his old soldiers, and they would follow him anywhere. The very sight of him was a
signal for cheers.
        —*One of Jackson's Foot Cavalry*, 1912.

5   [Lee] believed in his men and thought they could do anything that mortals could do.
His men worshipped him, and I think the greatest man the world ever saw was
Robert E. Lee.
        —*One of Jackson's Foot Cavalry*, 1912.

Wright, Ambrose R.

CS BRIGADIER GENERAL

6   The trouble is not in going there. . . . The trouble is to stay there after you get there,
for the whole Yankee army is there in a bunch.
        —quoted by Douglas Southall Freeman in *R. E. Lee: A Biography*, vol. 3, 1934.

    ★ This wise statement, made to the artillerist, Colonel E. P. Alexander, concerned the
Confederate charge at the battle of Gettysburg on July 3, 1863.

Yancey, William L. (1814–1863)

US CONGRESSMAN AND CS SENATOR FROM ALABAMA

The man and the hour have met.   **1**
> —quoted by Hudson Strode in *Jefferson Davis: American Patriot*, 1955.

★ Yancey was introducing Jefferson Davis to a crowd in Montgomery, Alabama, on February 16, 1861, two days before his inauguration as president of the Confederacy.

The sentiment in Europe is anti-slavery, and that portion of public opinion which   **2** forms, and is represented by the government of Great Britain, is abolition. They will never recognize our independence until our conquering sword hangs dripping over the prostrate heads of the North.
> —quoted by Shelby Foote in *The Civil War*, vol. 1, 1958.

★ Yancey had just returned from a trip to England in 1862 to seek support for the Confederacy.

Index

Page numbers are followed by a colon and an entry number. Page ranges in **bold** indicate certain prominent individuals' collected quotations.